D0616796

WITHDRAWN
FONDREN LIBRARY CENTER

Justice and Gender

JUSTICE AND GENDER

Sex Discrimination and the Law

Deborah L. Rhode

HARVARD UNIVERSITY PRESS
Cambridge, Massachusetts
London, England
1989

Printed in the United States of America
10 9 8 7 6 5 4 3 2 1

This book is printed on acid-free paper, and its binding materials have been chosen for strength and durability.

Library of Congress Cataloging-in-Publication Data

Rhode, Deborah L.
Justice and gender : sex discrimination and the law / Deborah L. Rhode.
p. cm.
Bibliography: p.
Includes index.
ISBN 0-674-49100-9 (alk. paper)
1. Sex discrimination against women—Law and legislation—United States—History. I. Title.
KF4758.R48 1989
342.73'0878—dc19 89-30854
[347.302878] CIP

Designed by Gwen Frankfeldt

For Ralph

Acknowledgments

This book has been in every sense a collaborative venture. It owes greater debts to a greater number of individuals than I can ever adequately acknowledge. Only through their insights, assistance, and support has this work been possible.

I hope these individuals will forgive me for not acknowledging each of them personally. My reluctance to do so stems only from a concern that the list of those who deserve credit is so long and extends over so many years that I would inadvertently omit some who deserve recognition. Many colleagues gave generously of their time and talents in reading parts of the manuscript. Research assistants provided invaluable help at all stages. Students and participants in working seminars offered insights that I have tried to incorporate throughout the book. Stanford Law School librarians tirelessly pursued large volumes of materials from inaccessible sources. Financial support was contributed by the Stanford Legal Research Fund, made possible by a bequest from the Estate of Ira S. Lillick, and by gifts from Roderick E. and Carla A. Hills and other friends of the Stanford Law School. Staff and affiliates of the Institute for Research on Women and Gender at Stanford provided unfailing wisdom and support.

There are, however, a few colleagues who have suffered through so many aspects of this work that I cannot fail to single them out for special thanks. Barbara Allen Babcock and Jan Clifford Costello offered essential guidance and encouragement. Lindsay Waters at Harvard University Press patiently shepherded me through various drafts. Matthew Dubuque, Dee Gustafson, and Marilyn Hershey provided incalculable help in preparing the manuscript for publication. Most of all, Ralph Cavanagh offered support, insight, and judgment beyond what I can ever express.

To each of these individuals I am deeply grateful. My greatest desire is that all those who have given so much to the process are able to recognize something of their contributions in its outcome.

D.L.R.

Stanford, California

Contents

Justice and Gender

Introduction

It is ironic that gender discrimination has become more obvious in a society seeking to make it less so. This book explores the law's responses to such discrimination within their broader cultural context. A primary objective is to reorient legal doctrine from its traditional focus on sex-based difference toward a concern with sex-based disadvantage. By examining how the law reflects, reinforces, or challenges persistent patterns of inequality, we may gain a better understanding of both the cultural construction of gender and the most promising strategies for cultural change.

Throughout the last century, the dominant strategy of the women's rights movement has been to emphasize gender difference in order to reduce its importance. Yet this strategy points up central tensions in feminist theory and practice. The dominant ideals of the women's rights movement have built on liberal individualist values; sex should play no role in constraining personal opportunities. However, by definition, feminism presupposes some recognition of women's common interests and concerns. In that sense, liberal feminism assumes the very sense of shared identity it seeks in large measure to transcend.

Related tensions involve the nature of that common identity. Feminist theory derives its coherence from an understanding of women's collective experience. Yet such an understanding presupposes sensitivity to variations in this experience across class, race, ethnicity, age, religion, and sexual preference. The more adequate the acknowledgment of differences among women, the more difficult it is to represent common perspectives or concerns. These tensions became increasingly visible during the 1970s and 1980s as critics from all points on the political spectrum began reexamining fundamental questions about the meaning of gender equality and the strategies needed to attain it. The radical left and New Right found themselves in curious agreement about the importance, if not the consequences, of sex-based differences—an importance that liberals had often challenged. An equally eclectic constituency began raising doubts about the effectiveness of conventional legal strategies in achieving equality for women.

The reasons for that skepticism were clear. Although the last quarter-century witnessed considerable changes in gender roles, certain patterns of gender inequality remained evident. In some respects, this was a period of extraordinary achievement in areas including education, employment, reproductive freedom, and political representation. However, substantial disparities between the sexes persisted. Women were still dramatically underrepresented in the highest positions of economic and political power, and equally dramatically overrepresented in the lowest socioeconomic sectors. In the late 1980s over 85 percent of all elective officeholders were male and over two-thirds of indigent adults were female. Full-time women workers earned less than two-thirds of the annual salary of men, and fewer than half of all women employees held full-time positions. Sexual violence remained common, and reproductive freedom was by no means secure. Women of color were doubly disadvantaged; they constituted a grossly disproportionate share of those experiencing poverty, unemployment, sexual violence, and restrictions on reproductive liberty. Yet few minority women were in positions that shaped public policy in these areas. So too, whatever our progress in gaining women access to roles traditionally occupied by men, we have been less successful in encouraging men's access to roles traditionally occupied by women.[1]

This book seeks to expand our understanding of such inequalities. Law is an important social text, which illumines as well as influences the cultural construction of gender. To provide a fuller account of this process, the chapters that follow place legal issues within broader historical, philosophical, and socioeconomic frameworks. Analysis focuses on the law's role in both institutionalizing and challenging inequality. Much of the difficulty in conventional frameworks stems from two fundamental limitations: the law's traditional preoccupation with gender difference rather than with gender disadvantage; and its focus on abstract rights rather than the social context that constrains them. To challenge these limitations, we need a better sense of legal development in various historical and substantive settings.

The law's conventional approach to gender issues has focused on gender difference. American equal-protection doctrine has drawn heavily on Aristotelian traditions, which define equality as similar treatment for those similarly situated. Within this framework, sex-based discrimination remains justifiable if the sexes are different in some sense that is related to valid regulatory objectives. For example, women's distinctive reproductive capacities have served to validate a wide array of restrictions in employment, family, and educational settings. However, this difference-oriented approach has proven inadequate in both theory and practice. As a theoretical matter, it tends toward tautology. It permits different treatment for those who differ with respect to legitimate purposes but provides no standards for determining what differences are relevant and what counts as legitimate. As a practical matter, this approach has both over- and undervalued gender differences. In some instances, biology has determined destiny, while in other contexts, women's particular needs have gone unacknowledged or unaddressed. Too often courts have treated gender as a matter of immutable difference rather than as a cultural construct open to legal challenge and social change. Reliance on "real difference" has deflected attention from the process by which differences have been attributed and from the groups that are underrepresented in that process. Such an approach has often done more to reflect sex-based inequalities than to challenge them.[2]

Related problems stem from the focus on individual rights that has dominated both gender discrimination law and the liberal feminist traditions from which it draws. Such a focus has, to be sure, played a crucial role in gaining women access to existing educational, employment, and political institutions. However, it has been less successful in making those institutions change in ways necessary to accommodate women's interests, values, and concerns. Formal mandates of similar treatment for individuals similarly situated have failed to confront the social forces underlying women's dissimilar and disadavantaged status. Debates over rights often simply restate rather than resolve fundamental tensions in cultural ideals; reliance on formal entitlements may obscure the broader institutional structure that constrains them. So too, the concept of an autonomous, self-interested individual that is paramount in liberal legal ideology is at odds with the more caring notion of personhood underpinning much contemporary feminist theory.

The alternative proposed here is not to abandon rights discourse, but to reimagine its content and recognize its limitations. The central strategy is to shift emphasis from gender difference to gender disadvantage. A determination that the sexes are not "similarly situated" only begins the discussion. Analysis turns on whether legal recognition of sex-based differences is more likely to reduce or to reinforce sex-based disparities in political power, social status, and economic diversity. Such an approach entails a more searching review than has been customary in cases involving gender. Its focus extends beyond the rationality of means, the legitimacy of ends, and the guarantee of rights. Rather, this alternative requires that governmental objectives include a substantive commitment to gender equality—to a society in which women as a group are not disadvantaged in controlling their own destiny.

That commitment presupposes a better understanding of the harms of sex-based classifications and the complexity of strategies designed to address them. It assumes greater sensitivity to the diversity of women's interests and the tradeoffs that may be required among them. To take a representative example, protective legislation that makes it more expensive to hire female employees may benefit one group of women at the cost of preempting opportunities for another. Preferential policies that offer concrete advantages to women in the short term may carry a less obvious price in the long term. Sex-based classifications often reinforce sex-based stereotypes, and thus help perpetuate sex-based inequalities. In these cases, any adequate legal analysis will require close attention to context. Shifting focus from gender difference to gender disadvantage will not always supply definitive answers, but it can at least suggest the right questions: which women benefit, by how much, and at what cost. Reframing the issue in these terms also points up the limitations of traditional rights-oriented strategies, which have too often promised equality in form but not in fact.

This book explores such traditional legal approaches within their broader social context. Part I provides a brief historical synthesis, beginning with the political and legal efforts of an emerging women's movement to challenge the sexes' "separate spheres." Discussion then centers on the postsuffrage period, roughly 1920–1960, with special attention to disputes surrounding gender difference and protective legislation that provide illuminating parallels to contemporary debate. These debates are the remaining focus of the book. Part II continues the chronological account by describing the emergence of the contemporary women's movement, the campaign for an Equal Rights Amendment to the United States Constitution, and the general evolution of sex-discrimination doctrine during the 1970s and 1980s. Part III explores critical contemporary issues, including welfare policies, family law, employment discrimination, reproductive rights, sexual exploitation and violence, and single-sex schools and clubs. The concluding chapter places these issues in the context of broader trends in feminist theory and their implications for cultural ideals and legal ideology.

Any discussion that relies on concepts such as feminism and gender confronts problems of definition. The term "feminism" did not come into common use until the early part of this century, and its meaning remains inconsistent and imprecise. Conventional definitions encompass any theory or activity on behalf of women's equality. However, in particular historical and cultural contexts the term has been more or less inclusive and has carried different connotations. This analysis seeks to avoid semantic tangles by using the term in its most general sense, and by distinguishing where appropriate among distinctive strands of feminist thought or activity.[3]

The concept of gender presents similar definitional problems. Many contemporary feminist theorists use the term "sex" to refer to biological differences between men and women and "gender" to refer to culturally constructed differences. Although for some purposes it is useful to distinguish between attributes that seem more related to culture than chromosomes, this distinction is not common in legal discourse. Jurisprudential discussions of sexual differences have typically encompassed social as well as physiological characteristics, and have used the term "gender," if at all, interchangeably with "sex." Moreover, as recent feminist theory has emphasized, the two concepts have been inextricably linked. Sexuality as commonly understood has been dependent on social relations, while gender has been grounded in biological differentiation. Where possible, this book attempts to avoid confusion by using "gender" when referring to predominantly cultural dynamics and "sex" when referring to clear biological classifications. However, in areas where the law has employed the terms synonymously, that usage should be understood to encompass the interlocking patterns of biological and cultural differences between men and women.[4]

Those patterns demand greater attention from individuals concerned with legal policy. Given the centrality of gender differences in American society, it is striking to find so little consensus or clarity on certain fundamental issues. Are any sex-linked roles or attributes important to preserve? How might such roles coexist with egalitarian ideals? What legal strategies are most likely to challenge the difference gender difference makes?

In exploring such questions, this book reflects the limitations inherent in any broad-scale survey. It cannot capture the full diversity of women's experience or the complexity of any particular topic. However, it can offer some sense of the continuities of gender disadvantage over time, and illumine the relation between legal doctrine and social change. To that end, the analysis shares the commitment to contextual analysis explicit in most feminist methodology. By focusing on particular legal issues within their broader historical, social, and economic settings, the following discussion seeks to build a theoretical framework from the ground up. The objective is to stengthen the connections between theory and practice, between our understandings of gender and the legal implications that should follow from it. Through that process, we may deepen our perceptions of justice and the strategies for achieving it.

Part One

HISTORICAL FRAMEWORKS

Chapter 1

Natural Rights and Natural Roles

The American women's movement emerged against a backdrop of fundamental social, political, and economic inequalities between the sexes. One of its primary objectives was to challenge the laws that reflected and reinforced such inequalities. Many of the tensions confronting feminists, particularly tensions between women's rights and social roles, took similar form in legal settings. Focusing on those similarities can provide a fuller understanding of the relationship between legal texts and cultural context on issues involving gender.

Domesticity as Destiny

American feminism developed in response to a social structure in which male and female roles were largely separate and anything but equal. From its very beginning, this nation inherited a tradition in which gender defined the geography of social life. For the most part, men occupied the "public" sphere of political and commercial activity, women occupied the "private" sphere of domestic life, and the law respected those boundaries. Women of color were, of course, subject to vastly more restrictive formal and informal codes. However for purposes of understanding the general evolution of sex-discrimination law, it makes sense here to focus on mandates applicable to women as a group, outside the particular context of slavery.

Metaphorical understanding of the sexes' "separate spheres" had firm ideological foundations. Until the mid-nineteenth century, virtually every major theologian and philosopher relegated women to a subordinate role.

That hierarchy was apparent in early Anglo-American common law. Married women were subject to coverture, a doctrine based in part on biblical notions of the unity of flesh between spouses. As described by William Blackstone's influential eighteenth-century legal treatise, coverture regarded husband and wife as "one person in the law."[1]

As a practical matter, the "one" was the husband. Throughout the seventeenth, eighteenth, and early nineteenth centuries, various common-law restrictions prevailed. Wives generally could not hold, acquire, control, bequeath, or convey property, retain their own wages, enter into contracts, or initiate legal actions. Although a married woman received a one-third or one-half dower interest in her husband's estate after his death, she had no legal claim to marital property during his lifetime. In the celebrated phrase of Alfred, Lord Tennyson, a wife stood in legal relation to her spouse as something just "better than his dog, a little dearer than his horse." Barred from higher education, public office, the professions, and most other vocations outside the home, women had few economic options apart from marriage.[2]

The extent to which these formal disabilities constrained women's daily experience remains a matter of considerable dispute. Drawing on different sources and different criteria, historians have offered varying interpretations of women's status in seventeenth- and eighteenth-century America. Most available evidence suggests that women had somewhat greater freedom than Blackstone's interpretation of the common law implies. Some wives, particularly those in upper-class families, managed to retain a degree of control over their property through various equitable exceptions to common-law constraints. Women also participated in commercial activity by acting as their husband's agents or by obtaining authorization to proceed as independent "fem[me] sole traders." Since labor was relatively scarce and few occupations required legal licenses in the pre-Revolutionary era, some wives and widows engaged in a variety of vocations ranging from butcher to lawyer. During a period in which much commercial activity centered in the home, and much welfare assistance occurred through women's charitable efforts, the boundaries between the sexes' "separate spheres" often blurred.[3]

The seventeenth and eighteenth centuries should not, however, be taken as some Golden Age of American history for women. In many jurisdictions exceptions to common-law restrictions were difficult and expensive to obtain. Separate equitable estates protected some wives' property from outside creditors but left control under male trustees. Recent research also suggests that after the Revolution certain employment and contractual options narrowed, particularly in more settled geographic areas. The growing influence of Blackstone's *Commentaries* contributed to that trend, as did the emergence of a cult of domesticity in early-nineteenth-century thought.[4]

During a period when industrialization and urbanization were forcing more productive and social activities outside the home, popular ideology sought to reaffirm the centrality of domestic life. In the process, women acquired an exalted, though still circumscribed, status. The message emerging from press and pulpit alike was that women, though intellectually inferior to men, were morally and spiritually superior. Within their separate empires wives reportedly reigned supreme; from the "throne of the heart," they shaped the character of their infants and thus "dictat[ed] national morality." To preserve their influence, women should not stray from their "domestic altar" to mingle in sordid commercial or political affairs.[5]

This "cult of true womanhood" bore little resemblance to the daily lives of many nineteenth-century women, particularly the racial and ethnic minorities and lower-class whites whose domestic experience was that of slave or servant rather than empress. And ironically enough, as historian Barbara Welter observed, the concept "carried within it the seeds of its own destruction. For if woman was so very little less than the angels, she should surely take a more active part in running the world, especially since men were making such a hash of things." Those charged with shaping the minds and character of future generations required better instruction than the "tinsel and trappings" available in early female academies, and more rigorous alternatives gradually emerged. Women's increasing education helped draw into further question the boundaries of their traditional role.[6]

To preserve the sanctity of the domestic sphere, early-nineteenth-century homemakers began to organize in maternal, temperance, social-purity, charity, and related societies. The skills and self-confidence these women gained, together with the discrimination they often experienced in seeking social reforms, fueled a desire for greater civil rights. By generating a sense of common identity and purpose, the ideal of domesticity laid foundations for an organized women's movement. Ultimately, the celebration of femininity contributed to a revolution of rising expectations, which found feminist expression.[7]

The Emergence of a Feminist Movement

The early women's movement was both a rebellion against, and a refinement of, the ideology that preceded it. Throughout its first century, roughly the period between 1830 and 1920, American feminism never quite came to terms with femininity. As a consequence, it could never generate a coherent theory of equality. In what sense women were the same as men, and in what sense different was an issue on which activists remained deeply divided. Feminists sometimes demanded equal status on the basis of natural rights, but they also claimed it on the ground of natural roles. Although this strategy was at times politically expedient, the limitations of both arguments, and the tensions between them, resulted in enduring difficulties.

The Rhetoric of Rights

American feminism is rooted in various intellectual traditions, but the most dominant influence has been liberalism. Early advocates of women's rights drew heavily on the ideals of individual liberty and autonomy that inspired classic liberal theory and nineteenth-century political struggle. That influence was apparent at the outset of the feminist movement, when discrimination within abolitionist societies fueled a campaign for sexual as well as racial equality. The exclusion of women from the floor of a London antislavery conference was a catalyst for Elizabeth Cady Stanton's and Lucretia Mott's organization of the first women's rights conference in Seneca Falls, New York, in 1848. The Declaration of Sentiments, adopted at that conference, proceeded from liberal premises set forth in the Declaration of Independence. Women were "created equal," with "certain inalienable rights," including the right to occupy any "station in society as [their] conscience shall dictate."[8]

This emphasis on individual choice was not unique to American feminists. Their views built on influential European works such as Mary Wollstonecraft's *Vindication of the Rights of Women* (1792) and John Stuart Mill's *The Subjection of Women* (1869). Such works emphasized women's right to educational and vocational opportunities that would permit individual self-determination. A primary objective was to free women from the constraints of an ascribed status and separate sphere. To theorists like Mill, "individual choice [must be] our model now." Similarly, Elizabeth Cady Stanton made clear that "[i]n discussing the rights of woman, we are to consider what belongs to her as an individual, in a world of her own, as the arbiter of her own destiny . . . Her rights under such circumstances are to use all her faculties for her own safety and happiness."[9]

This vision, while liberating in some respects, also reflected an egoistic understanding of human fulfillment as limited as the self-sacrificing ideals that it sought to replace. The kind of "possessive individualism" underlying this tradition cast each person as the proprietor of his or her own capacities, with little responsibility to others and with little concern for the broader socioeconomic forces that shaped such capacities and confined their exercise. All too often, constraints of birth apart from gender were overlooked, and the effects of formal rights were overstated.[10]

In particular, early feminists often ignored the practical problems of reconciling liberal premises with gender roles. Although some activists such as Stanton tended to dismiss as "mysterious twaddle, the sentimental talk about the male and female element," virtually no leading nineteenth-century feminist argued that women should cease to be the primary caretakers of home and family. Nor did any leaders advocate making methods of birth control (apart from abstinence) generally available. Like Mill and Wollstonecraft, American feminists generally wanted every woman to be capable of self-support and self-actualization, but they failed to imagine a redefinition of family responsibilities that would permit it. Even some of the most radical activists, such as Angelina Grimké, emphasized that feminists were not "ruined as domestic characters" and that the work "nearest and dearest before the eyes of average womanhood [remained] work within family boundaries, work within a sphere which men [could] not enter."[11]

How to reconcile the demands of domestic and public spheres was an issue that most early feminists simply finessed. Some, like Mill and Wollstonecraft, appeared convinced that only women of "exceptional" abilities would seek to combine careers in and outside of the home. Other theorists assumed away conflicts by hypothesizing utopian technological innovations or the growth of a professionalized domestic work force. Few of these solutions were likely to be affordable options for those who most needed to work—poor and minority women. But there was little enthusiasm for more practical initiatives such as the cooperative kitchens and childcare arrangements proposed in the late nineteenth and early twentieth centuries by feminists such as Charlotte Perkins Gilman. Even these individuals generally stopped short of envisioning major changes in the male roles and workplace structures that constrained women's alternatives.[12]

As a practical matter, the liberal legalist approach of early feminists offered limited scope for personal choice. Removing formal legal barriers was necessary but not sufficient to expand women's actual options. For most nineteenth- and early-twentieth-century women, marriage and paid labor-force participation remained mutually exclusive alternatives. As late as 1920 approximately four-fifths of the female work force was unmarried. For wives without servants, the liberal rhetoric of autonomy remained out of touch with daily realities. Married women with paid employment often worked at least ten-hour days outside the home, and then cooked, cleaned, laundered, and sewed. Such commitments left little time for the self-actualization to which liberal feminism was committed.

Moreover, as the campaign for women's rights gained momentum, proponents increasingly relied on arguments that undercut a broader social vision.[13]

The Rhetoric of Roles

In seeking to widen their appeal, many nineteenth- and early-twentieth-century feminists muted the rhetoric of natural rights in favor of the rhetoric of natural roles. In tones that echoed the cult of domesticity of the antebellum era and prefigured the relational feminism of the 1970s and 1980s, activists often celebrated the gender differences that liberal feminism challenged. Woman's special attributes thus became a rationale for including, rather than excluding, her from public life. Jane Addams, one of the leading proponents of this position, cast women as municipal housekeepers, who must venture outside the home in order to preserve it. Other feminists similarly maintained that the traditional wife and mother, with her "high code of morals," would "yet purify politics."[14]

Some historians have analyzed this shift in argumentative terrain in chronological terms, with the rhetoric of rights dominating the first phase of the women's movement and the rhetoric of roles the later period. However, both sorts of claims appeared throughout the nineteenth and early twentieth centuries, and many advocates alternated between them. Yet the coexistence of such arguments was not entirely comfortable. An emphasis on essential feminine attributes tended to confuse and subvert the egalitarian premises on which liberal feminism rested. Claims about women's purifying role had sexist as well as sentimental roots and perpetuated the stereotypes that antifeminism invoked. Such arguments did, however, serve important expressive and instrumental functions. For some feminists this ideology of role may have been a means of reaffirming their sense of self-worth and extending their public power. Others undoubtedly found appeals to femininity the most effective means of countering their opponents and capturing mainstream public support.[15]

Although antifeminists' activity was sporadic, their ideology was significant; it helped "defin[e] the context within which suffragist ideas developed [and] posed the problems suffragists had to solve." While invoking a broad arsenal of claims, antifeminists relied primarily on two arguments: the ballot would seriously jeopardize traditional values, and it would produce no significant political gains for women.[16]

In opponents' view, female enfranchisement ran counter to the dictates of biology, the experience of evolution, and the will of the Creator. Women lacked the "rational capacity" for political participation. Either they would vote as their husbands, in which case suffrage was unnecessary, or they would not, in which case domestic disaster would follow. Sexual intermingling in public pursuits would prove equally disastrous. Oddly enough, the dangers ran in opposite directions. Contact between the sexes could readily produce promiscuity or celibacy. Interaction in workplace or civic forums would either provoke constant sexual liaisons or else provide enough economic independence to tempt those "best equipped for . . . motherhood [to refuse] its sacred call." Accordingly, antisuffrage cartoons and editorials depicted women heading merrily off to work while men coped with chaos in the nursery. By encouraging women's specious independence, enfranchisement would reportedly pave the way not only for domestic discord but also for still greater assaults on civil society, such as socialism, anarchism, free love, and "mental abnormality."[17]

As the suffrage campaign wore on, much of this rhetoric seemed increasingly removed from reality. In the late nineteenth and early twentieth centuries, a variety of forces converged to encourage women's entry into the public sphere, including industrialization, urbanization, declining birthrates, increasing divorce rates, expanding educational opportunities, growing demands for female labor, and World War I. Yet what is perhaps most striking about antisuffragist claims concerning gender difference is their persistence. Most reemerged in various forms throughout the next century.[18]

In historical context these arguments were profoundly conservative. They generally issued from women of means who feared any change in the established social order. Ironically enough, many opponents joined Queen Victoria in condemning the "wicked folly of women's rights," but failed to confine their own activities to the narrow domesticity they celebrated. Other antifeminists used prophesies of domestic devastation as rhetorical camouflage for opposition based on different sentiments. Organized antisuffrage activity often received financial support from the leaders of the liquor industry, who feared that enfranchisement would pave the way for prohibition. Similar assistance came from political conservatives and elected officials who were concerned about any influx of voters that might disturb existing power structures or provide support for progressive social reforms.[19]

Yet from a contemporary vantage, certain aspects of the antisuffragist ideology have less regressive implications. Nineteenth-century antifeminists expressed concerns now central to twentieth-century feminists: that the demands of public life would prove difficult to reconcile with family values and would ultimately force assimilation to a male model. Like many contemporary feminists, antisuffragists feared the loss of woman's "independent identity" and the devaluation of her traditional roles. Most doubted that feminine nature would "develop better under masculine conditions of life." If a woman's professional advancement required "making a man of herself," the enterprise then, as now, required reexamination.[20]

Premises and Priorities

Antisuffragists' other major premise—that enfranchisement would have less political impact than supporters claimed—also contains a partial truth that most contemporary feminists acknowledge. As the rhetorical exuberance of the suffrage campaign escalated, it was often opponents who offered the more credible view of formal rights and their relation to social policy.

Given the amount of effort invested in seeking the ballot, it may have been inevitable that supporters lost some perspective on its likely effect. In the course of orchestrating close to nine hundred campaigns before state and federal legislators, party officials, and referendum voters, suffragists increasingly tended toward overstatement. Women would not only purify politics, they would prevent wars and curtail poverty. The first issue of *Revolution,* the weekly journal published by Stanton and Anthony, predicted that the ballot "will secure for woman an equal place and equal wages in the world of work; . . . will open to her the schools, colleges, professions, and all the opportunities and advantages of life."[21]

There were, to be sure, less sanguine assessments. Indeed, a subsequent issue of *Revolution* somewhat inconsistently maintained that "we are not dreamers or fanatics, and we know that the ballot when we get it will achieve for women no more than it has achieved for men." But by and large antisuffragists had the more realistic views on enfranchisement. As they noted, in Western states where women obtained the vote in the late nineteenth century, the millennium had not yet arrived. Nor had reforms that significantly improved women's circumstances.[22]

In any event, the difficulty was not simply the naivete of the proponents' predictions. Rather, it was that feminists' increasing focus on enfranchisement deflected attention from the broader economic and social forces that shaped women's lives. At its outset the women's movement endorsed a broad reform agenda. The vote figured in only one of nine resolutions adopted at Seneca Falls. The remainder focused on educational and employment opportunities, family-law reforms, the double standard of morality, and related concerns. Yet as women began securing more formal rights—to enter the professions, to hold property, to obtain higher education—their political disabilities assumed increasing prominence. And efforts to secure mainstream support for enfranchisement encouraged greater conservatism among proponents.

The suffrage and feminist movements should not, of course, be equated. Other progressive causes, including pacifism, socialism, unionization, protective labor legislation, divorce reform, and settlement houses, had substantial feminist involvement. It was, in part, some leaders' commitment to an array of social reforms, apart from enfranchisement, that contributed to a major split within the suffrage camp during the 1870s and 1880s. However, with the increase in women's political activity, the concrete and symbolic effects of their disenfranchisement attracted growing attention. By the 1890s the rival suffrage organizations had merged, and a united National American Women's Suffrage Association (NAWSA) came to fix its efforts ever more single-mindedly on the ballot. Without denying the legitimacy of single-issue movements in general, it is important to note the limitations of this one in particular.[23]

Although highly sensitive to constraints of gender, most leading suffragists were relatively unconcerned with constraints of race or class. To be sure, early women's rights advocates also tended to be abolitionists who emphasized analogies between racial and sexual oppression. But that emphasis gradually weakened, as became apparent during the 1870s, when one faction of the suffragist camp refused to support any formulation of the Fourteenth and Fifteenth Amendments that did not include women. Moreover, as the campaign for the ballot escalated, exploitation of racial and ethnic prejudices became more common. Black women were excluded by some suffrage organizations, unenthusiastically received in others, and segregated in many public demonstrations. Other minority groups were similarly marginalized. Leaders of the American women's rights movement were also less concerned with issues of class than many of their European counterparts. For example, at the height of early-twentieth-century organizing campaigns among female factory workers, NAWSA leaders maintained a position of studied neutrality; their policy was neither to "stand for labor or against it."[24]

In seeking conservative support, leading suffragists too often lost sight of the liberal principles on which many of their own arguments rested. Even some of the most ardent supporters of natural rights, such as Stanton and Anthony, advocated denial of such rights to the uneducated. In effect, their proposal was to enfranchise women and establish literacy tests. The result, conservative audiences were assured, was that female suffrage would stand as a bulwark against rule by "brutish . . . ignorant Negro men," and "unlettered and unwashed" immigrants. After the turn of the century such arguments occurred more frequently. Their tone was apparent in a 1913 banner:

> For the safety of the nation to
> Women give the vote.
> For the hand that rocks the cradle
> Will never rock the boat.[25]

These conservative ideological currents were not always matched by conservative political strategies. Under the leadership of Alice Paul, the more militant National Women's Party (NWP) pursued tactics of escalating pressure, including parades, White House pickets, and hunger strikes. But like its more moderate counterpart, NAWSA, the NWP sought to avoid divisiveness by focusing exclusively on suffrage. These strategies finally had the desired effect. Growing support for the suffrage campaign, together with women's increasing participation in public life and gratitude for their efforts during World War I, helped prompt congressional passage of a suffrage amendment in 1919. State ratification came in the following year.

Yet in order to broaden their political appeal, suffragists had narrowed their social vision. As the time for celebration approached, there was less to celebrate. By struggling so single-mindedly for one formal guarantee, suffrage advocates failed to confront the other social and economic forces that constrained women's independence. In avoiding issues such as divorce, birth control, poverty, employment discrimination, working conditions, racism, and domestic violence, the major women's rights organizations remained one step removed from the problems and priorities of most women.

Of course, to have focused on such potentially divisive issues risked compromising support, diluting energies, and delaying enfranchisement. And in the long run, the ballot was crucial to securing women's influence on all of the other issues that affected their lives. Thus, suffrage leaders faced a difficult strategic dilemma, and any resolution would carry a cost. Yet the price of their single-issue approach turned out to be greater than they may have anticipated. Like the cult of domesticity that had preceded it, the suffrage campaign laid the foundations for its own demise. By placing such faith in a single formal guarantee, suffragists had little to offer the postsuffrage generation. As a result, many feminists found victory "hardly less demoralizing than defeat"; the vote was poor compensation for the energies, expectations, and emotions it displaced.[26]

Worse still, the immediate effects of enfranchisement were highly disillusioning. Access to the ballot had far less impact on public policy or women's social and economic status than suffragists had predicted. Although passage of the Nineteenth Amendment prompted a brief flurry of attention to issues such as maternal health care and equal rights to jury service, this gender sensitivity soon eroded. Female voters did not vote as a bloc on "women's issues" or support female candidates. Nor did they purify politics or demand the sweeping social reforms that suffrage leaders had linked with enfranchisement. To some commentators, this absence of immediate practical consequences exposed the fallacy of feminist priorities. According to one prominent account, the movement for reform in women's dress, a cause that suffragists abandoned as too controversial, proved more liberating than the ballot.[27]

Such assessments miss a broader point. However limited its immediate effects, the Nineteenth Amendment did mark a crucial advance. It gave women a voice in defining the terms of their existence, a voice that gradually came to be heard. Moreover, what was equally critical about the suffrage movement was that it was a movement, one in which some two million women actively enlisted. The recognition, self-esteem, and political skills that these individuals acquired, quite apart from the abstract right they received, helped lay the foundations for a more egalitarian social order.[28]

But the sources of the suffrage movement's strength were also the causes of its dissolution. The ballot was tangible enough to activate women and abstract enough to unite them; once attained, it proved impossible to replace. Under its banner a variety of competing ideologies could find common ground. Suffragists could avoid taking consistent positions on contested issues, such as the relevance of gender difference. They could thus appeal both to natural rights and natural roles, to ideals of justice and prejudices of class. But with victory came defeat. After passage of the Nineteenth Amendment the coalition foundered. Not until the 1960s did the women's rights movement again enlist substantial popular support. Moreover, throughout the nineteenth and early twentieth centuries the issues of sexual difference that feminists had managed to finesse came squarely to the fore in a variety of legal settings.

Nineteenth-Century Legal Ideology: Separate and Unequal

The United States inherited a common-law tradition in which women were more separate than equal. Feminists' challenge to that tradition echoed themes of the suffrage campaign, and met with comparable rejoinders. Appeals to natural rights alternated with appeals to natural roles, and liberal egalitarian sentiments were tempered with subtle racist undertones. The judicial decisions of the period reflected these same rhetorical currents as well as broader cultural understandings about gender difference and gender roles. What is notable about virtually all of these decisions is the utter lack of self-consciousness with which an exclusively male judiciary interpreted texts written by exclusively male assemblies to determine issues of male power and exclusivity.

Throughout their first two centuries, American legal institutions permitted few challenges to women's subordinate status. When the framers of America's founding documents spoke of men—of "men . . . created equal" and "endowed . . . with certain unalienable rights"—they were not using the term generically. Although subject to the Constitution's mandates, women were unacknowledged in its text, uninvited in its formulation, unsolicited for its ratification, and, until the late twentieth century, largely uninvolved in its official interpretation. The *Federalist Papers,* which provides the intellectual justifications for the nation's governance structure, mentioned women only once. The reference, by Alexander Hamilton, is a warning about the perils to the state from the intrigues of courtesans and mistresses. For almost two centuries, the judiciary remained unwilling to remedy women's status of constitutional neglect through a broad interpretation of constitutional values. Nor were courts prepared to vest women with the political rights to challenge that status. Rather, as one 1874 Supreme Court decision made clear, the privileges and immunities of citizenship did not include suffrage and states were free to extend that "important trust" to men alone.[29]

By the mid-nineteenth century, although explicit discussion of women's issues was relatively rare, traditional assumptions about gender difference were apparent in a variety of cases concerning female political and professional activities, married women's property acts, and family relationships. Nineteenth-century jurisprudence both exaggerated and essentialized sex-linked attributes and did so from a male reference point. Men set the norm against which women appeared different and deficient. This framework implied a circumscribed role for both women and the law. The sanctity of domestic life generally called for female exclusion from public pursuits and the law's exclusion from private disputes. Paradoxically, the paternalism that justified confining women to the home did not extend to protecting them within it.

The following discussion focuses on three areas involving the most sustained legal challenges to gender inequality: women's exclusion from the professions, particularly law; married women's property rights; and marital relationships. Subsequent chapters will review the law's evolution as it relates to other specific substantive issues. What bears emphasis here are certain general currents in legal ideology, and the problems arising from the law's concern with gender differences rather than gender disadvantages.

Women and Professional Pursuits: Access to the Bar

One of the clearest discussions of the separate-spheres ideology appeared as the bar contemplated women's intrusion into its own professional sphere. Efforts to secure women's access to the professions aroused the same concerns as their efforts to gain the ballot. In the eyes of many nineteenth-century observers, the prospect of female breadwinners threatened an insidious "assault upon the home" and an invitation to "unsexed" wives and indolent husbands. For many nineteenth-century judges female legal practitioners posed a particularly worrisome example of these general dangers.[30]

Although in certain European countries, a few women had served as jurists and judges as early as the eighth century, the bar generally resisted female practitioners until the mid-1800s. In America, women occasionally had acted in the capacity of attorney during the colonial period, but the formalization of licensing standards after the Revolution barred their admission. And despite the almost complete erosion of other restrictions during the Jacksonian era, females and felons continued to be unwelcome.[31]

After the Civil War, women's increasing education, employment, and political activities encouraged challenges to such sex-based discrimination. In 1869, Iowa became the first state to license a woman attorney, Arabella Mansfield, and female applicants began seeking entry in other jurisdictions. The litigation that these efforts provoked offers an illuminating case study of the relation between nineteenth-century feminist thought and legal ideology.

A representative example is that of Belva Lockwood. According to her own account, after marriage failed to cure her "mania for the law," she sought formal legal education in the District of Columbia. Although rejected by a number of institutions on the stated ground that women lacked the "mentality" for legal study or would "distract the attention of young men," Lockwood managed to complete the program at the National Law School. Following her graduation, she encountered another series of rejections. It began with the United States Court of Claims, which refused her papers in 1873 with the announcement "Mistress Lockwood, you are a woman." Although acknowledging her "crime," Lockwood felt it was "too late to put in a denial." She had a similar response to the Virginia Supreme Court's determination that she was not a "person" within the meaning of the state bar licensing statute. The result was two decades of litigation and lobbying efforts that eventually secured her admission before various tribunals.[32]

A year earlier, Myra Bradwell, publisher of a prominent Chicago legal newspaper, began a similar campaign. In an argument typical of the period, her attorney invoked rhetoric of both rights and roles, together with subtle racist innuendos. Insofar as women were the same as men, he argued, they should enjoy the same inalienable right to enter the professions. And, insofar as they were different, their special skills warranted representation in legal arenas. Under some circumstances, women's "silver voice . . . would [doubtless] accomplish more than the severity and sternness of men." If the Fourteenth Amendment prohibited states from excluding their "colored citizens" from the bar, surely it should extend the same protection to "our mothers, our sisters and our daughters."[33]

The argument was unsuccessful, first in Illinois and then in the United States Supreme Court. In the federal case, the majority relied on an earlier, though distinguishable holding to find that Bradwell had no constitutionally protected right to practice law. However, three concurring Justices saw the issue in broader terms. Speaking for this group, Justice Bradley embraced an ideology of difference and vested it with constitutional as well as spiritual significance: "The natural and proper timidity and delicacy which belongs to the female sex evidently unfits it for many of the occupations of civil life. The constitution of the family organization, which is founded in the divine ordinance, as well as in the nature of things, indicates the domestic sphere as that which properly belongs to the domain and functions of womanhood . . . [and] is repugnant to the idea of a woman adopting a distinct and independent career from that of her husband."[34]

That Mrs. Bradwell, apparently unaware of the Creator's mandates, had already launched a successful independent career was a matter the Court politely overlooked. Similarly, that other women applicants might not be married was of no importance; after all, they should be married. Single women were "exceptions to the general rule. The paramount destiny and mission of women are to fulfil the noble and benign offices of wife and mother. This is the law of the Creator."[35]

Although the precise method of divine communication was never elaborated, it was apparently accessible to other nineteenth-century jurists. So, for example, an 1875 Wisconsin court rejected the application of Lavinia Goodell, an unmarried candidate, as "treason" against the "order of nature." Although acknowledging the "cruel chances of life" that sometimes kept women from performing the "peculiar duties of their sex," the court nonetheless felt bound to recognize the role of womanhood in general, as opposed to that of its "superfluous members." The legal profession should not "tempt women from the proper duties of their sex," particularly since the "peculiar qualities of womanhood, its gentle graces . . . its purity, its delicacy, [and] its emotional impulses" were not qualifications for "forensic strife."[36]

Such rhetoric was only one step removed from popular antifeminist caricatures of the times, which depicted women as fainting, crying, or experiencing labor pains in court. Yet never did courts explain why woman's gentle graces, delicacy, and reproductive responsibilities should bar her from all the more prestigious professions but not from certain more grueling or indelicate vocations such as field or factory labor. Not only were arguments based on gender differences selectively invoked, they were also inconsistently applied. By the late nineteenth century, some judges saw females' distinctive attributes as an argument for their admission to the bar. As was true in medical contexts, when cases involved "questions of delicacy," a female patient or client might "rather suffer injustice and wrong than confer with a man."[37]

Yet if assumptions about difference could argue either for women's qualification or disqualification for professional practice, the evidence concerning their expanding public role was less ambiguous. As the century drew to a close, more women were entering the labor market, obtaining higher education, and pursuing political activities. More state legislatures were also expanding married women's property rights and authorizing departures from their domestic destiny. Within five years after courts denied licenses to Myra Bradwell, Lavinia Goodell, and Belva Lockwood, the Wisconsin and Illinois legislatures and the United States Congress authorized woman's entry to the bar. In 1870 five women lawyers reportedly were practicing in the United States. By the turn of the century there were just over a thousand, and twenty states had allowed them admission.[38]

This influx of female practitioners was not received with equanimity in all quarters. Some states prevented their entry until the 1920s, and some courts were less than open-minded about those who did gain admission. One District of Columbia judge welcomed Belva Lockwood into the bar in 1873 with the challenge: "Bring on as many women lawyers as you choose; I do not believe they will be a success." Major law schools continued to resist the distracting influence and offensive "clack of these possible Portias." "No woman," declared one Columbia trustee in 1870, "shall degrade herself by practicing law especially if I can save her." Nineteenth-century Harvard Law School administrators similarly found it "impracticable" to admit women, given the temptations of unchaperoned intellectual intercourse in the library. Subsequent administrations identified other difficulties, and Harvard remained inviolate until 1950. Discrimination by universities and employers persisted throughout most of the twentieth century. Male-female salary differentials were pronounced, and until the late 1960s women constituted only 2–3 percent of the bar and a smaller percentage of judges and elite practitioners. For women of color the barriers were even more substantial. Although the first woman to receive a law degree was black (Charlotte Ray, Howard, 1873), most programs remained closed to minority female applicants for the next half-century. Throughout this period no more than twenty-five black women were reportedly in legal practice.[39]

Nor was the situation different in most other professions. Apart from elementary school teaching and nursing, where women's special maternal attributes were thought particularly relevant, sex-based discrimination was common in hiring, salary, promotion, and educational practices. Explanations varied, but many reflected the same assumptions about difference underlying the *Bradwell* decision and its analogues: woman's "delicate organization," emotional instability, and domestic obligations would leave her unfit for the "fatigue and mental shocks" of professional practice. Drawing on prominent medical theories, employers and educators also worried that female energies needed for reproduction would be diverted to cognitive pursuits; the result would be to deform and eventually deplete America's superior breeding classes. To avoid the deadly "brain-womb" conflict, a bovine placidity during critical reproductive years was strongly recommended.[40]

In some professional contexts almost no excuse for male exclusivity was too trivial. The leaders of a wide range of distinguished institutions including the Princeton graduate school, the Yale Medical School, and the Brooklyn and Bronx bar associations all justified their ban on women by an alleged inability to afford a separate lavatory. Subsequent chapters on employment and education review some of this history in greater depth. As they reflect, assumptions about difference served to legitimate a vast range of gender disadvantages throughout the nineteenth and early twentieth centuries.[41]

Married Women's Property Acts

So too, the most significant improvements in women's formal legal status during this period, those resulting from married women's property acts, were more limited in intent and effect than their language suggests. Much of the legislative support for such statutes arose neither from a desire to encourage married women's advances in the public sphere nor to equalize their position in the private sphere. Statutory provisions reflected this fact, and restrictive judicial interpretation further blunted their progressive impact.

Beginning in 1839, state legislatures launched a series of reforms that removed the most blatant restrictions on women's legal capacity. Over the next three decades, twenty-nine jurisdictions enacted married women's property acts, which typically granted wives certain powers to make contracts, to hold and convey property, and to retain their separate earnings. By the turn of the century, such statutes were in place in three-quarters of the states. After passage of the post-Civil War amendments, coverage extended to black women as well.[42]

Although the content and background of this legislation varied, certain common forces were at work. The doctrine of coverture, which had developed in a feudal agricultural society, was ill-suited for an expanding commercial economy. The legal disabilities of married women, particularly deserted wives, impeded land and credit transactions. Moreover, courts of equity had recognized a tangled set of exceptions to common-law rules, such as antenuptial agreements or separate estates that provided some protection against profligate husbands. But these devices were too cumbersome and expensive for general use, and confusion surrounding their terms impaired market functions. Married women's statutes were a means of regularizing equitable principles and extending them to the general public. Accordingly, such legislation appealed both to Jacksonian populists and to legal rationalists who sponsored codification movements in a variety of substantive fields. In some states insulating wives' separate property from husbands' creditors also served to buffer the risks of a volatile economy.[43]

In other jurisdictions, improvements in married women's status became a focus of feminist concern. Although historians have disputed the influence of women's rights advocates in securing statutory reforms, it is clear that many legislators' arguments closely paralleled feminist claims. While some politicians inveighed against coverture as a violation of natural rights, others stressed its effect on natural roles and sought to assure a more decent domestic life for women with "improvident . . . [and] intemperate" husbands.[44]

In general, however, even the most liberal legislators had no desire to transform wives into economic competitors of their husbands. Sponsors of codification often took pains to assure their more conservative colleagues that abandoning coverture would not "unsex" their spouses or unleash a tribe of Amazons in the marketplace. Statutory modifications would simply afford some protection to "credulous" heiresses and victimized homemakers.[45]

Sponsors were correct in their predictions. Married women's property acts fell far short of equalizing spousal status. Such statutes did not disturb husbands' power to manage or deplete family assets, and many acts did not grant wives full control over earnings or capacity to contract without spousal consent. Moreover, the distaste with which many nineteenth-century judges greeted this legislation rendered it even less effective than sponsors may have intended. Such distaste was not unique to married women's property acts. Legislative meddling with the common law often met with considerable judicial resistance. Nonetheless, the form such hostility assumed in marital property cases suggests that part of the resistance grew out of traditional assumptions about gender difference.[46]

Statutory reforms abolishing coverture forced the judiciary to recognize women as separate, but not necessarily as equal. By viewing the disabilities of married women as "general" and the capabilities created by statute as "exceptional," courts not only stemmed the flow of marketplace Amazons, but also severely impaired women's ability to obtain economic independence. For example, statutes recognizing women's right to their separate earnings were typically interpreted to exclude domestic tasks, such as operating a boardinghouse or selling home products and services. The apparent theory was that such work was performed by the male head of the household through his spouse. In addition, since the husband was entitled to determine the household's needs, his wife's separate property could be charged for his purchases, even if the items were for his exclusive use.[47]

To be sure, most of these holdings did not arise in the context of marital disputes. The typical case involved creditors' claims, and it was often not in the individual wife's interest to assert the rights that statutory reforms appeared to provide. Nonetheless, the effect of judicial rulings was to legitimate a marital hierarchy that restricted women's power and access to credit. Statutory reforms did make it easier for wives to buy, sell, bequeath, and borrow. But most nineteenth-century married women had no significant separate assets apart from their own domestic labor, which fell outside the statutes' scope. These wives remained totally dependent on their husbands' support, a dependency compounded by courts' refusals to inquire into the adequacy of support provided.

Marital Relationships

Laws concerning marital relationships in the nineteenth and early twentieth centuries reflected a somewhat selective endorsement of the cult of domesticity. Legal ideology sanctified the domestic realm but declined to grant women sovereignty within it. In cases such as *Bradwell* and *Goodell*, courts talked reverently of the wife's "custody over the home" while restricting her opportunities outside it. But once her custody was in fact at issue, the rhetoric suddenly shifted. It was the husband's right to determine the couple's domicile and standard of living. Except with respect to custody of small children, wives enjoyed few legal prerogatives, and not until the close of the century did mothers officially gain equal guardianship rights. Although married women doubtless exercised more power in marital relationships than formal doctrine acknowledged, laws governing support, domestic violence, and divorce tended to reinforce gender hierarchies.[48]

Although husbands were under a legal obligation to support their families, courts almost never enforced that obligation in the context of ongoing marriages. Not only were judges unprepared to scrutinize the adequacy of a husband's family expenditures, they also declined to enforce even those support obligations that he had voluntarily assumed. *Miller v. Miller* is a case in point. There, the husband, in apparent atonement for squandering money on other women while neglecting his wife's needs, agreed in writing to pay her an annual allowance. In declining to enforce the agreement, the Iowa Supreme Court rhetorically inquired, "what element could be introduced into a family that would tend more directly to breed discord than this contract?" To which the answer might have been Mr. Miller's continued breach of the agreement.[49]

A comparable judicial attitude was apparent toward domestic chastisement, the common-law euphemism for wife-beating. Early English law recognized the husband's right to discipline his spouse, provided that he "neither kill[ed] nor maim[ed] her," and judicial intolerance for brutality was slow to develop. During the early part of the nineteenth century, a few American courts explicitly recognized the husband's right to whip his wife provided he used a switch no thicker than his thumb. The more typical approach was to repudiate the common-law right of chastisement but to decline to hear "trivial" complaints. "Trivial," as some courts defined it, included all assaultive behavior short of "permanent or malicious injury" or "intolerable conditions." Formal sanctions were rare and were disproportionably visited on poor and minority groups. In most cases of "mere . . . impulsive violence," parties were left to "forget and forgive. For, however great are the evils of ill temper . . . they are not comparable with the evils that would result from raising the curtain, and exposing to public curiosity and criticism, the nursery and the bed chamber."[50]

Such Victorian sentiments were highly selective. While demurely averting their eyes from all but egregious cases of spousal brutality and nonsupport, courts willingly probed the sordid details of domestic life in other contexts, most notably divorce. Here, early Anglo-American jurisprudence built on canon law traditions, which had adopted a textual purist's approach to Matthew 19:6: "What therefore God hath joined together, let not man put asunder." In practice, however, both church and state were prepared to temporize somewhat. By the mid-nineteenth century most American jurisdictions had expanded the grounds of divorce to include not just bigamy, impotence, and adultery, but also desertion and cruelty. All but a few states had also broadened the justifications for legal separations and reformed procedures for altering martial status. America's original system of legislative bills of divorcement had proven arbitrary and expensive. In an effort to reduce those difficulties, states transferred power to the courts and allowed them to grant marital dissolutions or separations for specified reasons.[51]

This reform effort was not entirely successful, and women bore a disproportionate share of the resulting misery. Part of the problem stemmed from the limited grounds available for divorce and from gender biases in their application. For example, not all nineteenth-century statutes recognized cruelty as a basis for marital dissolution, and not all courts were prepared to label physical brutality as cruel. An extreme case is *English v. English,* in which a husband had repeatedly forced sexual intercourse upon his wife, whose medical condition made the act extremely painful. Although censoring the husband for his "selfish" and "unkind" conduct, the court found the wife's charges "insufficiently grave and weighty" to justify divorce, given Mr. English's apparently sincere plea for forgiveness. In a similar mid-nineteenth-century case, a Connecticut court rhetorically inquired: "Are we to allow nothing to the frailty of human nature excited by passion?"[52]

Such tolerance rarely extended to female frailty. According to many courts, a wife who provoked her husband's assault by scolding or rudeness was not entitled to divorce for cruelty. Nor was she entitled to separate maintenance if she stepped out of her prescribed role by failing to cook supper, attending dances contrary to her husband's wishes, refusing sexual intercourse without adequate medical reason, or declining to live under the control of in-laws.[53]

Judicial and legislative attitudes toward divorce did become somewhat more liberal as the century progressed, partly in response to feminist activity. Yet the restricted circumstances under which dissolution was available imposed particular hardships on women, especially those who lacked funds for judicial proceedings. Although husbands could frequently escape intolerable marriages by desertion, their wives lacked comparable opportunities for economic independence. Gender biases in application of divorce statutes further restricted women's independence. Trial courts were often willing to grant divorces upon a showing that a wife was idle, frivolous, neglectful of her household duties, or "contemptuous" of her husband's "rightful authority."[54]

The evolution of divorce reform was typical of general legal developments during this period. Although the latter half of the nineteenth century witnessed the removal of certain formal barriers to women's advancement, their position in fact remained much the same. Opportunities for professional achievement and economic independence were highly limited, and access was skewed by class, race, and ethnicity. For the vast majority of women, legal doctrine did little to ameliorate the inequalities of domestic life. Although suffragists often attributed this fact to disenfranchisement, its causes were more fundamental.

The law to which nineteenth-century women were subject was designed, interpreted, argued, and administered almost entirely by men. Its content reflected that fact, but the immediate effects of enfranchisement did little to alter it. Legal doctrine both reflected and reinforced a highly sex-stratified social order that feminist ideology only partially challenged. The ambivalence toward natural roles and faith in natural rights provided an inadequate response to legal norms. Courts' assumptions about gender difference and their insensitivities to gender disadvantage helped sustain a social order in which women remained more separate than equal.

Chapter 2

The Fragmentation of Feminism and the Legalization of Difference

The Postsuffrage Women's Movement

By conventional indexes, the organized women's rights movement declined during the half-century following enfranchisement. There was, to be sure, no lack of organized women. Suffragists drifted off in different directions, some to various progressive causes, others to a burgeoning social-club movement. The National American Women's Suffrage Association reconstituted itself as the League of Women Voters, but with only a small fraction of its former membership. The more liberal women's rights group, the National Woman's Party (NWP), remained even smaller. Its efforts focused on recapturing the momentum of the suffrage campaign under another constitutional banner, the Equal Rights Amendment. For the next half-century that effort proved unavailing.[1]

In part, the erosion of feminist support in the United States reflected broader social currents. Most progressive causes lost momentum during the politically conservative and culturally hedonistic 1920s, and accusations of Communism took a toll in some feminist organizations. The Depression and World War II displaced attention from women's special needs, and the postwar baby boom revived assumptions about their domestic destiny.[2]

The decline of organized women's rights activity during this period should not, however, be taken to imply an absence of feminism in its broadest sense. Many women participated in social and political organizations that, by contemporary definition, fostered feminist values or experiences. Yet, while conventional accounts too often equate the decline in women's rights activity with a decline in feminism, there is clearly some decline that requires explanation. Impetus for equality in the sexes' legal status diminished, while inequality in their social status remained pronounced. Although the extent to which women's position advanced or regressed between 1920 and 1960 is a matter of historical dispute, there is no doubt that substantial disparities persisted in the sexes' political, educational, and economic attainments.[3]

On a political level, women's organizations registered some significant victories on social-welfare initiatives, but achieved relatively little progress on issues of sex-based discrimination. They were similarly unsuccessful in integrating established power structures. According to one representative survey, at no point prior to the 1960s did women hold more than 2.4 percent of key federal offices. The only governmental level at which female candidates attained substantial representation was local library and school boards.[4]

Data concerning educational progress are mixed also, but are not, on the whole, encouraging. The percentage of women attending college and receiving advanced degrees peaked in 1920 and then fell for several decades. Surveys generally reflected that few female college graduates had long-term vocational aspirations, and the rate of women's entry into careers actually declined after enfranchisement. Although women made some gains in business and managerial occupations, their representation in the professions declined in the postsuffrage decades. As late as 1960 only 7 percent of the nation's doctors and less than 5 percent of its lawyers, scientists, architects, and engineers were female. The underrepresentation of women of color was even more dramatic.[5]

Changes in women's general economic circumstances reflect a more varied picture and require a complex analysis of shifting labor-force patterns. Although census data remain an imperfect index of women's employment, given the vast amounts of unpaid domestic labor and of undercounted part-time workers, the figures reported do suggest a significant cultural trend. The percentage of women in the paid labor force rose from approximately 23 percent in 1920 to 29 percent in 1940, and peaked temporarily at 38 percent during World War II. After a dip during the postwar baby boom, the rate climbed back to 37 percent in 1960. The growth of female-dominated occupations (particularly clerical, sales, and service work), coupled with increased life expectancies, declining birth rates, and rising expectations about living standards propelled larger percentages of women into the work force for longer periods. Ironically, certain factors contributing to women's subordinate status ultimately helped to undermine it. Many employers began to prefer women over men for some low-level positions. Female employees appeared cheaper, more quiescent, and less likely to unionize than their male counterparts.

The very characteristics that worked against job parity between the sexes also opened greater opportunities for female labor-force participation. And that participation eventually helped lay the foundation for a more egalitarian social order.[6]

Throughout the first half of the twentieth century, however, most women viewed their paid employment as intermittent and supplemental. Such perceptions were especially pronounced during the Depression. Public-opinion surveys during the 1930s disclosed that between three-quarters and four-fifths of respondents disapproved of working wives, who were variously denounced as "thieving parasites" and "pin-money employees." According to George Gallup, this was an issue on which Americans were "about as solidly united as on any subject imaginable including sin and hay fever." In response, state, local, and federal legislators enacted a variety of restrictions on wives' employment opportunities.[7]

Discrimination against women of color was even more pervasive. During the first part of the century, between 70 and 90 perecent of all black female workers were engaged in poorly paid agricultural and domestic service occupations that remained exempt from minimum wage and Social Security requirements. Hardships were particularly severe during the Depression, and governmental responses were grossly inadequate. Indeed, National Recovery Codes encouraged segregation, since some employers felt that the minimum wages required under the Codes were "too much money for Negroes." Native Americans, Mexicans, and Asian immigrants often faced similar discrimination, and the quarantine of Japanese Americans during World War II had devastating economic consequences for its victims. Throughout the first part of the century, minority women remained in the most menial, hazardous, and low-paid occupations, and the small percentage in professional or white-collar jobs were paid considerably less than whites of both sexes.[8]

Prior to World War II a woman's economic status tended to be inversely correlated with the amount of paid or domestic labor she performed. Few of her vocational opportunities were "nearly as lucrative as marrige," and the more lucrative the marriage, the less likely she was to enter the work force or perform household tasks unassisted. The war, however, marked a significant turning point in women's and minorities' economic progress. The demand for labor, coupled with an executive order forbidding racial discrimination in hiring by defense industries, helped erode formal barriers to employment. The national mobilization brought well over six million women into the work force, many in jobs formerly occupied by men.[9]

After the war, however, discriminatory policies and cultural biases returned to curtail employment opportunities. Fewer than a fifth of Americans surveyed in the late 1940s expressed unqualified approval of a wife's working if her husband was capable of supporting her. These attitudes, together with veterans' preferences, protective labor restrictions, rising birth rates, suburban living patterns, and the absence of childcare, helped oust women from the labor force or relegate them to traditionally female, low-paid occupations.[10]

Many of those ousted, however, gradually wedged themselves back into the labor force during the 1950s and 1960s. Former "wenches with wrenches" returned to take new clerical and service positions. But they encountered substantial discrimination in hiring, salaries, and promotion. Throughout the first half of the century, official job segregation and salary differentials were common; women's earnings remained between one-half to two-thirds of men's. Even during the war years, despite wage and price controls, equal pay mandates, and the decline in male competitors, this disparity in earnings persisted and helped reinforce other gender inequalities.[11]

Sameness and Difference

Feminists' difficulties in challenging such gender subordination can be attributed in part to ambivalence about gender roles. There was no consensus within the movement on the extent to which women were different from men and required different treatment. Nor was there agreement on the extent to which women faced common problems requiring common action.

Without a unifying issue such as suffrage, these tensions became quickly apparent. In some circles, the individualistic premises of liberal ideology worked against a feminist conception of shared identity. During the twenties, a group of largely left-activist women founded a "post-feminist" journal called *Judy,* which announced: "We're interested in people now—not in men and women." Moral, social, economic, and political standards "should not have anything to do with sex." Similarly, the flapper image that dominated the 1920s reinforced a view of liberation that stressed personal self-assertion rather than common purposes. More women came to "embrace the [liberal] principle of the women's movement—individualism," and the result ironically worked against participation in the movement itself. As in the 1980s, talk of emancipation and entitlements appeared to many younger women as "stale stuff," a preoccupation of unfeminine "frumps in non-descript tweeds," who "antagonized men with their constant clamor about maiden names, equal rights, [and] women's place in the world."[12]

To many older feminist "frumps," this younger generation had equally little to commend it. As Jane Addams noted, the "modern" woman's "preoccupation with personal freedom and self-development" helped displace concerns for equal justice. That preoccupation with individual achievement also diverted attention from the social forces that constrained it.[13]

Not only was the early feminist leadership unable to generate a unifying sense of women's commonality with each other, it provided no coherent account of their differences from men. The "separate-spheres" ideology that suffragists alternatively denounced and embraced proved even more divisive in the postsuffrage decades. While the most liberal constituencies, such as the National Woman's Party membership and the founders of *Judy,* tended to renounce gender differences, the more common approach was to affirm their value. Except during the Flapper era and war years, much of the writing for and about women celebrated femininity. Its tones echoed both the cult of domesticity, which had reigned a century earlier, and the validation of women's "different voice," which emerged several decades later.

Part of the problem, as Nancy Cott has argued, is that feminists during this period had to "shadow box with two opposing yet coexistent caricatures"; they were denounced both for "harping on definition by sex and . . . [with] dangerously (although futilely) trying to obliterate sex-based distinctions." The social, political, and economic forces noted earlier contributed to antifeminist sentiments. For much of the pre- and post-World War II era, warnings against careerist "female celibates" and "a-maternal feminism" emerged from various directions. Exposure to masculine education and pursuits was an invitation to "coarsened sensibilities," sexual frigidity, and race suicide. Ironically enough, it was often professional women who deplored women professionals. Labor Secretary Frances Perkins, for example, never "recommen[ded] a public career for women," because she believed that the "happiest place for most women [was] in the home."[14]

The popular media offered endless variations on that same theme. Women were barraged by information about finding a husband and feathering his nest. During the postwar period this affirmation of domesticity reached new heights. Feature articles avoided "ideas or broad issues of the day" and focused their attention instead on practical matters such as how to create a "Poet's Kitchen," or have a baby in an atom bomb shelter. As the title of a 1956 *New York Times* article on Radcliffe doctorates ominously warned, "Even a Ph.D. can't escape the kitchen."[15]

Increasing numbers of colleges also began offering courses in home economics in response to criticism that their female students received poor preparation for family duties. When surveys indicated that many graduates experienced discontinuities between the concerns dominating their academic experience and the domestic tasks occupying their later lives, the response of most administrators was to press for changes in women's education rather than women's roles. In 1950, for example, Lynn White, president of Mills College, urged women's institutions to shake off their subservience to masculine career-centered values and create a distinctively feminine program. Why not courses in basketry, garden design, and "the theory and preparation of . . . a well-marinated shish kebab" rather than "post-Kantian philosophy"? Even Radcliffe's president urged that educational objectives shift away from preparation for male vocational patterns that would simply "equip and encourage women to compete with men."[16]

Except during World War II, women who rejected their maternal missions were often dismissed as neurotic and irresponsible. Why should a normal woman want "to run a silly old steel corporation when [she could] influence the emotional, intellectual, and artistic life of a nation?" Psychiatrists and medical experts writing for the popular press during the 1950s provided new insights into feminist neurosis. With Freudian insight, it became abundantly clear that the quest for women's rights by feminists such as Mary Wollstonecraft was in reality a desire for male castration, the product of early childhood rejection and sibling rivalry. ERA supporters risked caricature as "cranks, queers, and old maids," and the association of feminism with lesbianism inhibited organization around women's issues. Challenges to established gender roles allegedly threatened the "normal" adjustment not only of women but also of their children. According to prominent experts such as Dr. Benjamin Spock, maternal careers were incompatible with child-rearing responsibilities.[17]

Most married women heeded such advice. Although their labor-force participation steadily increased, in 1940 less than a fifth and in 1960 less than a third of all wives had any paid employment. Far fewer held full-time positions. For most homemakers, domestic tasks expanded to fill the time available. Despite the introduction of numerous labor-saving conveniences such as washing machines and processed foods, the time spent on housework by nonemployed wives actually increased between 1924 and 1966.[18]

Not until the early 1960s did this refurbished cult of domesticity provoke substantial feminist challenge. And not until almost two decades later did any significant feminist constituency begin to articulate some of the concerns on which antifeminist rhetoric of the 1950s turned. Indeed, Lynn White's view—that women would save themselves from a sense of inferiority "only by recognizing and insisting on the importance of [their] differences"—is a perception that many contemporary feminists share, although they draw quite different conclusions about its implications.[19]

Equal Rights, Protective Policies, and Feminist Priorities

One dimension of the sameness-difference dispute that assumed particular importance during the postsuffrage period involved a proposed constitutional equal-rights amendment. After obtaining the ballot, the National Women's Party turned its attention to another constitutional campaign: passage of an amendment providing that "equality of rights under the law shall not be denied or abridged by the United States or any state on account of sex." Supporters proposed some version of that amendment in every congressional term between 1923 and 1972. Yet conceived as a measure to unite women, it served largely to divide them. Controversies centered primarily on the amendment's effects on protective labor legislation, but they had deeper ideological roots. In effect, the issue was whether women would gain more by recognition of their equal entitlements or their different needs, and whether emphasis on securing formal rights was adequately responsive to social realities.

In part, dispute centered on the focus of the feminist agenda. Left activists such as lawyer Crystal Eastman predicted that "nobody who has a thread of modern feminism [would] care a rap" for the National Women's Party if it remained wedded to the "old fashioned aim to remove formal disabilities." Minority and lower-class women found it difficult to support an organization that made little effort to include them and gave no priority to problems of racism, poverty, education, and voting rights. Despite such critiques, the NWP, mainstay of the women's rights movement, remained relatively unconcerned with the most pressing issues for those with the most pressing needs. Nor did the Party develop any coherent position on many matters that structured women's daily lives, such as marriage, divorce, birth control, occupational segregation, domestic violence, health, and childcare.[20]

While leftist feminists criticized the NWP's agenda as too narrow, more moderate constituencies attacked it as too sweeping. The immediate focus of the controversy was the ERA and protective labor legislation, but certain underlying issues provoked continuing dispute. The acrimony resulting from this conflict further contributed to the fragmentation of feminism during the postsuffrage decades. Worse still, the controversies over rights deflected attention from controversies over power and the broader societal forces that perpetuated women's subordinate status. Organizations such as the Women's Trade Union League spent so much of their budget battling threats to gender-based protective statutes that few resources remained for union-organizing among female workers. As in some contemporary contexts, women too often ended up fighting each other over the value of protective legislation rather than uniting to challenge the conditions that made protection so valuable.[21]

The controversy originated during the late nineteenth century, as state legislatures began passing a series of regulations governing maximum hours, minimum wages, and working conditions. A major setback to such efforts occurred in 1905, when the Supreme Court's *Lochner* decision struck down a sex-neutral maximum-hour law for bakery workers as an unreasonable restriction on freedom to contract. Three years later, however, in *Muller v. Oregon,* the Court upheld hourly restrictions for female laundry workers; it distinguished *Lochner* on the ground that women's special vulnerabilities justified special protection. This pairing of precedents laid the foundations for a wave of gender-specific protective statutes and an enduring feminist dispute.[22]

Although many women's rights advocates actively lobbied for such statutes, most activists were too preoccupied with suffrage at the time *Muller* was decided to consider adequately the implications of sex-based regulation. Indeed, the *Muller* opinion received surprisingly little public attention. No account of the case appeared in the *New York Times* on the day following the decision. To the editors of the *Times,* an issue of apparently greater significance to women was the scene at Mrs. Waldorf Astoria's charity ball, when one of the guests draped a boa constrictor over her shoulder.[23]

By the early 1920s the prevalence and consequences of gender-based labor regulations attracted greater attention. The liberal rights-oriented wing of the women's movement, particularly NWP members who supported a constitutional amendment, became convinced that neither the rationale nor the result of statutory protections served women's long-term interest. As long as female workers appeared different, dependent, and in need of special solicitude, they could never achieve the equal treatment as individuals that liberal principles demanded. In addition, sex-based regulation, by making women employees more expensive than men, could too readily become "a polite euphemism for covert discrimination." Thus, ERA proponents sought not "to wipe out protective legislation" but rather to "secure its extension to both sexes and insure that no handicap is placed on women."[24]

Yet this approach often ignored the political obstacles to obtaining adequate gender-neutral statutes, as well as other potential costs of undermining preferential legislation. *Equal Rights,* the NWP's journal, blithely concluded one editorial with the observation that, however the courts might interpret a constitutional amendment, "we can rest serene on our reliance on the principle of Equal Rights for men and women and not worry as to the details of how it will work out. The establishing of a righteous principle will certainly bring good results."[25]

Other feminists, particularly those who had struggled to obtain protective legislation, were less sanguine about the "details." Mary Anderson, head of the newly created Women's Bureau, Florence Kelly of the National Consumer League, and activists in trade unions and the League of Women Voters charged that NWP leaders were ignorant of, or indifferent to, the enormous cost of eliminating protective statutes. To ERA opponents the goal was not equality in form but equality in fact. "True equality" was obtainable only through measures that took into account the "actual biological, social, and occupational differences between men and women." In general, female workers had greater domestic burdens and less bargaining leverage than their male colleagues. By ignoring these disparities, the liberal women's rights agenda appeared to embrace a "laissez-faire individualism" that lacked "humanism." According to these protective-labor advocates, the women's movement should abandon campaigns for a sweeping constitutional mandate and seek specifically tailored measures challenging "invidious" but not "benign" discrimination.[26]

If ERA sponsors seemed inattentive to the difficulties of obtaining gender-neutral protective statutes, ERA opponents seemed equally insensitive to the difficulties of securing piecemeal antidiscrimination initiatives. Prevailing legal codes were riddled with provisions disadvantaging women, and the process of individual challenges seemed both futile and unending. In 1925 the NWP prepared 125 statutory reform bills, of which 39 were introduced and only 9 enacted. Equal difficulties surrounded efforts to aid women who were "protected" out of higher skilled and better paying employment.[27]

The desirability of sex-based labor legislation depended on a complicated series of tradeoffs involving health, income, family responsibilities, and opportunities for advancement, which affected women differently depending on their particular circumstances. The complexity of these tradeoffs and the ideological premises on which they turned were seldom fully explored by either wing of the feminist community.

This lack of close contextual analysis had both political and legal costs. On a political level, the protective-labor controversy demanded energies that, if mobilized for other causes, might have reduced the need for protection. This is not to understate the broader economic and ideological forces working against a united front. Nor is it to overlook the contexts in which women's groups were able to unite around feminist objectives. A number of coalitions on federal, state, and local levels lobbied for expansion of employment, contractual, and citizenship rights. This activism not only helped secure some significant legislative victories and political appointments, but also created networks and laid foundations for an expanded feminist movement in the 1960s.

Yet throughout this period, the women's rights agenda remained limited in scope and class-biased in orientation. Its premises and priorities were unable to enlist support from those women most in need of assistance. By focusing so single-mindedly on the goal of formal equality, conceived ever more abstractly, early ERA proponents lost sight of the method most likely to achieve that goal: a broad-based movement that could reach diverse grassroot constituencies and speak to their most pressing needs.

There were also legal as well as political costs in the way the ERA–protective-labor dispute polarized. Feminists failed to provide informed advocacy in judicial and legislative forums and to focus on the full implications of gender-based preferential treatment. Such advocacy was not forthcoming from other sources. The result was a line of decisionmaking that could neither protect nor promote women's long-term interests.

Separate Spheres and Legal Thought

Protective-Labor Legislation

One crucial gender-related issue that confronted courts during the first part of the twentieth century involved protective-labor statutes. This issue implicated various concerns apart from sex discrimination. The economic conservatism, social Darwinism, and judicial activism that characterized this line of decisionmaking have been the subject of extensive other commentary that need not be reviewed here. Rather, the following discussion focuses on the gender dimensions of legal ideology during this period, for the ways in which judges and legislators alternately ignored or exacerbated gender differences in employment contexts left an enduring legacy.[28]

The central difficulty lay in the inability of decisionmakers to recognize *both* that working women faced special disadvantages and that sex-based protections often perpetuated those disadvantages. Gender-specific regulations did curb some of the exploitative conditions to which female employees were especially vulnerable. But the price was substantial. Sex-linked statutes made it more expensive to hire women and thus limited their entry into occupations desirable to male competitors. The result was to lock female workers into crowded, sex-segregated employment and further depress their bargaining power. In both rationale and result, sex-based legislation reinforced the stereotypes that impeded women's advancement in commercial spheres and discouraged men's assumption of responsibilities in domestic spheres.

Maximum-Hour Regulation. Most early protective-labor cases involved legislative efforts to curtail the eleven-to-fourteen-hour days and night-shift requirements that were common for working women during the late nineteenth and early twentieth centuries. Despite claims that such employment was a means of discouraging "idleness and its inseparable attendants, vice and guilt," between 1870 and 1910 many states began passing restrictive statutes. Legal challenges to such legislation met with varying responses, but evidenced little understanding of the complexity of women's underlying interests.[29]

Prior to the *Muller* decision some state courts had struck down protective statutes as an unreasonable restraint on women's liberty, as guaranteed by the due process clause of the Fourteenth Amendment. Although this approach paralleled the Supreme Court's *Lochner* decision, its application to women was notable on several grounds. For example, in 1895, the Illinois Supreme Court concluded that maximum-hour laws infringed women's "inalienable" and "natural right to gain a livelihood," a right that the same court had rejected two decades earlier in affirming Myra Bradwell's exclusion from the bar. With similar reasoning, the New York Court of Appeals in 1907 struck down prohibitions on female night work. "Men and women," the court announced, "now stand alike in their constitutional rights. There is no warrant for making any discrimination between them with respect to the liberty of personal contract." Such egalitarian rhetoric was quite selective. Woman's ostensibly equal constitutional standing did not entitle her to a host of other rights, most notably enfranchisement.[30]

Moreover, the concept of contractual equality that these decisions exalted bore little relation to industrial realities. Neither male nor female workers were able to bargain on equal footing with most employers. Nor did men and women "stand alike" in workplace settings. In general, female workers were more vulnerable to exploitation than their male counterparts. They were younger, less experienced, and less likely to be unionized or to be permanent employees with a substantial stake in collective organizaion. Oppressive working conditions encouraged job turnover, which in turn impeded unionization and minimized opportunities for benefits associated with seniority.[31]

These inequalities reflected not only female workforce patterns but also male attitudes. Sex-based discrimination by employers and educational institutions restricted women's occupational choices and crowded them into the least desirable working environments. Prominent labor leaders typically perceived women workers more as competitors than colleagues, and often excluded them from union membership or declined to help organize predominantly female occupations.[32]

Judicial and public attitudes during the early twentieth century were often similarly unreceptive. For example, during the first large-scale women's strike, a walkout by garment workers in 1909–10, the participants received stiff sanctions and lengthy lectures on their natural destiny. Curiously enough, the divine will that once had relegated aspiring female workers such as Myra Bradwell and her contemporaries to the domestic sphere now dictated their departure from it. In view of one magistrate, garment employees were "on strike against God and Nature, whose firm law is that man shall earn his bread . . . [by] the sweat of his brow." Despite the use of the generic, the court appeared particularly affronted by woman's audacity. Apprised of this judicial wisdom, George Bernard Shaw cabled back: "Delightful. Medieval America always in intimate personal confidence of the Almighty." On the whole, however, commentators sympathized with the magistrate; many women trade unionists faced ridicule as "unsexed female incendiaries." Given these social and judicial constraints, women's efforts at collective organization met with little success. Data from the 1920s indicate that female employees comprised over 20 percent of the labor force, but only 8 percent of the unionized workers.[33]

Not only were women at a competitive disadvantage in the paid labor force, they also bore special burdens in the unpaid one. Household obligations, when coupled with extended working days, could impose crushing burdens. For women with family responsibilities, a typical day began at 5:30 A.M., preparing breakfast, and ended with cleaning, mending, and washing well after 10:00 P.M. This double day discouraged married women from working and created enormous hardship for those who had no choice.[34]

Yet while the decisions exalting woman's freedom to contract were unsatisfying in their formalism, those restricting her liberty were equally disturbing in their paternalism. Exaggerated deference to contractual rights ignored contractual realities; exaggerated assumptions about gender differences helped perpetuate gender disadvantages. Such assumptions received constitutional moorings in 1908 in *Muller v. Oregon.* The case was significant not only for its result but also for its reasoning, and for the litigation strategy that it inaugurated. Louis Brandeis and co-counsel Josephine Goldmark of the National Consumer League defended Oregon's ten-hour legislation with the first of what became known as "Brandeis briefs," which detailed social and economic conditions underlying the legal dispute. Brandeis' involvement came about somewhat by chance, and it was not an altogether happy development. The League had initially requested former ABA president Joseph Choate to defend the Oregon statute. Choate declined on the ground that he "could see no reason why a great husky Irish woman should not work in a laundry more than ten hours a day, if her employer wished her to do so."[35]

Brandeis and Goldmark took a more liberal view, but their argument hinged on an exaggerated and essentialist view of gender difference. That strategy was not the only alternative available. Since one of the crucial members of the *Lochner* majority had retired by the time *Muller* was argued, counsel might have pressed for reexamination of that precedent. Instead, they offered a rationale for distinguishing it. Their focus was on the effect that overwork might have on women's reproductive capacities, domestic obligations, and temptations to indulge alcoholic or other "degenerate" inclinations. What escaped notice was that overwork might also prevent male employees from assuming family responsibilities or expose them to comparable temptations.[36]

It also escaped the attention of the Supreme Court, which sustained the Oregon statute. Writing for the *Muller* majority, Justice Brewer embraced a "maternal mission" ideology only one step removed from that in *Bradwell* a half-century earlier. History disclosed that "woman has always been dependent on man," and biology insured that she always would be: "That woman's physical structure and the performance of maternal functions place her at a disadvantage in the struggle for subsistence is obvious. This is especially true when the burdens of motherhood are upon her . . . The physical well-being of women becomes an object of public interest and care in order to preserve the strength and vigor of the race."[37]

Although between 70 and 80 percent of the female workforce was single, the maternal-mission ideology dominated protective-labor decisions for the next half-century. It was "known to all men," the Illinois Supreme Court confidently announced in 1910, that male employees could work ten-hour days without injury, but that potential mothers of the race could not. Curiously oblivious to such universal male knowledge were the legislators who declined to extend statutory protection to some of the most grueling occupations, including domestic service and agricultural labor, as well as the husbands who declined to share the major household chores that prolonged their wives' working days. As one critic of the *Muller* decision noted, women routinely labored long hours at physically demanding tasks without pay and without objection; "the pay [was] the new feature."[38]

What was "known to all men" was often uninformed by any inquiry into what was desired by most women. As far as courts and counsel were concerned, female employees' preferences generally were beside the point. If some women might prefer long hours to extreme poverty or to exclusion from all occupations requiring overtime or night shifts, that preference was generally overlooked. Affidavits from female employees should be discounted, Brandeis assured one state court, because "[i]gnorant women [could] scarcely be expected to realize the dangers not only to their own health but to that of the next generation from such inhuman [night work]." Whatever the preferences of women workers, the state had a valid interest in safeguarding them from their own "indifference, error . . . recklessness" or "cupidity."[39]

In fact, that characterization bore little resemblance to the concerns of working women, most of whom reportedly supported protective labor legislation. For the majority of those women, crowded into predominantly female occupations, maximum-hour laws (when enforced) were a welcome restraint on exploitative conditions. In these industries most employers adjusted to the statutory scheme without substantially reducing take-home pay or finding cheaper male replacements for female workers.[40]

But the improvements that resulted from maximum-hour restrictions should not be overstated. Enforcement resources and sanctions were grossly inadequate, and exemptions for some of the most oppressive occupations were common. The protection that did result came at substantial cost. Male unions were often successful in obtaining gender-specific statutes that ousted female competitors from the most desirable positions. Some evidence also suggests that sex-based legislation significantly increased unemployment among the most marginal female workers, particularly racial and ethnic minorities, and frequently forced them to moonlight at second jobs without overtime pay. For women who had voluntarily chosen evening shifts in order to care for children or invalid relatives during the day, bans on night work prevented the domestic caretaking that the statutory schemes were designed to foster. By visiting the burden of excessive hours or night shifts solely on men, gender-specific legislation also discouraged husbands' assumption of family obligations.[41]

Moreover, as progressives increasingly realized, a ceiling on hours without a floor for wages left many women without adequate protection. In the aftermath of *Muller,* support for minimum-wage requirements intensified.

Minimum Wages. Throughout the nineteenth and early twentieth centuries, the vast majority of working women failed to obtain either wage parity with men or what economists then termed a living wage—the rough equivalent of what would now provide for subsistence just above the poverty line. Female employees generally received between one-third and two-thirds of prevailing male salaries for the same work, and black women averaged one-third to one-half of white women's pay. In 1914, about the time when state legislatures began passing minimum-wage laws, an estimated one-quarter of working women made a living wage. Legislative efforts to improve the situation met with mixed judicial responses. As with maximum hours, the decisions on both sides of the minimum-wage issue were unresponsive to the complexity of interests at stake.[42]

In cases concerning sex-based wage regulation, lower courts generally applied the logic of *Muller* to protect women from substandard pay scales that drove female workers into the "clutch of sin" or the health hazards of overwork. But in 1921 the Supreme Court struck a blow for what contemporary critics termed the "inalienable right of women to starve." The case was *Adkins v. Children's Hospital,* which involved a challenge to the District of Columbia's minimum-wage law. To a majority of Justices, wage restrictions appeared but "one step" from socialism. Such regulation also seemed inconsistent with modern "legislation, thought, and usage," which had emancipated woman from "the old doctrine that she must be given special protection or be subject to special restraint in her contractual and civil relationships."[43]

Such language was not readily reconcilable with precedents such as

Muller or a host of other legal restraints in employment and family law. And however egalitarian in rhetoric, the majority's decision was less so in results. In some jurisdictions, women's wages fell an estimated one-third to one-half after the decision, and maximum-hour laws restricted workers' ability to make up the difference.[44]

Subsequent efforts to reduce such hardships proved equally problematic. In 1937, just after President Roosevelt announced plans to counter the Supreme Court's conservatism by enlarging its membership, *Adkins* was overruled. In *West Coast Hotel Co. v. Parrish,* a narrowly divided Court resurrected the logic of *Muller* to protect women, whose bargaining power was "relatively weak," and whose wage scales reflected that vulnerability. Missing from the majority's opinion, however, was any attention to the possibility that gender-specific wage regulations in some contexts might amplify rather than ameliorate women's workplace inequalities. Although comprehensive data are lacking, some evidence suggests that such regulation substantially increased female unemployment in certain jurisdictions. Much of the "protection" that resulted was also considerably less than what proponents expected. Enforcement was grossly inadequate, and salary levels were rarely sufficient to provide necessities for a single woman, let alone one with dependents.[45]

Still, tangible benefits often did flow from minimum-wage requirements. For the most exploited women workers, particularly those in female-dominated occupations, even minor increases in take-home pay made an appreciable difference in the quality of life. But where male competitors were available, sex-linked protections exacerbated the gender disadvantages they were meant to address.

The point is not, however, that the outcomes in *Muller, West Coast Hotel,* or their state analogues were indefensible. Courts in those cases lacked systematic evidence as to the effects of protective-labor legislation for women. In circumstances involving uncertain economic tradeoffs, judges may justifiably be wary about substituting their views for those of more politically accountable branches. Yet it is also appropriate in such circumstances for the bench and bar to seek adequate information and to focus attention on the full costs and benefits involved. Moreover, in the protective-labor context, the costs at issue were in large part attributable to courts' initial hostility toward gender-neutral regulations, regulations that could have reduced workplace exploitation without adverse competitive consequences for women.

Ultimately, the Supreme Court did reverse its position. In 1917 it upheld maximum-hour laws for male workers. Two decades later the Court sustained the Fair Labor Standards Act, which prescribed minimum wages and overtime pay for both men and women in specified occupations. But although the constitutional rationale for sex-based wage and hour laws disappeared, the laws did not. In 1960, 39 of 42 state statutes restricting hours were applicable only to women, and 19 states had gender-specific night-work limitations. About half the states also had minimum-wage laws, only four of which were equally applicable to men. This approach to protective-labor decisionmaking was problematic in reasoning as well as result. Judicial paternalism spilled over into a variety of contexts in which women's need for protection was far less apparent.[46]

Occupational Exclusions

The other major type of protective-labor cases confronting the courts during the first half of the twentieth century involved women's exclusion from various occupations. Almost without exception, courts sustained such exclusions. Unlike racial classifications, which triggered "strict scrutiny" and virtually never survived it, sex-based exclusions had only to satisfy minimum standards of rationality. Under traditional difference-oriented approaches to gender discrimination, almost any differential treatment appeared "rational." Women were, after all, different. The same reasoning that had once legitimated woman's protection from the "forensic strife" of legal careers continued to oust her from various other occupations of equal apparent danger.[47]

During the late nineteenth century, legislatures began passing an increasing volume of exclusionary laws, and by the mid-twentieth century, women in half the states were banned from work ranging from shining shoes to legislative service. The most common restraints involved occupations presenting threats to health or morals, and the factual predicate for both was dubious. Where safety was at issue, the concerns should have encompased both sexes. Yet in some instances gender restrictions may have impeded safety improvements, since it was cheaper to ban women than to install protections for all employees. Where gender exclusions ostensibly served moral objectives, the consequence generally was to protect male paychecks rather than female virtue.[48]

Bans on women in liquor establishments are a case in point. Although women had often run taverns without apparent incident in colonial and frontier societies, many early-twentieth-century legislatures were unwilling to permit women's presence in locations where the "worst passions [were] aroused." Such legislation reflected the dual stereotypes common in Anglo-American culture. From one perspective, woman appeared as a pure and delicate creature who must be shielded from sordid influences; alternatively, she figured as a brazen seductress who threatened innocent males. In effect, these liquor ordinances cast every female as either "Eve or Little Eva and either way she los[t]." Worse still, she lost without any serious constitutional inquiry. Typically, courts deferred to legislators' authority over liquor regulation without pausing to consider whether their objectives could be more narrowly achieved. If elected officials chose not to prohibit immoral conduct, but simply ascribed it to one sex, that was their prerogative.[49]

The most disquieting performance in any of these cases was the Supreme Court's decision in *Goesaert v. Cleary.* At issue was a 1945 Michigan statute that prohibited women from bartending unless they were the wives or daughters of male bar owners. Other jurisdictions had enacted comparable legislation around the same period, usually after lobbying efforts by bartenders' associations that excluded women and included returning war veterans ill-disposed toward female competitors. At trial in *Goesaert,* the plaintiffs submitted extensive and uncontested proof that female employees in bars had experienced no significant safety risks; that their presence was a "civilizing" influence on patrons; and that the Michigan statute worked a substantial and arbitrary hardship on women who could serve drinks as low-paid cocktail waitresses, but could not mix drinks as higher-paid bartenders unless related to a male bar owner.[50]

None of this evidence appeared relevant to a majority of Justices. Rather, the Court summarily dismissed due process and equal protection claims with the observation that they presented one of those rare instances where "to state a question is in effect to answer it." After all, the Constitution did not require legislators to act from the "latest sociological insight" or "shifting social standards." Since the Court could not cross-examine these elected officials as to motive, it refused even to entertain the "suggestion that the real impulse for the statute was an unchivalrous desire of male bartenders to . . . monopolize the calling."[51]

Other judges proved equally deferential even where, as one court acknowledged, a "selfish" motive "[stood] out in the statute like a sore thumb." In 1956, the Oregon Supreme Court upheld women's exclusion from wrestling with the observation that they had already "invaded practically every activity formerly considered suitable and appropriate for [man] only . . . [and] . . . in many instances had outdone him. In these circumstances, is it any wonder that the legislative assembly . . . [sought] to halt this ever increasing feminine encroachment upon what for ages had been considered strictly as manly arts and privileges?"

Once again, to state the question was to answer it, and the abdication of judicial oversight became complete. The court assumed the worst possible legislative motive and added its blessing. Under this approach, the entire inquiry into legislative intent was largely beside the point since any intent would do.[52]

Although unusual in its unregenerate sexism, this kind of opinion cannot be dismissed as an engaging eccentricity. As a practical matter, it is unlikely that women who brought or considered bringing such suits found the court's tongue-in-cheek rhetoric amusing. And on a theoretical level, the holding was a logical extension of the separate-spheres ideology that characterized other judicial decisions of the period.

Roles and Rules

Comparable deference to legislative mandates was apparent in most other gender-discrimination contexts, such as those involving education, welfare, jury qualifications, family responsibilities, criminal conduct, and licensing fees. As in preceding decades, courts often leapt from the fact of gender difference to the appropriateness of differential treatment without any intermediate premises. The leading example of this approach in the Supreme Court involved a licensing-fee statute that provided exemptions for women but not men in laundry establishments with less than two employees. Writing for the majority in *Quong Wing v. Kirkendall*, Justice Holmes declined even to hypothesize a plausible justification for the exemption. Rather, he dismissed plaintiff's challenge with the observation that discrimination on the basis of sex was "not without precedent" in family and protective-labor laws. Such an approach was difficult to square with one of Holmes's most celebrated observations, that "it is revolting to have no better reason for a rule of law than that so it was laid down in the time of Henry IV." And despite his equally celebrated maxim that "abstract propositions do not decide concrete cases," Holmes rested his analysis in *Quong Wing* with the unelaborated declaration that the "Fourteenth Amendment does not interfere [with state regulation] by creating a fictitious equality where there are real differences."[53]

Following Holmes's example, a 1915 Utah court sustained a road poll tax imposed on men only with the laconic observation that sex-based classifications had "always been made and enforced from time immemorial," and unless expressly prohibited by the Constitution were "natural and proper . . . to make." In a similar vein, the United States Supreme Court subsequently sustained Georgia's one-dollar poll-tax exemption for women on the theory that the "special burden necessarily borne by them for the preservation of the race" somehow justified the state's largesse. Somewhat inconsistently, the Court also noted tht the ultimate beneficiaries of the legislative preference were not necessarily those who bore the "special burdens." Rather, since "the laws of Georgia declare[d] the husband to be the head of the family," subjecting his wife to the tax would add to his burden.[54]

Under this form of analysis, virtually any sex-based classification could pass muster. No rational linkage between gender differences and differential treatment was required. The arbitrariness of this approach was apparent not just in economic regulation but also in criminal statutes, where the argument for close constitutional scrutiny has traditionally been strongest. For example, in upholding gender classifications in sentencing laws, some state courts echoed the biology-as-destiny views popularized by mental-health experts. According to the Kansas Supreme Court, "In structure and function human beings are still as they were in the beginning. 'Male and female He created them.' It is a patent and deep-lying fact that these fundamental anatomical and physiological differences affect the whole psychic organization. They create the differences in personality between men and women, and personality is the predominating factor in delinquent careers." Similarly, the Massachusetts Supreme Court found it "too plain for discussion" that sex-based differences justified different sentences. Yet it was rather less plain which way the differences cut. To some decisionmakers, women's greater amenability to custodial regulation or lesser ability to withstand punishment justified shorter sentences. Conversely, other legislative and judicial authorities were convinced that unspecified gender differences dictated longer periods of penal supervision for women.[55]

Double standards also were apparent in substantive criminal provisions. In some states, only women were punishable for "lascivious carriage" or for "manifesting the danger of falling into habits of vice," while only men were liable for "impugning the chastity of the opposite sex." Several jurisdictions recognized a complete defense to murder or manslaughter for men but not women who stumbled on their spouses having sexual intercourse with someone else. Prostitution laws generally penalized only women, and even facially neutral statutes were rarely enforced against men.[56]

Welfare and family laws incorporated analogous double standards. Under the "man in the house" rule that prevailed in many states until the late 1960s, a female welfare recipient caught cohabiting with an "able bodied man" could lose all aid to her dependent children, irrespective of whether or not her partner provided or was obligated to provide an alternative means of support. Cohabitation was somewhat loosely defined. Since it could consist of infrequent sexual relations, "night raids" by welfare investigators were often a condition of state assistance.[57]

A substantial number of states also permitted husbands but not wives to obtain a divorce based on their spouses' unchaste character before marriage or on single acts of adultery after marriage. A mother's "extramarital sex experimentation" could be sufficient grounds for denying her alimony or child custody. Even those courts willing to overlook such moral lapses often did so on the basis of rigid stereotypes about parental roles. An adulteress might be "unfit for heaven," but she was still more fit for child-rearing than a divorced father.[58]

As the last example suggests, some stereotypical assumptions favored women in family law. Throughout the early twentieth century, wives were entitled to alimony, widows' benefits, dower interests in one-third or one-half of their husband's estates, and presumptions favoring them as custodial parents. In many cases, however, the statutory preferences were insubstantial or unenforceable. For example, widows' benefits in some states consisted of trivial tax exemptions or rights to clothing and cooking utensils. Alimony was infrequently granted, child support woefully inadequate, and fewer than half of the divorced women who obtained financial awards collected them regularly.[59]

Although the husband typically had exclusive or primary support obligations, his duties were not subject to review in the context of ongoing marriages, even in cases of severe hardship to the wife. The extent of this laissez-faire ideology was apparent in a 1954 Nebraska case. In *McGuire v. McGuire,* an eighty-year-old farmer with substantial assets had failed to provide his sixty-year-old wife with money for clothing, household necessities, indoor plumbing, or even an occasional movie ticket. In reversing the trial court's award of a modest monthly allowance to the wife, the Nebraska Supreme Court made clear that such judicial intrusiveness was impermissible: "As long as the home is maintained and the parties are living as husband and wife it may be said that the husband is legally supporting his wife and the purpose of the marriage relation is being carried out. Public policy requires such a holding."[60]

Such ostensible policy imperatives worked substantial hardships, particularly given the array of legal restrictions on married women's financial independence. Throughout the first half of the twentieth century a husband generally had exclusive power to manage joint marital property, and some states presumed him to be its sole owner. Other jurisdictions required judicial or spousal approval before married women could open their own businesses, and demanded extensive information concerning the would-be entrepreneur's "character, habits, education, and mental capacity." Men frequently received statutory preferences as guardians, trustees, executors, and administrators; not until 1970 did such gender distinctions receive serious judicial scrutiny.[61]

Similar patterns were apparent in one final area where feminist challenges were most persistent and most unsuccessful: jury service. Early common law had limited women's participation on juries to certain capital-punishment cases, in which a special female panel was convened to determine whether to execute a pregnant defendant before or after she gave birth. Even then, women's judgments were not necessarily controlling. In some instances all-male juries had authority to decide whether their female counterparts had reached the correct result. Abolishing gender discrimination in jury selection was one of feminists' earliest demands, and passage of the Nineteenth Amendment inspired a sustained litigation campaign for that objective. Since many states linked jury service to eligibility for voting, litigants often contended that enfranchisement necessarily qualified women as jurors. In addition, advocates invoked the familiar pairing of arguments based on sameness and difference. To the extent that women were like men, they should enjoy the same benefits and burdens of citizenship. To the extent that women were different, their distinctive "elevating and refining influence" would enhance the quality of justice available to all citizens.[62]

Such arguments met with mixed success. Typically, the issue arose as a question of statutory construction, and judges sometimes strained to find ways around the plain meaning of the legislation. One Massachusetts court, for example, reasoned that a provision allowing "any person qualified to vote" to sit as a juror excluded women because the Nineteenth Amendment had created a "new class of human beings" who somehow were not "persons." Other judges found history, rather than text, controlling. Women's initial exclusion from "the ancient mode of trial by jury" became a sufficient rationale for perpetuating that status.[63]

In justifying their statutory interpretations, judges often invoked the same policy considerations that had bolstered bans on women in the professions. The lack of suitable lavatory facilities was apparently an insurmountable obstacle, as was the absence of homemaker exemptions. The spectacle of "baby . . . in a fury" with "mama . . . on the jury" became a rationale for excluding all women, whatever their maternal status. Other judges were anxious to shield feminine sensibilities from the references to "loathsome" language, "indecent conduct," or "intimate sex relationships" that might emerge in trial proceedings. To accommodate such concerns, some states provided exemptions for women in cases involving crimes against chastity or morality, exemptions which occasionally persisted into the 1980s.[64]

Rarely did any of these early jury cases involve federal constitutional claims, perhaps because dicta in a nineteenth-century Supreme Court case involving race discrimination appeared to foreclose them. Not until the mid-twentieth century did the Court modify its position, by requiring federal courts to allow women jurors in states that permitted their participation. Yet as late as 1961, a majority of Justices were still willing to uphold state statutes that effectively excluded women from the jury rolls by exempting any female who did not specifically register a desire to serve.[65]

Hoyt v. Florida involved a challenge to one such statute by a woman convicted of the second-degree murder of her husband. Her defense was temporary insanity, which allegedly resulted from a "marital upheaval" involving the suspected infidelity of her husband and his refusal of reconciliation. In contesting the fairness of Hoyt's trial, her counsel introduced empirical research reflecting sex-based differences in male and female juror decisionmaking and suggested that women might have been more sympathetic in assessing the insanity defense. But the issue before the Court was not limited to whether the defendant could show prejudice from Florida's exclusion of women jurors. No such showing had been required in cases involving racial bias in jury selection procedures. As an ACLU *amicus* brief made clear, *Hoyt* involved not only defendants' rights but also women's status as citizens. Florida's counsel similarly perceived the role of women to be at issue. According to the state's brief, despite recent changes in gender roles, the basic feminine destiny remained unaltered and unalterable. "Ever since the dawn of time," child-rearing had remained the "prime responsibility of the matriarch." The "advent of 'T.V.' dinners" had not removed woman's domestic burdens, and those burdens should preempt civil obligations.[66]

The Supreme Court agreed. Writing for the majority, Justice Harlan observed that, even after her "enlightened emancipation," woman was "still regarded as the center of home and family life," and could appropriately be absolved from jury service. Rather than creating a system that exempted homemakers with particular hardships, the state was free to attribute those disabilities to all women. This holding, however, had an unusually limited life. Within a few years, some lower courts were reaching contrary conclusions, and in 1975 the Supreme Court effectively reversed its view at the request of a male defendant. Thus, *Hoyt* was significant less for its effect on jury classifications than for its articulation of prevailing legal ideology, for its assumptions about gender difference, and its tolerance of gender bias.[67]

Tolerance for legislative prejudice was not, of course, unique to cases involving gender. The activism of the *Lochner* era, in which courts invoked substantive due-process theories to strike down a vast range of progressive legislation, gave way to a period of judicial passivity. Many dubious classifications survived challenge under prevailing "rational basis" standards of review. What was distinctively disturbing about gender cases during this period was the judiciary's unwillingness to review such discrimination with at least some of the heightened scrutiny that classifications involving race or alienage evoked. Although color was as "natural" a difference as sex, and discrimination based on race and nationality was as "long-standing a custom" as discrimination based on gender, legal decisionmakers declined to recognize the parallels. It was, in part, this insensitivity to the relation between gender distinctions in law and gender disadvantages in society that helped rekindle the modern women's movement.

Part Two

EQUAL RIGHTS IN RETROSPECT

Chapter 3

Feminist Challenges and Legal Responses

To a striking extent, the resurgence of feminism during the 1960s paralleled the development of the first women's rights campaign a century earlier. Both movements were in part the outgrowth of a cult of domesticity that laid the groundwork for its own demise. The celebration of women's domestic destiny during the early nineteenth and mid-twentieth centuries occurred when technological and economic forces were reshaping that role. As traditional gender stereotypes became increasingly out of step with demographic patterns, the framework for a new social order developed. In both periods, the idealization of maternity gave rise to individual frustrations and collective activism. Such responses were also fostered by a climate of general social reform. Women's involvement in the nineteenth-century abolition and twentieth-century civil rights campaigns not only inspired egalitarian demands, but also provided experiences of discrimination that encouraged feminist sentiments.

The Growth of the Contemporary Women's Movement

By the early 1960s, an increasing proportion of American women were finding traditional roles less fulfilling or enduring than prevailing ideology assumed. The isolation and tedium of many household tasks contributed to increasing disaffection with full-time domesticity. National surveys revealed that only about 10 percent of interviewed women wanted their daughters to lead the same sort of life they had led. By almost all indices of mental health, married women appeared worse off than married men or single women.[1]

Other cultural trends made clear that marriage and motherhood were becoming less stable foundations for an entire lifetime. Although official divorce rates have never revealed the extent of informal separations, statistical trends are instructive. At the turn of the century one in five hundred marriages ended in divorce; in 1940 the ratio was one in six, and by the 1980s it was one in two. The number of women who would never marry also began to increase, rising to an estimated 10 percent in the late eighties, while the percentage of single-parent families headed by a woman grew to almost twice that figure. The decline in stability of marital relationships was matched by a decline in the duration of women's child-rearing responsibilities. At the turn of the century, the average woman's life expectancy was forty-eight, and she could contemplate living only ten to fifteen years after her last child left home. By the 1960s, increased longevity and access to effective birth control had helped to alter those patterns: the typical mother had her last child at the age of twenty-six or twenty-seven and could anticipate spending about two-thirds of her adult years with no children younger than eighteen.[2]

This discontinuity between traditional roles and demographic realities was reflected in women's increasing employment and education. The rising demand for workers in female-dominated occupations, together with families' growing economic needs and expectations, propelled more women into the labor force. Of course, as the preceding chapters indicated, substantial percentages of minority women had always worked, and World War II had already introduced large numbers of white women into paying jobs. But the 1960s marked a more widespread and enduring trend. In 1960, 38 pecent of all women were in the workforce; a quarter-century later, over 50 percent had paid employment. Nine out of ten women could expect such work at some point in their lives. Although much of that employment was part-time or intermittent, growing numbers of women were preparing themselves for long-term careers. The percentage of college degrees granted to women increased from a postwar low of 25 percent to over 50 percent in the mid-1980s, and the number of female graduate and professional students also rose dramatically.[3]

Women's increasing educational attainments and labor-force participation reflected ideological as well as demographic trends. Among the motivating forces was an increasing sense of what commentators have labeled "status deprivaton," a perception that women had less opportunity for social recognition than men with comparable talents and training. Those perceptions were the product of a complex set of interactions. For some individuals, particularly white middle- and upper-middle-class homemakers, Betty Friedan's *The Feminine Mystique* was a critical catalyst. By describing the cultural underpinnings of women's domestic disaffections—of the "problem that had no name"—Friedan's work helped inspire collective action.[4]

For other women, direct experience with discrimination fueled feminist concerns. Despite their increasing labor-force involvement, women remained crowded into relatively low-paying, low-status positions. Full-time female workers in the 1960s earned about sixty cents for every dollar earned by males, and only a tiny percentage gained access to upper-level jobs in business, professions, or government. Such patterns were not of course new; what changed in the 1960s was not the extent of gender discrimination but consciousness of it.[5]

Women's experience in the legal profession is a representative example. Despite the bar's rhetorical commitment to equality under law, the reality for women was often quite different. All too common was the situation facing Sandra Day O'Connor. Despite her distinguished academic record at Stanford Law School, no major firm was willing to employ her—except as a legal secretary. An extensive survey of law school graduates and administrators in the mid-1960s reported almost two thousand separate occasions on which employers had disclosed policies against hiring women. Close to two-thirds of the surveyed administrators believed that discrimination against female graduates was a significant problem, and the study's objective data regarding salaries, placement, and promotion confirmed that perception. During the early 1960s, women constituted less than 3 percent of the profession, and women of color numbered only a few hundred of the nation's approximately 300,000 attorneys.[6]

Studies of other employment contexts revealed similar patterns and provided an extended public record of private prejudices. Of course, such a record was hardly unique to the 1960s. What helped to rekindle a feminist movement was not only the increasing number of women in the work force who might experience discrimination, but also the increasing number of women who perceived it as such.

Gender prejudice in political organizations had similar consequences. Like early women's rights advocates, who were excluded from public participation in abolitionist conventions, female activists in the 1960s found themselves excluded from the leadership of civil rights and student political organizations. When some of these women protested their relegation to subordinate (often clerical) roles, their complaints provoked frequent ridicule, including Stokely Carmichael's now-infamous response that "the only position for women in SNCC [Student Non-Violent Coordinating Committee] is prone." Another celebrated example involved the 1967 New Politics Convention, where the chair refused to recognize advocates of a women's rights resolution and called instead on someone to speak on behalf of the "forgotten Americans," Native Americans. When several participants demanded an explanation, the chair responded by patting one of them on the head and advising, "cool down little girl. We have more important things to talk about than women's problems." The "little girl" was Shulamith Firestone, future author of *The Dialectic of*

Sex, who declined the advice. Women who were part of the "forgotten Americans"—Native Americans, Chicanas, Puerto Ricans—often fared no better in either minority or predominately white political organizations.[7]

Despite such disparagement, and in part because of it, women increased their protests. During the mid-1960s, activists founded separate women's liberation groups. A common focus was consciousness-raising, a practice often linked to strategies of Chinese revolutionary organizations, but one that also had antecedents in American feminist groups in the nineteenth and early twentieth centuries. By sharing experiences and providing mutual support, participants sought to understand their individual problems as part of broader societal patterns requiring broader collective responses. The goal was both to politicize the personal and personalize the political.[8]

Other feminist organizations also formed during this period, often in response to discriminatory attitudes within more established political networks. To understand the evolution of these women's rights groups, it is necessary to understand the governmental action (and inaction) that encouraged their formation.

Governmental Rejoinders

Two major catalysts of the contemporary women's rights movement were, ironically, political actions designed for other ends: the creation of a national Commission on the Status of Women, and the addition of a ban on sex discrimination to the 1964 Civil Rights Act. In 1961, President Kennedy established the Commission under a mandate to recommend ways to "combat the prejudices and outmoded customs [that] act as barriers to the full realization of women's basic rights." The evidence available, however, suggests a notable disparity between the Commission's stated mandate and the primary motives for its creation. In part, the body was designed to discharge political obligations to Kennedy's female campaign workers, none of whom obtained significant executive posts outside the Labor Department's Women's Bureau. In addition, administration officials hoped that the Commission might reject the need for an equal rights amendment to the Constitution, and thereby allow the President to finesse a controversial issue.[9]

Somewhat paradoxically, the Commission managed to fulfill both its official and unofficial mandates. As expected, its membership found no current necessity for a constitutional enactment, on the ground that the Fifth and Fourteenth Amendment guarantees of equal rights already afforded sufficient authority for banning discrimination against women. Since the Supreme Court had not yet invoked either amendment to that end, the Commission's logic was not entirely persuasive. Nonetheless, its report did recommend further antidiscrimination initiatives, including the 1963 Equal Pay Act, which requires equal salaries for men and women who perform equal work. The Commission's major contribution was not, however, its substantive recommendations but rather the organizations it helped to spawn. On the federal level, it generated a series of task forces and a Citizens Advisory Council that began documenting gender discrimination in a wide array of legal provisions, public policies, and employment practices. By 1969, all fifty states had established comparable commissions which, for the first time in a half-century, placed women's issues squarely on the legislative agenda. The establishment of such formal organizations created an informal network of women's rights activists. As a result, the Commission played a highly significant role in fostering the egalitarian demands it was intended to finesse.[10]

A second political impetus for the women's rights movement was also partly unintended. When Congressman Howard Smith of Virginia proposed extending Title VII of the pending Civil Rights Act to bar employment discrimination on the basis of sex as well as race, religion, or national origin, few observers believed that fervent feminist commitments had inspired his action. Although Smith had been a sponsor of the Equal Rights Amendment, he had opposed civil rights legislation in general and the Equal Pay Act in particular. The tenor of debate at "Ladies Day in the House" left little doubt that his amendment was designed to increase opposition to Title VII. For that reason, some legislators most sympathetic to women's rights joined forces with some of those least sympathetic in order to block the proposed modification. Edith Green, author of the Equal Pay Act, became an ally of Emanuel Celler, who announced that women didn't need any legal guarantee of civil rights since they already had "lots of them."[11]

However, some feminists were unwilling to endorse the same kind of prudential strategy that had previously excluded explicit sex-based protections from the Fourteenth and Fifteenth amendments. Had Smith not introduced a gender-discrimination provision, other legislators might well have done so; at least one representative indicated that intention in House debates. Once the amendment was put forward, a curious coalition of women's supporters and civil rights opponents banded together to secure its passage. In 1964, Congress enacted the amended version of Title VII, which prohibited certain employers from discriminating on the basis of sex, race, religion, or national origin, and empowered an Equal Employment Opportunities Commission to conciliate complaints and recommend cases for federal litigation.[12]

Although many Congressional sponsors regarded Title VII's prohibition of sex discrimination as inadvertent, inconsequential, or both, many of its beneficiaries felt otherwise. In its first year, over a third of the complaints received by the Equal Employment Opportunity Commission involved sex-based discrimination. Comparable complaint ratios persisted, despite a notable lack of enthusiasm among early Commission officials regarding gender grievances. The EEOC's first director characterized the prohibition on sex discrimination as a statutory "fluke," "conceived out of wedlock." In 1966, House Representative Martha Griffiths informed her colleagues that Title VII's enforcement officials "had started out by casting disrespect and ridicule on the law," but that their "wholly negative attitude had changed—for the worse."[13]

Among the most tangible evidence of Commission insensitivity to gender issues was its position on sex-classified help-wanted advertisements. Initially administrators permitted such advertising, on the theory that it maximized responses. The Commission had, however, rejected comparable justifications for racially classified advertising, and the inconsistency did not pass unnoticed among feminists. In the spring of 1966, some women's rights leaders received confidential advice from liberal government officials that the best way to pressure the administration would be through a national women's organization comparable to the major civil rights groups. The upcoming National Conference of State Commissioners appeared to be an appropriate occasion for testing interest in that proposal.[14]

The initial reception was unenthusiastic. Many state commission members believed that their organizations already provided adequate leverage on women's issues. However, after learning that the Conference was not legally authorized to pass resolutions or take any collective action, including measures directed at the EEOC, a number of these individuals reassessed their views. At a separate luncheon table, twenty-eight disaffected Conference participants each paid five dollars to join a group that Betty Friedan spontaneously christened NOW, the National Organization for Women. Its purpose, as recorded on the most accessible napkin, was "to bring women into full participation in the mainstream of American society now, assuming all the privileges and responsibilities thereof in truly equal partnership with men."[15]

Friedan became NOW's first president and the EEOC was its first target. An expanding membership engaged in various forms of protest, and ultimately the Commission reversed itself, declaring that sex-segregated employment advertising violated Title VII. The battleground then shifted to the courts, where publishers argued that banning such advertisements might well result in "fewer jobs for women because men would be applying for them." The Supreme Court was unpersuaded and, in 1973, rejected an extended array of justifications for the practice. In the interim, a rapidly expanding network of women's organizations began focusing on a broad range of issues.[16]

Liberalism and Liberation

When tracing the political developments of the 1960s and early 1970s, it is useful to distinguish between two strands of the women's movement, which have typically been categorized as liberal rights-oriented feminism and radical feminism. The former constituency included organizations such as NOW and the National Women's Political Caucus, which primarily focused on achieving equality through litigation and legislative reform. By contrast, radical feminist groups tended to be more eclectic and more interested in changing consciousness than changing laws. This left wing of the women's movement encompassed a wide range of participants, including women's liberationists, lesbian separatists, and Marxist-feminists. Such typologies should not, however, obscure either the diversity of views within each camp or their common commitments and memberships.[17]

Although some liberation groups shared members, objectives, and projects with women's rights organizations, others were critical of the hierarchical structure and "minor and meliorist" strategies of their less radical counterparts. The left's organizational priorities varied, but raising public consciousness ranked high among them. In the most celebrated of a series of street-theater events, some women protested the 1968 Miss America pageant by depositing oppressive undergarments in trash cans and crowning a sheep as surrogate queen. For the first time, the national press gave feminist issues front-page coverage. Although no lingerie was in fact incinerated, the media took some poetic license, and "bra-burners" suddenly became a recognized political constituency.[18]

During these formative years, women's rights and women's liberationist camps split over ideological as well as tactical issues. Mainstream organizations such as NOW were committed to working in partnership with men to attain goals traditionally valued in male-dominated societies: power, status, and financial independence. These groups also sought opportunities for men to have the kind of family involvements that conventional roles and workplace structures discouraged. Despite occasional concessions that not all males would, in the short run, willingly relinquish their advantaged positions, it was commonly assumed that in the long run they would realize their equal stake in eradicating gender stereotypes. Men were not "the enemy but . . . fellow victim[s]" of the current structure. As Wilma Scott Heide, then chairman of NOW's board of directors, urged in her congressional testimony on the Equal Rights

Amendment, "There are no women's interests and men's interests. There are only human interests."[19]

To the more radical fringes of the feminist movement, this analysis misperceived the problem and misled as to the solution. According to some women's liberationists, men were less victims than beneficiaries or "agents of . . . oppression," who received "economic, sexual and psychological rewards from male supremacy." Patriarchy, as theorists such as Kate Millett and Catharine MacKinnon argued, was the governing archetype in Western civilization. It provided the most enduring and rigid form of stratification and was unlikely to be dislodged by incremental legal reforms. Similarly, Shulamith Firestone linked gender hierarchy to women's reproductive role and the nuclear family structure. In her view, artificial reproduction, communal living arrangements, and egalitarian political structures were prerequisites for true liberation.[20]

Other radical feminists drew heavily from Marxist and socialist theory. Their analyses linked sexism with capitalism, and maintained that women's emancipation required a broader transformation of economic structures and class relationships. From this perspective, liberal capitalism's values of individual autonomy and competition were incompatible with feminist priorities of caretaking and cooperation. Many of these critics were wary of legal rights-oriented strategies that might deflect attention from feminism's broader revolutionary potential. The point was to "destroy positions of power," not to increase women's access to them.[21]

Women of color raised additional criticisms. A common perception, confirmed by sociological profiles during the mid-1970s, was that about 90 percent of those in women's rights organizations were highly educated middle- or upper-middle-class whites. Minority women leaders frequently doubted whether their concerns could be adequately represented by this seemingly elitist and ethnocentric movement. Some found it difficult to identify with a constituency that, in their view, had profited from or participated in racist practices. Others dismissed feminist struggles as essentially "family quarrel[s] between white women and white men," and resented "simplistic" analogies between racial and sexual oppression. Ironically enough, black women as a group appeared more receptive to the feminist movement than many of their leaders. According to a 1972 national poll, 67 percent of black, but only 37 percent of white female respondents expressed sympathy with the efforts of women's liberation groups. Nonetheless, the founding of a National Black Feminist Organization in 1973, and the subsequent formation of other minority associations made clear that many activists were dissatisfied with existing women's groups.[22]

This barrage of criticism provoked both confession and denial among liberal feminists. Most women's organizations made greater attempts to include minority leaders and concerns. However, other radical critiques were often dismissed as "unreal sexual fantasies." In the 1970s, many liberal leaders, including Friedan, assumed that they must "talk in terms of what is possible." In her view, it was a "profound misreading of the women's movement to believe that most women in America would strike 'against the system.' To want equality, a voice in the mainstream, to be part of the action of the system, that is what the women's movement is about." One of Friedan's central concerns was to avoid "overfocus on sexual . . . politics," on "man-hatred" and on visible affiliation with gay liberation (the "lavender menace"), which might alienate potential allies and "immobilize the movement politically." Yet to other more leftist leaders, any abandonment of lesbian issues or of demands for sweeping cultural changes was inconsistent with feminism's most fundamental principles.[23]

These conflicts, reminiscent of earlier controversies within the suffrage movement, took a political toll. As the following discussion of the contemporary ERA campaign makes clear, radical critiques and tactics reduced mainstream support for certain feminist objectives and compromised efforts to build a broad political base. Yet the strategies of left-wing feminists expanded the terms of debate and captured public attention in a way that more moderate approaches had not. Moreover, radical critiques encouraged mainstream organizations to extend their agendas beyond liberal legal reforms. As the decade progressed, schisms within the feminist movement became less apparent. The leftward drift of liberal women's rights organizations, coupled with the general decline in radical political movements, led to a greater sense of cohesiveness.

The growing unification of purpose was evident in 1977 at the first National Women's Conference. Some 2,000 delegates elected from diverse racial, ethnic, and socioeconomic communities gathered in Houston, Texas, to chart an agenda for change. Its list of demands suggested the extent to which the women's movement had broadened its concerns since the 1848 Seneca Falls Convention. Priorities included:

- full employment, with increased opportunities for flexible and part-time schedules;
- an adequate standard of living for all individuals, including income transfers labeled as wages, not welfare, for indigent homemakers with dependent children;
- abolition of all gender discrimination in education and employment;
- federally funded childcare services accessible to families at all income levels, with adequate opportunity for parental involvement;
- reproductive freedom;

- a "national health security program" insuring comprehensive medical and reproductive services;
- revision of criminal and family laws regarding marital support, consensual homosexual activity, and rape;
- governmental support for battered women and displaced homemakers;
- nonsexist portrayals of women in the media; and
- increased representation of women in elective and appointive public offices.[24]

The scope of this agenda testified to both the expanded vision and limited attainments of the resurgent women's movement. It was, in part, this gap between women's ideals and experience that helped revive the campaign for a constitutional guarantee of equal rights.

Chapter 4

The Equal Rights Campaign

An objective common to much legal and historical research is, in L. B. Namier's phrase, "to achieve an intuitive sense of how things do not happen." From this perspective, the campaign for an Equal Rights Amendment to the United States Constitution is a particularly illuminating case study. As preceding chapters indicate, the difficulties surrounding the campaign are not entirely of recent vintage. For a half-century supporters introduced some variant of a constitutional prohibition against sex discrimination in every congressional term. When, in 1972, the House and Senate finally passed an amendment, the struggle for state ratification foundered on much the same conflicts that have plagued American feminism throughout its history. In part, the dispute involved concerns about preferential treatment that had crystallized during the protective-labor debates of the 1920s. Underlying those controversies were more fundamental questions about the importance of formal rights and sexual differences—questions on which the women's movement has always been divided. Like the suffrage campaign a century earlier, the ERA struggle presented issues not only of constitutional entitlements, but also of cultural dominance. The question was whose vision of women's destiny should prevail and on what terms.[1]

After its initial introduction in the early twenties, the Equal Rights Amendment provoked sporadic legislative disputes and opposition from such unlikely bedfellows as the John Birch Society, the Communist Party, the AFL-CIO, Calvin Coolidge, and Eleanor Roosevelt. An equally eclectic coalition of supporters gradually increased; by the early 1970s it included the ACLU, the Teamsters Union, the Women's Christian Temperance

Union, George Wallace, and George McGovern. According to public-opinion polls, a solid majority of Americans supported the amendment, although many appeared uninformed or unenthusiastic about some of its likely consequences.[2]

The growth in support was both explicable and somewhat ironic in light of other governmental action. There was less need for a constitutional provision and correspondingly less logic in opposing it, given the proliferation of state and federal statutes, executive orders, and judicial decisions prohibiting sex discrimination. Against this legal backdrop, the 1972 Congress overwhelmingly endorsed an amendment providing that "[e]quality of rights under the law shall not be denied or abridged by the United States or any state on account of sex." At that point, the prospects for early and uneventful state ratification appeared promising. Within months after congressional approval, some twenty state legislatures had ratified the provision, often with only minutes of perfunctory debate.[3]

In Illinois, the momentum suddenly ceased. Phyllis Schlafly, a conservative resident with no national prominence, launched a "Stop ERA" campaign that succeeded, first in Illinois, and then in enough other states to block ratification. Despite a three-year extension, the ratification deadline expired without the necessary endorsements from three-quarters of the states. Fifteen states never endorsed the amendment and five attempted to rescind their ratification.[4]

That reversal is instructive both about the status of American women and the dynamics of constitutional change. At issue in the ERA campaign were fundamental questions about the meaning of sexual equality and the means of attaining it. Those questions had both an instrumental and symbolic dimension. On an instrumental level, the issue was whether the amendment's ban on gender classifications would in fact improve women's legal status. On a symbolic level, the campaign became a referendum on a host of other issues concerning sexual differences, social roles, and feminist politics.

That is not to imply a sharp disjuncture between these levels. Many of those who stressed the ERA's symbolic significance did so because they believed that it would have tangible, if indirect, effects on legal institutions and cultural patterns. It was also commonly assumed that the amendment's practical consequences would carry a broader symbolic message and ultimately affect actions beyond the reach of constitutional scrutiny. However, to understand the evolution of the ERA campaign, it is useful to separate these claims and to focus on the way opponents reframed debate on both instrumental and symbolic levels. As was true in the battle for suffrage, antifeminist activity was sporadic, but its ideology was significant; it helped "defin[e] the context within which [feminist strategies] developed and pose[d] the problems [feminists] had to solve." As is apparent from recent accounts of the ERA struggle, including those of Mary Frances Berry, Janet Boles, Jennifer Mansbridge, and Joan Hoff-Wilson, the difficulties that activists encountered offer more enduring lessons for the women's movement.[5]

Many of the problems that emerged in the ERA campaign reflected problems in the law's traditional approaches to discrimination. Far too often the debate focused on gender difference rather than gender disadvantages and granted too much importance to formal rights rather than to their social context.

Instrumental Claims

Proponents' primary argument in support of a constitutional amendment was that it would provide the most effective means of combating sex-based classifications in areas such as employment, education, welfare, credit, pensions, domestic relations, and military service. To seek piecemeal legislative or judicial remedies against each discriminatory action could result in interminable delay and inordinate expense, while offering no protection against future abuses. It would, as one supporter put it, be like "enforcing the Emancipation Proclamation plantation by plantation."[6]

Moreover, court decisions under existing statutory and constitutional provisions had produced "uneven developments marked by sharply divided opinions." According to many proponents, that result stemmed from the Supreme Court's unwillingness to view sex, like race, as a "suspect classification" triggering "strict scrutiny." Such scrutiny requires that the challenged classification serve a "compelling" state interest that cannot be achieved by less burdensome means. Few discriminatory practices have survived this test. Accordingly, proponents hoped that an equal-rights amendment would mandate a comparable level of scrutiny for sex-based classifications and thus promote a more egalitarian social order.[7]

There were a number of difficulties with this argument. As opponents often pointed out, the volume of antidiscrimination legislation, administrative regulation, and judicial intervention was already increasing without a constitutional catalyst. Many legal developments that anticipated the consequences of an equal-rights amendment were making it appear less essential and less worthy of political struggle. Moreover, passage of the ERA would not eliminate the need for piecemeal litigation to interpret its meaning and secure its enforcement. Analogies to the Emancipation Proclamation also missed the mark. By the 1970s, the evils of slavery were self-evident. The need for an equal-rights amendment was not. According to one representative public-opinion survey of the early seventies, 75 percent of male respondents and 71 percent of females considered the position of women in American society to be either "excellent or good." Once Schlafly and her followers raised concerns about the ERA's effects on laws advantaging women, doubts about the necessity of constitutional change grew stronger.[8]

The loss of preferential treatment was one of the opposition's most effective themes. While supporters appealed to women's aspirations, opponents appealed to women's fears. According to Schlafly, a constitutional mandate of equal treatment would jeopardize a host of "precious rights," particularly those related to family and military service obligations. Opponents claimed, for example, that wives would lose entitlement to support during or after marriage and would have a "*legal obligation* to go out to work to provide half the family income." Such predictions evoked broad concerns. Wives with unstable marriages or few marketable skills complained that the amendment might be "all right for a younger woman," but that they were unsure how to support themselves and their children under an equal-rights amendment. To traditional homemakers, a constitutional mandate seemed to offer an unnecessary and unwelcome exchange: they would pay the price of expanding some abstract set of opportunities that they had never experienced and would never enjoy.[9]

Opposition arguments concerning family law were among those most irritating to ERA proponents. Given Schlafly's training as a lawyer, her claims appeared somewhat disingenuous. As supporters pointed out, the amendment would cover only state action; it would not dictate families' private financial arrangements or require wives to work. Nor would it materially alter husbands' support obligations. Under current laws, courts virtually never enforced such obligations in ongoing marriages; and once a marriage terminated, judges would still be free under sex-blind provisions to require support for dependent homemakers. Even without the ERA, most state legislatures were already enacting gender-neutral family laws, and judicial decisions barring sex-based alimony statutes were accelerating that trend. As proponents noted, such statutory modifications had not produced the "radical" upheavals in family life that Schlafly predicted.[10]

These rejoinders were not entirely effective in allaying public concerns. As discussion in Chapter 7 indicates, traditional homemakers have not always fared well under gender-neutral family law reforms. Although such provisions have avoided sex-based stereotyping, they have also failed to address sex-based disadvantages. The real weakness in Schlafly's claim was that most wives already were, and always had been, less secure than she implied, and gender-neutral mandates were not the cause. The difficulty was not with reforms such as those replacing "wife" with "spouse" in alimony statutes that authorized "equitable" awards. Rather the difficulty lay in decisionmakers' interpretations of what "equity" meant, interpretations that undervalued domestic work and its effect on an individual's earning potential. Such judicial biases were as apparent under sex-specific statutes as under their gender-neutral replacements. But that message was unwelcome in many quarters. Many homemakers were more inclined to reject the messenger than to acknowledge their own vulnerability.[11]

Opponents' other most effective argument involved military service. Equality in the workplace was one thing; equality in the trenches was quite another. Throughout state capitols, legislators visualized their daughters sharing barracks, bunkers, or latrines with hardened combat troops, and having their "fair forms blasted into fragments" by "bayonets, bombs, [and] bullets." The issue was not only the future of womanhood but the security of the nation. According to politicians such as Illinois Representative Webber Borchers, women's "inadequate hip structure . . . tender [feet]," and inability "to press the attack" would "hamstring" the infantry.[12]

On this issue, proponents never developed a consistent response. The most common rejoinder—that Congress already had power to draft women—was hardly adequate to the occasion. According to Schlafly, the ERA would require women to assume the same military obligations as men, including combat service. The legal basis for that assertion was, however, open to dispute, as a subsequent Supreme Court decision permitting sex-based draft registration suggested. Thus, some proponents took the position that the ERA would not mandate women in combat; under the Constitution's War Powers clause, judges could properly defer to military leaders' resolution of the issue.[13]

Other ERA supporters, including the authors of a highly influential *Yale Law Journal* article, maintained that the amendment would mandate sex-neutral treatment in the armed forces. This position was consistent with Congress' refusal on several occasions to endorse an equal rights amendment with exemptions for military service. Proponents also cited evidence indicating that women were capable of performing many combat jobs and that their exclusion from such positions had adverse effects on military and civilian opportunities. From this perspective, until women were prepared to accept the full responsibilities of citizenship, including the draft, they would have difficulty claiming its full entitlements. Most Americans, however, took a different view. According to public-opinion polls, a majority of respondents opposed equal treatment for men and women in the military, and state legislators did not appear to be an exception.[14]

A final cluster of arguments that proved effective with some groups involved sexuality, reproduction, and privacy. Catholic and fundamentalist leaders often linked the ERA with legalized abortion, homosexual marriage, and the related evils of a "singles society." Although proponents generally denied those connections, their position was not unproblematic. Supporters were, of course, correct in noting that the Supreme Court had based abortion rights on considerations of privacy rather than equality. However, as opponents also pointed out, feminists had invoked state equal-rights amendments and federal equal-protection guarantees as a justification for governmental funding of abortion. On issues of sexual preference, proponents often noted that courts generally had not interpreted legal mandates against gender discrimination to bar discrimination against gays or lesbians as long as males and females were treated similarly. But some feminists opposed those rulings and were reluctant to relinquish the ERA as a potential ground for challenging them.[15]

Opponents' privacy arguments had less legal substance, though many members of their audience may not have recognized as much. The most notorious example involved Schlafly's account of the ERA's effects on public bathrooms. In her view, "the only reason that this nation has separate restrooms for men and women and boys and girls is sex. Consequently, being a distinction based on sex, the ERA would abolish the power of the Federal Government and the power of the 50 states to require separate facilities of this nature for persons of different sexes." With comparable logic, other opponents projected the demise of sex-segregated locker rooms, saunas, hospital facilities, and homes for wayward girls.[16]

Such arguments ignored the legislative history of the amendment, which clearly preserved an exception for privacy-related regulation. Moreover, the triviality of the argument invited ridicule. Within some constituencies, opponents' resort to "potty politics" was counterproductive. ERA supporters capitalized on the fact that Schlafly herself had apparently managed to survive the ordeal of undifferentiated restrooms during her frequent airline excursions to testify against the amendment. Other proponents claimed that women's greatest risk concerning single-sex bathrooms was that women would be cleaning them. Yet the persistence of some privacy-related claims suggests that they may have touched deeper nerves than proponents generally acknowledged. Although the particular examples opponents cited may not have had great independent significance, when taken together, they evoked a vision of androgyny that threatened core American values.[17]

Symbolic Underpinnings

For both sides in the ratification campaign, the ERA became a stand-in for more fundamental concerns and a battleground for symbolic politics.

To proponents, the amendment represented a significant affirmation of equality as well as a means for attaining it. To opponents, the ERA appeared as a "unisex" mandate, a tool to "nullify . . . distinction[s] between the sexes," and to transform the United States into a "gender-free society." Thus, Ronald Reagan maintained, "I do not want to see sex and sexual differences treated as casually and amorally as dogs and other beasts treat them. I believe this could happen under the ERA." From opponents' perspective, the amendment's egalitarian premises ignored sex-linked characteristics that were biologically determined or culturally desirable.[18]

Once again, the nineteenth-century cult of domesticity found adherents. In the world as ERA opponents conceived it, men and women assumed unique roles, dictated by nature and sanctified by scripture. Or, as Schlafly succinctly put it, "Women have babies so men should support them." Despite the fact that over half of all women were in the workforce, "marriage and the home [remained] the greatest liberation for women."[19]

The claim was not without irony, particularly given the source. The Supreme Court had, a century earlier, invoked precisely the same argument about women's maternal mission when it denied female applicants entry to Schlafly's chosen profession. Indeed, as ERA supporters occasionally noted, America's preeminent defender of woman's "God-given right to stay home" rarely exercised that right. Schlafly was a lawyer with a Harvard master's degree, the author of several books, the editor of a prominent conservative newsletter, and a political organizer with a national following.[20]

Other ERA opponents were in less anomalous positions. Many of these women were traditional homemakers who felt embattled and embittered by feminist rhetoric. Once "women's libbers" had been cast as the driving force behind the amendment, opponents were often preaching to the converted. Public-opinion polls throughout the 1970s indicated that most Americans did not view the organized feminist movement in a favorable light, even though many supported certain central feminist objectives. Opposition to that movement galvanized opposition to constitutional change. To members of groups such as the Feminine Anti-Feminists, Gigi Gals Galore Against the ERA, Winsome Wives and Homemakers, and Women Who Want to Be Women, Schlafly's message appeared flattering and reassuring. It exalted their values and ennobled their station. By contrast, much feminist rhetoric implied that these women had made the wrong choices and demanded reappraisal of their self-image, priorities, and daily lives.[21]

That message was understandably unwelcome in many quarters. For some, it seemed to come too late. Those who had followed traditional paths resented the assault, and the anti-ERA campaign offered a way to vent their frustration and reaffirm their sense of importance in a changing social order. Once family and feminism were fixed as the symbolic poles of debate, many women could be expected to rally around the symbol by which they had ordered their own priorities.[22]

For other women whose lives were less traditional, but whose opportunities appeared limited, the assumptions of the women's movement appeared to be out of touch with daily realities. Among those who lacked adequate skills, mobility, or employment opportunities, the feminist agenda seemed elitist and irrelevant. Particularly among minority women, many of whom confronted constant problems of racism, poverty, and violence, a campaign for constitutional symbols seemed largely beside the point.[23]

Women with unsatisfactory employment opportunities often measured their status and self-worth by traditional feminine standards. By devaluing these standards, the "liberation" movement appeared to endorse an alternative as limited as the domestic stereotypes it sought to supplant. According to one New York opponent, "I know [feminists] are intelligent women but I don't [think] they put enough value on the feminine role in the home. The woman who stays home is preparing the next generation but that's not respected. They don't even value volunteer work. I just don't [think] they've tried to reach women in general."[24]

These problems in the equal-rights campaign mirrored the problems of feminism over the last two decades. While radical rhetoric played an important role in expanding public consciousness on women's issues, it also alienated some constituencies who were most in need of assistance. For many women, it was Schlafly who gave dignity and significance to a domestic role that society as a whole has undervalued.

Other grounds for opposition included resistance to change in general and to women's advancement in particular. Within some conservative constituencies, the amendment became an all-purpose symbolic scapegoat. According to many opponents, the ERA, by weakening women's traditional role, would also weaken traditional values. In tones reminiscent of antisuffragist rhetoric, opponents predicted that the ultimate result of equal rights would be an array of social problems including increased "divorce . . . desertion . . . alcoholism, suicide, and possisble deviation." The principal beneficiaries of constitutional change would be "offbeats and deadbeats": the "homosexual who wants the same rights as husbands, the husband who wants to escape supporting his wife and children, the coward who wants to get out of military service by giving his place to a woman."[25]

Extremist right-wing organizations imbued the amendment with even more subversive overtones. Despite the Communist Party's long-standing opposition to the ERA, the John Birch Society perceived the amendment as an integral part of "Communist plans . . . at work in a now vast effort to reduce human beings to living at the same level as animals." Other opponents, less certain about the ERA's conspiratorial origins, nonetheless perceived it as promoting a "communistic way of life." In Southern states, conservative leaders also identified the amendment as yet another assault on states' rights and recalled the federal government's enforcement of comparably open-textured mandates in civil rights cases.[26]

Although proponents often dismissed these claims as pretextual, their underpinnings may have been more complex. For example, while arguments regarding states' rights may not have been decisive for many legislators, neither were such claims as patently disingenuous as was sometimes assumed. Schlafly and her associates framed the question as one of power: "Who's going to have it, the states or the feds?" To some state legislators, the amendment represented yet another blow to their declining status.[27]

Among conservative constituencies the ERA fell victim to a general backlash against the radicalism of the 1960s. Calls for emancipation rekindled fears, if not of revolution, of severe dislocations in a congenial way of life. Some legislators found the amendment threatening in a more fundamental sense. To conservative male politicians, it often loomed as the embodiment of an ideology that was personally offensive and socially pernicious. Women's liberation, with its claims of oppression, challenged not only these legislators' values, but also their self-esteem. Under the more radical feminist view, many of the domestic arrangements and professional achievements of these politicians were neither desirable nor deserved but rather a product of illicit subjugation and false consciousness. Not surprisingly, some legislators viewed the ERA as an opportunity to respond in kind, to vent their spleen against the "bra-less brainless broads" who had demeaned their status and relationships.[28]

Of course antifeminist sentiments were also common among women opposed to the ERA. But the rhetoric issuing from state capitols had a different resonance. On the whole, Schlafly and her female allies depicted a social order in which women were separate but equal. Many conservative legislators seemed less certain about the "equal." A surprising number were quite explicit on the point. One Montana legislator informed his colleagues that if God had wanted "women to be equal," he would have had "six female apostles." A wife's destiny was to "serve her husband"; she would rather be "loved than liberated." According to a poem read into the record by one Illinois lawmaker with literary aspirations,

> Just to be needed is more sweet says she
> Than any freedom in this world could be.[29]

Such sentiments did not receive universal critical acclaim. In the view of the *Chicago Daily News* editors, the ERA was blocked by a "prim little covey of legislators convinced that females were put on this earth for kuchen and kinder and, by cracky, not much else." These press accounts, if somewhat simplistic, nonetheless captured a significant point about political discourse. Tributes built on group stereotypes carry different symbolic baggage depending on their source. When mothers exalt the mystique of motherhood, it appears as an affirmation of personal identity and group status. When such tributes originate with males opposed to equal rights, the stereotypes may be the same but the effect is different. As Simone de Beauvoir suggested, we should regard with some skepticism the "enthusiasm for women's destiny manifested by men who would not for the world have any part of it."[30]

What is revealing about the anti-ERA rhetoric is not only what it discloses about the biases of particular legislators but also what it suggests about the ideological climate in state capitols. The record hardly reaffirms the Founding Fathers' vision of the ratification process as "the most likely means of drawing forth the best men in the states" to resolve fundamental issues of constitutional governance. That so many politically accountable officials felt free to couch their objections in phrases like "loved not liberated" or "bra-less brainless broads" demonstrates more than a flair for alliteration or a facility for grandstanding. Rather, it testifies to the perceived legitimacy of certain core attitudes about women's roles and feminist ideology. By the 1970s it would have been difficult to visualize even the most racist politician publicly objecting to civil rights legislation on the grounds that blacks would rather "serve than be served," or that proponents were "nagging noxious Negroes." Sensitivities to racism and sexism remained on qualitatively different levels.[31]

Yet ironically enough, the candor of conservative legislators proved one of proponents' most effective organizational assets. It was the rhetoric as well as the results of state ERA campaigns that enlisted large numbers of supporters. Sexist sentiments generated a backlash of financial and lobbying support that gave proponents enormous organizational advantages. A recurring question is why supporters could not capitalize on those advantages and convince enough legislators that equal rights, if not ideologically congenial, were at least politically expedient.

Political Strategies

Again historical parallels are evident. During the suffrage campaign, antifeminists generally were not credited with great rhetorical effectiveness; "their arguments seemed too puerile. [But their] appearances in hearings and in print did furnish legislators with the excuse that a body of respectable women did not want the vote." A century later, the emergence of a female anti-ERA lobby similarly helped to legitimate male legislator's opposition. Politicians became less wary of the label "oppressor" once they could present themselves as bowing to the demands of those allegedly oppressed.[32]

The ability of opponents to mobilize a campaign reflects remarkable tactical astuteness given the obstacles confronting them. At the outset of the ratification struggle, before the issue had attracted significant media attention, those obstacles were substantial. As one Illinois opponent explained, "People like us have very limited time and it would be against our nature to go out and organize because our main job-priority is the fact of staying in the home. If we put that aside . . . we're in effect doing just what we're fighting against." Many members of anti-ERA organizations were more committed in principle than practice. One frustrated Illinois organizer recalled that while she participated in one of the crucial early lobbying campaigns in Springfield, "No one else from my group was able to go. They all had excuses—child care, one woman's husband refused to let her go, another was having a rug delivered." Opponents' reluctance to accord politics a high priority created continuing practical problems for their leadership.[33]

In attempting to surmount such obstacles, Schlafly and her followers relied on two main techniques. First, they vested the ERA with instrumental and symbolic dimensions calculated to arouse even the most phlegmatic homemaker. Second, opposition organizers developed lobbying strategies that were both attractive to conservative constituencies and effective with state representatives. Among the most successful of these techniques was the mass-mail campaign. Letter-writing is the ideal vehicle for a constituent with limited time, mobility, and lobbying experience. By enlisting conservative women's organizations and supplying sample correspondence for the uninspired, opposition leaders were able to demonstrate broad-based political strength.[34]

For personal lobbying, Schlafly and her colleagues devised a uniquely domesticated approach that captured both public and legislative attention. ERA opponents arrived in state capitols bearing gifts of identifiably feminine manufacture, most often home-baked bread and similar culinary offerings. These strategies were effective in several respects. Not only were they a relatively inexpensive means of arousing media attention, they also appealed to women who lacked experience and interest in more conventional forms of political persuasion. Such approaches helped offset proponents' financial resources and organizational support from well-established women's associations.[35]

In addition, the anti-ERA leadership's emphasis on feminized lobbying strategies confronted their adversaries with an unhappy choice. If proponents did not respond in kind, they forfeited media coverage and left unchallenged claims that the battle was between feminine and feminist camps. Yet to the extent that they descended to opponents' level of discourse, supporters risked perpetuating a trivialized contest that they could never win. In response to that dilemma, women's rights advocates proposed two strategies. In the words of NOW's legislative vice-president, "[i]f it takes white gloves, we'll use white gloves. If it takes combat boots, we'll wear combat boots. If it takes white gloves and combat boots, we'll wear both." Proponents tried both but never found a satisfactory fit.[36]

Difficulties with the white-glove approach became apparent during the early Illinois ratification struggle. For example, in 1973 Chicago's ERA Central organized a press conference with an eye to counteracting assertions that its proponents were a bunch of "man-eating harpies." To this end, they scheduled brief pro-ERA statements by three suburban housewives, an airline stewardess, and a Playboy bunny. It is doubtful that the event accomplished its stated objectives. Journalists predictably treated it as a lark. The *Chicago Daily News* account, titled "A Bunny Hops on Rights Issue," opened its narrative by noting that the "first Playboy bunny to speak out on the Equal Rights Amendment went hop hop hop Wednesday for ERA." Worse yet, when a reporter inquired of the bunny, who ostensibly was present to exemplify positive sentiments toward men, whether she ever discussed equal rights with her customers at the Playboy Club, she replied: "No, they are a perfect example of pigism."[37]

A similar strategy, more inspired in theory than in practice, was to meet opponents on their own terrain and counter the assertion that traditional homemakers opposed equal rights. Accordingly, the more moderate pro-ERA leaders mounted their own culinary campaign, matching their foes muffin for muffin. Shortly after the bunny's debut, seventy-five mature housewives assembled to serve Eggs Benedict to Illinois Representatives and Senators. Neither the opposition nor the press let the event pass unnoticed. The day before the brunch, Schlafly and her followers distributed to all legislators small loaves of home-baked bread labeled "Let us stay in the kitchen." Not surprisingly, this juxtaposition proved irresistible to reporters. In their accounts the affair became a playful contest among rival hausfraus. "Rights Battle Booms From Kitchens" chortled the *Chicago Daily News*. The *Tribune*'s narrative, "Women Try to Cook Up Votes," began: "Women on both sides of the fight over ratification of the Equal Rights Amendment appear to have decided that the way to a legislator's vote is through his stomach." In response to a reporter's query, an irate ERA supporter observed that "this brunch was planned a month ago and was not an attempt to show that liberated women can cook as well as unliberated ones. Whatever the event was originally designed to show was lost in the translation."[38]

Undaunted by such jocular press reviews, proponents continued to offer variations on the same theme. Legislators across the nation received a barrage of breads, pastries, valentines, tea roses, forget-me-nots, and the like. Many recipients appeared more bemused than moved. The gestures seemed "unprofessional" and, as caricatured by the press, made the amendment appear unworthy of serious substantive debate. An inevitable, if unintended, consequence of these quiche and cookie crusades was to trivialize the issue and deflect attention from serious questions of gender inequality.[39]

Moreover, supporters taking this feminine approach were repeatedly upstaged by their more radical colleagues. Some feminists remained unconvinced that the most direct route to a legislator's vote was through his stomach They pursued a different path, with public denunciations in animal blood or spray paint and gifts such as chicken manure and a child's potty. Such gestures, however cathartic for the converted, did little to persuade those most in need of persuasion.[40]

Although more moderate ERA proponents attempted to dismiss these tactics as the harmless antics of a few extremists, that effort received a significant setback in 1977. Live on national television, delegates to the International Women's Year Conference in Houston endorsed the ERA—along with subsidized abortion, gay rights, and a host of other controversial planks and placards (such as "Mother Nature is a Lesbian"). Just in case any legislators from a nonratifying state had missed the festivities, Schlafly thoughtfully mailed them all a full account. Other anti-ERA leaders brought home conference souvenirs for display in state capitols, to ensure that no one could overlook the connection between equal rights, vibrators, and sex education in the public schools. The point was widely taken. According to one Illinois representative, who switched his vote after the conference, "the resolutions adopted there [show] what these people think the ERA stands for . . . I can't tolerate those things—and neither can my constituents."[41]

The problems surrounding the Houston Conference were emblematic of a deeper set of difficulties confronting ERA proponents. As the conference roster reflected, the women's movement brought together heterogeneous constituencies, with many common concerns but not necessarily common priorities. Participants varied considerably in the significance they attached to constitutional change and the sacrifices they were prepared to make in its behalf. Many of the movement's leftist members were unwilling to rank the ERA high on the feminist agenda, particularly if it required soft-pedaling principles for which, in their view, feminism stood. Thus, while highly successful in other respects, the Houston event raised problems of competing priorities. At the same time movement leaders were investing enormous energy and financial resources to secure mainstream support for the ERA, they were also sponsoring mass events that undercut such efforts.

As the campaign wore on, these political lessons became increasingly apparent to ERA supporters. Supporters became more adept at the less flashy aspects of interest-group politics. Pro-ERA leaders focused more on boycotts and ballots, less on brunches and Playboy bunnies. According to an Illinois organizer, "We've learned we must hit our legislative opponents where it hurts—their candidates, their bills." But in key states that lesson came too late. One New York organizer acknowledged: "[w]e didn't focus on all the Byzantine stuff that goes on in state legislatures."[42]

In part, the problem was tunnel vision. From some proponents' vantage, none of the major obstacles to ratification was their responsibility. "What went wrong," according to the president of NOW's New York chapter, "had nothing to do with image . . . [o]pponents used fear, distortion, outright lies and scare tactics." Other supporters variously ascribed blame to the Republican party, "big business," private insurance companies, right-wing extremists, self-hatred or stupidity among female opponents, and rank sexism among male legislators.[43]

Such explanations, although not without basis, obscured other forces at work. Too often, proponents assumed that the public was simply deceived. In fact, it was deeply divided. The opposition that conservative leaders mobilized reflected not only misunderstanding and prejudices, but also fundamental ambivalence about the nature of gender difference and the role of constitutional entitlements. The most effective aspect of opposition strategies was not the deception they practiced on the public, but the misperception they sometimes encouraged among proponents. The efforts of Schlafly and other scapegoats deflected feminists' attention from the problems in their own strategies and from the roots of ERA opposition.

That is not to imply that different strategies would necessarily have produced different results. Some influential lawmakers were unmistakably ill-disposed toward the concept of gender equality and its feminist pedigree. Once opponents had established respectable grounds for resistance, these legislators were unlikely to retreat. But especially during the early ERA campaigns, many politicians had limited personal investment in the issue and represented constituencies that were uninformed, unconcerned, or divided. These votes were negotiable. The inability of ERA sponsors to bargain effectively for support within this group proved a critical barrier in ratification struggles.

Part of the problem was inadequate leadership. By choice or necessity, proponents found themselves relying on legislative sponsors who lacked either parliamentary finesse or strong commitment to the issue. In some instances, powerful male legislators avoided involvement with the amendment, particularly after controversies arose. Much of the burden fell on female sponsors, many of whom lacked experience or leverage in parliamentary maneuvers.[44]

But blame for these difficulties cannot rest primarily at sponsors' doorsteps. The failures of women legislators reflect a prolonged exclusion from the political mainstream, for which they are not accountable. And, as other analyses of the ERA's difficulties have emphasized, the point is not to allocate fault but rather to identify strategies for altering such patterns of exclusion.

Requiems and Revivals

To those most intimately involved, the ratification struggle had all the makings of a medieval morality play. For the opposition, the allegorical references were unambiguous. In a contest between decency and deviance, the champions of femininity took arms against a radical fringe. To opponents, the result was culturally and spiritually appropriate, if not, indeed, preordained.

For many proponents the moral landscape was equally flat; the roles were simply reversed and the narrative was as yet incomplete. At the close of Act I, the vanguard of liberation suffered a setback at the hands of a small reactionary cadre. The 1982 ratification deadline marked only an intermission; the amendment will be revived repeatedly and, in the final scene, the forces of darkness will be dispersed and equality will at last become the law of the land.

Yet even at this limited historical distance, the narrative seems less banal, the motivations richer, and the outcome more indeterminate than those scripts acknowledge. Viewing the drama not as a single performance but as part of a continuing tradition, the denouement raises broader issues that do not readily yield allegorical truths. From a historical perspective, the ratification campaign seems a relatively small part of an ongoing struggle over the redefinition of social status and gender roles. The results of that process will depend on economic, technological, demographic, and ideological forces to which the ERA's fate will make at best a modest contribution.

Even so, the constitutional campaign remains significant as a cultural text. From a political and jurisprudential standpoint, the debate has offered insights about the dynamics of constitutional change. Most significantly, it has illustrated the difficulty of achieving informed public analysis of legal issues carrying substantial symbolic freight. From a more sociological vantage, the dialogue has illumined cultural assumptions and aspirations; in particular, it has exposed the lack of consensus regarding social institutions that seek to reinforce or suppress sex-linked differences. And finally, from an instrumental perspective, the results may have exerted some short-term influence over the continuing reformulation of women's legal rights and social status.

At this juncture, the shape of future ERA campaigns remains in doubt. One disquieting possibility is that the same morality play will be revived, with much of the original script unaltered. Having spent a decade snarling past each other, proponents and opponents face obvious difficulties reconceptualizing their interaction. Throughout the ratification struggle opponents flailed against their own caricatures of a unisex society, and that strategy shows signs of persistence. The reintroduction of the amendment in the 1983 congressional term evoked the perennial parade of horribles: necessary protective laws eroded, traditional homemakers imperiled, combat forces disabled, and sexual distinctions obliterated. According to witnesses at committee hearings, passage of a constitutional mandate would result in a "social revolution imposed from above." Wives and mothers would be "forced out of the home," governmental funding of abortions would be required, homosexuals would be entitled to marry, and boy scout troops would be ousted from public facilities. Despite decades of contrary experience with state ERAs, predictions of an androgynous apocalypse have continued. Many opponents are still unable to acknowledge that the feminist demon is at least partly their own fantasy.[45]

Some proponents have similarly oversimplified the sources of their own difficulties. After allocating blame among disingenuous opponents and sexist legislators, supporters have too often discounted problems in their own strategies and assumptions. In the 1983–84 rounds of congressional debates, proponents again presented the Equal Rights Amendment as an all-purpose prescription for varied social ills: the plight of displaced homemakers, the increasing feminization of poverty, the disparity in male-female earnings, and the lack of women's political power. How exactly a formal prohibition against sex discrimination by governmental entities would solve these problems was not explained. Nor was the less encouraging experience with state equal rights provisions acknowledged. According to many supporters, a federal constitutional mandate was "the only way" to secure "real progress" toward social equality. From their perspective, anti-ERA forces remained nothing more than "a lunatic fringe," incapable of adjusting to cultural imperatives.[46]

But the campaign that proved so divisive in the short term may have more constructive repercussions. By the close of the decade, it had become increasingly apparent that neither side in the ERA campaign could achieve its underlying objectives without broadening its appeal. If opponents are to preserve what is valuable in feminine traditions, they must confront the consequences of social change. By choice or necessity, an increasing number of women have become full-time workers and single heads-of-households. Many of these individuals experience substantial hardships, which are in part attributable to inadequacies in employment, welfare, and family policies. These are critical social problems that ERA opponents as well as supporters have an interest in addressing. To become a more constructive political force, conservatives must offer plausible strategies for enabling the working woman and single parent to fulfill, at least partially, the role they idealize.

If proponents are to become more successful advocates for social progress, they must work to retain the valuable aspects of traditional roles. Many women find the "liberated" alternative, grounded in male-oriented professional paradigms, either inaccessible or just as confining as the domestic mystiques it has sought to supplant. By the 1980s, increasing sensitivity to these concerns was apparent in both feminist theory and politics. The validation of women's differences, discussed more fully in Chapter 12, is one illustration. Others include thoughtful accounts of the ERA campaign published in the mid-1980s and the increased feminist attention to issues such as childcare, parental policies, and enforcement of child support.

According to several ERA proponents attending a 1988 Atlanta conference on women and the Constitution, "We didn't win in the ratification struggle, but we also didn't lose." Like the suffrage campaign that preceded it, the ratification effort provided important opportunities for political education and engagement. Many women gained experience, credibility, self-confidence, and networks that will be of continuing importance. The difficulties proponents encountered also offer lessons that could guide future efforts to mobilize around women's issues and candidates. In particular, the struggle has underscored women's need to build broader coalitions at the grassroots level; to seek greater involvement in the less visible aspects of the political process such as redistricting, voter registration, and party caucuses; to identify strategies and causes that can engage disempowered groups; and to convince individuals that they can influence issues that make a difference to their lives.

If the ratification debate continues to bring these points home, and to help women to make their perceptions felt, then the process itself may be more significant than either side's immediate objectives. A twenty-four-word constitutional amendment is more a catalyst than a source of change. Mandates of formal equality cannot adequately address the fundamental social inequalities that persist between the sexes. Substantial progress will require a fundamental reordering of American institutions and values. Such a reconstruction will depend on sustained political as well as legal commitments. Had the ERA sailed smoothly through state capitals, supporters would have missed valuable instruction in the mechanics of realpolitik and the limits of their own influence.

At various points in American history, prolonged constitutional conflict has provided an opportunity to clarify issues and to lay the foundations for broader social change. The conflict over social-welfare legislation during the early part of this century was one example; the campaign for an Equal Rights Amendment could prove to be another. The political truths distilled from this latest ratification struggle are likely to prove more enduring than the fruits of an early symbolic victory. If there is a further optimistic lesson from the ERA campaign, it is that the vast majority of women on both sides of the issue want equality in some sense: equality in social status, economic security, and vocational opportunities. The challenge remaining is to draw from these common aspirations the basis for a common struggle and an expanded legal vision.

Chapter 5

The Evolution of Discrimination Doctrine

The resurgence of a feminist movement in the 1960s drew into question central tenets of legal ideology. The increase of statutory mandates and state constitutional provisions banning sex discrimination were both a catalyst and consequence of changing attitudes toward gender roles. Against this new legal and cultural backdrop, courts began reassessing what standards should apply to sex-based discrimination and what forms of differential treatment should count as discrimination. An overview of judicial grapplings with gender during this period is instructive not only about women's rights but also about the complex relations between cultural norms and doctrinal development.

On the whole, this development has revealed substantial progress toward gender equality. The quarter-century following passage of the 1964 Civil Rights Act witnessed a tightening of legal standards for gender classifications, and a declining tolerance for gender stereotypes. Yet the unevenness of that doctrinal evolution has also suggested limitations in conventional approaches to discrimination law.

As this volume's introduction noted, American equal-protection analysis has developed largely within an Aristotelian tradition that defines equality as similar treatment for those similarly situated. Under this approach, discrimination presents no legal difficulties if the groups differ in ways relevant to a valid regulatory objective. During the 1970s and 1980s increasing challenges to gender classifications underscored the theoretical and practical limitations of this approach. On a theoretical level, it verges on tautology. It allows different treatment for those who are different with respect to legitimate purposes, but offers no criteria for determining which differences matter and what counts as legitimate. On a practical level, the focus on difference has failed adequately to raise, let alone resolve, the problems it seeks to address.[1]

The inadequacies in modern equal protection analysis are not unique to cases involving gender. However, the particular difficulties that emerge in sex discrimination contexts stem in part from courts' attachment to paradigms developed for other objectives. A framework that arose from concerns about "discrete and insular" racial minorities has proven inadequate to deal with concerns of a diffuse majority.[2]

Contemporary gender-discrimination analysis has presented difficulties along several dimensions. At the most basic level, traditional approaches have failed to generate coherent or convincing definitions of difference. All too often, modern equal-protection law has treated as inherent and essential differences that are cultural and contingent. Sex-related characteristics have been both over- and undervalued. In some cases, such as those involving occupational restrictions, courts have allowed biology to dictate destiny. In other contexts, such as pregnancy discrimination, they have ignored woman's special reproductive needs. The focus on whether challenged classifications track some existing differences between the sexes has obscured the disadvantages that follow from such differences.

Although discourses of difference must sometimes have a place, they should begin, not end, analysis. As deconstructionists remind us, women are always already the same and different: the same in their humanity, different in their anatomy. Whichever category we privilege in our legal discourse, the other will always be waiting to disrupt it. By constantly presenting gender issues in difference-oriented frameworks, conventional legal discourse implicitly biases analysis. To pronounce women either the same or different allows men to remain the standard of analysis.[3]

Significant progress toward gender equality will require moving beyond the sameness-difference dilemma. We must insist not just on equal treatment but on woman's treatment as an equal. Such a strategy will require substantial changes in our legal paradigms and social priorities. The alternative framework offered here shifts emphasis from gender differences to gender disadvantages. It builds on the work of other contemporary feminist legal scholars including Katherine Bartlett, Mary Becker, Ruth Colker, Kim Crenshaw, Clare Dalton, Lucinda Findley, Ann Freedman, Mary Jo Frug, Kenneth Karst, Herma Hill Kay, Sylvia Law, Christine Littleton, Isabel Marcus, Carrie Menkel-Meadow, Martha Minow, Frances Olsen, Ann Scales, Elizabeth Schneider, Nadine Taub, Robin West, Stephanie Wildman, Pat Williams, and Wendy Williams. This framework is responsive to two enduring strands of feminist jurisprudence: approaches that stress women's fundamental equality with men, and those that demand accommodation of women's differences from men. A disadvantage approach also incorporates the insights, though not the formulation, of the dominance-oriented paradigm that critics such as Catharine MacKinnon have advocated.[4]

As the introductory chapter reflected, a disadvantage framework is concerned not with difference but with its consequences. The legitimacy of sex-based treatment does not depend on whether the sexes are differently situated. Rather, analysis turns on whether legal recognition of gender distinctions is more likely to reduce or to reinforce gender disparities in political power, social status, and economic security. This alternative model focuses not only on the rationality of means and legitimacy of ends in governmental policies. It demands also that such policies include a substantive commitment to gender equality.

What that commitment requires in particular legal settings cannot be resolved in the abstract. Rather, it demands close attention to context, and to the complexity of women's interests. While this approach shares the concerns of feminist theories phrased in terms of gender dominance, it relies for most purposes on an alternative formulation that can command greater support in legal settings.

Although they differ in other respects, dominance frameworks generally begin with two central premises. The first is that the "relation between the sexes is organized so that men may dominate and women must submit." A second premise, accepted in varying degrees, is that this relation constitutes the most fundamental social hierarchy across time and culture, and that all male-female interactions reflect its structure. From such a perspective, traditional legal doctrine may have talked in terms of gender difference, but only as a means of legitimating gender dominance. As MacKinnon puts it, differences are "inequality's post hoc excuse for itself. They are the outcome presented as origin."[5]

This framework has been important to the development of feminist theory and politics in several respects. By emphasizing the subordination that women encounter as women, it offers a sense of shared identity and a powerful rationale for common action. Such an approach makes clear that the discrimination individuals experience is not an isolated instance of irrational prejudice or anachronistic stereotypes, but part of a systematic social hierarchy. By stressing the cumulative significance of gender differentiation, this paradigm demands focus on fundamental causes. In this sense, it deepens our understanding of sex-based dynamics and of the strategies necessary to change them.

Yet the sources of this theory's strengths are also the sources of its limitations. A we/they world view sharpens our perceptions of women's common inequalities but only by obscuring other critical dynamics. As a foundation for an alternative legal framework, dominance paradigms are too often theoretically reductive and strategically counterproductive. A top-down analysis presents a limited view of relations both within and between gender groups. Part of the difficulty stems from the paradox common to most feminist theory and practice. Feminism gains its power from the claim to speak on behalf of women and to identify common values, perceptions, and interests growing out of women's experience. Yet that experience also teaches that gender is mediated by other patterns of inequality involving race, class, age, ethnicity, and sexual orientation. On a descriptive level, dominance-oriented paradigms that divide the world solely along gender lines ignore the ways that common biological constraints are experienced differently by different groups of women. On a prescriptive level, no theory adequate to challenge gender subordination can avoid addressing the other forms of inequality with which it intersects.

If dominance cannot capture the complexity of women's experience in relation to each other, it is also limited in its account of women's relation to men. Hierarchical analyses often discuss power in undefined ways and understate the influence women can exercise individually and collectively. Power is a contested concept, and in legal settings its meaning needs to be explored rather than assumed.[6]

Even if one passes over these conceptual questions and proceeds with some commonsense understanding of central theoretical terms, dominance frameworks remain more problematic than their advocates often acknowledge. Dynamics of age, class, race, ethnicity, and sexual orientation can be as powerful as gender in ordering social relations. To take an obvious example, a wealthy woman's relations with her young sons or nonwhite male domestic staff do not fit easily within perspectives that stress only gender hierarchies. As theorists such as Cherri Marada, Audre Lorde, and Bell Hooks remind us, our frameworks must challenge the constraints affecting both sexes and acknowledge their joint role in patterns of subordination. Gender dominance is too crude a label for the mutual dependencies and complex power dynamics that characterize certain male-female relations.[7]

For legal purposes, these limitations in dominance approaches pose both strategic and substantive difficulties. As a practical matter, most individuals, including those who exercise lawmaking authority in this society, do not perceive themselves as oppressor and oppressed. To dismiss their perceptions simply as the product of "false consciousness" is to ignore critical questions about the process by which such labels are attached and altered. It is not sufficient to maintain, as dominance approaches generally do, that the public's failure to perceive the extent of gender inequalities is itself a product of such inequalities. If that is the case, the crucial question becomes how best to challenge such patterns under current social conditions and perceptions. For legal settings, the answer is likely to require frameworks that can command greater consensus than those cast in terms of oppression.[8]

Indeed, liberals have even doubted that disadvantage-oriented approaches will be acceptable to a judiciary "deeply invested in viewing itself as neutral and non-interventionist." Yet it is far easier to fit disadvantage than dominance within American jurisprudential traditions; compensatory approaches have, after all, been familiar in some equal-protection contexts such as affirmative action. The rhetoric of disadvantage is also less easily contested and less readily dismissed than the rhetoric of dominance. Disadvantage invites a dialogue about consequences, not motivations; it can speak in terms of statistical facts and frequencies that take account of differences as well as commonalities among women. Such a framework avoids sweeping causal claims about gender hierarchies that in legal settings are often unnecessary and unproductive. There is less conceptual commitment to identifying agents of oppression, and less risk of understating women's opportunities for social influence and social change. As a strategy for enlisting support among men as well as women, disadvantage has some clear advantages. Its rhetoric is less likely to deflect attention from the fact of inequality and the social initiatives necessary to address it.[9]

This is not to suggest that disadvantage is always a preferable paradigm or to overstate its potential in recasting legal analysis. For some theoretical, political, and legal purposes, dominance remains a crucial organizing principle; one does not, for example, speak of rape or pornography as questions of disadvantage. What again bears emphasis is the importance of contextual analysis. Rather than framing the issue as either/or—disadvantage vs. dominance—we should focus on issues of when and why. Each paradigm has its place. Not all historical patterns or contemporary issues fit tidily under any single scheme. The choice of formulation is less important than the conceptual commitment that both imply. Underlying each approach is a sensitivity to patterns of inequality that conventional legal traditions have failed to address.

The importance of reformulating legal analysis should be neither overstated nor undervalued. Some of the difficulties in conventional equal-protection approaches reflect deeper cultural ambivalence about sexual roles and judicial review. Whatever our formal standards, those difficulties will persist. Moreover, as some skeptics argue, if feminists often cannot agree on what disadvantages women in particular cases, it is implausible to suppose that judges will be "closer to the mark." A disadvantage framework confronts many of the same difficulties in assessing women's interests that plague other approaches. How to remain sensitive to individuals' felt preferences while recognizing that they have been socially constructed and constrained is a dilemma for all contemporary political theory.[10]

Yet it does not follow from such critiques that any doctrinal reformulation is in vain. The strategy proposed here at least minimizes difficulties by limiting its aspirations. It does not advocate any universal theoretical structure, but rather suggests an approach that will be useful in a particular context under current social conditions. We need not attempt to determine what women's ultimate or "authentic" interests may be; we know more than enough about what they will not be to provide a current legal agenda. By challenging the structural inequalities of men and women in political power, economic resources, and social status, this framework can lay foundations for a richer human existence than traditional gender roles have permitted.

Changes in law will not of themselves ensure our arrival at any predetermined destination, but they can change our pace and direction of travel, and our awareness of choices along the way. A disadvantage framework imposes no fixed and final determinations of women's interests. But it can do more to ensure that the fundamental problems facing women are acknowledged and addressed. To explore the advantages of disadvantage as an alternative analytic structure, the following discussion traces the evolution of contemporary theories of gender equality in three contexts: the Supreme Court's initial difficulties in establishing a standard of constitutional review for sex-based classifications; judicial efforts to develop a related standard in statutory contexts; and problems in applying those standards in the context of ostensibly "real" differences between the sexes.

The Search for Standards

The 1960s and early 1970s were a period of considerable confusion in the development of sex-discrimination law. As Chapter 2 indicated, the U.S. Supreme Court's sole contribution during the period did little to advance analysis. Rather, its 1961 decision in *Hoyt v. Florida* sustained women's exemption from jury service with the kind of domesticity-as-destiny reasoning characteristic of decisions a century earlier. In the absence of further guidance, lower federal and state courts issued judgments that were inconsistent in rationale and result.[11]

The Supreme Court's initial pronouncements on the subject did little to clarify matters. As one beleaguered federal judge put it, trial courts searching for guidance in the early 1970s were like players "at a shell game who [are] not absolutely sure there is a pea." Part of the problem stemmed from ambiguities about the appropriate standard for assessing sex-based classifications. By the mid-twentieth century, equal-protection analysis had crystallized into a two-tiered scheme of review. For cases involving general economic regulation, courts applied a "rational basis" test, which required only that the distinctions at issue be rationally related to a legitimate state purpose. For cases involving "fundamental interests" (such as speech or voting) or "suspect classifications" (race, alienage, or national origin), the reviewing court engaged in "strict scrutiny" and required that states establish a compelling interest that could not be achieved by less discriminatory means. Since gender classifications had traditionally triggered the more relaxed standard, women's rights groups in the 1970s directed much of their effort toward doctrinal or constitutional changes that would subject gender cases to more rigorous scrutiny.[12]

One opportunity to press for such modifications arose in 1971, when the Supreme Court first held that a gender classification violated the equal-protection clause. Speaking for a unanimous Court, Chief Justice Burger declared in *Reed v. Reed* that an Idaho statute preferring males as estate administrators was unconstitutional. Ironically, this landmark decision was directed at a statute no longer in force. The Idaho legislature had repealed it several months before the case was argued, and the Court's analysis was not particularly enlightening about the fate of other gender classifications. Indeed, the Chief Justice's opinion avoided any analysis of the appropriate standard of judicial review. Although the petitioner as well as various *amici curiae* had argued that sex-based distinctions should be subject to strict scrutiny, and a leading California Supreme Court decision had recently followed that approach, the *Reed* decision purported to apply a version of the more relaxed standard: gender classifications had only to bear a "fair and substantial relation" to statutory objectives. Yet, once having articulated that standard, the Chief Justice proceeded to ignore it. Without further analysis, his opinion dismissed the Idaho Supreme Court's conclusion that a sex-based preference was a reasonable method of minimizing expense and controversy in estate administration. Given the likelihood that more males than females would have business experience, the statutory preference was not self-evidently irrational, at least within the loose sense of rationality that the Court had previously accepted. But none of those equal-protection precedents, nor any prior cases upholding gender classifications, were even mentioned in the Chief Justice's opinion.[13]

Also missing from the Court's analysis was any exploration of the harm of gender stereotypes such as those reflected in the Idaho scheme. The problem in *Reed* was one of inequality, not irrationality. Women arguably were "different" in a relevant sense, but codifying such differences would perpetuate the disadvantages they reflected. Statutory presumptions that females are less qualified than males for administrative positions lends legal validity to a division of roles that is separate but scarcely equal. Although abandoning such stereotypes may involve some administrative costs, affirming their legitimacy carries a higher social price.

While courts and commentators were still poring over the entrails of *Reed,* the Supreme Court decided a second gender case that further complicated the interpretative process. *Frontiero v. Richardson* concerned a federal scheme that allowed male but not female members of the armed forces automatically to claim their spouses as dependents for purposes of gaining various benefits. An initial difficulty in *Frontiero,* which was to recur with some frequency in gender cases throughout the decade, involved identifying the primary victim of discrimination. The plaintiffs, an Air Force lieutenant and her husband, were represented by the ACLU's fledgling Women's Rights Project, and its brief sought to leave no doubt that the statutory scheme penalized female members of the armed forces. By contrast, the government's brief and the lower-court decision maintained that the statute's principal consequences affected male spouses who were not deserving of special protection. In dismissing servicewomen's claims, the trial judge invoked much the same logic that had led to the Supreme Court's celebrated legitimation of "separate-but-equal" racial segregation statutes a century earlier. To the majority in *Plessy v. Ferguson,* if such legislation appeared to "stamp the colored race with a badge of inferiority," it was "solely because the colored race [chose] to put that construction on it." So too, from the trial judge's perspective in *Frontiero,* any "subtl[e]" injuries experienced by servicewomen were "mistaken wrongs, the results of a misunderstanding."[14]

If so, it was a misunderstanding that eight members of the Supreme Court apparently shared. All but one Justice voted to strike down the statute as unconstitutional discrimination against females, but there was no consensus on the underlying standard. Four Justices joined a plurality opinion concluding that classifications based on sex should be subject to the same heightened scrutiny as classifications based on race. Their five colleagues, however, were unprepared to endorse a standard that would effectively accomplish the objectives of a constitutional Equal Rights Amendment, an issue then pending before state legislatures. The majority's reluctance may have stemmed in part from the premise that Justice Powell later advanced in the *Bakke* affirmative-action litigation: the "perception of racial classifications as inherently odious stems from a lengthy and tragic history that gender-based classifications do not share."[15]

Whether sex sould be treated like race for purposes of legal scrutiny has provoked continuing debate among courts and commentators, much of which has obscured the issues it seeks to address. Arguments like Justice Powell's tend to undervalue parallels between different forms of discrimination. Both sex and race are immutable, involuntary, and readily identifiable attributes. Both have served historically to deprive individuals of fundamental civil rights and have exposed them to systematic brutalities. It should not be necessary to draw a full bill of particulars—including prolonged disenfranchisement, educational and occupational constraints, and sexual violence—to establish the "lengthy and tragic" consequences of sexual subordination.

Comparable difficulties arise with the other argument most often advanced for treating sex less stringently than race. In a celebrated footnote to its 1938 *Carolene Products* decision, the Supreme Court suggested that "discrete and insular" minorities" may require special judicial protection because they are vulnerable to the tyranny of the majority. Building on that observation, theorists such as John Hart Ely have emphasized that women are not a minority. Since female voters are in principle able to assert their interests through majoritarian political processes, heightened protection by the nonmajoritarian branch of government is allegedly unnecessary.[16]

It would, however, follow logically from this analysis that all constitutional problems surrounding gender discrimination were solved in 1920 with passage of the suffrage amendment. What such accounts overlook is that numerical majorities can—and in American culture do—assume the functional characteristics of minorities. Women, no less than racial or ethnic groups, have been singled out for subordinate treatment on the basis of ascribed attributes and have internalized many of the social values that perpetuate such subordination. As a consequence, women also have been disempowered in the political process, despite their numerical strength. In fact, under a pluralist democratic system, status as a discrete and insular group has given minorities organizational advantages that women have lacked. It has, in part, been female voters' lack of self-identification and segregation that has impeded political mobilization around women's issues.[17]

To underscore the common injuries of racial and sexual discrimination is not to endorse the kind of unqualified analogy drawn by the plurality opinion in *Frontiero*, or by other courts and commentators in similar contexts. Women as a group have not been subordinated and stigmatized in the same way as racial and ethnic minorities. Most white females have lived on terms of intimacy with members of the dominant group, and many have enjoyed economic and social privileges traditionally denied to individuals of color. Racial discrimination has, on the whole, been perceived as degrading and disempowering. Gender discrimination has reflected a more complicated set of motives, including a desire to preserve privacy and protect women from the consequences of seemingly distinctive physical attributes. To take only the most obvious examples, sex-segregated schools or restrooms do not carry the same cultural meaning as racially segregated facilities. While color-blindness is now widely accepted as a social ideal, attitudes toward gender distinctions are more mixed.[18]

Part of courts' and commentators' difficulties in constructing an adequate analytic framework for sex-based discrimination has stemmed from a reliance on prior race-based paradigms that cannot capture the complexities of gender. One lesson of the feminist movement in the 1960s is that efforts to establish women's equal place in an oppression sweepstakes are rarely fruitful and often divisive. Comparisons that proceed as if race and sex are dichotomous categories ignore the experience of women of color and obscure relationships between the causes and consequences of various forms of subordination. To advance analysis we need closer attention to the continuities and discontinuities in different patterns of discrimination. Rank-ordering their severity or invoking the kind of selective analogies put forth in *Bakke* and *Frontiero* is unlikely to help.

In 1976, the perceived inadequacies of rational-basis and strict-scrutiny standards led the Court to a new "intermediate" approach. The occasion for that announcement was somewhat ironic, given the clear significance of the legal principle and the relative insignificance of the legislation in dispute. At issue in *Craig v. Boren* was the constitutionality of an Oklahoma statute prohibiting the sale of "non-intoxicating" 3.2 beer to males under the age of twenty-one and females under the age of eighteen. Although the Supreme Court assumed *arguendo* that the legislative objective was enhancement of traffic safety, a majority of Justices concluded that the correlation between sex and driving under the influence of alcohol was too tenuous to justify the statutory prohibition. None of the state's traffic studies purported to measure either the effect of 3.2 beer (as opposed to alcohol generally) or the effectiveness of legislation banning only sale (but not consumption). Accordingly, the Court concluded that Oklahoma's scheme failed to satisfy the new intermediate standard for sex-based classifications: that they be "substantially related" to "important" governmental objectives.[19]

Craig remains a troubling decision less for what the Court said than for what it left unsaid. The majority failed to require, as it did in subsequent cases, that states establish that their objectives could not be met by less discriminatory means. At no point did the Court attempt to justify the intermediate standard it applied, or even to acknowledge the departure from traditional two-tiered equal protection analysis. Nor did the majority explain why a classification burdening males should, for the first time, be subject to a heightened measure of scrutiny. Had the Court considered such questions, it might have provided a more satisfactory account of the harms of gender classification in general and of the Oklahoma statute in particular.

The difficulty with the challenged legislation was not just the weakness of the evidence linking gender, beer, and intoxicated driving, but also the state's failure to establish that such evidence had in fact motivated the statutory scheme. Rather, the Court was all too willing to "leave for another day" concerns that counsel had selected a "convenient but false post hoc rationalization," for the challenged legislation. This approach also preempted scrutiny of the stereotypical assumptions underlying the statutory scheme—assumptions about how the sexes mature, socialize, drink, and drive. Attention to such stereotypes could also have provided a response to the challenge posed by Justice Rehnquist's dissent and by other critics of the *Craig* holding: Why was special scrutiny appropriate for a statute burdening men, who scarcely constituted a disadvantaged or disempowered group.[20]

One answer to that question could rely on research concerning gender stereotypes. On the whole, such data confirm that beliefs about appropriate masculine and feminine behavior have significantly constrained individuals' aspirations and achievements. By attaching significance to gender, state regulation can reinforce stereotypes and promote acculturation to confining social roles. As the ACLU brief in *Craig* noted, even seemingly benign assumptions such as those underlying the Oklahoma beer statute can be part of a cultural message that presents men as dominant leaders and women as quiescent companions. Ironically enough, that message emerged in the male plaintiff-appellant's argument in *Craig*. His brief described at some length the insult that Oklahoma's statute visited on a hypothetical combat-eligible male artillery lieutenant ("with all the power and responsibility that entails [sic] in such a position"), who was forced to idle his jeep while his eighteen-year-old date, a noncombat-eligible WAC clerk-typist, purchased a six-pack for him.[21]

The harm of such gender stereotypes for both men and women is not well-captured by traditional equal-protection analysis. A theory that developed in response to invidious discrimination against discrete, insular, and disempowered minorities has coped poorly with certain more subtle injuries that affect both disadvantaged female majorities and privileged male minorities. This is not to imply indifference to male grievances in gender litigation. An overview of the first decade and a half of Supreme Court sex-discrimination decisions reveals that men have been more successful than women both in gaining access to the Court and in obtaining favorable results. A perception common among women's rights litigators has been that cases involving male plaintiffs with whom male Justices could identify have often appeared more sympathetic than cases involving female claimants. Yet the Court's understanding of the harms to both sexes has remained incomplete in both its analytic and its practical dimensions. The doctrinal legacy of the 1970s is an intermediate standard that recognizes the legitimacy of some gender classifications without a theory about which are legitimate and why.[22]

The significance of that standard in shaping litigation outcomes should not be overstated. Indeed, the most important consequence of the Court's intermediate approach may have been to fuel the campaign for a constitutional Equal Rights Amendment. According to its supporters, such an amendment was necessary to establish sex as a suspect classification. Yet it is scarcely self-evident, as those supporters typically assumed, that a different standard would produce different results. To be sure, the scrutiny of racial classifications has been "strict in form and fatal in fact"; almost no nonremedial discrimination has passed muster. But those results indicate attitudes that are reflected in, rather than compelled by, the formal standard of review.[23]

The indeterminacy of standards emphasized in much realist and critical legal scholarship has seldom been more apparent than in contemporary gender cases. A review of decisions under state equal-rights amendments reinforces that point; no systematic relation between result, rationale, and formal standard emerges. Some gender classifications have survived strict scrutiny under state ERAs, and federal litigation could have readily generated comparable consequences even if sex had been elevated to a suspect classification. It is the courts' understandings of gender differences, rather than the formula such differences must satisfy, that has most impeded progressive legal change.[24]

Separate Spheres Revisited: Bona Fide Occupational Qualifications

In exploring contemporary doctrine on gender difference, it is important to consider statutory as well as constitutional developments since they evolved in mutually reinforcing patterns. One of the first and most significant statutory issues involved defenses to employment discrimination claims under the 1964 Civil Rights Act. Of particular importance was the Title VII defense for "bona fide occupational qualification[s] [BFOQs] . . . reasonably necessary to the normal operation of [a] particular business or enterprise." Such a defense was available for discrimination involving sex, religion, and national origin, but not race. Given the sparse and equivocal nature of the legislative history on BFOQs, there was considerable latitude for judicial and administrative interpretation.[25]

Early Title VII litigation met with mixed results. Some lower courts sustained state-mandated or employer-initiated restrictions under rationales analogous to that in *Muller v. Oregon.* Such approaches viewed women's special physical vulnerabilities and reproductive responsibilities as justifications for special "protection" regarding working conditions and exclusion from certain jobs. Under this framework, biological differences served to perpetuate occupational disadvantages. Other judges demanded proof that most women were unable to perform the duties at issue safely or effectively, and some courts required that individual female employees be given opportunities to demonstrate their abilities. In 1969, after pressure from women's groups, the Equal Employment Opportunities Commission issued guidelines indicating that state protective-labor laws should no longer provide a valid BFOQ defense to sex-discrimination claims. That action, together with further litigation and lobbying efforts, resulted in substantial change and encouraged requirements of individual testing for job applicants. In certain areas, however, BFOQ defenses provoked more sustained controversies.[26]

Among the most frequently litigated and ideologically freighted issues were those concerning "sex-plus" restrictions, which coupled gender with some other attribute such as maternity, marriage, or grooming standards. The first such case to come before the United States Supreme Court did little to clarify the legal question presented. *Phillips v. Martin Marietta Corporation* involved a policy that barred job applications from women but not men with preschool children. A divided appellate court sustained the policy on the theory that Congress could not have been so irrational as to prohibit "consideration of the differences between the normal relationships of working fathers and working mothers to their preschool age children." In a brief 1970 *per curiam* opinion, the Supreme Court reversed. Although finding that the employer's policy constituted sex discrimination within the meaning of the statute, the Court remanded for two determinations: whether conflicting family obligations were "demonstrably more relevant to job performance for a woman than a man"; and, if so, whether that difference would constitute a BFOQ defense for the employer's policy.[27]

This summary disposition, while a substantial improvement over the appellate opinion, remained troubling on both practical and theoretical grounds. The Supreme Court's willingness to remand the case implied that employers might under some circumstances legally rely on gender stereotypes about parental roles. Yet those stereotypes have perpetuated the disadvantages Title VII seeks to prevent. To deny mothers responsible job opportunities because of disproportionate family obligations creates economic hardship for female-headed households and encourages married couples to replicate patterns of inequality. Families will benefit financially from assigning priority to husbands' careers and allocating most domestic tasks to wives. That allocation reinforces cultural assumptions about gender roles and the cycle becomes self-perpetuating. By invoking a theoretical framework that asked only if the sexes' different circumstances were relevant to their different treatment, the Court ignored more fundamental questions concerning the legitimacy of that treatment: What were the social costs of penalizing individuals for their parental status and of imposing special disadvantages on mothers?

Similar gender stereotypes and theoretical limitations were apparent in other "sex-plus" cases throughout the late 1960s and 1970s. The most graphic illustrations involved the airline industry, which subjected female but not male employees to an array of restrictions ranging from no-marriage to no-eyeglass rules. The stated rationales for such requirements varied, but omitted from the list were their economic and promotional advantages. Under the age and marriage rules of the 1960s, about 40 percent of stewardesses left each year, reducing the number with enough seniority to qualify for raises and retirement benefits. Although airlines were often adamant that sex appeal played no role in the formulation of gender-based policies, this posture did not readily square with many challenged requirements including physical attractiveness, good complexions, and age limitations of thirty-two. Nor did many employers' stated explanations seem consistent with advertising campaigns depicting flight attendants as "sky bunnies."[28]

Some courts, steeped in the logic of "similarly situated" doctrine, declined to find such policies discriminatory where there were no men occupying precisely the same positions. The absence of male flight attendants thus served to insulate the very policies concerning physical attractiveness that made the job seem inappropriate for males. Other courts were unable to perceive "fat as a feminist issue." Since "tubbiness" was not an immutable characteristic, nor one utterly unrelated to agility in job performance, some judges sustained highly restrictive weight policies, despite evidence of their disparate economic and symbolic impact on women.[29]

As the 1970s progressed, judicial tolerance of such policies declined. It was, however, litigation brought by male rather than female plaintiffs that most clearly exposed the sexist underpinnings of airline practices. The two most celebrated cases—*Diaz v. Pan American* and *Wilson v. Southwest Airlines*—involved bans on hiring male flight attendants. Again the defenses for such discrimination varied. Pan American attempted to demonstrate that women were better suited to the position because of their maternal capacities. According to one psychiatrist's trial testimony, female employees were more able to provide reassurance to passengers anxious about a "sealed enclave" environment. Southwest Airlines, by contrast, presented woman as temptress rather than nurturer. Female flight attendants in hot pants and high boots allegedly were necessary to personify Southwest's "sexy image" and take passengers "skyward with love."[30]

Although neither the flying womb nor the flying bordello defenses passed muster, the logic in *Diaz* and *Wilson* raised as many difficulties as it resolved. In both cases, the courts reasoned that the "essence" of the airline's business was safe transportation, and that other employment attributes were "merely tangential" to that "primary" function. Yet nothing in the statute or its legislative history restricted the BFOQ defense to primary job attributes. Nor did the judge in *Wilson* adequately explain his dismissal of uncontroverted evidence that Southwest's advertising of "female allure and sex appeal" had played an "important role" in the airline's recent economic recovery.[31]

In qualifying its holding, the *Wilson* court emphasized that it was not attempting to eliminate "the commercial exploitation of sex appeal," nor suggesting that customer preference was incapable of establishing a bona fide occupational qualification. What the decision failed to do, however, was develop any convincing distinction between permissible and impermissible forms of commercial exploitation or deference to consumer desires. Nor did the opinion adequately distinguish other cases upholding BFOQs for employees such as Playboy bunnies. According to the *Wilson* court, sexuality was reasonably necessary for bunnies, whose "dominant" function was "forth-rightly to titillate and entice male customers." Yet it was surely arguable that the "essence" of a cocktail waitress' job was to serve alcohol, and that "titillation" was as dominant a part of Southwest's job descriptions as it was of Playboy's. That is not to deny distinctions between the two occupations, but rather to suggest that "essence" analysis is inadequate to identify them. What was needed was a framework linking gender stereotypes with gender disadvantage.[32]

Such a framework was also missing from the Supreme Court's other early BFOQ case, *Dothard v. Rawlinson* (1977). At issue were Alabama prison regulations that prevented women from serving as guards in positions requiring close physical contact with inmates. The Court began its analysis by suggesting that Congress intended the BFOQ defense to be "an extremely narrow exception" to general prohibitions on job discrimination, and that in the "usual case" female employees should have the right to decide for themselves whether to assume certain safety risks. However, the majority went on to uphold Alabama's restrictions in light of "substantial" trial testimony indicating that women would pose a "substantial" security problem because of their special vulnerability to sexual assault.[33]

The factual basis for that testimony, however, was somewhat less than substantial. It consisted mostly of one administrator's speculations and two prior disturbances involving women, neither of whom were guards. Never did the state explain why *sexual* assaults, as opposed to assaults in general, posed a particular threat to prison safety—an omission particularly notable given studies suggesting that women are generally more successful than men at defusing violent situations. Nor did the Court explain its refusal to credit equally "substantial" evidence indicating that properly trained female guards had not presented risks in other states' maximum security prisons. By accepting what Catharine MacKinnon has characterized as the "reasonable rapist" perspective, the *Dothard* decision ignored a range of countervailing social costs. Alabama's regulation perpetuated stereotypes of women's inability to protect themselves and penalized female job applicants for the "barbaric" prision conditions that allegedly placed them at particular risk.[34]

Dothard's conflicting signals—its rhetoric limiting BFOQs and its rationale affirming them—complicated the development of sex-discrimination law in both statutory and constitutional contexts. The decision has served to justify gender classifications in a wide variety of unrelated cases, including everything from bans on male nurses to disparate penalties in criminal-sentencing statutes. It has also guided analysis in other occupational safety areas where exemptions from antidiscrimination mandates have been most prevalent.

Under conventional difference-oriented frameworks, courts in these cases have too often asked only whether gender is relevant to the job as currently structured, not whether the job could reasonably be restructured to make gender irrelevant. Thus, when upholding height restrictions that exclude more female than male applicants, judges have focused on how tall employees must be to operate existing equipment safely, not how feasible it would be to adjust that equipment. In cases implicating privacy interests, inadequate attention has focused on ways of accommodating such interests by modifying job descriptions and facilities rather than banning women.[35]

In the interests of maternal and fetal health, courts have sanctioned layoffs of pregnant employees and bans on employing fertile women in potentially toxic workplaces. Yet to preserve equal opportunity as well as maximize occupational safety, analyses should focus on reducing hazards for both sexes and on providing equivalent employment opportunities for those at risk. A growing body of research suggests that working conditions that involve reproductive dangers can harm men as well as women. Moreover, fetal protection policies, like other forms of protective-labor legislation, have frequently limited women's opportunities in male-dominated industries, while providing inadequate safeguards in female-dominated sectors. Since some twenty million jobs may potentially involve reproductive risks, it is crucial that legal decisionmakers demand responses that reduce workplace hazards rather than restrict women's employment.[36]

An adequate analytic framework would neither deny nor amplify gender differences, but would take greater account of gender disadvantage. That sex but not race has constituted a permissible occupational qualification suggests limitations both in our commitment to eradicating gender discrimination and in our understanding of its origins. If, for example, a state were to demonstrate that black prison guards were more likely than white guards to provoke assaults by white prisoners, that evidence would not provide legal justification for racially based hiring. Under such circumstances, we are prepared to pay the price of color blindness but not of gender blindness. Those different degrees of commitment may, in part, stem from a failure to identify the full countervailing costs of gender consciousness. No matter how "bona fide," sex-based occupational qualifications perpetuate the stereotypes and segregation that contribute to women's unequal labor force status. Challenging this inequality requires challenging the legal ideologies that sustain it, and further legislative or judicial curtailment of the BFOQ defense would be a useful step in that direction.

Objections to abolishing the defense have been in part conceptual and in part pragmatic. As a theoretical matter, it seems awkward to disregard occupations that one sex is biologically incapable of performing, such as wet nurse or semen donor. And, as a practical matter, it is difficult to ignore certain deeply rooted expectations about privacy, sexuality, and artistic authenticity that have made gender appear to be a relevant occupational attribute. It does not, however, follow that all those expectations are worth sustaining or that a BFOQ approach is essential to that end. For example, where one sex is biologically unable to perform the required task, neither a categorical employer policy nor an elaborate statutory edifice is necessary. The individualized-inquiry approach that is already applicable to jobs requiring particular physical capacities, such as strength or height, is theoretically adequate to deal with the largely theoretical difficulty of the would-be male wet nurse. Exceptional cases should not define the standards for occupational equality.

Similar arguments are applicable to other rationales for BFOQ exemptions. As with the Equal Rights Amendment, a narrow privacy exception could be incorporated without undercutting the statute's overall objective. For occupations requiring what EEOC guidelines term "authenticity or genuineness," no categorical exemption appears necessary. In the unusual circumstances where a particular male actor is able authentically to play a female role, surely the entertainment industry would survive a rule requiring fair consideration of his suitability for the part. The absence of race as a BFOQ has not demonstrably hampered casting practices. In some cases, it may also be possible to redescribe the job. The exploitation of sex appeal may be, as some courts put it, "a fact of life," but the exploitation of segregated work forces is not. In the mid-1980s, the sexual integration of the Playboy bunny force turned out to be no more unimaginable than the sexual integration of the legal profession had been a century earlier.[37]

A more satisfactory theoretical framework for employment litigation would take neither gender nor jobs as fixed. The question should not be simply whether women are, or are not, "like men" with respect to a given occupation. Of greater significance is whether that occupation can be redefined to accommodate biological differences and whether gender as a social construct can be redefined to make those differences less occupationally relevant.

Definitions of Difference

Similar questions arise in other major areas where the Supreme Court has confronted sex-based difference as a rationale for sex-based discrimination. In the first two decades following enactment of Title VII and the emergence of constitutional remedies in gender cases, the Court's efforts to define "real" differences yielded a set of chaotic characterizations. Cases involving military service, statutory-rape laws, and employer-affiliated insurance programs again point up the limitations of traditional analytic frameworks. Taken together, these cases reveal inadequate understandings of the relationship between biological difference, gender stereotypes, and social disadvantages.

The best-known illustration involves military service. Throughout the nation's history, cultural expectations and legal restrictions have severely limited female involvement in the armed forces. Until the early 1970s, women constituted less than 2 percent of the American military, and discrimination in placement and promotion, particularly for minorities, was widespread. Enrollment was limited through quotas on female applicants; exclusion from combat positions, military academies, and training programs; and disqualification of women who became pregnant or had minor children. After most of these restrictions were modified or withdrawn during the mid-1970s, female participation in the armed forces substantially increased, reaching 10 percent by the late 1980s. However, such changes occurred largely without judicial intervention. The prevailing view was apparent in one 1968 federal district court opinion: "In providing for involuntary service for men and voluntary service for women, Congress followed the teachings of history that if a nation is to survive, men must provide the first line of defense while women keep the home fires burning."[38]

By the late 1970s, although close to half of all women were in the workforce, this separate-spheres legacy lingered on in both legislative and judicial decisionmaking. In 1977, Congress enacted a compulsory draft registration system excluding women. Seven years later, the Supreme Court in *Rostker v. Goldberg* sustained that exclusion with little attention to its underlying justifications and broader social implications. Once again the focus on difference obscured analysis. Speaking for the majority, Justice Rehnquist reasoned that the purpose of the registration system was to prepare for a draft of combat-eligible troops. Since women were not permitted in combat, they were differently situated from men and could be treated differently in the registration system as well.[39]

This analysis presented a number of difficulties, not the least of which was its patent disregard of relevant precedents and legislative history. Under the prevailing intermediate standard for gender classifications, it was hard to see how exempting women served substantial governmental interests that could not be more narrowly achieved. Even if one assumed the legitimacy of excluding women from combat, their exclusion from registration did not follow. According to government estimates, about a third of those drafted during a national mobilization would not need combat skills. The registration system at issue included noncombat-eligible males, and the Joint Chiefs of Staff had been united in their desire to include females as well. Uncontroverted Defense Department studies suggested that some 80,000 women draftees could serve without administrative difficulties in a total draft of 650,000, and there appeared to be no insurmountable obstacle to inducting fewer females than males. Although some cost would be involved in registering more women than necessary in a system that precluded their combat service, prior Supreme Court decisions had often rejected administrative expense as a rationale for gender classifications.[40]

Moreover, by analyzing the case purely in terms of asserted registration needs, both the majority and dissenting opinions in *Rostker* sidestepped the more fundamental values at issue. Although Justice Rehnquist's analysis made much of the need for judicial deference to military judgments, a review of the legislative record left little doubt that Congress had based its conclusions on political rather than military considerations. In an illuminating passage, which none of the *Rostker* opinions quoted, the Senate Report concluded that a draft of women "would place unprecedented strains on family life . . . A decision which would result in a young mother being drafted and a young father remaining home with the family in a time of national emergency cannot be taken lightly, nor its broader implications ignored. The committee is strongly of the view that such a result, which would occur if women were registered and inducted under the administration plan, is unwise and unacceptable to a large majority of our people."[41]

Legislative debates concerning registration, like those involving military service under an equal rights amendment, reflected an extended array of gender stereotypes. To many politicians, conscription connoted combat, and the prospect of females in battle was unpalatable to congressional as well as military leaders. The concerns were manifold: women could not fight well and men would not fight well in mixed units; the nation would be reluctant to mobilize if its daughters were at risk; sexual proximity would invite sexual promiscuity, and so forth. Former Army Commander William Westmoreland was convinced that if a man and a woman occupied the same foxhole, they'd be "making love not war," and other military and political officials worried about related problems ranging from pregnancy leaves to urinary-tract infections. Despite the declining importance of hand-to-hand combat under modern technology, discussion focused on the specter of females who became too competent or remained too incompetent in physical confrontations; Amazons with hand grenades or Shirley Temples toting bayonets appeared equally unattractive. For women to be killed while serving in combat zones as nurses or support personnel was one thing; for them to engage in killing was quite another. Without proof of the effectiveness of sexually mixed fighting units in the United States, decisionmakers wished to err on the side of excluding women. Yet as long as that policy remained in effect, such proof would not be forthcoming.[42]

Given this deep-seated opposition to women in warfare, the Justices' reluctance to probe the issue in *Rostker* doubtless seemed prudent, particularly since the male plaintiff had not directly challenged female combat exemptions. The Court's political capital is not without limits, and its members might well have assumed that most women did not place conscription high on their list of social priorities. But as a matter of principle, the *Rostker* decision remained troubling. In declining to address the underlying rationale for gender-based registration, the Court left unchallenged certain highly stereotypical assumptions. Yet the available evidence about female performance in combat, simulated-combat, and related police and military contexts has afforded little support for such assumptions. Millions of women here and abroad have served with distinction in these contexts, and serious problems have yet to be demonstrated. As in civilian settings, military positions requiring particular levels of strength or agility can be allocated under gender-neutral guidelines that match individual capacities with job requirements.[43]

How actively to demand the benefits and burdens of military service has been a matter of considerable controversy within the women's movement. Among some constituencies, the objective is to end conscription for both sexes, not to allocate its burdens equally. Many feminists have seen little to be gained from inclusion in a national defense system so dominated by male values and male decisionmakers. Other feminists, though not necessarily disagreeing about the need for change in military structures and service requirements, view women's equal participation as a means to that end. As these commentators also note, sex-based combat restrictions have long served to limit women's entry into the armed forces; their access to desirable jobs, training, and benefits; their opportunities for promotion; and their chance to capitalize on military service in subsequent private and political positions.[44]

Whatever the practical effects of full female participation in the military, there remain powerful symbolic reasons to seek that objective. As subsequent discussion of "benign" discrimination will suggest, it is difficult for women to attain equal respect and equal treatment as citizens while exempt from one of citizenship's central obligations. The stereotypes underpinning such exemptions are not easily confined. Assumptions about females' physical incapacities and maternal responsibilities spill over to other areas of social life and reinforce traditional expectations about gender roles and hierarchies. The issue in *Rostker* was far more fundamental than the Court's analysis acknowledged. And the result of its decision was to legitimate assumptions for which both men and women have paid a heavy price.

A similar point is applicable to the Court's first gender-related decision in the criminal context. The case, *Michael M. v. Superior Court,* involved California statutory-rape legislation that imposed criminal penalties on males who had sexual intercourse with females under the age of eighteen, but placed no liability on underage females or on females over eighteen who had intercourse with underage males. In sustaining the statute against equal-protection challenges, a divided Court relied on biological differences to justify differential treatment.[45]

Justice Rehnquist's plurality opinion began by acknowledging that the legislative motives underlying the prohibition were doubtless mixed and somewhat murky. But at least one of the purposes of the statute appeared to be prevention of pregnancy. As both his opinion and Justice Stewart's concurrence emphasized, men and women were "not similarly situated" with respect to that purpose. By the plurality's reasoning: Only women may become pregnant, and they suffer "disproportionately the profound physical, emotional, and psychological consequences of sexual activity . . . Because virtually all of the significant harmful and inescapably identifiable consequences of teenage pregnancy fall on the young female, a legislature acts well within its authority when it elects to punish only the [male] participant who, by nature, suffers few of the consequences of his conduct." A gender-neutral statute that penalized underage females might compromise the state's objectives by discouraging complainants. Moreover, in the plurality's view, the statute discriminated only against males, a class not entitled to "special [judicial] solicitude" because of past discrimination or "peculiar disadvantages."[46]

Michael M.'s analysis is problematic on several counts. As a threshold matter, it stands in sharp contrast to the Supreme Court's approach in prior decisions regarding pregnancy discrimination, discussed more fully in Chapter 6. For example, when upholding the exclusion of childbirth expenses from disability programs, the Court declined even to view such practices as gender-based; the distinction was, in the majority's now-celebrated phrase, "between pregnant women and non-pregnant persons." By contrast, in sustaining California's statutory-rape law, the Court justified sex-based classifications on the theory that women, unlike men, were all potentially "pregnant persons," and therefore entitled to special treatment.[47]

Although *Michael M.*'s recognition of pregnancy as gender-related was an advance over earlier decisions, its understanding of that relationship remained inadequate. In effect, the Court confused nature and nurture; it assumed that the harmful consequences of pregnancy are "by nature" visited only on women, when in fact much of that asymmetry is culturally constructed. What makes sexual activity such a special risk for female adolescents is, in large measure, a particular set of social understandings about contraception, abortion, promiscuity, sexual aggression, and parental responsibility. The *Michael M.* decision, and the statute it sustained, took as biologically "inescapable" what is, and should be, subject to cultural redefinition.

The Court's opinion is equally problematic on other levels. Contrary to the plurality's assertion, the statute at issue did not discriminate only against men. Like other ostensibly "benign" gender classifications, sex-specific statutory-rape legislation disadvantages women in several respects. The history of such legislation suggests that it originated in concerns about chastity rather than pregnancy. As feminists such as Frances Olsen and Wendy Williams have argued, the assumption that only underage women lack capacity to consent is both demeaning and confining. To the extent that statutory-rape provisions are known and enforced, they risk legitimating stereotypes of male aggressiveness and female vulnerability, as well as double standards of morality that traditionally have served to repress women's sexual expression. Yet such adverse consequences escaped notice in all four of the Court's opinions.[48]

Moreover, the plurality's treatment of legislative purpose stands in sharp contrast to its approach in other contexts. In an extended footnote, Justice Rehnquist suggested that even if preservation of female chastity were conceded to be one of the state's objectives, the Court would not "strike down an otherwise constitutional statute on the basis of an alleged illicit legislative motive." Not only is that statement hard to reconcile with the Court's practice in other discrimination cases, it renders the entire quest for legislative intent superfluous. In any event, even assuming *arguendo* that prevention of unwanted pregnancy had in fact been the legislature's dominant objective, it is difficult to perceive gender-specific statutory rape prohibitions as substantially related to that goal. The infrequency of prosecution and the frequency of adolescent sexual activity do not point to criminalization as a rational strategy for controlling reproduction.[49]

Nor was there any evidence in *Michael M.* that the majority of states with sex-neutral prohibitions experienced greater enforcement difficulties than those with sex-specific provisions. As a practical matter, prosecution is most likely in contexts like *Michael M.*, where it would be difficult to meet the stringent standards of coercion applicable in adult rape cases, but where there is evidence of nonconsent. Although the complainant in *Michael M.* had "willingly participated" in kissing the defendant, she had also told him she didn't want to have intercourse and let him "have his way" only after he had hit her several times.[50]

Those facts point up the difficulties with current statutory rape prohibitions, including gender-neutral ones. Any bright-line age distinction will inevitably prove both under- and overinclusive, and gender neutrality may obscure factual asymmetries in sexual relationships. In this culture, men and women are not equally vulnerable to coercive sex, and age is an imperfect proxy for capacity to consent. Exploitation exists on a continuum, and ability to resist reflects a variety of physical, social, psychological, and economic factors that are related to both age and gender but not fully captured by either.

Given these complexities, the most defensible approach is to extend some protection to both underage males and females from sexual contact by adults, but to adopt a flexible penalty and enforcement structure that focuses on consent rather than chastity. To assume, as did the Court in *Michael M.*, that gender-based criminal prohibitions can significantly reduce the harms of adolescent pregnancy is to misdescribe the problem and mislead as to the solution. Appropriate social strategies will not emerge from frameworks such as *Michael M.*'s, which attribute all the hardships of unwed pregnancy to biological differences rather than social institutions.[51]

A final area in which courts have confronted "real" differences between the sexes has involved employer-affiliated insurance policies. During the late 1970s and early 1980s, leading decisions in this area provoked heated disputes in which participants spoke past each other on most of the major issues. Underlying the controversy are certain sex-related patterns that have affected insurance underwriting. In modern American society, women on the average live longer, have fewer automobile accidents, and incur greater health costs than men. As a consequence, most insurance programs have distinguished between the sexes in rates or coverage. Such distinctions demand tradeoffs of efficiency, equity, and equality not readily resolved under conventional discrimination doctrine.[52]

After passage of the 1964 Civil Rights Act, female litigants began challenging the legality of sex-based classifications in employer-sponsored or administered insurance programs. In the first of these cases to reach the Supreme Court, *Los Angeles Department of Water and Power v. Manhart*, a majority of Justices concluded that Title VII of the Act prohibits employers from requiring women to contribute approximately 15 percent more in premiums to obtain the same pension protection that men received. Five years later, in *Arizona Governing Committee v. Norris*, the Court extended its logic to prohibit employers from offering optional pension coverage through plans that pay women lower benefits than men who have made equal contributions.[53]

According to the *Manhart* majority, reliance on sex to predict longevity violates the basic principles of Title VII. In the Court's view, employers must treat their employees with "thoughtful scrutiny as individuals," not as "simply components of a racial, religious, or sexual or national class." Neither the *Manhart* nor *Norris* majority found anything "inherently unfair" about requiring male policyholders to subsidize their longer-lived female counterparts. In insurance contexts, "the better risks always subsidize the poorer risks . . . and nothing more than habit makes one subsidy seem less fair than [another]."[54]

Although both decisions carefully restricted their application to prospective relief in an employer-affiliated plan, their reasoning was not so readily limited. It quickly became the basis for proposed state and federal legislation that would prohibit sex-based premiums and payouts by all insurance companies. The potential costs of gender-neutrality in such contexts galvanized immediate opposition.[55]

That opposition found a number of easy targets in the reasoning of *Manhart* and *Norris*. Much of the majority's analysis appeared inconsistent with prior Title VII principles or settled actuarial practices. The rationale banning sex-based insurance classifications did not fit easily within the Court's conventional difference-oriented approach to gender discrimination. Since the sexes were not similarly situated with respect to insurable risks, why should they be entitled to similar treatment? As the *Manhart* dissent noted, the Court's refusal to allow discrimination on the basis of longevity was difficult to reconcile with prior decisions upholding discrimination on the basis of pregnancy. Insurance classifications premised on life span scarcely appeared less "fair" than those premised on reproductive capacity.[56]

Moreover, the Court's focus on fairness to individuals rather than classes obscured certain basic facts about insurance underwriting. Life expectancy is not some fixed individual attribute, but a prediction based on past experience with groups. Such a prediction presupposes judgments about what sorts of group characterizations are most equitable and efficient. In that sense the Court's assertions about inherent fairness assumed the point at issue. For purposes of insurance classifications, "thoughtful scrutiny" of individuals requires assumptions about classes. It was never clear from *Manhart*'s and *Norris'* cursory analyses why assumptions based on gender were necessarily inequitable for either sex, since women would benefit from such assumptions in certain contexts and men would benefit in others.

What constitutes fairness in insurance underwriting depends on a far more complex set of normative and empirical premises than either the Court or its critics have generally acknowledged. Any adequate analysis requires attention to at least three concerns: the efficiency costs of substituting factors other than sex in predicting risk; the distributional consequences of that substitution; and the nonquantifiable social values that would be served by disregarding sex when determining payouts and premiums. The difficulty in developing coherent national policy is that there is little consensus within the public or scholarly community on any of these issues.

Much of the dispute among commentators centers on the significance of gender as a predictive device. According to many critics, replacing sex with other risk-related factors correlated with sex, such as smoking or automobile mileage, would increase monitoring costs and offer insufficient predictive power to justify the expense. Drawing on an array of data, including mortality studies of various lower mammals, some analysts have argued that female longevity is biologically based and therefore particularly justifiable as an actuarial tool. Disregarding gender, they have claimed, could increase the costs of insurance coverage by as much as one to two billion dollars. Many of those costs would ultimately be born by women—those who purchase automobile and life insurance, and those who partially subsidize or receive benefits from their husbands' policies.[57]

Yet as defenders of the *Manhart-Norris* approach have noted, these claims are problematic on several grounds. Gender is not a stable predictor of insurance risks. Research purporting to establish biological explanations for mortality differentials is methodologically questionable and impossible to reconcile with the enormous variation in the sexes' relative longevity rates over time and place. Women's longer life span is a fairly recent and culturally contingent phenomenon, and changes in gender roles and smoking behavior over the last two decades suggest that past correlations between sex and mortality may no longer be valid. Although underwriters will concededly incur some costs in replacing gender with other factors that more directly bear on risks, the costs of that replacement often have been inflated. Most estimates fail to take into account the long-range efficiency savings from developing ways to monitor more stable and precise predictive criteria. Employers who provide insurance coverage directly have seldom used sex as a classifying device, and neither they nor the private companies that have moved to gender-blind policies have experienced the financially devastating consequences that insurance-industry analysts have typically projected.[58]

How much women would gain in economic terms from the elimination of sex-based underwriting practices is difficult to assess. It is possible that insurance companies would develop proxies for sex that have disproportionate effects on female consumers. Nonetheless, studies by women's rights organizations have maintained that female policyholders on the whole would be better off under a gender-blind system. According to such research, any cost increases in automobile and life insurance for women would be more than offset by savings in medical and pension coverage. However, if the inquiry is broadened to include wives of male policyholders, the net tradeoff is much less clear, since many of these women would bear indirect losses from their husbands' increased premiums or narrowed coverage.[59]

Given the uncertainties surrounding the efficiency costs and distributional consequences of gender-neutral insurance practices, it makes sense to focus on nonquantifiable values. From that perspective, the argument for banning sex-based classifications is stronger than the Court's difference-oriented framework makes apparent. Attitudes about the legitimacy of group treatment in one context tend to spill over into others. Practices that reinforce perceptions of gender difference usually have not worked to women's advantage, and insurance decisionmaking does not promise to be an exception. A more egalitarian social order is unlikely to result from the attitudes that underlie insurers' lobbying campaign against the Equal Rights Amendment and against legislation mandating sex-neutral underwriting structures. For example, full-page advertisements in the 1983 *New York Times* relied heavily on arguments about the "unfairness" of compelling "single men to buy maternity benefits." It is such claims about gender roles and responsibilities that have institutionalized unfairness toward women.[60]

These are also claims that the Court's traditional legal framework is ill-suited to confront. The results in *Manhart* and *Norris* appear more vulnerable because they occur within an analytic structure that focuses on gender differences rather than disadvantages. Such a focus carries particular costs in circumstances like insurance, where the extent of differences is readily exaggerated. About 80 percent of all women have life spans equivalent to those of men. Males and females who drive comparable amounts present comparable risks, and both sexes have an equal interest in obtaining protection for medical and retirement expenses. Mandating some internal subsidies by private insurers may be cheaper or more politically acceptable than providing adequate public insurance. In the final analysis, the rationale for supporting gender-blind insurance need not turn on abstract appeals to individual rights. It can rest on deeper understandings of joint responsibility, in which men and women share risks and recognize common values and concerns.

Part Three

CONTEMPORARY ISSUES

Chapter 6

False Dichotomies

For over a century, sex-discrimination law has foundered on definitions of difference. It has had comparable problems with dichotomies. Questions involving benign versus invidious classifications, special versus equal treatment, and public versus private spheres have plagued the feminist movement almost since its inception. During the 1970s and 1980s, a series of lawsuits began bringing such dichotomies into sharper focus. Part of the difficulty surrounding these issues has stemmed from the tendency of legal systems to seek bright lines, and the unwillingness of social problems to fit neatly into conceptual cubbyholes. But that difficulty is compounded by decisionmakers' failure to acknowledge its complexity, and to resist frameworks that distort the issue they purport to describe. Only by recognizing the blurred boundaries of these dichotomies can we fully address their underlying concerns.

An alternative strategy is especially crucial for issues that intersect welfare, work, and family policies. The law's sensitivity to gender inequality in matters such as social security, parental leave, childcare, and poverty initiatives has both theoretical and practical importance. Traditional analysis, which lacks such sensitivity, has remained unable to reconcile the principle of formal equality with the fact of social inequality.

As in other contexts, many limitations in conventional approaches are attributable to a preoccupation with gender difference rather than with the disadvantages that follow from it. Too much attention has focused on whether there are disparities between men's and women's social experience and too little on whether a legal classification reflecting such disparities exacerbates or mitigates them. As much contemporary feminist theory suggests, a more satisfactory approach will require closer attention to context than conventional legal analysis has encouraged. By focusing more concretely on the way distinctions such as benign versus invidious, special versus equal, and public versus private have been applied, we may gain a better understanding of their limitations.

Benign and Invidious Discrimination in Welfare Policy: Elderly Women and Social Security

As the history of the ERA and protective-labor campaigns makes evident, one of the most divisive issues confronting feminists throughout this century has involved "benign" discrimination, that is, practices purporting to benefit women. The following analysis focuses on social welfare decisions dating from the mid-1970s that established a general framework for preferential policies. Other chapters touch on related issues of benign discrimination, for example, those concerning military service, affirmative-action programs, and single-sex education.

In 1974, the Supreme Court issued the first of these preferential-treatment decisions. *Kahn v. Shevin* involved a challenge to a Florida tax exemption for property worth less than five hundred dollars belonging to widows or disabled residents, but not to widowers. Writing for the majority, Justice Douglas sustained the statute. As the son of a widow in straitened circumstances, he may have been especially sensitive to the special "financial difficulties confronting the lone woman in Florida." Under his analysis, states could respond to gender disparities in income and job opportunities through tax exemptions. That holding received mixed reviews. To some commentators, the Supreme Court appeared to be granting women the best of both worlds by distinguishing invidious and benign discrimination. Many feminists, however, found cause for concern, more in the Court's reasoning than its results.[1]

One obvious difficulty involved the majority's assumptions about legislative purpose. It strains credulity to believe that the state legislators who designed the exemption in 1885 and reauthorized it in 1941 intended the statute to compensate for the "inhospitable" job market confronting women. A more credible explanation for Florida's exemption was that legislators assumed that widows were more likely than widowers to have been dependent on their spouses and were more in need of economic assistance. Yet stereotyping wives as dependent carries a cost. Moreover, as subsequent cases made evident, that cost is amplified by standards that permit courts to hypothesize benign legislative motives, however improbable. Yet never did such concerns figure in *Kahn*'s assessment.

Nor did the majority's opinion acknowledge certain facts necessary to place the Florida statute in proper context. The exemption was worth only about fifteen dollars a year under prevailing tax rates, and its application was both over- and underinclusive. A provision intended to remedy past discrimination or the feminization of poverty would not have affected all widows, whatever their economic circumstances. If the state's primary objective had been compensatory, why did the exemption exclude women who had never married or who had been divorced? Such individuals would have been more likely than widows to have worked substantial periods and to have suffered job bias. Alternatively, if the legislature's primary concern had been poverty, why were benefits available to wealthy heiresses and not to indigent widows who lacked real property? As Justice Brennan's dissent noted, Florida's statutory approach scarcely seemed consistent with the new intermediate standard applicable to gender classifications, which required that they be precisely tailored to serve substantial objectives not available through less discriminatory means.[2]

A more contextual analysis in *Kahn* would have focused not only on the statute's historical origins and concrete consequences, but also on its relation to broader ideological patterns. Justice Douglas' approving quotation from *Muller v. Oregon* suggests a striking insensitivity to the price of paternalism. Despite extensive references in *amici* briefs to the cultural consequences of stereotyping, no such considerations figured in any of the Justices' opinions. Although each expressed concerns about the legacy of sex discrimination, none discussed whether token gestures like Florida's contributed more to the problem than to the solution. Unlike other remedial efforts, such as affirmative-action programs, tax abatement responds only to the symptoms of gender bias, not to its underlying causes. And when the response is restricted to the kind of underinclusive, underfunded benefit at issue in *Kahn*, the line between benign and invidious discrimination begins to blur.[3]

The fuzziness of that boundary became even more apparent three years later in *Califano v. Goldfarb*. At issue was a provision of the federal Old Age Survivors and Disability Insurance Benefits program that extended survivors' benefits to a widow, but not to a widower, unless he had been receiving at least one-half of his support from his wife prior to her death. Although a majority of Justices found the statute unconstitutional, they reached no consensus on a rationale for that conclusion. Four members of the Court viewed the statute as invidious discrimination against women, whose Social Security contributions would not buy the same level of support for a surviving spouse as would the contributions of a similarly situated man. Four other Justices voted to sustain the legislation as permissible benign discrimination in favor of widows. Following *Kahn*, these dissenting Justices reasoned that surviving wives were far more likely to have been dependent than surviving husbands. From this perspective, it appeared reasonable for the government to avoid administrative costs by assuming the dependency of women but not men. Nor did that approach seem unfair to female wage earners, since the Social Security system had never apportioned benefits solely by reference to the level of individual contributions; it also took into account beneficiaries' needs. Justice Stevens, who provided the crucial fifth vote to strike down the statute, agreed with his dissenting colleagues that the statute did not unconstitutionally penalize women contributors, but he disagreed that Congress had acted from a considered judgment about administrative costs. In his view, the legislation reinforced a "traditional way of thinking about females," which unreflectively and inappropriately equated widowhood with dependency.[4]

Although the *Goldfarb* decision received sharp criticism for its inability to identify the true victims of discrimination, commentators were no less divided. Ruth Bader Ginsburg, the ACLU Women's Rights Project attorney who litigated the case, viewed the result as a feminist triumph. It was the "first successful gender discrimination equal protection case carrying a substantial price tag," estimated at five hundred million dollars. Yet from the standpoint of class, the decision had other costs that its supporters failed to acknowledge. Under statutory requirements unaffected by the *Goldfarb* holding, husbands or wives could benefit as survivors only to the extent that benefits available from their spouses' account exceeded benefits available from their own. The only men who profited from the Court's determination were those who could not prove dependency and who were also not significant contributors to the Social Security system. These men, like the *Goldfarb* plaintiff, were typically part of other pension plans.[5]

Thus, as William Simon has argued, a holding "designed to vindicate the rights of [working] women . . . actually affected only a small and adventitiously defined subset of [their] families," few of whom were among the most economically vulnerable classes. Given these distributional consequences, the decision's price tag was scarcely grounds for rejoicing. In a Social Security system subject to budgetary constraints, increased costs may be absorbed not by some abstract governmental entity but by other participants, most of them women.[6]

By focusing solely on the equitable claims of contributors, and ignoring the economic circumstances of beneficiaries, the *Goldfarb* majority endorsed a regressive income distribution. In aggregate terms, that approach could only serve to disadvantage women. The Social Security Administration has estimated that female contributors provide just over a quarter of all program revenues, but receive over half of all benefits; thus, women will not benefit economically from a gender-neutral, contributor-oriented framework that seeks to equalize the returns to men's and women's tax payments. Nor is the issue of gender stereotypes as simple as the *Goldfarb* majority implied. If women suffer from a system that assumes their dependency, the best response may involve not only a denial of sex-based assumptions, but also a challenge to the underlying causes and pejorative connotations of dependency. As much contemporary feminist theory suggests, the objective should not be universal conformity to some rugged individualist model of autonomous wage earners. Rather, social policy should support varied social roles and the interdependence that accompanies them.[7]

The complexity of tradeoffs involving preferential treatment and gender stereotypes became more apparent in the decade following *Goldfarb,* and the Supreme Court's benign-invidious distinction did little to clarify the issue. In a series of subsequent welfare cases, the Court summarily struck down various sex-based dependency provisions, but it sustained certain other classifications that appeared to have remedial objectives. Again, the decisions met with mixed responses. Some leading women's rights advocates, including Ginsburg, applauded the Court's efforts to ensure "general rule[s] of equal treatment while leaving a corridor open for genuinely compensatory classifications." Other feminists found that corridor paved with the same overbroad and disabling generalizations about female dependency that had characterized *Muller* and its modern analogues.[8]

Underpinning this dispute are broader disagreements about the relation between preference and paternalism and between feminist commitments and class priorities. According to some commentators, benign discrimination is a contradiction in terms. Almost all gender classifications have purported to serve women's true interests, and legal doctrine has been consistently inadequate in sorting among them. Group-based treatment poses a special risk when the group itself lacks power in the processes by which its concerns are evaluated. Yet at this historical juncture, a categorical rejection of all preferential treatment would pose greater risks. For example, as Chapter 8 suggests, we cannot afford to jettison those forms of affirmative action most likely to challenge the stereotypes on which disabling discrimination rests. So too, in welfare contexts, an insistence on formal equality comes too early and too late. We need an alternative framework that focuses less on gender differences and more on gender disadvantages. The issue should not be whether women are more likely to be dependent, or to have lacked the same economic opportunities as men. The more critical question is whether classifications reflecting such disparities are likely to reduce them.

That determination requires close attention to context. The difficulty in many social-welfare cases is that women's interests point in multiple directions. There are tradeoffs not only among objectives, such as preserving protection and challenging stereotypes, but also among beneficiaries. As long as certain entitlements are financed from fixed revenues, increasing payouts for one group of women (for example, female wage earners) can reduce the resources available to another (for example, female survivors). Such distributional concerns are implicated not only by cases like *Goldfarb* but also by Social Security reform proposals supported by some feminist groups. Many of these proposals would help reduce sex-based disparities among contributors, but would also redirect resources away from the neediest female recipients.[9]

These conflicts cannot be resolved simply through reform of the Social Security system; they underscore the need for a wider array of support structures that respond to women's varying circumstances and concerns. Although the last quarter-century has witnessed substantial improvement in programs for the elderly, fundamental inadequacies remain. Older women are the fastest growing segment of American society, and many of them are in serious need. In the late 1980s, almost three-quarters of the elderly poor were female. Almost one-fifth of women over sixty-five were living in poverty, and over a third of older black and Hispanic women were indigent. As a group, elderly females have been much less likely than males to have adequate income because of lower earnings, more discontinuous work histories, and greater representation in part-time low-level employment positions without pension and medical coverage. Women have also been disproportionately represented among the very elderly, those over seventy-five, who suffer most from inadequacies in this nation's medical, nursing, and welfare programs. Without significant reforms, these inadequacies are likely to increase as the baby-boom generation reaches retirement. At a minimum, a humane social policy for the elderly will require more vigorous enforcement of prohibitions against age discrimination; expansion of subsidized health care, pension, and related social services; more comprehensive, cost-effective programs for individuals requiring long-term or in-home assistance; and Social Security reforms that promote equitable treatment of women's paid *and* unpaid domestic labor.[10]

Such initiatives will require more than ad hoc judicial intervention. Yet while most litigation permits only tinkering at the edges of highly inadequate public programs, it does provide opportunities to clarify the values at issue. The problem with contemporary gender decisions is that they have tended to describe only one side of the balance sheet, and to overlook distributional consequences across class as well as sex. To emphasize earners' entitlements deflects attention from beneficiaries' needs. To strike down all vestiges of gender stereotypes discounts hardships to which those stereotypes have contributed. However, codifying such generalizations also risks reinforcing them. If, as feminist legal scholars have frequently emphasized, we cannot always "have it both ways, we need to think carefully about which way we want to have it."[11]

A more satisfactory approach to benign-invidious distinctions will require dismantling the dichotomy. Gender preferences are a mixed blessing and should be analyzed as such. To sort out the competing concerns will require attention to a broad range of issues. What is the amount, duration, and distribution of the preference? Is it more likely to expand women's social roles or to reinforce gender stereotypes? Does it direct significant levels of support to those most entitled to compensation or assistance? How great a role do "preferred" groups play in determining their own interests?

The danger with any such contextual approach is that it leaves considerable discretion with judicial and legislative bodies that have exercised it poorly in the past. The problems characterizing the Supreme Court's approach have been equally apparent in the lower branches of the state and federal systems, where the *Kahn* framework has served to legitimate everything from gender-based alimony and support statutes to discrimination against mothers in the armed forces. But the progress in some areas of sex-discrimination law over the last half-century leaves hope that a more searching set of questions will lead to a more convincing range of responses.[12]

Special Treatment or Equal Treatment: Pregnancy, Maternal, and Caretaking Policy

During the late 1970s and 1980s, another dimension of the benign-discrimination debate sparked particular controversy within the women's movement. The issue involved "special" treatment for pregnant workers and employed mothers, and it raised many of the same protective-labor questions that had divided feminists for decades. It also pointed up the advantages of a framework focused on disadvantages rather than difference.

The origins of the special-treatment dispute are in part attributable to courts' initial confusion about how to cope with pregnancy discrimination. That legal issue evolved against a cluster of social constraints that discouraged accommodation of women's productive and reproductive roles. Although historical and cross-cultural research leaves no doubt about most women's capacity to work during much of the period surrounding childbirth, the reigning ideology of nineteenth- and early-twentieth-century America assumed otherwise. A pregnant woman should avoid "needlessly publishing her sacred secret" in workplace settings and should decline any labor-force activity that might distract colleagues or compromise her maternal mission.[13]

The prevailing and self-perpetuating assumption was that women were provisional workers who would (or should) not have paid employment during early child-rearing years. That assumption, in turn, discouraged development of maternity policies that might enable women to become less provisional. Until the mid-1970s, employers routinely dismissed pregnant workers once their condition became apparent and frequently failed to reinstate those who wished to return. Most state unemployment and insurance programs excluded pregnancy from coverage, leaving an estimated three-quarters of the work force without paid maternity leave. Such policies reinforced stereotypes that locked women into low-paying, dead-end jobs that did not require continuous commitment.[14]

By the mid-1970s, the disparity between traditional assumptions and labor-force patterns had become increasingly apparent. About 85 percent of female employees could expect to become pregnant at some point in their working lives, and a rapidly increasing group was likely to remain in the workforce. A decade later, close to two-thirds of those in prime child-bearing years were in the paid labor force and half of all mothers were returning to work within a year after childbirth. In this context, the lack of adequate maternity provisions brought increasing concern. Prompted by the growing consciousness of gender discrimination and the increasing availability of legal remedies, female litigants began challenging various forms of pregnancy discrimination. Given the broad social, economic, and ideological implications of maternity policies, the Supreme Court's initial responses to such challenges were highly unsettling. What enshrines these decisions as landmark sex-discrimination cases is the Court's unwillingness to treat them as such.[15]

Indeed, in the first of a series of pregnancy-related decisions, the Justices' majority opinion relegated the entire discussion of discrimination to a footnote. *Geduldig v. Aiello* upheld the constitutionality of a California program that excluded pregnancy from insurance coverage, but included disabilities affecting only men. According to a footnote in Justice Stewart's opinion, the challenged classification did not even involve "gender as such." Rather, California had simply drawn a distinction between—in the Court's memorable phrase—"pregnant women and non-pregnant persons." While the first class was exclusively female, the second was not exclusively male. Two years later, in *General Electric Co. v. Gilbert,* the Court extended this analysis by rejecting a Title VII challenge to pregnancy exclusions in a private employer's benefits program. According to the *General Electric-Geduldig* rationale, no discrimination was present since pregnancy posed an "additional risk, unique to women," and female employees as a group already received payments exceeding their relative contributions to the plan.[16]

By focusing on biological differences rather than societal disadvantages, the Court ended up with characterizations that were incoherent, inconsistent, and ultimately indefensible. The notion that distinctions based on pregnancy were not distinctions based on "gender as such" obscured the most basic physical, cultural, and historical meanings of reproduction. To characterize pregnancy as "unique" both assumed what should have been at issue and made that assumption from a male reference point. Men's physiology set the standard against which women's claims appeared only "additional."[17]

Nowhere in these cases did the Court give any coherent account of what makes female reproduction "unique" for purposes of medical coverage. It is true, as the majority noted in *General Electric,* that pregnancy is often a voluntary and desired condition. But that is not universally the case. Nor was the Court's characterization sufficient to justify the disability policies in *General Electric* and *Geduldig,* both of which included other voluntary conditions and male sex-related disabilities, such as vasectomies and prostatectomies. Although women did not receive lower benefits than men relative to overall contributions, female workers had greater risks of noncovered disabilities. Failure to address such risks exacerbated women's economic inequality and legitimated the stereotypes that perpetuated it. Such costs were of particular concern to the increasing number of families dependent on female wage earners.[18]

Following these Supreme Court decisions, intensive lobbying prompted passage of the 1978 Pregnancy Discrimination Act. The Act amended Title VII to provide that "women affected by pregnancy, childbirth, and related medical conditions shall be treated the same as other persons not so affected but similar in their ability or inability to work." Although that amendment has brought significant improvements in maternity policies, it has not effectively addressed the tensions between women's productive and reproductive roles. This is one of the contexts in which equality in form has not yielded equality in fact. The Act does not require the provision of adequate disability programs, and, in the absence of statutory requirements, such programs have been slow to develop. A decade after passage of the Act, about a third of the female work force still lacked job-protected leaves, and even those with such protection could not count on returning to their same position at the time they wished. Three-fifths of female employees were not entitled to wage replacement for the normal period of disability. The United States remained alone among major industrialized countries in its failure to guarantee such benefits.[19]

Efforts by some states to improve the situation gave rise to battles over maternity leave that again resulted in Supreme Court litigation. The case arose when Lillian Garland, a Los Angeles bank receptionist, challenged her employer's noncompliance with the California Fair Employment Practices Act. Like legislation in several other states, the Act required reasonable leaves of absence for pregnant workers, but it did not mandate comparable protection for other temporarily disabled workers. Garland's employer claimed that the California statute was preempted by the federal Pregnancy Discrimination Act, which requires that pregnancy be treated the "same" as other disabilities.[20]

In 1987, a divided Court rejected that claim and sustained the state statute. The majority acknowledged that the legislative history of the Pregnancy Discrimination Act was not entirely conclusive, but reasoned that policies such as California's were consistent with congressional intent, which was to guarantee women's right to "participate fully and equally in the workforce." By contrast, three dissenting Justices found nothing in the legislative record to authorize a departure from the clear language and design of the federal Act, which required equivalent treatment for pregnancy and other disabilities.[21]

Although most leaders of the women's movement publicly claimed *California Federal* as a victory, private reactions were more mixed. Some celebrations were tempered by a subsequent Supreme Court decision, which held that states may deny unemployment compensation to women whose employers would not reinstate them after "voluntary" pregnancy leaves. Other feminists found little to celebrate in the first instance. Indeed, the case had sparked controversy from the beginning, and women's rights organizations had filed briefs on both sides of the litigation. In many respects, the controversy paralleled the protective-labor dispute a half-century earlier. Although most feminists were united in their desire for job-secure leaves for any temporary disability, they differed sharply over whether the proverbial half a loaf for pregnant women was worth the cost. As long as this nation fails to mandate comprehensive maternity, parental, unemployment, and disability protection, the special treatment – equal treatment disagreement is likely to persist. This controversy highlights limitations in prevailing difference or dominance-oriented approaches to gender issues.[22]

Defenders of maternity protections generally begin from the premise that working men and women are different with respect to reproduction. Although a no-leave policy creates hardships for both sexes concerning the disabilities they share, it places an additional burden on female employees. As long as fetal development occurs *in utero* and breast-feeding proves advantageous for newborn infants, mothers will experience a conflict between their productive and reproductive roles that fathers will not. Building on the theoretical frameworks of scholars such as Lucinda Finley,

Herma Kay, Sylvia Law, Christine Littleton, and Reva Siegel, these feminists often distinguish childbearing from child-rearing and argue that gender-specific childbirth policies are appropriate, while gender-specific parental policies are not. From this premise, many commentators draw two further conclusions: that the absence of disability leaves has a disparate impact on women in violation of Title VII; and that states or employers may respond to this disproportionate effect through policies requiring job reinstatement after pregnancy.[23]

This rationale for preferential treatment rests on arguments of both principle and prudence. As a matter of principle, pregnancy should not have to seem the same as male disabilities in order to gain adequate protection. Comparative frameworks risk requiring female assimilation to male norms rather than fair recognition of women's separate capacities and commitments. In some feminists' view, even to speak of pregnancy in terms of disability distorts its meaning. From a prudential perspective, as long as policymakers fail to require adequate protection for all workers, partial coverage can be a useful interim strategy. As was true with protective legislation in the early twentieth century, a "women and children first" approach can lay the groundwork for broader gender-neutral regulation.

The danger is that settling for intervention on behalf of the most politically sympathetic constituency may erode impetus for more comprehensive approaches. Even with the benefit of hindsight, it is impossible to know whether protective-labor regulation for all workers might have occurred sooner if its proponents had avoided arguments based on women's maternal mission. Predicting which strategy will be most effective in the current political climate is no less difficult.

Other risks from preferential policies are equally hard to assess. As Chapter 2 suggested, gender-based protective legislation has often served to reinforce roles that are more separate than equal. Although pregnancy differs from other disabilities in an important sense, emphasizing that difference in employment contexts has often proved an ingenuous or disingenuous response to women's special concerns. Claims that pregnancy is a unique condition have been used to rationalize its exclusion from employment benefits programs. Maternal responsibilities have also served to justify courts, legislatures, and unions in barring women from a vast range of occupations during the first half of this century. By making female employees more expensive, much gender-based protective-labor legislation "protected" them out of jobs sought by male competitors. Comparable results could follow from policies that emphasize differences rather than commonalities between male and female workers. The perception among employers will remain that at the bottom line, "women cost you more."[24]

Yet one of the lessons we learn from history is that there are limits to what other lessons we can draw from it. The adverse consequences of protective statutes earlier in this century occurred in a society that lacked significant legal and social sanctions against gender discrimination. The current regulatory climate is different, although, as subsequent discussion will indicate, the difficulties of enforcing antidiscrimination mandates can be substantial. The consequences of contemporary maternity policies are likely to depend on a variety of factors including scope, financing, and the political context of implementation. Programs that do not require private employers to bear the full cost are an obvious way to mitigate the risk of discrimination against women of childbearing age. Without further experience and research, it is difficult to assess how many female workers at what income levels would benefit from maternity protections, and how many would pay the price in terms of lower wages or fewer employment opportunities.

What complicates the issues still further are the mixed ideological consequences of preferential policies. In one sense, job-protected maternity leaves may help to break the stereotype of childbearing women as provisional employees, with higher turnover and lower work commitment than men. Yet to require that employers offer maternity but not necessarily paternity or parental leaves is to reinforce, both in fact and appearance, unequal allocations of family responsibilities.

Such inequalities may be especially pronounced with policies that relegate mothers to special slower career paths. "Mommy tracks" often become "mommy traps"; they risk curtailing individual opportunities and reinforcing traditional gender stereotypes. Sex-based child-rearing policies pose concerns on several levels. The implication that infants are a mother's responsibility deters men from seeking, and employers from accommodating, full parental commitments. Paid paternity leaves remain highly unusual. According to contemporary surveys, only about a third of major private-sector companies and far fewer smaller organizations provide even unpaid leaves. In companies that formally extend such an option, men seldom take it, and the ones who do are rarely absent for more than a brief interval. Those patterns are in part a function of organizational climate. According to one representative survey of companies providing paternity leaves, over 40 percent of personnel directors indicated that the appropriate amount of time for a father to take off at childbirth was "no time." The barriers to more sustained commitments are even greater; the perception persists that men who assume equal nurturing responsibilities have "lace on their jockey shorts." Moreover, female employees who have entered traditional male fields feel considerable pressure to assimilate its norms and forgo the sustained parent-infant bonding that more generous child-rearing policies would permit.[25]

Such attitudes limit both male and female experience. They jeopardize infant development, impair fathers' formation of nurturing relationships, and force many mothers to choose between caretaking commitments and occupational advancement. Not only do working women's unequal burdens in the private sphere translate into unequal opportunities in the public sphere, the feminization of family responsibilities helps perpetuate the socialization on which such inequalities rest. If, as much recent psychoanalytic theory suggests, men develop better capacities for parenting by having significant attachments to their fathers during early childhood, then it is critical to develop policies that encourage paternal as well as maternal commitments.[26]

The complexity of this issue underscores the need to move beyond the dichotomies in which it has generally emerged. As in other contexts, a sameness-difference approach is ultimately unilluminating. Women are both the same and different. They are different in their needs at childbirth but the same in their needs for broader medical, child-rearing, and caretaking policies. To determine which side of the sameness-difference dichotomy to emphasize in legal contexts requires some other analytic tool.

A dominance-oriented framework is inadequate for that role. By inviting analysis in terms of zero-sum transfers from "us to them," it may misconstrue the problem and misconceive the solution. Women and men have neither monolithic nor competing interests. As was true earlier in the century, female employees experience and value the tradeoffs of preferential protections differently, depending on their own particular circumstances. Men have lined up on both sides of the maternity-leave debate, and it is possible to view either their support or opposition as an expression of patriarchal interests. Some conservative male legislators have supported special maternity leave requirements to help women who assume "traditional roles in the family and in society." Other male employers and politicians have opposed such requirements as an unduly expensive accommodation to women's personal choices and an inappropriate "interference" with market processes. The theory is that if a female employee places a high priority on maternity or disability policies, she can go to work for an organization that offers them.[27]

Yet to suppose that employees can effectively restructure workplace practices by "voting with their feet" is to ignore the history that necessitated a vast array of governmental regulation, including safety requirements, maximum-hour legislation, and antidiscrimination mandates. Fearing covert discrimination, many job applicants may not convey concerns about parental policy when seeking employment. Nor will they always anticipate future disability needs when applying for a particular position. To oppose state "interference" with the market is to ignore the effects of noninterference on family relationships. The absence of adequate caretaking policies in the United States diminishes opportunities for both sexes, as children, as parents, and as elderly dependents.

For issues such as preferential treatment, the advantage of focusing on disadvantage is that it can acknowledge complexity and encourage contextual inquiry. It can avoid entrapment in unproductive disputes over male motivation or female "difference." Rather, attention can center on identifying strategies most likely to promote gender equality in a given set of social, political, and economic circumstances.

From a disadvantage-oriented perspective, the preferable approach is to press for the broadest possible maternal, parental, and medical coverage for all workers. Sex-neutral strategies pose the least risk of entrenching stereotypes or encouraging covert discrimination and offer the widest range of protections for disadvantaged groups. The distinctive consequences of pregnancy should not be overlooked, but neither should they be overemphasized. More employers provide job-protected childbirth leaves than other forms of assistance that are equally critical to workers and their dependents. Pregnancy-related policies affect most women workers for relatively brief intervals. The absence of broader disability, health, child-rearing, and caretaking policies remains a chronic problem for the vast majority of employees, male and female, throughout their working lives.

Even if that problem is assessed solely in economic terms, our current approach appears misguided. As a late 1980s study noted, the costs resulting from the absence of a national disability policy, in terms of lost earnings, additional public assistance, and reduced productivity, substantially exceed the projected cost of requiring short-term leaves. Moreover, recent public-opinion polls indicate that a majority of Americans are sympathetic to such claims and favor some form of statutory leave requirements. Both men and women stand to gain if we press for more by refusing to settle for less.[28]

The details of an effective approach for disability and dependent care have been addressed elsewhere. What bears emphasis here is the importance of the issue and the need for less divisive responses. With respect to pregnancy, the objective is not just job-secure leaves, which help only those who can afford to take them, but also adequate health insurance, pre- and postnatal care, and wage replacement by employers or unemployment-compensation programs. With respect to parental policies, subsequent discussion reveals critical needs for more quality childcare, meaningful part-time work, and flexible scheduling. As commentators including Nancy Dowd, Sheila Kamerman, Nadine Taub, and Wendy Williams have emphasized, pregnancy leaves are only one aspect of an adequate parenting policy, and provisions for working parents are only one aspect of an adequate strategy for dependent care. Elderly relatives, sick children, and disabled spouses or domestic partners have needs that are difficult if not impossible to accommodate within traditional workplace structures.[29]

These concerns call for less dispute over preferential policies and greater efforts to obtain gender-neutral ones. More attention should focus on workplace organizing and collective bargaining, and on policies that can unite the broadest range of constituencies. From this perspective, even the formulation of the "special treatment – equal treatment" debate is misconceived. To view childbirth-related policies as "special" assumes that male needs establish the norm. And to label only one camp "equal" assumes the conclusion. Feminists on both sides of the debate seek equality. The challenge remaining is to keep disagreements over interim strategies from obscuring common long-term goals. We cannot afford a repetition of earlier struggles over preferential treatment, in which women spent too much of their energy fighting each other over the value of protection, rather than uniting to challenge the conditions that made protection so valuable.

At its most fundamental level, contemporary debate over preferential policies raises issues not only of gender equality but of cultural priorities. The question is not simply how well society accommodates women's particular biological capacities, but how highly it values intimate human relationships and the care-related obligations that such relationships entail. On that question, both sides of the "special treatment – equal treatment" debate can find common ground.

Public and Private: Social-Welfare and Childcare Policies

One final dichotomy that requires reassessment is the conventional distinction between the "public" sphere of political and commercial life and the "private" sphere of intimate association. This distinction has been central to American legal thought and the philosophical traditions from which it grows. A defining feature of liberal political theory has been its commitment to spheres of individual autonomy free from state intrusion. Although the family is generally presented as the most significant of these spheres, its dynamics have received relatively little philosophical attention. Classic liberal theory has been largely unconcerned with inequalities in domestic settings. While some prominent early theorists, such as John Stuart Mill, have defended asymmetrical roles in family life, most contemporary commentators, such as John Rawls, have simply avoided discussing its structure or significance. One central objective of contemporary feminist theory is to place such issues at the forefront rather than at the periphery of political discourse, and to challenge the premises that underpin such public-private distinctions.[30]

The boundaries between these "separate spheres" have always been murkier than much liberal jurisprudence acknowledges. The state is inevitably implicated in defining whose rights will be enforced and on what terms, and in contributing to patterns of individual wealth and power that are backed by governmental authority. Public norms also play a critical role in shaping ostensibly private social affiliations and family relationships. Laws affecting the terms of marriage and child custody; the structure of the workplace; the availability of contraception, abortion, welfare, and childcare; and the tax, inheritance, welfare, or property implications of various living arrangements—all have an important effect on domestic arrangements. Moreover, a dichotomous framework masks other connections between private roles and public opportunities. Individual achievements in the marketplace are highly dependent on family resources and socialization patterns. A society truly committed to liberal ideals of equal opportunity in the public sphere could not tolerate the kind of unequal opportunities in the private sphere that characterize contemporary American life.[31]

A vast body of social science research, reviewed more fully in Chapter 8, makes clear that family and role allocations have been major barriers to women's vocational advancement. By the same token, gender subordination in the marketplace encourages analogous patterns in the home. Studies of power relationships in white, nonwhite, professional, and blue-collar families consistently suggest that the greater the disparity in economic resources between husbands and wives, the greater the husband's dominance in decisionmaking. Women's unequal employment status also fosters an unequal distribution of domestic burdens, which further constrains occupational opportunities.[32]

Those interrelated inequalities, coupled with shifting marriage, employment, and fertility patterns, have contributed to an increasing feminization of poverty. Although official classifications of poverty are an imperfect index of actual need, they can measure relative status. Current data reveal striking gender disparities. Women of all ages are twice as likely as men to be poor, and women who are single parents are five times as likely. Two-thirds of all indigent adults are female, and two-thirds of the persistently poor live in female-headed households. Some 90 percent of single-parent families are headed by women, and half of those families are below the poverty line. Among minorities, the situation is worse; women head three-quarters of all poor black families and over half of all poor Hispanic families.[33]

Welfare programs have offered grossly inadequate responses to these problems and the public-private distinction has contributed to their failures. Americans traditionally have viewed the basic conditions of life largely as a family responsibility; the public's obligation has been seen as supplemental, limited to "deserving" candidates. The distinction between "worthy" and "unworthy" poor, a legacy of seventeenth-century English statutes, has long served to limit assistance to those conforming to conventional roles and values, and to license intrusive and demeaning regulations.[34]

For women, these conventional values have worked against humane welfare initiatives. Throughout most of this nation's history, policies governing public assistance reflected assumptions that domesticity was women's proper destiny. Such assumptions, coupled with pervasive employment discrimination, penalized all husbandless women, although the degree of penalty varied by the perceived "fault" of the individual. Greatest sympathy flowed to "deserving" white widows and their children; they were the principal beneficiaries of the meager state and local assistance available before the 1930s. Divorced, abandoned, unmarried, or "unfit" women were often excluded from coverage. Some definitions of unfitness were quite expansive, particularly for racial and ethnic minorities. Extramarital relations, the presence of a "man in or around the home," the failure to attend church, or even the use of tobacco could be grounds for denying aid.[35]

The growth of welfare programs during the Depression expanded the class of beneficiaries and created the federal structure now titled Aid to Families with Dependent Children (AFDC). However, such initiatives also reinforced a dual welfare system that distinguishes social insurance and public assistance. This structure has made insurance a matter of entitlement, granted primarily under criteria other than means (for example, age, disability, and work history). By contrast, public assistance has been available largely for those falling beneath a certain income level. Although some insurance programs have incorporated elements of redistribution (such as Social Security) and some have disproportionately benefited women (such as Medicare), welfare's dual structure has, on the whole, perpetuated gender disadvantages. Individuals with a continuous history of paid labor (primarily men) have obtained comparatively generous benefits (unemployment, Social Security, workers' compensation) and have suffered comparatively little social stigma. By contrast, individuals who have devoted much of their effort to unpaid domestic labor (primarily women) have received substantially less financial assistance (AFDC) and endured greater societal disapproval and degrading bureaucratic procedures. Welfare policies also have discouraged female caretakers from attempting to improve their status by entering the workforce. Benefit restrictions have deterred paid employment, and vocational training programs have traditionally been available largely to male "breadwinners." Women who have managed to gain access to these programs have often received "work experience" in occupations such as dishwashing and heavy cleaning.[36]

During the late 1960s various forces converged to reorient official AFDC policy toward requiring employment. The rise in eligible beneficiaries, particularly among unwed mothers and minority groups, contributed to a political backlash against subsidized "shirkers" and "brood mares." Women's escalating labor-force participation also legitimated work requirements. However, despite virtually unceasing reform efforts, the next two decades witnessed little progress toward policymakers' announced goals of reducing welfare dependence among those able to work, while providing an adequate safety net for those who were not.[37]

A large part of the problem stems from a misconception of what the problem is. The problem is poverty and the broader socioeconomic forces that perpetuate it. But debates over welfare reform have traditionally proceeded as if the principal difficulty lies in the welfare system itself. Conservative critics, including then-President Ronald Reagan and his Working Group on the Family, have claimed that the "easy availability of welfare" has encouraged female dependence, marital break-up, and out-of-wedlock births, while eroding males' sense of family responsibility. Liberal critics often share similar concerns, but they tend to locate the problem less in the availability of welfare than in its terms, including the inadequacies of vocational programs and misguided incentive structures. The public generally remains ambivalent. Survey data indicate that most Americans want to do more to assist the poor but do not want to increase welfare. Voters are reluctant to force single mothers with young children to work full time, but are equally reluctant to provide a decent economic alternative. Such ambivalence has been reflected in recent reform measures that require many AFDC mothers to participate in work or job-training programs, but that fail to ensure sufficient employment opportunities, training funds, or childcare.[38]

Some of the problems surrounding welfare policy stem from tension in its objectives and confusion about its dynamics. It has appeared difficult to provide adequate assistance without diminishing incentives to work, and to target assistance to the most needy individuals without eroding broad-based political support. Those difficulties have been compounded by widespread misperceptions about the extent and effect of current programs. The popular image of indolent welfare drones living high on the dole and relying on frequent pregnancies to avoid work bears little relation to reality. Extensive research indicates that levels of public assistance do not significantly affect out-of-wedlock births. The average AFDC family has only two children under the age of eighteen, and three-quarters of the states provide cash and food stamp assistance at less than 75 percent of the poverty level. The majority of AFDC recipients are not able to work; 65 percent are children, 11 percent are incapacitated, and those remaining generally cannot obtain jobs that pay enough to cover the costs of childcare and related employment expenses. Over half of all poor children live in families that receive no cash assistance.[39]

Contrary to conventional assumptions, welfare programs do not entrench large-scale dependency. Experience both here and abroad makes clear that most individuals prefer employment to assistance. Recent data reveal that the majority of recipients have obtained benefits for less than three years. Children whose parents receive welfare are no more likely to need public assistance as adults than other individuals. Many recipients need aid because of inadequacies in other social programs such as child support (which is widely unenforced), health care (which leaves 15 percent of the nation without coverage), or unemployment programs (which offer inadequate training and exclude part-time workers or those who "quit" for family-related reasons). The notion that most of the poor fall into a perpetual underclass unwilling to work misconceives the problem and misleads as to the solution.[40]

A more effective approach to poverty must begin from different premises. Our focus must be treating the causes of impoverishment rather than selectively mitigating its symptoms, and our strategies must dismantle conventional distinctions between public and private responsibilities. One critical need is for continuing research on the dynamics of poverty and the programs that can best address it. As experts often note, we are "swamped with facts" about the poor, but still surprisingly uninformed about the most cost-effective strategies for assisting them.[41]

Yet we also know more than enough to suggest fundamental changes in our current policies. Despite our rhetorical commitment to encouraging self-sufficiency among low-income populations, prevailing programs create precisely the opposite incentives. Benefit structures and bureaucratic procedures discourage the kind of work that most recipients are able to obtain. Expanded employment, training, and support services are essential to reduce persistent poverty. As subsequent chapters also suggest, progress will depend not only on changes in the welfare system, but also on sustained social initiatives in related areas. Proposals concerning pay equity, minimum-wage increases, job creation, vocational training, health insurance, birth control, family allowances, tax credits, and enforcement of child-support awards all must be part of any effective antipoverty initiative.[42]

Similar points are applicable to one final context where conventional public-private distinctions have yielded gender disadvantages. National policy toward childcare has been notable largely for its absence. What little governmental support has been available for childcare has been for highly circumscribed time periods, such as World War II, or for limited populations, such as poor immigrants and wartime factory workers. Although in recent decades parents have received increasing assistance through tax credits, such subsidies have not met national needs. Nor have employers been willing to fill the gap. Contemporary surveys indicate that fewer than 1 percent of private-sector employers provide childcare assistance. The traditional attitude has been that public initiatives are too "communal" or "communistic" for American families, and that private-sector support is unnecessary or unaffordable.[43]

During the late 1980s, such attitudes began to change, partly in response to mothers' increasing labor-force participation, and to growing evidence of productivity losses from childcare problems. But the extent of those problems remains in dispute. Not only are there inadequate data on which to ground informed assessments, there is little underlying agreement on critical normative questions. What constitutes "quality" care, what trade-offs between cost and quality are appropriate, and who should make such judgments?[44]

However one resolves those questions, the limited research available suggests several grounds for concern. Since over half of all women with small children work outside the home, America can ill afford a system of childcare that is not in fact a system but a series of ad hoc arrangements. National surveys have revealed that between a quarter and a third of interviewed mothers express dissatisfaction with their childcare arrangements or cite inadequate childcare as a major barrier to employment. Other data indicate chronic shortages of certain kinds of care, such as infant and sick-child programs and after-school supervision. High costs are an additional problem, especially for poor women, who spend between one-fifth and one-quarter of their income on childcare expenses and have little choice in types of service and benefit least from tax credits. A related concern involves quality: the ability of existing care arrangements to ensure children's basic health and safety and contribute to their cognitive, social, and psychological development. The absence of comprehensive research concerning quality is itself cause for concern, particularly in light of the structure of existing services. For example, 95 percent of the nation's childcare providers are unregulated; childcare workers are among the nation's poorest-paid employees, have high turnover rates (between 35 and 60 percent per year), and only 20 percent of them are required to have any training.[45]

Despite such evidence, existing and proposed legislation concerning childcare assistance remains seriously deficient. Federal and state regulation has fallen far short of standards that most child-development experts recommend. To meet even the most basic standards, the United States needs far more substantial subsidies for low-income families; expanded progressive tax credits; greater incentives for employer assistance and flexible benefit programs; more comprehensive public school involvement (expanded kindergarten, after-school, before-school, and summer programs); more aid to providers seeking to improve their services; and more support for research comparing various regulated and unregulated arrangements.[46]

Given its relative wealth, the United States compares poorly with other developed nations in family services. The costs fall disproportionately on women and children. Some of the inadequacies lie in the extent of the programs themselves. Not only must the level of insurance and assistance increase, they must reach larger percentages of the population. But it would be a mistake to believe that we can solve our social-welfare "problem" simply by improving the welfare system. That system is necessary because of other socioeconomic forces, institutional failures, and a political structure unwilling to address them. To make significant progress, our discourse about welfare must encompass a broader set of problems, including employment, education, housing, health, child support, day care, drug abuse, and birth control.

It is true that talk is cheap and welfare programs are not. Yet we also cannot overlook the costs of traditional approaches. Those costs must be measured not only in terms of equality between the sexes, but also in the quality of life for their children and the legacy left to future generations. Our private lives and public policies are intimately connected across generations. In our later years most of us will depend upon the productivity and compassion of those who are now children. To protect their futures as well as our own we must reassess our welfare policies.[47]

Chapter 7

Competing Perspectives on Family Policy

For the past century, political and legal rhetoric has placed the family at the foundation of American society. Presidents and Supreme Court Justices alike have consistently presented the domestic sphere as the cornerstone of social life and social progress. At that level of abstraction, few feminists would disagree. But on virtually any other question surrounding family policy, consensus quickly fades. As in other contexts, the controversy has often proceeded in dichotomous terms that obscure critical issues and obstruct effective change. On a symbolic level, the dispute has invoked competing visions of the contemporary family as haven or as hell, neither of which captures the complexity of intimate relationships. On a policy level, the controversy has involved many of the same problems of public and private, and special treatment-equal treatment at issue in debates over welfare and parental policies.[1]

A more fruitful public dialogue must transcend these dichotomies. A richer analysis would have both theoretical and practical significance. Almost 90 percent of the noninstitutionalized American population lives in some form of family, and few structures are more critical in shaping gender roles and social values. Nor has any institution been more inundated by official introspection. By the late 1970s, the federal government alone was annually funding over 2,500 research projects on family issues, and many of those issues had become lightning rods for cultural conflict. Yet as the last half-century's spate of commissions, conferences, and committees makes evident, effective policy is unlikely to emerge until we cope more rationally with our points of dispute and build on our points of commonality.[2]

One dispute that requires reassessment involves the basic functions of family life. On a metaphorical level, the controversy centers on the domestic sphere either as a source of women's oppression or an arena for women's values. This controversy has provoked some peculiar ideological alliances. New-Right conservatives, joined by some radical leftists and revisionist feminists, have variously portrayed the domestic realm as a haven from the crass, commercial, and competitive relationships of the marketplace. In this rendering, the family emerges as the primary focus of women's traditional values, identity, and authority. Domestic relationships also provide a critical buffer between the individual and the state, and a shelter for diverse racial, ethnic, and religious heritages.[3]

Those who share this vision have drawn different conclusions about the gender dynamics underlying it and the state's responsibility to sustain it. As discussion of the Equal Rights campaign reflected, most conservatives have revered the traditional nuclear family, with its hierarchy of male breadwinners and female nurturers, and have argued that public policy should support this structure. Such sentiments appeared in the proposed federal Family Protection acts of 1979 and 1981, which would have limited male-female "intermingling" in school activities and banned the use of federal funds for educational materials that could "denigrate, diminish, or deny the role of the sexes as it has been historically understood in the United States." By contrast, leftist defenders of the family have generally favored a more equal division of responsibilities, although some contemporary feminists have wished to retain women's special caretaking role but enhance its status.[4]

A competing perspective emphasizes the dark side of domesticity. To many Marxists and radical feminists, the family is a source of commercialization, not a refuge from it. Traditional structures foster egocentric consumerism and encourage private loyalties at the expense of broader community concerns. Rather than encouraging full development of human identity, the family enforces heterosexual conformity. Women who curtail their careers after marriage too often become "wedlocked wives." Male physical violence and female economic dependence reinforce patriarchical patterns. Over time, the asymmetrical allocation of domestic roles perpetuates the gender stereotypes that perpetuate subordination. To break this cycle, some radical feminists have proposed a variety of responses ranging from the abolition of marriage to test-tube reproduction.[5]

A richer understanding of family life must move beyond romanticization or renunciation. The conservative vision of domesticity is internally inconsistent and incomplete. It not only ignores the repressive aspects of traditional family structure but also offers competing views of that structure's broader social significance. The private sphere appears as both a cornerstone of, and refuge from, the existing public order; it inculcates the very egoistic and competitive values it implicitly challenges. Much leftist romanticism has an equally ironic twist. As Chapter 12 suggests, the celebration of women's maternal mission among some feminists in the 1970s and 1980s bears a striking resemblance to the claims of antifeminists a century earlier and presents similar risks. Women's presumed centrality in the private sphere has traditionally worked to restrict their influence outside it and to deny members of both sexes the chance to explore their full human potential.

As the preceding discussion of "benign" discrimination suggests, this history should not be overlooked, but neither should it be overstated. By emphasizing only the dark side of domesticity, radical polemics ignore much of value in women's experience. The homemaker role has been empowering and enriching as well as confining. Especially for minorities, the family has also been a foundation for cultural identity. Although the domestic sphere has been a source of female oppression, the same is true of state and community institutions that would assume increasing authority in the absence of significant family ties. If those public institutions can be transformed, why should private relationships be different? Politically and technologically we remain a fair distance from a test-tube society. The traditional pattern of family life—a permanent marital union between two heterosexual adults—has weakened. Yet our needs for close personal attachments remain.

How to accommodate those needs in a highly individualistic culture is an issue of enormous social importance. Yet that issue has often been obscured by the terms of political and legal debate. As in social-welfare contexts, part of the problem stems from a misconception of the problem. Conservatives have emphasized departures from traditional family norms: the increase in divorce, illegitimacy, open homosexuality, and nonmarital cohabitation, as well as the decline in social disapproval for such conduct. The following discussion suggests that the problem lies more in the norms themselves and in the absence of public support for varied domestic structures. The alternative framework envisioned here would seek a better accommodation of our multiple needs—our needs for autonomy and equality, for independence and interdependence, for stability in child-rearing attachments and for flexibility in adult relationships. To promote that vision, legal rules must focus more on gender disadvantage rather than gender difference, and resist conventional public-private distinctions.

Form and Substance: The Marital-Nonmarital Divide

For the last century, most legal commentators have shared the view of Sir Henry Maine that social progress occurs through the movement from "status to contract"—from the replacement of obligations that are socially imposed with obligations that are voluntarily assumed. In recent years, however, enthusiasm for that trend has weakened, particularly as it affects nonmarital relationships. One central dispute involves the treatment of individuals who have the social and economic but not the legal characteristics of a spousal unit. Underlying this dispute are many of the concerns that have long plagued the women's movement: the tension between autonomy and equality, and between formal and substantive justice.[6]

The controversy came to the fore during the 1970s, sparked by the increasing incidence of cohabitation and the inadequacy of conventional legal responses. Some studies estimated that the number of individuals living together in nonmarital units grew by as much as 700 percent between 1960 and 1970, and tripled again in the next decade. By the 1980s statistical surveys reported that almost two million couples were cohabiting. Most scholars believed that adjustments for unreported relationships might bring the total closer to twice that number. Explanations for such increases reflect a broad range of demographic and ideological trends, including society's changing attitudes toward sexuality, marriage, fertility, and gender roles.[7]

Given the decline in cultural taboos against cohabitation, the law's traditional treatment of such issues became increasingly anomalous. For most of this nation's history, American courts have been unsympathetic to "meretricious relaionships"—the legal term of art for living in sin—although penalties have varied widely. Early English common law vacillated between stringent prohibitions (including death) for fornication and no prohibitions whatsoever. During the Colonial period many jurisdictions devoted a great deal of effort to ferreting out fornicators for criminal prosecution. Although such efforts declined in the post-Revolutionary era, official prohibitions lingered on. Surveys from the mid-1970s have revealed that about one-third of the states still made nonmarital intercourse a criminal offense and occasionally put such statutes to use. Seldom has the contemporary objective been to discourage promiscuity. Rather, prosecutors typically have brought fornication or adultery charges to coerce a plea to other offenses, to obtain acknowledgment of paternity, or to give irate landlords, neighbors, or creditors further leverage against those who have offended commercial as well as sexual mores. Cohabitation has sometimes served as a basis for terminating employment opportunities, reducing alimony awards, or assessing fitness for child custody. Discrimination against gays and lesbians has been particularly debilitating.[8]

Initially many jurisdictions that criminalized fornication recognized common-law marriage, the traditional legal concession to such human frailty. Under a variety of statutory provisions or common-law presumptions, couples who were eligible to marry, agreed to marry, and lived as if they were married obtained that legal status. Such indulgence of immorality was commonly justified less by a spirit of human forgiveness than by a desire to avoid injury to otherwise illegitimate children or to unsuspecting creditors. However, by the late nineteenth century, most jurisdictions had begun to abolish or limit common-law marriage on the grounds that it encouraged as much unfairness as it prevented, particularly when claims were made after one member of the couple had died or disappeared. Except for "putative spouses"—those who believed incorrectly but in good faith that they were married—the law generally announced its intent to leave sinners in the situation they had themselves chosen.[9]

In practice, however, some judges were prepared to temporize when the equities were sufficiently compelling. For example, in the all-too-familiar situation where the parties had lived as if married and the man had placed jointly financed assets in his name alone, courts were sometimes willing to intervene under standard contract, trust, or partnership principles. One common device was to find an express agreement by the parties to share and share alike, which was enforceable if it did not explicitly rest on "meretricious" considerations. Yet such legal remedies remained inadequate since, under the probing eye of a puritanical judge, the vast majority of cohabitators' agreements appeared to contemplate sex, and parties often had no shared understanding about would happen if they did not live happily ever after. Although judicial policies against condoning sin purported to be gender-neutral, their effects were not. Typically the only member of the deviant couple who suffered was the woman, who had contributed more homemaking services than income to the relationship and who could not prove an explicit agreement.[10]

Those inequities became increasingly visible in litigation beginning with the California Supreme Court's celebrated decision *Marvin v. Marvin*. In 1964, Michelle Triola, a nightclub singer, gave up her somewhat precarious career to become a full-time homemaker for actor Lee Marvin, who was then in the process of an acrimonious marital break-up. Seven years later, Lee's experience of disillusion and dissolution repeated itself, with one important variation. Although Michelle had changed her last name to Marvin, she had done so without benefit of marriage. When Lee left her for another woman and discontinued voluntary support payments, he had no obligations under applicable divorce statutes. The legal issue in dispute was whether Michelle had any other basis on which to claim part of the $3.6 million dollars in property accumulated during their relationship. According to the majority in *Marvin,* courts could promote equity in such circumstances through various legal doctrines: express and implied agreements; implied partnerships; constructive trusts; or *quantum meruit* payments for the value of services rendered in order to prevent "unjust enrichment." After establishing that range of potential remedies, the California Court remanded the case for trial.[11]

The aftermath of *Marvin* pointed up a number of difficulties in bridging the marital-nonmarital divide. The trial involved eleven weeks of testimony by sixty witnesses concerning the most intimate and indelicate aspects of the Marvins' relationship, including Lee's alcoholism and Michelle's infidelities. In effect, the litigation reintroduced all the costs—financial and psychological—that no-fault divorce reform was meant to curtail. Legal fees for Michelle alone totaled half a million dollars, and the cumulative efforts of counsel pointed to no clear resolution of the questions at issue: whether Lee's "idle male promises" were binding and whether he had been unjustly enriched by Michelle's services. In an attempted Solomonic gesture, the trial court found no agreement between the parties but granted Michelle $104,000 in "rehabilitative" support to enable her to acquire new job skills. Lee, who by that point in the process was more disposed to pay such sums to his current lawyer than his former lover, contested the award. He prevailed in California's appellate court, and its Supreme Court declined to reenter the fray.[12]

The decades following *Marvin* witnessed increasing controversy over cohabitation in legal, political, and academic circles. Litigated cases generated an array of conflicting results and rationales. Decisions that followed the California Supreme Court's approach attracted opposition from all points on the ideological spectrum. In the view of many conservative courts and commentators, extending legal remedies to cohabitants would only encourage such behavior and threaten the foundations of stable family life. By contrast, left-wing critics claimed that decisions like *Marvin* would not jeopardize traditional marital values but would in effect impose them on couples who had deliberately chosen an alternative lifestyle. Such "repressive benevolence" would compromise individual autonomy, encourage female dependence, and commercialize intimate relationships.[13]

These criticisms, both from the right and left, were unsatisfying on several grounds. State courts that restricted recovery to cohabitants in order to encourage marriage permitted substantial injustice for dubious reasons. In some jurisdictions, women were left without legal recourse even after maintaining stable marriagelike relationships for fifteen years and making financial as well as homemaking contributions to the family. In avoiding state "repression," these courts licensed private oppression. Yet it is extremely unlikely that other heterosexual cohabitants in these jurisdictions were aware of, let alone materially influenced by, such holdings in deciding whether or not to marry. It is equally implausible to suppose that denying remedies to gay or lesbian couples can deter their relationships; research on the biological and psychological origins of sexual identity clearly suggests the contrary. Whatever limited effect cohabitation doctrine has on the institution of marriage, the result is likely to be mixed. If rules denying recovery to cohabitants create an incentive for the less well-off partner to marry, they also give an economic incentive to the other partner to avoid marriage. However strong the state's interest in encouraging marital commitments, penalizing weaker parties in nonmarital relationships is not an effective means of pursuing that objective.[14]

Nor is it self-evident, as critics of *Marvin* typically assumed, that granting legal remedies to cohabitants would impose a marriagelike regime on couples who had deliberately decided to avoid it. What little empirical evidence is available suggests that cohabitation generally is not the result of a conscious choice. Rather, individuals tend to drift into such relationships without focusing on the future or its legal implications. Most heterosexual couples do not seem to have rejected the possibility of marriage. Nor is it clear that those who have done so reached their decision on the basis of mutual choice. If, as some research suggests, explicit determinations not to marry often reflect the preference of only the stronger (generally male) partner, denying all remedies to disadvantaged parties and their children may impose substantial hardships. Comparable hardships arise for gay and lesbian couples, who lack marital alternatives.[15]

That is not, however, to underestimate the difficulties in *Marvin*'s approach. As that litigation demonstrated, inviting courts to decipher parties' intent frequently entails a costly and conjectural enterprise, particularly since intent may change over time. Uncertainties surrounding a couple's status can create a host of difficulties concerning property, support, inheritance, insurance, pensions, government benefits, and other third-party rights and obligations. Moreover, the broader the range of remedies for unmarried couples, the greater the temptations for *in terrorem* litigation. Among the less appealing offspring of the *Marvin* line of cases were unsuccessful but highly publicized suits against Billie Jean King by her former lesbian lover and against the Bloomingdale estate by a disaffected, albeit "well-paid," mistress.[16]

In the late 1970s, a growing number of states began responding to these competing concerns by granting cohabitants some remedies but limiting their scope. One common approach has been to enforce only written or explicit oral agreements. Yet such half-measures have raised as many problems as they resolve. Unless a written document is required, the expense and indeterminancy of legal proceedings will remain substantial. As a practical matter, the vast majority of cohabitants are unlikely to formalize any agreement. Those who draft contracts are generally the well-educated, higher-income, self-assertive individuals least in need of judicial protection. And as a policy matter, it may not be desirable to push all unmarried parties into explicit contractual frameworks. For some couples, such an approach implies precisely the sort of formalization that they seek to avoid. At the outset of a relationship, it can be difficult to anticipate precisely what obligations should follow from it, and few individuals will continue modifying their agreements in light of changed circumstances.[17]

The circumstances under which contractual frameworks make most sense are not typical among cohabitants. Standard market models assume two independent agents, bargaining more or less at arm's length, making rational self-interested choices that do not have significant third-party effects. By definition, cohabitants are not dealing at arm's length; emotional ties and pressures often work against reasoned decisionmaking. Nor is the bargaining behavior characteristic of commercial settings necessarily appropriate for intimate associations. It would be difficult, and by no means desirable, for parties seeking to build a trusting relationship constantly to redefine its economic premises from a self-interested perspective. If, as Hegel submitted, marriage is a "contract to transcend the standpoint of contract, the standpoint from which persons are regarded . . . as self-sufficient units," the same is true of many nonmarital relationships.[18]

Since over a quarter of all unmarried couples have children living with them, the costs of inequitable settlements will not always rest with the parties alone. Given such considerations, there is much to be said for abandoning requirements of explicit agreements and assuming, as did California's Supreme Court in *Marvin,* that cohabitants intend to "deal fairly with each other."[19]

The difficulties surrounding public policy in this area are in part empirical, in part normative. To frame a coherent set of legal norms that will further justice in the typical case, we need to know more about what is in fact typical. What are most parties' expectations about their relationship and its legal consequences? How clearly do couples communicate those expectations and how equally do they share decisionmaking? To what extent do unmarried partners' understandings about property and support conform to those of married partners? What effects are court decisions having on out-of-court behavior? What are the variations across class, race, ethnicity, and sexual preference?[20]

Effective policy in this area will also require a better accommodation of competing values—a better balance between liberty and equality in intimate associations, between flexibility and certainty in legal rules, and between tolerance for diversity and encouragement of stability in family life. To strike that balance, it will, in turn, be necessary to transcend the dichotomies that have traditionally dominated analysis. The tradeoff between liberty and equality becomes less stark if liberty is defined not as freedom to do what we want when we want, but rather as freedom to form relationships of mutual trust and commitment, relationships that presuppose some obligations of honesty and fair dealing. Flexibility and certainty are more readily reconciled if we do not demand a single framework for all intimate associations, but rather search for legal guidelines that will distinguish casual from committed relationships. In the absence of explicit agreements, criteria such as the duration of the relationship, the degree of parties' financial interdependence, and, most importantly, the presence of children, could help provide some consistency across cases. Such criteria could also guide parties "bargaining in the shadow of the law" to achieve out-of-court settlements.[21]

A shift in focus from preserving "the Family" to protecting its functions suggests a number of other points at which marital-nonmarital distinctions should blur. As subsequent discussion suggests, gay and lesbian couples should have the right to express the public commitments and obtain the legal entitlements that matrimony entails. Invoking legal sanctions to coerce compliance with traditional domestic forms is less likely to preserve important values than to stunt their evolution. As sociologists and anthropologists repeatedly have emphasized, the conventional family structure that has become such an icon in contemporary policy debates is not the most "natural" or necessarily the most functional arrangement for all individuals. Our concern should not be to privilege one exclusive form of intimate association but to ensure that the various associations individuals now choose can meet basic biological, social, psychological, and economic needs. Relationships other than conventional marriage that effectively serve these needs should receive legal recognition.[22]

Eroding distinctions between marital and nonmarital regimes will not be a costless enterprise. But too much attention has focused on cataloging the costs, and too little on ways they might be minimized. Alternative forms of dispute resolution could reduce some of the financial and emotional expenses that have traditionally accompanied adversarial processes. Increased sanctions against frivolous lawsuits might also help deter undeserving claims. For some purposes, such as establishing rights to governmental benefits, it may be helpful to follow the example of other countries that have established presumptions concerning couples who have children or who live together for a specified interval. For gay and lesbian couples, registration under domestic partner laws is another option.[23]

To be sure, such strategies can only constrain, not eliminate, the price of legal disputes. But in deciding whether that price is worth paying, we should focus less on the litigated cases that attract our attention—the *Marvin* or the *Billie Jean King* litigation—and more on the far larger number of relationships that will end without formal legal intervention. For the vast majority of cohabitants, the law will be relevant only in defining the context in which private ordering occurs. The standard that courts will employ if couples fail to reach agreement is significant largely in allocating bargaining leverage out of court. The greater the willingness of judges to make equitable adjustments among cohabitants, the greater the likelihood that weaker parties will be able to insist on such adjustments without judicial intervention. Given the inequalities in bargaining resources between men and women, extending remedies for nonmarried couples may help minimize gender disadvantages.

A related step is to expand remedies for married individuals. For some purposes, marriage should be treated more like cohabitation, just as cohabitation should be treated more like marriage. Where spouses deal with each other in fairness and good faith, their contractual agreements warrant greater legal respect. So too, the law's traditional refusal to provide any recourse for breach of obligations within marriage warrants reexamination. It remains anomalous that, in the 1980s, the duties of spousal support imposed by marriage were available only when a marriage ended. Opportunities for informal dispute resolution between husbands and wives should be available prior to the point of dissolution.[24]

A more coherent approach toward intimate associations requires more complex analysis than conventional public-private frameworks have encouraged. The movement of progressive societies is not, as commentators have argued, some simple linear advance from status to contract, but a continuing dialectic between them. To promote both liberty and equality in personal relationships, we need to focus less on the form than the substance of intimate relationships.

Lesbian-Gay Rights and Social Wrongs

This alternative perspective requires restructuring laws concerning sexual preference. As a theoretical matter, conventional approaches to discrimination on the basis of sexual preference and discrimination on the basis of sex reflect comparable problems. Too much attention has centered on gender-related differences and too little on the disadvantages that follow from those differences. As a practical matter, the limitations of the traditional framework have immediate and highly injurious consequences for lesbian women and their gay male counterparts, estimated at about 2–5 percent of the adult female population and 5–13 percent of the adult male population. Moreover, the ideology that permits discrimination on the basis of sexual preference has indirect implications for a much broader constituency. Prejudice against "effeminate" men and "unfeminine" women grows out of the same gender-role assumptions that have limited opportunities for all individuals, irrespective of their sexual preference. Feminists who have challenged those gender assumptions have often been falsely stigmatized as lesbian, and that label has long served as a means of discouraging or discrediting activism on women's issues. This history helps account for some individuals' tendency to renounce feminism while supporting its premises. "I'm not a feminist, but" is one strategy for avoiding the risks of a lesbian label. From a societal perspective, however, a better strategy would be to challenge the prejudices underlying that label. All women have a stake in fighting discrimination against lesbians and gay men.[25]

Such discrimination has been a pervasive but by no means uniform practice. Although conservatives typically claim that homosexuality has been "universally condemned as immoral," the historical record suggests otherwise. Sexual relations between men were acceptable in ancient Greek society and sanctified by some Mid- and Far-Eastern religions. Lesbianism was sacred in areas of North Africa for extended periods. By contrast, Judeo-Christian traditions have tended to condemn such practices. Under early English common law, sanctions were intermittent but sometimes draconian. Penalties for the crime "not fit to be named" included death by fire and castration.[26]

Early American jurisprudence built on that legal heritage, fortified by an ideology that linked sexual expression with reproductive responsibility. In seventeenth- and eighteenth-century society, cooperative labor of parents and children was essential to survival, and the heterosexual family served as the centerpiece for productive activity. In that context, reported instances of same-sex erotic behavior were sporadic, and were treated as a crime and sin rather than an organizing feature of social identity. Early Colonial law made sodomy a capital offense and punished other homosexual behavior under prohibitions against "lewd and lascivious conduct." Although most states abolished the death penalty for sodomy in the half-century following independence, it remained a felony in all but two jurisdictions until the 1950s.[27]

During the late nineteenth century, industrialization and urbanization enabled more individuals to live outside family structures and permitted greater freedom for homosexual activity. The growth of all-women's associations and educational institutions further contributed to the trend. Between the 1870s and 1930s a growing subculture of individuals sought intimate involvement with members of their own sex. Then as now, this constituency remained heterogeneous. It included all classes, races, and ethnic groups. Some homosexuals were married, some lived in relative isolation, and some formed lasting partnerships within a network of gay and lesbian friends. Particularly among women, the boundaries between affection and eroticism often blurred, and it is impossible to characterize many nineteenth- and early-twentieth-century relationships in terms of dualistic sexual categories.[28]

Legal responses to this emerging subculture were intermittent and inconsistent. A mid-1950s survey revealed that the same homosexual conduct could receive penalties ranging from life imprisonment to a hundred-dollar fine. Although relatively few men and virtually no women suffered the full penalties provided by law, a significant number experienced harassment and prosecution for public conduct. Patronage of gay and lesbian bars presented particular risks. Obscenity laws suppressed homosexual art and advocacy, and social sanctions fortified these legal restrictions. Further reinforcement of repressive ideologies came from the medical community. By the late nineteenth century the consensus was that homosexuality was a congenital disease, which threatened "natural laws" of evolution and family structure. Prescribed treatments included hysterectomies, clitoridectomies, lobotomies, and electroschock. Yet to some extent, medical authority validated the very behavior it sought to eliminate. Disease-oriented frameworks presented homosexuality not as a moral transgression warranting punishment, but as an involuntary condition that defined an individual's entire sexual nature. This articulation of a gay-lesbian identity made it easier for some men and women to accept their sexual preferences.[29]

The trend toward openness was accelerated by World War II and by Alfred Kinsey's landmark research on sexuality. The war years promoted greater sexual segregation and sexual permissiveness, which enhanced opportunities for gay and lesbian relationships. Kinsey's studies, which revealed substantial levels of homosexual experience, eventually helped some individuals accept their sexual inclinations and provided arguments for decriminalization. At the time, however, his research also encouraged backlash against homosexuals by exposing their prevalence. The increasing visibility of a gay and lesbian subculture in the postwar years sparked a wave of repression. During the McCarthy Era, revelations that most government officials dismissed for "moral turpitude" were homosexuals encouraged further crackdowns against "sexual perverts." Employment purges and mass arrests became more common.[30]

Yet once again, strategies that aimed to suppress homosexual activity ultimately proved self-defeating. Repressive law enforcement encouraged social solidarity and political organization among gays and lesbians. These early organizing efforts laid the foundations for the mass movement that began in the wake of 1960s civil rights activism. In 1969, police efforts to close the Stonewall Inn, a Greenwich Village gay bar, prompted riots and encouraged formation of the Gay Liberation Front. Further organizing efforts quickly followed. By the close of the 1970s, gay and lesbian organizations numbered in the thousands.[31]

Partly in response to this movement, as well as to new research and new interpretations of previous research, the American Psychiatric Association in 1973 removed homosexuality from its list of mental illnesses. The decline in stigma that this action reflected and reinforced led to further gay-rights activism. One consequence was exposure of what Adrienne Rich has labeled pressures toward "compulsory heterosexuality" in American society; another consequence was the first sustained legal challenge to discrimination on the basis of sexual preference. This litigation campaign, together with other scholarly and educational initiatives, began to expose the pervasiveness of such discrimination in areas that included employment, domestic relations, housing, child custody, taxation, insurance, immigration, military service, and criminal law.[32]

During the 1970s and 1980s, this legal campaign yielded some significant victories, particularly for interests that the courts had previously recognized as fundamental, such as association and expression. As a result of lobbying and litigation, half the states also eliminated sodomy statutes from their penal codes. On the whole, however, progress was limited. Part of the problem stemmed from a lack of legislation. Although the number of local antidiscrimination ordinances steadily increased, federal and state legislatures were not willing to authorize similar initiatives. Nor were courts prepared to hold that existing statutes or state equal-rights amendments prohibiting discrimination on the basis of sex also encompassed discrimination on the basis of sexual preference. As long as male and female homosexuals were treated equally adversely, the mandates of formal equality were satisfied.[33]

Most courts have been similarly unwilling to provide federal constitutional remedies against discrimination. As in other contexts, a fundamental problem has involved the focus on sex-linked differences rather than on the disadvantage they promote. Under conventional approaches, analysis has been circular, conclusory, or both. The fact that homosexuals are different, are perceived as different, or historically have been treated as different, has been sufficient justification for differential treatment.

The Supreme Court's 1986 decision in *Bowers v. Hardwick* is a case in point. At issue was a challenge to Georgia's sodomy statute by a gay male; his offense had been discovered in his own bedroom by police searching for evidence of other crimes. Although the statute was not limited to homosexual activity, a majority of Supreme Court Justices voted to uphold the legislation only as applied to homosexuals. In so holding, the Court rejected Hardwick's argument that his private, consensual conduct fell within the interests protected in other privacy cases involving intimate relationships and sexual autonomy: for example, cases involving contraception, abortion, and in-home use of obscene materials. To a majority of Justices, those cases were different because gays and lesbians were different. Distinguishing its prior decisions on the basis of facts rather than principles, the Court explained that homosexual activity stood on different footing; "proscriptions against that conduct [had] ancient roots." Such an approach was reminiscent of gender-discrimination cases a century earlier, in which courts had upheld women's exclusion from certain occupational and civic contexts on the ground that women had always been so excluded. So too, in *Bowers,* a history of discriminatory treatment was sufficient reason to perpetuate it.[34]

State supreme court decisions have been similarly preoccupied with difference and similarly inattentive to disadvantage. Among the most influential illustrations are opinions denying homosexuals the right to marry. As in gender-discrimination cases a half-century earlier, judges have often leapt from the fact of difference to the appropriateness of differential treatment without benefit of intermediate premises. For example, in *Baker v. Nelson* (1972), the Minnesota Supreme Court concluded that denying homosexuals the right to marry did not violate equal-protection mandates because the "Constitution does not require things which are different in fact or opinion to be treated in law as though they were the same." With similar reasoning, the Washington Supreme Court in *Singer v. Hara* concluded that since homosexual couples were different from heterosexual couples in their capacity to procreate, and since a primary purpose of marriage was procreation, the state could deny marriage licenses to gays and lesbians.[35]

This logic leaves out all the ways homosexuals are the same as heterosexuals concerning other interests that marriage serves—such as intimacy, affection, care, and mutual support. The state does not condition marriage licenses on intent or capacity to procreate. Nor are all gay and lesbian couples childless; surveys report that about a quarter of all female and almost a fifth of all male homosexuals live with their own or their partners' offspring. Decisions like *Baker* and *Singer* deny individuals in functioning family units not only formal recognition of their relationships but also a host of economic benefits that follow from marital status, including tax, inheritance, insurance, welfare, support, Social Security, and pension entitlements. A framework preoccuppied with difference has thus served to perpetuate disadvantage.[36]

This approach is impossible to reconcile with long-standing principles of constitutional interpretation. Under contemporary Supreme Court precedents, marriage is a fundamental right that states may not infringe unless they demonstrate a compelling interest that cannot be more narrowly achieved. None of the homosexual marriage opinions makes even a pretense of explaining how denial of marriage licenses to homosexuals will promote compelling interests. It is implausible to suppose that the unavailability of marriage will impel individuals to abandon committed homosexual relationships in favor of heterosexual alternatives. Nor is there any evidence that legal recognition of gay and lesbian lifestyles will impair traditional family life. Studies of countries that have legalized homosexuality do not find an increase in homosexual activity or a decline in heterosexual marriage rates following legalization.[37]

Similar criticisms are applicable to a broad range of other decisions upholding discrimination on the basis of sexual preference. Many of the stated justifications for differential treatment involve precisely the kind of archaic stereotypes and arbitrary prejudices that courts have disapproved in other contexts involving gender. For example, telephone-book publishers have been allowed to exclude listings of homosexual services on the unsubstantiated ground of reader discomfort. Employers have been allowed to dismiss gays and lesbians whose "socially repugnant" conduct would offend their co-workers or "embarrass" and "reflect discredit" on their employing institutions. Homosexual parents have been denied child custody because of their "deviant" lifestyles. Cases involving the armed forces' exclusion of gays and lesbians have been particularly instructive; virtually all of the justifications supporting that policy have been, or are still being, used to support restrictions on women. Military officials have claimed, for example, that subordinates would be unwilling to take orders from homosexual officers and that the presence of such individuals would cause disruption, discomfort, discredit, tension, and the potential for sexual coercion or promiscuity.[38]

What is striking about these opinions is courts' failure to recognize the circularity of their own arguments. By allowing prejudice to justify prejudice, such reasoning encourages the discrimination it claims only to describe. These results are particularly disturbing in light of the judiciary's special obligations to protect insular minorities against majority hostility. For gays and lesbians, that hostility remains substantial. Moreover, the AIDS epidemic has contributed to increasing levels of harassment and violence. In this context, the inadequacies of legal remedies carry considerable social costs.[39]

A principled approach to discrimination on the basis of sexual preference will require different premises. Disadvantage rather than difference must be the central concern, and evidence of prejudice must not be allowed to justify its continuation. The same principles that apply to discrimination on the basis of sex should be equally applicable to discrimination on the basis of sexual preference. A legal order truly committed to values of liberty and equality, respect and responsibility, cannot tolerate the senseless degradation that current case law permits. No individuals should be forced to disfigure their fundamental needs for intimacy, affection, and consensual sexual expression. Nor should legal institutions be allowed to ignore the social wrongs that make gay rights so essential.[40]

Equality and Equity in Divorce Reform

The ideology privileging traditional marriage at the expense of other family structures has had other social costs. Divorce law is a case in point. Here again, legal developments have not been linear; in fact, in some sense they have been circular. The no-fault reforms of the 1960s effectively reinstated practices of earlier eras. Before the Catholic Church established marriage as a sacrament subject to ecclesiastical jurisdiction, Roman law and Anglo-Saxon custom permitted consensual divorce. However, as Chapter 1 indicated, by the time of America's settlement, religious and secular doctrine severely limited the grounds for marital dissolution. Yet even under the most restrictive regimes, desertion and collusive proceedings remained common remedies for those willing to risk their status in the divine kingdom for harmony in this one.[41]

By the mid-twentieth century the disparity between the law in form and the law in fact, between divorce for the rich and divorce for the poor, had become increasingly apparent. Those with sufficient means often subverted their state's requirements by establishing temporary domicile in a more permissive jurisdiction or by staging a courtroom charade closer to home. The latter approach produced certain standard scripts. In New York, for example, where adultery remained the only ground for divorce until 1966, court records revealed countless enactments of the same sordid melodrama, with the same supporting cast of paramours rented for the occasion. For those without sufficient resources to stage such productions, and without access to extremely limited legal-aid programs, informal separation was the only alternative. Despite the fault-based facade, relatively few marriages terminated with meaningful allocations of blame.[42]

By the late 1960s, the financial and psychological costs of such a system, coupled with increased demands for divorce, sparked a series of reforms. Over the next two decades, every state instituted a no-fault procedure based on irretrievable breakdown of the marriage or on some other no-fault criterion, such as separation for a relatively short interval. Although some commentators have blamed feminists for the costs of this "divorce revolution," women's rights groups were not active in the campaign and their interests were not well-represented. To the extent that gender equality figured at all on the reform agenda, the concerns typically involved equality for men. Debate focused on the plight of beleagured ex-husbands, crippled by excessive alimony burdens and threats of blackmail. No-fault reforms also failed to challenge traditional public-private distinctions. Divorce was still viewed as an essentially private matter; the public's responsibility was largely limited to providing an efficient means of dispute resolution.[43]

This no-fault campaign ultimately coincided with legislative and judicial efforts to insure gender neutrality in family law. Such efforts obtained firmer constitutional foundations in 1977, with the Supreme Court's decision in *Orr v. Orr.* There, a majority of Justices struck down a Texas statute that made alimony available only to wives. Of greater practical significance were reforms in most of the forty-two common-law-property states, which, unlike community-property jurisdictions, treated spouses' earnings and services during marriage as separate property rather than joint assets. Traditionally, courts in common-law jurisdictions allocated property of divorcing spouses to the party who held title or had made financial contributions to the purchase of the asset. Such an approach significantly disadvantaged female homemakers. With the 1970 Uniform Marriage and Divorce Act as a guide, increasing numbers of legislatures enacted provisions requiring "equitable division" of marital holdings or presumptions favoring equal division between husband and wife.[44]

The effects of such changes remain a matter of dispute. A number of studies, including Lenore Weitzman's path-breaking account, *The Divorce Revolution,* concluded that women's relative economic position worsened in the aftermath of reform. According to this research, the move from fault-based standards, although effective in reducing the expense and acrimony associated with divorce proceedings, also reduced the bargaining leverage of many women. Wives could no longer obtain financial concessions by threatening to contest the grounds for divorce or to expose evidence of abuse or infidelity. Also, the removal of presumptions favoring maternal custody of young children, although an important symbolic affirmation of gender equality, carried a substantial price. In order to avoid expensive, traumatic, and perhaps unsuccessful custody fights, many mothers traded away property and support claims. Studies comparing pre- and postreform eras have often found that divorcing women receive alimony and child support less frequently, in lower amounts, and for shorter periods.[45]

This does not, however, imply the existence of some golden era in which divorcing women fared well. During the heyday of fault-based frameworks, alimony was awarded in fewer than one-fifth of all cases, child-support orders were grossly inadequate and widely evaded, and wives who deviated from conservative moral standards received punitive property decrees. Family-law experts disagree about how much women's plight worsened in the postreform era and how much causal responsibility no-fault legislation bears for any change.[46]

That debate can never be definitively resolved, and, at this juncture, may be somewhat beside the point. Since virtually no one wishes to return to the fault-based era, attention should focus less on issues of causation and more on strategies for change. It is rarely if ever possible to isolate the effects of legal reform from the social forces that produced it. The decade of no-fault legislation witnessed significant realignments in gender roles that the law in turn refracted. The ideology of women's rights and the fact of women's increased labor-force participation affected attitudes toward divorce and husband's support obligations.

In the vast majority of states, reform legislation did not significantly reduce judicial discretion over property awards, and the changing social climate clearly affected the way courts exercised their discretion. Among some judges, feminist strategies provoked an ill-disguised backlash. For example, in 1972, in reversing a modest alimony award to a forty-eight-year-old homemaker, the Florida Supreme Court made plain its view that woman could now be regarded "as fully equipped as [man] to earn a living and provide for her essential needs." Indeed, the Justices added, "In this era of women's liberation we now have almost universally come to appreciate the fallacy of treating the demure members of our society as anything but on a basis of complete equality with the opposite sex." Yet in avoiding that "fallacy," the Court embraced another. What apparently escaped notice were the inequalities in men's and women's status following divorce.[47]

These inequalities carry substantial economic and ideological significance. Policies concerning marital dissolution have always given important signals about gender roles and cultural priorities. With the doubling of the divorce rate between the mid-1960s and 1970s, those signals became increasingly evident, and their financial implications increasingly problematic. According to current projections, about half of all contemporary marriages will end in divorce, and 60 percent of all children will spend time in single-parent homes. Contributing to these trends are both sexes' increasing expectations for marital satisfaction and women's decreasing economic dependence. Ironically enough, as the emotional bonds of marriage have strengthened, its legal bonds have grown more attenuated, and "serial polygamy" is rapidly becoming the national norm. Yet it is a practice not all individuals, particularly women, can readily afford. By the late 1980s half of all single-parent families lived in poverty, and 70 percent of those families were headed by divorced or separated women.[48]

That bleak economic situation was partly attributable to inequities in divorce settlements, problems in their enforcement, inadequacy in the resources subject to division, and limitations in women's employment opportunities. Some of the difficulty stemmed from the "clean break" approach that came to dominate judicial decisionmaking under divorce-reform legislation. Under this approach, codified in the Uniform Marriage and Divorce Act, spouses were to become self-sufficient as quickly as possible. No-fault standards sought to limit "alimony as well as acrimony"; spousal maintenance was to be avoided entirely or limited to brief rehabilitative periods. In theory, equity between the parties would be accomplished through distribution of existing assets rather than future income. In practice, this approach has produced a rather skewed concept of equity, since less than one-half of divorcing couples and even fewer minority couples had any significant assets, and most judges have felt husbands should receive a "fair share" of the property to which they had contributed. In the majority of jurisdictions, "fair" generally has worked out to about two-thirds of the marital assets, a figure that acknowledges men's disproportionate monetary contributions but undervalues women's homemaking services and career sacrifices.[49]

Even in the minority of states that presumptively mandate equal property division between the spouses, the result has seldom been equal. Most couples' assets are primarily intangible, consisting of professional licenses, insurance, pensions, and related benefits not traditionally subject to marital property division. Given women's unequal family responsibilities and labor-force opportunities, men have a disproportionate share of these assets. Moreover, the judiciary's declining tendency to award the home to custodial parents has increased their economic hardships and eroded friendship networks at a time when needs for continuity are most intense.[50]

The inadequacies of spousal maintenance and child-support awards have compounded the problem. All too often, legal and legislative decisionmaking has been skewed by assumptions about "alimony drones," the mythical legions of women living in a "perpetual state of secured indolence" who become a "drain upon society and menace to themselves." In fact, contemporary studies reveal that only about a sixth of all divorcing women have received maintenance and that two-thirds of the awards have been for limited duration, averaging about two years. Amounts have been modest and, together with child support, have seldom exceeded one-third of the husband's income.[51]

The hardships have been particularly severe for wives with extended marriages; two-thirds of these women have obtained no support. Many are displaced homemakers, whose principal work has been caring for their families, and whose experience after divorce reflects a substantial loss of social status and a significant risk of poverty. The majority of women over forty-five will not remarry, have no significant savings, are ineligible for substantial government assistance until the age of sixty-five, and lack the education, experience, and training to find decently paid work. Yet in the wake of women's liberation, many judges have determined that these women should be "forced to be free," often within highly unrealistic time periods. Husbands who built their careers with spousal assistance or prevented their wives from working suddenly have acquired more egalitarian expectations in the divorce court. For many older women, the sacrifices involved in raising a family have had permanent repercussions. If virtue is its own reward, it is hardly adequate to the occasion.[52]

Child-support law has been similarly inadequate. Much of the inequality in contemporary family policy turns on one central fact. After divorce, most men become single and most women become single parents. Three-fifths of all divorces involve minor children, and mothers receive custody in 90 percent of all cases. Few of these women have obtained child-support awards sufficient to meet the actual costs of child-rearing. In one survey, two-thirds of fathers had support obligations that were less than their monthly car payments. Not only have support awards been set at unrealistically low levels, their value has quickly fallen through inflation and noncompliance. Over half of all divorced men have failed to meet their spousal and child-support obligations. Arrearages have averaged between one-half and three-fourths of the amounts due. Few decrees have required assistance for children over eighteen, and fathers have been less likely than mothers to provide it voluntarily, despite higher income levels. For many women, the legal cost of enforcing awards has been prohibitive. Only when nonpayment reaches substantial levels have formal proceedings made sense, and at that point many judges have been willing to forego penal sanctions or reduce amounts due in order to secure limited compliance. Because few courts have required husbands to pay their wives' attorneys' fees, legal remedies have often cost more than they are worth.[53]

This scandalous situation regarding child support has prompted increasing, but still inadequate, legislative action. Beginning in the late 1970s, the federal government began to expand assistance in locating recalcitrant parents and intercepting their assets. Subsequent congressional legislation, the 1984 Child Support Amendments, and the Family Support Act of 1988 require state implementation of various procedures including child-support guidelines and automatic wage withholding for most parents. Although these procedures represent substantial progress, they do not adequately address either gender inequality or child poverty. States retain discretion in defining the amount of support enforceable under their guidelines, and most current approaches fail to allocate the burden equitably between custodial and noncustodial parents. The dominant framework has been an "income shares" model, which provides a formula for first combining the parents' income and establishing support based on the family's resources and the number of children, and then dividing the obligation between parents. This approach does not seek to equalize mothers' and fathers' relative contribution to child-rearing expenses, or to secure rough parity in their postdivorce standards of living. Where family resources are insufficient to meet a child's needs, only one state,

Wisconsin, is willing to provide income supplements. In most jurisdictions, implementation of enforcement procedures has also been plagued by widespread shortages of staff and related resources.[54]

The inadequacies in current child-support approaches are exacerbated by divorced mothers' limited employment opportunities. The responsibilities of single parenting often prevent women from working the kind of hours or obtaining the skills that would permit labor-force participation on what many judges have assumed is "a basis of complete equality." The low wage rates in most female-dominated occupations compounds the problem. In Lenore Weitzman's study, one-third of all divorced women working full time could not support themselves and their children above the poverty level.[55]

The cumulative effect of these factors translates into substantial gender disparities. Unless and until they remarry, divorced men's discretionary income rises, while that of their former wives' declines. Contemporary studies have varied in their assessment of the extent and duration of this decline, but they consistently reveal significant inequalities. Although most younger women eventually remarry, their hardships during the period of single parenthood cannot be measured in dollars alone. Divorced women experience more psychological distress than persons of any other marital status, a condition that is strongly linked to financial insecurity. The economic and psychological burdens common among divorced mothers may compromise their ability to cope with the emotional needs of their children, which usually increase after marital breakdowns.[56]

A central tenet of feminism in the 1960s was that the personal is the political. A quarter-century later, the lesson was that the personal had not become political enough. In this, as in other contexts, equality in form has not yielded equality in fact. Achieving greater equity for divorcing couples will require redirecting the focus of reform. Case studies of state legislative processes suggest that too much attention has focused on limited doctrinal issues, such as whether divorce statutes should presumptively mandate "equal" division of marital assets, or whether courts should retain discretion to make "equitable" allocations. In theory, either formulation is defensible; in practice neither has been. Both have proved to be misnomers. "Equitable" distribution is more aptly understood as "discretionary distribution," and state court studies reveal that judges have exercised that discretion in idiosyncratic, gender-biased fashion. "Equal" division as currently applied ignores the unequal needs, responsibilities, and opportunities confronting divorced men and women in contemporary American society.[57]

What this suggests is less preoccupation with text and more with context in reform efforts. Better education about the real costs of homemaking is necessary for judges and legislators. Recent studies have revealed startling ignorance, not only about the day-to-day expenses of child-rearing but also about the permanent loss in earning potential for most primary caretakers. This educational process should also involve challenging traditional concepts of marital obligations. As much modern feminist theory suggests, conventional approaches to family law have placed too much emphasis on rights and too little on relationships, and have relied too heavily on private rather than public resources. The alternative framework proposed here focuses less on individual entitlements and more on family needs. Where minor children are involved, their welfare should be the central concern.[58]

This alternative focus points up the necessity of other, more specific, reforms. Child-support guidelines should seek to allocate burdens equitably between parents. As in Scandinavian programs (which Wisconsin has recently followed), the government should provide subsidies where parental resources are inadequate. Conventional notions of marital property also require reassessment. Many couples lack significant tangible assets that can be divided on divorce, and both spouses have often contributed to the development of future sources of income. Yet all too often, courts have viewed such potential income as a personal entitlement rather than a collective effort. According to many judges during the 1970s and 1980s, resources such as pensions or professional degrees should not be divisible in divorce since they lacked the "traditional" attributes of property: they could not be sold on the open market, and they represented the cumulative product of education, effort, ability, and financial expenditures for which spouses assertedly did not expect compensation.[59]

Such approaches, by treating property as a tangible object rather than as a legal construct, seek to deny judicial responsibility even as it is exercised. "Traditional" features of ownership have always been open to redefinition, and spouses' expectations are in part a function of what courts provide. The point is not that professional degrees should be singled out as joint "property" while other career assets remain individual entitlements. It is rather that all vocational capabilities should be evaluated in determining what spouses need, deserve, and are able to pay. Efficient enforcement mechanisms, such as automatic wage withholding now available for child support, should also be routinely available for spousal maintenance.

The needs of older displaced homemakers warrant special recognition. Women whose lives fit within traditional gender roles ought not to be punished simply because those roles have begun to change. These homemakers have made societal contributions warranting societal recognition; they should receive more education, training, job placement, and related services targeted to their special needs. So too, extended marriages may justify extended rather than temporary spousal support, particularly where homemakers have sacrificed their own earning potential to meet family obligations. In mandating one such award, the California Supreme Court concluded that where wives' actual job prospects were minimal, husbands must assume long-term financial responsibilities. In the court's view, "This has nothing to do with feminism, sexism, or male chauvinism. It is ordinary common sense, basic decency, and simple justice." The court was half right. Such determinations have a great deal to do with feminism, as well as with the broader moral values that underlie it.[60]

Gender neutrality in family law cannot be achieved simply through gender neutrality in formal standards. Nor will broad mandates calling for equality in the allocation of marital property achieve their objectives without a more realistic understanding of the gender inequalities in social experience. If we wish to encourage sharing relationships, we cannot continue to penalize sharing behavior. Nor can we continue denying public responsibility to reduce the private suffering that divorce entails. Many couples lack adequate assets to maintain two separate households. Most men remarry, usually within a few years after divorce, and incur new family obligations. When the pie is sufficiently small, changing the size of the slices is an inadequate approach. As experience in other countries suggests, even with more equitable property-allocation standards and efficient child-support enforcement mechanisms, many single-parent families will still need governmental assistance. The difficulties of divorcing women cannot be met solely through divorce law. They reflect broader societal problems calling for broader societal responses concerning employment, welfare, childcare, and related issues.[61]

Text and Subtext in Custody Adjudication

Debates over child custody offer variations on a similar theme. Much of the controversy centers on the value of formal equality in circumstances of social inequality. An adequate understanding of that issue again requires transcending the equal-special treatment framework in which it is typically presented. Dismantling that dichotomy will require greater sensitivity to the relation between legal texts and social subtexts in custodial disputes. Few situations present more agonizing choices than these disputes, and no legal formula can adequately resolve them. Yet we can make more informed choices between the inherently imperfect alternatives available.

Early Anglo-American doctrine built on ideologies of parental entitlement rather than caretaking relationships. Under English common law, as William Blackstone summarized it, the father was entitled to sole custody of all minor children; the mother was "entitled to reverence and respect." During the latter part of the nineteenth century, American doctrine gradually evolved from paternal preferences to maternal presumptions. Although traditional standards and treatises gave priority to fathers' rights, trial courts increasingly focused on the children's "best interest." The celebration of maternity that figured in so much nineteenth-century judicial as well as popular discourse gradually reshaped custodial premises. Courts became unwilling to "snatch" a child of "tender years" from the "bosom of an affectionate mother and place it in the coarse hands of the father," except in cases of maternal unfitness. For older children, the growing tendency was also to focus on parental fitness. Since social conventions favored husbands acting as the guilty parties in fault-based divorce actions, wives were more likely to appear as the better custodians. Economic forces also may have been at work. The industrial revolution and compulsory school attendance reduced the value of child labor and removed some incentives for fathers to insist on guardianship. Studies of court records indicate that in the late nineteenth and early twentieth centuries, mothers were obtaining custody in the vast majority of cases, typically around 80 to 85 percent. Over the next decades, that percentage continued to climb, leveling off at contemporary rates of about 90 percent.[62]

At the time, most feminists viewed the rise of maternal preference as a progressive step, but its legacy now appears more mixed. In one sense, the doctrinal evolution did favor women: it made it easier for them to leave an abusive relationship without losing custody, and affirmed their status and centrality in child-rearing. Yet like other forms of preferential treatment, the presumption was double-edged. Tributes to women's maternal mission served to confine as well as to celebrate. They perpetuated an ideology of separate spheres that denied male responsibility for parenting and female opportunities for employment. By assuming that women's nature was to nurture, courts helped stigmatize those who deviated from prescribed roles.

The selectivity with which courts invoked maternal preferences further circumscribed female roles. The "fit" mother presumptively entitled to custody was a chaste and closeted soul, innocent not only of sexual indiscretion but also of intellectual independence. The welfare of the child justified policing the conduct of the parent; abortion, adultery, or association with unpopular causes were all sufficient grounds to sever maternal ties. Under this framework, enforcement of a double standard appeared a necessary concession to prevailing mores. In the eyes of the Lord, the sins of adulterous parents might be comparable, but "in the opinion of society it was otherwise," and a mother "reduced to utter and irredeemable ruin" could not provide an acceptable home for her child. Potential wives should not grow up under the influence of women who had "immoral" understandings of marital obligations. Even those wives who satisfied a male judiciary's vision of female propriety were sometimes unable to take advantage of that fact in custody determinations. Child support did not become widely available until the 1920s, and awards generally were so low and so sporadically enforced that some mothers were deterred from seeking custody. Many women without independent economic resources found formal preferences an insufficient answer to practical exigencies.[63]

With the rise of the feminist movement in the 1960s and 1970s came the decline of maternal preference. Borrowing feminist rhetoric, a growing number of fathers'-rights groups joined forces with other constituencies seeking gender-neutral family laws. Their collective efforts generally succeeded, although more often in legislative than judicial arenas. When faced with equal-protection challenges, most state courts sustained maternal presumptions, typically on tenuous grounds. The Utah Supreme Court, for example, concluded in 1974 that a father's petition for his four-year-old daughter would be entitled to equal treatment if men were "equally gifted in lactation." Alabama courts sustained the "tender years" preference on the theory that it was "not a classification based upon gender, but merely a factual presumption based upon the historic role of the mother." Nonetheless, by the early 1980s, two-thirds of the states had officially abolished maternal preferences. In an effort to promote more equal parental involvement following divorce, two-thirds had also enacted some form of joint-custody legislation.[64]

The extent to which these doctrinal changes altered social practices is difficult to assess. In some jurisdictions, courts openly favored mothers with small children despite legislation guaranteeing equal parental rights. In other jurisdictions, judges did not talk in terms of preferences but continued to apply them. Well after California abolished its tender-years presumption, 81 percent of surveyed judges and 98 percent of surveyed attorneys believed that it was still in force. As one judge put it, "Even though the law says there isn't a presumption, I think mothers make better mothers." Yet particularly for older children, changes in formal standards reflected and reinforced changes in social expectations. Almost nine out of ten attorneys in Lenore Weitzman's study believed that fathers were having an easier time obtaining custody as a result of changes in legal doctrine (42 percent) or public attitudes (46 percent). The limited data available suggest that by the 1980s, although women were still retaining physical custody in about 90 percent of divorce cases, men were winning one-third to one-half of contested proceedings. A significant number also prevailed through extralegal coercion, by forcibly abducting their children or by threatening physical violence, public humiliation, or economic sanctions.[65]

Changes in formal standards concerning joint custody also had an impact, although again the consequences are difficult to measure with precision. Part of the problem stems from ambiguity in legal labels. Joint-custody legislation and decrees encompass a wide variety of practices. Some statutes have recognized courts' option to grant both parents custodial rights; other legislative and judicial mandates have incorporated a preference for such arrangements in all cases, or a presumption that it is in children's best interest if both parents agree to the arrangement. In practice, joint custody can mean sharing in either a legal or residential sense. Under the former approach, which is by far the most common, parents have equal rights to make important child-rearing decisions, but only one has physical custody. Under joint-residential decrees, the child lives for a substantial part of each week or year with each parent.

Early studies have left unclear whether fathers who obtain joint legal entitlements behave much differently from those with only liberal visitation privileges. Traditionally, most divorced men have evidenced little willingness to exercise parental responsibilities. Survey data from the mid-1970s to the mid-1980s indicates that under conventional single-custody arrangements, about half of all children have had no contact with their divorced father in the past year; frequent contact is rare. However, there has been little long-term research and no consensus on the extent to which formal changes in custodial responsibility have prompted changes in custodial behavior.[66]

Although the rise of a maternal preference was a mixed blessing, so was its demise. Its replacement with a best-interest standard or joint-custody preference has disadvantaged women in several respects. Most obviously, the loss of a tender-years presumption has made it easier to discriminate against women who do not conform to conventional norms or to the idiosyncratic expectations of particular judges. Some trial courts have been affronted by any extramarital sexual liaisons. Others have singled out lesbian relationships for special disapproval on the basis of empirically unsupported premises; common assumptions have been that homosexual women are mentally unstable or will interfere with the "normal" sexual and moral development of their children. Either having a career or not having a career has been prejudicial. Some judges have been hostile to "ambitious" mothers whose "outside interests" conflict with domestic duties. Men with "normal working fathers' hours" have not been similarly penalized, particularly if they can afford live-in help or have mothers or second wives willing to serve as full-time caretakers. Yet divorced mothers who have wanted to remain at home with their children have also risked judicial disapproval, since they have been unable to provide the same kind of financial security as their former husbands. Women subject to such prejudices have risked losing not only custody, but also their sense of identity, influence, and self-esteem.[67]

Another effect of the move away from maternal preference has been to increase inequalities in bargaining power between divorcing husbands and wives. The more indeterminate the standards, the more credible are men's threats to seek custody. The high emotional and financial costs of such litigation have encouraged many women to sacrifice financial claims rather than risk courtroom battles. Ironically, the greater the mother's attachment to her children, the more susceptible she is to this form of leverage. As a result, women often have ended up with the responsibilities of child-rearing but without the resources to fulfill them.[68]

Related probems have faced mothers in states with strong joint-custody preferences. In some instances, husbands have sought joint legal (though not physical) custody in an effort to reduce their support obligations, or to assert continuing control over their wives' lifestyle. Despite the fear of physical or emotional abuse, many women have accepted such arrangements to avoid custody disputes in which they would appear unreasonable. Pressure to make these agreements has been particularly intense in states with "friendly parent" provisions, which grant custodial preference to the party who demonstrates greatest willingness to promote contact by the other. Joint-custody arrangements negotiated under such constraints have frequently perpetuated the oppression that women initiated divorce proceedings to avoid.[69]

In response to these concerns, many feminists have increasingly advocated primary caretaker presumptions in cases involving young children. Such presumptions, which some states began adopting in the early 1980s, have granted preferences to the parent who has been primarily responsible for meeting a young child's daily needs. By reducing the indeterminacy of "best interest" standards, these preferences have reduced the credibility of custody threats as a means of achieving financial concessions. In addition, many advocates of this approach have emphasized its consistency with certain psychological theories that assert mothers' special caretaking capacities, or that stress young children's need for continuous, stable attachments to one individual.[70]

Although gender-neutral in form, these presumptions have not worked out that way in fact. And they came at a cost. As long as the vast majority of primary caretakers are women, privileging their custodial rights reinforces the assumption that parenting is largely the mother's responsibility. This assumption has circumscribed opportunities for both sexes. It has also helped to perpetuate unequal burdens on mothers who obtain sole custody and has fostered the guilt and social ostracism that discourage women from declining that role.

Although rigorous long-term research is not yet available, most existing studies do not find men performing primary caretaker roles less adequately than women, regardless of who assumed such responsibilities before divorce. Some, although not all, small-scale research has suggested that where the parents have cooperative relationships, children benefit economically and emotionally from maintaining attachments to both mother and father. Continued contact can provide emotional advantages for adults as well. Yet how many divorced couples are capable of continuing cooperation remains in doubt. To the extent that children have seemed better off under existing joint-custodial arrangements, it may be because the parties who have agreed to such dispositions are especially committed to maintaining parental involvement. Findings based on largely self-selected samples provide limited guidance about the appropriateness of particular standards for the public as a whole. Moreover, the available data make it clear that neither parents' nor children's interests are well served by imposing joint-custody arrangements on couples who do not want, or cannot cope with, that level of interaction.[71]

The current debate over custody presents inadequate alternatives with inadequate evidence on which to choose between them. Best-interest standards yield highly indeterminate, idiosyncratic, and ingenuous decision-making. They assume that courts are competent to make accurate predictions about future custodial arrangements, an assumption flatly inconsistent with empirical evidence. Both joint custody- and primary-caretaker preferences carry a price, and we have little basis on which to compare their magnitude. Enough variation in state custody standards now exists to permit more systematic study with larger, more representative samples. Issues to be investigated should include the effects of various custodial arrangements on day-to-day parental involvement, child development, and financial dispositions. What legal and social structures can best promote healthy parent-child relations? How criticial are the sex and age of the children involved, as well as the race, class, and ethnicity of the families? To what extent do primary caretaker presumptions reduce women's disadvantages in financial negotiations and to what extent would effective child-support requirements accomplish similar results?[72]

This is not to imply that more research will resolve such questions. It is impossible fully to isolate the effect of legal standards from the societal forces that produced them. What constitutes the "best" outcome following divorce is a normative as well as an empirical question; its resolution may involve tradeoffs between the interests not only of mothers, fathers, and their children, but also of second families and extended kin. A richer understanding of custodial arrangements in daily experience can inform our analysis, but it will not eliminate the need for choices based on imperfect knowledge and competing concerns.

In making those choices, it is critical to move beyond the equal-special framework that has traditionally constrained them. As conventionally applied, neither neutral nor preferential custody standards will promote true equality between the sexes. A primary caretaker preference may reduce existing disparities in bargaining power, but it also reinforces the stereotypes on which such disparities rest. A joint-custody standard affirms a desirable ideal, but it should not be imposed on parents who cannot meet its demands. The challenge is to find approaches that better accommodate these ideological and practical concerns. We should seek to promote equal responsibilities, while recognizing our current distance from that ideal.[73]

That objective demands reassessment of both the standards and the structures for resolving divorce-related disputes. Before resorting to primary caretaker presumptions as a check on coercive bargaining, we should exhaust other alternatives with fewer adverse side effects, such as the mandatory support standards proposed earlier. Before imposing joint-custody presumptions, we should be sure that adequate safeguards are in place; parties should not be forced into arrangements that are likely to enhance friction or offer one parent opportunities for control without responsibility.

Measures for improving the dispute-resolution process are of equal importance. A threshold step is to insure better judicial education in areas where misperceptions are greatest. It should also be possible to foster less combative frameworks for private ordering and more effective means of public intervention. State-supported mediation and counseling services could help divorcing couples work toward agreements that best accommodate the interests in question. That is not to endorse conciliation as an all-purpose prescription for family disputes. Mediation between parties with unequal negotiating skills, information, and power can perpetuate those disparities. But the same has also been true of adversarial settings. The current system alternates between inadequate judicial oversight in uncontested cases and unnecessarily expensive battles in contested ones. The point is not to discard conciliation but rather to improve its procedures, make them accessible in appropriate circumstances, and challenge the other social conditions that entrench inequality.[74]

Finally, and perhaps most significantly, we must broaden our frame of reference in assessing reform proposals. An approach truly informed by feminist values cannot proceed solely from the vantage of divorcing wives. A commitment to caretaking implies a concern for all parties affected by marital dissolution. The interests of women seeking total disengagement from prior relationships may need to be tempered by the interests of children who would benefit from continued involvement with both parents. If feminism is to have influence as a normative vision, it must resist capture by parochial perspectives. The concerns of this generation must not displace the needs of the next.

Chapter 8

Equality in Form and Equality in Fact: Women and Work

For economists in the 1970s and early 1980s, Leviticus 27:3–4 was a familiar text. Its teaching, as reported in innumerable scholarly and popular articles, was that women of working age in biblical times were valued at 30 silver shekels and men at 50. After 2,500 years, that ratio had not fundamentally changed. The difference was that, for the first time, many societies were actively attempting to do something about it. By the end of the 1980s, progress was apparent.

The rebirth of an American feminist movement in the 1960s witnessed a broad array of legislative, administrative, and judicial mandates against gender discrimination. The result has been a large measure of equality in formal treatment between the sexes, but a continued disparity in actual status. Women have more opportunities for economic independence than ever before in history, but certain obstacles persist. Law has played a critical role in breaking barriers to entry for those seeking nontraditional employment, but most occupations have remained highly gender-segregated or gender-stratified. While legal mandates have entitled men and women to equal pay for the same work, relatively few males and females have in fact performed the same work. If domestic and paid labor are combined, the average woman works longer hours and receives substantially less income than the average man. Although women have entered elite professions in significant numbers, they have tended to cluster at the lowest levels. Most female employees, and a disproportionate number of minority female workers, have remained in relatively low-status, low-paying, female-dominated vocations.[1]

Explanations for the lack of progress have varied, but any convincing analysis reveals fundamental limitations in conventional legal responses. These limitations of current employment policy reflect inadequacies in the theoretical traditions on which it draws. In part, the difficulty stems from the law's customary focus on gender differences rather than gender disadvantages. Its primary objective has been to secure similar treatment for those similarly situated; less effort has centered on remedying the structural factors that contribute to women's dissimilar and disadvantaged status. A related difficulty involves the individualist premises that have traditionally restricted legal policies. All too often a focus on maximizing individual choice has deflected attention from the social forces and workplace values that constrain choice. Enforcement of equal opportunity, pay equity, and affirmative-action mandates has been hampered by a preoccupation with individual victims and villains—with a demand for evidence of intentional discrimination and a reluctance to penalize innocent third parties. Too much concern has focused on the conscious motivations of decisionmakers and too little on the cumulative disadvantages that their actions impose.

Significant progress toward social justice will require alternative frameworks. Our objectives must include not only access to, but also alteration of, existing employment structures. Equal opportunity is insufficient as a means and an end; we need fundamental changes in workplace practices, premises, and priorities.

Occupational Inequality

Women's labor-force participation and opportunities increased substantially during the latter half of the twentieth century. That progress was accelerated by the enactment of the Equal Pay Act of 1963, which prohibits sex-based discrimination in wages; Title VII of the 1964 Civil Rights Act, which prohibits sex-based discrimination in hiring, advancement, termination, training, and related terms of employment; Title IX, which prohibits such discrimination in educational programs requiring federal assistance; and Executive Order 11375, which requires federal contractors to establish affirmative-action programs for women.[2]

Despite such enactments and the broader cultural changes they reflected and reinforced, wide disparities have persisted in the sexes' vocational status. In 1950 the annual wages of full-time women workers were 64 percent of the annual wages of males. Over the next two decades that percentage declined, dipping to 58 percent in 1968 before returning to 64 percent in annual wages two decades later (70 percent in weekly wages). However, those ratios have always understated gender disparities in earnings, since fewer than half of all employed women have worked full time for the full year and disproportionate numbers have lacked employment-related benefits such as health and pension coverage. Data from the late 1980s indicated that even among full-time workers, the average female college graduate still earned significantly less than the average male with a high school degree. The average black female graduate in a full-time position received 90 percent of the average white female's salary, a figure roughly equivalent to the pay of a white male high school dropout. Women also experienced disproportionate levels of involuntary part-time work or unemployment, and such rates were particularly high among minorities.[3]

These salary and unemployment disparities have reflected broader patterns of occupational segregation and stratification. Most women employees in the 1980s were crowded into a small percentage of prevailing job categories, and about three-fifths were in occupations comprised of at least 75 percent female workers. Although the level of segregation in occupations has decreased over the last two decades, the level of segregation within industries has not. Most jobs have been stratified by race and ethnicity as well as by sex, and women of color have remained at the bottom of the occupational hierarchy. Even in gender-integrated occupations, men and women generally have held different positions, with different pay and promotion opportunities. Despite significant trends toward greater integration, most projections suggest that at current rates of change it would take between fifty and one hundred years to achieve a sexually balanced workplace.[4]

The most dramatic progress to date has been in the professions, where women now constitute a majority of workers. However, few have obtained the positions of greatest power, prestige, and economic reward. Taking law, management, and academia as representative illustrations, significant sex-based disparities remain. Although women's representation grew from 3 to 7 percent in the early 1960s to 20 to 40 percent in the late 1980s, they were only half as likely to be partners in major law firms and held only 2 percent of corporate executive positions, 13 percent of tenured academic slots, and 8 percent of state and federal judgeships. Underrepresentation was even greater among women of color. Female lawyers earned approximately 20 percent less than men, and women vice presidents and presidents about 50 percent less. A "glass ceiling" on women's advancement was particularly noticeable in corporate hierarchies. In the late 1980s, of some 6,500 public corporations, only 15 had female chief executives. Gender disparities persisted even among those with comparable age, experience, and occupational qualifications.[5]

Gains in blue-collar employment have been less pronounced. Although the overall number of women in blue-collar jobs increased significantly in the 1970s and 1980s, their proportionate representation did not change substantially. Female employees have constituted an increasingly visible presence in certain formerly male-dominated occupations such as bus driving (49 percent) and bartending (48 percent), but reports in the late 1980s placed their share of skilled trade positions at only about 20 percent. Moreover, women's increasing interest in "men's work" has not been accompanied by a comparable increase of men's interest in "women's work." In the most heavily female-dominated job sectors, such as clerical work, male representation has not significantly changed.[6]

Defenders of the conventional equal-opportunity approach to employment discrimination typically dismiss these inequalities as artifacts of cultural lag or employee choice, and in either case, as matters beyond the scope of legitimate legal concern. From this perspective, the absence of women in upper-level positions and relatively well-paid occupations is a transitory phenomenon, the result of conduct no longer permissible under contemporary antidiscrimination doctrine. Formal prohibitions on gender bias in educational and employment practices, coupled with the retirement of a few last-ditch defenders of the ancien régime, are thought to be sufficient guarantees of equal opportunity. Given the available remedies for discriminatory treatment, any remaining disparity in employment status can be attributed to individual choice, capabilities, and commitment, and is not a ground for further legal intervention.

Yet most research suggests that the obstacles confronting women workers are considerably more intransigent than the equal-opportunity approach acknowledges. In identifying these obstacles, it is important to note at the outset certain complexities in the concept of occupational equality. It is not self-evident that proportional representation in all employment sectors is the ultimate ideal. To assume that under conditions of full equality women will make precisely the same occupational choices as men is to adopt an assimilationist perspective that many feminists renounce. Yet as long as there remains a strong negative correlation between the concentration of women in a given occupation and its relative earnings and status, the persistence of gender-segregated structures is a major concern. We can leave open questions about the precise degree of gender differentiation in the ideal society without losing sight of the disadvantages confronting women in this one.

In assessing those disadvantages, it is useful to distinguish two sorts of problems. Workforce inequalities reflect the relatively low status and pay scales in female-dominated occupations and the factors that discourage women's entry and advancement in alternative employment contexts. These phenomena in turn depend on complex interrelations between individual choices, social norms, discriminatory practices, and institutional structures.

Individual Choice and Socialization Patterns

Although individual choice plays an important role in virtually all theories of occupational inequality, the nature of that role sparks considerable controversy. According to human capital models of labor-force participation, gender differences in earnings and occupational status are largely attributable to differences in career investments. In essence, these models assume that women seek to balance work and family commitments by selecting female-dominated occupations that tend not to require extended training, long hours, inflexible schedules, or skills that deteriorate with absence. Under these theories, the solution to women's workplace inequality lies with women themselves. In their crudest form, human-capital approaches lead to a kind of Marie Antoinette response to occupational stratification. If women want positions with greater pay, prestige, and power, they should make different career investments; if female nurses want pay scales equivalent to male hotel clerks, let them become hotel clerks.[7]

There are a number of difficulties with this theory. Estimates have varied widely concerning the percentage of the wage gap that is attributable to human capital factors such as education, experience, and hours worked. However, according to a comprehensive National Academy of Sciences review, most studies have concluded that these characteristics cannot account for more than half of current gender disparities. On the whole, women who make comparable investments in time, training, and experience still advance less far and less quickly than men. Even in their most sophisticated forms, human-capital approaches leave a vast range of questions unanswered. What accounts for cross-cultural variations and historical changes in occupational segregation? Why do females choose to be nurses rather than hotel clerks—or for that matter, truck drivers, where job skills are even less likely to deteriorate with absence? Why do unskilled clerks earn more than highly educated nurses? Why don't male employees with family responsibilities choose jobs requiring shorter hours? Answers to these questions require a more complex account of cultural norms and institutional constraints.[8]

At the turn of the century Charlotte Perkins Gilman warned against making assumptions about the kinds of work men and women would freely choose until generation after generation could grow up under equal conditions. American society remains a considerable distance from that ideal, and occupational choices have been colored by cultural expectations. At early ages, children begin absorbing cues about appropriate sex-role traits and occupations, and only recently has that socialization process prompted serious concern. For example, not until the 1970s did public attention focus on stereotypes in children's books. What then became apparent was the crudest form of generalization. In the world traditionally presented to preschoolers, homemaking was women's sole occupation; in one representative survey, fairies and water maidens were the only apparent alternatives. Most fictional stories centered on males. Female characters appeared mainly in supporting roles; boys had adventures, while girls went shopping or lost bunnies that boys found. Despite substantial progress during the last decade, the legacy of Dr. Dick and Nancy Nurse persists. Most research has indicated that by early adolescence, males and females have acquired different career expectations. In general, women have expressed lower expectations for occupational success than men and have attached greater priority to the relational aspects of employment (such as opportunities for helping or working with others) than to opportunities for recognition (money, status, and power).[9]

Many career decisions have been less the product of fully informed and independent preferences than the result of preconceptions about "women's work," which are shaped by cultural stereotypes, family and peer pressure, and the absence of alternative role models. Individuals who have deviated from traditional norms in job selection usually have received less social approval than those who have not. Many families also have discouraged career choices that would conflict with domestic duties, require geographic mobility, or provide greater prestige or income for wives than for husbands. Such patterns can be especially pronounced among some minority groups, where males' education often carries greater priority than females'. Job-training, counseling, and recruitment networks have channeled many women toward conventional occupations, and socioeconomic barriers have limited employment aspirations. Although increasing numbers of women have expressed the same vocational preferences as men, a majority have still chosen traditional female-dominated occupations. Once having made such choices, many women have found it too costly—financially, psychologically, or logistically—to shift careers in response to fuller information about other options. Family obligations, seniority structures, and financial constraints have converged to entrench the effects of sex-role socialization.[10]

These socialization processes are further reinforced by the mismatch between characteristics associated with femininity and characteristics associated with vocational achievement. The aggressiveness, competitiveness, dedication, and emotional detachment thought necessary for advancement in the most prestigious and well-paid occupations is incompatible with the traits commonly viewed as attractive in women: cooperativeness, deference, sensitivity, and self-sacrifice. Similar discontinuities have been apparent in blue-collar contexts requiring physical strength, "toughness," or other seemingly masculine attributes. Despite substantial progress toward gender equality over the last several decades, these sexual stereotypes have been remarkably resilient. Women remain subject to the familiar double-bind. Those who conform to traditional definitions of femininity have often appeared lacking in the assertiveness necessary for occupational success, while those who conform to masculine models have appeared bitchy, aggressive, or difficult to work with. A "third sex" in vocational contexts has yet to emerge.[11]

Individual choices have also been constrained by different family responsibilities, discriminatory practices, and workplace structures. The result is a convergence of self-perpetuating signals that reinforce occupational inequalities. Males' and females' different career investments have been heavily dependent on their perceptions of different opportunities. Women have long faced relatively low wages in traditional vocations and substantial barriers to advancement in nontraditional pursuits. Under such circumstances, it has been economically rational for working couples to give priority to the husband's career, to relocate in accordance with his job prospects, and to assign wives a disproportionate share of family obligations. The gender division of labor in the home and workplace have been mutually reinforcing patterns. Women's unequal occupational status has encouraged them to make lower career investments and to assume greater domestic responsibilities, both of which help perpetuate that inequality. To break this cycle will require treating individual choices not as fixed and independent phenomena, but as responses to cultural forces that are open to redirection.[12]

Discriminatory Practices and Occupational Dynamics

Attempts to move beyond individual-choice-based models of occupational inequality have proceeded on several levels. One approach has focused on occupational segregation. Some commentators, drawing on dual labor-market theories, have stressed men's concentration in the primary and women's in the secondary sector of the workforce. The primary sector, generally characterized by high capital investment, advanced technology, unionization, opportunities for promotion, and low employee turnover, also has relatively high wages and benefits. The secondary sector, with the converse characteristics, tends to have lower pay scales and benefits, which in turn encourage higher turnover and provide fewer options for advancement. Other commentators have stressed more general effects of occupational crowding. Because women have remained clustered in a relatively small number of female-dominated occupations, the oversupply of labor in those fields has depressed wage rates and increased unemployment.[13]

Such approaches, although useful to a point, have proved too reductive or restrictive to provide a full account of occupational inequality. In part, their limitations reflect the level of analysis on which they proceed; their focus on surface explanations of gender disparities tends to leave fundamental causal questions unaddressed. Why have women remained crowded into certain sectors of the labor market and why have those sectors commanded relatively low status and prestige? Why do females in predominately male occupations have lower pay scales and fewer promotion opportunities despite comparable qualifications?[14]

In seeking answers to such questions, commentators have accumulated increasing evidence concerning discrimination of various forms: deliberate, statistical, and unconscious. On the most overt level, as economists such as Gary Becker have argued, competitive market forces do not necessarily discourage deliberate bias against women or minorities where employers have developed a "taste for discrimination." Such tastes, founded on personal prejudice, customer or co-worker preference, or favoritism toward male "breadwinners," have been identified in a wide range of contexts. Before passage of antidiscrimination legislation in the early 1960s, many employers were surprisingly public about their private biases. During the nineteenth century, intermingling between male and female workers was often viewed as "actively operative for evil." Although twentieth-century employers have appeared less concerned about the moral dimensions of occupational integration, many have viewed it as economically inefficient or culturally inappropriate. Before the mid-1960s, some job advertisements openly specified "males preferred," and many workplaces had separate job titles, pay scales, and promotion channels for men and women performing substantially the same work.[15]

Assumptions persist that male workers will resent female colleagues or supervisory personnel; that male consumers of certain services or products will not relate well to female employees; and that most women lack the capacity or commitment for positions calling for physical strength, extended training, or managerial skills. Similar biases against racial and ethnic minorities have left women of color doubly disadvantaged.[16]

Although changing attitudes and statutory mandates have made such overt discrimination increasingly rare, some of its legacy remains. Litigation in the late 1980s still revealed claims such as those advanced by owners of tuna fishing boats that excluded women. According to these owners, the presence of female employees would "destroy morale and distract the crew"; their boats would "catch fewer fish with women on board."[17]

In theory, a well-functioning free market should erode such discriminatory patterns, since employers who do not indulge arbitrary prejudices will have a competitive advantage. In practice, however, occupational segregation and differential reward structures, once established, can be highly resistant to change. For example, even after protective-labor statutes were declared illegal, the employment patterns they helped perpetuate remained largely unaffected. The more insulated the labor market from competitive forces, the more resilient these biases may prove. Even reasonably competitive markets will permit what economists label "statistical discrimination," that is, discrimination premised on generalizations which are inaccurate in a large percentage of cases but are cheaper to indulge than ignore. For example, if an employer believes female workers have a higher turnover rate than males and that it is expensive or difficult to screen for job commitment in advance, then it makes sense to channel women into lower-status, lower-paid positions where they can be easily replaced. Although recent data suggest that men and women with comparable qualifications holding comparable jobs do not generally have different turnover rates, the residual effects of statistical discrimination often linger. Once jobs become typed as male or female, socialization processes tend to perpetuate those labels.[18]

A final, and in contemporary society perhaps the most intransigent form of discrimination, operates at unconscious levels. Employer decisionmaking has reflected the same gender stereotypes that have constrained employees' vocational choices. An increasing array of studies has revealed unconscious bias on three levels: prototypes, the images associated with members of a particular occupation; schema, the personal characteristics and situational factors that are used to explain conduct; and scripts, the patterns defining behavior appropriate in a given situation. Thus, when a female applicant for a given position (for example, senior manager) does not fit the evaluator's prototype (for example, authoritarian male), her credentials will be judged with greater skepticism. Many explanatory schema embody similar stereotypes. Men's successes are more likely to be explained in terms of ability and their failures in terms of luck, while women's achievements are more often attributed to luck or effort, and their failures ascribed to inability. Since evaluations of ability are critical in promotion and salary decisions, these biases help entrench occupational hierarchies.[19]

So too, scripts defining appropriate social behavior often reflect patterns of gender dominance, deference, and accommodation. For example, in group conversation, male participants tend to speak longer and more often. Women are expected not only to talk less but to acquiesce in interruptions; those who deviate from their accustomed role provoke negative evaluations. Once again, these perceptual prejudices create a double bind. Women are criticized for being "too feminine" or "not feminine enough." Those who conform to accepted stereotypes appear to lack ideas or initiative, while women who take a more assertive stance are judged arrogant, aggressive, or abrasive.[20]

These unconscious gender biases have been apparent in a variety of contexts. Psychological research suggests that decisionmakers rate more positively those who conform to gender stereotypes than those who do not. Individuals are also more likely to recall evidence that supports rather than challenges assumptions about appropriate masculine or feminine behavior. Given the discontinuities between traits associated with femininity and those associated with vocational achievement, female performance is often undervalued. Since research involving racial bias reveals similar patterns, women of color face special obstacles.[21]

More specific clinical and longitudinal research makes the point directly. For example, surveys involving male managers, business students, and chairs of university psychology departments have revealed that identical resumes are rated significantly lower if the applicant is a woman rather than a man. In some, though not all studies, both male and female subjects have given lower ratings to the same artwork or scholarly articles when the artist or author is thought to be a woman. Other evidence has indicated that college students evaluate male professors more favorably than female professors, and that decisionmakers are more likely to hire, promote, or provide training opportunities for men than for equally qualified women. An illuminating example of such unconscious bias at work appeared in a 1970s survey of letters of recommendation for female graduate school applicants. Comments included: "Pretty she's not, but pleasant and sparkly and energetic she is . . ."; "She is a quiet yet personable young woman, rather neat and attractive though not likely to unduly distract male graduate students . . ."; "She is task-oriented, self-starting, non-neurotic. An unusual girl graduate student."[22]

Such unconscious bias affects not only opportunities for individual employees, but also reward structures for women as a group. This point was well illustrated by a survey of the federal government's *Dictionary of Occupational Titles,* which rates the complexity of tasks in some 30,000 jobs and which has influenced many public and private employers' compensation schemes. Among the occupations rating lowest in the 1975 *Dictionary* were foster mother, nursery-school teacher, and practical nurse—all of which were thought equally or less demanding than parking-lot attendant and "offal man," whose respective responsibilities were to park cars and to "shove[l] ice into [a] chicken offal container." Although repeated critiques prompted substantial progress in a later *Dictionary* edition, the legacy of earlier biases have been difficult to eliminate. Anthropological studies make the point most dramatically. Although cultures vary considerably in the tasks they allocate to each sex, their valuation patterns have been consistent. As Margaret Mead once noted, there have been villages in which men fish and women weave and villages in which women fish and men weave, but in either type of village the work done by men is valued higher than the work done by women.[23]

Unconscious gender prejudices not only affect evaluation of female performance, they also affect the performance itself. Low expectations of achievement frequently become self-fulfilling prophecies. Those who predict inadequate performance tend to signal their assumptions in subtle ways, and this negative feedback leads to anxiety, mistakes, and diminished aspirations. Such consequences then reinforce the initial adverse expectations, and a self-perpetuating cycle continues. Preconceptions about female employees' lower career commitment create similar patterns. A common assumption remains that many women will "stop being productive when [they] become reproductive." Decisionmakers who expect higher turnover among female employees structure their jobs to minimize the costs of replacement. In effect, that means minimizing challenge, training, and responsibility, which in turn encourages boredom, frustration, and high turnover.[24]

More overt, although often unintentional, forms of collegial bias have similar consequences. Many women workers remain outside the informal networks of support, guidance, and information-exchange that are critical to advancement. Such exclusion often begins in educational or job-training programs and increases in workplace environments. Women have disproportionate difficulties "fitting in" and forging the kind of collegial, mentoring, and client relations necessary for advancement. Sexual harrassment and the social isolation resulting from all-male clubs and activities reinforce women's subordinate status and the attitudes that perpetuate it.[25]

All of these problems are particularly acute for women of color, who face unconscious discrimination on two fronts, and whose small numbers make mentoring and role-modeling especially difficult. Moreover, individuals who seek to fit in by changing the culture rather than themselves face additional problems. The woman who "make[s] too much of the 'woman' issue" is subject to significant risk.[26]

As long as women constitute small minorities in nontraditional employment contexts, these problems are likely to remain pronounced. The presence of a few token females does little to alter underlying stereotypes, and the pressures placed on such individuals make successful performance less likely. Members of underrepresented groups perform under a special spotlight; their performance is heavily scrutinized and often assessed under particularly rigorous standards. In addition, the scarcity of other women and minorities may impose special burdens such as increased committee assignments or counseling responsibilities that decrease the time available for tasks more central to advancement.[27]

Given these barriers and biases, women must work harder to succeed and, when they do, must deal with the envy and anxiety that success arouses. Those who do not advance under such circumstances, or who become frustrated and opt for different employment, confirm the adverse stereotypes that had worked against their advancement in the first instance. The perception remains that women cannot make it by conventional standards, or are less committed to doing so. In either event, they do not warrant the same investment of training, assistance, and promotion opportunities as their male counterparts. Again, the result is a subtle but self-perpetuating cycle in which individual choices are constrained by discriminatory practices.[28]

Taken as a whole, this body of clinical, theoretical, historical, and empirical research leaves no doubt about the latent and lingering effects of gender bias. Not only has such bias shaped employment opportunities and salary patterns, it has also affected the way workplace structures have adapted to women's participation.

Institutional Constraints

Just after the turn of the century, in *Muller v. Oregon,* the Supreme Court acknowledged the "obvious" respects in which performance of woman's "maternal functions place[d] her at a disadvantage in the struggle for subsistence." Three-quarters of a century later, the most fundamental of those disadvantages remain. Most women work in occupational environments designed by and for men. The ways in which the workplace has been structured, advancement criteria defined, and domestic responsibilities allocated have all tended to perpetuate gender inequalities.[29]

In contemporary American society, any individual who seeks to balance significant work and family commitments confronts substantial obstacles. One of the most obvious involves the absence of support structures for domestic obligations. Inadequacies in childcare programs and parental leave provisions remain chronic problems. Tax, housing, and urban-development policies also discourage individuals from sharing family tasks. Little support has been available for residential complexes that provide joint dining facilities, housekeeping services, and care for young, sick, and elderly inhabitants.[30]

The demands of work and family life are exacerbated by the length and rigidity of most working schedules. By the early 1980s, 80 percent of nonfarm employees were holding full-time jobs, and about 85 percent of those jobs required a fixed forty-plus-hour workweek. The small number of positions that have permitted flexible schedules generally have done so within narrow bounds. Opportunities for permanent part-time work have been constrained in a different sense. The demand for such jobs has greatly exceeded their availability, despite the relatively low pay and benefits that most part-time positions command. Although public support for reduced hours, job sharing, and home-work sites has been steadily increasing, most of the options available have been in low-level, female-dominated areas that lack adequate benefits or opportunities for advancement.[31]

Resistance to more flexible structures has come from a variety of sources. Despite empirical findings to the contrary, many employers have overestimated the difficulties and underestimated the benefits of such innovations. Decisionmakers often have been unwilling to risk resentment among co-workers and coordination problems resulting from absent employees. Union leaders have been similarly unenthusiastic about the erosion of full-time positions. Many clients and employers have been put off by the seeming lack of commitment among part-time workers, and those attitudes have affected assignment and promotion decisions. For example, surveys involving upper-level business and professional contexts reveal widespread disparagement of anything less than full-time work. Even women who have come back "faster than a speeding bullet" after childbirth have been subject to risks; honorary males should not need maternity leave.[32]

Moreover, what passes for "normal" working hours in many of these contexts has posed special problems for women. A puritan ethic run amok can make life unmanageable for those with significant family commitments. Extended hours, unpredictable schedules, or protracted travel mesh poorly with child-rearing responsibilities. Yet for women "on the road to success" no detour from standard workplace obligations is advisable. Rather, the conventional wisdom has been to avoid vacations or extended leaves, to work longer and later hours than male colleagues, and, above all, to refrain from "ever mak[ing] excuses based on the needs of a spouse or children." If a woman feels she must go home to prepare dinner, at least she should never cook and tell. Of equal importance is to satisfy traditional measures of productivity, no matter how narrowly defined. For example, in academic contexts that means publishing research, not counseling students. Commentary for the aspiring woman generally makes clear that she should never present herself as "anything but a hard driving, capable [professional]" for whom productivity is always the "top priority." The model employee is built on the male model—with a vengeance.[33]

This is not to imply that men are unqualified beneficiaries of such cultural norms. Prevailing workplace structures have imposed costs for all individuals with family commitments. But women face special problems, both because of the time and the allocation of domestic demands. The foundations for professional development are often laid between the mid-twenties to mid-thirties, a period which coincides with women's peak childbearing years.

For women in nonprofessional contexts, work-family conflicts can be equally serious, though somewhat different in nature. Working hours are shorter but also more rigid, and less easily adjusted to cope with unexpected domestic dislocations. The low salaries prevailing in most female-dominated occupations reduce options for unpaid leaves, adequate child-care, and housekeeping assistance. All of these problems are especially pronounced for the growing number of single parents, who are overwhelmingly women, and who experience high rates of poverty.[34]

The conflict between productive and reproductive rhythms is amplified by the skewed allocation of family responsibilities. Contemporary studies indicate that those committed to equality in the abstract are not always equally enthusiastic in the concrete. One representative national opinion poll revealed that close to three-fourths of respondents believed that men and women should have equal responsibility for tasks such as housecleaning, but that only 29 percent of the surveyed men frequently performed such tasks. Representative studies indicate that in an average household women have remained responsible for about 70 percent of the housework, and that working wives have spent twice as much time on homemaking tasks as have working husbands. When paid labor and domestic labor are combined, employed males have averaged two hours less per day than employed females, and a disproportionate amount of men's homemaking contributions has involved relatively enjoyable activities, such as playing with infants rather than changing their diapers. Only about one husband in twenty has made the bed in which he slept. Over half of all working women, but only 1 percent of working men, have reported dropping out of the work force at least once for family reasons. Although younger couples tend toward somewhat more equal distributions of family responsibilities, wide disparities persist even within this group.[35]

Absent changes in domestic patterns and workplace structures, women confront difficult alternatives. The most common choice—a partial or complete withdrawal from the labor force when child-rearing demands are greatest—often carries a substantial personal as well as professional price. Most research indicates that paid labor generally increases women's sense of well-being and competence, reduces their feelings of social isolation, and enhances their power and satisfaction within marriage. For an increasing proportion of women with families, particularly single mothers, full-time work is also an economic necessity. Although at higher socio-economic levels a prolonged leave of absence presents fewer financial hardships, it also imposes greater professional costs. As economists have often noted, many women who defer career investment find that they have "gained a ticket to ride" after the train has left the station.[36]

Another option, one growing in popularity in recent years, is to remain single and/or childless. This trend reflects complex interrelations between cultural norms, demographic patterns, and employment-related constraints. The consequences have been particularly apparent among women in demanding occupations. Studies of lawyers and business executives during the 1980s revealed that almost a third of the women, but only 6–8 percent of the men, had never married. The vast majority of males in upper-level corporate positions have had children and a nonworking spouse. Most successful female executives have had neither. One need not be a Social Darwinist to find such patterns disturbing.[37]

Equally disturbing is the failure of conventional legal frameworks to address these asymmetries. As long as sex-discrimination doctrine focuses only on promoting equal treatment within the existing workplace, not on challenging its underlying structures, women's opportunities are likely to remain limited. For most individuals, the choice is to curtail either employment or family commitments, and whichever option they elect, the result is to perpetuate a decisionmaking structure insulated from their concerns. Those who advance to the positions with greatest power over policies governing parental leaves, working schedules, childcare, and related issues are those least likely to have experienced significant work-family conflicts. To promote equality between the sexes, and improve the quality of life for both of them, we must recast traditional strategies.

The Legal Response

The law's conventional approach to women's occupational disadvantages, like its approach to other gender issues, has focused on gender difference. Its primary objective has been to prevent those with comparable abilities from being treated differently because of sex. Under the equal-protection guarantee of the Fourteenth Amendment, courts have prohibited various forms of intentional discrimination. Under Title VII of the Civil Rights Act, they have banned intentionally discriminatory actions as well as certain facially neutral conduct that has a disproportionate adverse impact on women. Legislative and administrative regulations have required those receiving governmental contracts or assistance to implement affirmative-action policies.

Attempts to quantify the effectiveness of these legal strategies, like attempts to quantify the discrimination they address, have yielded varying results and common methodological difficulties. In explaining the increase of women in male-dominated occupations over the last two decades, it is impossible to disentangle the impact of changes in legal mandates from changes in cultural attitudes. But with a few notable exceptions, most studies involving regression analysis and case histories have suggested that active enforcement of antidiscrimination and affirmative-action requirements has played a critical role in expanding women's employment opportunities.[38]

Given the occupational inequalities that remain, however, it is equally critical to understand the limitations of conventional legal strategies. Although they have been highly significant in challenging the most overt forms of gender discrimination, traditional equal-opportunity frameworks have not confronted the deeper institutional and ideological forces that contribute to gender disadvantage.

The Quixotic Quest for Discriminatory Intent

One central limitation in contemporary antidiscrimination doctrine arises from its focus on motivation. The doctrinal emphasis on individual intent in both constitutional and statutory proceedings has unduly limited legal remedies. While these limitations have been most frequently explored in contexts involving race, they are no less applicable in cases involving gender.

To understand the limitations of this analytic framework, it is useful to focus first on constitutional doctrine, where motivational theories have been particularly critical. Although most employment discrimination cases now fall under Title VII, which has restricted the need to prove "invidious intent," constitutional standards remain significant. As a practical matter, they govern cases that fall outside statutory mandates (such as those involving public-sector employers and private institutions with fewer than fifteen employees). As a conceptual matter, constitutional theories of intent have influenced proof requirements in other contexts as well.

Modern intent requirements developed in chaotic fashion as litigation in the 1960s and 1970s revealed a wide range of governmental policies that were neutral in form but not in fact; that is, policies that did not incorporate explicit racial or sexual classifications but that worked to disadvantage members of one race or sex. Whether such de facto discrimination should require the same level of constitutional scrutiny as de jure discrimination became a point of major dispute among courts and commentators. By the late 1970s, after some unconvincing efforts to distinguish prior cases, the Supreme Court settled on an approach that would sustain facially neutral practices having disproportionate impact, unless they were demonstrably motivated by discriminatory intent. Although acknowledging that disparate effects might be relevant evidence of intent, the Court declined to view them as the "sole touchstone" of an equal-protection violation.[39]

For plaintiffs in sex-discrimination cases, the doctrine of discriminatory purpose has created major difficulties. The problems were clearly evident in a 1979 case, *Personnel Administrator of Massachusetts v. Feeney,* which involved challenges to veterans' preferences in public employment. Although neutral in form, such preference systems in practice have posed significant barriers to women's vocational opportunities. Approximately

98 percent of veterans are male, and about 40 percent of males over eighteen (as compared with fewer than 1 percent of females) are eligible for veterans' benefits. Among the most substantial of these benefits are preferences in civil-service hiring, promotion, and retention. Such entitlements affect a substantial part of the labor force. Approximately 20 percent of American employees work for federal, state, or local governments, almost all of which extend some form of veterans' preference for the vast majority of positions. The Massachusetts statute at issue in *Feeney* provided one of the most generous entitlements. It granted a preference in civil-service employment to any veteran with minimum qualifications over any nonveteran with higher qualifications. According to the trial court's findings, this lifetime preference system, although not established in order to discriminate against women, inevitably had that consequence. It effectively foreclosed female applicants from any civil-service position sought by a male veteran, and left them clustered in the lowest sectors of public employment.[40]

Despite these consequences, a divided Supreme Court upheld the preference system. According to the majority, the plaintiff had not sustained her burden of establishing that the statutory scheme was enacted "'because of,' not merely 'in spite of,' its adverse effects on women." Given the lower court's determination that the legislature's prime objective was to benefit veterans, "simple logic suggest[ed] that an intent to exclude women from significant public jobs was not at work in [the] law."[41]

The "simplicity" of the Court's logic ignored the complexity of the phenomena it sought to describe. In its attempt to isolate intent and impact, the majority misperceived both. Its assumption that discrimination requires an intent to harm misreads the dynamics of gender prejudice. Since bias often operates on a subconscious level, it may reflect selective indifference or stereotypical assumptions rather than overt misogyny. A premise of much contemporary psychological and social theory is that actions frequently are neither intentional, in the sense of being consciously sought, or unintentional, in the sense of being random or uninfluenced by belief structures. Although legislators may not have enacted a preference statute because of its effect on women, that does not exclude the possibility of prejudice. Given the state's wide variety of means to assist veterans, its choice of policies that reserve the upper echelons of state employment exclusively for men can scarcely be regarded as gender-neutral. Rather, that choice reflects insensitivity to women's opportunities for economic advancement and political influence.[42]

Yet the problem in *Feeney* was not simply the majority's confusion of legislative intent with legislative animus. A more fundamental difficulty arose from the Court's adherence to a framework that has proved untenable in theory and unworkable in practice. Attempts to isolate subjective purposes from their objective consequences, or to understand the meaning of a given text solely in terms of its author's conscious intent, run counter to the basic tenets of almost all modern schools of human psychology, analytic philosophy, and literary theory. Since interpretations of other individuals' motives and language are necessarily contingent on context, it makes little sense to treat intent as an independent phenomenon separable from its effects. Nor is there any practical advantage in doing so. As cases like *Feeney* demonstrate, many of the injuries arising from disproportionate impact exist irrespective of conscious purpose. The consequences of a given decision are generally the most probative, and often the only available evidence of motivation. As a result, arguments over intent almost inevitably collapse into arguments about impact. To frame the constitutional standard solely in terms of motivation deflects attention from the more central issue: What sorts of disadvantageous consequences should invalidate a facially neutral classification?[43]

Not only does an intent-oriented framework obscure that issue, it enmeshes courts in a highly indeterminate and unnecessarily devisive enterprise. In any context where multiple decisionmakers act from multiple motives with limited information, attributions of intent will remain conjectural. It is often impossible to aggregate the mixed views of a changing group or to ascertain politicians' true subjective states. As commentators have frequently noted, focusing on motivation places a "very heavy burden of persuasion on the wrong side of the dispute," on those who are the victims of disproportionate impact and who have least access to information about its origins. Given judges' understandable reluctance to impugn the motives of government officials, few litigants can sustain that burden. To force parties into debates over personal integrity rather than social inequality may diminish opportunities for constructive settlements or reinforce the insensitivities that gave rise to the dispute.[44]

That is not to suggest that legislative intent should be entirely irrelevant in assessing constitutional claims. Society has an interest in ensuring unbiased decisionmaking processes, whatever their ultimate outcome. In the rare instances where evidence of prejudice is clear and evidence of impact is not, constitutional relief should be available. But in more conventional circumstances such as *Feeney*, relief should also be forthcoming without a showing of misogynist motives.

What showing should be required is an issue frequently canvassed in recent constitutional scholarship. Although that entire debate need not be rehearsed here, one central difficulty demands concern: how to keep any alternative standard within manageable bounds. As the Supreme Court has noted in the context of racial discrimination, if every action having a disproportionate impact were subject to strict scrutiny, the result could be invalidation of a vast range of tax, welfare, and other regulatory statutes. Of course, as long as sex discrimination is subject to less than strict scrutiny, an impact test might present fewer risks. The danger, however, is that such a test could expand still further the range of permissible sex-based discrimination. The more governmental actions become open to challenge because of disproportionate impact, the more pressed courts will be to find legitimate justifications. Given the vast range of official policies that affect men and women differently, some further limiting principle is appropriate.[45]

As in other gender-discrimination contexts, a more satisfying theoretical framework would make gender disadvantage the focus of concern. Such an approach would shift analysis from intent to injury, and shift the burden of proof from those injured to those responsible for the injury. For example, when policies with disproportionate impact reflect prior de jure discrimination and reinforce current gender disadvantage, the state should have to demonstrate the importance of its objective and the unavailability of alternative means to secure it. Such an approach, which parallels Charles Lawrence's approach to unconscious racial discrimination, has the advantage of focusing attention on the cultural meanings of government decisionmaking. It offers a principled way of limiting legal intervention to unjustifiable gender-related consequences.[46]

Under this framework, policies such as those at issue in *Feeney* could not survive scrutiny. Without question, the disparate impact of veteran-preference reflects previous overt discrimination within the military. Moreover, the state has a wide array of alternative means to achieve its objectives. Health, tax, education, and qualified employment preferences can reward military service and facilitate veterans' transition to civilian life without dramatically curtailing women's economic opportunities.[47]

That is not to deny either the limitations or the costs of more expansive judicial oversight. No impact standard is readily confined; virtually any effects adverse to women can be said to reflect prior de jure discrimination if one is willing to trace the chains of causation back far enough. The selection of stopping points will inevitably prove indeterminate. Moreover, according to some critics, requiring public officials to predict what sorts of impact are constitutionally permissible could encourage precisely the kind of gender-conscious decisionmaking that constitutional safeguards are intended to prevent.[48]

Yet the way to secure gender blindness in the long run is not always to demand it in the short run. Allowing decisionmakers consciously to minimize gender disadvantages may be far less costly than leaving those disadvantages unchallenged. The indeterminacy involved in judicial assessments of impact is no greater than in judicial assessments of intent, and the social benefits are substantial. To promote not simply equality in form but equality in fact, constitutional analysis must become less preoccupied with decisionmakers' demonstrable intent and more attentive to the consequences their actions impose.

A similar point applies to intent inquiry in the most common form of employment-discrimination cases, those arising under Title VII. In interpreting that statute's antidiscrimination mandates, courts generally have distinguished between two sorts of claims: disparate impact and disparate treatment. Facially neutral practices having a disparate impact on women will not survive challenge, irrespective of intent, unless they are job-related, justified by business necessity, and unattainable through less discriminatory alternatives. In addition, courts have prohibited disparate treatment on the basis of sex, that is, intentional discrimination where sex is not a bona fide occupational qualification.[49]

As a practical matter, the distinction between impact and treatment cases sometimes blurs, and plaintiffs have often been forced to supplement statistical profiles with evidence of discriminatory intent. One of the most celebrated examples involved an Equal Employment Opportunity Commission (EEOC) suit against Sears, Roebuck, alleging a pattern and practice of discrimination against women in commission sales positions. Although EEOC statistics reflected substantial underrepresentation in such jobs, a federal district court accepted Sears's claim that female employees preferred lower-paying noncommission positions. According to Sears's managers, women were unfamiliar with major product items and unwilling to accept the irregular hours and competitive pressures that commission selling entailed.[50]

What gained the case unusual notoriety was further testimony by a prominent feminist scholar, Rosalind Rosenberg, to the effect that female employees have often elevated traditional values of caretaking and noncompetitiveness over opportunities for maximizing economic gain. Despite substantial rebuttal evidence, including testimony by another equally prominent feminist historian, Alice Kessler-Harris, concerning women's interest in nontraditional employment alternatives, the trial judge found the EEOC case unpersuasive. Without overt evidence of bias, the court was unwilling to assume that the disparate impact of Sears's promotion policies was attributable to anything other than women's own choices. Yet even if the government had identified a respectable number of unequivocal victims—an expensive and time-consuming burden—management could readily have denied the relevance of isolated incidents over a period of years in which the company processed more than a million female job applicants.[51]

Such litigation illustrates the dangers of difference-frameworks in legal settings; even approaches that validate women's traditional concerns risk contributing to women's economic marginalization. These cases also suggest the difficulties of presenting historical complexities in legal settings that demand single categorical explanations. As the result in *Sears* reflects, even plaintiffs who seek to focus on impact often end up having to argue about intent. Yet the judicial preoccupation with individual opportunity can deflect attention from the forces that constrain it. Too often the issue is only whether women are interested in and qualified for advancement under current institutional structures. Too little concern centers on how those structures must change to accommodate women. For example, what forms of training could increase female employees' familiarity with major product items, and what forms of flexible scheduling or childcare assistance would make higher-paying jobs accessible to them?

Similar limitations in traditional approaches are apparent in disparate treatment cases, where the pool of qualified applicants may be too small to demonstrate disproportionate impact. In such cases, after the plaintiff makes a *prima facie* showing of circumstances suggesting intentional discrimination, the defendant need only articulate an alternative nondiscriminatory explanation. The ultimate burden of persuasion remains with the plaintiff, who must demonstrate that this explanation is pretextual. That burden often has required aggrieved parties to prove that, but for their sex, they would have gained the employment in question. Particularly in cases involving subjective criteria or multiple decisionmakers, that requirement is extraordinarily difficult to meet.

Again law, management, and academia provide representative examples. Often there is no consensus on what qualifications are most critical for employees in these fields, or on how to identify those qualifications in a particular case. What counts as outstanding scholarship or an effective managerial style is open to dispute. Analogous disagreements center on the relative importance of particular skills: the quality of legal analysis as against the ability to attract legal business, or the effectiveness of teaching as against the subject-matter needs of an academic department. In the face of such indeterminacy, courts have generally been reluctant to second-guess employer decisionmaking. That reluctance has been particularly pronounced in contexts where upper-level positions or academic freedom are at issue; litigation success rates in those cases are exceptionally low.[52]

From a legal realist perspective, such judicial solicitude is hardly surprising. Many members of the bench may feel special sympathy toward decisionmakers with whom they identify and selection processes from which they have benefited. Upper-level employment litigation "confronts courts with their own worlds." To many judges, the more important the position, the more substantial the costs of intrusiveness. Such sentiments were unusually apparent in a 1980 federal district court decision involving sex-discrimination charges against a prominent Atlanta law firm. From the trial judge's perspective, Title VII should not apply to a professional partnership, which is "nothing less than a business marriage, for better or worse." In partnerships, as in matrimony, "worthy and desirable qualifications are not necessarily divided evenly among applicants according to race, age, sex or religion"; thus, statutory mandates should not coerce "shotgun weddings." Although the Supreme Court reversed and held that partnerships were subject to Title VII mandates, prevailing standards of proof insure that involuntary marriages will be rare. In upper-level employment litigation, plaintiffs rarely gain assistance from a judicial shotgun without first producing unequivocal "smoking gun" evidence of their own.[53]

Such evidence of overt prejudice is difficult to come by. Given the increasing legal and social sanctions that attach to sex-based discrimination, its most obvious manifestations are rarely expressed. Nor is it easy to demonstrate in litigation; many prospective witnesses are reluctant to come forward for fear of alienating colleagues and placing their own careers at risk. Even in cases presenting relatively clear evidence of sexist stereotypes, defendants and trial courts have frequently failed to recognize it as such. During the 1970s and 1980s, justifications for denying promotion to female managers, lawyers, and professors included "argumentative," "aggressive," and "ambitious" office styles; overly "reserved and intellectual" demeanors; "troublesome" or "old-fashioned" attitudes; inadequate transcription of minutes at faculty meetings; an absence of "give and take" on academic committees; "rigidity" in character (evidenced by concern for the height of window shades); "personalization of professional matters"; insufficiently "feminine" appearance and manner; support for the women's movement; and scholarship focusing on women's issues. The difficulty of course is that gender prejudices frequently accompany legitimate concerns. The more subjective the decisionmaking criteria, the harder it is to sort out the influence of illicit considerations. The pure villains and victims that make for convincing legal narratives are increasingly difficult to identify.[54]

In the absence of such *dramatis personae,* the barriers to successful litigation are considerable. As a threshold matter, victims of discrimination may not perceive themselves as such. Both clinical and empirical evidence suggests that women tend to devalue their own performance, undervalue their labor, and to ascribe their failures to internal rather than external causes. Even those convinced of the injustice of their treatment may see little advantage from contesting it. The costs of litigation, in both personal and financial terms, are considerable. Class actions are enormously expensive; some have dragged on for over a decade, consuming millions of dollars in legal fees. Individual cases can be similarly burdensome. A suit by one female professor denied tenure at the University of Pittsburgh required seventy-four days of in-court proceedings and produced seventy-three witnesses. Given the difficulties of proving gender discrimination and the low level of public interest or governmental funding for such litigation, many grievances will remain unremedied.[55]

Nor should the personal price of this form of legal intervention be underestimated. Plaintiffs are placing their conduct, character, and capabilities at issue, and the portraits that emerge are not always entirely flattering. The attorney who sued her Atlanta firm found her personal foibles splashed across the front pages of national periodicals, and even less celebrated cases generally receive considerable attention within the relevant community. An equally powerful deterrent is the risk of collegial hostility, retaliation, and blacklisting that can accompany litigation. In some circles even talking to a lawyer appears to be "professional suicide." All too often, even if the plaintiff wins, she loses. To be victimized first by the fact of discrimination, then by the process of proving it, is beyond the tolerance of most potential claimants.[56]

Thus, conventional antidiscrimination mandates offer a highly limited response to occupational inequality. If law is to become a more effective strategy, particularly for upper-level employment positions, it will require a different analytic focus. Less effort should center on reading the mind of the decisionmaker, and more on restructuring the processes of decision. In disparate treatment cases, plaintiffs should not have the burden of proving but-for causation. It should be enough to establish that discrimination was one factor in the decisionmaking process. The responsibility should then shift to the employer to establish that unlawful considerations did not affect the outcome of the process. That employment criteria are subjective is an inadequate rationale for judicial deference. For unless those practices are challenged, they remain self-perpetuating. Few women will rise to positions from which they can affect the way merit standards are defined and applied.[57]

Not only do we need a better antidiscrimination framework and greater public resources for its enforcement, we need a clearer sense of its limitations. No matter how we tinker with doctrinal formulations, equal-opportunity law cannot secure equal opportunity in fact. Sex-neutral hiring and promotion mandates do not begin to address the structural barriers concerning childcare and working schedules that impede women's full participation in the labor force. Given the high costs of litigating discrimination, and all the evidentiary barriers to finding it, much gender bias will escape judicial notice. This is not to minimize the significance of litigation in deterring abuses, empowering victims, and encouraging voluntary change. But it is to suggest that additional strategies are crucial to securing full equality for women in the workforce.

Affirmative Action

One of the most important responses to occupational inequality and the forces underlying it has been affirmative action. The concept dates to the Reconstruction period following the Civil War. Although preferential-treatment programs secured some advances for Southern blacks, support for such initiatives had eroded by the close of the century and did not reemerge to any significant degree until the early 1960s.[58]

Contemporary affirmative-action strategies have taken various forms. Some have been implemented under court order, based either on findings of discrimination or on negotiated settlements formalized in consent decrees. About one-third of the labor force works for employers subject to Executive Order 11246, which requires federal contractors to take "affirmative action to ensure that [individuals] are employed . . . without regard to their race, color, religion, sex, or national origin." Another substantial group of employees works for national, state, and local governmental entities subject to comparable mandates, or for private employers who have instituted voluntary affirmative-action programs.

How "affirmative" the action must be has varied. In its weaker form, the term encompasses largely process-oriented requirements, such as revised screening, recruitment, education, and training procedures to expand opportunities for underrepresented groups. In its stronger, more substantive form, affirmative action refers to preferential treatment for members of such groups if they are basically qualified for a given position. There is a range of intermediate alternatives, including tie-breaking procedures that favor underrepresented candidates whose qualifications are equal to their competitors. In practice, such distinctions often blur, since what constitutes equal or basic qualifications is open to dispute. For conceptual purposes, however, it is useful to focus on programs incorporating some form of preference, since these approaches have proven most effective and most controversial.

According to contemporary public-opinion polls, most Americans, including a majority of women, have opposed preferential treatment for women and minorities. In the Reagan administration, critics gained a new ally. By the mid-1980s, federal officials had adopted a far less activist stance in civil rights enforcement. Justice Department attorneys had stopped seeking numerical goals in employment-discrimination settlements and had filed suit seeking to overturn quotas in some fifty affirmative-action decrees. In defense of that position, prominent administration and congressional leaders launched a vitriolic attack on preferential treatment, analogizing it to evils ranging from slavery to heroin. Although much of the debate concerning affirmative action has centered on race rather than gender, the arguments have been closely related, and most of the following discussion is applicable to both women and minority men.[59]

Opposition to preferential treatment has turned on moral principle and practical consequences. As a matter of principle, critics contend, sex- and race-based remedies subvert the premise they are seeking to establish. Assigning preferences based on immutable, involuntary characteristics that bear no necessary relation to job performance reinforces precisely the kind of differences society should seek to eliminate.

In critics' view, such an approach also compromises concepts of individual responsibility and entitlement that are central to American values. Whatever obligation society now has to remedy the effects of past discrimination, the costs of that remedy should not fall solely on individual white males who are not accountable for prior injustice. Nor are affirmative-action programs appropriate vehicles for compensation since they seldom reach individuals who have suffered most from discrimination—the aged, the infirm, and the uneducated. To many observers, the case for compensatory treatment for white women is particularly weak since they have not been subject to the same economic, educational, and employment deprivations as racial minorities.[60]

These normative objections are vulnerable on several grounds. It is of course true that affirmative action compromises rights to be treated on the basis of individual rather than group characteristics. But arguments that make such rights preeminent come several generations early and several centuries late. Group treatment has been a pervasive feature of America's social, economic, and political landscape and has exposed women as well as minorities to systematic deprivations. We need not ignore the distinctions between race- and sex-based discrimination to recognize that both have left a legacy of disadvantages that neutral mandates have failed to address. In light of that history, it is more arbitrary to ignore than to acknowledge racial and gender differences. As in other contexts, our attention should center on disadvantage rather than difference.

That is not to deny the importance of spreading the burdens of affirmative action or providing other types of assistance to women and minorities who are most in need. But it is to challenge critics' assumption that all racial or gender preferences are, from a normative perspective, similarly objectionable. To equate discrimination against privileged and nonprivileged groups is to obscure the most basic cultural meanings and consequences that flow from such treatment. Disfavoring women serves to stigmatize, stereotype, and subordinate; disfavoring white men does not.

Nor does differential treatment of these male employees reinforce cumulative disadvantages or infringe preexisting rights to treatment solely on the basis of individual merit. As a factual matter, most employment decisions incorporate concerns that do not reflect merit in any objectively measureable sense. Veterans' preferences, personal connections, gender stereotypes, and innumerable other factors unrelated to performance shape employer choices. From a moral standpoint, individuals cannot credibly claim that they "deserve" a particular position for which they are objectively qualified. Merit is a social construct that reflects a range of factors over which the individual has no control, including natural talent, family background, educational environment, economic resources, and gender-role socialization.[61]

In critics' view, however, even if affirmative action is defensible as a matter of principle, it is objectionable as a matter of policy. From opponents' perspective, singling out women for special assistance risks reinforcing the assumptions of inferiority that society is striving to dispel. Selection of those who cannot succeed by conventional criteria risks compromising organizational efficiency and entrenching adverse stereotypes. Alternatively, critics contend, even when women or minorities perform effectively in a context of preferential treatment, their performance is likely to be devalued. As long as the beneficiaries of affirmative action appear unable to advance without special favors, latent prejudices will remain unaffected.

Of equal concern is the effect that such appearances have on women themselves. If members of these groups cannot be sure whether their position results from preference rather than competence, their self-esteem is likely to suffer. Such self-doubt may yield insecurity, stress, and diminished aspirations that translate into occupational disadvantages. As critics also emphasize, white female employees have not experienced the kind of educational and economic deprivations that affect minorities. Given the demonstrated ability of many women to succeed in male-dominated occupations without preferential treatment, why should they be burdened with the implications of inferiority that attach to affirmative action? To the extent that female employees cannot successfully compete under neutral criteria, critics' response is not to suspend the criteria but to propose educational and training programs that will redress competitive disadvantages.[62]

Even if preferential treatment promised greater benefits for disadvantaged groups, opponents argue that its price would be too high. Included in that price are a variety of factors: risks of incompetent performance;

resentment from white male employees; administrative costs in monitoring affirmative-action mandates and complying with governmental red tape; and compromise of other values such as those related to seniority rights and academic freedom.[63]

Such claims are problematic on several levels. Since virtually all preferential-treatment programs assist only those candidates who are basically qualified for the jobs at issue, the extent of efficiency loss remains speculative. Of course for some positions, such as brain surgeons or airline pilots, health and safety considerations argue for selecting the most demonstrably capable applicants. However, in most employment sectors, the costs of settling for basic competence are far less substantial. What counts as excellence and which candidates are likely to possess it is open to considerable dispute. Objective qualifications such as school grades are notoriously poor predictors of occupational success. Nor has there been any systematic evidence of significant declines in job performance as the result of affirmative-action programs.[64]

What most critics also overlook is that women and minorities often make contributions that are inadequately reflected in conventional criteria. To take an obvious example, female academics may offer different perspectives on traditional intellectual paradigms than their male counterparts; the contributions of women's studies programs over the last two decades underscore this point. Participation by those with different historical experiences can enrich the standards by which performance is measured. Moreover, women who compile similar objective records to their male counterparts, but do so under less supportive settings, often have skills beyond those recognized in traditional evaluation processes. As Martha Minow and Mary Becker have noted, even to characterize these cases as affirmative action is misleading. What critics often present as a thumb on the scale for "less qualified" individuals may in fact reflect only necessary adjustments in the way the scale is calibrated.[65]

Other costs of preferential treatment are equally open to question. At least some of the resentment associated with preferential treatment has been unnecessary. All too often, employers seeking excuses for rejecting white male candidates have seized on affirmative action as a convenient scapegoat. Training programs can help discourage such subterfuges and reduce backlash among employees. Although the stigma attaching to affirmative-action beneficiaries cannot be overlooked, neither should it be overvalued. The current underrepresentation of women in positions of influence is also stigmatizing. Many members of underrepresented groups find it demeaning to be denied affirmative action on the ground that they will experience it as demeaning. Barbara Babcock, an Assistant Attorney General in the Carter administration, made a similar point. When asked how she felt about gaining her position because she was a woman, Babcock responded, "It feels better than being rejected for the position because you're a woman."[66]

In assessing the price of preferential treatment, the question is always: compared to what? Yet omitted from many critics' calculations are the consequences of living with the discrimination that equal-opportunity approaches fail to address. Whether conscious or unconscious, such discrimination exacts a heavy toll. Not only does it create substantial efficiency losses by artificially restricting the pool of available talent, it subverts the values of human dignity and autonomy to which critics themselves profess commitment. As Ronald Dworkin has suggested, at this historical juncture equal treatment is not sufficient to secure treatment as an equal.[67]

To attain a social order in which wealth, power, and status are not distributed along racial, ethnic, or sexual lines, we must first dispel the stereotypes contributing to this unequal distribution. Affirmative action can be crucial to that effort by placing a critical mass of women in nontraditional positions. Only by insuring their presence beyond token levels can we expect to counteract the latent biases and socialization processes that have perpetuated occupational inequalities. Although positive effects are difficult to quantify, social science research suggests that role models have helped expand women's aspirations. Experience with female colleagues beyond token levels can also reduce adverse stereotypes among male decisionmakers.[68]

In the face of these considerations, the judiciary has steered an ambivalent course. In some affirmative-action cases, the Supreme Court has been at pains to avoid the difficult questions, even after accepting extended briefs and argument on point. In other contexts, the Court has vacillated between sustaining and invalidating fixed numerical standards. Percentage "set aside" provisions favoring minority-owned businesses, minority employees in consent decrees, and minority trainees in voluntary affirmative-action plans have survived scrutiny. Yet comparable preferences in educational programs and in layoff plans implicating seniority rights have not passed muster.[69]

Two of the clearest illustrations of the Court's uncertain search for equipoise have involved university admissions and public employment. In *Regents of the University of California v. Bakke,* five members of the Court voted to strike down numerical quotas in medical school admissions at the University of California at Davis, but five members also voted to sustain some form of preference for minority candidates. According to Justice Powell, who provided the swing vote, affirmative-action programs that barred white applicants from competing for a fixed number of places denied rights to be treated as a "unique individual" and therefore could not withstand strict scrutiny. By contrast, he was prepared to sustain programs that provided no numerical quotas but that attached positive weight to minority status in order to secure a diverse student body.[70]

Nine years later, in *Johnson v. Transportation Agency,* five Justices again voted to uphold a voluntary affirmative-action program. The program at issue allowed decisionmakers to consider sex as one factor in selecting among qualified applicants for positions in which women were significantly underrepresented. Although none of the Court's opinions so indicated, the facts in *Johnson* raised questions about its characterization as a case of preferential treatment. The woman who received a contested promotion appeared "less qualified" than her rival male candidate only if one ignored (as did the lower courts) certain biases in the evaluation process. Her promotion interviews were conducted by three men who had never recommended a woman for the position in question or any comparable position. One of the three interviewers had previously provoked a grievance charge from the female candidate for sexual harassment; another had characterized her as a "rebel-rousing [sic] skirt-wearing person." The woman promoted had compiled a performance score within two points of her male competitor and had done so as the first and only female road maintenance worker out of 110 employees (many of whom resisted her presence.)[71]

Nonetheless, four dissenting Justices found the case to involve impermissible preferential treatment, and Justice O'Connor, who provided the majority's essential fifth vote, wrote separately to make clear her opposition to strong forms of affirmative action. In particular, she would have struck down any program: that was not justified by underrepresentation sufficient to make a *prima facie* showing of illegal discrimination; that was designed "automatically" to promote "marginally qualified candidates falling within a preferred race or gender category"; or that could be equated with a "permanent plan of proportionate representation by race and sex."[72]

Such approaches toward affirmative action are generally defended on prudential grounds. A program that attaches positive weight to a range of attributes including race or gender may be less likely to entrench stereotypes and arouse resentment than rigid quotas ensuring proportionate representation. For similar reasons, layoff policies that spread burdens evenly through job-sharing may be more acceptable than the suspension of seniority systems that disfavor women and minorities. Where numerical quotas result in a "body count" approach to affirmative action, they may deflect attention from the need for more fundamental restructuring of jobs, training, and evaluative criteria.[73]

Yet the preference-not-quota compromise is problematic on both theoretical and practical levels. As a theoretical matter, there appears no principled distinction between a policy that handicaps white male applicants and one that restricts their eligibility for a specified number of places. As a practical matter, neither rhetorical camouflage nor structural accommodations will always be feasible. In some contexts, percentage set-asides and temporary suspension of seniority protections may prove the only means of securing progress. Yet existing legal frameworks have failed adequately to identify those contexts. The limitations courts have placed on affirmative action reflect a "perpetrator perspective" that ill serves broader social goals. To focus on the sins of individual employers and the innocence of white male applicants deflects attention both from the disadvantage of prior victims and from the strategies best designed to prevent its recurrence. At this juncture we need a less individualistic, more forward-looking framework, one less preoccupied with original sin and more committed to social change.[74]

The greatest risk of affirmative action is not the one that conservatives generally invoke. The most fundamental concern is that preferential treatment in some contexts will serve as window dressing. If its consequence is merely token representation, perfunctory interviews, or entry-level positions for the most upwardly mobile women, affirmative action may help more to legitimate than to challenge existing organizational values. As one applicant put it, after participating in repeated search processes designed only to satisfy affirmative-action requirements, the "next time the form asks about sex, I'm going to write 'occasionally' rather than 'female.'" The danger of token representation is especially pronounced for minorities, where the presence of a few highly visible successes may obscure the remaining barriers. To minimize that risk we need more comprehensive policies, which receive strong governmental and managerial backing and which are designed to employ a critical mass of underrepresented groups. Affirmative action is not the only strategy necessary to secure workplace equality, but it is one of the most critical.[75]

Pay Equity

By the close of the 1970s, as the limitations of conventional antidiscrimination approaches became increasingly apparent, women's rights organizations sought new strategies to secure greater pay equity between the sexes. A primary objective was to obtain comparable pay for jobs of comparable worth.

As a conceptual framework, comparable worth has historical analogues in medieval notions of a "just price," and in early twentieth-century theories of the British Fabian Sidney Webb. As a practical strategy, the concept emerged in this country during World War II. Although the federal government had made earlier intermittent efforts to reduce sex-based wage discrimination in the civil service, it was not until the national mobilization of the 1940s that prominent officials first identified such discrimination as a serious problem. To the War Labor Board, some legal intervention seemed necessary to preserve the morale not only of female workers, but also of their male counterparts at home and on the front who worried that feminization of the work force would undermine existing wage structures. Accordingly, the Board decreed that there should be "no discrimination between employees whose production [was] substantially the same on comparable jobs." However, since Board enforcement efforts proved woefully inadequate to secure equal pay even for identical jobs, standards governing comparability never developed.[76]

In any event, Board directives lost force once the war was over. Subsequent congressional proposals in the mid-1940s that would have prohibited "paying female employees at a lower rate than males for work of comparable quality or quantity" failed to reach a vote. Although similar language reappeared in the initial drafts of the Equal Pay Act during the early 1960s, it met with a similar fate. Neither sponsors nor their critics were prepared for the spectacle of federal intruders "trooping all around the country harassing business with various interpretations of the term 'comparable.'"[77]

Two decades later that caricature no longer seemed so disquieting, particularly if the alternative was reliance solely on market forces to determine wage hierarchies. Many manifestations of the invisible hand appeared visibly gender-biased. Feminists cited hosts of examples not readily squared with merit principles: schoolteachers who earned less than liquor-store clerks; nurses who earned less than tree trimmers or sign painters; and librarians who earned less than crossing guards and water-meter readers. Given the vast body of research pointing to undervaluation of women's work, particularly work done by women of color, market forces appeared unreliable guardians of equitable compensation structures.[78]

The most frequently proposed alternatives fall into two basic categories, often lumped under the generic title of comparable worth. Both rely on formal systems of job evaluation in establishing salaries. Such approaches have become increasingly prevalent since World War II, and an estimated two-thirds of employees are currently subject to some formal evaluation system. The methodologies vary, as does decisionmaking authority. Participants in the evaluation process may include outside consultants and worker representatives as well as management. Although the technical aspects of evaluation require more extended analysis than is possible here, it is useful to distinguish two basic frameworks that bear on pay-equity strategies.[79]

The commonest job-evaluation system involves a "policy-capturing" approach. This technique focuses on the *relative worth* of particular positions under existing wage scales, either the employer's own rates or those of similarly situated employers. Through this approach, decisionmakers identify factors relevant to existing compensation scales and score jobs in terms of those factors (such as skills, responsibility, and working conditions). Then statistical regression techniques are used to assess the relative importance of such factors in predicting current wages and to establish a weight for each factor. Each job receives a rating based on its weighted characteristics. This ranking can serve as the basis for adjusting pay scales or setting salaries for new jobs, although decisionmakers may make further modifications in response to market forces. To pay-equity advocates, such a policy-capturing approach is primarily useful in identifying racial or gender biases in the employer's own evaluation system. For example, statistical analysis can indicate the importance an employer attaches to particular factors in male-dominated or gender-integrated jobs and can determine whether the same factors command the same financial reward in female-dominated positions. When used in this fashion, such a method often reveals underpayment of "women's work" in terms of the employer's own criteria for compensation.[80]

For pay-equity advocates, the strengths of this system are also the source of its limitations. By relying on the employer's own standards to establish relative value, a policy-capturing technique avoids more subjective and divisive issues about the intrinsic value of particular jobs. Such a framework takes no position on what weight specific employment characteristics should assume. It demands only that employers be consistent in application of their own weighting system across job categories, regardless of the gender, race, and ethnicity of employees and the pay at which they are willing to work. Yet while this approach is consistent with antidiscrimination principles reflected in existing legislation, including Title VII, it does not accomplish one central objective of pay-equity proponents: to challenge societal devaluations of women's work. Since a policy-capturing system uses existing wage rates to assess the relative importance of job characteristics, it will reflect gender and racial biases that have traditionally affected those rates.

A more fundamental challenge to current norms is possible through techniques that focus on *intrinsic worth*. Under such an approach, decisionmakers generally define a priori the set of factors *and* factor weights that should serve as the basis for salary differentials. Typically, this system will rank job characteristics such as skill, effort, responsibility, and working conditions, and then assign points to particular jobs based on their weighted characteristics. Compensation levels can then be adjusted to insure parity between different jobs with similar ratings. By valuing job characteristics without explicit reference to employers' existing salaries or market rates, such techniques often expose underpayment of predominantly female occupations. Although employers can further adjust their internal compensation structures in light of market scales, an a priori system has the advantage of making such adjustments visible.[81]

To varying degrees, relative- and intrinsic-worth approaches can call into question current wage structures. By the mid-1980s one or both frameworks were influential in shaping comparable-worth litigation, legislative lobbying, and collective-bargaining strategies. From the perspective of critics, however, comparable worth presents a range of problems. The central difficulty centers on how to define worth. Salaries are not based solely on objective factors such as the skill, responsibility, and working conditions a job entails; the most cursory comparison of income levels for cabinet officials and fashion models makes the point directly. Any evaluation system involves subjective judgments, and they are especially prevalent in a priori intrinsic-worth approaches. Gender biases can enter at any number of points: in the choice and weighting of factors to be compensated, in their application to a given job, and in the standards for determining exemptions. How much weight should evaluators accord to particular skills or working conditions, and how should "skills" be defined?[82]

Given the inherent subjectivity of job-assessment techniques, it is scarcely surprising that different evaluators and evaluation systems have attached different values to identical positions. This subjectivity presents possibilities for the kind of bias apparent in a recent salary reevaluation study for New York public employees. The study concluded that acquired (and hence compensable) abilities were necessary for zookeepers in charge of baby animals, but that only innate (and hence noncompensable) abilities were necessary for day-care attendants responsible for human infants.[83]

A related criticism of both intrinsic and relative worth approaches concerns issues of supply and demand. To take a favorite illustration of economists, the reason water is cheaper than diamonds has more to do with its abundance than its "worth" in the sense that pay-equity advocates generally use the term. An evaluation system that considered only job content might, for example, dictate paying similar salaries to professors of male-dominated disciplines such as law and more gender-integrated disciplines such as English, even if legal academics were in shorter supply and could command much higher wages for alternative uses of their skills. Such evaluative approaches might make it difficult for a particular employer to attract and retain workers in areas of tight labor supply, and might distort signals to potential employees about labor needs.

The experience of a General Electric plant in the mid-1980s illustrates critics' concerns. That plant reportedly had three thousand women on a waiting list for openings as assemblers of radio components, a female-dominated occupation. No such labor supply was available for certain male-dominated packaging positions which had comparable rankings in terms of job characteristics. Since GE paid the female assemblers less than the male packagers, but eight times more than workers who performed the same assembling functions in Japan, the competitive consequences of revaluing women's jobs were significant. Lowering or freezing male wages could cause labor shortages, increased turnover, and worker resentment. Increasing female wages could require higher prices, which might eventually result in lower sales, production, and employment. If, under the threat of legal liability or other government mandates, other domestic employers had to make comparable wage adjustments, the resulting price escalations would contribute to inflation and, in some sectors, could diminish American industry's ability to compete with producers from abroad. Alternatively, if employers responded to the higher costs of female employees by substituting foreign workers or less labor-intensive processes, the result would be increased domestic unemployment. And the greater the government's involvement in the wage-setting process, the greater critics' concerns about overtures to a centrally planned economy.[84]

Critics have also questioned whether these costs would be offset by gains in social justice. One concern is that higher wages might simply encourage women to stay in traditional female-dominated jobs, thus reinforcing the problems of occupational crowding and stereotyping that underlie current sex-based disparities. Moreover, according to some commentators, comparable worth as a distributive principle would often prove regressive. The primary beneficiaries would be white middle-class women and the primary losers would be lower-class minority men. A familiar charge has been that the "maintenance man will be paid less so the librarian can be paid more."[85]

Both the magnitude and distribution of such adverse consequences is open to question. Estimates of the aggregate price of comparable worth have ranged between 2 and 150 billion dollars, and projections of efficiency and GNP losses reflect similar variations. On the whole, available research suggests that critics have overestimated the costs and underestimated the potential benefits of pay equity. Objections concerning unemployment, inflation, foreign competition, and socialist oversight have been voiced about virtually every form of employment regulation over the last century. Such concerns were common in early debates surrounding child labor, occupational safety, minimum wage, and collective-bargaining restrictions. Mucking about with the free market earlier in this century did not cause chaos or communism then, and it is unlikely to do so now.[86]

Criticisms of the "subjectivity" of comparable-worth procedures tend to ignore the biases of existing wage structures. Current pay differentials reflect a legacy of discrimination that already distorts responses to labor supply and demand. Subjectivity is what we now have; the fact that it is embedded in existing market dynamics does not render it morally just or economically essential. Critics' adverse projections have also incorporated assumptions about the efficiency and competitiveness of current markets, assumptions that do not hold in many public and private sectors of the economy where pay equity initiatives have centered. Gradual pay-scale revisions in these areas could help drive up women's compensation in other contexts.

Although comprehensive long-term data are lacking, comparable-worth reforms here and abroad have not appeared to trigger the kinds of inflation, inefficiency, and unemployment that critics generally predict. The typical cost of the reforms has been around 5 to 10 percent of employers' total wage rates, phased in over a number of years. Recent case studies of local and state comparable-worth initiatives have not found evidence of increased unemployment or reduced interest in nontraditional jobs among female workers. Moreover, even if the immediate effect of increasing pay in some female-dominated job contexts were to reduce the number of positions available, the eventual result might be to encourage women's entrance into alternative male-dominated occupations. That, in turn, could reduce occupational segregation and gender disparities in reward structures. Any adequate analysis of comparable worth must take into account not only its short-term costs but also its long-term benefits.[87]

Such an analysis must also remain sensitive to the distribution of those costs and benefits. Contrary to critics' suggestions, it is by no means clear that comparable-worth reforms disadvantage minorities or impose disproportionate burdens on blue-collar workers. Women of color are overrepresented in public-sector female-dominated occupations where such reforms have been most common. Minority male workers are similarly overrepresented in female-dominated jobs that have benefited most from pay-equity initiatives. Moreover, the same procedures that have exposed evidence of gender bias often have revealed evidence of racial bias as well, and the resulting adjustments have aided groups disadvantaged on both counts. Although evidence regarding class is more mixed, some comparable-worth initiatives have suggested that overcompensation is most likely with male-dominated white-collar, not blue-collar, jobs. Whatever short-term losses some workers sustain as a result of job revaluations may be offset by the potential long-term gains of making compensation criteria explicit and a subject for collective bargaining and organizing strategies.[88]

So too, much of the objection to pay equity could be minimized if implementation occurred gradually, with some sensitivity to its costs and to the respective competencies of various decisionmakers. It is well within courts' capabilities and statutory authority to enforce principles of relative worth, and to hold employers accountable for salary discrimination that cannot be justified by their own evaluative criteria. Issues of intrinsic worth—that is, judgments as to what criteria are most important and how such judgments should be made—are best addressed through political and collective-bargaining processes.

Such an allocation of responsibility could do much to clarify existing law. Part of the confusion stems from the United States Supreme Court's determination to sidestep the issue. In the first decade and a half of pay-equity litigation, the Court accepted review of only one case, *County of Washington v. Gunther*. There, a majority of Justices carefully disclaimed any view on the "controversial concept of comparable worth." In fact, the case involved a straightforward application of relative-worth principles. The plaintiffs, female jail guards, alleged that county officials had intentionally discriminated on the basis of sex, by setting their pay scales below those of male guards and below what county surveys indicated was appropriate. In concluding that such allegations stated a claim under Title VII's antidiscrimination mandates, the majority noted that its holding would not force a court to make "its own subjective assessment of the value of the male and female guard jobs" or to quantify the impact of discrimination. Rather, plaintiffs were seeking remedies for a departure from their employer's *own* evaluation of relative worth.[89]

In the aftermath of *Gunther*, lower court decisionmaking has remained confusing and confused. In contexts analogous to *Gunther*, some judges have rejected relative-worth claims on the dubious assumption that they would open a "Pandora's box" and disrupt "the entire economic system of the United States of America." Similar concerns were apparent in a celebrated federal court of appeals decision involving Washington state employees. The litigation arose in the mid-1970s after the state's own survey found that women's jobs paid an average of 20 percent less than men's jobs with comparable rankings. Despite that finding, the state did not seek to reduce the disparity until six years later, after the American Federation of State, County, and Municipal Employees (AFSCME) filed a sex-discrimination suit. In the view of the federal trial judge, such inaction (coupled with other evidence of gender bias) constituted proof of intentional disparate treatment in violation of Title VII. The court further concluded that the state's salary practices had a disparate impact on predominately female job classifications, and that no business necessity could justify those practices. Accordingly, the trial judge's decree ordered the state to raise female wages and provide back pay of some 838 million dollars. Since estimates of the total costs of compliance ran as high as a billion dollars, the case aroused considerable public attention.[90]

Its notoriety was short-lived. In 1985 the Ninth Circuit Court of Appeals reversed the trial judge's decision. Under the appellate panel's analysis in *AFSCME v. State of Washington*, compensation schemes based on market forces did not constitute "specific . . . employment practice[s]" for purposes of establishing disparate impact. Nor was the state's reliance on market-wage rates rather than job-evaluation surveys sufficient evidence of discriminatory intent to establish disparate treatment. Underlying the court's judgment were concerns about both the indeterminacy of job evaluation and the likelihood that few employers would undertake it if Title VII liability could follow. Before further appeals, the parties reached a settlement under which the state allocated 480 million dollars over six years to raise salaries in female-dominated occupations.[91]

Yet it is possible to address the concerns of the appellate court in *AFSCME* without denying legal remedies in all comparable-worth contexts. Where decisionmakers have commissioned an evaluation and endorsed its results, the accuracy of survey procedures need not become an issue. If holding employers to the results of their own job reassessments discourages these initiatives, federal, state, or local governments could mandate such evaluations either directly or as a condition of receiving governmental contracts or assistance. Courts also could minimize disincentives for comparable-worth reviews by following precedents from other sex-discrimination contexts and considering certain evidence of gender bias only for purposes of granting prospective relief, not back pay. In addition, employers' refusal to undertake evaluation procedures could serve as a basis for liability at least under circumstances that suggest a violation of relative-worth principles. Where employers receive evidence indicating that the same characteristics command higher pay in predominately male jobs than in predominately female jobs, a refusal to take corrective measures could serve as grounds for legal intervention.[92]

This approach would have the advantage of providing some recourse for demonstrable gender or racial bias in relative-wage rates, but would not enmesh courts in disputes over intrinsic value. Such a strategy would allow scope for market considerations in establishing job-evaluation criteria, but would not allow employers to depart from those criteria simply because they could hire female or minority employees for less. To recognize market forces as a complete defense in wage-discrimination cases is to perpetuate the problems antidiscrimination law was designed to address. Just as we do not tolerate such excuses in other equal-pay or Title VII contexts, we should not tolerate them here.[93]

This approach would also respond to legitimate concerns about judicial capacity and the lack of principled standards for resolving issues of intrinsic worth. If, for example, employers commission job-evaluation surveys that attach high importance to skills disproportionately associated with male-dominated positions (for example, heavy lifting), on what grounds would courts challenge those assessments? Judges would have to arbitrate battles among experts, with very little basis on which to choose between them. Although such battles would not be unique to comparable-worth litigation, the implications of staging them under judicial oversight raise significant concerns. Indeterminate standards often result in substantial uncertainties, inconsistencies, and legal costs.

Of still greater concern are the potential economic dislocations that litigation over intrinsic worth could entail. If courts were to require that evaluation systems focus only on job content, how could variations in labor supply be accommodated? As litigation in the early 1980s indicated, examples such as academics with differential pay scales present more than hypothetical problems. Had courts in those cases required compensation to reflect only intrinsic job characteristics, with no allowance for wage rates sensitive to supply and demand, universities would have faced an unhappy choice. In the likely event that budget constraints would have prevented raising all salaries, administrators would have been forced to reduce the compensation for faculty in male-dominated, high-paying disciplines such as law and medicine, and accept whatever loss in quality or quantity of instructors resulted. While the world might well be better off with fewer law professors, it is by no means clear that we wish courts to make that determination.[94]

Such objections do not, however, apply with equal force to pay-equity strategies in legislative and collective-bargaining contexts. These forums have the advantage of allowing wider participation and more flexible implementation than is generally possible in litigation. Pay equity as a political issue presents opportunities not only to challenge workplace values but also to expand the participants in workplace decisionmaking. As contemporary union campaigns reflect, comparable worth can be a powerful mobilizing force among women. One significant contributor to wage disparities between the sexes has been the lack of organization among female employees. In the mid-1980s female workers were only half as likely as men to belong to unions, and unionized women earned, on the average, 20 percent more than nonunionized women. Comparable disparities exist for minorities, and historically unions have paid too little attention to the interests of these groups. Pay equity presents new opportunities. By raising the expectations, self-esteem, and sense of relative deprivation of women and minorities, comparable worth can aid workplace organizing and bargaining efforts.[95]

It might also perform similar functions in political campaigns at the national, state, and local levels. Pay-equity initiatives can challenge not only the undervaluation of women's work but also women's underrepresentation in evaluation processes. One objective of these initiatives could be to vest greater responsibility for job reassessment in committees or task forces with broad-based worker and management representation. The more inclusive the evaluative process, the less likely that it will reflect gender, racial, and class biases.[96]

All too often, both critics and supporters have treated comparable worth as a generic concept, without regard to variations in evaluation strategies and decisionmaking contexts. In many debates pay equity figures as the first step on the path either to socialism or salvation. Critics, including some prominent Reagan administration officials, frequently present comparable worth as ludicrous or lunatic; it becomes either the "'looniest' idea since 'Looney Tunes,'" or a serious overture toward a centrally planned economy. To proponents, it is these criticisms that border on the fanciful.[97]

A more productive dialogue requires less loose rhetoric and more contextual analysis, sensitive to the varying implications of legal, legislative, and bargaining strategies. Enough public- and private-sector initiatives are now in place to allow more comprehensive review of different job-reevaluation procedures and their effects on unemployment, inflation, turnover, occupational segregation, worker satisfaction, and income distribution. Where adverse consequences of comparable worth have emerged, we need further analysis of policies that might best cushion such effects, such as job retraining, affirmative action, and expanded unemployment compensation. Our research agenda should also explore broader questions surrounding markets, merit, and money. How much consensus is there concerning the relative importance of factors that influence compensation? How closely do public attitudes about what salaries should be correspond to what salaries actually are? What evaluation procedures are most likely to seem just to the broadest number of constituencies?

As with affirmative action, the most substantial risks of comparable worth are not those invoked by conservatives. The danger is not that it will prove too radical, but that it will not prove radical enough. One disquieting possibility is that some narrow vision of pay equity will prevail, and that concerns about gender will displace concerns about race, class, and ethnicity. If we rest with narrow incremental reform strategies, the result could be a modified compensation hierarchy under which the "haves" still come out far ahead—but with more women among them. A related concern is that short-term political objectives could obscure broader normative issues. By cloaking job evaluation with a mantle of seemingly "scientific" objectivity, comparable-worth adjustments could insulate wage hierarchies from more searching review.

A more hopeful alternative is that pay-equity initiatives will focus attention on fundamental questions not only of gender equality but of social priorities. How should we reward various occupational and worker attributes and how much differentiation across salary levels is appropriate? Are we comfortable with a society that pays parking attendants more than childcare attendants whatever the male-female composition of these jobs? Exploring the dynamics of comparable worth can enrich our understanding of class and gender inequities and of the strategies best able to reduce them. Inspired by a social vision that emphasizes collective responsibility rather than individual competition, job reevaluation could become a strategy for narrowing economic inequality. It could also prompt a reassessment of paid and unpaid work traditionally done by women. From that vantage, comparable worth is indeed a radical concept, but not in the sense most critics claim. It need not invite the kind of centralized planning reflected in current state-run economies, which have scarcely dispensed with wage hierarchies or insured gender equality. Rather, pay-equity initiatives could help spark a rethinking of the scope of inequality and the ideologies that sustain it.

Employment Policy and Structural Change

If occupational equity is to become a serious national commitment, expressed in social policy as well as in political rhetoric, we need an array of strategies that extend beyond antidiscrimination, affirmative action, or pay-equity mandates. Women's subordinate labor-force status is a function of various factors, including sex-role socialization, workplace structures, and domestic constraints. Effective policy responses require an equally varied set of public- and private-sector initiatives, and a more systematic attempt to assess their relative success.

Although law has limited influence on socialization processes, it could play a more constructive role. Government-funded education, counseling, vocational, and job-training programs can affect occupational choices. Yet despite formal mandates of gender equality, such programs have often served more to perpetuate than to counteract sex-role stereotypes. Vocational education, which prepares well over half the work force for entry-level jobs, remains highly gender-segregated, as do placements under government-sponsored job-training programs. Efforts to improve women's math and science skills, and to interest men in traditional female vocations, have been at best sporadic. Too few financial incentives have been available to private employers for programs that challenge occupational segregation through recruitment, training, counseling, and restructured promotion ladders that bridge male- and female-dominated job sectors. All of these areas require greater governmental resources and more systematic study.[98]

Similar observations are applicable to other workplace structures. More incentives should be available for employers to offer part-time and flexible schedules. Adequate parental leaves and childcare should become social priorities. Finally, and perhaps most fundamentally, employment-related issues must be conceived as part of a broader political agenda. Men's and women's positions in the market are affected by a wide network of public policies concerning education, housing, welfare, tax structure, and social services. Too many of these policies reflect outmoded assumptions about women's secondary labor-force status; too few address the structural problems that still confine many women to that role. For almost a century some feminists have sought programs designed better to accommodate public and private life: cooperative residential housing; childcare and homemaker services; and integrated urban planning sensitive to the needs of single parents and dual-career couples. Current demographic trends have invested such policies with new urgency, not only to promote gender equality in this generation, but to provide decent environments for the next.

Chapter 9

Reproductive Freedom

Birth-control techniques have been in existence for over four millennia, but only during the last two centuries has their use prompted intense public controversy and organized political activity. Although few issues are more central to women's self-determination and sexual expression, it was not until the 1960s that the feminist movement began to attach high priority to reproductive freedom. Moreover, as with the Equal Rights Amendment, the campaign for reproductive freedom has provoked heated opposition from those whose freedom is at stake. Questions surrounding abortion and reproductive technology have acquired deep symbolic significance for women on both sides of the contemporary debate. At issue are fundamental concerns about individual liberty and sexual equality.

The Historical Legacy

Cultures have varied considerably in their attitudes toward controlling fertility, but few have invested the practice with the kind of moral significance that it began to acquire in the mid-nineteenth century. Most ancient societies, including Greece and Rome, were reasonably tolerant of abortion and contraception, and folk wisdom about different techniques has been passed down over centuries. Since many of the more effective preventive strategies required male cooperation or technical knowledge that was not widely available until the 1900s, abortion remained of critical significance. Although early Christian theologians generally condemned birth control, they disputed abortion's moral status. Between the eleventh and thirteenth centuries the controversy abated as a consensus formed around the doctrine of quickening. According to that theory, the fetus did not acquire a soul until it "quickened," that is, moved, in the woman's body. Prior to that point, abortion was permissible. Early English and American common law followed the view.[1]

This doctrinal development had practical as well as spiritual underpinnings. Until the point of fetal movement, medical knowledge was not sophisticated enough to determine whether a woman was definitely pregnant. The first American statutes, enacted between 1820 and 1840, typically codified case law and prohibited only post-quickening abortions. Although a second wave of legislation between 1840 and 1860 was more inclusive, enforcement remained lax. Since early court decisions placed high burdens of proof on prosecutors, even statutes that did not distinguish in theory between early and late abortions often did so in practice.[2]

Various cultural trends that began in the mid-nineteenth century contributed to a more stringent regulatory climate. Increased advertising of birth control and abortion made these practices more visible; expanded opportunities for women outside the domestic sphere made such techniques more desirable. The shift from rural to urban industrial society meant that large numbers of children were no longer an economic asset but rather an impediment to a family's rising standard of living. As middle- and upper-middle class Protestant wives increasingly turned to abortion and contraception as a means of limiting fertility, the resulting decline in birth rates sparked widespread concern. At the end of the century, estimates suggest that almost three-quarters of women practiced some method of fertility control, and that the ratio of abortions to live births was between one to three and one to five. As a result, the birth rate was about half what it had been in 1800.[3]

Opposition to these abortion and contraceptive practices reflected various concerns. Some critics feared that any separation of sex from procreation would result in increased venereal disease, psychological "derange[ment]," and social instability. The decline in fertility among the "better" classes, coupled with substantial population growth among immigrants, prompted fears of "race suicide." According to one nineteenth-century observer, nature "fortunately kills off the woman who shirks motherhood, but unfortunately it takes her a generation to do it." Meanwhile, some of civilization's "best breeding stock," who had married these shirkers, would lose out in the evolutionary struggle.[4]

In addition to concerns about the decline of their own class, leaders of the organized medical profession had special reasons for mobilizing against abortion. The issue provided doctors with a means of asserting technical, ethical, and social superiority over their competitors, particularly midwives and other practitioners who had not graduated from approved educational programs. Licensed physicians could claim special knowledge of the continuity of fetal development, special commitment to preserving human life, and adherence to the Hippocratic Oath, part of which forbids abortion. In the process, they could promote their own authority and economic monopoly. By lobbying for statutes that prohibited abortions unless necessary to save the life of the mother, the organized medical profession could criminalize much of its competition.[5]

This crusade was largely effective. Physicians' efforts coincided with those of other moral reformers interested in restricting all forms of birth control and obscene materials. In 1873 Congress passed the Comstock Law, which prohibited dissemination of information about abortion or contraception. Over the next several decades, all but one state made abortion a felony, and such statutes remained largely unchanged until the late 1960s. These developments were ironic in several respects. Although physicians often justified their campaign in terms of protecting maternal health, their success occurred just as medical advances had reduced the risks of abortion, making it substantially safer than childbirth. While many physicians presented the issue in moral and spiritual terms, religious leaders were relatively uninterested in the crusade. During the latter part of the nineteenth century, the Catholic Church did revise its position and began condemning abortion at all stages of fetal development irrespective of the risks to the mother or her potential child. The theory, as one bishop put it, was that two deaths were preferable to one murder. Yet despite that theological shift, the Catholic Church was not a major participant in the nineteenth-century American abortion campaign.[6]

Nor did the feminist movement actively support abortion reform despite the obvious significance of the issue for women's independence. To some movement leaders, reproductive issues were "too narrow . . . and too sordid." For others, they were too threatening. Legalizing contraception appeared to reduce the risks of extramarital sex and thus to jeopardize traditional domestic relationships. For the vast majority of late-nineteenth- and early-twentieth-century women, marriage and motherhood were the best sources of economic security and social status. Any threat to the family was not worth provoking, particularly if the major gain was to license sexual activity that many women had experienced as duty rather than pleasure. In the view of feminist leaders such as Carrie Chapman Catt, "to make indulgence safe is not enough." Continence, not contraception, was their solution. Although most of these leaders were committed to "voluntary motherhood," they wished to ensure it through abstinence rather than "degrading" birth-control methods.[7]

As a result, the initial struggle for reproductive freedom remained largely independent of the organized women's movement. Margaret Sanger, founder of the early-twentieth-century birth-control campaign, began with feminist principles, but they became less visible as her campaign intensified. Her first manifesto emphasized women's right to control their own bodies, and her early socialist affiliations reflected sympathy toward issues of class as well as gender. According to Sanger's autobiography, the catalyst for her crusade was the death of an impoverished East Side New Yorker from a self-induced abortion. For that woman, the only medical advice available about how to avoid a life-threatening pregnancy was to have her husband sleep on the roof.[8]

Yet as Sanger attempted to broaden her movement's appeal, her feminist arguments faded, her class sympathies diminished, and her emphasis shifted to eugenics. "More children from the fit and less from the unfit—that is the chief issue of birth control," she asserted in 1919. Although Sanger was generally careful to avoid explicit racist or ethnic slurs, her definition of unfit was highly inclusive and encompassed illiterates, epileptics, unemployables, and "dope fiends." Many of her disciples were even less restrained, and their publications often stressed the usefulness of contraception in reducing welfare expenditures and social deviance through selective breeding. In order to enlist support from the medical profession, the movement focused on strategies that gave physicians control over the distribution of birth-control materials. Sanger and her followers also disavowed any support for abortion and presented their preventive approach as a sufficient alternative. The growing conservatism of the movement was exemplified in its embrace of the term "family planning" in the 1940s. As Linda Gordon has noted, that terminology shifted focus from women's autonomy to family hygiene and carried as few sexual or feminist connotations as possible.[9]

In many ways, the evolution of the early reproductive-rights movement paralleled that of the suffrage campaign. In broadening their political appeal, birth-control advocates narrowed their social vision. Moreover, appeals to eugenics helped fuel the campaign for sterilization practices that resulted in involuntary fertility control for thousands of slightly retarded or impoverished women, particularly among minority groups. During the 1890s, the development of reasonably safe surgical techniques laid the foundations for a wave of compulsory sterilization laws, which received Supreme Court blessing in 1927. In *Buck v. Bell,* the Court permitted the sterilization of Carrie Buck, an institutionalized and assertedly "feeble-minded" daughter of a feeble-minded mother, after the daughter had given birth to an illegitimate feeble-minded child. Writing for the majority, Justice Holmes concluded that "three generations of imbeciles are enough." Subsequent evidence exposed the risks of such decisionmaking. Carrie Buck does not appear to have been mentally deficient; she was institutionalized to hide a pregnancy resulting from rape by one of her foster relatives.[10]

In the late 1930s and 1940s, the eugenic sterilization movement began to decline, partly in response to scientific evidence undermining its premises, and partly to the lessons of Nazi Germany. Without overruling *Buck*, the Supreme Court cast doubt on its reasoning and limited its application in a subsequent decision that invalidated mandatory sterilization laws for habitual criminals. However, family planners, public hospital administrators, and welfare officials continued to condition assistance on "consent" to sterilization by poor and minority women, who were assumed to lack competence or motivation for other techniques. Coercive and uninformed sterilization remained a major problem until the 1980s, when highly publicized litigation and the promulgation of federal regulations finally began to curb abuses.[11]

Throughout the early twentieth century, the birth-control movement reflected both class and racial biases. Fertility control emerged as a right for the privileged and a duty for the poor. Strategies that repudiated abortion and emphasized physicians' authority over contraceptive distribution had the effect of restricting access for many women who needed it most. The movement's earliest legal victories involved reinterpretations of federal statutes to permit prescription and distribution of birth control materials where permissible under state law (for example, in order to prevent disease). The result was that women who could afford a sympathetic private physician usually could obtain contraceptives. Similarly, those with sufficient resources were sometimes able to establish a physical or psychological justification for a legal abortion. Alternatively, they could afford a relatively safe illegal one, or travel to a more permissive jurisdiction. For the poor, uneducated, or unsophisticated, the options were far more limited. Misconceptions about conception, as well as deaths from self-induced abortions, were common.[12]

Legal restraints on birth control gradually weakened in response to various cultural forces. As was true with liquor, official prohibition of contraceptives was ineffective in curbing sales. The military's distribution of condoms to prevent venereal disease during World War I increased the supply and ultimately the demand for such products. Liberalization of sexual mores in the post-World War I era further expanded the market. Other factors contributed to that trend: opportunities for nonmarital sexual contacts in automobiles, dance halls, and the like during the 1920s; greater economic pressures to curtail fertility during the Depression in the thirties; and increased female labor-force participation in the forties and fifties. After 1960 the availability of an oral contraceptive helped liberalize public attitudes and practices, and concerns about global overpopulation had similar effects. Although President Eisenhower declared in 1959 that he could imagine no subject that was less a matter for government involvement than birth control, just eight years later federal agencies were spending close to 30 million dollars on contraceptive programs at home and abroad.[13]

Beginning in the mid-1960s, the Supreme Court issued a series of decisions that reflected and reinforced these trends. In *Griswold v. Connecticut* (1965), a majority of Justices interpreted the due process clause to protect private use of contraceptives by married couples. Decisions in 1972 and 1977 extended that right to unmarried minors. Although the Justices' reasoning differed, a majority found constitutional grounding for a right of privacy in matters related to procreation. That right in turn provided the doctrinal foundation for some of the Court's most significant and contested decisions—decisions involving abortion.[14]

Abortion

During the 1960s, many of the same forces underlying liberalized contraception policy also encouraged abortion-law reform. Women's increasing sexual activity and labor-force participation increased the number of unwanted pregnancies. As improvements in medical technology reduced the circumstances in which abortion was necessary to preserve a mother's life, the rigidity of existing statutes became more apparent. Physicians faced growing pressure to evade both the letter and spirit of the law, and that pressure was reflected in abortion rates. By the 1960s, most estimates indicated that about a million abortions were occurring annually: one abortion for every three to four live births. At the close of the decade, projections suggested that a quarter of American women would have an abortion, few of them legally. Abortion was the most frequent form of criminal activity after gambling and narcotics, and its perpetrators were also its victims. Procedures could be quite painful and dangerous if performed hastily by unskilled practitioners. Somewhere between 1,000 and 10,000 individuals died each year as a result of botched abortions, and more suffered permanent physical or psychological injuries. Predictably, those most at risk were poor and minority women. These human costs were a catalyst of reform activity.[15]

Other forces were also at work. The 1960s witnessed a new consciousness about population control and women's rights, and activists in both campaigns placed high priority on liberalized abortion laws. In their view, a certain number of unwanted pregnancies were unavoidable. Fear, ignorance, lack of planning, or pressure from male partners made many females, particularly teenagers, ineffective contraceptive users. Side effects deterred some women from taking the pill, and other devices had significant failure rates. Neither individual nor societal interests would be well-served by coercing birth in such cases. For many women, the consequences of an unwanted pregnancy could be devastating. Lost employment and educational opportunities or the stigma of out-of-wedlock birth often had permanent repercussions. Given the enormous physical, psychological, and socioeconomic consequences of an unwanted child, abortion was crucial to women's control over their own destiny. During the 1960s the issue assumed increasing importance. "Men don't get pregnant, they just pass the laws," became a rallying cry within the women's movement.[16]

Growing concern about fetal deformities also expanded public support for abortion reform. During the early 1960s, defects resulting from the use of thalidomide, an antidepressant drug, and a German-measles epidemic crystalized sympathy for women who terminated abnormal pregnancies and for the doctors who provided illegal assistance. Capitalizing on such sympathies, feminists increased their lobbying and litigation campaigns against restrictive abortion laws.

Changes in public sentiment were apparent both in state legislative initiatives and in national opinion surveys. Reform bills began to surface in 1961, usually modeled on an American Law Institute proposal that allowed abortion in certain compelling circumstances: where the physical or mental health of the mother might be seriously impaired; where the child might have grave physical or mental defects; or where the pregnancy resulted from rape, incest, or felonious intercourse. In the five years preceding the Supreme Court's 1973 landmark abortion decision, *Roe v. Wade,* one-third of the states had liberalized their statutes. However, on the eve of that decision, half the states still prohibited termination of pregnancy except where necessary to preserve maternal life, even though substantial evidence indicated that such restrictive statutes were out of step with public opinion.[17]

Although polls on abortion are unusually difficult to interpret, given the way slight changes in wording or question sequence affect results, it is clear that attitudes changed significantly during the 1960s. In the decade prior to *Roe v. Wade,* the number of individuals who approved of abortion in the most compelling circumstances—rape, incest, fetal abnormalities, or threats to maternal health—climbed to between 80 and 90 percent. Public support for termination of pregnancy in other cases—such as where the mother was unmarried, the family was poor, or the couple did not want further children—increased to around 50 percent. In 1972, just prior to *Roe,* two national surveys reported that between 50 and 57 percent of Americans thought abortion decisions should be left to a woman and her physician.[18]

So the Supreme Court held, at least with respect to the first trimester of pregnancy. *Roe v. Wade* involved the constitutionality of a statute prohibiting abortion except to save the life of the mother. A companion case, *Doe v. Bolton,* raised similar challenges to legislation modeled on the ALI proposal. Speaking for the majority in *Roe,* Justice Blackmun concluded that the Fourteenth Amendment's guarantee of personal liberty implied a fundamental right of privacy "broad enough to encompass a women's decision whether or not to terminate her pregnancy." Restrictions on that fundamental right required justification by a compelling state interest. In the Court's view, one such interest, protecting maternal health, became compelling only after the first trimester, the point at which mortality rates from abortion became higher than mortality rates from childbirth. As to the state's interest in protecting fetal life, the compelling point was at viability, when the fetus had the capability of meaningful life outside the womb. After that point, which generally occurred in the third trimester, the state could prohibit abortion except when necessary to protect the health or life of the mother.[19]

The *Roe* decision set off some of the most strident and sustained criticism that the American judiciary has ever experienced. Objections came from all points of the political spectrum. To most conservatives, the decision appeared utterly without moral foundation; many moderates found it lacking in constitutional justifications; and the left complained that the Court had offered the wrong justifications.

Part of the controversy stemmed from the Court's explicit attempt to avoid "resolving the difficult question of when life begins." Yet in determining that the fetus was not entitled to legal protection prior to viability, the Court necessarily concluded that the unborn were not "persons" within the meaning of the Constitution. This conclusion was unacceptable to many individuals, particularly Catholics and Fundamentalists, who believed that life begins at conception. In their view, as Ronald Reagan expressed it, society could not "diminish the value of one category of human life—the unborn" without devaluing all life. In addition, many critics who did not personally subscribe to this "right to life" position nonetheless believed that the Court gave it too little recognition in *Roe,* and thereby provided a strong impetus for the antiabortion campaign. According to these scholars, had the Court proceeded more cautiously in *Roe,* and given more latitude to legislatures, much of the hostility that resulted from *Roe* could have been averted or directed at other targets.[20]

To some of these commentators the Supreme Court's holding was equally problematic on doctrinal grounds. Critics frequently contended that *Roe* was without support in the Constitution's history, text, or structure, or in principles derived from them. From this perspective, not only was *Roe* bad constitutional law, it was "not constitutional law at all." Of particular concern was the Court's trimester framework. In these commentators' view, *Roe* provided insufficient justification for why viability should be the "magic moment" at which abortion could be prohibited. Nor did the Court adequately explain what viability meant. What constituted a reasonable likelihood of survival outside the womb? Ten percent? Fifty percent? Why should individual physicians have authority to determine which probability was reasonable? And why should the likelihood of fetal survival, which depended on the technology and resources available in a particular locality, be granted overwhelming moral or constitutional significance?[21]

Even those who supported the result in *Roe* were critical of a framework that made women's privacy interest depend on an unstable technological rationale. Within a decade after *Roe,* medical advances were calling into question its trimester framework; viability was occurring earlier and abortions were safer than the decision had envisioned. What would happen if, as Justice O'Connor predicted in a subsequent case, medical advances permitted fetal survival much earlier in a woman's pregnancy, even during the first trimester? So too, by the mid-1980s abortion was safer than childbirth through the twenty-second, not the twelfth week, of pregnancy. Such developments eroded the maternal-health justification for restrictions on abortion during the second trimester. Yet once the Court had allowed such restrictions, it had difficulty retreating from that position. As a result, the Justices remained enmeshed in controversies over regulations designed to deter abortions while purporting to offer maternal-health protections, such as consent requirements, waiting periods, bans on outpatient clinics, and limitations on the type of procedures available. Related disputes arose concerning mandatory testing for fetal viability and use of public funds and facilities for abortion-related services.[22]

In assessing criticisms of *Roe,* it is important to focus on the context in which the litigation arose. Whether a more cautious approach by the Supreme Court would have reduced the conflict surrounding abortion, or resulted in a more defensible accommodation of competing interests, is by no means clear. To some religious groups, the issue implicates fundamental moral principles that permit no compromise. Also, for many conservatives, legalized abortion, like the proposed Equal Rights Amendment, has come to assume profound symbolic significance. As Kristin Luker's study suggests, right-to-life advocates perceive any move toward liberalization as an assault on traditional family values and gender roles. To this constituency, abortion undermines marriage, morality, and motherhood. Given the uncompromising intensity of their convictions, antiabortion activists can disproportionately influence a pluralist political process. Moreover, the groups that suffer most from restrictive legislative policies have little power in legislative arenas: poor, nonwhite, and adolescent women.[23]

One critical function of judicial review is to safeguard the interests of such minorities. A primary reason for granting federal judges life tenure, and entrusting them with the interpretation of broad constitutional provisions, is to ensure some protection for evolving principles of liberty and equality. Control over reproduction implicates both of these principles, and its importance for women has long been undervalued by majoritarian political processes. If these concerns are taken seriously, the difficulty in *Roe* is not the result but the rationale. The problem rests in the Court's failure adequately to define the interests at issue and establish some coherent accommodation.

Neither of the primary governmental interests surrounding abortion can justify *Roe*'s trimester framework. The state's first concern, protecting maternal health, is both broader and narrower than the Court has acknowledged. It surely exists prior to the point at which abortion is riskier than childbirth. Yet now that abortion is safer than childbirth until the third trimester of pregnancy, the original health justification for distinguishing first and second trimester procedures has disappeared.

As to the state's second concern, preserving fetal life, the viability-nonviability distinction is similarly problematic. With some modification, however, it seems preferable to the commonly suggested alternatives. From a technological standpoint, the distinction is by no means as vulnerable as some critics have asserted. Contrary to Justice O'Connor's suggestion, most experts do not anticipate imminent medical advances that will sustain fetal life outside the womb at substantially earlier points. Certainly there is no immediate prospect of developing artificial wombs that could preserve embryos during the first trimester of pregnancy, when over 90 percent of all abortions occur.[24]

From an ethical standpoint, the viability-nonviability distinction is by no means as arbitrary as is sometimes supposed. Nor do preferable alternatives suggest themselves. If, as many conservative critics argue, life begins at conception and abortion is murder, it becomes impossible to justify procedures that the vast majority of Americans find morally defensible: abortion in cases of rape, incest, or jeopardy to maternal health; and contraceptive methods that prevent implantation of a fertilized egg. Similarly, the position that life does not begin until birth fails to capture what most individuals find to be an intuitively important moral distinction. In postviability procedures, where removing a fetus from the womb does not entail its extinction, the process of deliberately allowing death seems much closer to infanticide than does abortion prior to viability. Society's interest in affirming the value of human life and minimizing physical and psychological complications argues for ensuring that abortions occur before the point of fetal survival, except under limited extenuating circumstances. Those interests have been furthered by the viability framework. By the mid-1980s, 99 percent of all abortions occurred in the first twenty weeks; only 0.01 percent occurred after twenty-four weeks, the point at which a fetus has a substantial chance of surviving outside the womb.[25]

Aside from viability, the only alternative position between conception and birth that has commanded substantial support is fetal brain consciousness. Such a standard would have the advantage of symmetry with contemporary standards for determining death, now defined as the absence of brain activity. Yet that approach would present other problems. The development of brain consciousness, unlike its cessation, is a continuous process, occurring most rapidly between the nineteenth and thirtieth week of pregnancy. Singling out any particular stage as the point at which abortion becomes impermissible would be more arbitrary than maintaining the viability distinction.[26]

Yet one difficulty with the viability distinction as currently formulated involves its application to a small category of cases involving gross fetal defects that cannot be diagnosed prior to viability. Supreme Court decisions have allowed states to prohibit abortions whenever the fetus is capable of "meaningful" life, unless the mother's life or health is in danger. What constitutes "meaningful," or a substantial risk to health remains unclear. Surely it would not diminish our commitment to life to recognize that, in some instances, a life is likely to be so bleak, and to exact such a heavy toll on the immediate family, that artificial support should be withdrawn. What sorts of fetal defects fall into that category is a complex question, but one that cannot be resolved by any rigid viability-nonviability distinction, or by an abstract appeal to women's "privacy." Once a fetus can survive outside the womb, other public interests are obviously implicated.

A more fundamental difficulty with the *Roe* framework lies in its doctrinal foundations. Privacy is too limited a concept to capture what is at stake for women, either as individuals or as a group. What critics too seldom acknowledge and the Court failed adequately to explain is the fundamental importance of reproductive choice in shaping individual destiny and promoting gender equality. The principal harm of abortion restrictions has little to do with those emphasized in *Roe:* invading the privacy of doctor-patient or family relationships. Rather, as Sylvia Law and Robin West have suggested, the primary harm involves "invading the physical boundaries of the body and the psychic boundaries of a life." At issue is not simply intimacy but identity—women's capacity to define the terms of their existence. To deny individuals that capacity would impose a burden unique in its combination of physical intrusiveness, psychological trauma, and career impairment. From this perspective, the moral issue of "when life begins" becomes less critical. Even if the fetus were assumed to be a person, it would not follow that its interests must assume primary importance. Just as we do not compel individuals to serve as Good Samaritans in other contexts, we ought not to expect women at all stages of pregnancy to sacrifice their own destiny to embryonic life. State efforts to coerce childbirth do violence to the values of care and commitment that should underpin mother-infant attachments. If the due process clause is to play an adequate role in safeguarding basic values "implicit in the concept of ordered liberty," reproductive freedom must rank among the protected concerns.[27]

Moreover, access to abortion implicates equal-protection interests as well. Although only two of many *amici* briefs argued the point in *Roe,* equality concerns were central to a number of earlier lower court cases and emerged clearly in subsequent Supreme Court litigation. The issue is not simply individual rights but social roles. Unless women are able to control their childbearing capacity, they can never assume positions of full equality. By casting abortion issues solely in terms of individual autonomy, the Court has obscured their collective implications, and reaffirmed the public-private dichotomy that feminism challenges.

The focus on privacy also has helped rationalize the Supreme Court's subsequent decisions upholding withdrawal of public funds for abortion services. In 1977, in *Maher v. Roe,* a majority of Justices affirmed the right of states to deny Medicaid funding for nontherapeutic abortions, while fully subsidizing childbirth. Three years later, in *Harris v. McRae,* the Court extended its reasoning to uphold Congress' ban on federal support even for abortions necessary to protect the mother's health, unless her life was in danger or she was the victim of rape or incest. Underlying those decisions was a revived form of the much discredited distinction between benefits and burdens. In the view of a majority of Justices, the state had "place[d] no obstacles—absolute or otherwise—in the pregnant woman's path to an abortion . . . By making childbirth a more attractive alternative, the state may have influenced a woman's decision but it has imposed no restriction on access to abortion that was not already there. Although government may not place obstacles in the path of a woman's exercise of her freedom of choice, it need not remove those not of its own creation . . . The financial constraints that restrict an indigent woman's ability to enjoy the full range of constitutionally protected freedom of choice are the product not of governmental restrictions on access to abortions, but rather of her indigency."[28]

This reasoning is problematic on several levels. The notion that the state has played no role in creating economic constraints on choice suggests an extraordinary degree of myopia: welfare, education, employment, tax, and innumerable other public policies have contributed to cycles of poverty. It is of course true that indigency limits the exercise of many fundamental rights. Yet it is also the case that the right at stake in *Maher* and *Harris* was as significant as others for which the Court has required state assistance, such as court costs in divorce proceedings or free transcripts for defendants in criminal cases. Moreover, the usual justification for the government's failure to provide such assistance—conserving scarce resources—was unavailable in *Maher* and *Harris*. When those cases arose, the average cost of subsidizing childbirth was close to ten times that of underwriting abortions. Since many indigents' children would also require continuing welfare support, the statutes in question were inexplicable as revenue-saving measures. Rather, the government had sought to accomplish indirectly what it could not do directly: coercing women into completing unwanted pregnancies.[29]

The targets of such coercion were women least able to protect themselves through conventional political channels, and least able to provide adequate support for an additional child. Although in the aftermath of *Maher* and *Harris* the vast majority of indigent women continued to receive some funding through state or private sources, surveys indicate that a significant number were unable to afford abortions. Another substantial percentage of low-income individuals could do so only at extraordinary sacrifice, often with extended delays that increased physical risk and psychological trauma. At the time of the Court's funding decisions, the average expense of an abortion exceeded the average monthly welfare payment to an entire family, and in some states it was three to four times greater. When questioned about the justice of this selective attempt to coerce childbirth, then-President Jimmy Carter replied that "life's unfair." However true, that observation was utterly unresponsive to concerns about the government's complicity in such unfairness. As this line of cases evolved, it illustrated the inadequacy not only of the Court's privacy framework, but also of a liberal rights-oriented approach to gender equality. The bottom line has been that, in Catharine MacKinnon's phrase, "women with privileges get rights."[30]

A decade after the *Roe* decision, some one-and-one-half-million legal abortions were occurring annually in the United States, yet women's reproductive liberty remained at risk. Threats emerged from varied sources: proposed constitutional amendments to prohibit abortion; state, local, and hospital restrictions on access; funding cut-offs; bans on abortion counseling by publicly funded agencies; repeated terrorism against clinics; and new appointments to the Supreme Court. Potential curtailment of constitutional protections threatens to return the issue to the states and expose women to the dangers of the pre-*Roe* era. In this climate it has become increasingly crucial to reconceptualize the abortion question, in both political and legal terms. As with other issues, we need less preoccupation with abstract rights and more concern with the context in which they are exercised. It has been a mistake to allow the debate over abortion to proceed under "pro-life" and "pro-choice" labels. The issue must be reframed to encompass not only the fetus' abstract entitlement to life but also the quality of that life, and of the lives of those surrounding it. Conservatives who seek to compel childbirth but who oppose adequate social services for children and their parents are not "pro-life." Feminists must reappropriate that label, and claim abortion as a means of insuring the quality of existence for women and their children.

This claim to abortion cannot rest with some narrow abstract understanding of a "right to choice." No adequate notion of reproductive freedom can exclude the public benefits essential for its exercise. Nor can feminists who advocate choice limit their claims to abortion on demand. Their objectives must encompass broader societal support for contraceptive research, education, counseling, and distribution that will make abortion less necessary. Experimentation is currently under way with a new French drug that might prove to be a safe abortifacient; funding for further innovations could yield important advances. As cross-cultural and historical comparisons make clear, abortion rates are much more closely related to the availability of birth-control information and techniques than to repressive laws.[31]

Removing barriers to abortion, although critical, will not make women's choices truly free. Just as some individuals are unable to afford abortion, others are unable to afford childbirth. American society provides woefully inadequate health services, maternity policies, childcare, welfare assistance, and related family-support structures. The decision whether to terminate a pregnancy still remains heavily constrained. Our public and private choices are interrelated, and we should not lose sight of the entire range of social conditions that must change before reproductive liberty is possible.

Adolescent Pregnancy

Teenage pregnancy raises similar issues. Traditional policy approaches were punitive, and current strategies still reflect this legacy. Prior to the 1960s, out-of-wedlock births resulted in ostracism and public sanctions. Many schools excluded unwed mothers, although not fathers, a practice ultimately discontinued after judicial challenges in the late 1960s and early 1970s. At that point, the rate of adolescent sexual activity and single parenthood was increasing sharply. By the late 1980s the United States had the highest teen pregnancy rate in the developed world. Approximately 45 percent of adolescent females were sexually active before marriage, and a substantial number of them used contraceptives intermittently or ineffectively. The result was about a million teen pregnancies each year, and around four-fifths were unintentional. An estimated four out of every ten female adolescents were becoming pregnant at least once before age twenty; about half of that group were carrying their pregnancy to term, and half of those who did so were unmarried.[32]

If such trends continue, all but a tiny percentage of these adolescent mothers will keep their children, and the costs of that decision will be substantial. For most women, the price of teenage pregnancy has been disrupted education, reduced employment opportunities, increased likelihood of poverty, and heightened medical risks. Although some recent longitudinal data suggest that the vast majority of teen mothers are eventually able to obtain a high-school education, secure full-time employment, and avoid welfare dependency, a significant number experience enduring poverty, and many face prolonged periods of severe hardship. The consequence for children of adolescent mothers has been a greater likelihood of physical, psychological, cognitive, and educational problems, as well as a greater possibility of becoming teenage parents themselves. These risks have been especially pronounced among minorities. Contemporary studies have found that the rate of teen childbirth among blacks is almost two and a half times greater than among whites; among Hispanics the rates are almost twice as great. Over a quarter of single black women have had at least one child by the age of eighteen.[33]

Adolescent pregnancy has prompted increasing national concern but no coherent policy. As with other gender-related issues, much of the problem stems from dispute over the nature of the problem. Is the primary issue morality, fertility, or poverty? Although most liberals "begin with the premise that teenagers should not have babies, [most conservatives] begin with the premise that single teenagers should not have sex." Policymakers generally fault unmarried mothers for wanting "too much too soon" in a sexual relationship, but counselors in the field generally fault government for offering those mothers "too little too late": too little reason to stay in school, too little opportunity for childcare or decent jobs, and too little information about contraception, abortion, and the costs of single parenting.[34]

These disputes have resulted in a patchwork of programs with conflicting social signals. One representative survey found that three-quarters of all high schools and junior high schools offered some sex education, but only about a fifth identified reducing adolescent motherhood as an objective. In 1978, Congress amended an earlier family-planning act to require that federally funded contraceptive services (excluding abortion) be available to adolescents. Three years later, however, the first federal legislation specifically designed to deal with adolescent pregnancy, the Adolescent Family Life Act, placed emphasis on encouraging "sexual self-discipline" rather than providing contraceptive services, and banned any use of federal funds for abortion counseling. Many of the programs receiving AFLA funds have been religious. Their instruction has included distribution of pamphlets on "Reasons to Wait"—with reasons such as "God wants us to be pure." Despite substantial evidence of church-state entanglement, a 1988 Supreme Court decision sustained the Act.[35]

Parental-consent policies have reflected similar conservatism. A 1981 regulation by the Department of Health and Human Services required parental notification for adolescents seeking contraceptives in all federally funded clinics. Although lower federal courts enjoined enforcement of that "squeal rule," subsequent surveys indicated that about a fifth of hospitals and well over a third of private physicians voluntarily have required parental consent before prescribing contraception. Some states and localities have similarly mandated parental involvement for all unemancipated minors seeking abortions, while over a third of hospitals and about a fifth of surveyed clinics have voluntarily adopted comparable rules.[36]

Legal challenges to parental notification and consent policies have resulted in compromises that make little long-term sense. In a series of cases during the late 1970s and early 1980s, the Supreme Court held that states could require parental consent or notification for abortion services to unemancipated minors on one condition: that an adjudicative procedure be available to permit bypassing such requirements under certain circumstances. An adolescent should be able to avoid parental involvement by establishing in court either: that she is sufficiently mature and well-informed to make an independent decision concerning abortion; or that even if she is immature, the abortion would be in her best interest.[37]

On a symbolic level, this resolution is understandable. It affirms the value of parental involvement in matters that call for mature guidance. It also acknowledges that in some instances, such involvement may result in punitive or otherwise counterproductive measures, and that birth-control services may be clearly appropriate. Yet on a practical level, this compromise has been unworkable. Given the absence of standards for determining maturity, courts are generally hard-pressed to deny abortions to minors willing and able to navigate bypass procedures. They have been equally reluctant to identify circumstances under which an immature minor's best interest involves having a child that she does not want. Not surprisingly, the limited data available suggest that virtually all bypass petitions are granted. However, these legal obstacles impose considerable costs, particularly among young, minority, low-income, and unsophisticated adolescents. Consent requirements for abortion result in additional psychological trauma, life-endangering delays, and, according to at least one major study, increased risks of an unwanted child.[38]

These limitations on adolescent reproductive rights reflect two primary concerns. Conservatives typically argue that providing birth control for teenagers undermines parental authority and legitimates sexual promiscuity. According to Senators Orrin Hatch and Jeremiah Denton, "the most effective oral contraceptive yet devised is the word 'no.'" In their view, any outreach program designed to prevent pregnancy rather than sex is counterproductive; it encourages the activity that creates the problem. Available research, however, suggests that the issue is far more complicated. Making contraceptive services less accessible discourages contraception, not sex. Studies of birth-control programs find no evidence that their availability has increased sexual activity. The vast majority of adolescents seek assistance only after they are engaging in such activity. Comparative data underscore the point. Many European countries have rates of adolescent sexual relations similar to those in the United States, but substantially lower rates of adolescent pregnancy and abortion.[39]

That is not to deny the indirect influence that birth-control programs may have on adolescent attitudes. Nor is it to suppose that more vigorous outreach programs would leave sexual mores unaffected. Few adolescents in their early teens have been adequately prepared to deal with the consequences of sexual intercourse, and it is difficult to prevent materials designed for older adolescents from filtering down to their younger counterparts. But granting that risk, it nonetheless makes sense to attempt more effective birth-control programs than have been available to date. Even if it were clear that the absence of such programs has helped deter some teens from sexual activity, the price has been too great. To reduce the enormous personal and social costs that flow from adolescent pregnancy, we need a different strategy.

A critical first step is to direct more systematic research and social resources to teen parenting. As a special panel of the National Research Council noted, there has been little reliable evaluation of existing programs, including contraceptive services, school-based clinics, peer counseling, media outreach, sex education, and mentoring strategies. Nor have sufficient resources been available for those programs that appear most effective in preventing unplanned pregnancy or providing assistance for adolescent parents. Education, employment, health, childcare, welfare, and related services could do much to minimize the costs that early parenthood now exact. We cannot respond effectively to teenage motherhood without responding also to the broader range of social problems that make motherhood seem to be a teen's best option.[40]

In designing more effective programs for adolescents, it is critical to include both sexes. One of the striking deficiencies in most research and policy is the inattention to male attitudes and behavior. Too little work focuses on the roles and dynamics of adolescent fatherhood, or the social initiatives necessary to encourage greater contraceptive and parental responsibility among young men. While the AIDS epidemic has underscored the need for better sex-education programs for males, it should not obscure the broader role that such education must serve. Encouraging men to exercise greater responsibility in sexual relationships from an early age is a crucial part of reproductive freedom for women.[41]

Given the disproportionately high rates of adolescent childbearing among women of color, it is essential to focus on issues of race and ethnicity as well as gender. Although some of the differentials in teen fertility and family stability among whites and nonwhites are decreasing and some appear attributable to relative economic disadvantage, significant disparities persist, even controlling for class and other demographic variables. More work is necessary to explain the interaction of race and other factors, and to develop counseling programs and other social initiatives responsive to minority needs.[42]

Finally, and most fundamentally, an adequate response to adolescent pregnancy requires broader changes in our cultural landscape. Few if any societies exhibit a more perverse combination of permissiveness and prudishness in their treatment of sexuality. The United States tolerates pervasive sexual appeals in entertainment, literature, music, fashion, arts, and advertising. Sex sells everything from automobiles to laundry detergent. Yet we have been unable to deal frankly with the consequences of such messages among our nation's adolescents. Coherent policies on teenage pregnancy require a more searching analysis of adult values and priorities, one that encompasses men's attitudes as well as women's rights.

Reproductive Technology

Technological Developments

That women have assumed so much of the responsibility for birth control is a function not only of biology but also of technology, and of the cultural attitudes that have shaped its direction. The low priority historically given to male contraception, except as a means of controlling venereal disease, cannot be explained solely in physiological terms. Although researchers report greater technical difficulties in developing safe oral contraceptives for men than for women, relatively little work has focused on these difficulties until recently. Other strategies for male birth control, such as reversible vasectomies, have fared no better.

This skewed allocation of reproductive responsibility is something for which women have paid an emormous price. But it is also an area where they have been ambivalent about relinquishing control. As long as women assume the physical burdens of childbearing and the primary social burdens of child-rearing, this desire for control remains justifiable. Legal regulations such as spousal-consent requirements for abortion or sterilization are objectionable on precisely that ground. However, if cultural and technological changes reduce the primacy of biological parenthood, expand opportunties for effective male contraception, and curtail gender asymmetries in child-rearing obligations, the dialogue about reproductive control will have to change.[43]

As the potential for technological development becomes more apparent, women must seek a greater role in shaping its direction. Among the most critical areas for inquiry are issues surrounding new reproductive methods and markets: artificial insemination, in vitro fertilization, embryo transfers, and surrogate motherhood. Interest in such techniques has grown dramatically over the last quarter-century, partly in response to demographic and socioeconomic changes. Only recently has involuntary childlessness emerged as a widespread social problem. In seventeenth- and eighteenth-century America, fertility rates were extremely high. By the mid-nineteenth century, as industrialization, urbanization, and abolition of slavery reduced the value of child labor, reproductive difficulties were more likely to involve unwanted infants than unwanted infertility. One result was baby farms, where "tradeswomen in tiny lives" accepted undesired offspring for a fee. In the early twentieth century, these patterns began to change. By the 1950s a congressional investigation revealed enough evidence of baby-buying by eager adoptive parents to justify comprehensive regulation.[44]

The next quarter-century witnessed growing demands for healthy (particularly white) infants available for adoption. Estimates in the later 1980s suggested that between 10 and 15 percent of American couples were involuntarily childless, a substantial increase over the preceding two decades. Women's exposure to environmental hazards, contraceptive side-effects, and sexually transmitted diseases, as well as delayed efforts at childbearing, have contributed to a growing rate of infertility. In addition, a larger number of unmarried women, both lesbians and heterosexuals, have sought to become mothers.[45]

While such patterns have increased the number of would-be adoptive parents, other factors have decreased the number of infants available for adoption. The increased accessibility of abortion and contraception, coupled with the decreased social stigma of unwed motherhood, has resulted in dramatic asymmetries; the contemporary ratio of potential adoptors to adoptees is about thirty-five to one. The wait ranges from three to seven years, and the expense is substantial. Individuals unwilling to accept an older or handicapped child or to navigate the complexities of third-world adoption procedures are often left childless. Many would-be parents, especially those committed to having some biological tie with their offspring, are turning to new reproductive technologies.[46]

The most common technique, artificial insemination, involves impregnating a woman by sperm injections. Although this technique has been available since the eighteenth century, its use among humans has not been widespread until recent decades. Aided in part by developments in freezing and storing sperm, the contemporary market for artificial insemination is increasing in size and selectivity. Specialized sperm banks are appearing for donors with certain traits, such as high IQs or exceptional athletic abilities. While most of the estimated 20,000 successful inseminations per year involve wives with infertile husbands, a growing number of unmarried women are also seeking assistance.

Two more recent medical advances present greater technical challenge. In vitro fertilization, first accomplished in 1978, involves uniting the sperm and egg outside the womb. Once fertilized, the developing embryo is implanted in the uterus of either the woman who provided the egg or another woman who agrees to carry the fetus to term. Success rates among different facilities have varied, but by the mid-1980s they were averaging between 10 and 20 percent. A related technique, embryo transfer, involves removing an embryo fertilized through intercourse or artificial insemination and placing it in another woman's womb. The first effective transfer occurred in 1983, but it was followed by frequent failures. Estimates of the success rate throughout the 1980s remained at about 2 to 5 percent. However, if that rate improves, and associated costs and health risks diminish, the transfer technique might provide an option for women who wish to conceive a child, yet avoid the burdens of pregnancy. This procedure, coupled with technologies for freezing and storing embryos, could effectively halt the female biological clock. Women could conceive in their twenties, preserve their potential offspring, and, with the aid of surrogates, become parents in their forties.[47]

The oldest of the "new" reproductive technologies involves surrogacy. The most celebrated example dates to the biblical account of Abraham, who with the consent of his infertile wife, Sarah, impregnated her handmaiden, Hagar. Under most modern surrogacy arrangements a woman agrees, for a substantial fee, to conceive and/or gestate a child through artificial insemination, in vitro fertilization, or embryo transfer. After birth she relinquishes the infant to the genetic father and, in case of in vitro fertilization and embryo transfer, the genetic mother. By the late 1980s there were six hundred recorded cases of surrogacy in this country, and some experts estimated the number of private arrangements at around five thousand. Other technologies are under development. Procedures are steadily improving for diagnosis and treatment of fetal disorders and may soon create opportunities to select a child's sex. In the less immediate but still foreseeable future is an artificial womb that would permit a fetus to evolve entirely outside a woman's body.[48]

The Cultural Implications of Technological Change

These reproductive technologies, although at different stages of development, pose certain common concerns. A threshold issue involves control. Technological advances that expand women's opportunities to control fertility create comparable opportunities for the state, and for the professionals it funds and licenses. One danger is that options will become obligations. Just as some courts have ordered women to undergo Caesarean sections for the sake of their offspring, other judges or legislatures might require prenatal therapies that present health risks to the mother but significant potential benefits to the fetus. If pregnant women's interests can be subordinated to fetal interests, similar logic might permit compromising women's right to an abortion by requiring the preservation of embryos.[49]

The possibilities for eugenic intervention available through new technologies are of equal concern. The easier it becomes to orchestrate and terminate fetal development, the easier it will be to determine the kind of life that survives. Would-be parents may feel increasing pressure to seek artificial methods in order to create the "perfect" child. Comparable pressures may encourage abortion of any fetus that might not measure up, and the definition of "perfect" remains deeply problematic. With expanded scope for parental choice comes expanded scope for governmental influence through tax, welfare, research, and other public policies. Moreover, the potential combination of in vitro fertilization and artificial wombs could permit almost total government control over reproductive processes. By regulating the storage and availability of sperm, eggs, and embryos, the state could effectively determine whose genetic legacies would survive. Given the class and racial biases that have historically colored eugenic intervention, any extension of governmental oversight carries substantial risks.[50]

Even without the specter of direct public intervention, the growth of artificial control over reproductive processes has certain obvious dangers, particularly in the area of fetal sex selection. In theory, giving parents the option to choose sons or daughters might appear desirable; it promotes population control and healthy parent-child relationships. In practice, however, the public costs of private choices could prove substantial. In some countries, where second-trimester screening procedures disclose fetal sex, many parents already use abortion to insure the birth of a son rather than a daughter. Various techniques to control a child's sex at conception or to reveal its sex earlier in pregnancy are under development. Their availability could seriously skew male-female birth ratios. Although surveys indicate that most couples want a child of each sex, almost all of those with gender preferences want sons rather than daughters. In addition, most fathers and mothers prefer their first child to be a boy. Because first-born children are likely to have higher social, economic, and educational attainments than their siblings, parental choices could reinforce gender inequalities.[51]

A related cluster of concerns involves access to reproductive technologies and their implications for family relationships. Traditionally, the medical profession has enjoyed substantial control over participants in artificial conception. The overwhelming majority of sperm donors have been doctors and their students, while recipients have been women judged acceptable by those professionals: women who are married, psychologically "stable," and financially secure. Despite legislative and administrative policies that permit single women to adopt, only 10 percent of physicians surveyed in the late 1970s would accept such patients for artificial insemination, and many clinics have continued exclusionary practices. When unmarried women have succeeded in giving birth through insemination, often with aid from feminist health organizations, some courts have vested paternity and visitation rights in the sperm donor. Such a practice contrasts with the treatment of married women, whose husbands have universally obtained exclusive paternal status. Medical professionals' fear of legal complications has also encouraged increasing anonymity in record-keeping, a policy that has prevented adequate research on potential problems resulting from artificial insemination.[52]

Distributional issues raise related concerns. By the late 1980s, surrogacy expenses typically ranged from $20,000 to $30,000; in vitro fertilization and embryo transfers could cost more than double that amount. Insurance carriers rarely cover such expenses, so access to these techniques has been severely limited by wealth. Although such distributional patterns are by no means unique, their presence merits special focus in view of the fundamental interests involved and the class and eugenic implications of market-based allocation. With technological improvements in embryo transplants and in vitro fertilization, the demand for these and related surrogate services is likely to increase. The result might be a pattern comparable to that prevailing in seventeenth- and eighteenth-century Europe, when women of wealth turned their infants over to lower-class wet nurses, who often had to sacrifice the interests of their own children to those of their employers.[53]

Investment in reproductive technologies also raises a broader set of distributional issues. American society has diverted substantial resources to developing fertility techniques for a relatively small number of couples able to afford such assistance. Yet at the same time, funding has been grossly inadequate for programs designed to reduce environmental causes of infertility or to address fertility related concerns among less affluent women: for example, genetic screening, pre- and postnatal care, nutrition, prevention of sexually transmitted diseases, and family health services.[54]

Surrogate Parents

By the late 1980s, the issues surrounding reproductive technology had begun to attract greater attention, partly in response to the well-publicized

Baby M. litigation. That case involved a surrogacy contract in which Mary Beth Whitehead agreed, for $10,000, to bear a child through artificial insemination and to relinquish the infant to its natural father, William Stern, and his wife, Elizabeth. After birth, Whitehead found herself unable to give up the child. A New Jersey trial court decision upholding the contract and denying her custody and visitation attracted widespread attention. On appeal, the state supreme court declared such surrogacy contracts unenforceable as against public policy, but allowed the Sterns to retain custody (which they had exercised pending judgment). Although Whitehead did receive rights of visitation, the compromise struck many observers as anything but Solomonic.[55]

Cases such as *Baby M.* present a host of social, moral, and legal issues on which the public is deeply divided. The result has been metaphorical warfare and legal chaos. Opponents of the practice stress its commercial underpinnings and exploitative potential. In the view of some feminists, surrogacy is a form of mercenary motherhood, procreative prostitution, and baby-buying, which compromises reproductive freedom among economically vulnerable women. Even the term appears objectionable; except in the relatively rare cases involving embryo transfer, the "surrogate" is the biological mother. Supporters of surrogate arrangements use a different moral discourse, which invokes metaphors of donation rather than commerce and stresses the expansion of reproductive freedom for infertile women and economic opportunity for childbearing women. These divergent moral perceptions have created problems in legal categorization. Should surrogate contracts be treated as a form of baby brokering, a practice long prohibited by adoption statutes? Alternatively, should such arrangements be analogized to sperm or egg donation, a practice for which donors have lawfully received financial compensation? In many respects, these arguments paralleled the debates about sameness-difference and special-equal treatment that have emerged in other contexts. Should women who wish to make such agreements be treated the same as other contracting parties or should the unique experience of pregnancy and childbirth entitle these women to special legal standards?[56]

Most proposals for regulating surrogacy arrangements have taken one of four approaches: (1) prohibit contracts involving payments for surrogacy services; (2) enforce surrogacy agreements and require the natural mother to relinquish the infant despite any change of mind after childbirth; (3) permit surrogacy arrangements and resolve custody disputes under the same "best-interest-of-the-child" standard applicable in divorce proceedings; (4) regulate surrogacy agreements and require that a "gestational" mother have a reasonable period after childbirth to reconsider her decision to give up an infant. Although all of these approaches are problematic, the final regulatory model appears the least-worst option, at least under the limited knowledge available.

The first proposal, banning surrogacy payments entirely, is the approach taken by most European countries and a number of states. It rests on several concerns. First and most fundamentally, many individuals find the prospect of commodifying childbirth abhorrent. In their view, the same reasons for prohibiting the sale of bodily organs or adoptive babies argue for prohibiting agreements to conceive a child for profit. Such arrangements threaten core notions of bodily integrity and human identity. Some courts and commentators also worry about the risk of long-range psychological injury to surrogate mothers who underestimate the power of maternal bonding and place a price tag on their offspring. Related concerns involve harm to surrogates' children, who eventually may learn of their contractual history, and harm to siblings, who might fear that they too will be relinquished for a fee. Even if these individuals escape injury, society has an interest in preventing the devaluation of human life and the exploitation of class advantages. This position, adherents note, does not foreclose opportunities for parenting. Rather, the result will be to encourage adoption of the many hard-to-place children living in an already overpopulated world: children who are older, have special needs, or are from developing countries. Ideals of interpersonal responsibility and gender equality will best be served by a vision of parenting that does not overly privilege genetic ties.[57]

Such arguments fail to acknowledge the diversity of women's interests and the full range of societal values at issue. For some women the opportunity to aid an infertile couple, while providing crucial financial assistance to their own family, constitutes an affirmation, not a devaluation of life. Given the absence of systematic research and the small number of reported cases in which a surrogate has changed her mind (5 of 600 in the late 1980s), assumptions about maternal harm remain speculative. Longitudinal data about surrogates' infants and siblings are also lacking, and it is not self-evident that concerns about abandonment will be more critical than perceptions of being wanted in affecting children's psychological development.

Moreover, these risks of injury must be weighed against the incontrovertible benefits to infertile couples who have no alternative way to conceive a child with genetic ties to at least one parent. Although an ideal world might not privilege such genetic connections, we remain a considerable distance from that vision. Under current cultural and legal norms, the desire to procreate has seemed as worthy of protection as the desire not to procreate; recognition of both is critical to many individuals' sense of identity and human fulfillment. To suppose that adoption is an adequate alternative ignores its practical difficulties and undervalues desires for a biological legacy—desires that have persisted across time, culture, race, and class. Just as we do not compel fertile couples to help mitigate overpopulation by adopting rather than reproducing, we ought not to try forcing that alternative on infertile or homosexual couples. Such an approach woud be unlikely to prove effective. Rather, it would force surrogacy underground and offer fewer protections for all concerned, including the child.[58]

To some commentators, such considerations argue for full enforcement of surrogacy contracts. In their view, as long as individuals make informed choices and bargain without fraud or misrepresentation, the law should uphold their agreements. Such an approach, proponents claim, is necessary to ensure full reproductive autonomy, maintain fundamental principles of contractual responsibility, reinforce father-child bonds, and minimize disputes that are costly for everyone involved. By giving full effect to surrogate contracts, including the gestational mother's obligation to relinquish the child, courts will discourage women with any ambivalence from making such agreements in the first instance.

Advocates of this free-market model see no reason to prefer the genetic or gestational mother who has changed her mind over the genetic father (and in cases of in vitro fertilization or embryo transfer, genetic mother). Any "disappointment" that the gestational "donor" feels in having to uphold her agreement has been thought less important than the "general utility in enforcing contracts per se, whether they be contracts . . . to buy a car or a house, to provide sperm, or be a host mother." Nor do these commentators have difficulty with enforcement of related contractual obligations designed to ensure healthy offspring. Unlike adoption cases, where allowing financial payments would add to the economic and social pressures already present for many unwed mothers, surrogates reach their decision prior to pregnancy, at a point involving far less stress and possible coercion. Also, unlike circumstances involving adoption, the parties offering financial assistance are not simply buying someone else's baby; they, too, have a biological relationship with the child.[59]

Such arguments, like those supporting the converse position, carry some force, but they fail to take adequate account of all the ethical and practical considerations at issue. Granting parties unrestricted contractual autonomy would invite exploitation and compromise fundamental moral principles. A mother forced to relinquish a child of her own flesh does not simply experience "disappointment," and the social "utility" of enforcing her agreement stands on different footing than enforcing sales agreements for automobiles. Just as we prohibit individuals from auctioning off their kidneys, we should ban some of the provisions common in surrogacy contracts. In the *Baby M.* case, for example, the surrogate mother, Mary

Beth Whitehead, consented to a variety of highly intrusive restrictions on her conduct during pregnancy; she agreed, for example, not to drink alcoholic beverages, not to take medication without a physician's consent (including nonprescription items such as aspirin), and not to abort the fetus unless it had a genetic or congenital abnormality *and* the genetic father, William Stern, requested it. Since the Supreme Court has struck down requirements of husbands' consent to abortion as a violation of women's fundamental rights of privacy, it is difficult to see why non-spouses should enjoy greater control over the decision than spouses. So too, long-standing contractual principles counsel against invasive judicial oversight of pregnant women's daily lives.[60]

Judges should be equally reluctant to enforce other provisions of contracts, like that between the Whiteheads and Sterns, which call for surrogate mothers not to "form or attempt to form a parent-child relationship" and to "surrender custody to [the father] after birth." The first of these provisions is not a matter that individuals can control, and the second is not one that courts should specifically enforce. Available research suggests that a woman generally forms strong attachments with her infant during pregnancy and childbirth. Such bonds cannot be set aside at will. Until the experience of birth, a mother cannot make an informed judgment about the psychological costs of severing these bonds. That is, in part, why adoption statutes grant a woman a specified time after delivery to determine whether to abide by any prior agreement to relinquish her child.[61]

A third approach is to resolve surrogacy-related disputes under the "best-interest-of-the-child" standard applicable in divorce proceedings. That was the approach of the trial court in *Baby M.;* indeed, the judge there explicitly refused to credit evidence concerning the psychological harm to mothers who give up their children, because such "testimony centers on adults and the only concern of the court is the child." However, that should not be the courts' only concern, particularly given their inability accurately to predict what will, ultimately, prove best for a given infant. As Chapter 7 indicated, existing research provides no basis for determining the effects of particular custodial dispositions except in extreme cases. Nor is there consensus about which, among a broad range of outcomes, are in fact "best." The standard invites decisionmaking that is intrusive, idiosyncratic, and class-biased.[62]

The *Baby M.* litigation illustrated as much. The issue, as the court framed it, was who could provide a better family environment. That inquiry seemed stacked from the outset. Mary Beth Whitehead was a high-school dropout and former delicatessen worker, married to an alcoholic who drove a sanitation truck and had financial difficulties. William Stern was a biochemist, married to a professor of pediatrics. Nonetheless, counsel found it necessary to produce evidence concerning virtually every aspect of Ms. Whitehead's life. Testimony focused not only on her conduct during the proceedings (her threats against the child and the Sterns, her dishonesty under oath, and her defiance of court orders), but also on the intimate details of her married life. "Expert" witnesses delivered opinions as to Whitehead's "preoccupation with grooming and remaining youthful," her "narcissis[tic]" decision to dye her hair, her inappropriate choice of toys for the infant (pandas rather than pots and pans), and her overly "enmeshed" involvement with her children. Nor did her opponents escape unscathed. Psychological profiles revealed Mr. Stern to have an "introverted" personality that suppressed hostility, while Mrs. Stern displayed some "conflict in handling instinctual drives." To the court, however, it was clear who could provide the "best" environment with the greatest opportunities for "athletic and music lessons" and a college education. While acknowledging Ms. Whitehead to be a good mother to her older children, the trial judge found her an inferior parent to the baby in dispute, and the State Supreme Court affirmed that judgment.[63]

In the view of many observers, this decision built on evidence that involved "hitting below the belt." In responding to such charges, counsel for the Sterns replied, "that's what the best interest test is all about, which side can better raise the child." What else the best-interest standard is about is money: who can not only provide the most economic advantages for that child but also hire the most effective attorneys and retain the most persuasive experts. Such costs can be substantial. In the *Baby M.* litigation, for example, Ms. Whitehead ended up not only with her own attorneys' fees, but with a court order to pay counsel for the Sterns (billed at half a million dollars), and the guardian *ad litem* (over $100,000). Yet ironically enough, Whitehead was also condemned by the court and commentators for publicity-mongering, the single strategy most likely to attract assistance in underwriting the costs of litigation.[64]

Problems with the best-interest standard also arise in divorce cases, but they are magnified in surrogacy disputes. In such disputes, courts have no extended history from which to infer who has been the child's primary caretaker. The infant cannot express a preference, and the court cannot allocate marital property or spousal-maintenance payments to reduce financial disparities between the parties. Moreover, given the critical importance of the first six months to a child's later development, delays in making final custodial placements carry special risks. Under these circumstances, the best-interest standard is often in the worst interest of all concerned.

A final alternative is to regulate surrogacy agreements in an effort to accommodate the various interests implicated. For example, the law could permit contractual arrangements but prohibit certain intrusive conditions, such as restrictions on a gestational mother's life-style during pregnancy or decision to have an abortion. It could also require opportunities for a woman to obtain independent psychological and legal counseling prior to signing an agreement. As in adoption cases, a mother could have a specified period (for example, thirty days) after childbirth during which she could change her mind, void the contract, and return the fee. To be sure, some women, particularly those suffering from postpartum depression, will not be ideally situated during this period to make irrevocable custody decisions. But such an approach would at least provide some recognition of the significance of maternal bonds, which may not be foreseeable at the point of contact, while also preventing costly litigation and delays in placing a vulnerable infant. Legislative frameworks could, in addition, insure further protections for the child, such as adequate record-keeping, screening for parental diseases, and requirements that the parties initiating such an arrangement accept a child with abnormalities. To prevent undue exploitation and commercialization, legislatures could also impose minimum restrictions concerning surrogate fees and set maximum third-party brokers' payments.[65]

Such an approach would not of course resolve all difficulties. Concerns about commodification, class exploitation, and psychological trauma will remain. But they are not unique to the surrogacy context. Nor will they be solved by legal prohibition. They call for a reassessment of broader social practices and priorities. We cannot let surrogacy become yet another vehicle for symbolic politics that deflects attention from the wider concerns it raises. Instead of fixation on a single poignant case like *Baby M.*, we must examine more carefully a host of less visible choices about research budgets and resource allocations. What kind of problems are we addressing, who is benefiting, and, most important, who is making the decisions? We cannot adequately address any single issue like surrogacy without confronting a more fundamental set of questions about how life is created, valued, and sustained.

The last quarter-century has witnessed profound changes in reproductive patterns and the next quarter-century promises developments that will be equally dramatic. In an era where children may be conceived, born, and raised by different sets of parents, our legal system must develop better strategies for supporting varied family relationships. Technology has brought us to the point at which sex need not involve procreation and procreation need not involve sex. Yet in the rush for "progress," we need to think more carefully about what precisely that means. As Jacques Ellul has suggested, "ours is a civilization committed to the quest for continually improved means to carelessly examined ends." Only by more searching inquiry into underlying cultural values and concrete social contexts can we begin to control technology before it controls us.[66]

Chapter 10

Sex and Violence

In 1853, Elizabeth Cady Stanton wrote Susan B. Anthony: "Man in his lust has regulated long enough this whole question of sexual intercourse. Now let the mother of mankind whose prerogative it is to set bounds to his indulgence, raise up and give this whole matter a thorough fearless explanation."[1]

For most of its first century, the American feminist movement declined Stanton's invitation. Although the evils of male licentiousness in general and female prostitution in particular were matters of concern, nothing approximating "fearless" or systematic scrutiny emerged until the latter part of the twentieth century. Issues surrounding the social construction of sexual coercion have remained relatively unexplored. As Catharine MacKinnon has noted, it has been "as if sexuality comes from the stork." At least some of this reticence is attributable to the reluctance of (typically male) policymakers to view sexual aggression and exploitation as a significant social problem. Until recently, there were no record-keeping procedures and no legal structures designed to deal with abuses such as sexual harassment or wife-beating. Laws concerning rape and prostitution, built on exaggerated notions of sexual difference and double standards of morality, often added to victims' victimization. Much of what women suffered remained unnamed, unreported, unchallenged, and unchanged.[2]

With the rise of the contemporary women's movement, issues concerning sex and violence have attracted greater attention. Harassment, domestic violence, rape, prostitution, and pornography have all become targets of feminist inquiry and organization. As the pervasiveness of these practices has grown more apparent, their continuity with accepted social norms has also become more obvious. Boundaries between flirtation and harassment, seduction and rape, erotica and exploitation have provoked increasing controversy. In the process, the relationship between sexual desire and sexual domination has emerged as a central feminist concern.

Law, in both its practical and symbolic dimensions, has played a crucial role in these developments. Changes in legal frameworks have validated women's sense of violation and challenged traditional rationalizations for sexual coercion. At issue has been the assumption, long reflected in legal ideology and law-enforcement practices, that many women subject to aggression somehow desire, deserve, or provoke it. A central objective of contemporary feminists has been to shift the blame from victims to aggressors, and to the cultural forces that encourage them. Such efforts have again called into question traditional legal assumptions about sameness and difference and public and private. These developments have, in turn, given new force to Stanton's demand, and sparked more searching inquiries into the relationship between sexual identity and social subordination.

Sexual Harassment

Sexual harassment—legally defined as the imposition of unwelcome sexual demands or the creation of sexually offensive environments—has been a perennial problem. Until the late 1970s, it was one that the law discreetly overlooked. The injuries stemming from harassment were internalized, institutionalized, and, for the most part, inaudible.

That was not for lack of conceptual categories. In theory, many acts constituting sexual harassment fit within standard criminal and civil prohibitions, such as assault, battery, blackmail, lewdness, breach of contract, and intentional infliction of emotional distress. In practice, however, judicial solicitude traditionally confined itself to intermittent Victorian moralisms, in contexts where they were least helpful. For example, according to one nineteenth-century court, every woman railroad passenger was entitled to assume that she would "meet nothing, see nothing, hear nothing to wound her delicacy or insult her womanhood." Female employees or students, by contrast, were generally left to fend for themselves, and minority women were especially subject to abuse. Individuals whose livelihoods depended on continued employment were also particularly vulnerable to exploitation. Historical research on domestic servants, factory workers, sales personnel, and clerical employees leaves no doubt of the debilitating effects of sexual harassment. Refusal of an unwelcome overture could result in retaliation, dismissal, and an unfavorable reference. In the long term, acquiescence presented comparable risks and carried additional social and psychological costs. Sexual abuses and advances also perpetuated occupational subordination. By creating offensive working environments, male colleagues were often able to oust female intruders.[3]

With the increase in contemporary women's rights activity and labor-force participation, sexual harassment became more visible. Surveys of individuals in various academic and work environments revealed that between one-third and two-thirds of respondents had experienced some form of abuse. Studies by the United States Merit Protection Board found that roughly 42 percent of women and 14–15 percent of men reported incidents of harassment on their current job, ranging from unwanted sexual overtures to actual or attempted rape. According to Board estimates, 85 percent of working women would be subject to harassing behavior at some point in their lives.[4]

Such conduct has carried a substantial price. Contrary to popular myths, current research finds that males' sexual advances have rarely led to female advancement. Rather, the typical consequences for individual victims have included economic and psychic injuries, job dismissals, demotions or transfers; anxiety, depression, or other stress-related conditions; and loss of status and self-esteem. For women as a group, harassment has served to perpetuate views of females as sexual objects, to intimidate them from entering nontraditional occupations, and to impair their educational and employment performance, all of which reinforce patterns of gender inequality. For employers and society as a whole, the costs of such behavior have included decreased productivity and increased turnover. Yet despite these consequences, many employers have been reluctant to institute grievance procedures. Most victims have been equally reluctant to use them, largely out of a conviction that it would do no good. They have largely been right.[5]

Despite the broad array of studies documenting sexual harassment, its status as a "problem" has remained problematic. Blaming the victim has been a national pastime. Many public- and private-sector officials have shared the assumptions about the gender difference and double standards that have traditionally obscured exploitative conduct. According to Phyllis Schlafly, testifying in 1981 congressional hearings, for the "virtuous" woman, harassing behavior has not been a problem except in the "rarest of cases." Those who conform to appropriate standards of feminine decorum need not worry. Corporate managers and university administrators have similarly assumed that women who are not "smart enough" to cope with unwelcome advances are not smart enough to be in environments that present such difficulties. Generalizing from their own experience, many male business executives have found it impossible to believe that female employees are really troubled by sexual overtures. As one respondent to a *Harvard Business Review* survey put it, "I have never been harassed, but I would welcome the opportunity."[6]

As in other contexts involving sexual aggression, women's complaints have been dismissed as vindictive fantasies or wishful thinking. An all-too-typical administrator's response to the claims of a female prison guard was: "I can't believe anyone propositioned her. Have you ever seen her? She just wishes someone would make an advance at her and is angry because no one did." Gender differences in sexual roles have contributed to gender differences in sexual perceptions. What men often experience as fun or flirtation, women often experience as degrading and demanding. And it is male experience that has shaped the law's traditional responses to sexual harassment.[7]

Legal responses have been inadequate in several respects, although receptivity has improved markedly since the first litigation of sexual-harassment claims during the mid-1970s. Much of the initial decision-making was inconsistent and incoherent. Federal district judges typically viewed harassing behavior as isolated and idiosyncratic, or as natural and universal, and, in either case, as inappropriate for legal intervention. To some courts, such conduct seemed attributable to aberrant "personal proclivities," for which employers should not be held accountable. Other judges took a converse view of similar behavior; it was "natural," not deviant, a "normal and expectable" consequence of the "attraction of males to females and females to males."[8]

As with other legal issues, courts often obscured analysis by focusing on sex-based difference rather than sex-based disadvantage. By considering physiological drives, abstracted from their cultural context, some federal judges were able to find harassment, like pregnancy, unrelated to "gender as such." From this perspective, sex-based exploitation did not constitute sex-based discrimination. Women workers allegedly were penalized not because they were women but because they refused to engage in intimate activity or become enmeshed in an "inharmonious personal relationship." Their sex seemed only "incidental to the claims of the abuse."[9]

Attempts to fit sexual harassment within traditional antidiscrimination paradigms also confronted a certain conceptual embarrassment. According to the conventional approach, harassment constitutes sex discrimination if the victim would not have suffered had it not been for his or her sex. Under such a framework, a bisexual who harassed both male and female subordinates would not be subject to liability. This apparent anomaly convinced some courts to bar relief to all claimants, despite the absence of any evidence indicating that such bisexual advances occurred in the case at issue or in other workplace settings. What remained unclear was why this purely hypothetical and presumably rare circumstance should set the terms for legal recovery. As feminists argued with increasing success during the late 1970s, why not simply permit a defense for those willing and able to prove that they harassed both sexes equally?[10]

Much of the doctrinal resistance to harassment claims weakened in

1980, when the Equal Employment Opportunities Commission (EEOC) issued guidelines characterizing sexual harassment as a form of unlawful sex-based discrimination under Title VII. In 1986, in its first decision on point, *Meritor Savings Bank, FSB v. Vinson,* the Supreme Court endorsed that characterization and provided firmer grounding for the two forms of liability that had been gaining recognition in the lower courts. Such liability, as defined by EEOC guidelines, involves "quid pro harassment," sexual advances and related conduct where the response affects employment decisions; and "work environment harassment," conduct that unreasonably interferes with an individual's work performance or that creates an "intimidating, hostile or offensive" working environment. However, the *Vinson* decision left unsettled the scope of employers' liability for acts undertaken without their direct knowledge, as well as the implications of their failure to establish adequate grievance procedures for harassment complaints. Even more disturbing was the Court's unqualified holding that a plaintiff's "sexually provocative" speech or dress was relevant to whether allegedly offensive conduct was in fact offensive.[11]

Absent from this analysis, and from similar lower court decisions, was any sensitivity to the costs of raising harassment claims. As in other civil and criminal contexts, allowing defendants broad scope to place the plaintiff's conduct on trial requires victims to intensify their injury in order to remedy it. For most complainants, the prospect of sweeping scrutiny of their own sexual relationships, behavior, and attire provides a substantial deterrent to litigation. This effect has been exacerbated by some courts' requirement that victims show that they resisted or complained about unwanted sexual demands, despite the risks of retaliation that such actions often entail. In essence, this approach prohibits harassment of those ill-positioned to refuse only if they in fact do manage to refuse. Women whose injury stems from being forced to submit are assumed not to suffer any injury at all.[12]

Even courts that have not imposed such evidentiary burdens have displayed attitudes likely to discourage litigation. Recoveries have remained quite limited. Habitual harassers have escaped with job suspensions or mandates to apologize, while victims have been transferred, ridiculed, and denied compensation for their psychic injuries. Courts have stigmatized complainants' "aggressive," "abrasive," and "antagonistic" conduct, while dismissing the harassment that provoked it as an inevitable byproduct of a society that "condones [vulgarity and] exploits . . . erotica." Most judges have refused to order reinstatement where it might cause continued friction, but have failed to explain why victims, not perpetrators, must forfeit their jobs.[13]

In some jurisdictions, the definitions of prohibited conduct have been as restrictive as the remedies provided for it. Courts have trivialized abusive behavior as a "dalliance," "flirtation," "game," or series of "minor physical intimacies." When finding liability, some judges have cast their decisions in cautionary or faintly apologetic tones. Remedies will not be forthcoming for "petty slights suffered by the hypersensitive," but only for "sustained, malicious, or brutal harassment." Title VII is not to function as a "clean language act," nor does it require employers "to extirpate all signs of centuries-old prejudices." What constitutes "malicious" ultimately depends on the perceptions of the judge rather than the victim, and the vestiges of long-standing prejudices do not seem entirely absent from judicial as well as workplace forums. The attitude conveyed by many of these decisions was expressed with unusual candor by one district court in the early 1980s: "So we will have to hear [your complaint], but the court doesn't think too much of it."[14]

Underlying these decisions are, of course, certain obvious concerns about frivolous or retaliatory lawsuits. Many individuals meet their future spouses in employment settings, and federal courts are not particularly desirable chaperones for courtship rituals. Not all consensual romantic conduct ends happily, and there are costs in adding litigation to the wounds of unrequited affection. Women experience considerable difficulty finding mentors in employment and academic settings, and it is often claimed that the threat of harassment charges can only amplify that problem. But given the financial and psychological costs of bringing such lawsuits and the limited remedies available, it is doubtful that unfounded claims will be more prevalent in this context than in any other. As with rape, empirical research discloses high levels of underreporting rather than the reverse, and substantial corroborating evidence is present in most cases actually filed.[15]

Despite significant progress, a wide schism remains between the way women experience and the way the law defines sexual harassment. Bridging that gap will require changes in doctrines that victimize victims and absolve employers. Implicit assumptions about gender difference and the double standard of morality they endorse should no longer shape legal proceedings. Again, we need less attention to difference and more to disadvantage. Plaintiffs should not be required to litigate the length of their hemlines in order to recover for conduct that a "reasonable person" in their position would find offensive. If the plaintiff is a woman, then "reasonable" should be assessed from the perspective of a woman; that is, after all, her position. Employers should also be liable for harassment whether or not they know of its occurrence. As courts have recognized in other employment-discrimination contexts, the primary objective of Title VII is to prevent and redress unlawful conduct. That objective is ill served by limiting recovery to instances where an employer directly condones such conduct. We do not require plaintiffs in race-discrimination cases to prove that management was aware of subordinates' racism; plaintiffs in sex-harassment cases should be treated no differently. Nor should we absolve defendants for sexually offensive behavior that seems a "natural" outgrowth of broader cultural norms. To make substantial progress toward gender equality, those norms must change.[16]

The doctrinal history of harassment points up the power and limitations of legal rights as a strategy for social change. The establishment of sexual exploitation as a legal claim has served both to confer and constrain power. Judicial recognition has been critical in legitimating the injuries that stem from harassment and transforming a personal problem into a political issue. Individuals' experience of injury is often shaped by whether they can "get anyone to do anything about it." Establishing a basis for legal liability thus can help reshape women's consciousness as well as men's behavior.[17]

Since the cost of such liability is generally more visible than the cost of harassment, instituting grievance channels creates new incentives for employers and educators to find less formal means of deterring as well as redressing complaints. A decade's worth of litigation has helped increase training programs, complaint procedures, and guidelines concerning sexual harassment, though much remains to be done and more research is required to identify the most effective approaches. But the prospect of legal liability has unquestionably nudged employers and educators in the right direction. Of equal, if not greater importance, is the public exposure that the threat of formal complaints entails. After the *New York Times* provided details of how one president of a major university fondled a female subordinate at a public function, the victim's point may have been made without legal intervention.[18]

Yet as critical legal theorists have often emphasized, overreliance on rights can disempower as well as empower. The price of legitimating victims' injuries can be to legitimate a framework that will not fully redress them. For most women, the embarrassment and evidentiary hurdles of complaint procedures and the financial expenses associated with litigation will be prohibitive. Developing a conceptual cubbyhole for harassment claims is a substantial advance, but it should not foster the illusion that the problem has been solved. We cannot respond adequately to harassment without responding also to the institutional conditions that sustain it—the gender stereotypes, occupational stratification, and remedial barriers that are endemic to American workplaces. Nor can we ignore the difficulties of educating judges about the costs of harassment as victims experience it.

In this, as in other contexts, legal rights must be taken as means, not ends. Sustained litigation can help establish sexual harassment as a social problem. It can also mitigate the economic losses of individuals prepared to bring formal proceedings, and the sense of degradation and self-doubt of individuals who are not. But law is only a first step in transforming the social realities that it has so long ignored.

Domestic Violence

Women have been battered for centuries, but it was not until the 1970s that their private experience became a public concern. Like sexual harassment, domestic violence has been an area where the force of law meddled little with the law of force. Until the emergence of the modern feminist movement, virtually no information was available concerning the frequency or severity of family assaults. This total absence of data about the problem was itself part of the problem.

Although systematic research has been limited and underreporting substantial, recent studies are beginning to sketch the dimensions of domestic brutality. In any given year, estimates suggest that 10 to 20 percent of American women are beaten by a man with whom they are intimately involved, and one-fourth to one-half of all women will experience such violence at some point in their lives. This form of abuse, often generically described as "spousal violence," also includes assaults by cohabitants and former spouses or lovers. It accounts for more injuries to women than any other cause and can result in death or permanent impairment. About one-third of all female homicide victims are killed by a male friend or family member, and the vast majority of these women had suffered previous beatings. Violence against the elderly is also a serious social problem and, given women's greater longevity, it is gender-related.[19]

Of course, men and children (particularly girls) are also victims of domestic abuse. Violence against women is part of a broader pattern of family conflict that historically has prompted too little concern. Yet for purposes of this analysis, it is important to focus on brutality against women. Most research indicates that domestic assaults by men are much more frequent and severe than assaults by women, and much less likely to occur in self-defense. Moreover, the abuse women experience in family settings reflects and reinforces other patterns of gender inequality. As theorists including Linda Gordon, Catharine MacKinnon, and Robin West have emphasized, domestic violence is culturally constructed in its definition and in its causes. What constitutes unacceptable brutality and appropriate responses has varied according to political moods and movements. The conflicts that give rise to domestic violence are rooted in broader power relations and social norms. An important contribution of contemporary feminist scholarship is to expose the violent dimensions of family conflict and its similarity to other criminal behavior, without losing sight of its distinctively gendered character.[20]

Wife-beating is deeply rooted in the religious, legal, and cultural heritage of Anglo-American societies. Early Christian theology explicitly sanctioned male assaults as a means of securing female submissiveness. It was preferable for husbands to "punish the [wife's] body and correct the soul than to damage the soul and spare the body." Ecclesiastical doctrine presumed no similar necessity with respect to male souls, and that asymmetry was reflected in social attitudes. Although by the Reformation, official theology disapproved of chastisement, it remained publicly acceptable if kept within "reasonable" bounds. That tolerance found expression in William Blackstone's influential eighteenth-century commentaries on the common law. In his view, since a husband was legally accountable for his wife's behavior, it was "reasonable to entrust him with the power of restraint by domestic chastisement." Some early nineteenth-century American courts similarly approved the husband's authority to administer "moderate" discipline without threat of "vexatious prosecution." From this perspective, "moderate" usually encompassed anything short of life-threatening or permanent injury.[21]

By the end of that century, various cultural trends, including the rise of a women's movement, had helped to establish wife-beating as a criminal offense. If sufficiently severe, it was also grounds for divorce in most jurisdictions. The most effective sanction, however, was usually community disapproval, sometimes buttressed by pressure from the wife's family. In the absence of informal controls, women's formal options were extremely limited. Divorce was unavailable if the wife had continued to live with an assaultive husband or had "provoked" his abuse, and definitions of provocation were expansive. "Passionate language" or refusal to have sexual relations could be sufficient legal justifications for physical reprisals.[22]

Even where grounds for divorce were present, the absence of adequate welfare, alimony, and child support often made separation impractical if not impossible. Although clients of nineteenth- and early-twentieth-century child-welfare agencies forced many social workers to confront issues of spousal as well as child abuse, available remedies were grossly inadequate. No assistance was thought appropriate for those who departed from middle-class norms—mothers who worked, drank, or remained unmarried. Yet women who conformed to appropriate gender roles had little chance to stop the abuse; effective intervention by law-enforcement officials was extremely unlikely.[23]

The inadequacy of remedies for spousal brutality, which often occurred under the influence of alcohol, accounted in part for widespread female support of the temperance movement. "Drinking" was often a code word for violence; the label allowed social reformers to attack male abusiveness obliquely, without appearing to attack men in general or marital hierarchies in particular. But this strategy ultimately misconceived both the problem and the solution. Empirical and cross-cultural data make clear that drunken behavior is learned behavior; alcohol is less a root cause of violent interactions than a facilitator and a rationalization for them.[24]

Inadequacies in legal responses stemmed from similar misconceptions. A major difficulty involved police attitudes and practices. Until the late 1970s, the general view was that assaults within families—euphemistically categorized as "domestic disturbances"—were relatively unimportant and that intervention was generally ineffective. Although studies during the 1970s indicated that such "disturbances" accounted for approximately one-third of the calls for police assistance, and a comparable percentage of police injuries, police training academies devoted less than 2 percent of program hours to the problem. The instruction that was available further trivialized the issue. According to an influential International Association of Police Chiefs' training manual, an officer's "sole responsibility" in domestic violence cases was to "preserve the peace." He should attempt to "pacify the parties," refer them to community agencies, and arrest only as "a last resort." Officers should "never create a police problem where there [was] only a family problem existing."[25]

Until the 1980s, police departments generally trained officers to conciliate in response to most domestic violence. Under the prevailing "stitch rule," arrest was appropriate only when the victim's injuries were so severe as to require surgical sutures. In other cases, the police typically instructed the parties to "break it up," "reason together," or "take a walk," and routinely failed to advise women of their right to file a complaint. Male officers often identified with male assailants and assumed that female victims provoked or subconsciously enjoyed their abuse. As one policeman put it, women "must like it or they wouldn't stay." Dispatchers attached low priority to domestic calls, an approach reinforced by other law-enforcement officials. It made sense to avoid "messing up someone's docket" as long as "nothing [would] happen" when such disputes got into court.[26]

Prosecutors traditionally worked on similar assumptions. Overburdened and underfunded district attorneys often resisted using courts for "personal quarrels." Such disputes did not, in their judgment, "deserve" a twelve-person jury. Everyone would be better off if the parties would simply "kiss and make up" and courts could focus on "real felons." Many judges took a similar view. In a representative case from the 1920s, the court, relying on psychiatric "insight," attributed a husband's brutality to his wife's "upset and undemonstrative" attitudes during menopause. The response was not criminal sanctions, but an admonition to the defendant to show more "tender care and affection particularly during this trying time of life." Such judicial and prosecutorial attitudes, together with fear of spousal retaliation, often deterred battered women from seeking legal remedies. The infrequency of formal complaints became a self-fulfilling prophecy. District attorneys who doubted that victims would cooperate established special requirements of credibility and tenaciousness that discouraged cooperation. Beginning in the late 1960s, studies of attrition rates indicated that fewer than 3 percent of the women who sought to file complaints succeeded in doing so, and that fewer than 10 percent of the complaints that police forwarded for prosecution resulted in formal proceedings. According to a 1982 United States Civil Rights Commission report, the odds of a spousal abuse case ending up in court were about one hundred to one.[27]

Some of this attrition resulted from diversion programs. Formalized in the late 1960s, such programs sought to provide a less costly and more therapeutic response to family violence than did criminal proceedings. As diversion alternatives evolved over the next two decades, they generally provided for withdrawal of charges against assailants who completed a specified number of mediation or counseling sessions. This strategy has proven problematic on several grounds. By suggesting that victims and assailants share responsibility for abuse and its prevention, a mediation-conciliation framework can perpetuate attitudes that perpetuate violence. Most contemporary research on batterers has emphasized one characteristic common to men with otherwise widely varying backgrounds and personality profiles: a tendency to blame their victims for causing violence and to minimize its severity. Those tendencies gain legitimacy through a legal response that avoids attaching criminal sanctions to assaultive behavior and instructs victims to modify their conduct in return for their assailants' promises to modify theirs; for example, the husband agrees to stop beating his wife if she agrees to keep the house tidier.[28]

Related problems stem from the power imbalance between the parties and the involuntary nature of their participation in diversion programs. The theory of mediation—that individuals can come together on a relatively equal footing to reconcile differences in a cooperative atmosphere—is ill-suited to the power dynamics of many domestic conflicts. Although research on diversion programs has been largely impressionistic, it suggests that many husbands have lacked the motivation to change and that wives have been caught in patterns of economic, physical, and psychological subordination that prevent effective mediating strategies.[29]

Whatever the problems with diversion programs, there have been at least equal difficulties with the alternative. Family court judges historically have been unsympathetic toward battered women who were prepared to "wash [their] dirty linen" in public. In some jurisdictions, temporary restraining orders to protect victims have been unavailable in "household disputes." First offenders have received lenient treatment, and second-

and third-time assailants have not fared significantly worse. Studies in the late 1970s and 1980s found that batterers routinely ended up with minimal fines and suspended sentences. In one survey of 350 abused wives, none of the husbands served time in jail. Two of the most notorious reported cases involved a convicted assailant whose fine was suspended on condition that he buy his wife a box of candy, and a habitual offender released five times on his promise to stop his abuse. In the second case, the wife lost an eye and part of an ear, and finally resolved the matter herself, by suicide.[30]

Despite increasing evidence of the serious consequences that follow from wife abuse, many judges' attitudes have remained unchanged; as a consequence, traditional boundaries between public and private have persisted. Contemporary task-force reports on gender bias in the courts have found repeated nonenforcement of protective orders, trivialization of complaints, and disbelief of female petitioners absent visible evidence of severe injuries. Some judges have instructed parties to "kiss and make up and get out of my court"; others have assumed that the problem would vanish if wives would just show a little initiative. Blame lies not with the men who batter but with the women who stay. "All they have to do," one judge explained, "is to get out of the house. It's as simple as that." In 1987 a Massachusetts trial judge castigated a battered wife for wasting his time with her request for a protective order. If she and her husband wanted to "gnaw" on each other, "fine," but they "shouldn't do it at the taxpayer's expense." A subsequent report noted that the wife is now dead and her husband awaits trial for murder, "at the taxpayer's expense."[31]

In response to such attitudes among judges, prosecutors, and police, some women have resorted to self-defense. Yet many of them have faced difficulties justifying their conduct under conventional legal principles. One study of Illinois women convicted of homicide revealed that 40 percent had been battered by the decedent and had sought assistance from the police. However, such women have often failed to meet the legal requirements for self-defense as traditionally applied; their force has appeared excessive and their danger less than imminent. In circumstances where wives can leave their husbands, standard legal doctrine has appeared to offer no excuse.[32]

Missing from that framework has been any sensitivity to the psychological and economic constraints confronting these women. By the late 1970s a growing body of research had begun to define the behavioral patterns that kept victims in abusive relationships. This "battered woman syndrome" has been most prevalent among individuals who identify themselves primarily as homemakers and who internalize blame for the violence they suffer. After a cycle of beatings that they cannot prevent, and a series of experiences that makes escape appear psychologically impossible, economically ruinous, or an invitation to further brutality, these women begin to perceive themselves as "helpless." This perception then "becomes reality and [victims] become passive, submissive, and helpless." Finding themselves unable to leave the relationship, some victims finally respond to extreme fear with extreme force.[33]

To escape that pattern, many women need support structures that have often been unavailable. Until the late 1970s, there were almost no shelters, counseling services, or vocational training programs for victims of domestic violence. Welfare and public housing were frequently unavailable, since officials counted husbands' assets in determining wives' eligibility. Such governmental policies reinforced women's sense of helplessness. They were unable to separate without financial assistance and unable to obtain it until they separated.[34]

During the late 1970s, the inadequacy of legal practices and social services involving battered women came under increasing challenge. The American women's movement, building on strategies developed by British feminists earlier in the decade, began establishing shelters, lobbying for legislation and financial assistance, and suing various law-enforcement officials. The central goal was to make legal decisionmakers treat domestic violence as a significant criminal offense and a pervasive social problem.[35]

Such efforts met with partial success. Several well-publicized litigation settlements, together with the first systematic research comparing police practices, convinced many policymakers that arrest was more successful than conciliatory approaches in preventing future abuse. Prosecutors and judges began to take domestic violence more seriously and to work with victim-assistance programs to improve legal responses. By the early 1980s, several hundred shelters were in operation. All but two states had developed coalitions of service-providers, and all but one had passed legislation expanding remedies for family assaults and imposing duties on law-enforcement officials. Most jurisdictions had also established funding mechanisms for battered-women programs, often through surcharges on marriage licenses.[36]

For assault victims, the law on self-defense gradually improved. Expert testimony on the battered-woman syndrome more frequently became admissible at trial to explain why defendants remained in abusive relationships. Although progress was uneven, standards for determining whether a woman's fear of injury and use of force were reasonable began to take into account her limited social options.[37]

As leaders in the batterd-women's movement have recognized, these developments can be double-edged. Theories of "learned helplessness" have aided in revealing the sources of women's disempowerment at the risk of obscuring their capacities for resistance. By emphasizing battered women's deviance and dependence, such theories can also reinforce gender stereotypes or divert attention from the frequency of domestic violence and the social conditions that encourage it. The challenge remaining is to use explanations of women's "victimization" in ways that avoid perpetuating that status. A central objective is to highlight the continuing inadequacies in legal responses, scholarly research, and social resources. We need, for example, increased judicial education and more effective, accessible procedures for temporary restraining orders, low-cost divorces, and child-support enforcement. Without more systematic studies, it is impossible to formulate appropriate strategies of legal intervention and treatment. Domestic violence is one area in which further data can make an enormous difference. Much of the progress since the early 1970s has been attributable to research that has exposed the dimensions and dynamics of battering; we have yet to identify effective strategies for ending it. Critical unresolved questions concern the effects of various mandatory arrest, determinate sentencing, incarceration, and counseling approaches.

Related issues involve victims' influence over prosecutorial decisions. Many battered women face continuing physical, psychological, and economic coercion, and are poorly situated to choose among alternative dispositions for their assailants. Accordingly, some feminists have opposed vesting these women with the kind of discretion that might subject them to intensified pressure and leave serious violence unpunished. Other feminists have argued with equal force that victims will be less likely to seek help if they have no control over the consequences. Since it is the woman's life and safety that are most affected by choices about disposition, many activists have sought to insure her power over the process. This controversy cannot be resolved in the abstract. Without better research on the consequences of victim control, it is difficult to assess the merits of alternative prosecutorial policies.[38]

The inadequacy of longitudinal data on various counseling and social-service approaches makes it equally difficult to establish resource priorities. What evidence is available, however, indicates that many effective programs are seriously underfunded. Battered-women's shelters have been able to meet only a small fraction of community needs, and policymakers have been unresponsive to the problem. Congressional opponents have blocked some funding initiatives for domestic abuse programs, in part on the ground that the government has "no business intruding into family disputes" or subsidizing "missionaries who would war on the traditional family." As one conservative Republican Senator warned, "what kinds of values and ideas" would homes for battered women advance? Although modest federal assistance became available in the 1980s, governmental leaders have remained more disposed to praise than to subsidize necessary services. For example, after stressing the importance of battered-women's shelters and related programs, the 1984 Attorney General's Task Force Report on Family Violence placed responsibility on each state to find "creative funding" for them.[39]

What the Task Force did not acknowledge is the need for strategies beyond those explicitly directed at victims and perpetrators. Family violence is a symptom as well as a cause of women's subordination. As long as women are economically dependent on men, and both sexes are socialized to accept male aggression and female passivity, abuse will remain pervasive. Changing the conditions that foster violence requires changing cultural perspectives and priorities. It demands sustained challenges to media presentations, educational programs, and social services. In order for women to leave an abusive relationship, they must be able to support themselves and their children. Ensuring opportunities for economic independence will require restructuring a vast range of social policies regarding employment, education, divorce, legal services, childcare, housing, and welfare. Only as women achieve equality in the public sphere are they likely to break patterns of aggression and submission in the private sphere.

Challenging these patterns must be a crucial part of any societal strategy to control violence. Most available research indicates that assaultive behavior is learned behavior, and that abuse against women builds on traditional assumptions about gender roles. Children's exposure to domestic violence and sex-based stereotypes socializes them to accept such violence as a legitimate response to stress. Studies of battered spouses consistently reflect that men who grow up in abusive home environments are far more likely to become abusive as adults. Failure to find more effective responses to domestic violence in this generation will intensify our problems in the next.[40]

Rape

Unlike domestic violence and sexual harassment, rape has long been recognized as a serious legal offense. Some forms of coercive sex have been unlawful for over two millennia. What is new is an understanding of such offenses that reflects women's experience. Rape has traditionally been defined by male views of male sexuality. To a considerable extent, prohibitions on force against women have functioned to protect men. Historically, rape has been perceived as a threat to male as well as female interests; it has devalued wives and daughters and jeopardized patrilineal systems of inheritance. But too stringent constraints on male sexuality have been equally threatening to male policymakers. The threat of criminal charges based on female fabrications has dominated the history of rape law. As a result, the offense has been hedged with substantive exceptions and procedural safeguards that leave considerable latitude for aggression.

Traditional understandings of rape have reflected a pronounced sexual schizophrenia. One form of abuse—intercourse achieved through physical force against a chaste woman by a stranger—has been treated as the archetypal antisocial crime. By contrast, coercive sex that has departed from this paradigm frequently has been denied or discounted. The attitude, well-captured by a popular army slogan, has been: "it never happened, and what's more, [she] deserved it." The criminal justice system has reflected this ideological oscillation. At the level of formal pronouncement, some sexual abuses have been subject to long-standing prohibition and severe (sometimes draconian) penalties. At the level of actual practice, most coercive sex has remained unacknowledged and unpunished.[41]

Anglo-American rape law builds on a history of class, race, and gender biases. In many ancient societies such as Babylonia and Assyria, the severity of the offense depended on the social and sexual status of the victim. Rape of a virgin was worse than rape of a married woman, but, ironically enough, the punishment was not directed solely at the aggressor. Rather, in some cultures the victim was required to marry her assailant, and her father was entitled to rape the aggressor's wife or sister. Early English law also graded offenses not by the brutality of the crime but by the status of the victim. Rape of a propertied virgin could result in castration or death; assaults against nuns, wives, or widows received lesser penalties. Since a woman's status was to a considerable extent derivative, the vindication of her injury often depended on her relationship to men. So, for example, rape of a nobleman's serving maid cost twelve shillings; rape of a commoner's maid only five.[42]

The social class of victims and assailants had a profound effect on subsequent law in fact if not in form. Just as medieval tracts for courtiers recommended a "little compulsion as a convenient cure for [peasant women's] shyness," many law-enforcement officials continued to look indulgently on gentlemen who followed such advice. In the United States, similar distinctions were based on race as well as class. Rapes of black women by white men were often discreetly overlooked, while black men accused of raping white women ran the risk of show trials, disproportionate sanctions, and lynch mobs. One Southern Senator's 1930 campaign pledge in support of lynching exemplified prevailing attitudes: "Whenever the Constitution comes between me and the virtue of the white women of the South, I say to hell with the Constitution." Between 1945 and 1965, a death sentence was eighteen times more likely for convicted black rapists with white victims than for any other racial combination. Despite evidence that rape has been an overwhelmingly intraracial crime, and its victims primarily black, visions of white women defiled by nonwhite "rape fiends" persisted.[43]

Although the punishments for certain forms of rape have remained severe throughout the nineteenth and twentieth centuries, only a tiny fraction of sexual assaults have resulted in such sanctions. Difficulties in defining the offense have made for difficulties in assessing attrition rates. It is, however, clear that relatively few rapes have been reported, and fewer still have been investigated and successfully prosecuted. Conservative estimates suggest that between 20 to 30 percent of females over the age of twelve will experience a violent sexual assault outside of marriage at some point in their lives. Recent studies suggest that rape is the most underreported of all violent crimes, although the precise extent of underreporting is subject to dispute. Estimates of the percentage reaching police attention range from 5 to 50 percent, and much appears to depend on how one surveys possible victims. Women have been reluctant to report sexual assaults to researchers as well as to police, and the history of racist enforcement practices has been an additional deterrent for minorities. So too, many victims of forcible sexual intercourse with acquaintances do not label it rape. To the question "have you ever been raped," the response is often something on the order of "well . . . not exactly." What happens in the pause between "well" and "not exactly" reflects the gap between the legal understanding and social experience of rape, between women's perception of force and their perception of whether the criminal justice system is likely to do anything about it.[44]

Even if only reported rapes are considered, the attrition rate from complaints to convictions is high. Prior to reform efforts in the late 1970s, the percentage of complaints considered "founded" (that is, meriting criminal charges) by the police, and the percentage of arrests thought worthy of prosecution by district attorneys, were unusually low. New York may have been the worst case, with 2,415 complaints, 1,085 arrests, and 18 convictions in 1969. Although some data suggest that attrition rates for rape are no longer disproportionately high in comparison with other major felonies, the likelihood of a complaint actually ending in conviction is generally estimated at 2 to 5 percent.[45]

At least some of the difficulties in obtaining convictions for rape have stemmed from its traditional definition and its evidentiary requirements. As with other issues of sexual coercion, legal ideology has incorporated stereotypical views of gender differences and double standards of morality. Early common law described the crime as a man's sexual intercourse with a woman not his wife against her will. As the offense evolved, it also came to require force or the threat of force by the assailant and physical resistance by the victim. Although many other offenses have depended on the absence of consent, they generally have not required physical force but have encompassed means such as deception, blackmail, or prior violence. Nor has any other offense required victims to respond with physical resistance, and thus to risk intensifying their injuries in order to prove them.[46]

These requirements have both limited the prosecution of sexual assaults and perpetuated sexual stereotypes. According to some national surveys, physical force is absent in over half of all rapes; a third involve no weapons. Most assaults occur through threats of force, and victims' most common response is verbal protest. Many are paralyzed with fear, while others decide not to risk provoking further brutality by a physical struggle. Such responses fail to satisfy resistance requirements. In these cases, the law compounds the woman's injury by denying its existence. Victims who fail to fight are invited to believe either that they haven't really been raped or that they ought to have prevented it. By contrast, women who follow the law's mandate and struggle with their assailant are more likely to suffer physical injuries than those who do not. It is a perverse dilemma, grounded in deeply sexist assumptions about female sexuality. The traditional requirement that women "resist to the utmost" reflected a kind of death-before-dishonor philosophy that has been only partially mitigated by modern demands of "reasonable" resistance.[47]

A related assumption is that rape victims have sent confused signals about their sexual desires. Building on crude Freudian analysis, legal scholars and policymakers have supposed that women often desire, and hence invent or invite, forced sex. John Wigmore, author of the nation's most influential treatise on evidence, relied on early-twentieth-century psychiatric insight for the proposition that "most" women at some point entertain "fleeting fantasies" of rape and that it was "easy for some neurotic individuals to translate their fantasies into actual beliefs and memory falsifications." In a similar vein, law review commentators throughout the 1950s and 1960s asserted that it was "customary" for a woman who desired intercourse to say "no, no, no," while meaning "yes, yes, yes." Since it was "always difficult in rape cases to determine whether the female really meant 'no'," she should be required to convey her resistance by more than "mere" verbal protest, or "such infantile behavior as crying." Although recent psychoanalytic research suggests that much of this scholarship has been grounded in male rather than female fantasies, its doctrinal legacy has endured.[48]

According to traditional legal ideology, not only have many women been unable to distinguish fact from fantasy, but an equally substantial number have been bent on deliberate fabrication. To guard against complainants motivated by spite, shame, guilt, or greed, courts have imposed a series of safeguards in addition to force and resistance requirements.

Some of these requirements are applicable in no other criminal contexts—that a victim's testimony be corroborated by other evidence, and that complaints be filed within three months of the alleged incident. For cases that managed to satisfy these mandates, courts traditionally instructed jurors to evaluate the testimony of a complaining witness with "special care in view of the emotional involvement of the witness and the difficulty of determining the truth with respect to alleged sexual activities carried out in private."[49]

The rationale for these requirements, expressed by a prominent eighteenth-century jurist, Matthew Hale, is that "rape is . . . an accusation easily to be made and hard to be proved and harder to be defended by the party accused though never so innocent." For two centuries Hale's observation has been cited with widespread approval but without empirical support. Although there have been celebrated cases of unjust convictions, particularly in interracial contexts, there is no systematic evidence that miscarriages of justice are more common for rape than for other offenses. Such evidence would, of course, be difficult to come by. However, empirical studies have consistently revealed that accusations of rape are less easily made and proved than accusations of any other serious offense. The stigma, intrusiveness, and risk of retaliation that accompany criminal charges have kept rape the most underreported major felony.[50]

For sexual coercion that departs from the traditional paradigm of chaste victim–violent stranger, the burden of proof has been exceptionally high. Lawyers and judges have tended to dismiss acquaintance or date rape as a "personal problem," rather than a criminal offense—as "felonious gallantry," or "assault with failure to please." Kalven and Zeisel's landmark study of jury behavior in the 1950s and subsequent surveys in the 1980s found ill-disguised hostility toward victims who had assertedly "assumed the risk" of attack by conduct such as drinking, wearing "seductive" clothing, or accepting a ride with their assailant. Women with unchaste reputations have met with similar treatment. The assumption, as expressed by nineteenth- and early-twentieth-century courts, was that the victim who was "spotless and pure," who preferred "death to pollution," was much less likely to consent than one who "incited by lust or lucre . . . ha[d] already submitted herself to the lewd embraces of another." Such attitudes have persisted. Surveys in the late 1970s and early 1980s reported that two-thirds of respondents believed that women provoked rape by their appearance and actions, and a majority of respondents agreed that victims in most rapes were promiscuous or had bad reputations.[51]

By this logic, it followed that evidence of a woman's prior sex life should be admissible, even under circumstances where the presence of force and absence of prior acquaintance made consent extremely unlikely. Until enactment of rape-shield statutes in the late 1970s, victims were twice assaulted, once by the assailant and once by the criminal justice system. Although inquiry into the defendant's sexual history or prior sexual offenses was generally impermissible on grounds of prejudice, the complainant could face cross-examination on all her previous intimate relationships, her methods of birth control, her attendance at bars, and even her children's erotic games.[52]

Not only did such cross-examination invite juries to believe that a woman who consented once would do so again, for anyone, anywhere, and anytime, but evidence of her "impurity" was relevant to issues other than consent. As one nineteenth-century court explained, "no evil habitude of humanity so depraves the [female] nature . . . as common, licentious indulgence. Particularly this is true of women whose character is virtue, whenever that is lost, all is gone; [their] love of justice, sense of character and regard for truth." To ensure that no one missed the significance of a victim's fall from grace, courts as late as the 1970s were routinely instructing juries that evidence of "unchaste character" was relevant in assessing credibility as well as consent.[53]

Such instructions invited confusion as to who exactly was on trial. As jury studies reflected, condemnation of the victim often meant acquittal for the assailant, even under circumstances clearly demonstrating rape. One of Kalvin and Zeisel's more memorable examples involved the exoneration of defendants who had kidnapped and sexually assaulted a woman whom the jury found unsympathetic because she had had an illegitimate child. Simulation studies have also found that rape of a divorcee results in shorter sentences than rape of a married woman, and interviews with trial judges in the 1970s and 1980s disclosed comparable biases. In their view, victims "asked for it" if they hitchhiked or dressed "provocative[ly]" by wearing short skirts, tight jeans, or no bras. In a series of Wisconsin cases in the middle 1980s, one judge described rape as a normal response to a permissive society, and another characterized a five-year-old victim "an unusually promiscuous young lady." A similar New York case, which ultimately resulted in a censure of the judge, began when a masked assailant broke into a woman's apartment, raped her, and passed out drunk in her bed. In response to protests against the minimal sentence the judge intended to impose, he explained to the press: "As I recall [the defendant] did go into [the victim's] apartment without permission . . . I think [the sexual intercourse] started without consent, but maybe they ended up enjoying themselves."[54]

As traditionally applied, rape law has declined to protect not only unchaste women but also chaste wives. During the late eighteenth century, husbands' exemption from liability for coercive intercourse became explicit. The initial rationale for the exception rested on two related theories. The first, according to Matthew Hale, was that by her "matrimonial consent and contract, the wife hath given up herself in this kind unto her husband which she cannot retract." Having promised to love, honor, and obey, a woman was obligated to submit; in addition, since common-law notions of marital unity held that husband and wife were one, a married man could not readily be found guilty of raping himself.[55]

As these rationales grew increasingly anachronistic, they were replaced by various policy arguments, many of them inconsistent. As with sexual harassment, the claim was that marital rape occurred so infrequently that legal remedies were unnecessary or, alternatively, that it occurred so frequently that any remedial structure would be overwhelmed with complaints. Defenders of the exemption also claimed that whatever minimal injury wives suffered, state oversight would be worse. Vindictive women assertedly would file complaints to blackmail their husbands or extort better settlements in divorce proceedings. State officials would become voyeurs of activity "behind the bedroom door," meddlers in "normal sexual relations."[56]

Much depends on one's view of "normal." During the 1970s, those views came under increasing challenge. The marital rape exception became a target for reforms less because feminists believed that its erosion would result in widespread prosecution than because its presence remained symbolic and symptomatic of gender domination. According to the most systematic studies available, between 10 and 15 percent of married women experience forcible sex with their husband, and many suffer severe physical or psychological injuries as a consequence. Attempts to criminalize such conduct have underscored both the pervasiveness of sexual coercion and the inadequacies of its legal definition. As researchers have increasingly noted, rape is "simply at the end of the continuum of male/aggressive female/passive patterns, and an arbitrary line has been drawn to mark it off from the rest of such relationships." The legality of forcible sex within marriage emphasizes that arbitrariness, particularly when it occurs in tandem with other physical abuse or among couples who are separated.[57]

In this context, concerns about marital privacy are often misdirected. It is not the recognition of wives' right to bodily integrity that threatens marital relations; it is the violation of that right. Contrary to popular assumption, spousal rape is not less harmful than violent sexual assaults. Indeed, marital rape victims report more long-term injuries than women raped by strangers. Given the extended history of prosecutorial and judicial skepticism regarding acquaintance rape, it is unlikely that any significant number of husbands would risk unjust conviction. Indeed, the experience of the few states and foreign countries that have abolished spousal exemptions suggests that criminal proceedings will be rare, and will generally occur only in circumstances of separation and/or brutality.[58]

Despite that experience, as well as lobbying efforts by women's organizations, surveys in the late 1980s found that most states retained some form of the marital exemption. In many areas legislators declined even to take the issue seriously. After all, as one state senator put it, "if you can't rape your wife, who can you rape?" Nonetheless, in the late 1970s and 1980s almost half the states amended their laws to permit prosecution in some instances, usually when the couple had formally separated. However, over a quarter expanded the spousal exemption to encompass cohabitants, and a few jurisdictions made changes prohibiting first-degree rape charges if the parties had previously engaged in consensual sexual activity. Thus, in many states, conventional public and private boundaries remain unchallenged and unchanged.[59]

Much other contemporary reform activity has taken a similarly uneven course. Between the mid-1970s and mid-1980s, the number of reform and victim-assistance organizations grew from a few dozen to over 1500. During the same period, almost every state made some changes in its laws governing rape. Over half the states recharacterized the offense in various ways. Some relabeled the crime as assault, in order to emphasize its violent rather than sexual character and to shed some of its distinctive symbolic and substantive baggage. Changes included redefinitions of consent; elimination of resistance and corroboration requirements; modification of jury instructions; expansion of coverage to include acts other than intercourse and to protect men as well as women; restrictions on references to the victim's prior sexual activities; and modifications in penalty structures to establish gradations of liability, mandatory minimum sentences for repeat offenders, and less stringent punishments (in the hope of increasing the likelihood of conviction).[60]

Assessing the effectiveness of these reforms is difficult, given the complexity of forces that affect criminal behavior and law-enforcement responses. Removing certain barriers to prosecution may account for some of the increase in rape complaints, which have doubled since 1970 and tripled since 1960. It is, however, unclear how much of that growth is related to increases in violent crime in general, how much to increases in rape in particular, and how much to increases in victim reports. Measuring the effect of reform statutes on complaint disposition is equally difficult, although for different reasons. Comparing statistics from before and after reforms gives only a partial perspective, since some of the changes in attitudes necessary to secure legal initiatives may have had an impact before formal modifications were implemented. Other effects may take longer to become apparent than the period of study reflects.

Even granting these difficulties, it remains significant that law reforms have produced so few measurable changes. Michigan, the state that feminists in the mid-1980s generally identified as having the most progressive legislation in the country, experienced a slight increase in its conviction rate, but few other objective effects. In Washington, which also made major statutory modifications, arrest and conviction rates remained largely unchanged. Legislation restricting trial evidence of victims' sexual history has had a limited impact, in part because most defense attorneys continue to seek information through pretrial disclosure rules, and in part because many judges continue to admit such evidence under statutory exceptions. Where consent is at issue, trial proceedings can still transform the victim into the accused. Other changes in form have not always translated into changes in fact. For example, even after removal of a corroboration requirement, prosecutors have often declined to proceed without it. Nonetheless, most studies on rape law reform have identified some positive changes, including less trauma for victims and more sensitivity on the part of the public and law-enforcement officials, particularly with respect to nonstranger cases.[61]

These mixed results are not surprising. Most factors affecting the likelihood of conviction and the gravity of punishment are beyond the scope of antirape initiatives—factors such as the availability of witnesses or other circumstantial evidence and the applicability of general felony sentencing and parole policies. That is not, however, to understate the importance of continued reform efforts. Cross-cultural research suggests that the most effective changes in criminal law are those that protect victims and encourage higher conviction rates through graded offenses that focus on the conduct of assailants, rather than victims.[62]

To secure such changes will require increased pressure in the many jurisdictions that have failed significantly to modify formal or informal rules governing resistance, corroboration, marital rape, and evidence of prior sexual activity. Efforts are also necessary in every state to expand legal understandings of coercion. The crime of rape must be reconceptualized as the product of power, which can be exercised in ways other than physical force. The injury of rape must be redefined to reflect the experience of fear, betrayal, and degradation that results from sexual coercion by social acquaintances as well as strangers. Attention must center on the coerciveness of the act rather than the relationship of the parties. Such redefinitions cannot occur only through statutes. They require other measures such as rape counseling and crisis centers and educational programs for judges, law-enforcement personnel, and the general public.[63]

The point of reform is not simply to improve remedies for reported rapes but to alter their preconditions. Regional and cross-cultural comparisons suggest that sexual assault rates are lower in societies where women have gained greater influence, respect, and socioeconomic status. Studies of American rapists' attitudes have revealed a striking absence of guilt and a consistent perception of their conduct as normal sexual behavior. One critical function of law reform campaigns is to politicize those perceptions and focus attention on their broader ideological roots.[64]

As with sexual harassment and domestic violence, legal doctrine can make a difference—in validating injuries, in altering societal perceptions, and in laying the groundwork for further cultural change. These consequences are of critical significance not only for women who are raped, but also for the greater number who fear it and structure their lives to avoid it. As Susan Brownmiller has noted, sexual assault is debilitating in part because individuals experience some of its effects even if they are never actually assaulted. The challenge remaining is to redefine rape and, in the process, to challenge the social understandings of sexuality that legitimate it.[65]

Prostitution

Unlike sexual harassment, domestic violence, and rape, prostitution has long been a focus of feminist concern. During most of its first century, the American women's movement viewed prostitution as the preeminent metaphor for sexual oppression. The "social evil," variously defined, became the symbol of female subordination.

In explaining that focus, historians have identified a complex set of forces. Until the antebellum period, prostitution remained an unobtrustive presence on the social and legal landscape. Early-nineteenth-century common law did not criminalize prostitution per se, although it could be prosecuted under other offenses such as lewdness, fornication, adultery, or disorderly conduct. The shortage of women and the tight-knit character of American communities worked against commercial vice. Much of the adult sexual exploitation that occurred involved slaves and domestic servants rather than an independent class of prostitutes. With industrialization and urbanization, as well as immigration from the East and migration to the West, prostitution became more visible. As single men moved to the frontier, they decreased the supply of eligible bachelors in established communities and increased the demand for sexual outlets in unsettled regions. Markets also emerged near military camps and seaports. Women, particularly immigrants, who could find neither husbands nor adequate employment, were increasingly likely to conclude that the "wages of sin" were better than any available alternative. The relative anonymity of urban areas, the growing secularization of American society, and the tacit tolerance of law-enforcement officials accelerated such trends. Despite occasional "whorehouse riots," in which an aroused citizenry torched local brothels, the tendency was toward peaceful coexistence as long as prostitutes kept within accepted geographic and social bounds.[66]

Part of that tolerance reflected stereotypical assumptions about men's and women's different sexual needs and moral natures. Although lacking in empirical support, the conventional wisdom was that prostitution was an inevitable manifestation of males' greater biological urge. A distinguished Philadelphia physician informed the American Medical Association in 1874 that sexual intercourse was an "imperious necessity implanted in our nature for . . . which man will brave any danger, however great to health and even life." To free virtuous women from excessive sexual demands, limited tolerance of prostitution seemed appropriate. In some municipalities, a de facto regulatory structure evolved. Police invoked criminal sanctions only as a means to keep prostitutes in certain districts, to control disease, and to restrict offensive solicitation or other criminal activities.[67]

This was the compromise that many early women's groups challenged. Their campaign began in the 1830s as part of the more general cult of domesticity, and accelerated during periods of religious revival throughout the century. Moral-reform societies organized to prevent "traffic in souls" and protect the family values that extramarital sexuality threatened. Emboldened by their cause, some members engaged in "pious harassment"; they prayed and proselytized among female sinners and organized vigils at known brothels in order to reveal, or threaten to reveal, "licentiousness in High Places."[68]

After the Civil War, this campaign intensified, fueled by proposals to control prostitutes through regulation rather than repression. Borrowing from European models, such as the short-lived British Contagious Diseases Act of 1864, coalitions of American health specialists and public officials proposed a system of compulsory licensing and medical examinations. Except for a four-year trial period in St. Louis, such proposals met with no success. They appeared unworkable in practice and abhorrent in theory to the growing women's rights movement. In feminists' view, medical checkups could provide a false sense of security, since any prostitute certified safe might be infected by her next contact. Worse still, state-sanctioned brothels would legitmate male debauchery, female debasement, and the double standard of morality. To dramatize the point, a group of young virgins clad in pure white gowns hand-delivered antiregulatory petitions to St. Louis legislators. Capitalizing on the issue, some suffragists popularized slogans demanding votes for women and chastity for men.[69]

By the turn of the century, the popularity of regulation proposals had diminished, but prostitution itself was flourishing. Virtually every major city had at least one red-light district, and increased public attention focused on the causes and consequences of venereal disease. This threat to public health as well as morality became a subject of growing concern. Fueled by lurid accounts of traffic in white slavery, various feminist, progressive, religious, and temperance organizations joined forces to combat the mounting "moral peril." Many of these accounts were highly exaggerated and catered to nativist and anti-Semitic prejudices. There were, to be sure, clearly documented instances of coercion connected with prostitution, particularly with Asian immigrants in the West. Lured by promises of marriage or sold into bondage by impoverished families, thousands of Chinese women found themselves in brothels. At the height of importation, "prostitute" was listed as the occupation of two-thirds of the 3,500 Chinese women in the country. However, systematic studies found little evidence for the typical *House of Bondage* narrative in which a small-town American ingenue fell into the clutches of a foreign-born procurer and ended up hostage in a brothel.[70]

Despite repeated studies denying the existence of a national organized white-slavery syndicate, the federal government passed a variety of statutes directed at this supposed underworld. The best known, the Mann Act of 1910, prohibited interstate transportation of women for any "immoral purpose." Under expansive Supreme Court interpretations, it became a vehicle for prosecuting fornication as well as prostitution.[71]

Between 1900 and 1920, feminist leaders, citizen organizations, and vice commissions in almost every major city proposed additional responses to commercialized sin. Although their proposals varied, many viewed prostitutes as victims rather than villains. While some nineteenth-century crusaders had denounced the "tribes of libertines" who initiated young men in licentious rites, progressive reformers tended to focus on the origins of that behavior. Female feeblemindedness, male profiteering, and social permissiveness were all popular explanations, but a substantial constituency also acknowledged poverty and lack of employment options as primary causes. There was increasing sympathy, if not unqualified agreement, with George Bernard Shaw's position in his preface to *Mrs. Warren's Profession:* "Prostitution is caused not by female depravity and male licentiousness but simply by underpaying, undervaluing, and overworking women. If, on the large scale, we get vice instead of what we call virtue, it is because we are paying more for it."[72]

Proposed responses were equally varied. Social hygienists stressed male continence; liberals called for minimum wages; socialists demanded the abolition of the capitalist system; local neighborhood associations advocated repression; and vice commissions recommended everything from providing chaperones for dance halls to banning prurient literature and "short skirts . . . or other improper attire" in public places. Yet those differing strategies generally sprang from a common premise: that prostitution was as much a social as a moral problem. There was also increasing recognition that much of this problem stemmed from male rather than female "immorality." As the Philadelphia Vice Commission noted, "commercialized vice is a business conducted largely by men and the profits go mainly to men."[73]

Despite this recognition, most Progressive-era responses to prostitution also ended up benefiting primarily men. Feminist efforts to visit sanctions on customers as well as practitioners met with almost no success. The most dramatic change was the widespread elimination of red-light districts, a result aided by the military's antivenereal-disease campaign and detention of suspected prostitutes during World War I. Whether this strategy had any effect on the overall incidence of commercial sexual contacts remains speculative, but it did change their form. Forcing prostitution underground strengthened its links with organized crime and subjected many practitioners to increasing hardships. Routine strategies of arresting, fining, and releasing prostitutes heightened their vulnerability. To pay their legal costs, many women had to work longer, rely on intermediaries, or engage in other criminal activity. Major beneficiaries were male defense attorneys, bail bondsmen, landlords, hotel operators, and pimps.[74]

This reform effort points up broader patterns, which are instructive for contemporary campaigns against prostitution and pornography. As with other forms of legislation designed to protect women, the consequences were double-edged. By politicizing the symbolic and practical effects of prostitution, feminists issued an important challenge to male exploitation, one that laid the foundations for more egalitarian social roles. Yet in transforming the prostitute from villain to victim, reformers reinforced stereotypes about gender difference that worked against egalitarian development. Strategies that cast the "fallen woman" as an unwitting, unwilling target of male coercion diverted attention from the social and economic circumstances that more fully explained her condition. Most accounts that stressed female impoverishment ignored prostitutes' own descriptions of their motivations; many women preferred commercial vice to "honest labor" or parental control. On an ideological level, reformist perspectives that equated female passion with social pathologies denied any affirmative role for sexual expression.

On a practical level, the feminist antivice campaign also invited coalitions and inspired statutes that were ultimately inconsistent with feminist objectives. The diversity of groups that joined the crusade provided its strength but also its limitations. By aligning themselves with conservative and religious leaders, nineteenth- and early-twentieth-century feminists attracted additional support for the antivice movement. But that alignment also defined the reform agenda in a way that preserved male access to prostitution, while increasing the costs for its female practitioners. Such a strategy reflected double standards that stigmatized female promiscuity and exposed the wayward to repressive adult criminal codes and to juvenile standards that punished female but not male sexual activity. In commenting on analogous British strategies, Sylvia Pankhurst noted that legislation "which was passed ostensibly to protect women [was] used almost exclusively to punish them."[75]

Prostitution did not resurface as a significant social issue until the 1970s, when the emergence of strong feminist, civil libertarian, and criminal law reform movements brought new attention to traditional prohibitions. In the interim, commercial sex remained illicit but accessible. Kinsey's study of white males in the late 1940s indicated that 69 percent reported experience with prostitutes. Although more recent systematic surveys are unavailable, it is likely that cultural changes in the 1960s and 1970s reduced the percentage of men with such experience. The decline of the double standard and the rise in divorce and premarital sex may have curtailed some of the demand for commercial outlets. These same trends toward permissiveness have expanded the supply of part-time prostitutes and left other market factors unaffected. Studies of male customers have revealed a variety of reasons for seeking commercial sex: unconventional desires, insecurity about performance, physical unattractiveness or disabilities, loneliness (particularly when traveling), and preferences for variety without emotional entanglement. Estimates of the number of full-time practitioners responding to those concerns have remained at a fairly stable level over the past half-century—around a quarter-million—and they reportedly have about 1.5 million customers per week. Recent estimates of the gross annual revenue from such activities have varied but generally cluster between seven and nine billion dollars.[76]

The renewed focus on prostitution during the 1970s had less to do with concerns about its frequency than about its ideological signficance and the inappropriateness of legal responses. Since approximately 90 percent of all convicted prostitutes are female, cultural understandings about the sale of sexuality assume particular importance for women. For some members of the contemporary feminist movement, as for their counterparts a century earlier, prostitution remains "the world's oldest oppression"; it objectifies women and expropriates their sexuality. To other constituencies, including those with the most direct personal experience, it is not the act of prostitution but its criminalization that is oppressive. Borrowing from nineteenth-century Marxist analysis, many contemporary feminists as well as prostitutes have echoed Friedrich Engels' point that the married woman differs little from the "common courtesan," except that she does not "sell her body on piece work but once and for all." Women have long exchanged sexual for nonsexual favors, including gifts, entertainment, companionship, job advancement, financial support, and marital status. In the view of some feminists, to single out cash transactions for criminal liability is both arbitrary and hypocritical. As Frances Olsen has argued, "the difference between what prostitutes do and what a lot of women do a lot of the time is that prostitutes get a decent wage for it."[77]

These differing perspectives within the women's movement attracted greater attention in 1971 at what organizers billed as the first feminist conference on the subject, titled "Toward the Elimination of Prostitution." One of its more memorable moments occurred when a member of the vocation under discussion assaulted a would-be sister-savior. Two years later, the National Organization for Women attempted a politic compromise by condemning both the conditions that encouraged exploitation of women's sexuality and the legal consequences that flowed from it. As an "interim measure," NOW advocated decriminalization of prostitution.[78]

The merits of that approach have attracted increasing attention. A growing body of academics, state legislators, bar-association committees, and civil-liberties organizations have joined feminist groups in seeking partial or full decriminalization, although with little political success. Only one state, Nevada, has granted counties the option to legalize prostitution, and those that have done so imposed the kind of invasive licensing requirements that women's groups had long opposed.

Opposition to decriminalization proposals has come from both ends of the ideological spectrum and has stressed a number of common themes. A primary objection has been the degradation of women that sale of sexuality implies. Concern has focused in part on injuries to individual sellers, and in part on injuries to women as a group. The moral predicate for the first concern was summarized by Immanuel Kant in his *Lectures on Ethics:* "to let one's person out on hire and to surrender it for the satisfaction of . . . sensual desire in return for money is the depth of infamy"—the alienation of moral personality. Two centuries later, many members of the radical left and radical right have taken a similar view. From their perspective, sex for hire is not a victimless crime. It is the exploitation of women by men—by customers, pimps, massage-parlor owners, and law-enforcement officials.[79]

This exploitation can have psychological as well as physical consequences. Contemporary research generally finds high levels of suicides, rapes, and beatings among surveyed prostitutes, as well as substantial risks of venereal disease, gynecological disorders, and, most recently, AIDS. However, such evidence requires qualification. Prostitutes are a heterogeneous group, and the experiences of part-time call girls, small-town brothel workers, and full-time urban streetwalkers can be quite dissimilar. Much of the empirical research on prostitution involves nonrandom subgroups and fails to control for variables such as race, class, and drug and alcohol addiction. It is also difficult to separate consequences that are endemic to prostitution from those that are a function of its criminal status.[80]

Nonetheless, as opponents of legalized prostitution note, life for women at the lower end of the professional spectrum has substantial physical risk and brings limited economic rewards. Although some prostitutes may be the highest paid women in the United States, many others fare poorly after losing most of their proceeds in legal expenses and payments to pimps, brothel-owners, and other third parties. Practitioners often face retirement in their mid-twenties or early thirties, with few savings and no benefits. To assume that women freely choose such vocational risks ignores the circumstances in which those choices often occur. Many prostitutes enter the trade as teenage runaways, with little opportunity to make informed judgments. Others lack decent alternative employment, and a small minority report physical and psychological coercion.[81]

Quite apart from the consequences to those who engage in prostitution, the practice has broader cultural implications. The sale of sexuality institutionalizes a view of women as objects for male gratification, a view that many feminists link with attitudes leading to rape and domestic violence. To drafters of the Model Penal Code, as well as conservative political leaders, prostitution represents a "significant fact in social disorganization," encourages "sex delinquency," and undermines "marriage, the home, and individual character." Despite numerous opportunities to modify its view, the United States Supreme Court has left undisturbed its 1908 judgment that the lives and examples of those who offer themselves to "indiscriminate intercourse with men . . . are in hostility to the idea of the family . . . [and] the holy estate of matrimony; the sure foundation of all that is stable and noble in our civilization, the best guarantee of that reverent morality which is the source of all beneficent progress in social and political improvement."[82]

Whether nonmarital sexuality poses such a threat has been questioned earlier. Discussion in Chapter 7 reviewed difficulties in conservatives' general rationale for regulating sexual intimacy among consenting adults. As to prostitution in particular, many commentators have long supposed that commercial outlets diminish the frequency of rape and marital difficulties. Subscribers to that view have included not only contemporary social scientists and health professionals, but also some revered moralists. Saint Augustine and Thomas Aquinas, for example, were convinced that suppressing prostitution would allow "capricious lust [to] overthrow society." Contemporary public-opinion polls suggest that many individuals remain equally unpersuaded that repression is the most appropriate social strategy. In a national Harris survey from the 1970s, only 43 percent agreed that prostitutes do more harm than good, and other recent research generally has revealed majority support for at least partial decriminalization.[83]

As to the injury to women who engage in prostitution, a substantial part may be attributable to its illicit status. The stigma of criminal liability can diminish self-respect, increase vulnerability to abusive pimps or customers, intensify alienation from friends and family, and preempt other employment opportunities. Yet, paradoxically enough, most surveys of prostitutes have not found high levels of occupational dissatisfaction or sexual impairment. Almost three-fourths of those surveyed in one mid-sized Midwestern city thought their lives were better after they became prostitutes; another study found that two-thirds had no regrets about their choice of work. Most research suggests that the average prostitute nets more than the average salary of working women—and substantially more than she would make in the other jobs open to her. Nor are economic concerns generally her sole motivation. A desire for variety and excitement, as well as control over her hours and her sexuality, are also considerations.[84]

Of course, many women enter prostitution without adequate alternatives or the capacity for informed judgment, and many experience substantial hardships as a consequence. Yet it does not necessarily follow that criminalization is an appropriate response. The issue is whether penal sanctions add more to the problem or to the solution. Defenders of such sanctions typically invoke three major justifications in addition to the general moral concerns summarized earlier: prevention of venereal disease, related criminal activity, and neighborhood nuisances.

The first of these concerns is, at least in contemporary American society, vastly overstated. Health studies have consistently revealed that prostitution accounts for fewer than 5 percent of venereal-disease cases. Public education and free medical treatment would be more promising responses than criminalization. While estimates of prostitutes' AIDS exposure are more speculative, their major risk appears to come from intravenous drug use. Here again punitive sanctions are a highly ineffective substitute for health and information programs.[85]

With respect to other illegal conduct, most research suggests that prostitution plays a "small and declining role" in organized crime. Although it is correlated with certain other illicit activities, particularly larceny and bribery, this correlation is less pronounced where prostitution is legal. Decriminalization diminishes the need to corrupt law-enforcement officials and reduces deterrents to prostitutes' and customers' reports of abuse. Removing liability also removes the legal fees and fines that pressure some prostitutes into committing other crimes. Finally, nuisance-related concerns can be addressed through zoning laws and prohibitions on harassing or disorderly conduct.[86]

Not only are the rationales for criminalizing prostitution unpersuasive, the costs of retaining that approach are prohibitive. Some cities have spent well over $2,000 to arrest and prosecute a single prostitute. As a crime-prevention strategy, that approach has been utterly unproductive. The legal expenses and stigma that accompany prosecution help entrap women in debt and dependence; imprisonment helps to socialize them into cultures of deviance. Seventy percent of the female prison population was first arrested for prostitution, and the recidivism rate for such arrests is even higher. These punitive strategies have been discriminatory as well as self-defeating. Statistical profiles generally indicate that fewer than 10 percent of those arrested for prostitution are male customers, and that they rarely receive any significant penalty. Despite such asymmetries, courts have rejected equal-protection challenges on the theory that purchase and sale are different crimes. Enforcement patterns are skewed by race and class as well as sex. According to NOW surveys, streetwalkers, who tend to come from the lowest socioeconomic group, account for 10 to 15 percent of all prostitutes and 85 to 90 percent of all arrests. Women of color account for 40 percent of streetwalkers, 55 percent of those arrested, and 85 percent of those receiving jail sentences.[87]

The situation for prostitutes is not substantially better in the single state that has partially decriminalized their activities. In Nevada, the brothel-licensure system applicable in the state's nonmetropolitan counties has brought more legitimacy for proprietors, but also more repressive working conditions for their employees. Women have no control over their hours or their choice of customers. They work extended schedules at modest wages and cannot leave their brothel except at certain times and under certain conditions. (For example, no fraternizing with husbands or boyfriends is allowed during the work week, and visits to nearby towns are limited to once a week.) Prostitutes' names and fingerprints appear on a permanent police record. Although the system has been fairly effective in controlling incidental crime and street solicitation within areas serviced by brothels, it has by no means curtailed illicit prostitution elsewhere in the state. Licensed prostitutes account for only 2 to 5 percent of those estimated to be working in Nevada. Experience with European licensure systems reveals similar patterns. Many customers and practitioners are unwilling to confine their activities to the restrictive atmosphere of state-regulated brothels.[88]

In this as in other contexts, the last century of feminist struggles over prostitution suggests the need for a less divisive framework. Unlike their predecessors, members of the contemporary women's movement have begun to develop a vision of female sexuality that could provide a unifying agenda. Regardless of their other differences, most feminists share a commitment to the fullest expression of individuals' sexual identity that is consistent with the same liberty for others. Implicit in that ideal is some notion of reciprocity, of mutual concern and respect, that excludes treating women as sexual objects.

While working toward that vision, it is critical to acknowledge our distance from it. In the current social order, selling sexuality offers many women a measure of psychological and economic independence not otherwise available. Under such circumstances, to single out a particular group of women for legal liability makes little sense. Prostitution is not a victimless crime, but criminalizing its most immediate victims is not the answer. A more productive strategy would involve diverting resources now spent on punishment to prevention, counseling, job-training, and health care. Many prostitutes are victims of child abuse, broken homes, or welfare systems that fail to provide even subsistence-level support. Programs in other nations suggest that substantial numbers of prostitutes, particularly juveniles, will respond to appropriately designed support services. So too, in the United States, efforts are under way to develop more humane alternatives than the European or Nevada licensure approach. For example, COYOTE (Cast Off Your Old Tired Ethics), a coalition under the leadership of Margo St. James, is seeking strategies to organize prostitutes and establish worker-owned collectives with decent working conditions.[89]

As an interim measure, the best legal strategy is decriminalizing the sale of sexual services, while retaining prohibitions against vexatious public solicitation, brokerage, recruitment, and advertising. Such a compromise would do much to avert the degradation and dangers of current approaches, but offer some safeguards against entrepreneurial initiatives. As Scandinavian experience suggests, removing all criminal sanctions is likely to increase not only the market for sexual services, but also the involvement of a managerial class intent on legitimating its activities and ensuring its control. A society in which sex was sold as freely and imaginatively as soft drinks, with price gradations for every characteristic of the seller, would have corrosive effects far beyond those involved in the immediate transaction. If our ultimate goal is to reduce sexual objectification, we cannot tolerate unrestricted commercial sex as a provisional strategy.[90]

Nor can we rest with measures directed only toward prostitution. That so many women find it so much more profitable to sell their bodies than anything else is an unmistakable indictment of current social structures. Any adequate analysis of prostitution invites us to reconsider not simply the rationale for its prohibition but the reasons for its persistence.

Pornography

Pornography raises related issues and has more complex historical and theoretical linkages with prostitution than is often acknowledged. Most scholars have traced the origins of the term pornography to graphic sexual writings or pictures (*graphos*) of prostitutes (*pornos*). The word eventually acquired a less restrictive meaning and came to encompass any sexually explicit material designed to produce sexual arousal. In the late 1970s and early 1980s, some leading feminists sought to focus attention on the term's earlier usage. From their perspective, it was important to distinguish between pornography, which involved scenes of degradation and dominance, and other forms of erotic material premised on equality and mutual respect. To activists such as Andrea Dworkin, pornography in this sense "strictly and literally conforms to [its] root meaning," the "graphic depiction of whores," since it defines women as sexual objects whose mission is to provide gratification for men.[91]

On a political as well as structural level, the linkages between pornography and prostitution bear emphasis. Both reflect a form of sexuality in which male dominance has been eroticized, commercialized, and institutionalized. And both have posed fundamental difficulties for the feminist movement. In historical and contemporary context, the campaign against pornography, like that against prostitution, has had progressive and repressive dimensions. Politicizing pornography has raised public sensitivity to fundamental relationships between human sexuality and gender subordination. It has also strengthened a conservative crusade with values likely to perpetuate that subordination.

Pornography has an extended historical lineage. It was common in Greek and Roman societies, and, even after the rise of Christianity, there was little effort at suppression. In the mid-sixteenth century, after the development of the printing press, English law required printers to secure licenses from the church and the state. However, censors' predominant concerns initially involved political, rather than sexual material. By the eighteenth century, although British licensing laws had become largely ineffective, governmental officials and members of private antivice societies were increasingly interested in prosecutions for distributing material falling under broad definitions of "obscene libel."[92]

Legal restrictions on sexually explicit material in America began in the early Colonial period. As in England, regulatory efforts occurred under the rubric of obscenity, and enforcement was initially sporadic. The prolonged absence of legal interest was in part attributable to the absence of a strong indigenous industry. Before the Civil War, only four states had statutes specifically directed at obscenity, and federal customs legislation prohibited the importation of indecent pictorial, but not printed, material.

However, during the late nineteenth century, as printing became more economical, the mass circulation of explicit books and pictures became possible. So too, the same forces of secularization, industrialization, and migration that enhanced demand for prostitution expanded the market for other sexually stimulating outlets and provoked a similar political response. During the late nineteenth and early twentieth centuries, antivice societies marshaled their efforts against the "satanic" literature that "defiles the body, debauches the imagination . . . and damns the soul."[93]

Such efforts met with limited success. Under the leadership of Anthony Comstock, a former Connecticut dry goods salesman, these organizations lobbied for the passage and enforcement of the 1873 federal Act for the Suppression of Trade and Circulation of Obscene Literature and Immoral Use. Over the next half century most states and many municipalities enacted similar ordinances. On the whole, early feminists supported these initiatives. Any complaints tended to focus on laxity, not overzealousness, among antivice crusaders. Feminists such as Julia Ward Howe regretted only that women had not been granted a more central role in the "guardianship of the press," since they would doubtlessly prove more "strict and scrupulous than the average of the other sex."[94]

By contemporary standards, however, male leadership was not lacking in vigilance. Initial definitions of "obscene" were expansive. In the late nineteenth and early twentieth centuries, the leading precedent, *Regina v. Hicklin* (1868), was a British case authorizing the suppression of any material that tended to "deprave and corrupt those whose minds are open to such immoral influences." Under that standard, authorities suppressed not only dime-store novels of seduction but also masterpieces by Aristophanes, Balzac, Shaw, Tolstoy, and Voltaire. Even isolated passages or discreetly worded descriptions of adultery were sometimes banned to spare the unsuspecting reader from "impurity in thought or deed." Sale and advocacy of contraceptive devices were similarly subject to prosecution, and, under the forty-year reign of Postal Inspector Anthony Comstock, so were almost any representations of the human body in a state of undress. By his own efforts, Comstock claimed, he had destroyed 160 tons of material, including everything from classical art to indecent playing cards.[95]

Following World War I, the influence of antivice societies began to wane, and courts became increasingly tolerant of explicit sexual material. Focus began to shift to the merits of the work as a whole and its erotic effect on the average, rather than the susceptible, reader. Nonetheless, the formal definition of obscenity remained expansive and its application idiosyncratic. Challenges to the vagueness of legal prohibitions met with little sympathy. To most judges and other officials involved in regulation, the target was unambiguous. As one Postmaster General put it, "filth is filth." Although enforcement was uneven, the threat of legal expenses induced substantial self-censorship by doctors, authors, educators, publishers, and distributors.[96]

In the 1950s the scope of suppression provoked greater challenge. Following World War II, the market for sexually explicit materials rapidly increased, fueled in part by small-scale entrepreneurs whose decentralized operations were difficult to repress. In response, various decency leagues renewed their efforts and a National Commission on juvenile delinquency targeted the diversion of school lunch money into "smut" as a major problem. The Supreme Court, in an effort to clarify the standard for obscenity, laid the foundations for enduring conflict and confusion. According to a majority of Justices in *Roth v. United States* (1956), obscene material was not within the zone of constitutionally protected speech. In determining what was obscene, the Court vacillated. Finally, in a 1973 decision, *Miller v. California,* a majority settled on a three-part test: whether an average person applying contemporary community standards would find that the work as a whole appealed to the "prurient interest"; whether the work depicted sexual conduct in a "patently offensive way"; and whether the work taken as a whole lacked serious literary, artistic, political, or scientific value. Material falling within that definition could be subject to prohibition.[97]

From a theoretical standpoint, many women's rights advocates have found that framework both under- and overinclusive. Depending on a particular judge's view of prurience, obscenity could encompass sexually explicit material that most feminists would view as erotic, but exclude sexually violent material that they would consider pornographic. From a practical standpoint, the *Miller* formulation has proved no less subjective than its predecessors, one of which prompted a now-notorious acknowledgment from Supreme Court Justice Potter Stewart. After confessing that he was unable to provide an intelligible description of hard-core obscenity, Stewart nonetheless insisted, "I know it when I see it."[98]

For one group of feminists active in the antipornography campaign, obscenity law presents concerns beyond those that have troubled liberals. The problem is not simply courts' indeterminate, idiosyncratic, and ill-considered applications. The difficulties lie deeper and stem in part from women's long-standing exclusion from the constituencies that have defined and enforced sexual prohibitions. Who is the assertedly gender-neutral "average" person envisioned by *Miller?* If, Catharine MacKinnon has argued, "I ask from the point of view of women's experience," does the male judge or legislator "know what I know when I see [it] . . . I doubt it, given what's on the newsstands." Part of the problem may also lie with the anomaly of *Miller*'s formulation, which can leave decision-makers reluctant to admit that material which they find patently offensive is also sexually arousing. In addition, some clinical research indicates that the more often individuals are exposed to pornography the less likely they are to find it offensive. In the view of antipornography activists, the *Miller* standard provides little protection against a gradual deterioration of community standards once a market for sexually degrading materials begins to mushroom.[99]

Clearly such a market has developed in the United States. In the decade following *Miller,* the pornography industry expanded rapidly. Part of the increase resulted from developments in home video films and cable television, coupled with Supreme Court decisions protecting the use of obscene materials in private homes. Although by the mid-1980s some evidence suggested that the industry's growth had leveled off, estimates of gross receipts remained highly speculative. Most ranged between six and eight billion dollars. Given the time, effort, and expense of enforcing obscenity prohibitions on an item-by-item basis, prosecution in most parts of the country had become minimal. Much of the enforcement involved zoning restrictions, which did little to curb market growth. During the post-*Miller* decade, the inadequacy of this legal framework began prompting responses from an unlikely coalition of radical feminists and right-wing conservatives, an alliance similar to that which had joined forces in the early antiprostitution campaigns.[100]

Initial efforts centered on politicizing pornography through organization, education, boycotts, and marches. Increasingly, interest turned to legal strategies as a means of controlling distribution and influencing attitudes. Quite apart from its other problems, existing law appeared to some feminists to miss the misogynist underpinnings of many pornographic displays. While obscenity prohibitions have been preoccupied with morality, these feminists have been concerned with inequality. From their vantage, the issue is not male arousal but female degradation, and the focus of law should not be prurience but power.

To that end, in 1983 Dworkin and MacKinnon drafted a model ordinance that was proposed first in Minneapolis, adopted in Indianapolis, and debated in various other localities. In the form enacted in Indianapolis, the ordinance defined pornography as the "sexually explicit subordination of women, graphically depicted in words or pictures" that debased women in various specified ways or presented "men, children, or transsexuals in the place of women." Among the contexts specified were women enjoying pain, rape, or humiliation; serving as sexual objects for domination, conquest, exploitation, and possession; or [appearing in] positions of "servility or submission or display." Under that ordinance, it would be a civil offense to "traffic" in pornography or to coerce participation in its making or use. Any aggrieved individual could claim injunctive relief and monetary damages under judicial or special administrative proceedings. These legislative initiatives have focused national attention on the harms of pornography and appropriate regulatory responses. Both issues have proven highly controversial.[101]

Some of the dispute dates back to 1970, when a presidential Commission on Obscenity and Pornography "found no evidence that exposure to explicit sexual material plays a significant role in the causation of delinquent or criminal behavior," and recommended legalization of such material. Subsequent analysis, however, revealed substantial problems with the studies on which the commission had relied. Most of this research posited a cathartic process, in which exposure to sexually explicit materials allowed individuals to release sexual aggression in a nonaggressive manner. However, those studies included little material that was violent as well as sexually explicit, and most subsequent research has documented substantial adverse consequences from that combination.[102]

Such inadequacies helped fuel demands for further review. In 1986, a commission appointed by President Reagan, under the leadership of Attorney General Edwin Meese, issued a report at odds with its predecessor. In essence, the 1986 report concluded that both sexually explicit violent material and nonviolent degrading material bore a causal relation to violent behavior, and that the production of such pornography posed a threat to models and actresses, particularly children. To combat those harms, the commission proposed more rigorous enforcement of existing obscenity standards rather than initiatives along the lines of the Indianapolis ordinance.[103]

Many social scientists, including some on whom the commission had relied, objected to its procedures, its reasoning, and its recommendations. Critics noted that the commission included a disproportionate number of members who had taken strong public positions against pornography; that it lacked the time, budget, or staff to conduct an adequate inquiry; and that its selection of evidence was systematically skewed. For example, commission hearings excluded feminist leaders opposed to censorship, but included testimonials such as that of a middle-aged born-again Christian who attributed his problems with drug dependence, prostate disease, and bestiality to the deck of pornographic playing cards he had discovered at age twelve. While the commissioners invited testimony from thirty women who alleged serious injury from pornography, it heard from none who had enjoyed sexually explicit material. Nor did its 2,000-page report mention the experience of sex therapists (some of whom had testified before the commission), concerning the educational and therapeutic value of such material. Moreover, in critics' view, even the most rigorous research on which the commission relied should have prompted qualifications absent in its report. Such qualifications should also have prompted reservations about enforcement of obscenity law.[104]

Although the commission study sparked some useful public debate, much of the surrounding controversy has obscured analyis of its two most critical issues: the nature of pornography's harms and the policy implications that follow from it. Evidence concerning the harms falls into three general categories. Some data are anecdotal. For example, reports by victims, police, and mental-health professionals indicate that pornography is often a model for sexual assault. Such accounts, while suggestive in their cumulative impact, provide no indication of the frequency with which pornography serves this function. Nor do they indicate the importance of pornographic materials in causing sexual aggression, as distinguished from shaping the forms that aggression assumes.[105]

A second category of evidence involves longitudinal and cross-cultural studies. Some research, for example, has found that reported rapes have increased in certain countries during periods when pornography laws have grown more liberal, while reported rapes have declined in other nations when laws have grown more restrictive. Such correlations, however, do not prove causation; other social factors may account for increases or decreases in pornography regulation and violence. Moreover, other research has failed to confirm such findings and suggests that the relationship between these phenomena is complex and inadequately understood. Some countries with low pornography consumption have high rates of violence against women; the converse is also true.[106]

A final category of evidence, the one on which the 1986 commission primarily relied, involves laboratory studies. Such research has found, for example, that exposing male subjects to depictions of sexual violence against women results in lowered sensitivity to the harms of rape and a greater expressed willingness to commit it. These effects are particularly pronounced with material suggesting that women enjoy aggression, and with certain subjects (for example, males whose motivation for sexual interaction is based more on power than affection). Such studies are consistent with others noted earlier, which indicate that violence is learned behavior and that repeated exposure increases its acceptability. Yet the extent to which these attitudinal changes affect behavior remains unclear. Laboratory research has the advantage of controlling for relevant variables in a way that field studies cannot. Its disadvantage is its inability to provide an adequate account of the duration or significance of pornography's influence when mediated by other factors in the outside world. Nor does existing work make clear whether changed attitudes following exposure to sexually explicit violence are related more to the sex than the violence. Some of the nation's leading experts believe that violence is the crucial variable. More research is necessary to test that judgment.[107]

Additional work must focus on the effects of nonviolent but degrading sexual materials, and on consequences other than sexual aggression. As feminists such as Dworkin and MacKinnon have noted, the harm resulting from pornography is not confined to discrete acts of aggression against individual women. It also extends to women as a group, by eroticizing inequality, by linking female sexuality with female subordination, and by making that subordination a powerful source of male pleasure. Pornography that objectifies and brutalizes women in order to entertain men cannot help but affect the social construction of gender. In testimony before the Meese Commission, MacKinnon noted that "women in pornography are bound, battered, tortured, humiliated and sometimes killed . . . hung from a meat hook, forced to eat excrement, penetrated by eels and rats and knives and pistols . . . Or merely taken through every orifice." In their cumulative force, such presentations eroticize hierarchy. Because it operates on a subliminal level, deeper than discourse, pornographic speech is not readily countered by more speech, the customary constitutional prescription for offensive verbal or visual material.[108]

On this reasoning, a coalition of antipornography activists have supported various regulatory initiatives. Although united against a common target, coalition members work from very different premises. Unlike feminists, who generally view pornography as speech—uniquely powerful speech—many conservatives view it as smut, without expressive content. And unlike antipornography feminists, who see its suppression as part of a broader assault on traditional gender roles, many conservatives view their efforts as helping to preserve those roles. According to the New York sponsor of an ordinance based on the Minneapolis model, such legislation would not only protect women, but would "restore them to what ladies used to be." So too, the Meese Commission report vacillated between radical feminist concerns about gender subordination and traditional conservative concerns about decency, promiscuity, hedonism, and marital infidelity.[109]

By contrast, many liberals, together with many women's rights activists of all political persuasions, have been sensitive to the abuses underlying the feminist antipornography campaign but unpersuaded by its proposed solution. Some of their reservations found expression in a federal court of appeals decision striking down Indianapolis's ordinance. Although accepting the MacKinnon-Dworkin premise that portrayals of subordination tend to perpetuate subordination, the court found that the legislation was unconstitutional per se, since it discriminated on the basis of viewpoint. Unlike content-neutral restrictions, which in some instances may be justified by a balancing of competing interests, the Indianapolis ordinance suppressed certain speech on the basis of its substance—its degradation of women. This, in the appellate court's view, was "thought control." The United States Supreme Court summarily affirmed, without argument or further analysis. Although some liberal and feminist constituencies deplored the absence of full review, many supported the result.[110]

Their concerns rested partly on traditional First Amendment grounds. Any judicial restraints on speech implicate values essential to a free and democratic society: self-expression, advancement of knowledge, and political participation. As the history of obscenity law amply demonstrates, the principles and enforcement structure assembled to combat one form of degrading speech cannot always be contained. The Supreme Court's fleeting, and much discredited, venture into the area of group libel makes the point directly. To suppress speech on the theory that it contributes to group subordination is a precedent that admits of no ready limiting principle. As First Amendment defenders note, women are not the only targets of vilification in this society.

Nor would legislation banning materials that degrade women be interpreted by progressive feminists. Rather, it would be enforced by the same mix of state and federal judges whose prior constitutional interpretations have been denounced repeatedly by antipornography activists. Accordingly, many prominent women's rights advocates have feared that the materials most vulnerable under such an enforcement structure would include not the well-financed (and, to a predominately male legal establishment, nonthreatening) men's magazines, but radical feminist and lesbian publications instead. By granting *any* aggrieved victim the right to initiate suit, the Indianapolis ordinance and its analogues also present constant opportunities for harassment. Since these ordinances contain no exception for works of redeeming literary or artistic value, classics that graphically depict domination could be subject to suppression.[111]

Moreover, by reinforcing views of women as victims and men as aggressors, such legislation risks perpetuating sexist stereotypes. Women no less than men find some depictions of female subordination arousing, as any cursory stroll into the world of Harlequin romances makes evident. Even if their enjoyment is largely a product of sexist cultural conditioning, it does not follow that what such women need "is more sexual shame, guilt and hypocrisy, this time served up as feminism." The impact of images is often complex, contradictory, and highly contextual. To make a largely male judiciary the arbiters of what degrades women would risk the kind of paternalism that has rarely worked in women's interests.[112]

Restrictions on pornography are more complicated than partisans on either side often acknowledge. First Amendment values do not preclude all forms of regulation. Many democracies, including the United States, have managed to tolerate constraints on expression. Material that is of "low value" in terms of traditional constitutional concerns—commercial speech, libelous speech, or "hard-core" obscenity—has been subject to restraint without compromising the nation's entire system of free expression. Works that most concern antipornography activists are not the centerpiece of First Amendment freedoms. It does not strengthen constitutional values to deny distinctions between political interchange and pornographic materials of the kind reviewed by the 1986 Attorney General's commission: "Asses and Ankles," "Pussy on a Stick," "Pregnant Dildo Bondage," "Slit Sucking Sluts," "Teen Twits and Twats," "Dorothy: Slave to Pain," "Cheerleader Gang Bang," and "Jap Sadists' Virgin Slave."[113]

Even certain highly political speech, such as speech by employers in the context of union elections, has been subject to some constraints without unraveling constitutional safeguards. Surely the government's interest in reducing sexual violence and subordination is no less substantial than the interests underlying other First Amendment restrictions. Nor is legislation targeted at pornography any more content-specific than some of these restrictions such as laws prohibiting commercial bribery or employers' threats of antiunion reprisals.

As in other contexts, we need to deconstruct dichotomies. Rigid speech-nonspeech categories distort what they pretend only to describe. Both expression and constraints on expression form a continuum and require assessment by reference not to categorical absolutes but to cultural values. The importance of the speech, the interests supporting its regulation, and the means chosen to further those interests all demand analysis.

Under such a framework, it should be possible to design legislation that would be more constitutionally and politically acceptable than the Indianapolis ordinance. An example would be criminal prohibitions against sexually explicit visual portrayals of force or violence that lack redeeming literary, artistic, political, or scientific value. Unlike the *Miller* standard, such legislation would require no showing of prurient appeal or patent offense. Yet unlike the Indianapolis ordinance, the prohibition would encompass only a small minority of pornographic materials, those which existing research has identified as most harmful. By leaving enforcement in the hands of publicly accountable officials, such legislation would present fewer risks of harassing litigation. And it would confront fewer constitutional and political obstacles. Such an approach would smack less of viewpoint discrimination than the Indianapolis legislation and have a greater chance of widespread adoption. According to public-opinion surveys in the mid-1980s, some two-thirds of Americans favored prohibitions on sexual violence in magazines and movies.[114]

Whether such targeted legislation would prove more effective than existing statutes in controlling consumption is unclear. Much would depend on the political forces that secured its passage. As the Attorney General's commission noted, existing obscenity provisions are chronically underenforced. If legislative campaigns served to galvanize popular and prosecutorial pressure against sexually explicit violent materials, that might be a useful step, whether or not the new statutory language was significantly more inclusive than its predecessors.

To many antipornography activists, any such limited initiative is unacceptable because it fails to address fundamental issues of inequality. But that is true also of their proposed ordinance. Experience with prohibitions on liquor and prostitution leave doubt that large-scale efforts at legal suppression would prove successful. Rather, they might simply force more pornography underground and strengthen its connections with organized crime. Images of less sexually explicit subordination would continue to pervade the mainstream media. As social scientists have often noted, such images may be of more concern than pornography, since they have greater public legitimacy. Yet if we are to avoid wholesale judicial regulation of our fantasy lives, the only way to alter such images is to alter the culture that makes them appealing. According to some experts, the most effective response to pornography is educating viewers. Given the costs of item-by-item crusades against particular materials, it would make sense to concentrate greater resources on public education and political organization—boycotts, protests, mass-media campaigns, workshops, and curricular materials for public schools.

That is not an ideal solution. While in theory, the best response to false and degrading speech may be more speech, in practice such an approach is limited by disparities in power, status, and money among the potential speakers. By definition, the First Amendment protects only those able to exercise the rights it secures. And, in the view of activists such as MacKinnon, "so long as pornography exists in the way it does, there will not be more speech by women." Yet the history of her own campaign suggests the contrary. In the course of a decade, a small number of feminists challenged some of the nation's most sacred legal iconography and most successful entertainment industries. As a result, there has been more speech by women, and it has been heard differently by men.[115]

Law has made a difference in that debate. The model ordinance that antipornography feminists crafted has been a powerful tool in raising sensitivity, encouraging organization, and fostering dialogue. But that has not come without costs. After a decade's division within the women's movement, it is appropriate to reconsider whether pornography is the issue on which so much energy should center. In some respects, the question is similar to that posed by the Equal Rights Amendment campaign. For radical feminists of the 1980s, the presence of pornography served the same symbolic purposes as the absence of a constitutional mandate for the liberal feminists of the 1970s. Both issues became condensed metaphors for male domination. Both served to divide as well as mobilize women, and to empower not only progressives but also their conservative opponents. In addition, both deflected attention from fundamental social and economic sources of subordination. The substance of our constitutional mandates and sexual fantasies reflect as much as promote gender inequality. In responding to that inequality, it is crucial to recognize not only the potential, but also the limitations of symbolic single-issue crusades.

Chapter 11

Association and Assimilation

In 1896, in *Plessy v. Ferguson,* the United States Supreme Court upheld a Louisiana law providing "separate but equal" railway cars for white and black passengers. In response to claims that such segregation "stamps the colored race with a badge of inferiority," the Court stated: "If this be so, it is not by reason of anything found in the Louisiana act, but solely because the colored race chooses to put that construction on it." While the *Plessy* reasoning no longer enjoys a respectable following in contexts involving race, its legacy for gender issues is more complex. Not all women resent all forms of separatism, and American society remains deeply divided over which forms count as invidious.[1]

A substantial constituency even denies that gender separatism involves gender discrimination. In 1982, three Justices of the Supreme Court insisted that Mississippi University's exclusion of male students from one of its nursing schools was "simply not a [case of] sex discrimination," and advocates of all-male clubs have frequently made analogous claims. To these defenders of separatism, the preeminent issue is not equal protection but association, and the values of individual freedom and cultural diversity that underlie it. So too, although many feminists view equality as the central question, they differ sharply on whether single-sex institutions promote or subvert it.[2]

In part, the dispute rests on competing Utopian premises. As the concluding chapter suggests, there is no consensus within society in general or the feminist community in particular over the role that gender differences and gender segregation should play in an ideal world. Under one vision of an egalitarian social order, sex becomes like eye color, a biological characteristic that does not significantly shape public opportunities, personal aspirations, or associational networks. Other theorists, more ambivalent about the importance of gender identity in the ideal society, might preserve institutions that are sexually separate but truly equal.[3]

Even those sharing a similar Utopian vision often differ on the role of gender-based affiliations in bringing us closer to that ideal. A threshold disagreement centers on what priority to attach to the entire issue. Those most affected by single-sex clubs and schools are generally not those who are most economically or socially disadvantaged. Only a small percentage of American educational institutions are segregated by sex, and the number of all-male clubs and schools has been gradually declining. Why then should separatism become a central legal concern? Moreover, some feminists question women's insistence on getting in, as opposed to doing in, sex-segregated clubs. From their perspective, an association that bans women is not an association that women should want to join, particularly if it means endorsing principles that could undermine all-female affiliations.[4]

Other observers have questioned women's focus on an issue that risks trivializing their antidiscrimination campaign. If, for instance, prominent business leaders and government officials view organizations like the Bohemian Club as an opportunity to "dress like a woman and make wee wee on trees," they should be left in peace. Or if substantial numbers of students want to attend all-female schools, feminists should not be on the front lines fighting to deny them that choice.[5]

For many women, however, the issues surrounding gender-segregated secular institutions are not so readily dismissed. As a practical matter, single-sex clubs constitute a substantial presence on the social landscape. Membership in the Elks, Moose, Lions, and Eagles totals well over five million, and smaller, more elite institutions provide forums for significant political and commercial interchanges. As a symbolic matter, the exclusion of women, like that of racial or religious minorities, carries a stigma that affects individuals' social status and self-perception. And as a theoretical matter, separatism poses questions that have shaped feminist legal struggles for the last century: questions about public and private, sameness and difference, formal versus substantive equality. In what contexts should the sexes' distinctive social experiences find expression? Under what circumstances is special treatment for women's affiliations necessary to secure equal treatment for women? How much public structuring of personal choices are we prepared to tolerate?[6]

These questions call for a richer understanding of the dual role of sex-segregated institutions in American culture. They have provided channels for expressing individual autonomy and fostering collective goals; they have also been vehicles for denying individual opportunity and perpetuating collective disadvantage. Their presence has served both to empower women and to exclude them from circles in which power is exercised. Such institutions have affirmed women's traditional values of care and connection, while reinforcing social hierarchies that work on opposite principles.

This complex legacy points up limitations in conventional constitutional doctrine, which seeks neutral principles, abstract categories, and sharp dichotomies. Judicial grapplings with gender-segregated clubs and schools over the last quarter-century reveal the inadequacy of efforts to differentiate public from private discrimination, or to distinguish associations that foster invidious stereotypes from those that promote a healthy pluralism. A more satisfactory framework must acknowledge the blurred character of our categories and the double-edged implications of our choices. Private institutions have public consequences, and legitimizing separatism in one setting often entrenches it in others. As with other issues, public-private dichotomies provide inadequate foundations for legal analysis.

If our approach toward separatism is to become more convincing, it must first become consciously contextual. It must begin not with abstract contested assumptions about the value of gender segregation in an ideal world, but rather with a clearer understanding of its mixed functions in this one. We may not be sure about the role gender ought to play in the good society, but we can share a sense of the role gender ought not to play. Here again, legal analysis must focus less on sex-based differences and more on sex-based disadvantages. From this perspective, we must distinguish between separatist institutions that on balance challenge or perpetuate such disadvantages. Any adequate analysis must become more attentive in theory to what is evident in fact. Associations of disempowered groups carry different social meanings than do associations of empowered groups, and associations of the disempowered vary in their capacity to alter that status. Under some circumstances, this approach will require preferential treatment for all-women's institutions. Only by seeking a frame of reference that focuses more concretely on the relation between gender separatism and gender disadvantages can we begin to deal adequately with associational issues.

Private Clubs and Public Values

Historical Perspectives

According to conventional wisdom, the United States has always been a nation of joiners. In no other country, Tocqueville asserted, "has the principle of association been more successfully used or applied to a greater multitude of objects." Later accounts suggest that society's increasing secularization, urbanization, and geographic mobility have heightened the desire for organized affiliations. With the erosion of kinship, community, and religious ties, other social networks are generally thought to have grown more prominent.[7]

What sketchy empirical research is available suggests that these accounts require certain qualifications. Correlations between urbanization, secularization, and association are by no means clear. Nor is it apparent how distinctive Americans are in their desire for affiliation. Most adults do not report active participation in nonreligious associations. These qualifications should not, however, obscure the importance of such organizations to large segments of the population or to the culture in general. For the last two centuries, a broad array of civic, social, political, and professional groups has provided opportunities for personal growth and public influence. Associations ranging from the Guild of Former Pipe Organ Plumbers to societies for Females who Have Deviated from the Paths of Virtue have organized around common concerns. Larger, more diverse groups have variously served to disperse power or to consolidate privilege; to conserve traditional values or to promote social change; to safeguard minority rights or to obstruct minority influence.[8]

Much of that work has proceeded through all-male or all-female affiliations. Although there are no reliable figures on the number of such organizations, historical research leaves little doubt about the sex-segregated landscape of American associations. Throughout the eighteenth and nineteenth centuries, men generally dominated the public sphere, while women occupied the domestic sphere, and their organizational affiliations reflected similar patterns. Early all-male associations served as forums for political debate, professional interchange, and social advancement; female groups tended to center on family, charitable, and religious activities. Most of the nation's influential political and legal theorists of this period apparently shared Thomas Jefferson's conviction that, in order to prevent "depravity of morals and ambiguity of issues, women should not mix promiscuously in gatherings of men." Organizations that permitted females to be present did not necessarily invite their active participation. Women could be seen but not heard in many early abolitionist and religious societies; in some instances, they were not even to be seen. In one of the most celebrated examples, female participants in the 1840 London Anti-Slavery Conference found themselves seated in the balcony, cordoned off by curtains from the formal floor proceedings.[9]

Such experiences fostered feminist sentiments. By the mid-nineteenth century the boundaries of the sexes' separate spheres came under greater challenge. As more women sought political, educational, and employment opportunities, their desire for formal organizations increased. Some of these organizations were committed to altering gender roles, but an even larger array formed to assert traditional female values in a broader political setting. Maternal, cultural, temperance, and social-reform associations provided channels for personal interchange and public influence. By 1914, the General Federation of Women's Clubs claimed over a million members.[10]

Typically these groups formed along class and race as well as gender lines. Barred from joining white women's organizations, black women formed their own local groups and their own national federation (the National Association of Colored Women). Although the organizations of minority and nonminority women filled many of the same needs and sought many of the same objectives, their agendas were not identical. Black women's groups were much more concerned with issues of racial discrimination and somewhat less interested in issues of gender discrimination than were their white counterparts. A relatively larger number of minority organizations appear to have been successful at bridging class barriers and focusing on issues of greatest importance to poor women.[11]

Although many all-female organizations never explicitly confronted the question of male membership, those that faced the issue were generally opposed. With some prominent exceptions, such as the National Association of Women's Suffrage, most groups proceeded on the assumption that female members could best gain self-confidence and organizational skills apart from the overpowering or "constraining presence of their more experienced brothers." In a few celebrated instances, these groups invited men to participate in club functions on the same terms women had enjoyed in male gatherings: guests could adorn but not participate in the proceedings.[12]

The growing popularity of women's associations met resistance from various quarters. Many commentators worried that women's organizational commitments, together with their increased access to educational and employment opportunities, would lure participants from their appointed sphere. The inevitable effect of female associations would be "homes . . . ruined [and] children neglected." Women's clubs were blamed for everything from the rise in feminist agitation to the decline of homemade pies.[13]

Such attributions were not wholly without substance, although the causal connections were more complicated than critics generally assumed. Like their educational counterparts, early all-female associations served both to challenge and to conserve traditional roles. By providing highly circumscribed channels for women's energies, some organizations may have deflected demands for more significant public involvement. Too often, women settled for the semblance rather than the substance of power. Moreover, club membership policies often reinforced class, race, ethnic, and religious prejudices that worked against coalitions on women's issues. Yet participation in collective activities also helped lay the foundations for a broader feminist consciousness. The confidence and competence that some members gained in organizational settings encouraged involvement in other public pursuits. Even the most traditional female associations often invited feminist speakers, debated feminist issues, or inadvertently became enlisted in feminist causes. For example, social-purity societies that began with the mission of rescuing women from sin sometimes found themselves denouncing the male sexual and employment practices that rendered sin a necessary vocation. The barriers that women's organizations experienced in pursuit of traditional women's interests often helped persuade members to define such interests more broadly. To preserve the sanctity of the home, organizations such as the Women's Christian Temperance Union came to support measures that ultimately expanded women's influence outside it.[14]

The dual role of single-sex institutions in challenging and in conserving traditional gender patterns persisted throughout the twentieth century. Particularly for full-time homemakers, such clubs often provided the most accessible channel for personal growth and public influence. And, like their nineteenth-century predecessors, some traditionalist organizations evolved in the 1960s and 1970s into forums for more active feminism. But, unlike all-male clubs, few all-female associations provided important career advantages. Organizations that formed in response to men's affiliations, such as the Jaycettes, Rotary-Anns, ladies' auxiliaries, or women's professional associations, failed to attain similar social status, and most of the prominent women's organizations, such as NOW and the League of Women Voters, admitted men.

Legal Challenges

Given this historical backdrop, it is not surprising that almost all legal challenges to gender-segregated clubs have been directed at all-male institutions. Such challenges have met with only partial success. Judicial and legislative decisionmaking has sought to establish a firm boundary between public and private associations, and sex-discrimination plaintiffs have managed only to chip away at the margins, not to challenge underlying premises.

Traditionally, the state-action requirement of the Fourteenth Amendment has insulated private clubs from constitutional scrutiny. Over the last century the Supreme Court has declined to extend equal protection requirements to a segregated association absent a showing either: that it performs a "public function" by offering goods or services historically provided by governments; or that the government is significantly involved with the association through regulation or enforcement of discriminatory practices. Conferral of a liquor license or state charter has not been thought a sufficient entanglement to meet the state-action requirement.

And although the availability of tax deductions and exemptions has been an adequate nexus of government involvement in cases involving race, it has proved inadequate in cases involving gender. This double standard is also reflected in Internal Revenue Code provisions and Supreme Court precedents that have made race—but not sex—discrimination a basis for denying tax deductions and exemptions to organizations.[15]

A comparable distinction is evident in many public-accommodations statutes. Acting under the commerce power, Congress drafted Title II of the 1964 Civil Rights Act to ban discrimination in public accommodations on the grounds of race, religion, or national origin, but not sex. Political leaders willing "to end the White Cafe [were] not prepared to close down the Men's Grill." State legislatures have been somewhat more receptive. During the two decades following the Civil Rights Act, about half the states passed public-accommodations laws that included prohibitions on gender discrimination. Yet these statutes, by express provision or judicial interpretation, have generally extended only to "public" institutions. Their effect on sex-segregated clubs initially was quite limited. In the 1980s, however, lobbying and litigation efforts began to expand conventional understandings of the term "public."[16]

Those efforts have received cautious approval from the Supreme Court, although the scope of its holdings has remained unclear. First in *Roberts v. United States Jaycees* (1984), and then in *Rotary International v. Rotary Club of Duarte* (1987) and *New York State Club Association v. City of New York* (1988), the Court held that state or local antidiscrimination laws could ban gender restrictions in club membership policies without infringing First Amendment rights of association. In so holding, the Court noted that associational interests have received constitutional protection in two contexts. One line of decisions has shielded certain intimate human relationships against state intrusion in order to preserve fundamental personal liberties. A second line of precedents has recognized rights to associate in order to engage in other constitutionally protected activities—speech, assembly, and religious expression. In analyzing the first interest, the Court concluded that neither Jaycee nor Rotary clubs could claim the kind of intimate attachments that warranted constitutional protection. Factors influencing that determination included the substantial size of some club chapters, the inclusiveness of admission processes apart from gender, and the participation of nonmembers and female associate members in many organizational functions. Although a "not insubstantial" part of club activities involved protected expression, admitting women as full members would not, in the majority's view, require altering or abandoning that expression.[17]

The Court reached a similar conclusion in the *New York State Club* case. At issue was a facial challenge to an antidiscrimination law applicable to nonreligious associations that had over four hundred members, provided regular meal service, and regularly received payment directly or indirectly from nonmembers "for the furtherance of trade or business." Since the legislation had not yet been enforced, the Court was unwilling to assume that the admission of women would impair associational or advocacy interests. However, the Justices left open the possibility that individual clubs subsequently could show such impairment under principles set forth in *Rotary* and *Jaycees*.[18]

If hard cases make bad law, easy cases sometimes do no better, and the private-clubs decisions are good examples. The organizational practices at issue in *Jaycees* and *Rotary* were not typical of most sex-segregated clubs, and the Court's opinions were careful to limit their holdings to those practices. The *New York Club* decision also offered no guidance on the application of constitutional principles to large but selective clubs. What is disturbing about this sequence of cases is not the results but the rationales, and the Court's continued adherence to a public-private framework that does not adequately capture the competing values at issue.

A threshold difficulty lies with the distinction between intimate and nonintimate associations. Under the analysis endorsed in *Jaycees, Rotary International,* and various lower court decisions, the ultimate question is whether an organization seems more an extension of home or market. That leaves many groups occupying an awkward middle ground, and neither of the principal criteria the Supreme Court identified, size and selectivity, yields satisfactory distinctions.[19]

For example, what level of protection should apply to the organizations that are large but more exclusive than the Minnesota Jaycees, which reportedly had rejected no male applicant in recent memory? Many selective groups have substantial memberships; some 2,000 individuals belong to the Bohemian Club, and restrictive luncheon and country clubs frequently number in the hundreds. It is not self-evident that gender prejudice is more deserving of protection in such elitist organizations than in their more democratic counterparts. So too, the relation between size and intimacy is more complicated than conventional doctrines have acknowledged. Some exclusive organizations, although not intimate in scale, can provide forums for developing intimate relationships.

Moreover, missing from the major associational privacy cases is any acknowledgment of the values that separatism might serve, whatever an association's size or exclusivity. The dynamics of mixed and single-sex organizations differ, and separatism in some contexts may present opportunities for self-expression and collective exploration that would be inhibited by gender integration. Many feminist associations have proceeded on that assumption. Indeed, much of the literature on single-sex affiliations suggests that subordinate groups can be empowered by the exclusion of dominant groups. The ability to choose associates or to determine who should share private information and social activities is an aspect of personal liberty warranting at least some constitutional recognition independent of size and selectivity. By granting individuals the right to structure their social relationships without state intrusion, the law can create spheres of solidarity that promote both private and public values. Such associations preserve opportunities for self-expression and mutual commitment, as well as constraints on governmental power.[20]

Equally disquieting has been the courts' treatment of expressive interests. In the *Jaycees* litigation, for example, the organization's counsel asserted that women would have different attitudes about various issues on which the group had taken a public position, particularly its campaign supporting President Reagan's economic policies. Without referring to that example, the majority dismissed such claims as resting on "sexual stereotyping" and "unsupported generalizations about the relative interests and perspectives of men and women." The problem with that analysis was not simply its willingness to overlook a wealth of gender-gap studies supporting the Jaycees' argument. A more fundamental difficulty was the implication that exclusion from an all-male institution could be permissible if the club had supported its generalizations and produced evidence suggesting that female members might challenge its prevailing values. If the price of women's admission is a promise of assimilation, that alternative is deeply problematic.[21]

The claims about "women's point of view" at issue in cases like *Jaycees* are analogous to arguments that have divided American feminism for decades. Suffragists in the nineteenth and early twentieth centuries alternated between asserting that women were fundamentally the same as men and therefore entitled to the same rights of citizenship, and contending that women were fundamentally different and that their distinctive perspectives warranted equal representation. Comparable disputes resurfaced in the 1970s and 1980s fueled in part by research of feminist theorists such as Carol Gilligan and Nancy Chodorow, discussed in the chapter that follows. The implications of much of this work run counter to the position that civil liberties and women's rights organizations generally took as *amici curiae* in *Jaycees*. Claims about gender-linked attributes and attitudes that arise from males' and females' different social experience are not easily reconciled with the rhetoric of many *amici* briefs, which rejected all "stereotypical assumptions" that "women as a group will express differing . . . views merely because of their sex."[22]

Yet the case for full female participation in all-male associations like the Jaycees or Rotary need not depend on denying either sex-linked differences or the value of single-sex associations. Instead, it entails a more contextual assessment of the significance of those differences and values. If men and women as groups tend to differ in their approach to certain moral or political issues, it does not necessarily follow that the particular men and women likely to join a given organization would differ. Nor does it follow that the organization should be entitled to use gender as a crude proxy for personal ideology. In a wide variety of other contexts, courts have declined to permit the use of sex-linked generalizations, however accurate, because the social costs are too high. The same result should hold for institutions where gender segregation has perpetuated gender disadvantages. Organizations could of course consider ideology in selecting their membership; they simply could not rely on sex-based generalizations to justify categorical exclusions. Given the availability of more accurate screening devices, sexual integration need not impair an association's expressive activities. Rather, it might enrich assessment of issues on which the sexes have a common interest.[23]

A framework more attentive to gender disadvantages than gender difference would focus more directly on the social costs that flow from single-sex affiliations. These costs are more extensive than conventional public-private distinctions and state-action doctrine have acknowledged. Although the *Jaycees, Rotary,* and *New York Clubs* holdings were an advance over earlier decisions, their reach remained quite limited. They permitted states to bar gender discrimination by certain organizations, but fell short of creating a constitutional remedy for such discrimination or of clarifying the organizations subject to regulation. These limitations in the Court's approach reflect more fundamental limitations in its public-private dichotomy. Such an approach obscures how women's exclusion from spheres conventionally classified as private contributes to their exclusion from spheres uniformly understood as public.

The perpetuation of all-male associations has worked to women's disadvantage on several levels. The most direct harms involve lost opportunities for social status, informal interchanges, and personal contacts. Although defenders of men's clubs have often presented them as refuges from commercial activity, the research available undercuts that characterization. Surveys of male executives as well as reports from business and professional women consistently emphasize the significance of men's associations. Such clubs have provided forums for exchanging information and developing relationships that generate business or career opportunities. In a society where men reportedly obtain almost one-third of their jobs through personal contacts, and probably a higher percentage of prestigious positions, the commercial role of social affiliations should not be undervalued. Nor should their political significance be overlooked. Elite all-male associations have often been the site for private discussions that later emerged as public policy.[24]

Women's exclusion from "private" associations also works in less direct ways to perpetuate their subordinate public status. When employers schedule business functions at discriminatory clubs, many female employees face an uncongenial choice: attendance will compromise personal principles, while boycotts will risk compromising collegial relationships. Moreover, as the Supreme Court has long recognized in the context of racial discrimination, the denial of equal access inevitably constitutes a "deprivation of personal dignity." Sex discrimination carries similar symbolic freight. The nineteenth-century practice of organizational bundling, of cordoning off women from the centers of activity, has had numerous twentieth-century analogues. Relegating females to separate dining rooms, separate entrances, or separate organizations is an affront to their integrity and sense of self-worth. That affront is no less substantial because women "choose to put that construction on it." Rather, these symbols of inferiority, once perceived and internalized as such, can become self-perpetuating.[25]

In responding to such arguments, defenders of all-male institutions frequently maintain that women do not experience separatism as degrading but enjoy having their own clubs or dining facilities. These rejoinders, which resemble the explanations often given for excluding racial or religious minorities, obscure a fundamental distinction. Separatism imposed by empowered groups has a different symbolic and practical significance than separatism chosen by subordinate groups. Given this nation's historic traditions and cultural understandings, the exclusion of males from women's liberation groups or garden clubs no more conveys inferiority than does the exclusion of whites from black associations or Protestants from Jewish social organizations. Nor does such exclusivity perpetuate political, social, or economic disadvantages.[26]

By contrast, the forms of institutional separatism chosen by dominant groups tend to reinforce their privileged position and the stereotypes underlying it. The explanations that private-club members commonly advance for excluding women leave little doubt about the lingering strength of such stereotypes. It is variously claimed that a female presence would alter associational demeanor and decor, that women "wouldn't fit in," or that men would feel embarrassed using crude language, telling off-color jokes, or encountering "last night's date at lunch." According to one club manager, "if a man has a business deal to discuss, he doesn't want to sit next to a woman fussing about how much mayonnaise is on her chicken salad." To like-minded members of other clubs, sexual integration threatens to transform their organization's atmosphere into that of a "henhouse . . . [with] all that cackling" or of "Macy's basement at a post-Christmas sales." And as a fall-back position, some separatists invoke the perennial excuse: Washingon Metropolitan Club officials have regretfully reported that, "much [as] we love the girls, we just don't have the lavatory facilities to take care of them."[27]

The rationale for male separatism thus appears less compelling in practice than in principle. The concerns that club members typically advance mesh poorly with the apocalyptic rhetoric that their legal advocates generally employ. It is difficult to perceive the alteration of club decor as a "chilling spectacle" or a prelude to totalitarian oversight. Moreover, when sexist stereotypes dictate associational policy, they tend to become self-reinforcing. No women are present to counteract the assumption that males' luncheon conversation centers on mergers, while females' fixates on mayonnaise. Men who are uncomfortable associating with women in such social settings are unlikely to become less so if discomfort remains a justification for exclusivity.[28]

Such discomfort is not readily confined. Those who have trouble treating women as equals at clubhouse lunches will not escape such difficulties in corporate suites or smoke-filled rooms. A substantial array of social science research indicates that individuals who seem "dissimilar" are often disliked and avoided in work-related contexts. As long as women do not "fit" in the private worlds where friendships form and power congregates, they will never fully "fit" in the public sectors with which the state is justifiably concerned.[29]

The boundary between public and private is fluid in still another sense that traditional state-action doctrine declines to acknowledge. Most "private" clubs depend heavily on public support, largely in the form of state and federal tax subsidies. Clubs gain tax exemptions by claiming to be private organizations in which "substantially all" activities are for pleasure, recreation, and other nonprofit purposes, while members (or their employers) deduct dues and fees as "ordinary and necessary business expenses." This privileged status points up the difficulties of seeking to label organizations as either commercial or noncommercial, public or private. Such rigid distinctions are further compromised by other forms of governmental support that state-action doctrine has discounted, such as federal grants, state liquor licenses, or municipal services.[30]

Alternative Frameworks

An alternative approach for sex-segregated associations must begin with a greater sensitivity to context, to the varying cultural consequences of particular institutional structures. If we distinguish between organizations that can reinforce and those that can challenge gender disadvantages, men's and women's groups will frequently stand on different footings. The point is not that values of choice and intimacy have less social importance for men than women, but rather that the social costs are different. In a male-dominated society, the price of male cohesiveness is substantial. At this juncture, we cannot maximize both intimacy for men and equality for women. Nor can we underestimate the hard choices that our regulatory policies will entail. What we can do is make our choices with greater sensitivity to the full range of values underlying them. Our analysis can depend not only on the benefits available in single-sex associations but also on the likelihood that experiences of comparable value are available in mixed environments with fewer social costs.

Such an alternative approach requires a reconceptualization of public and private. In this context, a familiar feminist maxim holds particular force; the personal is the political and warrants legal recognition as such. That recognition of course only begins analysis. The difficult task lies in drawing distinctions that adequately reflect the dual role of sex-segregated institutions in enhancing and in confining human relationships. We need not only a better set of rules, but also a better understanding of their capacity to express our social aspirations.

To this end, our statutory and constitutional analysis should focus not simply on an organization's intimate or expressive character, but also on the totality of its public subsidies and public consequences. Rather than looking to any single nexus of state involvement, courts and legislatures should consider the cumulative significance of the organization's governmental and commercial entanglements. Public grants, licenses, and tax benefits can serve as legitimate bases for regulation. For example, any association that receives a substantial percentage of its revenues through tax exemptions and business deductions could be considered "public" and hence subject to prohibitions against gender discrimination. Alternatively, the state could withdraw favorable tax treatment or liquor licenses from sex-segregated organizations. Employers who subsidize membership fees and business functions at such clubs could be denied governmental contracts or be held liable for discrimination under existing statutory prohibitions. Since employers provide an estimated one and a half billion dollars in annual support to private clubs and 40 to 50 percent of the revenues of certain selective men's associations, the cumulative effect of these strategies would be significant. Recent municipal ordinances that follow some of these approaches have already had major effects on club policies.[31]

Focusing on governmental support and commercial entanglements would avoid some of the idiosyncrasies of conventional balancing approaches. Associational liberty and equal opportunity are not commensurable values that can be calibrated and offset in a neutral, principled fashion. Without a more focused framework, we are left with the kind of inconsistent decisionmaking that has viewed the Bohemian and Kiwanis clubs as private, and the Jaycees and Princeton eating clubs as public. Moreover, an approach that ties public sanctions to public entanglements accommodates competing concerns; clubs willing to forego tax advantages, employer contributions, or state licenses could retain their separatist status. This strategy would leave scope for associational choices but would not purport to be neutral as to their content. Since women's organizations on the whole tend to be less commercially oriented and thus less dependent on employer support or business expense deductions than men's organizations, such strategies would target those groups with the greatest social costs.[32]

That is not to underestimate the price of such a regulatory approach. Subjecting associational policies to state oversight increases the risk of harassing litigation and narrows the range of private choice. In some contexts, penalizing separatism by dominant groups may undermine its legitimacy for subordinate groups. We have, however, managed to prohibit racial discrimination by private clubs and schools and sex discrimination by private employers without the disabling social consequences that critics have often envisioned. Private organizations that serve public functions do not provide the only opportunities for male bonding in this society.

Of course, the more categorical any regulatory strategy, the more over- and underinclusive it will prove. Of particular concern are all-female organizations that might be inhibited by the withdrawal of preferential tax treatment. Yet a law that explicitly differentiates between men's and women's associations, while theoretically defensible, may prove politically unpalatable. The problem is not, as advocates of all-male clubs have frequently argued, that such distinctions would be unprincipled. An approach that disadvantaged men's organizations but not women's would be asymmetrical with respect to sex but not with respect to social influence. And from the point of view of reducing gender inequality, it is influence that matters.

From a more prudential perspective, however, it is risky to argue for a policy that expressly grants rights to women's but not men's affiliations. In some contexts, such as single-sex colleges or athletics, it makes sense to assume those risks. As the following discussion suggests, the small and declining number of all-male educational institutions, together with the remedial justifications for all-female learning environments, offers a defensible case for preferential treatment. So too, some sports warrant special solicitude for all women's but not all men's teams. For most forms of association, however, it is better to rely on strategies that differentiate men's and women's affiliations in practice rather than in principle. That is in part the justification for an approach that focuses on commercial entanglements and public subsidies.

Even if such a strategy encouraged more women's groups to adopt formal positions of gender neutrality, many would find that their composition did not actually change. Nor is it apparent that change is undesirable. As women become more fully integrated into male organizations, the need for some all-female associations may diminish. To the extent that groups like the Jaycettes or local women's networks have functioned less as communities by consent than communities by imitation or exclusion, their passing is an acceptable by-product of a more egalitarian society. Their demise would also have compensating benefits. Male involvement in female-dominated organizations can erode gender stereotypes and enlarge understandings of women's concerns. At the very least, an increase in sex-neutral admission policies would help undercut one of the most convenient current rationalizations for male separatism: that women are happy with their own institutions.

A more basic problem lies in the inevitable underinclusiveness of any legal assault on sex-segregated associations. The law is too blunt an instrument to reach the most influential separatist networks. Golfing groups and luncheon cliques that form along gender lines may play a more substantial role in limiting women's opportunities than any of the organized entities susceptible to legal intervention. Moreover, even in formal organizations, access does not insure admission. Nor does admission guarantee acceptance. Getting women into the right clubs is far easier than getting them to the right tables. But access is a necessary first step. Although we cannot eliminate social segregation by legal fiat, we can at least minimize its crudest form and the social legitimacy that perpetuates it.[33]

Education

Single-sex education presents comparable issues and comparable complexities. Women's schools, like women's organizations, evolved against a backdrop of separatism that they helped both to challenge and to perpetuate. The history of female education reflects the same ambivalence about gender differences that has divided the women's movement throughout the nineteenth and twentieth centuries.

Historical Perspectives

Although equal education was one of the earliest feminist demands, it enjoyed little public support during most of this nation's early history. Arguments for joint or equivalent instruction of the sexes, such as those advanced by British feminists Mary Astell and Mary Wollstonecraft in the late seventeenth and eighteenth centuries, had relatively little influence in the United States until after the Civil War. Throughout the Colonial and post-Revolution periods, female education was rudimentary. It rarely progressed beyond instruction at home or in primary schools, generally in intermittent periods when boys were absent. Proposals for more systematic education often provoked extended tributes to "Mother's knee," which, as a site of female learning, allegedly rivaled the most distinguished universities in America and Europe. As John Trumbull suggested at the end of the eighteenth century:

> Why should girls be learn'd and wise?
> Books only serve to spoil their eyes.
> The studious eye but faintly twinkles
> And reading paves the way to wrinkles.[34]

In the late eighteenth and early nineteenth centuries, a small number of private women's schools began offering more advanced courses in academic disciplines and feminine accomplishment, and support grew for public elementary education of both sexes. By the latter part of the nineteenth century, amost all public primary schools were coeducational and a rising number of all-female secondary schools were offering a standard academic curriculum. Access to these institutions was highly restricted by class and race. Until the passage of compulsory-school-attendance laws and prohibitions on child labor in the late nineteenth and early twentieth centuries, education remained a luxury many poor families could not afford. Racial and ethnic prejudice, coupled with disparities in school finance systems, created barriers for minority and lower-class students at all educational levels.[35]

Nonetheless, the growing availability of elementary and secondary instruction in the mid-nineteenth century represented a significant advance. The increased demand for teachers, and the willingness of female employees to accept salary levels well below those of men, heightened the need for college-educated women. School administrations that had once excluded female applicants began to conclude that their "gentle," "unaspiring," and "compliant" natures, as well as heightened moral sensibilities, rendered them particularly suitable for working with children. The growing women's rights movement, the availability of better secondary institutions, and the declining enrollments of male students during the Civil War and Reconstruction era also helped expand opportunities for female college applicants. In 1837, some two hundred years after the founding of the first American college, Oberlin admitted the first women undergraduates, and Mount Holyoke Seminary began what eventually became an all-female baccalaureate program. Three decades later, approximately 3,000 female students were enrolled in four-year institutions. Slightly over two-thirds were in the nation's thirty-odd women's colleges, and the remainder were dispersed across forty private coeducational colleges and eight state universities.[36]

Progress for minorities was far slower. In 1862, Oberlin granted the first college degree to a black woman in the United States; a quarter-century later, blacks numbered only about 30 of the nation's 250 female graduates. De facto and de jure segregation, coupled with financial constraints, severely limited the numbers of minority students and confined most to predominately minority institutions. However, expanded opportunities for white women laid foundations for an eventual increase in options for women of color.[37]

This expansion in female education was not without resistance. Many constituencies doubted that women had the physical or mental capacity for serious study. Opponents compiled an array of "scientific" data: women's brains were too light, their foreheads too small, their powers of reasoning too inadequate for rigorous academic programs. Female students who ignored such limitations did so at their peril. Highly influential works by Dr. Edward Clarke and his disciples warned that women who diverted their scarce biological reserves to cognitive rather than reproductive organs risked "life-long suffering," perhaps permanent sterility. Equal education for women could only result in defeminizing, deforming, and eventually depleting America's superior breeding stock. Even those who escaped physical risk would remain psychologically vulnerable. "Bookishness" was a "bad sign" in female adolescents; a rigorous academic program might tempt them from the "duties of [their} station."[38]

On closer examination, most of the empirical foundations for such claims looked rather tenuous. Dr. Clarke's work was based on six dubious cases, and more systematic research about women's physical and academic performance in higher education suggested that their alleged infirmities were more a product of "corsets and cant [than] calculus or Kant." Statistical surveys did, however, indicate that college-educated women were less likely to marry and had lower reproductive rates. Although a few observers consoled themselves by noting that such celibacy was occurring among the selfish, career-oriented women least likely to make good mothers, not all members of the educated classes contemplated their decline with equanimity. Concerns about the relation beween education and domesticity continued to color public debates, not only about equal opportunities for collegiate instruction, but also about the content and context of women's entire academic experience.[39]

The extent to which education should reflect or challenge traditional roles provoked controversy throughout the nineteenth and early twentieth centuries. To some advocates of expanded female instruction, such as Catherine Beecher and Emma Willard, the primary objective should be "the preparation of woman for her distinctive profession as housekeeper, mother, nurse, and chief educator of infancy and childhood." Critics of the more rigorous nineteenth-century academies lamented the attention to algebra and astronomy among students whose primary mission was to "sew, darn, wash, [and] starch."[40]

In responding to such claims, defenders of intellectual rigor often took an ambiguous or ambivalent course. Some emphasized that the point of instructing women in traditional disciplines was both to "enlarge their spheres of thought" and to render them "more interesting companions to men." Chemistry might be significant in it own right, but its principles were also applicable in the kitchen. Early leaders of the Seven Sisters schools vacillated between denials that domesticity was women's "sole destiny" and reassurances that higher education would not divert her from traditional "womanly ways to serve," or make her "any the less woman." The tension was particularly apparent in Southern and church-affiliated institutions, which were sometimes chartered with the explicit intent of preparing women for conventional female roles.[41]

This ambivalence about educational objectives affected curricular debates throughout the nineteenth and early twentieth centuries. Even some of the more progressive coeducational colleges, including Oberlin, initially established a separate "ladies' course" or placed other restrictions on female students' opportunities. Although these constraints tended to lapse once the "ladies" had proven their ability to handle standard academic fare, many institutions continued to offer majors in subjects such as home economics, which were designed to bridge the gap between women's traditional roles and the university's traditional disciplines. As a result, the academic as well as extracurricular programs at coeducational schools frequently reflected patterns of de facto sexual segregation. Particularly in the more elite colleges, however, the trend was toward increasingly androgynous curricula. Even the revived cult of domesticity in the 1950s failed to reverse that progression. Despite repeated calls for a feminized program of study, with greater emphasis on haute cuisine and less on modern philosophy, few four-year colleges altered their traditional approach.[42]

This disdain for "female-oriented" courses came at a cost. One result was to obscure or devalue women's experience. In their attempt to establish academic credibility, leading women's schools tended to imitate rather than innovate. A prevailing assumption, as Bryn Mawr President M. Carey Thomas expressed it, was that a "men's curriculum" was essential for women if they were to "hold their own" in professional life after leaving the university. In Thomas' view, the role of women's colleges was to encourage such professional aspirations, a view reflected in her celebrated claim, "our failures only marry." Although a few institutions such as Sarah Lawrence and Bennington attempted to gear their programs to women's interests, most curricula appeared intent on providing an education "at least as bad as that given men."[43]

With certain brief exceptions, such as Vassar's flirtation with "Euthenics" (dominated by unreflective courses on marriage and motherhood), the elite women's colleges evidenced almost no interest in women's studies until the 1970s. The focus was on encouraging individual achievement, not identifying collective problems. Even in the less prestigious all-female institutions, where relatively few graduates pursued academic or professional careers, little effort was directed toward rethinking conventional curricula, challenging traditional paradigms, or preparing students for "living with people as well as paper." Administrators who targeted special courses for women tended to confine offerings to narrow "feminine" areas such as home economics. On the whole, such instruction reaffirmed rather than challenged gender roles.[44]

Ironically enough, many early presidents of women's colleges were openly hostile to the women's rights movement, as well as to the "mannish tastes and manners" or "bumptious" professionalism that it might foster. Some institutions refused even to permit suffragist speakers on campus, let alone extend academic credit for studying their ideology, and many student bodies were equally unreceptive until late in the suffrage campaign. Even those administrators more sympathetic to the feminist movement were unwilling to consider it worthy of serious intellectual interest. Nor did faculty members feel free to devote significant scholarly attention to those areas until the 1970s. Although many of these academics had experienced gender discrimination in their own careers, few focused research on the causes and consequences of such social practices.[45]

Since most of the leaders (and many of the followers) in women's education during the late nineteenth and early twentieth centuries resisted efforts to "feminize" curricula, the rationale for single-sex institutions had to rest on different footing. Initially the main justification was male exclusivity. Most women's schools were founded at a time when administrators of prominent collegiate and secondary programs were adamantly opposed to coeducation. The reasons varied, and consistency was not among their strengths. It was claimed, for example, that romance would be both bred and destroyed by institutionalized intermingling of the sexes. Proximity would invite promiscuity or else androgyny. Some believed carnal appetites would prove uncontrollable; campuses would become "matrimonial bureaus . . . dotted with couples billing and cooing." Other critics assumed that such appetites would wither away once daily interchange made males "unmanly," females "unwomanly," and marriage less "glamourous." Many commentators, drawing on the same arguments that had been launched against any higher education for women, maintained that coeducation ignored "natural" differences in the sexes' mental capacities and social roles. Joint instruction would compromise traditional academic standards and coarsen feminine sensibilities. Related concerns involved the declne in athletic achievement, alumni contributions, and academic inquiry that would reportedly follow from female intrusion; women could scarcely be expected to hold their own on the football field or in rigorous analysis of "delicate" subjects.[46]

Early supporters of coeducational programs met opponents on their own terrain. Males and females received instruction together in the family, proponents submitted, and what could be more "natural" than the family? Not all tendencies toward androgyny were disadvantageous; society would benefit when men became more "orderly [and] gentle," and women became "stronger and more earnest" through joint education. It was sexual segregation, not integration, that was most likely to corrupt manners and morals. To some observers, the connection between female academies and feminist agitation was painfully apparent. Presumably the kind of "mutual understanding" that grew from joint instruction of the sexes would prove a desirable preventative for "extremis[m] in the suffrage cause." Such contact might also curb the "morbid tendencies," anticapitalist sentiments, and inadequate fertility rates that Calvin Coolidge accused the Seven Sister colleges of encouraging.[47]

For those unmoved by considerations of sex, there were considerations of money. However attractive in theory, separate but equal turned out to be quite expensive in practice. Most private women's schools could not match the resources of their male counterparts. Nor were taxpayers and legislators prepared to establish truly equivalent men's and women's facilities. Coeducation was cheaper and could minimize financial difficulties at formerly all-male institutions during periods of sagging enrollment. For minority communities, the costs of separate institutions were generally prohibitive. Only two black women's colleges, Spelman in Atlanta and Bennett in Greensboro, were able to secure a substantial funding base.[48]

At the turn of the century, the force of these economic as well as ideological considerations was clearly evident. Between 1870 and 1910, the proportion of colleges that was coeducational grew from less than one-third to more than one-half. By 1957, the ratio was almost three-quarters. Student agitation fueled further interest in coeducation during the 1960s and early 1970s. Administrators' initial responses varied, but many were less than enthusiastic. Harvard's President Nathan Pusey made his sentiments abundantly clear in a comment about the relation between conscription and the university's graduate programs; the draft, he predicted, would leave Harvard with the "blind, the lame, and the women." In 1971, the director of Harvard Admissions added that it would be "unfortunate to reduce the number of men . . . in order to accommodate more women students," since that would mean "less diversity in the class and, as a result, fewer interesting people." But ultimately, even Harvard College succumbed. By the mid-1980s, single-sex schools accounted for only 2.3 percent of all college women and a much smaller percentage of men, and the trend in secondary schools was similar.[49]

Legal Challenges

Such trends developed largely without legal intervention. Gender separatism in public education did not attract significant attention until the 1970s, when debates over Title IX of the Civil Rights Act and the Equal Educational Opportunities Act raised the issue. At that point, qualified tolerance for sex discrimination became explicit national policy. In relevant part, these statutes prohibited such discrimination in federally funded educational programs, but created an exception for student admissions. Prior to a restrictive Supreme Court interpretation in the early 1980s, this legislation had significant effects, particularly in affirmative-action and athletic programs. On matters of student admissions, however, congressional sponsors claimed that they lacked sufficient factual information to pass judgment and declined to treat sex like race, color, or national origin as a prohibited ground for selection. Given the substantial academic research on the subject, these legislators' professed ignorance seems largely self-imposed. From the tenor of debate, it is by no means clear that such data would have influenced deliberations. Some legislators, whose wives or constituents reportedly received "a very fine education from A to Z" at women's schools, did not appear entirely open-minded on the subject. In any event, promises of further, more systematic congressional attention to the issue have not been kept.[50]

Most American courts have retained a similar distance from the subject. For three centuries, the exclusion of women from public and private education passed without judicial objection. Until the 1980s, the Supreme Court issued no full opinions on point; ironically, its first decision prohibited discrimination against male rather than female students. Prior to that decision, the Court declined certiorari or granted summary affirmances in several cases that merited more serious scrutiny. The first of these cases arose in 1960 and involved challenges to Texas A & M's exclusion of women. A parallel claim a decade later concerned the exclusion of men from Winthrop State College in South Carolina. In both instances, the lower courts upheld gender segregation despite evidence that the institutions offered courses unavailable at other schools and were more convenient for the plaintiffs. In neither case were the judges disturbed by the gender stereotypes reflected in the academic programs at issue. While Texas A & M required military training, Winthrop offered courses in stenography, typewriting, drawing, dressmaking, millinery arts, cooking, housekeeping, and other areas "suitable" for women. According to the courts' reasoning, however, such curricular differences justified rather than indicted sex-based admissions. Although the decisions in both cases purported to preserve individual choice, they displayed no recognition of the way in which gender stereotypes constrained that choice.[51]

A comparable lack of sensitivity characterized a 1977 federal court of appeals holding in *Vorchheimer v. School District of Philadelphia*, affirmed without opinion by an equally divided Supreme Court. At issue was Susan Vorchheimer's right to attend Central High School, a public all-male college preparatory institution, rather than Girl's High, an all-female preparatory school. Despite Central's conceded superiority in mathematics and science programs, the court found that the schools offered "similar" courses, "comparable" facilities, and hence "comparable" education. From whose perspective and by what criteria remained more problematic than the court acknowledged. Certainly the institutions did not appear comparable to the plaintiff, who excelled in mathematics and science. Nor did they appear equivalent to the Philadelphia court that, in subsequent litigation under the state Equal Rights Amendment, identified numerous inequalities in library, instructional, and computer facilities as well as scholarship resources. What the federal panel also overlooked was empirical research suggesting that coeducational secondary schools promote less stereotypical attitudes toward the opposite sex than gender-segregated institutions and provide better learning environments than do all-male schools. Such findings are not conclusive, but they suggest the need for a more comprehensive inquiry than is apparent in *Vorchheimer* or other leading decisions.[52]

In this respect, the Supreme Court's decisions have not proven exceptions. The Court chose, for its first full opinion on sex-segregated education, a case that was ill-suited to the occasion. *Mississippi University for Women* [*MUW*] *v. Hogan* involved Joe Hogan's claim to admission at the nation's only all-female nursing school. In the view of many women's rights organizations, the Court's acceptance of the case for review was improvident; as their *amicus* brief noted, any holding limited to nursing schools would affect just one institution and the record was "exceedingly sparse" on the broader issue of single-sex schools. Undeterred by such observations, a divided Court upheld Hogan's claim. Although Justice O'Connor's majority opinion confined itself to MUW's school of nursing, the decision's logic was not so limited. Given the uncertain scope and symbolic significance of its holding, the majority's cursory evaluation of the merits of single-sex education remains troubling.[53]

Contemporary justifications for sex-segregated schools usually take two forms. One rationale is remedial and applies only to all-female institutions. This line of analysis suggests that gender segregation, like gender preference in affirmative-action programs, serves a short-term objective of overcoming women's historic disadvantages in educational and vocational pursuits. A second and broader rationale, applicable to both male and female schools, involves pluralism; single-sex education promotes values of cultural diversity and personal association that have traditionally enjoyed First Amendment protection.

The *Hogan* majority chose to address only the first of these claims. In rejecting Mississippi's compensatory defense, Justice O'Connor reasoned that female students had not lacked opportunities for training or advancement in nursing. Nor had Mississippi demonstrated that gender-based admission was substantially related to any remedial objective. In 1980, women constituted about 97 percent of the nursing profession, and it has been discrimination against males, not females, that has helped to depress nurses' wages and status. According to the trial testimony of two witnesses, men do not dominate the nursing classroom and would not affect female students' performance. By continuing to exclude male applicants, the university's policies perpetuated archaic gender stereotypes about nursing as a women's profession. In the majority's view, such policies could not help but "penalize the very class the state purports to benefit."[54]

Particularly since this was the Court's first full opinion on single-sex schools, its analysis left much to be desired. As MUW's brief and Justice Powell's dissent pointed out, a substantial body of research suggests that certain all-female learning environments serve compensatory objectives. Compared with coeducational institutions, women's colleges reportedly have fostered greater verbal assertiveness, higher career aspirations, more intellectual self-esteem, expanded leadership opportunities, enhanced faculty-student contact, greater access to female role models, and more opportunities for women faculty and administrators. Presumably the state might have an interest in promoting some of these characteristics even for those in female-dominated professions. Why the Court declined even to mention this research and instead relied on two witnesses' more speculative opinions is not self-evident. It may be, as one brief suggested, that the university failed to introduce such research at trial. Alternatively, certain data regarding undergraduate programs may not be relevant for nursing schools because their students are older, the percentage of male enrollees is unusually small, and opportunities for female faculty and access to female role models are already present. In any case, the majority's analysis begs for qualifications missing from the opinion.[55]

Equally problematic was the dissenting opinion's unqualified embrace of the university's compensatory claim. In extolling the virtues of single-sex education, Justice Powell, joined by Justices Burger and Rehnquist, set forth a selective and superficial account of the available research. His dissent relied uncritically on studies such as those by Elizabeth Tidball, which found that all-female colleges had produced a higher percentage than had coeducational colleges of those listed in *Who's Who of American Women* between 1910 and 1950. In explaining this disparity, Tidball argued that women's level of achievement was attributable to the greater number of female role models in women's colleges. Yet as *amici* briefs noted, the methodology of Tidball's study poses substantial problems.[56]

As a threshold matter, to view *Who's Who* listings as an adequate measure of achievement is to accept what many feminists have criticized as an impoverished understanding of individual worth, an understanding that has historically devalued women's contributions. But even accepting *arguendo* such definitions of success, one cannot infer a causal relation from a correlation without controlling for a host of variables that Tidball's research failed to acknowledge. From her data, it is impossible to separate the effects of single-sex schools from the higher socioeconomic status and career orientation of their students. Had Ivy League institutions been open to women during the period of Tidball's study, the percentage of achievers from coeducational schools might have been substantially different; subsequent research replicating Tidball's methodology suggests as much. So too, other empirical work on which the dissent and its authorities relied are, in the words of a recent Women's Coalition Report, "outdated and generally insufficient to support a coherent argument." For example, it is unclear how attributes such as greater verbal assertiveness and intellectual self-esteem in single-sex environments affect women's capacity to function in mixed environments.[57]

The pluralist defense of single-sex schools raises similar difficulties. It is true, as Justice Powell noted in *Hogan,* that generations of distinguished Americans have found "distinct advantages" in sex-segregated education. However, a comparable claim was often made about racially segregated schools and clubs, and it rested on comparable stereotypes. Moreover, nothing in the standard pluralist argument distinguishes all-female from all-male schools as an antidote for "needless conformity." According to the president of one of the few remaining all-male colleges, educational separatism fosters much the same expressive interests as those advanced in association cases; it promotes a "directness, a relaxed informal exchange." If women gained admission to the late-evening beer sessions where male students sat around "talking about Thomas Wolfe, Bismarck, or girls, or whatever . . . what they talked about would be different." Yet it might also be better. Experience at other institutions does not suggest that coeducation banishes Bismarck from the intellectual landscape. Nor does it prevent students from continuing to congregate in other single-sex settings. It may, however, help to erode what some students and faculty of all-male colleges have acknowledged as part of their distinctive atmosphere: the tendency to regard women as "sex objects" rather than as potential equals.[58]

Thus, the enhancement of some students' choices can only come at the cost of restricting others, and history leaves little doubt about which sex has paid the greater price for segregation. Nor does limiting the pluralist defense to women's institutions entirely solve these difficulties. Contrary to the dissent's suggestion in *Hogan,* perpetuating such institutions does not unequivocally "expan[d] women's choices." To affirm the "honored traditions" of Mississippi University for Women, which focused on typewriting, teaching, nursing, and needlework, is to reinforce expectations that have constrained, not enlarged, female options. Lumping all women's schools into the same abstract category ignores the diversity in experiences that such institutions have fostered.[59]

The complexity in cases like *Hogan* is that no single constituency speaks for women's interests. Separatist education, like other separatist associations, offers the vices and virtues of a ghetto: it provides support, solidarity, and self-esteem for subordinate groups, but often at the price of perpetuating attitudes that perpetuate subordination. For some constituencies, such as the MUW alumnae association that filed an *amicus* brief supporting its alma mater, the direct personal benefits of gender segregation are worth the price. For organizations such as the National Organization for Women, which took the contrary position in *Hogan,* the costs of gender stereotyping are prohibitive.

In the face of such competing concerns and conflicting data, American courts have steered a muddled course, and the prospects for improvement do not appear substantial. Separate but equal as educational policy remains a perplexing misnomer. In some respects separate is better, in other respects worse, but never is it likely to be equal. Nor has the judiciary done an impressive job of sorting out the differences. Given the backdrop of inequality against which such issues arise, we might expect that doubts would be resolved in favor of all-female but not all-male schools. In that sense, the converse pattern emerging from *Vorchheimer* and *Hogan* carries an ironic symbolic message.

Alternative Frameworks

Men's schools, like men's clubs, have often been "witting or unwitting devices for preserving tacit assumptions of male superiority." The effect of women's secondary and undergraduate institutions has been more mixed and justifies a different degree of legal tolerance. At least in the short run, the most desirable result may be a return to the general pattern of noninvolvement that traditionally characterized the law's role in single-sex education. All-male secular schools are already verging on extinction, and all-female institutions seem destined to avoid that fate only as long as they provide advantages lacking in coeducational settings. Given the difficulties that courts have experienced in assessing those advantages, judicial restraint seems a generally prudent strategy. Only in contexts like *Vorchheimer* or *Hogan,* where the disparities in resources or the harms of stereotypes are so apparent and the adverse impact of integration is so minimal or uncertain, is legal intervention justifiable. At this historical moment, undermining all-female institutions through tax policies, funding cutoffs, or constitutional mandates is a dubious use of legal resources.[60]

In the long run, however, separatist education requires rethinking. Perpetuating segregated institutions is often a poor substitute for improving integrated ones. In all-female settings, it is more difficult to challenge the cultural attitudes that reinforce subordination; by definition, many of those most in need of such challenge are absent. One goal of contemporary women's schools should be to create a society in which their compensatory function is no longer required. To the extent that all-female institutions have been especially supportive for female students by providing role models, leadership opportunities, and positive teaching environments, those characteristics should become more dominant in coeducational settings as well.

To make existing educational structures truly coeducational we must focus not just on admissions policies but also on institutional priorities. Although women by no means speak with one voice on such issues, there are certain concerns that large constituencies share. A school genuinely hospitable to these concerns would have different relations with its internal and surrounding communities than those typical of existing institutions. Its working environment would have a less hierarchical and sex-segregated structure than the prevailing norm, in which female and minority support staffs dominate the lower reaches and white male tenured professors and senior administrators occupy the upper tier. Its student body would include a broader cross-section of American society, including more minorities and greater representation of older and part-time women enrollees with interrupted career patterns and competing family responsibilities. Its curricula, classroom climate, financial aid, and affirmative-action policies would be more responsive to the experiences of subordinate groups and to the need for challenging as well as transmitting dominant intellectual paradigms. And its wage-scales, working hours, leave policies, and childcare commitments would reflect greater sensitivity to the needs of working parents. The objective, as Virginia Woolf emphasized, is not for women simply to "join the [academic] procession." It is rather for both women and men to rethink the direction of that procession and the terms on which they are prepared to enter.[61]

Athletics

Gender discrimination in athletics presents similar concerns, and similar questions about priorities. Given the critical problems facing American women—poverty, sexual violence, reproductive liberty, occupational inequality, childcare—should getting girls into Little League baseball be a pressing feminist objective? Will equal access for women risk accepting a male model of athletic achievement, one preoccupied with competition, aggression, and profitability?

To those concerned with equity in sports, the answers involve both practical and symbolic considerations. Athletic activity promotes physical and psychological health; it reduces cardiovascular risks, provides coping mechanisms for stress and anxiety, and fosters personal skills and collegial relationships. In contemporary American society, athletic achievement also confers prestige, respect, and self-esteem, as well as educational and employment opportunities. Moreover, gender disparities in sports have been both a cause and a consequence of broader cultural stereotypes involving masculinity and femininity. Substantial progress toward gender equality will require challenging those stereotypes wherever they persist, and athletics is no exception.

Traditionally, athletic prowess has been far more valued in men than in women. Until the last century, the feminine ideal was inconsistent with strenuous physical competition. Standards of dress, complexion, figure, and behavior discouraged female sports. Any male-female interaction on the playing field involved largely noncompetitive or relatively sedate pastimes that could be pursued without acquiring an indelicate sweat. Most of these activities—riding, archery, or croquet—served mainly to provide respectable social encounters for the upper classes. During the late nineteenth and early twentieth centuries, those norms gradually changed, partly in response to efforts by physicians, educators, and women's rights advocates. After some all-female colleges introduced exercise regimens and team sports to balance their intellectual programs, other educational institutions gradually followed suit. The rising popularity of bicycles, the less restrictive trends in women's fashions, and the changing standards of female beauty all encouraged greater athletic activity.[62]

Women's increasing involvement in sport, like their involvement in education, provoked objections along two major lines. Women were allegedly unsuited for sport, and sport would make women unsuitable as women. The female physique and disposition would not bear the strain of competition. Some of the concerns were well expressed by a principal of an English women's college at the close of the nineteenth century. Her institution had become a "hotbed of hockey," and she could not help but register some misgivings when watching her first match. "The children will hurt themselves if they all run after one ball," she predicted. "Get some more balls at once."[63]

If women persisted in their "Amazonian ambitions," their efforts could drain "vital forces" necessary for reproduction (a threat that strenuous domestic work somehow failed to present). Sporting activities would both disfigure and divert women from their rightful roles; they would develop large feet, coarse hands, and "bicepts like a Blacksmith." As G. K. Chesterton put it, "let women play violent and confusing games if you think it will do them any good to be violent and confused."[64]

Partly in response to these objections, women's physical education developed along less competitive lines than men's. Female involvement in formerly male sports such as basketball was often defended as a way to enable participants to develop "poise and grace and become better ladies." In the late 1920s, the leaders of physical education for women in the United States formally rejected what they perceived as an increasingly competitive and market-oriented model of men's sports. Their alternative was a program based on educational values, widespread participation, and positive social interaction rather than competitive achievement.[65]

By the late 1960s, limitations in this model were provoking widespread dissatisfaction. No athletic scholarships were available to women, interscholastic programs were relatively rare, and many physical education departments stressed activities that required few skills (ring tossing or rhythmic hoola-hooping) or promoted vicarious roles (cheerleading and pep-club activities). Women who excelled in sports not traditionally associated with women risked being stigmatized as socially and/or sexually "deviant."[66]

Partly in response to these concerns, Congress passed Title IX of the Civil Rights Act (1972), which prohibited sex discrimination in educational programs receiving federal funds. Although the legislative history concerning its application to athletics is murky, congressional sponsors clearly did not envision full equality. As then-Senator Birch Bayh put it, "we are not requiring that intercollegiate football be desegregated."[67]

What exactly Congress was requiring, and what should be the standards for assessing equal athletic opportunity, have remained open to dispute. In 1975, the Office of Health, Education, and Welfare promulgated regulations clarifying that Title IX would permit separate teams for men and women in contact sports or in any activity where selection is based on "competitive skill." If a noncontact sport is available only to members of one sex, and athletic opportunities for the other sex have "previously been limited," members of the excluded sex must be allowed to try out for the team offered. Subsequent HEW regulations made clear that funding need not be equal for men's and women's programs. Nor does it need to be proportional to the number of male and female athletes at a particular institution, except in providing scholarships. Instead, the regulations somewhat ambiguously require "equivalent treatment" in order to provide "equal accommodation of the interests and abilities" of each sex.[68]

The decade following Title IX's enactment witnessed dramatic progress. The number of female athletes in interscholastic collegiate competition increased fourfold, even greater advances occurred at the secondary level, and litigation or legislation resulted in female access to many formerly all-male teams or programs, including Little League baseball. But major inequalities also persisted. The Civil Rights Commission's 1980 report noted that in colleges with major sports programs, budgets for female athletics were less than half those for males. Subsequent surveys of secondary as well as collegiate institutions revealed that fewer sports were open to women and that they experienced discrimination in coaching, facilities, equipment, practice schedules, competitive opportunities, and related areas. The merger of male and female sports programs that Title IX encouraged had an ironic effect on decisionmaking structures. Women lost key administrative and coaching positions, together with control over budget and personnel decisions.[69]

Beginning in the early 1970s, these discriminatory patterns prompted litigation under state and federal constitutional provisions as well as Title IX. Results have been mixed. Much of the difficulty has again stemmed from courts' focus on gender difference rather than on the disadvantages that have resulted from it. Early judicial decisionmaking provided striking examples of the very stereotypes that litigants sought to challenge. A case in point involved a 1971 Connecticut state court decision that girls could be excluded from a high school's only cross-country running team. In the court's view, "The present generation of our younger male population has not become so decadent that boys will experience a thrill in defeating girls in a running contest . . . With boys vying with girls in cross country running and indoor track, the challenge to win and the glory of achievement, at least for many boys would lose incentive and become nullified. Athletic competition builds character in our boys. We do not need that kind of character in our girls." In other cases involving equal-protection challenges, courts have assumed that "innate physical differences" justify excluding males from female teams or females from male teams, despite the lack of comparable opportunities for the excluded athletes. Thus one judge explained, the Constitution "does not create a fictitious equality where there are real differences."[70]

As in other contexts, courts have taken as innate and essential differences that are in part cultural and contingent. Physiological characteristics are heavily influenced by social norms governing diet, appearance, dress, behavior, and athletic opportunities. How much of males' advantage in most sports results from nature and how much from nurture remains unclear. It is, however, obvious that the differences in men's and women's capabilities are relatively small in comparison to the differences in opportunities now open to them. Since the most effective way to challenge assumptions of inherent female inferiority is to provide successful counterexamples, our athletic policies must become less preoccupied with gender differences and more concerned with gender disadvantages.

To address these disadvantages, courts and commentators have identified two basic approaches. The first is to unify all athletic programs and allocate opportunities for participation without regard to sex. Advocates of this approach generally begin from the premise that separate can never be equal, and that gender as a selection principle will inevitably prove under- and overinclusive. Under current circumstances, the difficulty with this strategy is that female athletes would be unable to qualify in large numbers for most teams. Until adequate remedial programs and competitive opportunities at all skill levels are available, gender neutrality in form will not yield gender equality in fact.[71]

A preferable approach is to permit separate teams but make them truly equal in terms of expenditures, practice schedules, equipment, coaching, and so forth. One way to insure greater equity would be to adopt an Olympic scoring method; separate teams would compete against those of their own sex, but scores would be combined to determine interscholastic rankings. Under such a system, economies of scale could result from having male and female teams share the same schedule and staff. If there is insufficient interest to justify a team for both males and females, HEW regulations specify a reasonable approach; members of the excluded sex must be allowed to try out for the team offered if athletic opportunities have previously been limited for that sex. Such a strategy has the advantage of being neutral in form but responsive to differences in fact. Those whose previous opportunities have been limited are overwhelmingly female. Allowing women to compete for places on men's teams would help redress sex-based disadvantages; allowing men to compete for places on women's teams would amplify those disadvantages.

One difficulty with this approach involves the exceptional female athlete who would prefer to forego competition with her own sex in order to work with males closer to her skill level. Although some courts and commentators have justified accommodating her preference, such an approach risks maximizing individual opportunity at the expense of broader social goals. Without the example, inspiration, and assistance that an outstanding teammate can provide, all-female programs are less likely to break the stereotypes of second-class status.[72]

However this particular issue is resolved, a more fundamental point deserves emphasis. The objective of maximizing women's participation in sports is not only to equalize opportunities but also to transform them.

As women increasingly become respected competitors and national leaders in athletics, they will have a greater chance to challenge its premises and priorities. These individuals will be in a position to develop alternative models that are less commercial, less combative, and less dangerous. As more women become participants rather than spectators, they must take the opportunity to rethink as well as master athletic demands.[73]

Different but Equal

Analogous claims could be made about female entrance into other institutions. If we are to make significant progress toward a more humane and egalitarian social order, our focus must be not simply on access to, but alteration of, existing structures. One danger is that women's gradual absorption into prevailing social networks will result in assimilation, not alteration. In attempting to become full "members of the club," women may lose the perspective or inclination to question its underlying premises. Once inside, female members may have less interest in challenging the closed networks of privilege that membership reflects and reinforces. How to avert that form of acculturation is one of the most critical issues confronting feminism. For women to attain equality without relinquishing difference, to ascend the hierarchy without losing commitment to change it, remain central objectives.

As we make progress toward these goals, our sense of separatism may change. At this juncture, it is impossible to assess what role single-sex institutions might play in a truly egalitarian society. It is hard enough to sort out their competing values in the current social order. For the present at least, separate is not equal. But neither can women entirely forego separatism without greater control over the terms of integration.

Conclusion: Principles and Priorities

After a period of enormous growth, American feminism in the 1980s showed signs of strain. In many respects, the difficulties paralleled those of an earlier era. The decades following enfranchisement witnessed considerable division and disaffection concerning women's issues. After gaining the ballot, suffragists were unable to unite around another cause, and most of the postsuffrage generation avoided feminist activity. The trend in the 1920s was toward increasing individualism, and those who remained interested in women's common problems could not agree about potential solutions. Deep theoretical and political disputes centered on whether women would gain more by stressing their differences or their commonalities with men.[1]

Comparable problems have emerged a half-century later. Although unsuccessful in their campaign for a constitutional amendment, women's rights advocates have secured legal prohibitions against most overt forms of gender discrimination. These victories have removed some of the impetus for feminist efforts, as has the country's generally conservative tilt. Whatever the movement's difficulties, they have been greatly exaggerated by the media, which makes news by declaring feminism dead, dying, or permanently disabled. Public figures have tended to avoid the feminist label, and others have often prefaced support for women's issues with the disclaimer: "I'm not a feminist but..."[2]

Yet at the same time feminism's political progress has slowed, its theoretical efforts have been flourishing. Women's studies programs have been growing in scope and strength, and gender has become an increasingly significant category of analysis across a wide array of disciplines. Contemporary feminist theory has placed long-standing questions in new perspective; it has not only recast debates about women's differences from men, it has also redirected concerns about women's differences from each other.[3]

These developments have obvious relevance for the law's approach to gender discrimination. What may be less obvious is that the converse is also true. Law can inform theory just as theory can inform law. Emerging currents in feminist jurisprudence can help shape conceptions of the just society and the priorities that it entails.

Differences over Difference

American feminists have always differed over difference. During the suffrage campaign, some activists stressed natural rights while others stressed natural roles. Building on the work of liberal theorists such as John Stuart Mill, many suffragists invoked basic similarities between the sexes as an argument for equal legal treatment. Other suffrage leaders emphasized woman's distinctive qualities as an argument for her full participation in public life. With their special nurturing capacities and moral sensitivities, women would "purify politics." Like its European counterparts, this second strand of feminism sought "equality in difference."[4]

In the postsuffrage era, this divergence in theoretical premises assumed greater political significance. Without a unifying objective such as the ballot, conflicts within the feminist movement increased. Its liberal wing focused major effort on a constitutional amendment providing that "equality of rights [would not be denied] on account of sex." Other feminists opposed that effort, largely because of its implications for protective legislation ostensibly favoring women. To ERA opponents, equality in fact was more critical than equality in form, and progress was possible only through measures responsive to social and biological differences between the sexes.[5]

A half-century later, these issues of sameness and difference reemerged. In the 1960s and early 1970s, the women's movement tended to emphasize similarities between the sexes and their entitlement to equal opportunities. Relatively few feminists outside the lesbian community focused on validating women's distinctive attributes.

By the late 1970s and early 1980s, however, increasing numbers of theorists were emphasizing the centrality of sexual difference, while disagreeing about its origins and consequences. From their perspective, gender inequality stemmed less from denial of opportunities available to men than from devaluation of functions and qualities associated with women. This tradition encompassed a broad range of methodologies and perspectives that do not readily coexist under any single label. Nor has there emerged any single term for this group of theorists. For the purposes of this discussion it makes sense to use "relational feminists." As Karen Offen has suggested, this phrase highlights the importance of relationships in explaining attributes historically linked with women. It also has the advantage of encompassing European as well as American theorists. Although the diversity among relational perspectives should not be understated, what bears emphasis here are the strengths and limitations of certain common themes.[6]

This group of feminists has focused attention on women's reproductive role and the responsibilities it has traditionally entailed. From the vantage of *The Second Stage* in the American women's movement, Betty Friedan identified a new "feminist mystique" as confining as the feminine version it sought to replace. According to her account, the problem in the 1950s was entrapment in the home; in the late 1970s and 1980s, the problem was entrapment in the world outside the home. In Friedan's view, the uncritical embrace of male standards of achievement had led women to devalue their own needs for intimacy and nurturance. The solution was a restructuring of social institutions that would permit better accommodation of work and family roles.[7]

A similar focus on maternity was apparent in other feminist work of the late 1970s and early 1980s. Psychoanalytic accounts, such as Nancy Chodorow's and Dorothy Dinnerstein's, stressed the developmental roots of gender differences and the importance of "mothering in reproducing mothers." According to these theories, children tend to develop a closer attachment to a primary caretaker of the same sex. Individuals who form a strong primary attachment early in life will be more likely in later years to define themselves in relation to others and to develop close nurturing relationships. Since most primary caretakers have been female, girls have disproportionately tended to grow up with the inclination and capacity for caretaking roles.[8]

Other feminists gave greater weight to biology. Although in the 1960s Alice Rossi had been a leading proponent of "socially androgynous" conceptions of gender roles, by the 1980s she was offering more sociobiological accounts of sexual differences. Theorists such as Susan Griffin, Jean-Bethke Elshtain, and Elizabeth Wolgast ascribed similar importance to women's innate capacity for child-rearing and the nurturing values associated with it. In work that paralleled or drew from strands in contemporary French feminism, a growing number of other American commentators stressed women's essential "specificity" rather than commonality with men.[9]

Some theorists, less wedded to biological or psychoanalytic explanations, emphasized women's distinctive experience as caretakers as the foundation for other gender differences. According to scholars such as

Sarah Ruddick, motherhood endowed women with a special capacity for "maternal thinking," an analytic style that privileged nurturing values. A related school of thought, popularized by Carol Gilligan, was noncommital about the origin of gender differences but insistent on their significance for moral theory. Gilligan's major work, *In a Different Voice,* merits particular attention, for it achieved wide public recognition, had substantial influence on legal scholars, and sparked many of the most heated theoretical debates.[10]

Gilligan's work drew from literary analysis, psychological theory, and field research. In part, her objective was to challenge Lawrence Kohlberg's influential six-stage theory of moral development. Based on empirical research involving only males, Kohlberg argued that the highest levels of moral maturity required a subordination of relationships to rules (stage four) and rules to universal principles of rights and justice (stages five and six). In Gilligan's study, these analytic styles were predominately, though not exclusively, displayed by male subjects. Women were more likely than men to reason in a "different voice," one that stressed responsibility and relationships. This voice corresponded most closely to Kohlberg's stage three, where subjects defined morality in interpersonal terms and emphasized aiding others.[11]

Building on this empirical work, Gilligan argued that conventional moral and legal theory had placed excessive weight on hierarchies of abstract rules and principles and had granted inadequate emphasis to responsibilities arising from concrete relationships. In tones that both echoed and influenced other relational feminists, she advocated an ethic of responsibility as well as rights, an ethic more attentive to care, cooperation, and context in the resolution of human problems.[12]

This strand of relational feminism has been influential in a number of respects. When a group has experienced substantial discrimination, an affirmation of group-linked traits and values is often critical in establishing collective self-esteem. For many women, relational feminism has served functions comparable to black separatism and to other work validating contributions of racial, ethnic, and religious minorities.

Such validation can provide an important counterweight to the dominant culture. The significance of that function for women became increasingly clear during the late 1970s and the 1980s, as more women began entering traditionally male occupations and institutions. Most popular advice for these new entrants has been to assimilate at almost any cost. If women didn't quite fit in, the strategy has been to change them, not the institution. Books, manuals, and magazines for working women have frequently appropriated feminist concerns but advocated strategies at odds with feminist commitments. The stated objective, which feminists have long shared, has been to help women gain personal fulfillment, economic security, social status, and public influence. Yet the means proposed are scarcely conducive to feminist process or principles: for example, an "absolute deference" to male superiors; avoidance of "personal" relationships with female subordinates; self-assertive behavior with colleagues; single-minded pursuit of occupational status; and recognition that "nice girls finish last and nice women come in second to nice guys." Yet individual efforts to "have it all" leave unchallenged the social forces that make having it all impossible. This "dress for success" feminism has been, at its core, profoundly antifeminist and has become more a symptom of women's problems than a solution to them.[13]

Relational feminist work has challenged these assimilationist impulses. Unlike much of the difference-oriented discourse that had preceded it, this strain of feminist theory has not merely celebrated values traditionally associated with women. It has insisted that these values *be valued* and has demanded changes in occupational structures, public policies, and male attitudes. The point has been not simply to celebrate women's experience but to change men's, to affect their conduct in work, family, and political contexts.

This body of theory has made similar contributions to the development of feminist jurisprudence. In particular, it has focused attention on the legal reforms necessary to accommodate caretaking values, reforms that will require fundamental changes in family, welfare, and employment policies. Among some constituencies, relational feminist work has provided a theoretical underpinnng and political catalyst for such changes. At the same time, it has underscored the limitation of a conventional rights-oriented strategy for achieving them. The inadequacies identified by scholars such as Gilligan have paralleled concerns of critical legal theorists, some of whom have directly incorporated relational approaches in their work. Taken together, this body of critical and feminist scholarship has helped reshape the analysis of gender-related issues. As women's representation in the legal profession increases, a body of work that speaks to their distinctive experience can have increasing influence.

While relational feminist theory has made significant contributions, they have not come without cost. Much of this work has provoked important criticism that has not been taken into account adequately in either popular or legal circles. In part, the critiques have been methodological and have emphasized the inattention to differences in women's experiences across culture, class, race, and ethnicity. Related concerns have involved the lack of focus on historical, social, and economic forces that mediate these experiences. Gilligan's work sparked particular objections, on the grounds that her approach replicated certain flaws that she had identified in Kohlberg's: universalizing from a small, unrepresentative sample and providing inadequate justifications of how she categorized moral responses. Such methodological difficulties have assumed greater significance in light of other research that cast doubt on how different the different voice really was. A review of some sixty studies involving Kohlberg's moral reasoning stages disclosed no tendency for males to score higher than females; in fact the majority of such studies revealed no sex distinctions at all.[14]

Of course, as Gilligan and her defenders have responded, such findings have their own limitations; "the fact that men and women are capable of the same level of justice reasoning on the Kohlberg scales has no bearing on whether women would choose to frame moral issues that way." Given the substantial body of research that has found some gender differences in reasoning styles, the issue should prompt further inquiry. It cannot be assumed, as Giligan has noted, that males' and females' different experiences in this culture leave "no psychological trace . . . [that is] significant for moral development." Nor can it be denied that the voice relational feminists have associated with women does resonate with many women.[15]

Yet at least some of that resonance may be the product of internalized gender stereotypes that have contributed to women's disadvantage. As the preceding historical material reflects, males' association with abstract rationality and females' with interpersonal nurturance reflect long-standing dichotomies that have restricted opportunities for both sexes. The celebration of women's maternal instincts by some relational feminists bears a striking resemblance to the assertions of antifeminists throughout the last several centuries. The claims that women's liberation does not lie in "formalistic" equality but in "the recognition of that specific thing in the feminine personality—the vocation of a woman to become a mother" reflects the phrasing of Pope Paul VI; it could as readily be drawn from work of the New Right or the feminist left.[16]

These different constituencies have of course drawn quite different political conclusions from their points of common emphasis. However, traces of conservative ideology have surfaced in the work of some relational feminists, including those with leftist backgrounds, who have advocated women's retention of primary caretaking roles. Other commentators, such as Friedan, have urged the women's movement to build support among more traditional voters by stressing family concerns and avoiding "diversionary" or "incendiary" issues such as lesbianism. As in the later stage of the suffrage campaign, this approach has invited activists to broaden their public appeal by narrowing their social vision.[17]

Moreover, feminist theory has reverberations outside feminist circles. Essentialist presentations of Woman may reproduce as well as reflect dominant gender stereotypes. Relational rhetoric is easily appropriated by right-wing leaders who have always known that "you girls think differently" and who have exaggerated the importance of such differences. Recent experiences such as the antipornography campaign leave no doubt about the repressive uses of progressive theories. So too, women supporters of Robert Bork's Supreme Court nomination credited him with speaking in "a different voice," and defendants in sex-discrimination cases have invoked relational theories about women's caretaking priorities to explain women's underrepresentation in well-paying occupations. The risk for feminists in validating gender difference is that it can reinforce the antifeminist premises they wish to oppose.[18]

Celebration of women's distinctive attributes also risks oversimplifying and overclaiming. Understandings of male and female characteristics have been heavily dependent on gender stereotypes and social constraints. Sex-linked traits have been profoundly affected by forces that are culturally contingent, not biologically determined. Our physiological inheritance can be expressed in a wide variety of ways; it reflects changing social conventions concerning the sexes' appearance and behavior. Gender is part of what constructs and constrains human identity, but it is only part. Its significance varies for different individuals and social groups under different social circumstances. Although some relational works have been careful to underscore that point, others have not. Nor have such qualifications appeared in summaries by the popular press.

If women do sometimes speak in a "different voice," it may be one that is more ascribed than intrinsic. It is, morever, a voice that speaks in more than one register. Missing from some relational work, particularly as it has figured in legal and journalistic accounts, is any attention to the dark side of the difference, to the less benign aspects of women's caretaking roles and values. Mother-child relations have resulted in physical and psychological abuse as well as care and concern. For some women, family ties have encouraged forms of dependence and parochialism that carry heavy individual and social costs. Although some relational work has acknowledged the downside of difference, the tendency too often has been to dismiss its significance or assume it will vanish automatically as structures of subordination erode.

That tendency is understandable. Much of what is theoretically and politically empowering about relational feminism comes from its insistence on the positive attributes of women's experience. But that emphasis carries a price, which increases when rhetoric outruns experience. Certain strands of relationalism risk the simplistic sentimentalism that marred the suffrage campaign. Just as some late-nineteenth- and early-twentieth-century activists claimed that woman's involvement would purify politics, contemporary theorists have often assumed that her participation will of itself reshape the structure and substance of public decisionmaking. That assumption finesses the difficult question of how women's voice will attain such influence. And it ignores the possibility that what will change most is the voice, rather than the context in which it is heard. Contemporary research on leadership styles and political values generally discloses less substantial sex-linked differences than relational theory suggests.[19]

Of course, much of that research was completed before significant numbers of women gained influence. But it may also be true that in most bureaucratic organizations and political structures, those who succeed, whether male or female, generally conform to prevailing values. An "add woman and stir" approach does not of itself ensure transformation of the existing social order. Nor is it clear that women are necessarily better off in societies that attach greatest importance to cooperative, caretaking values. By virtually any index of social, economic, and political status, women do not fare better in Japan than in the United States.

From a legal perspective, further difficulties arise from some relational feminist works, which present stark contrasts between reasoning based on abstract rights (a style predominately associated with men), and reasoning based on concrete responsibilities (a style predominately associated with women). In many contexts, rights impose responsibilities, and responsibilities imply rights. Often the concepts serve identical ends. For example, a right to freedom from sexual harassment imposes a responsibility not to engage in it. The converse is also true, and privileging one form of discourse over the other is unlikely to reshape the foundations of American law. As discussion of the special-equal and public-private debates suggested, we need a jurisprudence that can transcend such dichotomies. Conventional rights-oriented frameworks have often served more to restate than resolve fundamental social conflict. Yet women have also made substantial gains through a rhetoric of rights. Further progress is possible only through an approach that insists on integrating ethics of both autonomy and connection. Our problem is less a poverty of moral vocabulary than an absence of concrete strategies for accommodating the needs of self and other, of independence and interdependence.

Efforts to develop such strategies can profit from relational theory, but only if its use is more reflective and more attentive to the limitations previously noted. Too often, the attempt to incorporate feminist perspectives into legal scholarship has a disturbingly *deus ex machina* flavor. Women's different voice arrives just in time to supply whatever dimensions the author finds important and undervalued in contemporary legal discourse. Often these dimensions could just as easily be associated with humanism, socialism, or critical theory; the feminism shows up in the footnotes, in the selection of citations.

This implies a need for some revisions in relationism and the jurisprudence that borrows from it. To ignore sexual differences is to ignore human experience; to romanticize their value is to risk exaggeration. If women are to obtain adequate recognition of their distinctive experience, they must transcend its constraints. The difference dilemma cannot be resolved; it can only be recast. The critical issue should not be difference, but the difference difference makes.[20]

Differences over Sameness

Underlying the sameness-difference debate among contemporary theorists have been broader issues of cultural ideals. Although not all relational feminists have addressed the point directly, much of their work has raised basic questions about the importance of sexual identity in a just society. Is the objective an androgynous social order in which sex becomes, like eye color, a biological characteristic without broader significance? Or is the ideal more pluralistic, with room for sex-linked traits and values that do not translate into social disadvantages? And, most important, is continuing the sameness-difference debate in this form productive?

During the initial phase of the contemporary women's movement, many theorists assumed the desirability of breaking down linkages between sexual identity and social roles. Their vision implied an androgynous social order, although most commentators never used that term, and those who did so gave it varying content. From this work, two dominant understandings of androgyny emerged. One corresponded to the literal meaning of the concept: the best traits of man (andros) and woman (gyne) would exist side by side in the same person. This ideal type reflected a kind of Jungian approach that would infuse into each sex the distinctive qualities of the other. An alternative vision offered no single ideal, but rather a spectrum of traits and roles equally available to men and women. Apart from physiological differences, no sex-based distinctions would require social recognition. Implicit in both visions was a commitment to individual self-determination, unconstrained by gender. This philosophical commitment was reinforced by psychological research suggesting that men and women who combine masculine and feminine traits respond more effectively in a variety of situations than persons who conform to conventional male or female stereotypes. Androgyny offered both an ideal of human identity unconstrained by gender roles, and a vision of social relations unmarred by sex-based hierarchies.[21]

Such androgynous visions attracted little popular support. With the rise of relational work, enthusiasm declined in feminist circles as well. Some early proponents of the concept, such as Alice Rossi and Alison Jaggar, revised their views. Others became convinced that the vision was unlikely ever to "play in Peoria," and that its negative connotations signaled broader conceptual difficulties. These difficulties became more apparent during the contemporary Equal Rights Amendment campaign. The ratification struggle revealed considerable public resistance to the "unisex" society that the Amendment came to symbolize. For a substantial constituency, the proposed constitutional mandate appeared to deny important and inescapable differences between the sexes. Other observers, while rejecting that view of the ERA, were equally uncomfortable with an androgynous social vision. From their perspective, sex was not like social class; they could not imagine gender withering away as a significant fact in human life. Sexual difference and sexual desire seemed inextricably linked. Androgyny often conjured up threatening images of a homosexual, bisexual, or hermaphroditic world. Alternatively, the image was that of a heterosexual but homogenized social order, lacking in richness and variety.[22]

Many feminists also worried about the effort necessary to suppress sex-linked characteristics and questioned whether the result would be worth the cost. Androgyny seemed lacking in any coherent account of child development or any historically situated understanding of human subjectivity. Although in theory the androgynous ideal called for integration of masculine and feminine qualities, critics feared that in practice the consequence would be development of a predominately male archetype. As they noted, most of the change in gender roles that has recently occurred in American society has been asymmetrical. Females have assumed males' traits and occupations with much greater frequency than males have assumed females'. Women in pin-striped suits on Wall Street are no longer a novelty; men in aprons on paternity leaves are much rarer. Even if further changes in sex-linked attributes become more symmetrical, the results could remain stereotypical. Without deeper changes in cultural ideals, the new androgynous archetype could be some combination of two inadequate halves, a cross between "John Wayne and Brigitte Bardot." To many feminists, continued use of the term thus seems misconceived. It may perpetuate the norms of masculinity and femininity that it seeks to challenge. By assuming that the merger of sexual identities is the only secure foundation for social equality, androgyny may divert attention from the broader cultural forces that have made such equality unattainable.[23]

Within this framework, the debate about androgyny is unresolvable and unproductive. What is most problematic about current gender relations is disparities in power; it is impossible to resolve what gender would become in an ideal society where by definition such disparities did not exist. Defenders and opponents in the current debate have often been speaking past each other on the most crucial issues. Many criticisms fail to confront androgyny in the sense proponents mean it: as an ideal that balances both sexes' best qualities. Analysis of that vision cannot proceed in a vacuum. The question is always: compared to what? Equal if not greater difficulties arise with the pluralist vision that critics of androgyny have generally preferred. Under their pluralistic ideal, sex-based values, traits, and affiliations would remain, but would have equal social recognition in fact as well as form. In this pluralist vision, individuals would not be denied opportunities because of sex. Yet neither would society seek to interfere with gender differences that emerge from individual choice.[24]

This vision shares the limitations of liberal legalism described earlier. Most of what we know about personality development suggests that as long as sex-linked characteristics remain, socialization pressures will often restrict men and women to stereotypical patterns. Individual choices are in some measure socially constituted, and a "separate but equal" society would impose substantial constraints on human experience. Gender stereotypes prevent the exercise of socially desirable talents and preferences that violate conventional gender norms. It is not self-evident that a pluralist society in which such norms survived would promote greater richness and variety than a more androgynous alternative, if that alternative encouraged full self-expression rather than sex-typed roles.[25]

In any event, the critical issue is not the range but the content of choices available. Neither pluralist nor androgynous models adequately address the multiple ways in which preferences are created and constrained. A person's ability to choose is a function of various factors including racial and ethnic identity, family background, economic resources, and consciousness of alternatives. In any society that tolerates significant inequalities, provides grossly inadequate social services, and delegates childrearing to family units, an individual's choices will remain limited by the accident of birth. But to deny parents the right to raise children and to make financial decisions affecting their welfare also would impose substantial restrictions on choice.

These constraints are inherent in the liberal foundation of American feminism, whatever the response to disputes over difference. To make progress in theory and practice, we must move beyond frameworks that claim to maximize choice but remain neutral about outcome and the socioeconomic factors that restrict it. A central limitation of the American women's movement has been its inadequate attention to inequalities apart from gender. The focus on women's differences from men has often obscured consideration of women's differences from each other in class, race, ethnicity, and sexual orientation. One of the most significant developments in contemporary feminist theory has been an increasing sensitivity to that issue. Such sensitivity, aided by other postmodern intellectual insights, has suggested a way to dislodge the sameness-difference dilemma that has traditionally preoccupied the American women's movement.[26]

Theory about Theory

Feminism's theoretical limitations have stemmed in part from limitations in conceptual resources. Recent postmodernist currents across a wide range of disciplines have underscored the inadequacy of traditional universalist approaches in social criticism. Theories that have claimed such universal status have often proven too broad and abstract to explain particular ideological, material, and historical relations. Alternatively, these approaches have been too biased by class, race, gender, and ethnicity to yield generalizable insights and illumine broader patterns.

An obvious example involves Marxism. Analysis that centers on modes of production fails to explain common aspects of woman's subordination that cut across class and cultural boundaries. Gender inequality has never been limited to capitalist societies, and recent experience provides no assurance that women's interests and values are well-served by socialist revolution. Heidi Hartmann noted in the mid-1970s that the traditional marriage between Marxism and feminism was like the bond between husband and wife under early English common law: "Marxism and feminism are one, and the one is Marxism." It is time for a "healthier marriage or a divorce."[27]

Recent work provides some hope that the relationship is on sounder footing. Analysis of class conjoined with race and gender has offered an increasingly powerful critical tool. Yet whether Marxist traditions can yield any universal utopian ideal remains doubtful. The economic structure most responsive to the full range of human needs in a particular culture at a particular historical moment cannot be resolved in the abstract.[28]

Similar observations hold for other theoretical schemes. Inattention to gender is striking in much contemporary liberal work such as John Rawls's and Ronald Dworkin's, which rely heavily on universalist claims and disembodied subjects. A comparable gap is apparent in the critical legal and social theory that has sought to challenge liberal paradigms. Moreover, much of the legal analysis that has centered on gender issues suffers from problems of abstraction and specificity. All too often, courts and commentators have focused on narrow doctrinal questions abstracted from their broader social, economic, and historical context. Alternatively, when seeking a higher level of generality, they have jumped to conclusory concepts that do more to obscure than advance analysis. The search for elusive and ultimately illusory "real differences" is one illustration; the debates over "benign discrimination" are another.[29]

In essence, we need theory without Theory; we need fewer universal frameworks and more contextual analysis. Feminist methodology undercuts claims to any unitary foundational approach, including a feminist one. We need not, and should not, commit ourselves to a single vision of economic structure or gender differences in an ideal universe. Rather, we should retain a stance of self-critical agnosticism. Only by exposing inadequacies in the current social order can we create a more just alternative.

Contemporary feminist theory offers no single view of our appropriate destination, but it does suggest certain preferred means of travel. A crucial insight is that decisions about getting from here to there—wherever there might be—must be made not from the top down but from the bottom up. We need fewer abstract theoretical typologies and more historically and empirically grounded analyses. Detailed blueprints of the ideal structure are less important than strategies to engage more participants in the reconstructive enterprise. Utopian debate should seek to inform our understandings of existing institutions and help us imagine alternatives; it should not impose any single ideal that must inevitably change in the course of change.[30]

Although we cannot know a priori what the good society will be, we know more than enough about what it will not be to provide a current agenda. It will not be a society with wide gender disparities in status, power, and economic security. Nor will it be a society that limits women's reproductive freedom, tolerates substantial poverty, violence, and racial injustice, or structures its workplace without regard to family needs. Finally and most fundamentally, it will not be a society that denies many of its members substantial power over the terms of their daily existence. To realize its full potential, feminism must sustain a vision concerned not only with relations between men and women but also with relations among them. The commitment to sexual equality that gave birth to the woman's movement is necessary but not sufficient to express the values underlying that movement. Those values call for justice in its broadest sense and for richer understandings of what justice requires.

Legal Frameworks

This book has worked from the theoretical premises just outlined. It has built from the ground up, by focusing on the historical, social, and economic foundations of particular problems, rather than constructing abstract analytic models. The objective has been to understand legal texts in cultural context and to explore theoretical and policy alternatives.

These policy implications require new directions in a variety of areas, including employment, education, reproductive freedom, welfare, family law, and prevention of sexual abuse. Such proposals are interrelated, and all contribute to a reconstruction of gender that can inform and expand human experience. Specific legal mandates also cut across substantive areas. To take an obvious example, laws affecting women's access to birth-control measures also affect educational and employment opportunities, which in turn influence allocation of family roles. Those roles, and related legal policies, help shape labor-force participation, educational aspirations, and fertility decisions. Given these interrelations, it would be a mistake to conclude by singling out only a few issues as critical priorities. It is, however, possible to identify certain thematic concerns that span most substantive areas.

One set of concerns involves refocusing conventional legal doctrine from gender difference to gender disadvantage. As a century's experience makes clear, assumptions about difference have been indeterminate, inconsistent, and often indefensible. In some instances, courts have leapt from the fact of difference to the appropriateness of differential treatment without benefit of intermediate premises. In other contexts, physiological distinctions have become cultural imperatives. Women's "nature" has legally disqualified them from a vast range of pursuits, ranging from shoe-shining to legal practice and Little League baseball. At different times in different jurisdictions, the same "special" attributes of womanhood have dictated opposite results; the law has favored or disfavored mothers in child-custody disputes, and has specified longer or shorter prison sentences for female defendants than their male counterparts. Not only have sex-based differences been overvalued, they have also been overlooked. Cases involving pregnancy discrimination have been treated as not involving "gender as such," but simply different treatment for "pregnant and non-pregnant persons."[31]

In most of these cases, courts have simly assumed what should be at issue and made the assumption from male reference points. It is always woman's characteristics—her pregnancy, her child-rearing responsibilities, her physical or sexual vulnerability—that appear "special." Significant progress toward gender equality will require an alternative focus. The issue should center less on difference and more on disadvantage. Framing legal debate in terms of women's sameness or difference is merely two ways of using men as the standard. The central question in discrimination cases should not be whether gender is relevant, but how to make it less so.

Refocusing inquiry will not resolve all difficulties. Women's interests are not monolithic. Tradeoffs may be required between symbolic and concrete achievements, short- and long-term goals, and different groups of women. But while a disadvantage-oriented framework will not yield determinate answers, it at least centers attention on the right question: how best to reach a society in which sexual identity does not correlate with social inequalities.

A related set of issues involves the reconceptualization of public and private. Boundaries between family and market overlap to an extent that is poorly recognized under prevailing policies. The result has been mutually reinforcing patterns of subordination. Inequalities in employment encourage inequalities in family roles, responsibilities, and power. Asymmetries in domestic burdens promote asymmetries in career investment and advancement. Public policy shapes "private" conduct, and private conduct has public consequences in a wide range of areas, such as divorce, employment, sexual abuse, reproductive choice, sexual preference, single-sex institutions, and nonmarital cohabitation. These consequences call for an equally broad range of social initiatives. Without major structural change, many individuals will never realize an integrated work, family, and community life.

A final set of concerns involves the meaning of equality in various legal contexts. The law's traditional focus on equal treatment cannot cope with situations where the sexes are not equally situated. Policies affecting pregnancy, divorce, affirmative action, pay equity, and related issues require assessment in terms not only of formal principles but also of concrete consequences. To prevent gender differences from becoming social disadvantages, we need not simply mandates of equal treatment for women; we need strategies to secure women's treatment as equals.

This is not to imply unqualified support for laws purportedly advantaging women. Experience with protective-labor legislation, preferential-welfare statutes, child-custody presumptions, and maternity policies makes clear that "benign discrimination" is a mixed blessing. Evaluation of its benefits requires a less categorical, more contextual approach than conventional jurisprudence supplies. Any adequate alternative must recognize that "women's interests" often point in different directions. What protects one class of female workers from exploitative conditions may protect other employees out of opportunities desirable to their male competitors. Policies that provide concrete advantages for women in the short run may exact a less obvious price in the long run. Some individual women will benefit from gender-related preferences in parental-leave policies or child-custody presumptions, but for women as a group, the message that child-rearing is primarily a mother's responsibility perpetuates stereotypes that perpetuate subordination. Distinctions that appear benign in one context often spill over to others where the effect is less welcome.

Yet as the last two decades of affirmative action make clear, "special treatment" can also erode stereotypes, expand aspirations, and ensure the critical mass necessary to challenge gender hierarchies. Our preferences about preference should never be determined in the abstract. Whether benign discrimination is worth the price depends on a careful evaluation of which women benefit, how much, at what cost, and compared with what alternatives. Although we cannot measure those consequences with certainty, we can at least attempt more informed assessments.

To that end, we need not only more empirical research on legal mandates but also greater sensitivity to the limits of what that research can discover. One strength of contemporary feminist work in a variety of disciplines has been its attention to the constraints of social science methodology and to the insights of postmodernist theory. Legal analysis should reflect a similar understanding of the blurred boundaries between the knower and the known, and the ways in which data are constructed, not just collected. Yet to acknowledge the biases in empirical research is not to invite paralysis. We cannot cede the struggle for knowledge to those less respectful of its limitations. We can, however, make greater efforts to deconstruct our data. Our analysis can become more self-critical about the partiality of our understandings and more explicit about the values underlying them.

Effective strategies for gender equality require a reassessment of ends as well as means. The paradigmatic liberal prescription—equal opportunity—is a necessary but never sufficient social objective. The ultimate goal is not simply to ensure women's full participation in organizations that wield social, economic, and political power; it is rather to change the nature of those organizations and the way power is distributed and exercised. Our priority should be to empower women as well as men to reshape the institutions that are shaping them. At issue is not simply equality between the sexes, but the quality of life for both of them.

That priority has consequences for the process as well as substance of decisionmaking. Legal procedures often determine the extent to which social-policy objectives are realized. All too often, victims of employment discrimination or sexual abuse have been victimized twice: once by the injury and once by the process of proving it. Too much emphasis has centered on individual intent and too little on institutional practices. Our understanding of what constitutes a "legal" problem ought not to turn on whether a particular plaintiff is willing and able to demonstrate that she lost a position because of her employer's conscious prejudice. Rather, our concern should extend to contexts in which workplace structures and standards disadvantage women, in fact if not by design.

Similarly, the law's approach to rape, sexual harassment, and domestic violence must reach beyond the relatively rare circumstances in which an individual plaintiff comes forward with conclusive proof of injury. Analysis must focus more critically on the cultural conditions that foster sexual abuse and on the law-enforcement practices that discourage redress. We must also make major efforts to reduce the cost, complexity, and contentiousness of most dispute-resolution procedures. It is not enough to reformulate legal doctrine; we need to rethink our legal process, and the psychological and financial barriers that it imposes.[32]

In short, we need a deeper understanding of the way law relates to life. We need to know more about the effect of legal strategies on daily experience; for example, what forms of intervention most effectively deter domestic abuse, and what consequences follow from joint-custody awards or pay-equity initiatives? We need ways to ensure that women's concerns play a greater role in shaping research priorities. We must also become more sensitive to the potential of law as an organizational tool. What legal issues can bridge class, racial, and ethnic boundaries? How can women avoid fighting each other over the value of special treatment and unite to challenge the conditions that make such treatment so valuable? Many of the legal campaigns that have recently mobilized women—such as those involving family law, sexual violence, reproductive freedom, and pay equity—have done as much to change women as to change the law. We need to build on this experience in developing more systematic strategies for social change.

This is not a modest agenda. It requires a fundamental restructuring of social priorities and of the ideologies underlying them. It means translating our rhetorical support for equal opportunity and family relationships into financial commitments. At a minimum, such commitments will require major improvements in workplace structures, welfare policies, and related social services. We must insist not only on equal rights for women, but also on equal recognition of the values they have traditionally sustained.

These objectives require a richer appreciation of both the capacities and limitations of law as an instrument of public policy. Formal doctrine is mediated by a wide range of cultural factors, and the expense of legal remedies often is prohibitive. Mobilization for symbolic causes can divide women and discourage coalitions on more critical issues. Incremental legal reform can legitimate existing structures and deflect attention from the more basic economic and social problems that remain. But such reforms can also lay the foundations for more fundamental changes. Law can be a focal point for political organization and popular education; it can validate injuries and in some instances deter or redress them. It can also help redistribute power and increase the number of voices that are heard in distributive decisions. By reshaping legal policy, we can in some measure reshape social experience. By broadening our aspirations to justice, we may come closer to attaining it.

Notes

Introduction

1. For discussion of these disparities, see Chapters 6, 7 and 8, and "Women in Politics," *Los Angeles Times,* Nov. 30, 1987, III, 6.
2. See Chapter 5.
3. See Robert J. Stoller, *Sex and Gender,* pp. 9–10 (New York: J. Aronsen Press, 1974). For discussion of the problems with the sex-gender distinction, see, for example, Zillah Eisenstein, *Feminism and Sexual Equality* (New York: Monthly Review Press, 1984), p. 152, and Catharine A. MacKinnon, "Toward Feminist Jurisprudence," *Stanford Law Review,* 34 (1981–82): 703.
4. For historical overviews of the term "feminism," see Karen Offen, "Defining Feminism: A Comparative Historical Approach," *Signs,* 14 (1988): 119. For contemporary accounts, see Bell Hooks, *Feminist Theory: From Margin to Center* (Boston: South End Press, 1984), p. 17; Alison M. Jaggar, "Political Philosophies of Women's Liberation," in Mary Vetterling-Braggin, Jane English, and Frederick Elliston, eds., *Feminism and Philosophy* (Totawa, N.J.: Littlefield Adams, 1977).

1. Natural Rights and Natural Roles

1. For discussion of themes raised in this chapter, see Deborah L. Rhode, "Equal Protection: Gender and Justice," in Michael McCann and Gerald Houseman, eds., *Judging the Constitution: Critical Essays on Judicial Law-making* (Boston: Little, Brown, 1988); and "Gender Equality and Constitutional Traditions," in Leslie Cohen Berlowitz, Denis Donoghue, and Louis Menand, eds., *America in Theory* (Oxford University Press, 1988).

   See Susan M. Okin, *Women in Western Political Thought* (Princeton:

Princeton University Press, 1979); William Blackstone, *Commentaries on the Laws of England,* 15th ed. (1756; rpr. Oxfordshire: Professional Books, 1982), I, 442–445. For a critical overview of the concept of separate spheres, see Linda K. Kerber, "Separate Spheres, Female Worlds, Woman's Place: The Rhetoric of Women's History," *Journal of American History,* 75 (1988): 9.

2. United States v. Yazell, 382 U.S. 341, 361 (1966) (Black, J., dissenting); Alfred, Lord Tennyson, "Locksley Hall" (1842), 50. See generally Leo Kanowitz, *Women and the Law,* (Albuquerque: University of New Mexico Press, 1969), pp. 35–37.
3. For an overview of the historical dispute, see Suzanne Lebsock, *The Free Women of Petersberg: Status and Culture in a Southern Town, 1784–1860* (New York: W. W. Norton, 1984), pp. 48–50; and Norma Bash, "The Emerging Legal History of Women in the United States: Property, Divorce, and the Constitution," *Signs,* 12 (1986): 97. Colonial women's activities are chronicled in Elisabeth Dexter, *Career Women of America* (Clifton, N.J.: A. M. Kelley, 1972), pp. 139–175, 196; and Linda Kerber, *Women of the Republic: Intellect and Ideology in Revolutionary America* (Chapel Hill: University of North Carolina Press, 1980), pp. 149–153. For exceptions to common-law restrictions, see the subsequent discussion of married women's property acts.
4. For the Golden Age thesis, see, for example, Mary R. Beard, *Woman as a Force in History: A Study in Traditions and Realities* (New York: Collier, 1946), pp. 114–115. For critiques, see Elizabeth Bowles Warbasse, *The Changing Legal Rights of Married Women, 1800–1861* (New York: Garland, 1987); Marylynn Salmon, "The Legal Status of Women in Early America: A Reappraisal," *Law & History Review,* 1 (Spring 1983): 129–151. Post-Revolutionary changes are discussed in Norma Basch, "Invisible Women: The Legal Fiction of Marital Unity in Nineteenth Century America," *Feminist Studies,* 5 (Summer 1979): 346–366; and Warbasse, *Women,* pp. 1–5. Frontier societies were less restrictive; see Lillian Schlissel, Vicki Ruiz, and Janice Monk, eds., *Western Women: Their Land, Their Lives* (Albuquerque: University of New Mexico Press, 1988).
5. Mrs. A. J. Graves, *Woman in America: Being an Examination into the Moral and Intellectual Conditions of American Female Society* (New York: Harper and Brothers, 1847), p. 151; *Raleigh Register* (1850), quoted in Albert Coates, *By Her Own Bootstraps: A Saga of Women in North Carolina* (n.p., 1975), pp. 142–143. See generally Barbara Welter, "The Cult of True Womanhood, 1820–1860," *American Quarterly,* 18 (1966): 151–174.
6. Welter, "Cult of True Womanhood," p. 174. Throughout the nineteenth century the majority of working women were in domestic service. Mary Ryan, *Womanhood in America,* 3rd ed. (New York, Franklin Watts, 1983). For minority women's limited options, see generally Jacqueline Jones, *Labor of Love, Labor of Sorrow: Black Women, Work, and the Family from Slavery to the Present* (New York: Basic Books, 1985); Christine Stansell, *City of Women: Sex and Class in New York, 1789–1860* (New York: Alfred A. Knopf, 1986); Alfredo Mirande and Evangelina Enriquez, *La Chicana*

(Chicago: University of Chicago Press, 1979); Faye E. Dudden, *Serving Women: Household Services in Nineteenth Century America* (Middletown, Conn.: Wesleyan University Press, 1983). For historical material on education, see Chapter 11.

7. See generally Nancy Cott, *The Bonds of Womanhood: Woman's Sphere in New England, 1780–1835* (New Haven: Yale University Press, 1977); Gerda Lerner, *The Majority Finds Its Past* (New York: Oxford University Press, 1979), p. 27.
8. Declaration of Sentiments (1848), reprinted in Alice Rossi, ed., *Feminist Papers* (New York: Columbia University Press, 1973), p. 419.
9. John Stuart Mill, *The Subjection of Women,* in Millicent Fawcett, ed., *On Liberty, Representative Government, The Subjection of Women* (London: Oxford University Press, 1912); Mary Wollstonecraft, *A Vindication of the Rights of Women,* in Rossi, ed., *Feminist Papers;* Elizabeth Cady Stanton, "The Solitude of Self" (1892), quoted in Aileen Kraditor, *The Ideas of the Woman Suffrage Movement: 1890–1920* (New York: Norton, 1971), p. 40. The limitations of these theorists' visions are explored in Okin, *Western Political Thought,* in Zillah Eisenstein, *The Radical Future of Liberal Feminism* (New York: Longman, 1981), p. 95, and in Carol C. Gould and Marx Wartofsky, eds., *Women and Philosophy: Toward a Theory of Liberation* (New York: G. P. Putnam's Sons, 1976), pp. 97–112. For discussion of more cooperative visions and their influence on feminism, see William Leach, *True Love and Perfect Union* (New York: Basic Books, 1980), pp. 9–15, 347–351.
10. C. B. MacPherson, *The Political Theory of Possessive Individualism* (Oxford: Clarendon Press, 1962), p. 3. See Wendy McElroy, "The Roots of Individualism and Feminism in 19th Century America," in Wendy McElroy, ed., *Freedom, Feminism and the State* (Washington, D.C.: Cato Institute, 1982).
11. Elizabeth Cady Stanton, quoted in Leach, *True Love,* p. 147. Views on family roles are noted in Carl Degler, *At Odds* (New York: Oxford University Press, 1980), p. 345. For Grimké's arguments, see letter from Angelina Grimké to Anna Weston, July 15, 1838, Boston Public Library. See also Antoinette Brown Blackwell, "Relation of Women's Work in the Household to Work Outside" (1873), quoted in Aileen Kaditor, ed., *Up From the Pedestal: Selected Writings in the History of American Feminism* (Chicago: Quadrangle, 1968), pp. 150–151.
12. See Mill, *Subjection of Women,* pp. 484, 514–515; Wollstonecraft, *Vindication,* pp. 70–73 (comparing women in the "common walks of life," who would remain homemakers with women of a "superior cast" who could pursue professions). For a representative example of American feminists' efforts to finesse the problem, see Blackwell, "Relation of Women's Work," p. 158 (proposing that women defer vigorous personal achievement until age fifty, at which point everything, including the presidency, should be open to them). For proposals for cooperative management, see Charlotte Perkins Gilman, *Women and Economics* (Boston: Small, Maynard, 1898); Catherine Clinton, *The Other Civil War: American Women in the Nineteenth Century*

(New York: Hill and Wang, 1984), p. 193, and Dolores Hayden, *The Grand Domestic Revolution: A History of Feminist Designs for American Homes, Neighborhoods and Cities* (Cambridge, Mass.: MIT Press, 1981).

13. For estimates on the percentage of the female labor force that was unmarried, see Mary Ryan, "Femininity and Capitalism in Antebellum America," in Zillah R. Eisenstein, ed., *Capitalist Patriarchy and the Case for Socialist Feminism* (New York: Monthly Review Press, 1979), p. 175 (estimate of 90 percent); Winifred Wandersee, *Women's Work and Family Values, 1920–1940* (Cambridge, Mass.: Harvard University Press, 1981), p. 68 (77 percent). Working hours are discussed in chapter 2.
14. Jane Addams, "Why Women Should Vote," in Frances M. Bjorkman and Annie G. Porritt, *Woman Suffrage: History, Arguments, and Results* (New York: National Woman Suffrage Publishing Co., 1917), pp. 110–129; Jane Addams, "The Modern City and the Municipal Franchise for Women," in Susan B. Anthony and Ida Husted Harper, eds., *History of Woman Suffrage* (Indianapolis: Hallenback Press, 1902), IV, 178. See also ibid., pp. 39, 308–309 (purification), and Nancy Woloch, *Women and the American Experience* (New York: Alfred A. Knopf, 1984), p. 299.
15. For analysis of the rhetorical shift, see Kraditor, *Ideas;* Olive Banks, *Faces of Feminism* (New York: St. Martin's, 1981), p. 98.
16. Kraditor, *Ideas,* p. 12.
17. See Louise Michele Newman, *Men's Ideas/Women's Realities* (New York: Pergamon, 1985), pp. 197–219; Azel Ames, *Sex in Industry: A Plea for the Working-Girl* (Boston: J. R. Osgood, 1875), pp. 30–31; Caroline F. Corbin, "Suffrage and Industrial Independence," in *Why Women Do Not Want the Ballot* (New York State Association Opposed to the Extension of the Suffrage to Women, 1904), vol. II; statement of Franklin W. Collins, Nebraska, before the Senate Committee on Woman Suffrage, Senate Document No. 601, 62d Cong., 2d sess. (April 1912), p. 30. See also Anne F. Scott and Andrew M. Scott, *One Half the People: The Fight for Woman Suffrage* (Philadelphia: Lippincott, 1975), p. 27; Andrew Sinclair, *The Better Half: The Emancipation of the American Woman* (New York: Harper and Row, 1966), p. 323; A. Elizabeth Taylor, "The Woman's Suffrage Movement in Texas," in Kermit L. Hall, ed., *Women, the Law, and the Constitution* (New York: Garland, 1987) p. 475.
18. See particularly Chapters 2, 4, 11, and 12.
19. To make their influence felt, the most active women antisuffragists had to defy some of the conventions they exalted. See Viola Klein, "The Historical Background," in Jo Freeman, ed., *Women: A Feminist Perspective,* 2d ed. (Palo Alto, Calif.: Mayfield, 1979), p. 539 (quoting Queen Victoria). For discussion of forces underlying antifeminism, see Carrie Chapman Catt and Nettie Rogers Shuler, *Women Suffrage and Politics* (New York: Charles Scribner's Sons, 1969), pp. 132–159; Eleanor Flexner, *A Century of Struggle: The Woman's Rights Movement in the United States,* rev. ed. (Cambridge, Mass.: Harvard University Press, 1975), pp. 222–225, 256–261, 296–298.
20. "Feminine vs. Feminist," *Living Age,* March 9, 1912, pp. 587, 588–589;

Margaret C. Robinson, "The Feminist Program," *The Unpopular Review,* 5 (1916): 319–320; Ida Tarbell, quoted in Charlotte Perkins Gilman, "Are Women Human Beings? A Consideration of the Major Error in the Discussion of Women Suffrage," *Harper's Weekly,* May 25, 1912, pp. 11–12.

21. For feminist efforts, see Catt and Shuler, *Women Suffrage and Politics,* p. 107; For claims concerning war, see materials reprinted in Kraditor, *Up From the Pedestal,* p. 285, and Kraditor, *Ideas,* p. 50, n. 48. Stanton and Anthony's prediction appears in Elizabeth Cady Stanton, "The Ballot—Bread, Virtue, Power," *Revolution,* Jan. 8, 1868, p. 1.
22. Laura Bullard, "What Flag Shall We Fly?" *Revolution,* Oct. 27, 1870, p. 264. See also Flexner, *Century of Struggle,* p. 326 (quoting Catt). For discussion of antifeminist claims, see Degler, *At Odds,* p. 357, and William L. O'Neill, *Everyone Was Brave: A History of Feminism in America* (Chicago: Quadrangle, 1969), p. 60.
23. The National Women's Suffrage Association, under the leadership of Stanton and Anthony, took positions on a variety of causes and declined to support any formulation of the Fourteenth and Fifteenth Amendments that did not include women. The American Women's Suffrage Association, whose leaders included Lucy Stone and Henry Ward Beecher, maintained a distance from "side issues" and supported the Fourteenth and Fifteenth Amendments. See O'Neill, *Everyone Was Brave,* pp. 14–30, and Flexner, *Century of Struggle,* pp. 142–158, 222–231.
24. See Kraditor, *Ideas,* p. 141; Paula Giddings, *When and Where I Enter: The Impact of Black Women on Race and Sex in America* (New York: William Morrow, 1984), pp. 127–129, 153; Bell Hooks, *Ain't I a Woman: Black Women and Feminism* (Boston: South End Press, 1981), pp. 130–131. Philip Foner, *Women and the American Labor Movement* (New York: Free Press, 1980), I, 482; Rosalyn Terborg-Penn, "Discrimination Against Afro-American Women in the Woman's Movement, 1830–1920," in Sharon Harley and Rosalyn Terborg-Penn, eds. *The Afro-American Woman: Struggles and Images,* (Port Washington, N.Y.: Kennikat Press, 1978), p. 17.
25. Susan B. Anthony, quoted in Philip Foner, *Frederick Douglass On Woman's Rights* (Westport, Conn.: Greenwood, 1976), p. 30; Lerner, *Majority Finds Its Past,* p. 34.
26. O'Neill, *Everyone Was Brave,* p. 274.
27. For voting behavior, see William Henry Chafe, *The American Woman: Her Changing Social, Economic, and Political Roles, 1920–1970* (New York: Oxford University Press, 1972); Degler, *At Odds,* pp. 356–357; Ethel Klein, *Gender Politics* (Cambridge, Mass.: Harvard University Press, 1984), pp. 142–143; Woloch, *Women,* pp. 355–356; for comparisons with dress reform, see O'Neill, *Everyone Was Brave,* pp. 269–270, 391.
28. For assessments of the suffrage movement, see Estelle Freedman, "The New Woman: Changing Views of Women in the 1920's," *Journal of American History,* 61 (September 1974): 372–393; Ellen Du Bois, "The Radicalism of the Women's Suffrage Movement: Notes Toward the Reconstruction of Nineteenth-Century Feminism," *Feminist Studies,* 3 (Fall 1975): 65; Ellen Dubois, *Feminism and Suffrage: The Emergence of an Independent Women's*

Movement in America, 1848–1869 (Ithaca, N.Y.: Cornell University Press, 1978); Barbara J. Berg, *The Remembered Gate: Origns of American Feminism* (New York: Oxford University Press, 1978).

29. Alexander Hamilton, No. 6, *The Federalist Papers* (1788; rpr. New York: New American Library, 1961), pp. 54–55; Minor v. Happersett, 88 U.S. 162 (1874). See Rhode, "Gender Equality."
30. Edward O'Donnell, "Women as Breadwinners—The Error of the Age" (1897), in Rosalyn Baxandall et al., eds., *America's Working Women: A Documentary, 1600 to the Present* (New York: Vintage, 1976), pp. 168–169.
31. See Isabella M. Pettus, "The Legal Education of Women," *Albany Law Journal*, 61 (1900): 325, 326–327; Ada M. Bittenbender, "Woman in Law," in Annie Nathan Meyer, ed., *Woman's Work in America (New York: Henry Holt, 1891), pp. 220–221; Sophie Drinker, "Women Attorneys of Colonial Times," Maryland Historical and Society Bulletin,* 56 (December 1961): 461.
32. Belva Lockwood, "My Efforts to Become a Lawyer," reprinted in W. Elliot Brownlee and Mary M. Brownlee, eds., *Women in American Economy, A Documentary History, 1675–1929* (New Haven: Yale University Press, 1976), pp. 297–298, 304.
33. Bradwell v. State, 83 U.S. 130, 134, 135, 137 (1872); Brief for the Plaintiff in Error, quoted in Albie Sachs and Joan H. Wilson, *Sexism and the Law* (London: Robertson, 1978), p. 100.
34. Bradwell v. State, 83 U.S. 130, 137 (1872) (Bradley, J., concurring). The *Bradwell* majority relied on the Slaughter-House Cases decided earlier the same year, 83 U.S. 36 (1872). There the Court held that a state could confer monopoly privileges on certain butchers without violating the newly enacted Fourteenth Amendment; other butchers denied such privileges should seek relief from the legislature rather than the judiciary. Because aspiring female attorneys were disenfranchised, they lacked that legislative option. Compare Justice Bradley, dissent in *Slaughter-House* (arguing that deprivations of employment violated Fourteenth Amendment protections), with his concurrence in *Bradwell* (finding no comparable protection for women).
35. Bradwell v. State, 83 U.S. at 141–142.
36. In the Matter of Goodell, 39 Wis. 232, 244 (1875). For other cases, see Sachs and Wilson, *Sexism*, pp. 6–44.
37. The 1850 *New York Herald* gave an amusing account of Lucy Stone "pleading a cause, suddenly [taken] ill in the pains of parturition." See Ida Husted Harper, *The Life and Work of Susan B. Anthony* (Indianapolis and Kansas City: Bowen-Merril, 1899), I, 78–79. Stone was single at the time. For further examples, see Charles C. Moore, "The Woman Lawyer," discussed in Kelly Weisberg, *Women and the Law: A Social Historical Perspective* (Cambridge, Mass.: Schenkman, 1982), II, 236–237. For claims concerning female delicacy, see In re Kilgore, 17 Phila. 14, 17 (1884) (Pierce J., dissenting); Barbara Ehrenreich and Deirdre English, *For Her Own Good: 150 Years of Experts' Advice to Women* (Garden City, N.Y.: Anchor Press, 1978) (physicians).

38. Robert Bocking Stevens, *Law School: Legal Education in America from the 1850's to the 1980's* (Chapel Hill: The University of North Carolina Press, 1983), p. 82, n. 74.
39. Lockwood, "Lawyer," p. 301; Dean Henry Booth, quoted in Kathleen LaZarou, "Fettered Portias: Obstacles Facing Nineteenth Century Women Lawyers," *Women Lawyers Journal,* 64 (Winter 1978): 21, 22; Janette Barnes, "Women and Entrance to the Legal Profession," *Journal of Legal Education,* 23 (1970): 283 (quoting trustee); Stevens, *Law School,* p. 83, n. 86. See generally Karen Morrello, *The Invisible Bar; The Woman Lawyer in America* (New York: Random House, 1986); Barbara Allen Babcock, "Clara Shortridge Foltz," *Arizona Law Review,* 30 (1988): 801. Not until 1972 did all law schools with American Bar Association accreditation admit female students. Donna Fossum, "Law and the Sexual Integration of Institutions: The Case of American Law Schools," *ALSA Forum,* VII (1983): 22. For discussion of minority women, see Geraldine Segal, *Blacks in the Law* (Philadelphia: University of Pennsylvania Press, 1983), pp. 213–219.
40. Philadelphia County Medical Society Preamble, in Gerda Lerner, ed., *The Female Experience, An American Documentary* (Indianapolis: Bobbs Merrill, 1977), p. 409. See also Chapter 11.
41. For policies on rest rooms, see Cynthia Fuchs Epstein, *Woman's Place* (Berkeley: University of California Press, 1970), p. 185; Susan Baserga, "The Early Years of Co-Education at the Yale University School of Medicine," *Yale Journal of Biology and Medicine,* 53 (1980): 181–190. Yale changed its policy after the father of a would-be applicant offered to subsidize the expenses of suitable lavatory facilities. For discrimination against professional women, see generally Barbara J. Harris, *Beyond Her Sphere: Women and the Professions in American History* (Westport, Conn.: Greenwood, 1978); Rhode, "Perspectives on Professional Women," *Stanford Law Review,* 40 (1988): 1163; and discussion in Chapters 2, 3, and 8.
42. Linda E. Speth, "The Married Women's Property Acts, 1839–1865: Reform, Reaction, or Revolution?" in Weisberg, *Women and the Law,* II, 69, 70; Richard Chused, "Married Women's Property Law, 1800–1850," *Georgetown Law Journal,* 71 (June 1983): 1369, 1370.
43. See Lawrence Friedman, *A History of American Law* (New York: Simon and Schuster, 1973), p. 186; Norma Basch, *In the Eyes of the Law: Women, Marriage, and Property in Nineteenth Century New York* (Ithaca, N.Y.: Cornell University Press, 1982), p. 227; Speth, "Married Women's Property Acts," p. 72.
44. Sachs and Wilson, *Sexism and the Law,* pp. 79–80; Judge Thomas Hertell, quoted in Peggy Rabkin, *Fathers to Daughters: The Legal Foundations of Female Emancipation* (Westport, Conn.: Greenwood, 1980), p. 86. See sources cited in note 42.
45. Chused, "Married Women's Property Law," p. 1425; Basch, *Eyes of the Law,* pp. 153–154.
46. Chester Vernier, *American Family Laws* (Stanford, Calif: Stanford University Press, 1935), III, 193; John D. Johnston, "Sex and Property: The Common Law Tradition, The Law School Curriculum and Developments Toward

Equality," *New York University Law Review*, 47 (1972): 1033, 1070–1079, Warbasse, *Women*, pp. 243–244. For general resistance to codification, see Morton Horwitz, *The Transformation of American Law* (Cambridge, Mass.: Harvard University Press, 1979), pp. 253–266.

47. Reynolds v. Robinson, 64 N.Y. 589, 593 (1876); Hudson v. King Bros., 23 Ill. App. 118 (1876). See also Neasham v. McNair, 103 Iowa 695 (1897); (diamond studs) Blanche Crozier, "Marital Support," *Boston University Law Review*, 15 (1935): 28, 37–39 (and cases cited therein).
48. For discussion of early custody law, see Chapter 7.
49. Miller v. Miller, 78 Iowa 177, 182 (1889). See Runkle v. Runkle, 96 Mich. 493 (1893); and Coleman v. Burr, 93 N.Y. 17 (1883).
50. For early English law, see Julia O'Faolain and Lauro Martines, eds., *Not in God's Image* (New York: Harper and Row, 1973), pp. 175, 318; and Deckard, *Women's Movement*, p. 200. For early American cases permitting chastisement, see State v. Hussey, 44 N.C. (Busb.) 123 (1852); State v. Black, 60 N.C. (Win.) 266 (1864). For trivial complaints, and the language quoted in text, see State v. Oliver, 70 N.C. 60, 61 (1874), and State v. Rhodes, 61 N.C. (Phil. Law) 453, 454 (1868). See generally Elizabeth Pleck, "Wife Beating in Nineteenth-Century America," *Victimology*, 4 (1979): 60.
51. See generally Nelson Blake, *The Road to Reno: A History of Divorce in the United States* (New York: Macmillan, 1962), pp. 1–8; Max Rheinstein, *Marriage, Stability, Divorce and the Law* (Chicago: University of Chicago Press, 1972), pp. 26–47.
52. English v. English, 27 N.J. Equity Reports 71 (1876); Shaw v. Shaw, 17 Conn. 189, 190, 196 (1845). *English* and *Shaw* were not, however, typical. See Robert Griswold, "Sexual Cruelty and the Case for Divorce in Victorian America," *Signs*, 11 (1986): 529.
53. Such attitudes persisted throughout the nineteenth and early twentieth centuries. David v. David, 27 Ala. 222 (1855); Poer v. Poer, 8 N.H. Reports 307 (1836); Knight v. Iowa, 1 Iowa 452 (1871); Buchan v. Buchan, 201 Ill. App. 349 (1916); Nicholson v. Nicholson, 115 S.C. 326, 105 S.E. 700 (1921); Lindenschmidt v. Lindenschmidt, 29 Mo. App. 295 (1888); Cunningham v. Cunningham, 48 Pa. Super. 442 (1912).
54. See generally Chapter 7; Blake, *Reno*, pp. 49–50; Lynn Halem, *Divorce Reform: Changing Legal and Social Perspectives* (New York: Free Press, 1980) pp. 34–39; and Elaine Tyler May, *Great Expectations* (Chicago: University of Chicago Press, 1980) p. 41.

2. The Fragmentation of Feminism and the Legalization of Difference

1. At its height NAWSA had two million members, while League membership ranged from about 100,000 to 200,000 and NWP membership ranged from 50,000 to a few hundred. See William Chafe, *The American Woman: Her Changing Social, Economic, and Political Roles, 1920–1970* (New York: Oxford University Press, 1972), p. 114; Nancy F. Cott, *The Grounding of Modern Feminism* (New Haven: Yale University Press, 1987), p. 301, n. 5.
2. Susan Ware, *Holding Their Own: American Women in the 1930s* (Boston:

Twayne, 1982), p. 103; J. Stanley Lemons, *The Woman Citizen: Social Feminism in the 1920s* (Urbana: University of Illinois Press, 1973), pp. 204–227; Nancy McGlen and Ellen O'Connor, *Women's Rights: The Struggle for Equality in Nineteenth and Twentieth Century America* (New York: Praeger, 1983), pp. 285–286.

3. For works emphasizing women's attainments during this period, including their increased rate of labor-force participation, their social-welfare activity, and their positions in government, see Ware, *Holding Their Own,* pp. 68–69, 86–88, 105; Susan Ware, *Beyond Suffrage: Women and the New Deal* (Cambridge, Mass.: Harvard University Press, 1981); Dorothy Brown, *Setting a Course: American Women in the 1920s* (Boston: G. K. Hall, 1987); and Frank Stricker, "Cookbooks and Law Books: The Hidden History of Career Women in Twentieth Century America," in Nancy F. Cott and Elizabeth Pleck, eds., *A Heritage of Her Own: Toward A New Social History of American Women* (New York: Simon and Schuster, 1979), pp. 479–482. For more negative assessments, see Chafe, *American Woman;* William O'Neill, *Everyone Was Brave: A History of Feminism in America* (Chicago: Quadrangle, 1969); and Carl Degler, *At Odds: Women and the Family in America from the Revolution to the Present* (New York: Oxford University Press, 1980). See generally Cott, *Feminism.*
4. See Margaret Mead and Frances Bagley Kaplan, eds., *American Women: The Report of the President's Commission on the Status of Women and Other Publications of the Commission* (New York: Charles Scribner's Sons, 1965), p. 73; Carl A. Degler, "Revolution without Ideology: The Changing Place of Women in America," in Robert Lifton, *The Woman in America* (Boston: Houghton Mifflin, 1965), pp. 193, 204; Eleanor Flexner, *Century of Struggle: The Woman's Rights Movement in the United States,* (Cambridge, Mass.: Harvard University Press, 1975), p. 325; Jane De Hart Mathews, "The New Feminism and the Dynamics of Social Change," in Linda K. Kerber and Jane De Hart Mathews, eds., *Women's America: Refocusing the Past* (New York: Oxford University Press, 1982), pp. 397–425,
5. For discussion of educational trends, see O'Neill, *Feminism,* pp. 304–305; Jessie Bernard, *Academic Women* (University Park: Pennsylvania State University Press, 1964), pp. 40–44; Ware, *Holding Their Own,* pp. 24–25; National Manpower Council, Conference on Womanpower, *Work in the Lives of Married Women* (New York: Columbia University Press, 1957), p. 197; Mabel Newcomer, *A Century of Higher Education for Women* (New York: Harper, 1959), pp. 47–49; Nancy Woloch, *Women and The American Experience* (New York: Alfred A. Knopf, 1984), pp. 508–509. For survey data, see Susan Hartmann, *The Home Front and Beyond: American Women in the 1940s* (Boston: Twayne, 1982), pp. 179–180; Elaine Showalter, ed., *These Modern Women: Autobiographical Essays from the Twenties* (Old Westbury, N.Y.: Feminist Press, 1978), p. 8. For data on professional women, see Jack Pole, *The Pursuit of Equality in American History (Berkeley: University of California Press, 1978), p. 311;* Flexner, *Century of Struggle,* p. 327; Hartmann, *The Home Front and Beyond,* pp. 105, 108–109; Deborah L. Rhode, "Perspectives on Professional Women," *Stanford*

Law Review, 40 (1988): 1163. For increases of women in business, see Stricker, "Cookbooks," pp. 479–482. For minority women, see Jacqueline Jones, *Labor of Love, Labor of Sorrow: Black Women, Work, and the Family from Slavery to the Present* (New York: Basic Books, 1986); Julianne Malveaux, "No Images" (unpublished manuscript); Alfredo Mirande and Evangelina Enriquez, *La Chicana* (Chicago: University of Chicago Press, 1979).

6. U.S. Women's Bureau, Bulletin No. 294, *1969 Handbook on Women Workers* (Washington, D.C.: Government Printing Office, 1969), p. 10. See generally Winifred D. Wandersee, *Women's Work and Family Values, 1920–1940* (Cambridge, Mass.: Harvard University Press, 1981); Valerie Kincade Oppenheimer, *The Female Labor Force in the United States* (Westport, Conn.: Greenwood, 1970). Of equal importance was the compression of child-rearing years; see Chapter 3. Janet Zollinger Giele, *Women and the Future: Changing Sex Roles in Modern America* (New York: Free Press, 1978), p. 147. For discussion of employers' preference for women clerical workers, see Robert Smuts, *Women and Work in America* (New York: Schocken, 1959), p. 137; Margery Davies, "Women's Place Is at the Typewriter: The Feminization of the Clerical Labor Force," in Zillah Eisenstein, ed., *Capitalist Patriarchy and the Case for Socialist Feminism* (New York: Monthly Review Press, 1979), pp. 248–259.

7. Susan Becker, *The Origins of the Equal Rights Amendment, American Feminism Between the Wars* (Westport, Conn.: Greenwood, 1981), pp. 27, 125 (citing polls); Oppenheimer, *Labor Force,* p. 43 (citing polls); Chafe, *American Women,* p. 107 (quoting Frances Perkins and C. A. Darr); George Gallup, quoted in Ware, *Holding Their Own,* p. 27. During this period, some thirty states enacted laws restricting women's employment, including bans on hiring mothers. Section 213 of the Federal Economy Act barred from the government payroll any person whose spouse held a federal job. Ethel Klein, *Gender Politics* (Cambridge, Mass.: Harvard University Press, 1984), p. 18; Lois Scharf, *To Work and to Wed: Female Employment, Feminism and the Great Depression* (Westport, Conn.: Greenwood, 1980), pp. 45–48.

8. Ware, *Holding Their Own,* pp. 30–31; Phyllis Wallace, Linda Datcher, and Julianne Malveaux, *Black Women in the Labor Force* (Cambridge: MIT Press, 1980), p. 7 (1910: 70 percent, 1930: 90 percent); Jean Collier Brown, "The Negro Woman Worker: 1860–1890," in Gerda Lerner, ed., *Black Women in White America* (New York: Pantheon, 1972), p. 250. Philip Foner, *Women and the American Labor Movement* (New York: Free Press, 1979), II, 280; Jean Collier Brown, "The Negro Woman Worker," U.S. Women's Bureau Bulletin No. 165 (Washington, D.C.: Government Printing Office, 1938), p. 14; see generally Paula Giddings, *When and Where I Enter: The Impact of Black Women on Race and Sex in America* (New York: William Morrow, 1984), pp. 140–146; Mirande and Enriquez, *La Chicana;* Jones, *Labor of Love,* p. 208 (black female workers earned less than a quarter of the salaries of white males); Elizabeth Higgenbotham, "Laid Bare by the System: Work and Survival for Black and Hispanic Women," in Amy

Swerdlow and Hanna Lessinger, eds., *Class, Race and Sex: The Dynamics of Control* (Boston: G. K. Hall, 1983); Evelyn Nakano Glen, *Issei, Nisei, War Bride* (Philadelphia: Temple University Press, 1986).

9. Emily James Putnam, *The Lady* (Chicago: University of Chicago Press, 1970), p. 69. For discussion of wartime labor practices, see U.S. Women's Bureau Bulletin No. 211, *Study of Employment of Women in the Early Postwar Period* (Washington, D.C.: Government Printing Office, 1946), pp. 1, 8, and sources cited in Hartmann, *Home Front and Beyond,* pp. 90–91; Ruth Milkman, *Gender at Work: The Dynamics of Job Segregation by Sex During World War II* (Urbana: University of Illinois Press, 1987).

10. Hazel Erskine, "The Polls: Women's Role," *Public Opinion Quarterly,* 35 (Summer 1971): 275, 283–284 (citing Gallup poll); see Mary P. Ryan, *Womanhood in America* (New York: New Viewpoints, 1975), p. 319; Karen Anderson, *Wartime Women: Sex Roles, Family Relations, and the Status of Women During World War II* (Westport, Conn.: Greenwood, 1981); Sheila Tobias and Lisa Anderson, "What Really Happened to Rosie the Riveter? Demobilization and the Female Labor Force," in Kerber and Mathews, eds., *Women's America,* pp. 354–373. Edith Abbott, *Women in Industry: A Study in American Economic History* (New York: D. Appleton, 1918), pp. 311–316; Degler, *At Odds,* pp. 414–417, 424; U.S. Women's Bureau, *The Earnings Gap Between Women and Men* (Washington, D.C.: Government Printing Office, 1979), p. 6; Ware, *Holding Their Own,* p. 27; Chafe, *American Woman,* p. 185.

11. See Elizabeth Howe, *Why Women Cry: On Wenches with Wrenches* (New York: Reynal & Hitchcock, 1943); Hartmann, *The Home Front and Beyond,* pp. 24, 92; National Manpower Council, *Work,* pp. 158–159; Oppenheimer, *Female Labor Force,* pp. 157–168. A quarter of the National Recovery Act Codes expressly allowed sex-based salary differentials, and employers could often circumvent code requirements and National War Labor Board directives of equal pay through facially neutral policies that disadvantaged women. See Foner, *Labor Movement,* II, 279, 357; Chafe, *Women and Equality,* p. 93.

12. Cott, *Feminism* (quoting journal), p. 282; Ellen Key, *The Woman Movement* (New York: G. P. Putnam, 1912), p. 97; Miriam Allen de Ford, "The Feminist Future," *The New Republic,* Sept. 19, 1928, pp. 121, 123; Geoffrey Perrett, *America in the Twenties* (New York: Simon and Schuster, 1982), p. 158; Elaine Showalter, ed., *These Modern Women: Autobiographical Essays from the Twenties* (Old Westbury, N.Y.: The Feminist Press, 1978) p. 8; Dorothy Bromley, "Feminist, New Style," *Harper's,* 155 (October 1927): 552.

13. Jane Addams, *The Second Twenty Years at Hull-House* (New York: Macmillan, 1930), pp. 110–120; Leila Rupp and Verta Taylor, *Survival In the Doldrums: The American Women's Rights Movement, 1945 to the 1960s* (New York: Oxford University Press, 1987), p. 81.

14. Cott, *Feminism,* p. 271; Richard W. Wertz and Dorothy C. Wertz, *Lying-In: A History of Child Birth in America* (New York: Free Press, 1977), pp.

207–208 (quoting warnings); Lynn White, *Educating Our Daughters* (New York: Harper, 1950), pp. 91, 97; Marynia F. Farnham and Ferdinand Lundberg, *Modern Woman, The Lost Sex* (New York: Harper, 1947), p. 771; Banner, *Women in Modern America,* p. 197.

15. Rupp and Taylor, *Survival,* pp. 14–15, (describing articles such as "I'm Lucky, I'm Lucky" and "I'd Hate to be a Man"); Betty Friedan, *The Feminine Mystique* (New York: Laurel, 1983), pp. 34–37, 47–53; Hartmann, *The Home Front and Beyond,* p. 200.
16. Robert G. Foster and Pauline Park Wilson, *Women After College: A Study of the Effectiveness of Their Education* (New York: Columbia University Press, 1942), pp. 48–50, 113–118, 186–188 (citing surveys); White, *Educating Our Daughters,* pp. 77–78, 82, 85, 91; Mary Bunting, "The Radcliffe Institute for Independent Study in American Council on Education," *The Educational Record,* October 1961, p. 19. See also Chafe, *American Woman,* p. 103; and Chapter 11.
17. Becker, *Origins,* p. 64 (quoting Creighton Peet, 1934); Farnham and Lundberg, *Modern Woman,* p. 150; Rupp and Taylor, *Survival,* p. 22; Cott, *Feminism,* p. 159. For Spock's views, see Ryan, *Womanhood in America,* p. 350; Benjamin Spock, "Should Mothers Work," *Ladies Home Journal* (February 1963), p. 16.
18. U.S. Women's Bureau, *1969 Handbook on Women Workers,* p. 26, table 8; Helena Z. Lopata, *Occupation: Housewife* (New York: Oxford University Press, 1971), pp. 47–53. For data on housework, see John P. Robinson and Philip E. Cowen, *United States Time Use Survey* (Ann Arbor, Mich.: Survey Research Center, 1974), and Joann Vanek, "Time Spent in Housework," *Scientific American,* 231 (November 1974): 116–120. Among full-time homemakers, technological advances resulted in higher standards rather than decreased obligations. For example, after the introduction of washing machines, women bought more clothes, washed them more often, and used paid laundries less frequently.
19. White, *Educating Our Daughters,* p. 47. See also Chapter 12.
20. Crystal Eastman, quoted in Cott, *Feminism,* p. 70. See Bell Hooks, *Ain't I a Woman? Black Women and Feminism* (Boston: South End Press, 1981), p. 176; Giddings, *When and Where I Enter,* p. 166; Becker, *Origins,* p. 245; Hartmann, *Home Front,* p. 145; Banner, *Women,* p. 141; Rupp and Taylor, *Doldrums,* pp. 152–155; Rosalyn Terborg-Penn, "Discontented Black Feminists: Prelude and Postscript to the Passage of the Nineteenth Amendment," in Lois Scharf and Joan M. Jensen, eds., *Decades of Discontent: The Women's Movement 1920–1940* (Boston: Northeastern University Press, 1983), p. 261.
21. Foner, *Labor Movement,* II, 150; Susan Ware, *Beyond Suffrage: Women in the New Deal* (Cambridge, Mass.: Harvard University Press, 1981).
22. Lochner v. New York, 198 U.S. 45 (1905); Muller v. Oregon, 208 U.S. 412 (1908); Alice Kessler-Harris, *Out To Work* (New York: Oxford University Press, 1982), p. 188.
23. *New York Times,* Feb. 25, 1908. See Nancy Erickson, "Historical Back-

ground of Protective Labor Legislation: Muller v. Oregon," in D. Kelly Weisberg, ed., *Women and the Law* (Cambridge: Shenkman, 1982), II, 155, 164–166.

24. Editorial, *Equal Rights,* 23 (Jan. 19, 1937): 2; Harriet Stanton Blatch, quoted in Sheila Rothman, *Woman's Proper Place* (New York: Basic Books, 1978), p. 157. See Alice Paul, quoted in Foner, *American Labor Movement,* II, 140; Christine A. Lunardini, *From Equal Suffrage to Equal Rights: Alice Paul and the Woman's Party, 1910–1928* (New York: New York University Press, 1986).
25. "Interpretation of the Equal Rights Amendment by the Courts," *Equal Rights,* 20 (March 1, 1924).
26. Mary Anderson, *Women at Work* (Minneapolis: University of Minnesota Press, 1951), p. 115; Florence Kelley, quoted in Julia Johnsen, ed., *Special Legislation for Women* (New York: H. W. Wilson, 1926), p. 87; statement of Mrs. William J. Carson, Philadelphia, Chairman of the Committee on the Legal Status of Women of the National League of Women Voters, in *Hearings,* 71st Cong., 3rd sess., on Senate Joint Resolution 52, p. 45; Ethel Smith, National League of Women Voters, "Different Concepts of Sex Equality," Statement Presented to the Subcommittee of the Senate Judiciary Committee, Feb. 8, 1938, 75th Cong., Senate Joint Resolution 65, p. 90; Mary Beard, quoted in Chafe, *American Woman,* p. 127.
27. See Emma Wold, quoted in Becker, *Origins of the Equal Rights Amendment,* p. 130 (discussing NPW efforts). For legislative surveys of discriminatory laws, see statement of Burnita Shelton Matthews, in *Hearings,* 71st Cong., 3rd sess., on Senate Joint Resolution 52, pp. 5–14.
28. See Gabriel Kolko, *The Triumph of Conservatism* (New York: Free Press, 1963); Arnold M. Paul, *The Conservative Crisis and the Rule of Law* (Ithaca, N.Y.: Cornell University Press, 1960); Paul Murphy, *The Constitution in Crisis Times* (New York: Harper and Row, 1972), chaps. 1–4.
29. "Machine Industry and Plantation," in Mary Beard, ed., *America Through Women's Eyes* (New York: Macmillan, 1933), p. 133.
30. People v. Ritchie, 155 Ill. 98, 113, 115–116, 40 N.E. 454 (1895); New York v. Williams, 189 N.Y. 131 (1907). See also Chapter 1, and text at notes 47–67 below.
31. See Elizabeth Baker, *Protective Labor Legislation,* rev. ed. (New York: AMS Press, 1969), pp. 207–210; Robert Smuts, *Women and Work in America* (New York: Columbia University Press, 1959), pp. 44, 79, 85, 96, 118; Alice Kessler-Harris, *Women Have Always Worked* (Old Westbury, N.Y.: Feminist Press, 1981).
32. See James J. Kenneally, *Women and American Trade Unions* (St. Albans, Vt.: Eden Press, 1978), pp. 160–170; Rosalyn Baxandall, Linda Gordon, and Susan Reverby, eds., *America's Working Women* (New York: Vintage, 1976); Hartmann, "Capitalism, Patriarchy and Job Segregation by Sex," *Signs,* 1 (1976): 161–166.
33. Louis Levine, *The Women's Garment Workers: A History of the International Ladies Garment Workers Union* (New York: B. W. Huebsch, 1924), p. 159; Mimi Abramovitz, *Regulating the Lives of Women* (Boston: South

End Press, 1988), p. 189; Chafe, *American Woman,* p. 68; Alice Kessler-Harris, "Where Are the Organized Women Workers?" in Nancy Cott and Elizabeth Pleck, eds., *A Heritage of Her Own* (New York: Simon & Schuster, 1979), pp. 343–366.

34. See Baker, *Protective Labor Legislation,* pp. 186–188, 207; Alice Kessler-Harris, *Out to Work* (New York: Oxford University Press, 1982), p. 60; David M. Katzman, *Seven Days a Week: Women and Domestic Service in Industrializing America* (New York: Oxford University Press, 1978), chap. 3; Jane de Hart Matthews, "The New Feminism and the Dynamics of Social Change," in Linda K. Kerber and Jane de Hart Matthews, eds., *Women's America: Refocusing the Past* (New York: Oxford University Press, 1982), pp. 397–425; Paul Blanshard, "How to Live on Forty-six Cents A Day" (1929), reprinted in Gerda Lerner, ed., *The Female Experience: An American Documentary* (Indianapolis: Bobbs-Merrill, 1977), p. 290; Evelyn Nakano Glen, "Racial Ethnic Women's Labor: The Intersection of Race, Gender, and Class Oppression," *Review of Radical Political Economics,* 17 (1985): 17.
35. Ronald K. Collins and Jennifer Friesen, "Looking Back on Muller v. Oregon," (Part Two) *American Bar Association Journal,* March 1983, pp. 294, 296. In response to Choate's question, Florence Kelley reportedly replied, "Why not indeed?" (ibid.)
36. For the strategy of Brandeis and Goldmark, see Brief for the Defendant, pp. 34–38, 110, in *Muller v. Oregon,* 208 U.S. 412 (1908).
37. Muller v. Oregon, 208 U.S. 412, 421–422 (1908).
38. Joseph A. Hill, U.S. Bureau of the Census, Monograph No. 9, *Women in Gainful Occupations 1870 to 1920* (Washington, D.C.: Government Printing Office, 1929), p. 77; Ritchie & Co. v. Wayman, 244 Ill. 509 (1910); Blanche Crozier,"Regulation of Conditions of Employment: A Critique of Muller v. Oregon," *Boston University Law Review,* 13 (1933): 276, 289.
39. Facts of Knowledge, People v. Charles Schweinler Press, 214 N.Y. 395, 407 (1915), quoted in Judith A. Baer, *The Chains of Protection* (Westport, Conn.: Greenwood, 1978), pp. 79–84. See also Radice v. People, 264 U.S. 292 (1924).
40. See Baker, *Protective Labor Legislation,* pp. 351–353; U.S. Women's Bureau, Bulletin No. 65, *The Effects of Labor Legislation on the Employment Opportunities of Women* (Washington, D.C.: Government Printing Office, 1028), p. 53. Some employers raised wages to compensate for shorter hours; more often they speeded up the work process. Kessler-Harris, *Out to Work,* p. 195.
41. For discussion of enforcement and exemptions, see Baer, *Chains of Protection,* pp. 31–32; Scharf, *To Work and to Wed,* p. 114. Examples of women's foreclosure from desirable positions are discussed in Kessler-Harris, *Out to Work,* pp. 194, 211; J. Stanley Lemons, *The Woman Citizen: Social Feminism in the 1920s* (Urbana: University of Illinois Press, 1973), pp. 23–25; Foner, *American Labor Movement,* II, 94–96. For analysis of unemployment, see Elisabeth M. Landes, "The Effect of State Maximum Hours Laws on the Employment of Women in 1920," *Journal of Political Economy,* 88

(1980): 476. Women's reasons for moonlighting and for accepting night shifts are reviewed in U.S. Women's Bureau, *Effects of Labor Legislation,* pp. 172–173; "The Night Shift," in Baxandall et al., eds., *America's Working Women,* p. 160. For discussion of reinforcement of roles, see Susan Lehrer, *Origins of Protective Labor Legislation for Women* (Albany, N.Y.: SUNY Press 1987), p. 229. See generally Frances Olsen, "From False Paternalism to False Equality: Judicial Assaults on Feminist Community, Illinois, 1869–1895," *University of Michigan Law Journal,* 84 (1986): 1518.

42. Kessler-Harris, *Women Have Always Worked,* p. 63; Smuts, *Women and Work,* p. 10; Foner, *American Labor Movement,* I, 256, 265–269; II, 8–10; John R. Commons et al., eds., *Documentary History of American Industrial Society* (New York: Russell and Russell, 1958), VI, 1955.
43. See Woloch, *Women,* pp. 233, 385 (quoting Massachusetts Labor Board and Florence Kelley); Adkins v. Children's Hospital, 261 U.S. 525, 546–553 (1922).
44. Lemons, *The Woman Citizen,* p. 239; Foner, *American Labor Movement,* II, 146.
45. West Coast Hotel Co. v. Parrish, 300 U.S. 379 (1937); Chafe, *American Woman,* p. 124–128. Kessler-Harris, *Out to Work,* p. 196. Woloch, *Women and the American Experience,* p. 448.
46. 29 USC 201 et seq.; United States v. Darby, 312 U.S. 100 (1941); Babcock et al., *Sex Discrimination and the Law,* pp. 35–36; Lemons, *Woman Citizen,* pp. 22–25; U.S. Women's Bureau, *Summary of State Labor Laws for Women* (Washington, D.C.: Government Printing Office, 1965), pp. 13–44; U.S. Women's Bureau, *1969 Handbook on Women Workers,* pp. 261–279; Baer, *Chains of Protection,* pp. 16, 89; Becker, *Origins,* pp. 129–130; Chapter 5.
47. For bar admission cases, see Chapter 1. For standards of scrutiny, see Chapter 5.
48. Cott, *Feminism,* pp. 124–125; Baer, *Chains of Protection,* p. 31; Comment, "Are Sex Based Classifications Constitutionally Suspect?" *Northwestern University Law Review,* 66 (1971): 481, 490, n. 60; Baker, *Protective Labor Legislation,* p. 368.
49. Goesaert v. Cleary, 74 F. Supp. 735, 738–739 (E.D. Mich. 1947); Commonwealth v. Price, 123 Ky. 163, 164–165, 94 S.W. 32, 33 (1906). For discussion of various "B-Girl" (bar-girl) ordinances, see Baer, *Chains of Protection,* pp. 120–121; John Johnston, Jr., and Charles D. Knapp, "Sex Discrimination By Law: A Study in Judicial Perspective," *New York University Law Review,* 46 (1971): 675, 705 (Eve/Eva).
50. See Babcock et al., *Sex Discrimination,* pp. 277–280; Brief of Appellants, p. 23, Goesaert v. Cleary, 335 U.S. 464 (1948).
51. Goesaert v. Cleary, 335 U.S. 464, 465–467 (1948).
52. State v. Hunter, 208 Or. 282, 284–285, 300 P.2d 455, 457–458 (1956).
53. Quong Wing v. Kirkendall, 223 U.S. 59, 63 (1912); Oliver Wendell Holmes, "The Path of the Law," *Harvard Law Review,* 10 (1897): 457, 469; Lochner v. New York, 198 U.S. 54, 76 (1905) (Holmes, J., dissenting).
54. Salt Lake City v. Wilson, 46 Utah 60, 63, 148 P. 1104, 1107 (1915); Breedlove v. Suttles, 302 U.S. 277, 282 (1937).
55. State v. Heitman, 105 Kan. 139, 146–147, 181 P. 630, 633–634 (1919);

Platt v. Commonwealth, 256 Mass. 539, 52 N.E. 914, 915 (1926); Territory v. Armstrong, 28 Hawaii 88 (1924); Ex Parte Gosselin, 141 Me. 412, 442, 44 A.2d 882, 886 (1945).

56. See State v. Mattiello, 4 Conn. Cir. 55, 225 A.2d 507 (App. Div. 1966), appeal dismissed, 395 U.S. 209 (1969); Note, "Sex Discrimination in the Criminal Law: The Effect of the Equal Rights Amendment," *American Criminal Law Review,* 11 (Winter 1973): 469, 485.

57. The Supreme Court struck down such rules in 1968. King v. Smith, 392 U.S. 309 (1968). For discussion of the "night raids" by welfare investigators to determine cohabitation, see Jacobus ten Broek, "California's Dual System of Family Law: Its Origin, Development, and Present Status," Part III. *Stanford Law Review,* 17 (1965): 614, 667–668.

58. U.S. Women's Bureau, *Legal Status of Women: Analysis of Sex Distinctions* (Washington, D.C.: Government Printing Office, 1944), p. 5; Reimann v. Reimann, 39 N.Y.S.2d 489 (Sup. Ct. 1942); Bunim v. Bunim, 298 N.Y. 391, 83 N.E.2d 848 (1949); Maxine Virtue, *Family Cases in Court* (Durham, N.C.: Duke University Press, 1956), p. 102.

59. See Note, "Sex Discrimination," pp. 700–701; Wortman, *Women in American Law,* I, 291, and Chapter 7.

60. McGuire v. McGuire, 157 Neb. 226, 59 N.W.2d 336, 342 (1953).

61. National League of Women Voters, *A League of Women Voters Survey of the Legal Status of Women,* in Wortman, *Women in American Law,* pp. 376–381; Joan M. Krauskopf, "Partnership Marriage: Legal Reforms Needed," in Jane Roberts Chapman and Margaret Gates, *Women Into Wives: The Legal and Economic Impact of Marriage* (Beverly Hills, Calif.: Sage, 1977), pp. 39, 96; Comment, "Sex Based Classifications," pp. 490–493; Note, "Sex Discrimination," p. 712, n. 120.

62. See Ann Garfinkle, Carol Lefcourt, and Diane Schulder, "Women's Servitude Under Law," in Robert Lefcourt, ed., *Law Against the People* (New York: Random House, 1971), pp. 105–122; Jennie Loitman Barron, "Jury Service for Women," in Wortman, *Women in American Law,* I, 330.

63. Commonwealth v. Welosky, 276 Mass. 398, 177 N.E. 656, 661 (1931), cert. denied, 284 U.S. 684 (1932); State v. Emery, 224 N.C. 581, 31 S.E.2d 858 (1944). See also State v. Kelly, 39 Idaho 668, 229 P. 659 (1924).

64. Bailey v. State, 215 Ark. 53, 61, 219 S.W.2d 424, 428 (1949). See Commonwealth v. Welosky, 276 Mass. 398, 410–411, 177 N.E. 656, 662; State v. Kelly, 39 Idaho 668, 676, 229 P. 659, 662 (1924). The couplet is characteristic of the press accounts of women's jury service in the late nineteenth century. See Grace Raymond Hebard, "The First Woman Jury" (Wyoming Territory, 1870), *Journal of American History,* 7 (1913): 1302–1304, 1313.

65. Strauder v. West Virginia, 100 U.S. 303, 310 (1879); Ballard v. United States, 329 U.S. 187, 193–194 (1946); Hoyt v. Florida, 368 U.S. 57, 59 (1961).

66. Brief for Appellant, pp. 11, 19–20, Hoyt v. Florida, 368 U.S. 57 (1961). See Babcock et al., *Sex Discrimination,* p. 101; Reid Hastie, Steven D. Penrod, and Nancy Pennington, *Inside the Jury* (Cambridge, Mass.: Harvard University Press, 1984).

67. Hoyt v. Florida, 368 U.S. at pp. 61–62. See Edwards v. Healy, 363 F.Supp.

1110 (E.D. La.), vacated and remanded, 421 U.S. 772 (1975); White v. Crook, 251 F.Supp. 401 (M.D. Ala. 1966); Taylor v. Louisiana, 419 U.S. 522 (1975).

3. Feminist Challenges and Legal Responses

1. Helena Lopata, *Occupation Housewife* (New York: Oxford University Press, 1971), p. 217; Jessie Bernard, *The Future of Marriage* (New York: World, 1972), pp. 27–33, tables 11–23 (and sources cited therein); Betty Friedan, *The Feminine Mystique* (New York: Dell, 1974), pp. 282–283, 289–290.
2. Judith M. Bardwick, *In Transition: How Feminism, Sexual Liberation and the Search for Self-Fulfillment Have Altered America* (New York: Holt, Rinehart and Winston, 1979), p. 100; President's Commission on the Status of Women, *American Women, The Report of the President's Commission on the Status of Women* (1953), pp. 4–7; Mary P. Ryan, *Womanhood in America: From Colonial Times to the Present* 2d ed. (New York: Franklin Watts, 1979), p. 238; Ethel Klein, *Gender Politics* (Cambridge, Mass.: Harvard University Press, 1984), pp. 66–67; Alice Rossi, "Family Development in a Changing World" (1971), quoted in Gayle Graham Yates, *What Women Want: The Ideas of the Movement* (Cambridge, Mass.: Harvard University Press, 1975), p. 155.
3. President's Commission, *American Women,* p. 4; Caroline Bird, "The Androgynous Life," in Mary Lou Thompson, ed., *Voices of the New Feminism* (Boston: Beacon, 1970), pp. 178–198; Caroline Bird and the National Women's Conference, *What Women Want: From the Official Report to the President, the Congress and the People of the United States* (New York: Simon and Schuster, 1979), p. 106; Janet Zollinger Giele, *Women and the Future: Changing Sex Roles in Modern America* (New York: Free Press, 1978), p. 92; Ryan, *Womanhood in America,* pp. 195–198; Nancy Woloch, *Women and the American Experience* (New York: Alfred A. Knopf, 1984), p. 508.
4. Maren Lockwood Carden, *The New Feminist Movement* (New York: Russell Sage Foundation, 1974), pp. 154–155; Jane De Hart-Mathews, "The New Feminism and the Dynamics of Social Change," in Linda K. Kerber and Jane De Hart-Mathews, *Women's America: Refocusing the Past* (New York: Oxford University Press, 1982), pp. 408–409; Friedan, *Feminine Mystique*, chap. 12. For the limitations of Freidan's analysis, see Bell Hooks, *Feminist Theory from Margin to Center* (Boston: South End Press, 1984), pp. 1–3, 95.
5. U.S. Women's Bureau, *Fact Sheet on the Earnings Gap* (February 1971), p. 1; *Congressional Quarterly,* 24 (June 1963): 978.
6. James White, "Women in the Law," *Michigan Law Review,* 65 (1957): 1051, 1071–1095; Donna Fossum, "Women in the Legal Profession: A Progress Report," *American Bar Association Journal,* 67 (May 1981): 578, 582; Cynthia Fuchs Epstein, "Positive Effects of the Multiple Negative; Explaining the Success of Black Professional Women," *American Journal of*

Sociology, 78 (1973): 912, 917; Geraldine Segal, *Blacks in the Law* (Philadelphia: University of Pennsylvania Press, 1983), p. 213.

7. Jo Freeman, "The Origins of the Women's Liberation Movement," *American Journal of Sociology,* 78 (1973): 792, 798, 800–801; Sara Evans, *Personal Politics: The Roots of Women's Liberation in the Civil Rights Movement and the New Left* (New York: Alfred A. Knopf, 1979), pp. 84–87; Alfredo Mirande and Evangelina Enriquez, *La Chicana: The Mexican-American Woman* (Chicago: University of Chicago Press, 1979).
8. See the discussion of Heterodoxy, a feminist society, in Elaine Showalter, *These Modern Women: Autobiographical Essays from the Twenties* (Old Westbury, N.Y.: Feminist Press, 1978), p. 7; and Carden, *Feminist Movement.*
9. Executive Order 10980, Dec. 14, 1961, reprinted in President's Commission, *American Women,* p. 76; Judith Hole and Ellen Levine, *Rebirth of Feminism* (New York: Quadrangle, 1971), pp. 19–20; Cynthia Harrison, *On Account of Sex* (Berkeley: University of California Press, 1988), pp. 109–165 (describing divisions).
10. President's Commission, *American Women,* p. 37. See generally Hole and Levine, *Rebirth;* Ryan, *Womanhood;* Leila J. Rupp and Verta Taylor, *Survival in the Doldrums* (New York: Oxford University Press, 1987), pp. 188–194. See generally Harrison, *Sex.*
11. Rupp and Taylor, *Survival,* pp. 166–174; Statement of Rep. Emanuel Celler, Hearings on House Resolution 7152 before the House Committee on Rules, 88th Cong., 2d sess., p. 125 (1964).
12. Representative Frances P. Bolton, 110 *Congressional Record* 2578 (1964); Title VII, Civil Rights Act of 1964, 705, 42 U.S.C. 2000(e) (1981).
13. Edelsberg, quoted in Caroline Bird, *Born Female,* rev. ed. (New York: David McKay, 1970), p. 13; The EEOC's executive director also indicated that staff were "aware of the importance of not becoming known as the 'Sex Commission.'" N. Thompson Powers, quoted in Harrison, *Sex,* p. 187.
14. See generally Bird, *Born Female,* pp. 15–18, Hole and Levine, *Rebirth,* pp. 82–83.
15. See Freeman, "Origins of the Women's Liberation Movement," pp. 798–799; Carden, *Feminist Movement,* pp. 31, 59, 103–104. See generally Betty Friedan, *It Changed My Life* (New York: Random House, 1976).
16. Monroe Green, quoted in Martha Weinman Lear, "The Second Feminist Wave," *New York Times Magazine,* March 10, 1968, p. 24. See Pittsburgh Press Co. v. Pittsburgh Commission on Human Relations, 413 U.S. 376 (1973).
17. Jo Freeman adds some important qualifications to the distinction that appears in works such as Yates, *What Women Want,* and Hole and Levine, *Rebirth of Feminism.* See Freeman, "Origins of the Women's Liberation Movement," pp. 795–811.
18. See generally Barbara Deckard, *The Women's Movement: Socioeconomic and Psychological Issues* (New York: Harper and Row, 1975), pp. 355–356; Carden, *Feminist Movement,* p. 95; Woloch, *American Experience,* p. 518.

19. Statement of Wilma Scott Heide, chairwoman of NOW's Board of Directors, Equal Rights Amendment Hearings before the Senate Committee on the Judiciary, Subcommittee on Constitutional Amendment, 91st Cong., 2d sess., Senate Joint Resolution 61, pp. 569–570 (1970).
20. "Red Stockings Manifesto," reprinted in Robin Morgan, ed., *Sisterhood Is Powerful; An Anthology of Writings From the Women's Liberation Movement* (New York: Vintage, 1970), p. 534; Kate Millett, *Sexual Politics* (Garden City, N.Y.: Doubleday, 1970), pp. 15, 54–58; Shulamith Firestone, *The Dialectic of Sex: The Case for Feminist Revolution* (New York: William Morrow, 1970), pp. 256–274. See also "The Feminists: A Political Organization to Annihilate Sex Roles," in Ann Koedt, Ellen Levine, and Anita Rapone, eds., *Radical Feminism* (New York: Quadrangle, 1973), pp. 368–377.
21. See Catharine MacKinnon, "Feminism, Marxism, Method, and the State: Toward Feminist Jurisprudence," *Signs,* 8 (Summer 1983): 635; Margaret Benston, "The Political Economy of Women's Liberation," reprinted in June Sochen, *The New Feminism in Twentieth-Century America* (Lexington, Mass.: D. C. Heath, 1971), pp. 192–202; Eli Zaretsky, *Capitalism, the Family and Personal Life* (New York: Harper and Row, 1976); Ti Grace Atkinson, quoted in Janine Slade, "History of the Equality Issue in the Contemporary Women's Movement," p. 2, cited in Hole and Levine, *Rebirth,* p. 90. For a good overview of different feminist positions, see Alison Jaggar, *Feminist Politics and Human Nature* (London and Totowa, N.J.: Rowman and Allanheld, 1983).
22. Carden, *Feminist Movement,* p. 19 (profiles); Ida Lewis, quoted in Paula Giddings, *When and Where I Enter: The Impact of Black Women on Race and Sex in America* (New York: William Morrow, 1984), p. 309; Margaret A. Simons, "Racism and Sexism: A Schism in Sisterhood," *Feminist Studies,* 5 (1979): 384, 396. See Toni Cade, ed., *The Black Woman: An Anthology* (New York: New American Library, 1970), pp. 9–10; Bell Hooks, *Ain't I a Woman: Black Women and Feminism* (Boston: South End Press, 1981), pp. 129–179; Mirande and Enriquez, *La Chicana,* pp. 237–238; Gloria Hull, Patricia Scott, and Barbara Smith, eds., *All the Women are White, All the Blacks are Men, But Some of Us are Brave: Black Women's Studies* (Old Westbury, N.Y.: Feminist Press, 1982); Linda J. M. La Rue, "Black Liberation and Women's Lib," *Transaction,* 8 (November–December 1970): 61; Toni Morrison, "What Black Women Think About Women's Lib," *New York Times Magazine,* Aug. 22, 1971, p. 15. For survey data, see Lou Harris and Associates, *The 1972 Virginia Slims American Women's Opinion Poll* (1972), p. 4; Bonnie Thornton Dill, "Race, Class, and Gender: Prospects for an All Inclusive Sisterhood," *Signs* 9 (1983): 131, 133; Rayna Green, "Native American Women," *Signs* 6 (1980): 248 (describing organizations).
23. Friedan, *It Changed My Life,* pp. 484–487, 161, 396; "Critique of Sexual Politics, An Interview With Betty Friedan," *Social Policy,* 1 (November–December 1970): 38. For contemporary criticism of radical feminists' view, see Sylvia Hewlett, *A Lesser Life,* p. 185.
24. National Women's Conference, *What Women Want.*

4. The Equal Rights Campaign

1. This analysis draws on a more expansive analysis with fuller supporting authority in Deborah L. Rhode, "Equal Rights in Retrospect," *Journal of Law and Inequality*, 1 (1983): 1. For historical material, see Chapter 2.
2. For a fuller catalog of opponents and supporters, see Janet Boles, *The Politics of the Equal Rights Amendment: Conflict and the Decision Process* (New York: Longman, 1979). One poll during the mid-seventies found that only a bare majority (53 percent) of American women had heard of the amendment, and three-quarters did not know enough about it to have an opinion. Sharon Whitney, *The Equal Rights Amendment* (New York: Franklin Watts, 1984), p. 33. In June 1982, just as the deadline for ratification expired, a Gallup poll revealed that 58 percent of the respondents who had heard of the amendment supported it; 24 percent were opposed. See Nadine Brozan, "58% in Gallup Poll Favor Equal Rights," *New York Times*, April 10, 1975, p. 45. But see also George Gallup, "Public Support Grows for Reviving the Draft," *San Francisco Chronicle*, March 3, 1980, p. 12, col. 1 (noting that 39 percent of males and 50 percent of females opposed drafting women; 53 percent of males and 56 percent of females opposed women in combat).
3. Proposed Amendment to the United States Constitution, Section 1, Senate Joint Resolution 8, Senate Joint Resolution 9, and House Joint Resolution 208, 92d Cong., 1st sess. (1971). The remaining sections of the amendment provided: "Section 2. The Congress shall have the power to enforce, by appropriate legislation, the provisions of this article. Section 3. The amendment shall take effect two years after the date of ratification." The amendment was approved by a vote of 354 to 23 in the House of Representatives and 84 to 8 in the Senate.
4. In 1978 Congress extended the date for ratification to June 30, 1982. House Joint Resolution 638, 95th Cong., 2nd sess., 124 *Congressional Record* H8, 26, 264–265 (House), S34, 314–315 (Senate) (1978). A lower federal court judge held that extension invalid, but during the pendency of the appeal, the 1982 limit expired without the requisite state endorsements. Accordingly, the Supreme Court dismissed the case as moot. Idaho v. Freeman, 529 F.Supp. 1107 (D. Idaho 1981), stayed, 455 U.S. 918 (1982), dismissed as moot sub. nom. National Organization for Women, Inc. v. Idaho, 459 U.S. 809 (1982).
5. See Mary Frances Berry, *Why ERA Failed;* Boles, *Politics;* Jennifer Mansbridge, *Why We Lost the ERA* (Chicago: University of Chicago Press, 1986); Joan Hoff-Wilson, ed., *Rights of Passage; The Past and Future of the ERA* (Bloomington: Indiana University Press, 1986). For a critical review, see Catharine A. MacKinnon, "Unthinking ERA Thinking," *University of Chicago Law Review*, 54 (1987): 759.
6. *McNeil-Lehrer Report*, June 30, 1982, transcript p. 4 (Rep. Geraldine Ferraro quoting Rep. Barbara Mikulski). See Karen DeCrow, *Sexist Justice* (Vintage, 1975), p. 301.
7. Ruth Bader Ginsburg, "Sexual Equality Under the Fourteenth and Equal Rights Amendments," *Washington University Law Quarterly* (1979): 161,

171. See Barbara A. Brown et al., "The Equal Rights Amendment: A Constitutional Basis for Equal Rights for Women," *Yale Law Journal,* 80 (1971): 871–985; Norman Dorsen and Susan Ross, "The Necessity of a Constitutional Amendment, *Harvard Civil Rights–Civil Liberties Law Review,* 6 (971): 216.

8. Robert Cross, "Dialog: Phyllis Schlafly," *Chicago Tribune Magazine,* Nov. 9, 1975, p. 26 (quoting Phyllis Schlafly); "Slowdown Feared for Women's Rights," *Chicago Today,* March 1, 1973 (citing poll).

9. Phyllis Schlafly, "The Precious Rights ERA Will Take Away From Wives," *The Phyllis Schlafly Report,* 7 (August 1973): sec. 2, p. 11; Interview with Illinois State Senator Eugenia Chapman (Chicago, Aug. 13, 1973) (quoting constituent letters). See Ruth Murray Brown, "In Defense of Traditional Values: The Anti-Feminist Movement," *Marriage and Family Review,* 7 (Fall/Winter 1984): 19, 35 (quoting Oklahoma ERA opponents).

10. The proposed Uniform Marriage and Divorce Act, which many states have adopted in substantial part, incorporates sex-neutral standards, as did the Supreme Court's decision concerning alimony, Orr v. Orr, 440 U.S. 268 (1979). See Leo Kanowitz, "The ERA: The Task Ahead," *Hastings Constitutional Law Quarterly,* 6 (1979): 637, 648.

11. Thus, as Norman Dorsen observed in a statement before the Senate Judiciary Committee, opponents often seemed to be "trying to erect bridges which were [already] crossed." 117 *Congressional Record* 933 (1971). For discussion of family law reforms, see Chapter 7.

12. Mike Royko, "Borchers Hip to Girl Power," *Chicago Daily News,* March 26, 1973, p. 12. See 118 *Congressional Record* 9080, 9089, 9100, 9103, 9333, 9350, 9507 (1972).

13. See discussion of Rostker v. Goldberg, 453 U.S. 57 (1981), in Chapter 5. Even under strict scrutiny standards, women's exclusion from combat might have passed muster. See Senate Committee on the Judiciary, *Equal Rights for Men and Women,* Senate Report No. 689, 92d Cong., 2d sess., pp. 13–14 (1972); Mansbridge, *ERA,* pp. 60–89 (discussing War Powers clause).

14. Brown et al., "Equal Rights Amendment," p. 977. See also Mariclaire Hale and Leo Kanowitz, "Women and the Draft: A Response to Critics of the Equal Rights Amendment," *Hastings Law Journal,* 23 (1971): 199; Kanowitz, "The Task Ahead," p. 647. For poll data, see note 2.

15. For antifeminist positions, see Berry, *ERA,* p. 65; Phyllis Schlafly, *The Power of the Positive Woman* (New York: Jove, 1978), p. 89 and Phyllis Schlafly, "What's Wrong with Equal Rights for Women?" *The Phyllis Schlafly Report,* 5 (February 1972): 2, 4; David Brady and Kent Tedin, "Ladies in Pink: Religion and Political Ideology in the Anti-ERA Movement," *Social Science Quarterly,* 56 (1975): 564; Arlene Swidler, "Catholics and the ERA," *Commonweal,* 103 (1976): 585. For discussion of Massachusetts Civil Liberties Union efforts to enjoin abortion-fund cutoffs, see Carol Felsenthal, "How Feminists Failed," *Chicago,* June 1982, p. 157. For a representative decision upholding bans against homosexual marriage, see Singer v. Hara, 11 Wash. App. 247, 522 P.2d 1187 (Ct. App., 1974). See 118 *Congressional Record* 55 (1972).

16. See "Stop ERA," *What the Equal Rights Amendment Really Means,* p. 1;

Boles, *Politics,* p. 6; George Whittenberg, *The ERA and You* (New York: Vantage, 1975), pp. 41–42; "The ERA Loses Two More Rounds," *Time,* Feb. 1, 1982, p. 18.

17. Edith Mayo and Jerry K. Fry, "The ERA: Postmortem of a Failure in Political Communication," in Hoff-Wilson, *Rights of Passage,* 85; and 118 *Congressional Record* 9531 (1972) (Senator Cook).
18. "DAR Hits Satanism, Sex Equality," *Chicago Tribune,* April 18, 1974, sec. 2, p. 7 (quoting DAR); Henry Schipper, "The Truth Will Out: An Interview with Phyllis Schlafly," *Ms.,* January 1982, p. 88 (quoting Phyllis Schlafly); Barbara Rowes, *The Book of Quotes* (New York: E. P. Dutton, 1979), p. 34 (quoting Ronald Reagan). For general discussion of symbolic politics, see Jacob Murray Edelman, *Politics as Symbolic Action: Mass Arousal and Quiescence* (New York: Academic Press, 1971); Kenneth Burke, *Language as Symbolic Action* (Berkeley: University of California Press, 1966).
19. Diana Loercher, "Equality for Women Stalled?" *Christian Science Monitor,* Feb. 15, 1973, p. 6, col. 2 (quoting Phyllis Schlafly); Dale Wittner, "All Women's Liberationists Hate Men and Children," *Chicago Tribune Magazine,* May 20, 1973, p. 22 (quoting Phyllis Schlafly).
20. See Bradwell v. Illinois, 83 U.S. 130, 141–142 (1872) (Bradley, J., concurring), discussed in Chapter 1.
21. Other organizations included American Women Already Richly Endowed; Happiness of Motherhood Eternal (HOME); Humanitarians Opposed to Degrading Our Girls; Housewives and Motherhood Anti-Lib Movement; Right to Be a Woman; and Women for Maintaining the Differences Between the Sexes and Against the ERA. For a fuller catalog, see Boles, *Politics,* pp. 200–202.
22. See Lindsy Van Gelder, "The 400,000 Vote Misunderstanding," *Ms.,* March 1976, p. 67 (citing national survey findings that 65 percent of American women support "most of the efforts to strengthen and change women's status in society," but only 17 percent have a positive image of the women's movement and its major organizations); Louis Harris and Associates, *The 1972 Virginia Slims American Women's Opinion Poll* (1972), p. 4 (reporting that 39 percent of women described themselves as sympathetic and 49 percent as unsympathetic to the women's movement; men were evenly divided, with 42 percent on each side.)

    Lipset and Raab attribute engagement in right-wing politics to a reaction "against the displacement of power and status accompanying change" by groups that are declining in a "felt sense of importance, influence, and power as a result of secular endemic change in the society." Seymour Lipset and Earl Raab, *The Politics of Unreason: The Politics of Right-Wing Extremism in America* (New York: Harper and Row, 1970), pp. 3, 29. See also Joseph Gusfield, "Moral Passage: The Symbolic Process in Public Designations of Deviance," *Social Problems,* 15 (1967): 175, 185.
23. See generally Paula Giddings, *When and Where I Enter* (New York: William Morrow, 1984), p. 346; Sandra K. Gill, "Attitudes Toward the ERA," *Social Perspectives,* 28 (1986): 441; Cathy Sedwick and Reba Williams, "Black Women and the ERA," *Black Scholar,* 7 (July–August 1976): 25–26.
24. Van Gelder, "The 400,000 Vote Misunderstanding," p. 67 (quoting Lilly

Newman). See also Enid Nemy, "Feminists Reappraise Direction and Image," *New York Times,* Nov. 8, 1975, p. 32 (discussing criticism of NOW's "negative" attitude toward volunteerism). For contemporary complaints, see Mary Ann Mason, *The Equality Trap* (New York: Simon and Schuster, 1988), p. 26 (claiming that the ERA campaign drained "millions of dollars and millions of working hours into the attempt to pass an amendment which would have made little or no change in the fundamental conditions of women's lives").

25. "ERA—Selling Womenhood Short," *Christian Crusade Weekly,* 14 (March 10, 1974): 3 (quoting J. Pincus, Professor of Neurology, Yale Medical School); Whittenberg, *ERA,* p. 66 (quoting Phyllis Schlafly). See Rex Lee, *A Lawyer Looks at the Equal Rights Amendment* (Provo, Utah: Brigham Young University Press, 1980), pp. 64–65 (arguing that homosexuals could well prove to be "among the principal beneficiaries of the ERA"). For similar antisuffragist claims about the family, see Chapter 1.
26. Loercher, "Equality for Women Stalled?" p. 1 (quoting John MacManus, spokesman for the John Birch Society). See, for example, Berry, *ERA,* p. 65; Jane O'Reilly, "Big Time Players: Behind the Small Town Image," *Ms.,* January 1983, pp. 38, 59 (quoting Kenneth McFall, executive secretary of the Oklahoma Farm Bureau: "Civil rights was an area of states' rights until the 1950's. We didn't want Congress to have any more rights to enforce, especially this kind of vague [equal rights] law."). See also "DAR Hits Satanism, Sex Equality," *Chicago Tribune,* April 18, 1974, sec. 2, p. 7, col. 1 (statement of Daughters of the American Revolution); Boles, *Politics,* p. 170 (discussing fears in Georgia that the amendment would lead to more Supreme Court decisions like Brown v. Board of Education).
27. Felsenthal, "How Feminists Failed," p. 142 (quoting Phyllis Schlafly).
28. Boles, *Politics,* p. 160 (quoting Rep. Hanahan).
29. Boles, *Politics,* p. 6; David Gilbert, "Equal Rights Proposal Fails Twice in Assembly," *Chicago Tribune,* April 5, 1973, p. 1 (quoting Roscoe Cunningham [R., Lawrenceville, Ill.]); letter from Sen. Frank Ozinga to Martha Clark, May 2, 1973. See also "Trouble for ERA," *Time,* Feb. 19, 1973, p. 25 (quoting Sen. Guy Hamilton Jones, Ark., "Women are put on this earth to minister to the needs of miserable men").
30. Editorial, "The Mossbacks Win Again," *Chicago Daily News,* April 6, 1973, p. 12; Simone de Beauvoir, *The Second Sex,* trans. H. M. Parshley (New York: Vintage, 1952), p. xxvi.
31. Max Farrand, ed., *The Records of the Federal Convention of 1787* (New Haven: Yale University Press, 1966), p. 93 (James Madison quoting Rufus King).
32. Eleanor Flexner, *A Century of Struggle: The Women's Rights Movement in the United States,* rev. ed. (Cambridge, Mass.: Harvard University Press, 1975), p. 296. See also Chapter 1.
33. Boles, *Politics,* p. 123 (quoting unidentified ERA opponents).
34. In some jurisdictions, legislators reported mail running between 10 to 1 and 50 to 1 against the amendment. See Boles, *Politics,* p. 115; Hurling, "ERA Capitol Conflict"; "State Senate OK for Women's Rights," *Chicago Today,*

May 25, 1972. As the campaign wore on, however, some legislators became irritated at the large volume of standardized letters, which complicated the task of identifying and responding to individualized correspondence.

35. See generally Boles, *Politics,* pp. 113–133. For example, in the final year of the campaign, NOW reportedly spent some $15,000,000 nationally, where Schlafly acknowledged national expenditures of only $100,000, in addition to some $100,000 in PAC candidate contributions. O'Reilly, "Big Time Players," pp. 38, 59. Many other women's organizations, such as the National Women's Political Caucus, the League of Women Voters, and local business and professional women's associations, gave significant monetary and in-kind assistance. By contrast, anti-ERA efforts were frequently orchestrated from opponents' homes or church basements, and their financial outlays were far more modest. However, since some business organizations, particularly insurance companies, spent undisclosed amounts in lobbying against the amendment, aggregate resource comparisons are impossible to draw.
36. Ann Scott, quoted in Lisa Cronin Wohl, "White Gloves and Combat Boots: The Fight for ERA," *Civil Liberties Review,* 1 (Fall 1974): 77, 98.
37. "A Bunny Hops on Rights Issue," *Chicago Daily News,* Feb. 15, 1973, p. 34.
38. Hurling, "ERA Capitol Conflict"; "Rights Battle Booms from Kitchens," *Chicago Daily News,* March 15, 1973, p. 34; "Women Try to Cook Up Votes," *Chicago Tribune,* March 15, 1973. See also Sheila Wolfe, "ERA Given Boost at State Breakfast," *Chicago Tribune,* March 15, 1973, sec. 2, p. 9.
39. Bole, *Politics,* pp. 1113–1133; interview with Illinois State Senator Eugenia Chapman, *Chicago,* Aug. 13, 1973.
40. See Boles, *Politics,* p. 125; Lentz, "ERA Backers Pour Blood on Capitol Floors," *Chicago Tribune,* June 26, 1982, p. 2. See *MacNeil-Lehrer Report,* transcript p. 1.
41. O'Reilly, "Big Time Players," p. 59 (discussing Oklahoma anti-ERA organization's display of Houston materials); Felsenthal, "How Feminists Failed," p. 140 (quoting Illinois rep. Edward Blaihardt).
42. Susan Fraker, "Women Versus Women," *Newsweek,* July 25, 1977, p. 38 (quoting B. Feigen Fasteau). See also Enid Nemy, "Feminist Cause Looks Back to Grass Roots," *New York Times,* Nov. 8, 1982, p. B10.
43. Nemy, "Feminists Reappraise Direction" (quoting Carol De Saram); Marjorie Hunter, "Leaders Concede Loss on Equal Rights," *New York Times,* June 25, 1982, p. A13, col. 1 (quoting Eleanor Smeal); Elinor Langer, "Why Big Business Is Trying to Defeat the ERA: The Economic Implications of Equality," *Ms.,* May 1976, p. 64; NOW advertisements, "Will the ERA Be Sacrificed for the Insurance Numbers Game?" discussed in O'Reilly, "Big Time Players," p. 61. For proponents' dismissals of their opponents as "masochistic," "stupid," "naive," and "incapable of independent thought," see Van Gelder, "400,000 Vote Misunderstanding," p. 68; Boles, *Politics,* p. 87. See also "Rights Plan Advocates Assail Insurance Rates," *The New York Times,* June 2, 1982, p. 19; "ERA Dies," *Time,* July 5, 1982, p. 29.

44. See editorial, "ERA RIP," *The Nation,* July 3, 1982, p. 3; Bode, "Fellowship and Sisterhood," p. 4; see generally Boles, *Politics,* pp. 145–180; Rhode, "Equal Rights," pp. 64–65.
45. See 129 *Congressional Record* H9860–9864 (1983); Summary of Hearings before the Senate Subcommittee on the Constitution, on the Impact of the Proposed Equal Rights Amendment (Washington, D.C.: Government Printing Office, 1985), testimony of William Kristol (social revolution), p. 140; Lynn Wardle (wives forced out of home), p. 113; John T. Noonan (abortion funding); Raymond Marcin (homosexual marriage); Jeremy Rabin (boy scouts), p. 19; Eugene Hickok (homosexuality), p. 97; Eliot A. Cohen (military). Comment, "Equal Rights Provisions: The Experience Under State Constitutions," *California Law Review,* 65 (1977): 1068.
46. See 129 *Congressional Record* H9852–9855; testimony of Marna Tucker in Hearings, pp. 6–7 (only means of progress); Peter Navarro, "The Fire Next Time? The Future of the Equal Rights Amendment," *Savvy,* January 1985, p. 74 (lunatic fringe); see also testimony of Senator Packwood, Hearings, pp. 28–30. For a critical perspective, see Deborah L. Rhode, "Feminist Perspectives on Legal Ideology," in Ann Oakley and Juliet Mitchell, eds., *What is Feminism?* (Oxford: B. Blackwell, 1986) p. 151.

5. The Evolution of Discrimination Doctrine

1. Joseph Tussman and Jacobus Ten Broek, "The Equal Protection of the Laws," *California Law Review,* 37 (1949): 341; Catharine A. MacKinnon, *Feminism Unmodified: Discourses on Life and Law* (Cambridge, Mass.: Harvard University Press, 1987), pp. 32–45.
2. United States v. Carolene Products, 304 U.S. 144, 152, n. 4 (1938).
3. Kaja Silverman, *The Subject of Semiotics* (New York: Oxford University Press, 1983); Martha Minow, "The Supreme Court 1986 Term Forward: Justice Engendered," *Harvard Law Review,* 101 (1987): 10; and MacKinnon, *Feminism Unmodified.*
4. See, for example, Mary E. Becker, "Prince Charming: Abstract Equality," *Supreme Court Review* (1987): 201; Ann Freedman, "Sex Discrimination in the Supreme Court—A Comment on Sex Equality, Sex Differences, and the Supreme Court," *Yale Law Journal,* 92 (1983): 913; Sylvia Law, "Rethinking Sex and the Constitution," *University of Pennsylvania Law Review,* 132 (1984): 955; Kenneth Karst, "The Woman's Constitution," *Duke Law Journal* (1984): 447; Christine A. Littleton, "Reconstructing Sexual Equality," *California Law Review,* 75 (1987): 1279; Carrie Menkel-Meadow, "Portia in a Different Voice: Speculations on a Woman's Lawyering Process," *Berkeley Women's Law Journal,* 1 (1985) 39; Minow, "Justice Engendered"; Frances E. Olsen, "The Family and the Market: A Study of Ideology and Legal Reform," *Harvard Law Review,* 96 (1983): 1497; Elizabeth Schneider, "The Dialectic of Rights and Politics: Perspectives From the Women's Movement," *New York University Law Review,* 61 (1986): 589; Robin West, "Jurisprudence and Gender," *University of Chicago Law Review,* 55 (1988): 1; Stephanie Wildman, "The Legitimation of Sex Dis-

crimination: A Critical Response to Supreme Court Jurisprudence," *Oregon Law Review,* 63 (1984): 265. Patricia J. Williams, "Alchemical Notes: Reconstructing Ideas from Deconstructed Rights," *Harvard Civil Rights–Civil Liberties Law Review,* 22 (1987): 401. For works by Lucinda Finley, Herma Hill Kay, Nadine Taub, and Wendy Williams, see the discussion of maternity policy in Chapter 6.

5. See MacKinnon, *Feminism Unmodified,* pp. 3, 32–45, and Catharine MacKinnon, "Legal Perspectives on Sexual Difference," in Deborah L. Rhode, ed., *Theoretical Perspectives on Sexual Difference* (New Haven: Yale University Press, 1990).
6. For example, some theorists speak of power in terms of intentional effects and individuals' ability to carry out their own will. See, for example, Bertrand Russell, *Power: A New Social Analysis* (London: Allen and Unwin, 1938), pp. 25–34; Max Weber, *Economy and Society,* trans. Gunther Roth and Claus Wittich (Berkeley: University of California Press, 1978), pp. 941–948. Other commentators, including many Marxists, refuse to consider individual relations independent of wider class systems. See, for example, Nicos Poulantzas, *Political Power and Social Classes,* trans. and ed. Timothy D'Hagan (London: New Left Books, 1973). And some prominent theorists, such as Michael Foucault, emphasize power as a dynamic constituted through multiple processes rather than exercised by individuals, groups, or social classes. Michael Foucault, *Power/Knowledge: Selected Interviews and Other Writings, 1972–1977* (New York: Pantheon, 1976). For an overview, see Steven Lukes, *Power* (London: Basil Blackwell, 1986), and Jean Lipman-Blumen, *Gender Roles and Power* (Englewood Cliffs, N.J.: Prentice Hall, 1984). Dominance theorists, particularly those outside the socialist-feminist tradition, often ignore such definitional issues.
7. See, for example, Audre Lorde, *Sister Outsider* (Trumansburg, N.Y.: Crossing, 1984), pp. 114–123; Bell Hooks, *Feminist Theory From Margin to Center* (Boston: South End Press, 1984); and Cherri Moraga, "From a Long Line of Vendidas: Chicanas and Feminism in Feminist Studies," in Theresa de Lauretis, ed., *Feminist Studies/Critical Studies* (Bloomington: Indiana University Press, 1986), p. 180.
8. For example, public opinion polls over the last decade and a half have revealed relatively high levels of satisfaction concerning the status of women. See, for example, "Rosy Outlook Among Women Ages 18 to 44," *San Francisco Examiner,* Aug. 28, 1988 (nearly 90 percent of women of child-bearing age are satisfied with their lives). See also polls cited in Deborah L. Rhode, "Equal Rights in Retrospect," *Journal of Law and Inequality,* 1 (1983): 1, 18. For concerns about false consciousness in dominance theories, see Robin West, "The Difference in Women's Hedonic Lives: A Phenomenological Critique of Feminist Legal Theory," in *Wisconsin Women's Law Journal,* 3 (1987): 81 (criticizing MacKinnon for departing from her own methodological commitments in labeling other women's perceptions as false and resolving by "definitional fiat" what should be open to an individual's own self-scrutiny); Cass Sunstein, "Review of Feminism Unmodified," in *Harvard Law Review,* 101 (1988): 824, 837 (noting MacKinnon's failure

to examine the consequences of her framework in light of preferences and practices already in place), and Christine A. Littleton, "Feminism and Jurisprudence: The Difference Method Makes," *Stanford Law Review*, 41 (1989): 751 (arguing that dominance theorists such as MacKinnon fail to identify ways that women, if they are "a class constructed by and for men, can come to be a sex for [themselves]").

9. Wendy Williams, "American Equality Jurisprudence," in Sheilah L. Martin and Kathleen E. Mahony, eds., *Equality and Judicial Neutrality* (Toronto: Carswell, 1987), pp. 115, 122–123.
10. Williams, "Jurisprudence," p. 5; Nadine Taub, "Review of Catharine A. MacKinnon, Sexual Harassment of Working Women: Case of Sex Discrimination," *Columbia Law Review,* 80 (1980): 1686; Ruth Kolker, "Feminism, Sexuality and Self: A Preliminary Inquiry into the Politics of Authenticity," *Boston University Law Review,* 68 (1988): 321.
11. See discussion of Hoyt v. Florida, 368 U.S. 57 (1961), in Chapter 2, and John D. Johnston, Jr., and Charles L. Knapp, "Sex Discrimination by Law: A Study in Judicial Perspective," *New York University Law Review,* 46 (1971): 675.
12. Vorchheimer v. School District of Philadelphia, 400 F.Supp. 326, 340–341, rev'd, 532 F.2d 880 (3rd Cir. 1976), aff'd by an equally divided Court, 430 U.S. 703 (1977). See generally Gerald Gunther, "The Supreme Court 1971 Term Foreword: In Search of Evolving Doctrine on a Changing Court: A Model for a Newer Equal Protection," *Harvard Law Review,* 86 (1972): 1.
13. Reed v. Reed, 404 U.S. 71 (1971). See Sail'er Inn Inc. v. Kirby, 5 Cal. 3d 1, 485 P.2d 529 (1971). After an evidentiary hearing, the Boise probate court made the petitioner, Sally Reed, and her estranged husband coadministrators of their son's estate.
14. Plessy v. Ferguson, 163 U.S. 537 (1896); Frontiero v. Laird, 341 F.Supp. 201, 209 (M.D. Ala. 1972).
15. Frontiero v. Richardson, 411 U.S. 677 (1973); Regents of the University of California v. Bakke, 438 U.S. 265, 303 (1978).
16. Carolene Products, 304 U.S. 144, 152, n. 4; John Hart Ely, *Democracy and Distrust: A Theory of Judicial Review* (Cambridge, Mass.: Harvard University Press, 1980).
17. See generally Bruce Ackerman, "Beyond Carolene Products," *Harvard Law Review,* 98 (1985): 713; William Chafe, *Women and Equality: Changing Patterns in American Culture* (New York: Oxford University Press, 1977), pp. 76–78; Helen Mayes Hacker, "Women as a Minority Group," *Social Forces,* 60 (1951–52): 60; Arlie Hochschild, "Making It: Marginalities and Obstacles to Minority Consciousness," in Ruth B. Kundsin, *Women and Success: The Anatomy of Achievement* (New York: William Morrow, 1974).
18. See Nancy Gertner, "*Bakke* on Affirmative Action for Women: Pedestal or Cage?" *Harvard Civil Rights—Civil Liberties Law Review,* 14 (1979): 173, 189–195; Richard Wasserstrom, "Racism, Sexism, and Preferential Treatment: An Approach to the Topic," *U.C.L.A. Law Review,* 24 (1977): 581.
19. Craig v. Boren 429 U.S. 190, 199–200, n. 7 (1976).
20. Ibid., p. 219.

21. Brief for the American Civil Liberties Union as *amicus curiae* in Craig v. Boren, p. 22. See Alexandra G. Kaplan and Joan P. Bean, eds., *Beyond Sex Role Stereotypes* (Boston: Little, Brown, 1976); Barbara Lloyd and John Archer, eds., *Exploring Sex Differences* (New York: Academic Press, 1976); Inge K. Broverman et al., "Sex Role Stereotypes: A Current Appraisal," *Journal of Social Issues,* 28 (1972): 59.
22. Herma Hill Kay, "Models of Equality," *University of Illinois Law Review,* 10 (1985): 39.
23. Gunther, "Foreword," p. 8.
24. Note, "The Interpretation of State Constitutional Rights," *Harvard Law Review,* 95 (1982): 1324; Dawn Marie Driscoll and Barbara J. Rouse, "Through a Glass Darkly: A Look at State Equal Rights Amendments," *Suffolk University Law Review,* 12 (1978): 1282, 1308; Paul M. Kurtz, "The State Equal Rights Amendments and Their Impact on Domestic Relations Law," *Family Law Quarterly,* 11 (1977): 101.
25. 42 U.S.C. 2000e-2(e) (1982); see 110 *Congressional Record* 2718, 7212–15 (1964) (statement of representatives Bolton and Clark, and Case memorandum); Michael L. Sirota, "Sex Discrimination: Title VII and the Bona Fide Occupational Qualification," *Texas Law Review,* 55 (1977): 1025.
26. "Guidelines on Discrimination Because of Sex: Sex as a BFOQ," 34 *Federal Register* 13367 (Aug. 19, 1969); Caruthers Gholson Berger, "Equal Pay, Equal Employment Opportunity and Equal Enforcement of the Law for Women," *Valparaiso Law Review,* 5 (1971): 326, 361–362; Rosenfield v. Southern Pacific Co., 293 F.Supp. 1219 (C.D. Cal. 1968), aff'd 444 F. 2d 1219 (9th cir. 1971).
27. Phillips v. Martin Marietta Corporation, 400 U.S. 542 (1970).
28. Caroline Bird, *Born Female* (New York: D. McKay, 1970), 171; Denis Binder, "Sex Discrimination in the Airline Industry: Title VII Flying High," *California Law Review,* 59 (1971): 1091, 1105, n. 81; Kathleen Heenan, "Fighting the Fly-Me Airlines," *Civil Liberties Review,* 3 (December 1976): 48.
29. See Cooper v. Delta Air Lines Inc., 274 F.Supp. 781 (E.D. La., 1967); Binder, "Flying High."
30. Diaz v. Pan American, 442 F.2d 385 (5th Cir. 1971); Wilson v. Southwest Airlines, 517 F.Supp. 292 (N.D. Tex. 1981).
31. Wilson v. Southwestern Airlines, 517 F.Supp. at 295, 301–302.
32. Ibid., citing for example, St. Cross v. Playboy Club, App. No. 773, State Human Rights Appeal Bd. (N.Y. 1971).
33. Dothard v. Rawlinson, 433 U.S. 321, 334–336 (1977).
34. Catharine A. MacKinnon, "Unthinking ERA Thinking," *University of Chicago Law Review,* 54 (1987): 759, 769; Dothard v. Rawlinson, 433 U.S. 321, 342 (1977) (Marshall, J. dissenting). See sources cited in Lynn E. Zimmer, *Women Guarding Men* (Chicago: University of Chicago Press, 1986), pp. 163–164; Wendy Williams, "The Equality Crisis: Some Reflections on Culture, Courts, and Feminism," *Women's Rights Law Reporter,* 7 (1982): 175, 189.
35. Bohemian Club v. Fair Employment and Housing Commission, 187 Cal.

App. 3d 1 (1986) (reh. denied 1987); Note, "Balancing Inmates' Right to Privacy with Equal Employment for Prison Guards," *Women's Rights Law Reporter,* 4 (1978): 243, 247; Littleton, "Equality"; Taub, "Review."

36. See Hannah Arterian Furnish: "Beyond Protection: Relevant Difference and Equality in the Toxic Work Environment," *University of California–Davis Law Review,* 21 (1988): 1; Mary Becker, "From *Muller v. Oregon* to Fetal Vulnerability Policies," *University of Chicago Law Review,* 53 (1986): 1219, 1245; Wendy Chavkin, ed., *Double Exposure: Women's Health Hazards on the Job and at Home* (New York: Monthly Review Press, 1984); Wendy Williams, "Firing the Women to Protect the Fetus; The Reconciliation of Fetal Protection with Employment Opportunity Goals Under Title VII," *Georgetown Law Journal,* 69 (1981): 641, 703, and sources discussed therein. The EEOC's estimate of 20 million appears in EEOC, "Interpretive Guidelines on Employment Discrimination and Reproductive Hazards," 45 *Federal Register* 7514 (Feb. 1, 1980).
37. 29 C.F.R. 1604.4. See Kathleen Rockwell Lawrence, "Hers," *New York Times,* Nov. 21, 1985, p. 18 (describing addition of male rabbits to Playboy bunny force).
38. Martin Binkin and Shirley J. Bach, *Women and the Military* (Washington, D.C.: Brookings Institution, 1977); United States v. St. Clair, 291 F.Supp. 122, 125 (S.D. N.Y. 1968). For a discussion of minority women's experience, see Mary Frances Berry and John Blassingame, *Long Memory: The Black Experience in America* (New York: Oxford University Press, 1982), pp. 325–326.
39. Rostker v. Goldberg, 453 U.S. 57, 74 (1984).
40. Ibid. at 86–113 (Marshall, J. dissenting).
41. Senate Report No. 96–826, 96th Cong., 2d sess., rpr. in 1980 United States Code, *Congressional and Administrative News* 2612, 2649.
42. See Report of the Subcommittee on Manpower and Personnel of the Senate Armed Services Committee, 126 *Congressional Record* 13880; 126 *Congressional Record* S. 6530–6550 (June 10, 1980); Susan Estrich and Virginia Kerr, "Sexual Justice," in Norman Dorsen, ed., *The Rights of Groups* (New York: American Civil Liberties Union, 1984), p. 98; William Westmoreland, quoted in Sara Ruddick, "Women in the Military," *Report From the Center for Philosophy and Public Policy,* 4 (College Park, Md., 1984), p. 3. Also of concern were childcare requirements, single parenthood, and the assignment of military couples. See generally Lipman-Blumen, *Gender Roles;* and Chapter 4.
43. Lori S. Kornblum, "Women Warriors in a Man's World: The Combat Exclusion," *Law and Inequality: A Journal of Theory and Practice,* 2 (1984): 351; Helen Rogan, *Mixed Company; Women in the Modern Army* (New York: G. P. Putnam's Sons, 1981), p. 258; John L. Laflin, *Women in Battles* (New York: Abelard-Schuman, 1967), pp. 10–22, 62–79; Judith Stiehm, *Bring Me Men and Women: Mandated Change at the U.S. Air Force Academy* (Berkeley: University of California Press, 1981), pp. 129–130, 167, 199, 250. See generally Department of Defense, *Report, Task Force on*

Women in the Military (Washington, D.C.: Defense Department, January 1988).

44. For opposition to the draft, see Jean Yarbrough, "The Feminist Mistake: Sexual Equality and the Decline of the American Military," *Policy Review,* 33 (1985): 48; see also the discussion in Wendy Williams, "Equality Crisis," p. 189; Sarah Ruddick, "Women in the Military" and "Pacifying the Forces: Drafting Women in the Interests of Peace," *Signs,* 8 (1983): 471. For concerns about restrictions on women, see Janice Mall, "Military as a Ticket to the Mainstream," *Los Angeles Times,* Sept. 15, 1985, part IV, p. 8; Kornblum, "Warriors," pp. 369–389, 872, 968; Stiehm, *Bring Me Men,* p. 299; Owens v. Brown, 455 F.Supp. 291 (D. D.C., 1978). See generally Jean Bethke Elshtain, *Women and War* (New York: Basic Books, 1987), pp. 232–240.
45. Michael M. v. Superior Court, 450 U.S. 464 (1981).
46. Ibid. at 471–473 (plurality opinion); ibid. (Stewart J., concurring).
47. Geduldig v. Aiello, 417 U.S. 484, 497, n. 20 (1974).
48. Ibid., Brennan, J., dissenting. (See Statutes of Westminister, 13 Edw. 1, ch. 34 [1285]). For discussion of concerns regarding female chastity underlying such legislation, see Kenneth H. Karst, "Woman's Constitution," *Duke Law Journal* (1984): 447, 456; Frances Olsen, "Statutory Rape: A Feminist Critique of Rights Analysis," *Texas Law Review,* 63 (1984): 387, 417–420; Williams, "The Equality Crisis," p. 186.
49. Michael M. v. Superior Court, 450 U.S. 472 at n. 7; ibid., 450 U.S. at 488 (Brennan, J., dissenting).
50. Ibid., 450 U.S. at 483 (Blackmun, J., concurring).
51. Leigh B. Bienen, "Rape III—National Developments in Rape Reform Legislation," *Woman's Rights Law Reporter,* 6 (1981): 171, 193–197. See also Olsen, "Statutory Rape."
52. See generally Herbert S. Denenburg et al., *Risk and Insurance,* 2nd ed. (Englewood Cliffs, N.J.: Prentice Hall, 1974); Leah Wortham, "Insurance Classification: Too Important to be Left to the Actuaries," *University of Michigan Journal of Law Reform,* 19 (1986): 349.
53. Los Angeles Department of Water and Power v. Manhart, 435 U.S. 702 (1978); Arizona Governing Committee v. Norris, 463 U.S. 1073 (1983).
54. Arizona Governing Committee v. Norris, 463 U.S. 1073 (1983), quoting Los Angeles Department of Water and Power v. Manhart, 435 U.S. 702 (1978).
55. See, for example, George J. Benston, "The Economics of Gender Discrimination in Employee Fringe Benefits: *Manhart* Revisited," *University of Chicago Law Review,* 49 (1982): 489, 542; Spencer Kimball, "Reprise on *Manhart,*" *American Bar Foundation Research Journal* (1980): 915.
56. Los Angeles Department of Water and Power v. Manhart, 435 U.S. 702 (1978) (Blackmun, J., dissenting).
57. For general arguments about the inadequacy of sex-neutral predictive criteria, see Diane Kiesel, "A Matter of Policy: Sex Bias Insurance Attacked, Defended," *American Bar Association Journal,* 69 (July 1983): 875, 877.

For defenses of the biological underpinnings of longevity, see Madigan, "Are Sex Mortality Differences Biologically Caused?" *Milbank Memorial Fund Quarterly,* 35 (1957): 202, 206 (comparing Roman Catholic nuns and monks); Robert D. Retherford, *The Changing Sex Differential in Mortality* (Westport, Conn.: Greenwood, 1975); but see also sources cited in Lea Brilmayer, Richard W. Hekeler, Douglas Laycock, and Theresa A. Sullivan, "Sex Discrimination in Employer-Sponsored Insurance Plans: A Legal and Demographic Analysis, *University of Chicago Law Review* 47 (1980): 505.

58. See Lea Brilmayer, Douglas Laycock, and Theresa A. Sullivan, "The Efficient Use of Group Averages as Non-Discrimination: A Rejoinder to Professor Benston," *University of Chicago Law Review,* 50 (1983): 222, 227; National Insurance Consumer Organization, quoted in Ann C. Cicero, "Strategies for the Elimination of Sex Discrimination in Private Insurance," *Harvard Civil Rights–Civil Liberties Law Journal,* 20 (1985): 211; George Rutherglen, "Sexual Equality in Fringe-Benefit Plans," *Virginia Law Review,* 65 (1979): 199.
59. See Guido Calabresi, *Ideals, Beliefs, Attitudes and the Law: Private Law Perspectives on Public Law Problems* (Syracuse, N.Y.: Syracuse University Press, 1985), pp. 36–37 (proxy criteria); statement of Judy Goldsmith, president, NOW, HR-100 hearings, Commerce Subcommittee, Transportation and Tourism of the Committee on Energy and Commerce, U.S. House of Representatives, Feb. 22, 1983.
60. Advertisement sponsored by the Health Insurance Association of America and American Council of Life Insurance, *New York Times,* June 8, 1983, p. A24.

6. False Dichotomies

1. Kahn v. Shevin, 416 U.S. 351 (1974). For different perspectives on *Kahn,* see, for example, Catharine MacKinnon, *Sexual Harassment of Working Women: A Case of Sex Discrimination* (New Haven: Yale University Press, 1978), p. 117; Nancy S. Erickson, "*Kahn, Ballard,* and *Wiesnfeld:* A New Equal Protection Test in 'Reverse' Sex Discrimination Cases?" *Brooklyn Law Review,* 42 (1975): 1, and sources cited in note 5.
2. Kahn v. Shevin, 416 U.S. 351, 357 (Brennan, J., dissenting).
3. See Kahn v. Shevin, 416 U.S. 351, 356 n. 10 (citing Muller).
4. Califano v. Goldfarb, 430 U.S. 199 (1977); ibid., at 223 (Stevens, J., concurring).
5. Ruth Bader Ginsburg, "Sex Equality and the Constitution: The State of the Art, " *Women's Rights Law Reporter,* 4 (1978): 143, 146; William Simon, "Rights and Redistribution in the Welfare System," *Stanford Law Review,* 38 (1986): 1481, 1486.
6. See Simon, "Rights and Redistribution"; testimony discussed in Alicia H. Munnell and Laurie E. Stiglin, "Women and a Two-Tier Social Security System," in Richard V. Burkhauser and Karen C. Holden, eds., *A Challenge to Social Security: The Changing Roles of Women and Men in American Society* (New York: Academic Press, 1982).

7. Califano v. Goldfarb, 430 U.S. 199, 222–223 (Stevens, J., concurring). See sources cited in note 6.
8. Compare Ginsburg, "Sex Equality," p. 143, with Wendy Williams, "The Equality Crisis: Some Reflections on Culture, Courts, and Feminism," *Women's Rights Law Reporter,* 7 (Spring 1982): 175, 179, n. 35; and Nancy Gertner, "*Bakke* on Affirmative Action for Women: Pedestal or Cage?" *Harvard Civil Rights–Civil Liberties Law Review,* 14 (1979): 173, 187–188.
9. For different perspectives on various Social Security reform proposals, see Burkhauser and Holden, *Challenge to Social Security;* Office of Legislative and Regulatory Policy, "Report on Earnings-Sharing Implementation Study," *Social Security Bulletin* 48 (1985): 31, 35; Barbara A. Mikulski and Ellyn L. Brown, "Case Studies in the Treatment of Women Under Social Security Law: The Need for Reform," *Harvard Women's Law Journal,* 6 (1983): 29; Shelley Lapkoff and Edith Fierst, "Working Women, Marriage and Retirement" (Washington, D.C.: President's Commission on Pension Policy, 1980); Simon, "Rights," pp. 1477–1486.
10. See Sheila B. Kamerman and Alfred B. Kahn, *The Responsive Workplace* (New York: Columbia University Press, 1987), p. 51; Emily K. Abel, "Adult Daughters and Care for the Elderly," *Feminist Studies,* 12 (1987): 479 and *Love Is Not Enough: Family Care for the Elderly* (Washington, D.C.: American Public Health Policy Service, 1987); Congressional Caucus for Women's Issues, "Older Women's League," *Update,* May 31, 1988, p. 9; Jennifer Warlick, "Aged Women in Poverty: A Problem Without a Solution?" in William P. Browne and Laura Katz Olson, eds., *Aging and Public Policy: The Politics of Growing Old in America* (Westport, Conn.: Greenwood, 1983); Lois Grau, "Illness Engendered Poverty Among the Elderly," *Women and Health* 12 (1978): 103 (noting that Medicare covers less than one-half of the health costs of the elderly, and that stringent Medicaid eligibility rules exclude half of the nation's poor as well as the needy near poor); Cathy Stentzel, *Women, Work and Age* (National Commission on Working Women, 1987), pp. 12–22 (noting, for example, that four of five female retirees have no pensions; that inaccurate stereotypes about absenteeism, performance, and turnover restrict work opportunities; and that most age discrimination is unreported and unredressed); Older Women's League, *The Road to Poverty: A Report on The Economic Status of Midlife and Older Women in America* (Washington, D.C.: Older Women's League, 1988); U.S. Senate Special Committee on Aging, *Women in Our Aging Society* (Washington, D.C.: Government Printing Office, 1985).
11. Williams, "Equality Crisis," p. 96; Nancy Fraser, "Talking about Needs: Interpretive Contests as Political Conflicts in Welfare State Societies," *Ethics,* 99 (1989): 291.
12. See Murphy v. Murphy, 232 Ga. 353, 206 S.E.2d 458, 459 (1974): People v. Elliot, 525 P.2d 457, 459 (Ore. 1974); Dill v. Dill, 232 Ga. 231, 206 S.E.2d (6 Ga. 1974); Crawford v. Cushman, 378 F.Supp. 717 (D. Vt. 1974).
13. Harvey Green, *The Light of the Home* (New York: Pantheon, 1983), quoting a columnist in *The Household,* 12 (1879): 79. See also Sheila B. Kamerman,

Alfred J. Kahn, and Paul Kingston, *Maternity Policies and Working Women* (New York: Columbia University Press, 1983), p. 38, and discussion in Chapters 1 and 2.

14. See sources cited in Kamerman, Kahn, and Kingston, *Maternity Policies,* pp. 1–25; Linda J. Krieger and Patricia N. Cooney, "The Miller-Wohl Controversy: Equal Treatment, Positive Action and the Meaning of Women's Equality," *Golden Gate Law Review,* 13 (1983): 513, 518–521; Wendy Williams,"Equality's Riddle: Pregnancy and the Equal Treatment/Special Treatment Debate," *New York University Review of Law and Social Change,* 13 (1985): 325–385 (paid leaves, job security); Reva B. Siegel, Note, "Employment Equality Under the Pregnancy Discrimination Act of 1978," *Yale Law Journal,* 94 (1985): 929, 942, n. 63, 944, n. 76.
15. Kamerman and Kahn, *Responsive Workplace,* pp. 1–15.
16. Geduldig v. Aiello, 417 U.S. 484, 497 n. 20 (1974); General Electric Company v. Gilbert, 429 U.S. 125, 139 (1976).
17. See Katherine Bartlett, "Pregnancy and the Constitution: The Uniqueness Trap," *California Law Review,* 62 (1974): 1532; Nancy Erickson, "Women and the Supreme Court: Anatomy Is Destiny," *Brooklyn Law Review,* 41 (1974): 209.
18. For discussion of contraceptive failure, see Chapter 9; for discussion of female-headed families, see Chapter 7.
19. General Electric Co. v. Gilbert, 429 U.S. 125, 136; 42 U.S.C. 2000e (k) (1982); Kamerman, Kahn, and Kingston, *Maternity Policies;* Kamerman and Kahn, *Responsive Workplace;* Herma Hill Kay, "Equality and Difference: The Case of Pregnancy," *Berkeley Women's Law Journal,* 1 (1985): 1; Brief for the California Women's Lawyers Association et al., as *amici curiae* in California Federal Savings and Loan Association v. Guerra, 479 U.S. 272 (1987); Anne L. Radigan, *Concept and Compromise* (Washington, D.C.: Women's Research and Education Institute, 1988), p. 9 (citing survey data indicating that less than one-third of all firms offered paid maternity leave and tracing history of proposed parental leave and disability legislation).
20. California Federal Savings and Loan Association v. Guerra, 479 U.S. 272 (1987).
21. Ibid. (quoting Senator Williams), 123 *Congressional Record* 29658 (1977).
22. Wimberly v. Labor and Industrial Relations Commission, 479 U.S. 511 (1987); Among those defending state pregnancy leave statutes were Equal Rights Advocates, the Western Center for Law and Poverty, the Mexican American Legal Defense and Education Fund, the Legal Aid Foundation of Los Angeles, and the Coalition for Reproductive Equality in the Workplace. Organizations challenging such statutes included the ACLU, the National Organization for Women, the National Women's Political Caucus, the Women's Legal Defense Fund, and the National Women's Law Center. For an example of proposed federal legislation, which would have provided limited coverage for both parents, see Parental and Disability Leave Act, H.R. 2020, 99th Congress, 131 *Congressional Record* H 1942 (1985), discussed in Cynthia Harrison, "A Richer Life: A Reflection on the Women's Move-

ment," in Sara E. Rix, *The American Woman* (New York: Norton, 1988), pp. 53, 76.

23. Lucinda M. Finley, "Transcending Equality Theory: A Way Out of the Maternity and the Workplace Debate," *Columbia Law Review,* 86 (1986): 1118; Kay, "Equality and Difference"; Sylvia A. Law, "Rethinking Sex and the Constitution," *University of Pennsylvania Law Review,* 132 (1984): 955; Christine Littleton, "Reconstructing Sexual Equality"; Siegel, "Employment Equality," p. 929. See also Krieger and Cooney, "Miller-Wohl."
24. Sally O'Neill, "Baby Boom Hits Corporate America," *San Francisco Examiner,* July 20, 1987, p. C8; Frances Olsen, "From False Paternalism to False Equality: Judicial Assaults on Feminist Community, Illinois, 1869–1895," *University of Michigan Law Journal,* 84 (1986): 1518.
25. See Felice N. Schwartz, "Management Women and the New Facts of Life," *Harvard Business Review* (January–February 1989): 65 (advocating mommy track) Congressional Caucus for Women's Issues, *Fact Sheet on Parental Leave Legislation* (Washington, D.C., 1985); Catalyst, "Maternity/Parental Leaves"; David Wessel, "Working Fathers Feel New Pressures Arising from Child-Rearing Duties," *Wall Street Journal,* Sept. 7, 1984, sec. 2, p. 29 (reporting that, of Prudential Life Insurance Company's 60,000 employees, about a dozen men had taken paternity leave over five years); "Dads Ignore Paternity Leave," *San Francisco Examiner,* June 14, 1984, p. C12; interview with Patricia Schroeder, "Should Leaves for New Parents Be Mandatory?" *New York Times,* Dec. 29, 1985, p. E16; Gail Gregg, "Putting Kids First," *New York Times Magazine,* April 13, 1986, p. 47.
26. For discussion of infant needs, see Edward Zigler and Meryl Frank, eds., *The Parental Leave Crisis: Toward a National Policy* (New Haven: Yale University Press, 1988), pp. 44–45, 161–162, 36–51. For pressures on women to assimilate, see Chapters 8, 12, and "So Where's the Daddy Track?" *New York Times,* Aug. 25, 1988, p. A14. For psychoanalytic theories, see Nancy Chodorow, *The Reproduction of Mothering: Psychoanalysis and the Sociology of Gender* (Berkeley: University of California Press, 1978); Dorothy Dinnerstein, *The Mermaid and the Minotaur* (New York: Harper and Row, 1976). See Michael E. Lamb and Abraham Sagi, eds., *Fatherhood and Family Policy* (Hillsdale, N.J.: Lawrence Erlbaum Association, 1983); Scott Coltrane, "Father-Child Relationships and the Status of Women: A Cross-Cultural Study," *American Journal of Sociology,* 93 (March 1988): 1060–1095 (finding greater gender equality in societies where men participate significantly in child-rearing); and Chapter 12.
27. Legislators' concerns appear in an Interim Study by the Subcommittee on the Judiciary, "Equality of the Sexes" (Montana, December 1974), involving similar Montana legislation. For opposition to maternity leaves, see Williams, "Equality Crisis," p. 194, n. 109; Tamar Lewin, "Maternity Leave: Is It Leave Indeed?" *New York Times,* July 22, 1984, p. F23; Edward F. Zigler and Rita E. Watson, "Business Myopia About Children," *New York Times,* Nov. 19, 1987, p. A31.
28. Roberta M. Spalter-Roth, *Unnecessary Losses: Costs to Americans of the Lack of Family and Medical Leave* (Washington, D.C.: Institute for Wom-

en's Policy Research, 1988); "Family and Medical Leave Compromise Stirs Controversy Among Supporters," *National NOW Times*, September–November 1987), p. 8.

29. Nancy E. Daud, "Work and Family: The Gender Paradox and the Limitations of Discrimination Analysis in Restructuring the Workplace," *Harvard Civil Rights–Civil Liberties Law Review*, 24 (1989); 79; Kamerman, Kahn, and Kingston, *Maternity Policies,* pp. 4, 56–57, 74; Nadine Taub, "From Parental Leaves to Nurturing Leaves," *New York University Review of Law and Social Change,* 13 (1985): 381; Williams, "Equality's Riddle," p. 325; Family Policy Panel of the Economic Policy Council of UNA-USA, *Work and Family in the United States: A Policy Initiative* (New York, 1985).
30. See Chapter 1; John Rawls, *A Theory of Justice* (Cambridge, Mass.: Harvard University Press, 1971). For an exploration of how liberal theorists marginalize family issues, see Susan Moller Okin, "Justice and Gender," *Philosophy and Public Affairs,* 16 (1987): 42. For analysis of the dangers of such abstract public-private distinctions, see generally Fran Olsen, "The Politics of Family Law," *Law and Inequality,* 2 (February 1984): 1.
31. See Alison M. Jaggar, *Feminist Politics and Human Nature* (Totowa, N.J.: Rowman and Allanheld, 1983); Zillah R. Eisenstein, *Feminism and Sexual Equality: Crisis in Liberal America* (New York: Monthly Review Press, 1984), pp. 76–77; James S. Fishkin, *Justice, Equal Opportunity, and the Family* (New Haven: Yale University Press, 1983); Seymour Martin Lipset, "Social Mobility and Equal Opportunity," *Public Interest,* 29 (1972): 108–109.
32. See Janice M. Steel and Beth A. Tvretsky, "Marital Influence Levels and Symptomalogy Among Wives," in Faye J. Crosby, *Spouse, Parent, Worker: On Gender and Multiple Roles* (New Haven: Yale University Press, 1987), p. 79; Sandra L. Hofferth and Kristin A. Moore, "Women's Employment and Marriage," in Ralph E. Smith, ed., *The Subtle Revolution: Women at Work* (Washington, D.C.: Urban Institute, 1979), pp. 116–118; Mirra Komarovsky, *Blue-Collar Marriage* (New York: Vintage, 1962), pp. 221–234; Janet G. Hunt and Larry H. Hunt, "Male Resistance to Role Symmetry in Dual Earner Households," in Naomi Gerstel and Harriet Engel Gross, eds., *Families and Work* (Philadelphia: Temple University Press, 1987), pp. 192, 196; Lea Ybarra, "When Wives Work: The Impact on the Chicano Family," *Journal of Marriage and the Family,* 44 (1982): 169.
33. Congressional Caucus for Women's Issues, *Fact Sheet* (Washington, D.C., 1987), p. 4; Janice Peterson, "The Feminization of Poverty," *Journal of Economic Issues,* 21 (1987): 329; Margaret C. Sims, "Black Women Who Head Families: An Economic Struggle" (unpublished manuscript, 1988); Douglas J. Besharov and Alison J. Queen, "Not All Female-Headed Families are Created Equal," *Public Interest,* 89 (1987): 48. See Ruth Sidel, *Women and Children Last: The Plight of Poor Women in Affluent America* (New York: Viking, 1986); Isabel Sawhill, "Poverty in the United States: Why Is It So Persistent?" *Journal of Economic Literature,* 26 (1988): 1073, 1075 (noting difficulties in calculating economic need, resources, and income-

sharing units); Greg J. Duncan, *Years of Poverty, Years of Plenty* (Ann Arbor, Mich.: Institute for Social Research, 1984), pp. 35–45.

34. See Chapter 2, and Mimi Abramovitz, *Regulating the Lives of Women* (Boston: South End Press, 1988); Michael B. Katz, *Poverty and Policy in American History: Social Welfare Policy from Colonial Times to the Present* (New York: Academic Press, 1983); Sylvia Law, "Women, Work, Welfare and the Preservation of Patriarchy," *University of Pennsylvania Law Review,* 131 (1983): 1256.
35. Abramovitz, *Women,* pp. 193–203; Jacqueline Jones, *Labor of Love, Labor of Sorrow: Black Women, Work, and the Family from Slavery to the Present* (New York: Basic Books, 1985), pp. 266–267, 307–308; Michael B. Katz, *In the Shadow of the Poorhouse: A Social History of Welfare in America* (New York: Basic Books, 1986), p. 253; Irwin Garfinkel and Sara S. McLanahan, *Single Mothers and Their Children: A New American Dilemma* (Washington, D.C.: Urban Institute Press, 1986), pp. 91–94; Betty Lou Valentine, "Women on Welfare: Public and Institutional Racism," in Amy Swerdlow and Hanna Lessinger, *Class, Race, and Sex, and the Dynamics of Control* (Boston: G. K. Hall, 1983), p. 279.
36. See Law, "Welfare," pp. 1256, 1261–1266, 1325; Katz, *Poorhouse,* pp. ix–xi, 246–253; Diana Pearce and Harriette McAdoo, *Women and Children: Alone and in Poverty* (Washington, D.C.: Women's Research and Education Institute, 1982); Valentine, "Racism," pp. 281–282.
37. James T. Patterson, *America's Struggle Against Poverty, 1900–1980* (Cambridge, Mass.: Harvard University Press, 1981), pp. 172–173 (quoting Sen. Russell Long); Abramovitz, *Women,* pp. 335–341. See generally Blanche Bernstein, *The Politics of Welfare: The New York City Experience* (Cambridge, Mass.: Abt Press, 1982).
38. White House Working Group on the Family, *The Family: Preserving America's Future* (Washington, D.C.: Government Printing Office, 1986), p. 34; William P. O'Hare, *America's Welfare Population: Who Gets What* (Washington, D.C.: Population Reference Bureau, September 1987) p. 10 (quoting Ronald Reagan). See David T. Ellwood, *Poor Support: Poverty in the American Family* (New York: Basic Books, 1988), pp. 4–7 and 22–26 (polls); Family Support Act of 1988 (requiring welfare recipients to participate in JOBs program unless they are ill, incapacitated, or caring for children under three).
39. Ellwood, *Poor Support,* pp. 7–35; O'Hare, *Welfare Population,* pp. 5–10, 26–28 (profile); Duncan, *Years of Poverty,* pp. 60–65, 89–90 (profile and goals): L. Van DeVeer, "Adequacy of Current AFDC Need and Payment Standards," *Clearinghouse Review,* 21 (December 1987): 141, 144–145; Leonard Goodwin, *Causes and Cures of Welfare: New Evidence on the Social Psychology of the Poor* (Lexington, Mass.: Lexington Books 1983); but see Garfinkel and McLanahan, *Single Mothers* (Washington, D.C., Urban Institute Press, 1986), pp. 166–167 (arguing that small influence of benefits on unwed motherhood may multiply across generations).
40. O'Hare, *Welfare Population,* pp. 10–13; Duncan, *Years of Poverty,* pp. 64–

65, 90–91; Katz, *Poorhouse,* pp. 277–278 (correlation between children and adult welfare), pp. 290–291; Rhoda Schulzinger and Paula Roberts, "Welfare Reform in the States: Fact or Fiction," *Clearinghouse Review,* 21 (December 1987): 694–709; Law, "Welfare," p. 1277. See also Chapter 7 (child support); Kamerman and Kahn, *Responsive Workplace,* p. 45 (health); Karen Davis, "Women and Health Care," in Sara E. Rix, *The American Woman* (New York: Norton, 1988), p. 162.

41. Sawhill, "Poverty," pp. 1083–1084.
42. Mary Jo Bane, "Politics and Policies of the Feminization of Poverty in the United States," in Margaret Weiss, Ann Shola Orloff, and Theda Skocpol, *The Politics of Social Policy in the United States* (Princeton: Princeton University Press, 1988), p. 381 (describing work disincentives); see also Ellwood, *Poor Support,* pp. 232–239; Duncan, *Years of Poverty,* pp. 64–65.
43. For historical material on day care, see Bernard Greenblatt, *Responsibility for Child Care* (San Francisco: Jossey-Bass, 1977); Philip K. Robins and Samuel Weiner, eds., *Child Care and Public Policy: Studies of the Economic Issues* (Lexington, Mass.: Lexington Books, 1978); Sheila M. Rothman, "Other People's Children: The Day Care Experience in America," *Public Interest,* 30 (1973): 11, 13. For denunciations of proposed childcare programs by New York Governor Dewey and President Nixon, see Sylvia Ann Hewlett, *A Lesser Life: The Myth of Women's Liberation in America* (New York: Morrow, 1986), p. 245. For discussion of the inadequacy of current policies, see Hearings before Subcommittee on Employment Opportunities, Committee on Education and Labor, House of Representatives, 99th Cong., 2d sess., *Women in the Work Force: Supreme Court Issues,* Sept. 30, 1986, p. 7; National Commission on Working Women, *Working Mothers and Their Families—A Fact Sheet* (Washington, D.C., Fall 1984).
44. See U.S. Department of Labor, *Childcare: A Workforce Issue* (Washington, D.C.: Government Printing Office, 1988), pp. 1, 4, 7–10.
45. Myra H. Strober and Sanford N. Dornbush, "Public Policy Alternatives," in Sanford N. Dornbush and Myra H. Strober, eds., *Feminism, Children and the New Families* (New York: Guilford, 1988), p. 340; U.S. Commission on Civil Rights, *Childcare and Equal Opportunity for Women* (Washington, D.C.: Clearinghouse Publication, 1981), p. 9 (surveys), Department of Labor, *Childcare,* pp. 11–14. (shortages, training, salaries); United States Bureau of the Census, *Who's Minding the Kids? Child Care Arrangements: Winter 1984–1985* (Washington, D.C.: Government Printing Office, 1987); Hearings on Child Care Before the Subcommittee on Human Resources of the U.S. Commission on Education and Labor, U.S. House of Representatives, April 21, 1988 (testimony of Robert Rector), 100th Cong., 2d sess. (regulation); testimony of Heidi Hartmann (surveys, salaries).
46. Rogers, *Poor Women,* pp. 119–120; Hartmann, testimony; Zigler and Frank, *Parental Leave,* pp. 123–135; Karen Skold, "The Interests of Feminists and Children in Child Care," in Dornbush and Strober, *Feminism*, pp. 113–127.
47. Marian Wright Edelman and James D. Weill, "Status of Children in the

1980s," *Columbia Human Rights Law Review,* 17 (1986): 139, 153; Victor R. Fuchs, *Women's Quest for Economic Equality* (Cambridge, Mass.: Harvard University Press, 1988).

7. Competing Perspectives on Family Policy

1. For representative quotations about family, see Gilbert Steiner, *The Futility of Family Policy* (Washington, D.C.: Brookings Institute, 1981), pp. 14–17 (quoting presidents Carter and Johnson); Maynard v. Hill, 125 U.S. 190 (1888); Marvin v. Marvin, 18 Cal. 3d 660, 134 Cal. Rptr. 815, 557 P.2d 106 (1976).
2. Wakefield Washington Associates, Inc., *Family Research: Source Book, Analysis and Guide to Federal Funding* (Westport, Conn.: Greenwood, 1979).
3. Compare George Gilder, *Sexual Suicide* (New York: Quadrangle, 1973), and Jerry Falwell, *Listen America* (Garden City, N.Y.: Doubleday, 1980); Steven Goldberg, *The Inevitability of Patriarchy* (New York: William Morrow, 1974), with Jean Bethke Elshtain, *Public Man, Private Woman: Women in Social and Political Thought* (Princeton: Princeton University Press, 1981), pp. 323–329, and "Feminism, Family and Community," *Dissent,* 29 (Fall 1982): 442; Christopher Lasch, *Haven in a Heartless World* (New York: Basic Books, 1977). See generally Mary Jo Bane, *Here to Stay: American Families in the Twentieth Century* (New York: Basic Books, 1976); Working Group on the Family, Attorney General's Commission, *The Family* (Washington, D.C., November 1986).
4. The full texts of the Family Protection Act of 1979 and 1981 appear in S. 1808, 96th Cong., 1st sess. (1979), and S. 1378, 97th Cong., 1st sess., 127 *Congressional Record* 12694 (1981). See sources cited in note 3, and Sarah Ruddick, "Maternal Thinking," *Feminist Studies,* 6 (1980): 342.
5. Michelle Barrett and Mary McIntosh, *The Anti-Social Family* (London: NLB, 1982); Lee Comer, *Wedlocked Women* (Leeds, Eng.: Feminist Books, 1974); Eli Zaretsky, *Capitalism, the Family, and Personal Life* (New York: Harper and Row, 1976); Shulamith Firestone, *The Dialectic of Sex* (New York: Bantam, 1970); Alice Schwarzer, *After the Second Sex: Conversations with Simone de Beauvoir* (New York: Pantheon, 1984), p. 42.
6. Henry Sumner Maine, *Ancient Law* (New York: John Wiley, 1887), pp. 163–165.
7. Graham B. Spanier, "Married and Unmarried Cohabitation in the United States: 1980," *Journal of Marriage and the Family,* 45 (May 1983): 277; Michael D. Freeman and Christina M. Lyon, *Cohabitation Without Marriage: An Essay in Law and Social Policy* (Aldershot, Eng.: Gower, 1983).
8. See Sir William Blackstone, *Commentaries on the Laws of England,* ed. St. George Tucker (1803), Book IV, chap. IV, pp. 64–65; Kai Erikson, *Wayward Puritans: A Study in the Sociology of Deviance* (New York: John Wiley, 1966); Lawrence M. Friedman, *A History of American Law* (New York: Simon and Schuster, 1973); Martha L. Fineman, "Law and Changing Pat-

terns of Behavior: Sanctions on Non-Marital Cohabitation," *Wisconsin Law Review,* (1981): 275.

9. Ira Mark Ellman, Paul M. Kurtz, and Ann M. Stanton, eds., *Family Law: Cases, Text, Problems* (Charlottesville, Va.: Michie, 1986), pp. 20–24; Stuart J. Stein, "Common Law Marriage: Its History and Certain Contemporary Problems," *Journal of Family Law,* 9 (1969): 271; Walter O. Weyrauch, "Informal and Formal Marriage—An Appraisal of Trends in Family Organization," *University of Chicago Law Review,* 28 (1960): 88.
10. Ellman, Kurtz and Stanton, *Family Law;* cases discussed in Marvin v. Marvin.
11. Marvin v. Marvin, 18 Cal.3d 660, 134 Cal. Rptr. 815, 557 P.2d 106 (1976).
12. Marlene Marks, *The Suing of America* (New York: Seaview, 1981), p. 22; *National Law Journal,* April 16, 1979; *Marvin v. Marvin*; David L. Chambers, "The 'Legalization' of the Family: Toward a Policy of Supportive Neutrality," *University of Michigan Journal of Law Reform,* 18 (1985): 805.
13. Compare the concerns about marriage reflected in Grishman v. Grishman, 407 A.2d 9 (Me. 1979), Hewitt v. Hewitt, 77 Ill.2d 49, 394 N.E.2d 1204 (1979), and Rehak v. Mathis, 239 Ga. 541, 238 S.E.2d 81 (1977), with the concerns about repression and dependence discussed in Freeman and Lyon, *Cohabitation,* p. 205; Ruth L. Deech, "The Case Against Legal Recognition of Cohabitation," *International and Comparative Law Quarterly,* 29 (April 1980): 480.
14. See sources cited in note 13; Vern L. Bullough, *Sin, Sickness and Sanity* (New York: Garland, 1977); Donald West, *Homosexuality,* 3rd. ed. (London: Duckworth, 1968), and discussion in the text accompanying notes 28–30.
15. Grace Ganz Blumberg, "Cohabitation Without Marriage: A Different Perspective," *UCLA Law Review,* 28 (1981): 1125, 1168; Judith Lyness, Milton Lipetz, and Keith Davis, "Living Together: An Alternative to Marriage," *Journal of Marriage and Family,* 34 (1972): 305, 307–308; Eleanor D. Macklin, "Nonmarital Heterosexual Cohabitation," *Marriage and Family Review,* 1 (March–April 1978): 1; Jan Trost, *Unmarried Cohabitation* (Vasteras, Sweden: International Library, 1979), p. 75.
16. See "Oh, Billy Jean," *National Review,* May 29, 1981, p. 598; "Bloomingdale Mistress Loses on Palimony Issue," *San Francisco Chronicle,* Sept. 29, 1982, p. 1. King won her lawsuit but lost an estimated one million dollars in canceled promotion contracts. "Women Who Have Changed the World," *Working Women,* September 1988, p. 91.
17. For criticism of decisions and legislation requiring explicit agreements, see Blumberg, "Cohabitation," p. 1135; Susan Prager, "Sharing Principles and the Future of Marital Property Law," *UCLA Law Review,* 25 (1977): 1; Weyrauch, "Metamorphoses of Marriage," *Family Law Quarterly,* 13 (1980): 415.
18. Hegel, *The Philosophy of Right* (Oxford: Clarendon Press, 1962), p. 163; see also Kenneth L. Karst, "The Freedom of Intimate Association," *Yale Law Journal,* 89 (1980): 624, 640.

19. See Spanier, "Cohabitation"; Marvin v. Marvin, 18 Cal.3d 660, 134 Cal. Rptr. 815, 557 P.2d 106 (1976).
20. Cees J. Straver, Wim. C. J. Robert, and Ab M. van der Heiden, "Lifestyles of Cohabiting Couples and Their Impact on Juridical Questions," in John M. Eekelaar and Sanford N. Katz, *Marriage and Cohabitation in Contemporary Societies* (Toronto: Butterworths, 1980), p. 1.
21. See generally Robert Mnookin and Lewis Kornhauser, "Bargaining in the Shadow of the Law: The Case of Divorce," *Yale Law Journal,* 88 (1979): 950.
22. Ronald Dworkin, *Taking Rights Seriously* (Cambridge, Mass.: Harvard University Press, 1977), pp. 240–259; H. L. A. Hart, *Law, Liberty, and Morality* (Stanford: Stanford University Press, 1963); City of Berkeley, California, Domestic Partnership Policy, Dec. 1984; Note, "The Legality of Homosexual Marriage," *Yale Law Journal,* 82 (1973): 573 (and sources cited) and text accompanying notes 31–37. For anthropological perspectives, see Rayna Rapp, Ellen Ross, and Renate Bridenthal, "Examining Family History," *Feminist Studies,* 5 (1979): 174.
23. See Blumberg, "Cohabitation"; Freeman and Lyon, *Cohabitation,* pp. 167–170; J. Thomas Oldham and David Caudill, "A Reconnaissance of Public Policy Restrictions upon Enforcement of Contracts between Cohabitants," *Family Law Quarterly,* 18 (1984): 93, 123; and sources cited in note 22.
24. The appropriate scope of married couples' contractual rights is reviewed in Mary Ann Glendon, *The New Family and the New Property* (Toronto: Butterworths, 1981), p. 67, and note 60; Marjorie M. Schultz, "Contractual Ordering of Marriage: A New Model for State Policy," *California Law Review,* 70 (1982): 204; Lenore Weitzman, *The Marriage Contract: Spouses, Lovers, and the Law* (New York: Free Press, 1981); Judith T. Younger, "Perspectives on Antinuptial Agreements," *Rutgers Law Review,* 4 (1988): 1059.
25. See Judd Marmor, eds., *Homosexual Behavior: A Modern Reappraisal* (New York: Basic Books, 1980), p. 7; Rhonda R. Rivera, "Our Straight-Laced Judges: The Legal Position of Homosexual Persons in the United States," *Hastings Law Journal,* 30 (1979): 799, 800, n. 4 (20 million). For discussion of the stigmas on lesbians, see subsequent discussion, Chapter 2, and John D'Emilio and Estelle B. Freedman, *Intimate Matters: A History of Sexuality in America* (New York: Harper and Row, 1988), p. 317; Charlotte Bunch, *Passionate Politics* (New York: St. Martin's, 1987); Rayna Rapp and Ellen Ross, "The Twenties Backlash: Compulsory Heterosexuality, the Consumer Family, and the Waning of Feminism," in Amy Swerdlow and Hanna Lessinger, eds., *Class, Race and Sex: The Dynamics of Control* (Boston: G. K. Hall, 1983).
26. Brief for Petitioners, Bowers v. Hardwick, 478 U.S. 186 (1986), p. 19. See Roland Brinkley et al., *The Laws Against Homosexuality,* Criminal Justice Monograph, II (Huntsville, Tex.: Institute of Contemporary Corrections and the Behavioral Sciences, Sam Houston State University, 1970); Kenneth J. Dover, *Greek Homosexuality* (Cambridge, Mass.: Harvard University Press, 1978). For Christian traditions, see generally John Boswell, *Christianity,*

Social Tolerance, and Homosexuality (Chicago: University of Chicago Press, 1980); Judith C. Brown, *Immodest Acts* (New York: Oxford University Press, 1986), pp. 3–20; Blackstone, *Commentaries* IV, 216.

27. D'Emilio and Freedman, *Intimate Matters,* pp. 27–30. The liberalization proposed by Thomas Jefferson in Virginia, and enacted in Pennsylvania, replaced the death penalty with facial disfigurement for women and castration for men: see Jonathan Katz, *Gay American History* (New York: Avon, 1978), pp. 37, 200; John D'Emilio, *Sexual Politics, Sexual Communities: The Making of a Homosexual Minority in the United States, 1940–1970* (Chicago: University of Chicago Press, 1983), p. 10; Karl M. Bowman and Bernice Engle, "A Psychiatric Evaluation of the Laws of Homosexuality," *Temple Law Quarterly Review,* 29 (1956): 273.
28. D'Emilio, *Sexual Communities,* pp. 1–22; Carroll Smith-Rosenberg, *Disorderly Conduct* (New York: Alfred A. Knopf, 1985); see generally Katz, *Gay History.*
29. Bowman and Engle, "Laws," p. 278; D'Emilio, *Sexual Communities,* pp. 129–207, 16–17 (quoting Richard Von Krafft-Ebing), 21; Katz, *Gay History,* pp. 197–315; Dolores Klaich, *Woman + Woman: Attitudes Toward Lesbianism* (New York, Simon and Schuster: 1974). For historical material on obscenity enforcement, see Chapter 10.
30. Alfred Kinsey et al., *Sexual Behavior in the Human Male* (Philadelphia: W. B. Saunders, 1948), pp. 621–622; Alfred Kinsey et al., *Sexual Behavior in the Human Female* (Philadelphia: W. B. Saunders, 1953); D'Emilio, *Sexual Communities,* pp. 34–59; D'Emilio and Freedman, *Intimate Matters,* pp. 290–291.
31. See Nancy Myron and Charlotte Bunch, eds., *Lesbianism and the Women's Movement* (Baltimore: Diana Press, 1975), pp. 148–176; D'Emilio, *Sexual Communities,* pp. 41–123; Katz, *Gay History,* pp. 505–665; D'Emilio and Freedman, *Intimate Matters,* pp. 319–323; Toby Marotta, *The Politics of Homosexuality* (Boston: Houghton Mifflin, 1981), pp. 136 ff.
32. Ronald Bayer, *Homosexuality and American Psychiatry* (New York: Basic Books, 1981); Adrienne Rich, "Compulsory Heterosexuality and Lesbian Existence," in Adrienne Rich, *Blood, Bread, and Poetry: Selected Prose* (New York: Norton, 1986), pp. 23–75. For the range of discrimination, see Rivera, "Homosexual Persons," and Roberta Achtenberg, ed., *Sexual Orientation and the Law* (New York: C. Boardman, 1985).
33. *DeSantis v. Pacific Telephone and Telegraph,* 608 F.2d 327 (9th Cir., 1979); Smith v. Liberty Mutual Insurance Company, 395 F.Supp. 1098, 1099, n. 2 (N.D. 6a, 1975).
34. Bowers v. Hardwick, 478 U.S. 186, 189 (1986) (Blackmun, J., dissenting); See, for example, Chapter 2's discussion of jury-exclusion cases and Thomas B. Stoddard, "*Bowers v. Hardwick:* Precedent by Personal Predeliction" *University of Chicago Law Review,* 54 (1987): 648.
35. Baker v. Nelson, 291 Min. 310, 191 N.W.2d 18, Minnesota 1972; Singer v. Hara, 11 Wash. App. 247, 522 P.2d 1187 (1974).
36. Boddie v. Connecticut, 401 U.S. 371 (1971); Zablocki v. Redhail, 434 U.S. 374 (1978); Alissa Friedman, "The Necessity for State Recognition of Same

Sex Marriage: Constitutional Requirements and Evolving Notions of Family," *Berkeley Women's Law Journal,* 3 (1988): 134, 158–163; Del Martin and Phyllis Lyon, *Lesbian-Woman* (San Francisco: Glide, 1972), p. 103.

37. Friedman, "Same Sex Marriage," pp. 158–163; Note, "The Legality of Homosexual Marriage," *Yale Law Journal,* 82 (1973): 573; David A. Richards, "Sexual Autonomy and the Constitutional Right to Privacy: A Case Study in Human Rights and the Unwritten Constitution," *Hastings Law Journal,* 30 (1978): 957, 993, n. 158.

38. Loring v. Bellsouth Advertising and Publ. Corp., 339 S.E.2d 372, (Ga. App. 1985); Rivera, "Homosexual Persons," pp. 813–817, 852 (citing cases); Norton v. Macy, 417 F.2d 1161, 1164, 1167 (D.C. Cir. 1969); Singer v. U.S. Civil Service Commission, 530 F.2d 247, 530, n. 3 (4th Cir. 1976), *vacated* 429 U.S. 1034 (1977); McConnell v. Anderson, 451 F.2d 193 (8th Cir. 1971); Childers v. Dallas Police Department, 27 Employment Discrimination Reporter, Paragraph 23.54g; For military service cases, see Rivera, "Homosexual Persons," pp. 837–852; Beller v. Middendorf, 632 F.2d 788, 811, n. 22 (9th Cir. 1980); and Colin Williams and Martin Weinberg, *Homosexuals and the Military* (New York: Harper and Row, 1971).

39. James Kim, "Are Homosexuals Facing an Ever More Hostile World?" *New York Times,* July 3, 1988, p. 16e.

40. Richards, "Sexual Autonomy," p. 989; Sylvia Law, "Homosexuality and the Social Meaning of Gender," *Wisconsin Law Review,* 2 (1988): 187; Karst, "Intimate Association."

41. James Bryce, *Studies in History and Jurisprudence* (New York: Oxford University Press, 1901), II, 802; Sir Frederick Pollock and Frederick W. Maitland, *The History of English Law*, 2d ed. (Cambridge: University Press, 1968), II, 390; Gerhard Mueller, "Inquiry into the State of a Divorceless Society," *University of Pittsburgh Law Review,* 18 (1957): 545.

42. See Nelson Blake, *The Road to Reno* (New York: Macmillan, 1962); Max Rheinstein, *Marriage Stability, Divorce, and the Law* (Chicago: University of Chicago Press, 1972); Leon C. Marshall and Geoffrey May, *The Divorce Court* (Baltimore: Johns Hopkins University Press, 1933), I, 199–231; Lee Silverstein, "Eligibility for Free Legal Services in Civil Cases," *Journal of Urban Law,* 44 (1967): 549, 571–581 (discussing legal-aid limitations); Walter Gellhorn, *Children and Families in the Courts of New York City* (New York: Dodd, Mead, 1984), pp. 285–288 (collusive proceedings).

43. Mary Ann Mason, *The Equality Trap* (New York: Simon and Schuster, 1988) (blaming feminists); Herbert Jacob, *Silent Revolution: The Transformation of Divorce Law in the United States* (Chicago: University of Chicago Press, 1988) (tracing history of no-fault as a routine policy process and noting the absence of feminist involvement). See Martha Minow and Deborah L. Rhode, "Reforming the Questions, Questioning the Reform: Feminist Perspectives on Divorce Reform," in Herma Hill Kay and Stephen Sugarman, *Divorce Reform at the Crossroads* (New Haven: Yale University Press, 1990).

44. Doris Freed and Henry Foster, "Divorce in the Fifty States: An Overview," *Family Law Quarterly,* 14 (1981): 229, 241; Orr v. Orr, 440 U.S. 268 (1979), U.S. Commission on Uniform Laws, *Uniform Marriage and Divorce*

Act. See Glendon, *New Family*, p. 62. Herma Hill Kay, "Equality and Difference: A Perspective on No-Fault Divorce and Its Aftermath," *University of Cincinnati Law Review*, 56 (1987): 1.

45. Lenore J. Weitzman, *The Divorce Revolution* (New York: Free Press, 1985), winner of the American Sociological Association Award for a Distinguished Publication, 1986; Robert McGraw, Gloria Sterin, and Joseph Davis, "A Case Study in Divorce Law Reform and Its Aftermath," *Journal of Family Law*, 20 (1981–1982): 443; Elizabeth Peters, "Marriage and Divorce: Informational Constraints and Private Contracting," *American Economic Review*, 76 (1986): 437; James B. McLindon, "Separate But Unequal: The Economic Disaster of Divorce for Women and Children," *Family Law Quarterly*, 21 (1987): 351.
46. Research involving different jurisdictions has revealed different results concerning postdivorce inequalities. Some studies have relied on samples that are too limited in size or in geographic and demographic characteristics. Compare Weitzman, *Divorce Revolution*, p. 362, with studies discussed in Sara E. Rix, ed., for the Women's Research and Education Institute, *The American Woman: A Report in Depth* (New York: Norton, 1987), pp. 72–82. For critical reviews of Weitzman's findings, see Martha Fineman, "Illusive Equality: On Weitzman's *Divorce Revolution*," *American Bar Foundation Research Journal* (1986): 781. Herbert Jacobs, "Faulting No Fault: A Review of Lenore Weitzman, *The Divorce Revolution*," *American Bar Foundation Research Journal* (1986): 773. See generally Kay, "Equality," and Deborah L. Rhode, "Gender and Jurisprudence: An Agenda for Research," *University of Cincinnati Law Review*, 56 (1987): 521.
47. Beard v. Beard, 262 So.2d 269, 271–272 (Fla. 1972); Kevin Gray, *The Reallocation of Property on Divorce* (Abingdon, Eng.: Oxon Professional Books, 1977), pp. 286–287. See also sources cited in note 52.
48. For divorce and poverty statistics, see Alfred J. Kahn and Sheila B. Kamerman, "Child Support in the United States: The Problem," *Child Support* (Beverly Hills, Calif.: Sage, 1988), p. 10; Terry Arendell, "Women and the Economics of Divorce in the Contemporary United States," *Signs*, 13 (1987): 121; Weitzman, *Divorce Revolution*, p. xvii. Explanations for demographic trends are summarized in Rheinstein, *Marriage*.
49. Uniform Marriage and Divorce Act, sec. 308; Sylvia Ann Hewlett, *A Lesser Life* (New York: William Morrow, 1986), p. 56; *Household Wealth and Asset Ownership, 1984*, Current Population Reports, series p-70, no. 70 (Washington, D.C., 1986), pp. 4–9 (race). For discussion of the one-third rule, see Martha Fineman, "Implementing Equality: Ideology, Contradiction, and Social Change," *Wisconsin Law Review* (1983): 789, 866–887; and New Jersey Supreme Court, *Task Force on Women in the Courts* (June 1984), pp. 60–80.
50. See Weitzman, *Divorce Revolution*, pp. 30–36, 48–64, 69–75; Minow and Rhode, "Divorce Reform"; Ira Ellman, "The Theory of Alimony, *California Law Review*, 77 (1989): 1.
51. Sally F. Goldfarb, "Rehabilitative Alimony, the Alimony Drone, and the Marital Partnership," in *National Symposium on Alimony and Child Sup-*

port, American Bar Association, Family Law Section Publication (Chicago: American Bar Association, 1987) (quoting Judge Stanley Hofstadter); Terry Arendell, *Mothers and Divorce* (Berkeley: University of California Press, 1986); Weitzman, *Divorce Revolution,* pp. 33–35, 265–272, 284.

52. Frances Rathstein of the Displaced Homemakers Network, *A Status Report on Displaced Homemakers and Single Parents* (Washington, D.C.: Displaced Homemakers Network, 1987) (40 percent of displaced homemakers—divorced, separated, and widowed women—are living below the poverty level, and 20 percent just above it); Arendell, "Economics," pp. 120–122; Goldfarb, "Alimony"; Report of the New York Task Force on Women in the Courts (March 1986).

53. Sally Goldfarb, "What Every Lawyer Should Know About Child Support Guidelines," *Family Law Reporter,* 13 (1987): 3031 (discussing Colorado study); Mary Ann Glendon, *Abortion and Divorce in Western Law* (Cambridge, Mass.: Harvard University Press, 1987), pp. 81–111; Weitzman, *Divorce Revolution,* pp. 33–35, 265–284; Cynthia Harrison, "A Richer Life: A Reflection on the Woman's Movement," in Sara E. Rix, *The American Woman* (New York: Norton, 1988), pp. 53, 74.

54. For critiques of child-support guidelines, see *Essentials of Child Support Guidelines Development: Economic Issues and Policy Considerations* (Washington, D.C.: Women's Legal Defense Fund, 1987), and *Critical Issues, Critical Choices: Special Topics in Child Support Guidelines Development* (Washington, D.C.: Women's Legal Defense Fund, 1987); Wanda Johnson, "Do Minnesota Child Support Guidelines 'Support' Children?" *Law and Inequality: A Journal of Theory and Practice,* 3 (1985): 343; Statement of NOW Legal Defense and Education Fund on the Status of the 1984 Child Support Enforcement Amendments, Before the Subcommittee on Public Assistance and Unemployment Compensation, Committee on Ways and Means, House of Representatives, 100th Cong., 2d sess., Feb. 23, 1988.

55. See Weitzman, *Divorce Revolution,* p. 351, and Chapter 8.

56. For postdivorce income, compare Weitzman, *Divorce Revolution*, pp. 30–36, 79, 167–175, and Women's Research and Education Institute, *American Women,* pp. 88–89. For remarriage rates and psychological hardships, see Arendell, "Economics," pp. 120–124; Arthur J. Norton and Jeanne E. Moorman, "Current Trends in Marriage and Divorce Among American Women," *Journal of Marriage and the Family,* 49 (1987): 3; Graham B. Spanier and Linda Thompson, *Parting: The Aftermath of Separation and Divorce* (Beverly Hills, Calif.: Sage, 1984), p. 22; Judith S. Wallerstein and Joan Berlin Kelley, *Surviving the Breakup: How Children and Parents Cope with Divorce* (New York: Basic Books, 1980), pp. 1–23; Susan E. Krantz, "Divorce and Children," in Dornbush and Strober, *Feminism*, p. 249.

57. Doctrinal fights in New York and Wisconsin are reviewed in Fineman, "Implementing Equality"; Isabel Marcus, "Reflections on the Significance of the Sex/Gender System: Divorce Law Reform in New York," *Miami Law Review,* 42 (1987): 55, and Jessica Pincus, "How Equitable Is New York's Equitable Distribution Law?" *Columbia Human Rights Law Review,* 14

(1982): 433. For gender bias, see New York Task Force, *Courts,* New Jersey Supreme Court Task Force, pp. 64–80; and Glendon, *Divorce,* pp. 77–97; and Isabel Marcus, "Locked Out: Divorce Law Reform and Women's Legal Identity," unpublished manuscript (1988).

58. Judith Cassetty, "Emerging Issues in Child Support Policy and Practice," in Judith Cassetty, ed., *The Parental Child-Support Obligations* (Lexington, Mass.: Lexington Books, 1983), pp. 3, 4; Glendon, *Divorce,* pp. 97–103; Praeger, "Sharing Principles," Weitzman, *Divorce Revolution,* pp. 357–403.

59. See Glendon, *Divorce,* pp. 82–95; Peter Dopffell, "Child Support in Europe: A Comparative Overview," in Kahn and Kamerman, *Child Support,* pp. 182–207; David L. Chambers, "The Federal Government and a Program of 'Advance Maintenance' in the United States," in ibid., p. 343, and cases discussed in Note, "Family Law: Professional Degrees in 1986—Family Sacrifice Equals Family Asset," *Washburn Law Journal,* 25 (1986): 276.

60. *In re* Marriage of Morrison, 20 Cal.3d 437, 143 Cal. Rptr. 139, 573 P.2d. 41 (Cal. Sup. Ct. 1978) (quoting In Re Marriage of Brantner); Minow and Rhode, "On Divorce Reform."

61. See Gray, *The Reallocation of Property on Divorce;* Glendon, *New Family,* pp. 63–72; Weitzman, *Divorce Revolution,* pp. 48–61; Laurence D. Houlgate, *Family and State* (Totowa, N.J.: Rowman and Littlefield, 1988), pp. 67–68; and Chapter 6.

62. Blackstone, *Commentaries,* II, 435; Helmes v. Franciscus, 2 Bland 544; 20 Am. Dec. 402 (Maryland, 1830). See Michael Grossberg, *Governing the Hearth* (Chapel Hill: University of North Carolina Press, 1985); Olsen, "Family Law," pp. 12–15; Weitzman, *Divorce Revolution,* pp. 221–225; Katherine T. Bartlett, "Re-Expressing Parenthood," *Yale Law Journal,* 98 (1988): 291.

63. Carol Brauch, "Mothers, Fathers and Children: From Private to Public Patriarchy," in Lydia Sargent, ed., *Women and Revolution* (Boston: South End Press, 1980); Henry H. Foster and Doris Freed, "Life with Father: 1978," *Family Law Quarterly,* 11 (1978): 321, 326–327; Grossberg, *Governing the Hearth,* pp. 244–250; Olsen, "Family Law," pp. 16–19.

64. Arends v. Arends, 30 Utah 2d 328, 517 P.2d 1019 (1974), *cert. den.* 419 U.S. 881 (1974). See cases cited in Ex Parte Devine, 398 So.2d 686 (Ala. Sup. Ct. 1981); Annamay T. Sheppard, "Unspoken Premises in Custody Litigation," *Women's Rights Law Reporter,* 7 (1982): 229.

65. Phyllis Chesler, *Mothers on Trial* (New York: McGraw-Hill, 1986); Allan Roth, "The Tender Years Presumption in Child Custody Disputes," *Journal of Family Law,* 15 (1976–77): 423, 435–437; Weitzman, *Divorce Revolution,* pp. 234–239. For figures on women's success rate, see ibid., pp. 50, 310–380; J. Shear et al., "An Empirical Study of Custody Arrangements: Joint vs. Sole Legal Custody," in Jay Folberg, ed., *Joint Custody and Shared Parenting* (Washington, D.C.: Bureau of National Affairs, 1984), p. 151.

66. See sources cited in Weitzman, *Divorce Revolution,* pp. 246–255; and Frank F. Furstenberg, Jr., "Marital Disruptions, Child Custody, and Visitation," in Kahn and Kamerman, *Child Support,* p. 277.

67. For unsupported assumptions resulting in discrimination against gays and

lesbians, see Ellen Lewin, "Lesbianism and Motherhood: Implications for Child Custody," *Human Organization,* 40 (1981): 1; Comment, "Assessing Children's Best Interests When a Parent Is Gay or Lesbian: Toward a Rational Custody Standard," *UCLA Law Review,* 32 (1985): 852; "Lesbian Child Custody," *Harvard Women's Law Journal,* 6 (1983): 183. Examples of discrimination against employed and unemployed mothers appear in Nancy Polikoff, "Gender and Child Custody Determinations: Exploding the Myths," in Diamond, *Families, Politics, and Public Policy,* pp. 191–193, and Laurie Woods, Vicki Been, and Joanne Schulman, "Sex and Economic Discrimination in Child Custody Awards," *Clearinghouse Review,* 16 (April 1983): 1130.

68. See Mnookin and Kornhauser, "Bargaining in the Shadow of the Law"; Richard Neely, "The Primary Caretaker Parent Rule: Child Custody and the Dynamics of Greed," *Yale Law and Public Policy Review,* 3 (1984): 168.
69. Chesler, *Mothers on Trial,* p. 79; Jon Elster, "Solomonic Judgments Against the Best Interest of the Child," *University of Chicago Law Review,* 54 (1984): 1, 6; Bobette Adler Levy and Carole R. Chambers, "The Folly of Joint Custody," *Family Advocate,* 3 (Spring 1981): 6.
70. See sources cited in David L. Chambers, "Rethinking the Substantive Rules for Child Custody Disputes in Divorce," *Michigan Law Review,* 83 (1984): 477; and Ramsay Laing Klaff, "The Tender Years Doctrine: A Defense," *California Law Review,* 70 (1982): 335; Neely, "The Primary Caretaker Parent Rule," Joseph Goldstein, Anna Freud, and Albert Solnit eds., *Beyond the Best Interests of the Child* (New York: Free Press, 1979); Alice Rossi, "Gender and Parenthood," *American Sociological Review,* 49 (1984): 1. See also Chapter 12.
71. See research cited in Katharine T. Bartlett and Carol B. Stack, "Joint Custody, Feminism and the Dependency Dilemma," *Berkeley Women's Law Journal,* 2 (1986): 9; Chambers, "Child Custody Disputes," and Weitzman, *Divorce Revolution,* pp. 253–266; Marin Center for the Family in Transition, "Outcomes in Joint and Sole Custody Families: Findings from Different Populations and Social Policy Implications," (Corte Madera, Calif.: unpublished, 1988); For critical reviews of existing literature, see Martha L. Fineman and Annie Opie, "The Uses of Social Science Data in Legal Policymaking: Custody Determinations at Divorce," *Wisconsin Law Review* (1987): 107; but see David Chambers, "The Abuses of Social Science: A Response to Fineman and Opie," *Wisconsin Law Review* (1987): 159.
72. Chambers, "Child Custody Disputes"; Levy, "Custody Investigations," pp. 763–784; Robert Mnookin, "Child Custody Adjudication: Judicial Functions in the Face of Indeterminacy," *Law and Contemporary Problems,* 39 (1975): 226; Bartlett, "Re-Expressing Parenthood."
73. See Martha Fineman, "Dominant Discourse, Professional Language and Legal Change in Child Custody Decisionmaking," *Harvard Law Review,* 101 (1988): 727.
74. Joan Blades, *Family Mediation: Cooperative Divorce Settlement* (Englewood Cliffs, N.J.: Prentice Hall, 1985); O. J. Coogler, *Structured Mediation in*

Divorce Settlement (Toronto: Lexington Books, 1978); Howard Davidson, ed., *Alternative Means of Family Dispute Resolution* (Chicago: ABA, 1982). See Jay Folberg and Alison Taylor, *Mediation: A Comprehensive Guide to Resolving Conflicts Without Litigation* (San Francisco: Jossey-Bass, 1984); Carol Bruch, "And How Are the Children? The Effects of Ideology and Mediation on Child Custody Law and Children's Well Being in the United States," *International Journal of Law and Family,* 2 (1988): 106, 108–122; Jessica Pearson and Nancy Thoennes, "Mediating and Litigating Custody Disputes: A Longitudinal Evaluation," *Family Law Quarterly,* 17 (1984): 497; Janet Rifkin, "Mediation from a Feminist Perspective: Promise and Problems," *Law and Inequality: A Journal of Theory and Practice,* 2 (1984): 21, 59.

8. Equality in Form and Equality in Fact: Women and Work

1. For discussion of some of the same issues in this chapter, see Deborah L. Rhode, "Perspectives on Professional Women," *Stanford Law Review,* 40 (1988): 1163, and "Occupational Inequality," *Duke Law Journal* (forthcoming, 1989).
2. See Chapter 6. Equal Pay Act of 1963, Pub. L. 88-38, June 10, 1963, 77 Stat. 56 (Title 29, 206); Title VII of the 1964 Civil Rights Act, Pub. L. 88-352, July 2, 1964, 78 Stat. 253, 42 U.S.C. 2000 et. seq. (Title VII, 701); Executive Order 11375, 32 Fed. Reg. 14303, Oct. 13, 1967.
3. National Committee on Pay Equity, "Briefing Paper on the Wage Gap" (Washington, D.C., Sept. 18, 1987); Sara E. Rix, ed., Women's Research and Education Institute of the Congressional Caucus for Women's Issues, *The American Woman, 1987–88* (New York: W. W. Norton, 1987), p. 27; Julianne Malveaux, "No Images: Black Women in the Labor Force" (unpublished manuscript, 1988); Diana Pearce, "On the Edge: Marginal Women Workers and Employment Policy," in Christine Bose and Glenna Spitze, *Ingredients for Women's Employment Policy* (Albany, N.Y.: SUNY Press, 1987), pp. 197, 197–203 (unemployment and benefits).
4. Heidi I. Hartmann, Patricia A. Roos, and Donald J. Trieman, "An Agenda for Basic Research on Comparable Worth," in Heidi Hartmann, ed., *Comparable Worth: New Directions for Research* (Washington, D.C.: National Academy Press, 1985), p. 3; Rita Mae Kelly and Jane Bayes, "Comparable Worth and Pay Equity: Issues and Trends," in Rita Mae Kelly and Jane Bayes, eds., *Comparable Worth, Pay Equity and Public Policy* (New York: Greenwood, 1988), pp. 32–39; William T. Bielby and James N. Baron, "A Woman's Place Is With Other Women: Sex Segregation Within Organizations," in Barbara F. Reskin, ed., *Sex Segregation in the Workplace: Trends, Explanations, Remedies* (Washington, D.C.: National Academy Press, 1984), pp. 27–55; National Committee on Pay Equity, *Pay Equity: An Issue of Race, Ethnicity and Sex* (Washington, D.C.: National Committee on Pay Equity, 1987); Suzanne M. Bianchi and Daphne Spain, *American Women in Transition* (New York: Russell Sage, 1986). For projections on the

amount of time necessary to achieve an integrated workplace, see United States Commission on Civil Rights, *Comparable Worth: Issue for the '80s,* (Washington, D.C.: U.S. Commission on Civil Rights, 1984), II, 109 (statement of Joy Ann Grune).

5. *Employment and Earnings,* U.S. Dept. of Labor, Bureau of Labor Statistics (January 1987), p. 179; Rhode, "Perspectives" (reviewing "Women in the Law: the Glass Ceiling," *American Bar Association Journal,* June 1, 1988, pp. 49–75); Carolyn Dexter, "Women and the Exercise of Power in Organizations: From Ascribed to Achieved Status," in Laurie Larwood, Ann H. Stromberg, and Barbara A. Gutek, eds., *Women and Work: An Annual Review* (Beverly Hills, Calif.: Sage, 1984), p. 239, 251–253; Ann M. Morrison, Randall P. White, and Ellen Van Velson, *Breaking the Glass Ceiling* (Reading, Mass.: Addison-Wesley, 1987); David Stiff, "Women Lawyers Get Less Pay than Men and Less Respect," *Wall Street Journal,* Feb. 12, 1988, p. 1. Michael J. McCarty, "Women's Salaries Reflect Disparities in Executive Suites," *Wall Street Journal,* Dec. 1, 1986, p. 29; Betty M. Vetter and Eleanor Babco, eds., *Professional Women and Minorities; A Manpower Data Research Source* (Washington, D.C.: Scientific Manpower Corporation, 1986); Miriam Slater and Penina Middal Glazer, "Prescriptions for Professional Survival," *Daedelus,* 116 (1987): 119, 132 (10 percent tenured faculty at four-year institutions; the average American college has 1.1 women in senior administrative positions); Karen Fullbright, "The Myth of the Double Advantage: Black Female Managers," in Margaret C. Simms and Julianne Malveaux, eds., *Slipping Through the Cracks: The Status of Black Women* (New Brunswick, N.J.: Transaction, 1986) p. 33; Angela Simeone, *Academic Women* (South Hadley, Mass.: Bergin and Garvey, 1987).
6. Subcommittee on Civil and Constitutional Rights, House Judiciary Committee, "Hearings on Women in Non-Traditional Jobs," (1988); Kay Deaux, "Blue Collar Barriers," *American Behavioral Scientist,* 27 (1984): 287, 288; Hearings before the Subcommittee on Employment Opportunities, Committee on Education and Labor, House of Representatives, 99th Cong., 2d sess., *Women in the Work Force: Supreme Court Issues* (Sept. 30, 1986), p. 44 (testimony of Cynthia Marano); "A Decade of Change," *New York Times,* March 27, 1987, sec. 3, p. 11; Sylvia A. Law, "'Girls Can't Be Plumbers'—Affirmative Action for Women in Construction: Beyond Goals and Quotas," *Harvard Civil Rights–Civil Liberties,* 24 (1989): 175–178; William T. Bielby and James Baron, "Undoing Discrimination: Job Integration and Comparable Worth," in Bose and Spitze, *Employment Policy,* pp. 211, 228 (male preferences).
7. Gary S. Becker, *Human Capital* (Washington, D.C.: National Bureau of Economic Research, 1975); Francine D. Blau and Carol L. Jusenius, "Economists' Approaches to Sex Segregation in the Labor Market: An Appraisal," in Martha Blaxall and Barbara Reagan, eds., *Women and the Workplace: The Implications of Occupational Segregation* (Chicago: University of Chicago Press, 1976), p. 181; "Manufacturer Group Hits Comparable Worth in Pay," *Los Angeles Times,* Nov. 24, 1984, p. 24 (quoting representative

of National Association of Manufacturers to the effect that women should change occupations). See also Victor Fuchs, *Women's Quest for Economic Equality* (Cambridge, Mass.: Harvard University Press, 1988).

8. See Paula England, "The Failure of Human Capital Theory to Explain Occupational Sex Segregation," *Journal of Human Resources,* 17 (1982): 358; Francine D. Blau, "Occupational Segregation and Labor Market Discrimination," in Reskin, ed., *Sex Segregation,* pp. 117–129; Hartmann, Roos, and Trieman, "Agenda for Basic Research"; Mary Corcoran and Gregory J. Duncan, "Work History, Labor Force Attachment, and Earnings: Differences Between the Races and Sexes," *Journal of Human Resources,* 19 (1979): 3; Slater and Glazer, "Professional Survival," p. 132; Simeone, *Academic Women.*

9. See generally Charlotte Perkins Gilman, *Women and Economics* (Boston: Small, Maynard, 1898). For a discussion of children's literature, see Ann Oakley, *Woman's Work: The Housewife, Past and Present* (New York: Pantheon, 1975), p. 190; Judith Hole and Ellen Levine, *Rebirth of Feminism* (New York: Quadrangle, 1971), pp. 334–335. For accounts of sex-role socialization processes, see Sandra L. Bem and Daryl J. Bem, "Homogenizing the American Woman: The Power of an Unconscious Ideology," in Alison M. Jaggar and Paula Rothenberg Struhl, eds., *Feminist Frameworks: Alternative Theoretical Accounts of Relations Between Women and Men* (New York: McGraw-Hill, 1978); Bernard, "Sex Difference: An Overview," in Alexandra Q. Kaplan and Joan P. Bean, eds., *Beyond Sex-Role Stereotypes* (Boston: Little, Brown, 1976), p. 10; Eleanor Macoby and Carol Jacklin, *The Psychology of Sex Differences* (Stanford, Calif.: Stanford University Press, 1974). Research on women's differential expectations of success is summarized in Martha T. Mednick, "Women and the Psychology of Achievement: Implications for Personal and Social Change," in Mildred E. Katzell and William C. Byham, eds., *Women in the Work Force* (New York: Behavioral Publications, 1972), p. 48; Debra R. Kaufman and Barbara L. Richardson, *Achievement and Women: Challenging the Assumptions* (New York: Free Press, 1982), pp. 49, 96.

10. Pamela Stone Cain, "Prospects for Pay Equity in a Changing Economy," in Hartmann, *New Directions,* pp. 239, 155 (frequency of nontraditional career choices); John P. Fernandez, *Racism and Sexism in Corporate Life: Changing Voices in American Business* (Lexington, Mass.: Lexington Books, 1981); Alfredo Mirande and Evangelina Enriquez, *La Chicana: The Mexican American Women* (Chicago: University of Chicago Press, 1979), pp. 134–135. For a summary of research, see Barbara F. Reskin and Heidi J. Hartmann, eds., *Women's Work, Men's Work: Sex Segregation on the Job* (Washington, D.C.: National Academy Press, 1986), pp. 63–68; Benson Rosen, "Career Progress of Women: Getting in and Staying in," in H. John Bernadin, ed., *Women in the Workforce* (New York: Prager, 1982), pp. 70, 73. For an overview of institutional mechanisms concerning job-training, assignments, mobility, and retention, see Patricia A. Roos and Barbara F. Reskin, "Institutional Factors Contributing to Sex Segregation in the Work-

place," in Reskin, ed., *Sex Segregation,* pp. 235–260, and sources cited therein.

11. Cynthia Fuchs Epstein, *Deceptive Distinctions: Sex, Gender, and the Social Order* (New Haven; Yale University Press, 1988), pp. 83–88; Laurie Larwood and Marion Wood, *Women in Management* (Lexington, Mass.: Lexington Books, 1977); Patricia A. McBroom and Maria D. Guarnaschelli, *The Third Sex* (New York: William Morrow, 1986); Jane Prather, "Why Can't Women Be More Like Men? A Summary of the Socio-Psychological Factors Hindering Women's Advancement in the Professions," in Linda S. Fidell and John DeLamater, eds., *Women in the Professions: What's All the Fuss About?* (Beverly Hills, Calif.: Sage, 1971).
12. Donald J. Trieman and Heidi I. Hartmann, *Women, Work, and Wages: Equal Pay for Jobs of Equal Value* (Washington, D.C.: National Academy Press, 1981). For discussion of domestic obligations, see text at notes 34–35.
13. For dual market theories, see, for example, Alice H. Amsden, ed., *The Economics of Women and Work* (New York: St. Martin's, 1980), pp. 20–22. For crowding, see Blau, "Occupational Segregation," p. 126; Reskin and Hartmann, eds., *Women's Work, Men's Work,* pp. 10–13.
14. See Heidi Hartmann, "Internal Labor Markets and Gender: A Case Study," in Clair Brown and Joseph A. Pechman, eds., *Gender in the Workplace* (Washington, D.C.: Brookings Institution, 1987); Barbara F. Reskin, "Sex Differentiation and the Devaluation of Women's Work: Implications for Women's Occupational Progress and Comparable Worth," (unpublished manuscript, 1987).
15. Gary S. Becker, *The Economics of Discrimination,* 2d ed. (Chicago: University of Chicago Press, 1971). For nineteenth-century views, see, for example, Azel Ames, *Sex in Industry* (Boston, 1875; New York: Garland, 1986), pp. 30–31, quoted in Robert W. Smuts, *Women and Work in America* (New York: Columbia University Press, 1959), p. 118 (operative for evil); Claudia Golding, "The Earnings Gap in Historical Perspective," in Commission on Civil Rights, *Comparable Worth,* pp. 86–109; Julie A. Matthaei, *An Economic History of Women in America* (New York: Schocken, 1982), pp. 187–232. For "male preferred" advertisements, see Bernice Sandler, "Patterns of Discrimination in Higher Education in New York," in New York City Commission on Human Rights, *Women's Role in Contemporary Society* (New York: Avon, 1972), p. 567.
16. Valerie Oppenheimer, *The Female Labor Force in the United States,* Population Monograph Series No. 5 (Berkeley: University of California Press, 1970), pp. 107–109; Malveaux, *No Images;* Fernandez, *Racism and Sexism;* Elizabeth Higgenbotham, "Employment for Black Professional Women in the Twentieth Century," in Bose and Spitz, *Women's Employment Policy.*
17. Caribbean Marine Services v. Baldridge 844 F.2d 668 (9th Cir., 1988).
18. Bielby and Baron, "Undoing Discrimination," and "Sex Segregation"; Trieman and Hartmann, *Women, Work, and Wages,* p. 61; Edmund S. Phelps, "The Statistical Theory of Racism and Sexism," *American Economic Re-*

view, 62 (1972): 659. For turnover rates, see Linda J. Waite and Sue E. Berryman, *Women in Non-Traditional Occupations: Choice and Turnover* (Santa Monica, Calif.: Rand, 1985), pp. 75–76; Reskin and Hartmann, eds., *Women's Work, Men's Work,* p. 51.

19. See generally Epstein, *Deceptive Distinctions,* pp. 81–88; F. L. Geis, M. R. Carter, and D. J. Butler, "Research on Seeing and Evaluating People" (unpublished manuscript, University of Delaware, 1982), pp. 55–64; Sharon Toffey Shepela and Ann T. Viviano, "Some Psychological Factors Affecting Job Segregation and Wages," in Helen Remick, ed., *Comparable Worth and Wage Discrimination* (Philadelphia: Temple University Press, 1984), pp. 47–58. For attributions of success and failure, see Kay Deaux and Tim Emswiller, "Explanations of Successful Performance on Sex-Linked Tasks: What Is Skill for the Male Is Luck for the Female," *Journal of Personality and Social Psychology,* 29 (1974): 80; Madeline Heilman and Richard Guzzo, "The Perceived Cause of Work Success as a Mediator of Sex Discrimination in Organizations," *Organizational Behavior and Human Performance,* 21 (1978): 346.

20. Susan J. Frances, "Sex Differences in Nonverbal Behavior," *Sex Roles,* 5 (1979): 519; Geis et al., *Seeing and Evaluating,* p. 56; Cynthia Epstein, "Encountering the Male Establishment: Sex-Status Limits on Women's Careers in the Professions," in Athena Theodore, ed., *The Professional Woman* (Cambridge, Mass.: Schenkman, 1971), pp. 52–73; Morrison, White, and Van Velson, *Glass Ceiling,* pp. 61–62.

21. Kay Deaux, *The Behavior of Women and Men* (Monterey, Calif.: Brooks/Cole, 1976), pp. 24–34; David L. Hamilton, ed., *Cognitive Processes in Stereotyping and Intergroup Behavior* (Hillsdale, N.J.: Lawrence Erlbaum Associates, 1981); Randi Hagen and Arnold Kahn, "Discrimination Against Competent Women," *Journal of Applied Social Psychology,* 5 (1975): 362; Symposium, "Black Employment Opportunities: Macro and Micro Perspectives," *Journal of Social Issues,* 43 (1987): 1.

22. See Paula J. Dubeck, "Sexism in Recruiting Management Personnel for a Manufacturing Firm," in Rodolfo Alvarez, Kenneth G. Lutterman, and Associates, *Discrimination in Organizations* (San Francisco: Jossey-Bass, 1979), pp. 88–89; Philip Goldberg, "Are Women Prejudiced Against Women?" *Trans-Action,* April 1968, pp. 28–30 (articles); Marianne Ferber and Joan Huber, "Sex of Student and Instructor: A Study of Student Bias," *American Journal of Sociology,* 80 (1975): 949 (student evaluations); Bernice Lott, "The Devaluation of Women's Competence," *Journal of Social Issues,* 41 (1985): 43; Benson Rosen and Thomas H. Jerdee, "Effects of Applicant's Sex and Difficulty of Job on Evaluations of Candidates for Managerial Positions," *Journal of Applied Psychology,* 59 (1974): 511; Ruble et al., "Stereotypes," pp. 346–351. For tenure letters, see Patricia W. Lunneborg and Carol Lillie, "Sexism in Graduate Admissions: The Letter of Recommendation," *American Psychologist,* 28 (1973): 187–188.

23. Louise Kapp Howe, *Pink Collar Workers* (New York: G. P. Putnam's Sons, 1977), pp. 246–249; Ronnie Steinberg and Lois Haignere, "Equitable Compensation: Methodological Criteria for Comparable Worth," in Bose and

Spitze, *Employment Policy*, pp. 158, 165; Margaret Mead, *Male and Female: A Study of the Sexes in a Changing World* (New York: William Morrow, 1949). For discussion of Margaret Mead's findings, see "Paying Women What They're Worth," *Report from the Center for Philosophy and Public Policy* (College Park, Md., Spring 1983), p. 1.

24. Athena Theodore, *The Campus Troublemakers: Academic Women in Protest* (Houston, Tex.: Cap and Gown Press, 1986). For a discussion of "feedback discrimination," in which employers, by denying women training and reinforcing "feminine behavior," ensure that women will exhibit the characteristics attributed to them, see Kenneth J. Arrow, "The Theory of Discrimination," in Orley Ashenfelter and Albert Rees, eds., *Discrimination in Labor Markets* (Princeton: Princeton University Press, 1973), pp. 3–33; Francine Blau, "Discrimination Against Women: Theory and Evidence," in William Darity, ed., *Labor Economics: Modern Views* (Boston: Kluwer-Nijhoff, 1984); Kaufman and Richardson, *Achievement and Women,* pp. 109–110.

25. For academic environments, see for example, Nadya Aiesenberg and Mona Harrington, *Women of Academe* (Amherst: University of Massachusetts Press, 1988), pp. 7–8, 46–54; Simeone, *Academic Women;* and Roberta M. Hall and Bernice R. Sandler, *Academic Mentoring for Women Students and Faculty: A New Look at an Old Way to Get Ahead* (Washington, D.C.: Project on the Status and Education of Women, Association of American Colleges, 1985); Robert J. Menges and William H. Exum, "Barriers to the Progress of Women and Minority Faculty," *Journal of Higher Education,* 54 (1983): 123; For professional and business contexts, see, for example, American Bar Association Commission on Women in the Professions, *Report to the House of Delegates* (Chicago: American Bar Association, 1988), p. 7–12; Cynthia F. Epstein, *Women in Law* (New York: Basic Books, 1981), and *Woman's Place: Options and Limits in Professional Careers* (Berkeley, University of California Press, 1970), pp. 172–174; Rosabeth Moss Kanter, *Men and Women of the Corporation* (New York: Basic Books, 1977), pp. 18–25; Prather, "Why Can't Women Be More Like Men," pp. 14–24. For blue-collar contexts, see Deaux, "Barriers"; Mary Walshok, *Blue-Collar Women: Pioneers on the Male Frontier* (Garden City, N.Y.: Anchor, 1981); Lynn E. Zimmer, *Women Guarding Men* (Chicago: University of Chicago Press, 1986). For sexual harassment, see Chapter 10; for all-male clubs, see Chapter 11.

26. For special problems of minorities, see Fernandez, *Racism and Sexism,* and Malveaux, *No Images.* For penalties attached to feminism, see Morrison, White, and Van Velson, *Glass Ceiling,* p. 38, and George La Noue and Barbara A. Lee, *Academics in Court: The Consequences of Faculty Discrimination Litigation* (Ann Arbor: University of Michigan Press, 1987), pp. 55–58.

27. See Kanter, *Men and Women,* pp. 208–242; Rosabeth Moss Kanter, "Some Effects of Proportions on Group Life: Skewed Sex Ratios and Responses to Token Women," *American Journal of Sociology,* 82 (1977): 965; Ann Fehrer and Karen Maitland Schilling, "The Values of Academe: Sexism as a Natural

Consequence," *Journal of Social Issues,* 41 (1985): 29; Gwyned Simpson, "The Daughters of Charlotte Ray: The Career Development Process During the Exploratory and Establishment Stages of Black Women Attorneys," *Sex Roles,* 11 (1984): 113.

28. For research reflecting adverse reactions to successful women, see Irene Frieze et al., *Women and Sex Roles: A Social Psychological Perspective* (New York: Norton, 1978), p. 253; Hagen and Kahn, "Discrimination Against Competent Women"; Fernandez, *Racism and Sexism.*
29. Muller v. Oregon, 208 U.S. 412, 421 (1908).
30. See Dolores Hayden, *Redesigning the American Dream* (New York: W. W. Norton, 1984), and Chapter 6.
31. U.S. Department of Labor, Office of Information, "Ten Million Americans Work Flexible Schedules, Two Million Work Full-Time in Three to Four and a Half Days," News Release, Washington, D.C., Feb. 24, 1981. See Karen Holden and W. Lee Hanson, "Part-Time Work, Full Time Work," in Brown and Pechman, *Gender in the Workplace,* p. 241; Jerome M. Rosow and Robert Zager, *New Work Schedules for a Changing Society* (New York: Work in America Institute, 1981), pp. 124–128.
32. See sources cited in note 31, and Rhode, "Perspectives," pp. 1185–1186.
33. Nell B. Strachan, "A Map for Women on the Road to Success," *American Bar Association Journal,* 70 (1984): 94, 96; Stephen Brill, "Headnotes: The Women Problem," *American Lawyer,* February 1983, pp. 1, 9–10; Reskin and Hartmann, *Women's Work, Men's Work,* pp. 68–69.
34. See Karen Brodkin Sacks and Dorothy Remy, eds., *My Troubles Are Going to Have Trouble with Me* (New Brunswick, N.J.: Rutgers University Press, 1984); Barbara J. Bergmann, *The Economic Emergence of Women* (New York: Basic Books, 1987), p. 225, and Chapter 7.
35. Estimates vary in part because surveyed individuals are often unable to give accurate reports of their work and in part because patterns vary across race, class, age, and so on. See Epstein, *Deceptive Distinctions,* p. 172 (describing methodological problems and racial variations); Rosanna Hertz, *More Equal Than Others: Women and Men in Dual Career Marriages* (Berkeley: University of California Press, 1986), pp. 120–155, 191, 208–211; Maureen Dowd, "Many Women in Poll Value Jobs as Much as Family Life," *New York Times,* Dec. 4, 1983, pp. 1, 66; Marian Burros, "Women: Out of the House but Not Out of the Kitchen," *New York Times,* Feb. 24, 1988, p. A1; L. M. Boyd, "Grab Bag," *San Francisco Chronical,* March 8, 1986 (beds); June O'Neill, "Role Differentiation and the Gender Gap in Wage Rates," in Laurie Larwood, ed., *Women and Work* (Beverly Hills, Calif.: Sage, 1985), pp. 56, 56–60; Patricia Roos, *Gender and Work: A Comparative Analysis of Industrial Societies* (Albany, N.Y.: SUNY Press, 1985), pp. 16–29; Graham L. Staines and Joseph H. Pleck, *The Impact of Work Schedules on the Family* (Ann Arbor: University of Michigan Press, 1983), p. 63; "Status Report: Who Does the Work," *Ms.,* February 1988, p. 19; Tumultz, "Bias" (dropout).
36. Veronica F. Nieva and Barbara A. Gutek, *Women and Work* (New York: Praeger, 1981), pp. 44–47; Janet G. Hunt and Larry H. Hunt, "Male

Resistance to Role Symmetry in Dual-Earner Households," in Naomi Gerstel and Harriet Engel Gross, eds., *Families and Work* (Philadelphia: Temple University Press, 1987), pp. 192, 196.

37. Sylvia Ann Hewlett, *A Lesser Life: The Myth of Women's Liberation in America* (New York: William Morrow, 1986), p. 398; Fuchs, *Women's Quest for Economic Equality,* pp. 15–22; Janice Mall, "Facing a Choice: Marriage or Career?" *Los Angeles Times,* Nov. 25, 1984, part VI, p. 15; Susan Fraker, "Why Women Aren't Getting to the Top," *Fortune,* April 16, 1984, pp. 40–45; Helen Rogan, "Top Women Executives Find Path to Power Strewn with Hurdles," *Wall Street Journal,* Oct. 25, 1984, p. 35. See Martha R. Fawlkes, "The Myth of Merit and Male Professional Careers," in Gerstel and Gross, *Families and Work,* p. 347 (importance of wife in elite professional contexts).
38. Citizens' Commission on Civil Rights, *Affirmative Action: To Open the Doors of Job Opportunity: A Policy of Fairness and Compassion That Has Worked* (Washington, D.C.: Citizens' Commission on Civil Rights, 1984); Hartmann, *Women's Work, Men's Work,* pp. 84–119. But see also James P. Smith and Michael P.Ward, *Women's Wages and Work in the Twentieth Century* (Santa Monica, Calif.: Rand, 1984), pp. xvi, xiv.
39. Arlington Heights v. Metropolitan Housing Development Corporation, 429 U.S. 252 (1976).
40. Grace Blumberg, "De Facto and De Jure Sex Discrimination Under the Equal Protection Clause: A Reconsideration of the Veteran's Preference in Public Employment," *Buffalo Law Review,* 26 (1976): 3, 4–6; John H. Fleming and Charles A. Shanor, "Veterans' Preferences in Public Employment: Unconstitutional Gender Discrimination?" *Emory Law Journal,* 26 (1977): 13, 14–18. Personnel Administrator of Massachusetts v. Feeney, 442 U.S. 256 (1979).
41. Personnel Administrator of Massachusetts v. Feeney, 442 U.S. 256, 279 (1979). Id. at 277.
42. See Charles Lawrence, "The Id, the Ego and Equal Protection: Reckoning with Unconscious Discrimination," *Stanford Law Review,* 39 (1986): 317; and sources discussed in William T. Bielby, "Modern Prejudice and Institutional Barriers to Employment Opportunities for Minorities," *Journal of Social Issues,* 43 (1987): 79.
43. See Ludwig Wittgenstein, *Philosophical Investigations,* ed. G.E.M. Anscombe (Oxford: B. Blackwell, 1958); Hans Gadamer, *Truth and Method* (New York: Continuum, 1975); Stanley Cavell, *Must We Mean What We Say?* (New York: Cambridge University Press, 1977). The relevance of this body of theory to cases such as *Feeny* is explored in Edwin Baker, "Outcome Equality or Equality of Respect," *University of Pennsylvania Law Review,* 131 (1983): 933, 973–975; and Marjorie Weinzweig, "Discriminatory Impact and Intent Under the Equal Protection Clause: The Supreme Court and the Mind-Body Problem," *Journal of Law and Inequality,* 1 (November 1983): 277.
44. Paul Brest, "Palmer v. Thompson: An Approach to the Problem of Unconstitutional Legislative Motive," *1971 Supreme Court Review* 95 (1971): 95;

Paul Brest, "Foreword: In Defense of the Antidiscrimination Principle," *Harvard Law Review,* 90 (1976): 7; Kenneth Karst, "The Costs of Motive Centered Inquiry," *San Diego Law Review,* 15 (1978): 1163, 1165; Arthur Miller, "If the 'Devil Himself Knows Not the Mind of Man,' How Possibly Can Judges Know the Motivation of Legislators?" *San Diego Law Review,* 15 (1978): 1167.

45. Washington v. Davis, 426 U.S. 229, 248, (1976); John Hart Ely, "Legislative and Administrative Motivation in Constitutional Law," *Yale Law Journal,* 79 (1970): 1205.

46. Approaches that would permit courts to invalidate practices with disparate impact absent a direct finding of discriminatory intent are developed in Lawrence, "The Id, Ego, and Equal Protection"; Brest, "Defense of Antidiscrimination"; Theodore Eisenberg, "Disproportionate Impact and Illicit Motive; Theories of Constitutional Adjudication," *New York University Law Review,* 52 (1977): 36; Anne Freedman's testimony in *Equal Rights Amendment: Hearings on H.J. Res. 1 Before the Subcommittee on Civil and Constitutional Rights of the House Judiciary Committee,* 98th Cong., 1st sess. (1983), at 5–10; Michael Perry, "The Disproportionate Impact Theory of Racial Discrimination," *University of Pennsylvania Law Review,* 125 (1977): 540; Eric Schnapper, "Perpetuation of Past Discrimination," *Harvard Law Review,* 96 (1983): 828.

47. For discrimination in the military, see Chapter 5.

48. See Eisenberg, "Disproportionate Impact," p. 49; Ely, "Legislative and Administrative Motivation."

49. Griggs v. Duke Power Company, 401 U.S. 424 (1971). See generally Elizabeth Bartholet, "Application of Title VII to Jobs in High Places," *Harvard Law Review,* 95 (1982): 947, 949 (and sources cited therein).

50. Equal Employment Opportunity v. Sears, Roebuck & Co., 628 F.Supp. 1264 (N.D. Ill., 1986).

51. 628 F.Supp. pp. 1308, 1314–1315. See Jim Weiner, "Women's History on Trial," *The Nation,* September 1985, p. 176, Oct. 26, 1985, p. 41; "Statistics Have Become Suspect in Sex Discrimination," *New York Times,* Feb. 9, 1986, p. 8; Ruth Milkman, "Women's History and the Sears Case," *Feminist Studies,* 12 (1984); Joan W. Scott "Deconstructing Equality vs. Difference: or the Uses of Post Structuralist Theory for Feminism," *Feminist Studies,* 14 (1988): 33. See also the interchange between Alice Kessler-Harris and Thomas Haskell and Sanford Levinson in *Texas Law Review,* 66 (1988): 1629, and 67 *Texas Law Review,* 429 (1988).

52. See Bartholet, "High Places," p. 49; and sources cited in note 53. For the low level of success in tenure cases, see La Noue and Lee, *Academics;* Jennie Farley, "Women versus Academe: Who's Winning?" *Journal of Social Issues,* 41 (1985): 111.

53. See Bartholet, "High Places," p. 970; Hishon v. King and Spalding, 24 Fair Empl. Prac. Cas. (BNA) 1303 (N.D. Ga., 1980), 678 F.2d 1022, 460 U.S. 1050 (1982). For the low level of success in tenure cases, see La Noue and Lee, *Academics.*

54. Fogg v. New England Telephone and Telegraph Co., 346 F.Supp. 645 (D.N.H.

1972); Pace College v. Commission on Human Rights, 377 N.Y.S.2d 471, 339 N.E.2d 880 (Ct. App. 1975). Sweeney v. Board of Trustees, 604 F.2d 106, cert. denied, 444 U.S. 1045 (1979); Peters v. Middlebury College, 409 F.Supp. 857, 860, (D. Vt. 1976); Lynn v. Regents of the University of California, 656 F.2d 1337; Hopkins v. Price Waterhouse, 618 F.Supp. 1109, 1117–1118 (D. D.C. 1985), *aff'd in part, rev'd in part,* 825 F.2d 458 (D.C. Cir. 1987), rev'd and remanded U.S. (1989); Theodore, *Campus Troublemakers,* pp. 18–20, 50, 52; La Noue and Lee, *Academics,* pp. 55–59. In the *Hopkins* case, the accountant denied partnership was advised to "walk more femininely, talk more femininely, dress more femininely," and have her hair styled.

55. See Kristin Bumiller, "Victims in the Shadow of the Law: A Critique of the Mode of Legal Protection," *Signs,* 12 (1986): 421; Faye Crosby, "The Denial of Personal Discrimination," *American Behavioral Scientist,* 27 (1985): 371; Denise D. Bielby and William T. Bielby, "She Works Hard for the money," *American Journal of Sociology,* 93 (1988): 1031; Johnson v. University of Pittsburgh, 435 F.Supp. 1328, 1337 (W.D. Pa., 1977); Farley, "Women versus Academe," p. 113; La Noue and Lee, *Academics.*
56. Jane Brass, "Against the Odds," *New York Magazine,* June 6, 1985; Christine Cooper, "Title VII in the Academy," *University of California at Davis Law Review,* 16 (1983): 975, 1010; Kristin Bumiller, *The Civil Rights Society: The Social Construction of Victims* (Baltimore: Johns Hopkins Press, 1988).
57. See Mark Brodon, "The Standard of Causation in the Mixed Motive Title VII Action; A Social Policy Perspective," *Columbia Law Review,* 82 (1982): 292, 323; cf. Hopkins v. Price Waterhouse.
58. See United States Commission on Civil Rights, *Affirmative Action in the 1980s; Dismantling the Process of Discrimination* (Washington, D.C.: Clearinghouse, 1981), p. 38.
59. George Gallup, Jr., "Little Support for High Court Ruling on Hiring," *San Francisco Chronicle,* July 16, 1987; McGlen and O'Connor, *Women's Rights,* quoting Deborah Banor and Daniel Yankelovich, *Today's American Woman: How the Public Sees Her* (The Public Agenda Foundation, December 1980), p. 64; "Attorney General Meese Links Quotas to Slavery," *New York Times,* Sept. 22, 1985, p. E4; James R. Kluegel, "If There Isn't a Problem You Don't Need a Solution: The Bases of Contemporary Affirmative Action Attitudes," *American Behavioral Scientist,* 28 (1985): 761.
60. For overviews of such objections, see Alan H. Goldman, *Justice and Reverse Discrimination* (Princeton: Princeton University Press, 1979); Walter E. Block and Michael A. Walker, eds., *Discrimination, Affirmative Action, and Equal Opportunity: An Economic and Social Perspective* (Vancouver: Fraser Institute, 1982); Richard H. Fallon, "To Each According to his Ability; From None According to his Race; The Concept of Merit in the Law of AntiDiscrimination," *Boston Law Review,* 60 (1980): 815.
61. See Marshall Cohen, Thomas Nagel, and Thomas Scanlon, eds., *Equality and Preferential Treatment* (Princeton: Princeton University Press, 1979); Robert K. Fullinwider, *The Reverse Discrimination Controversy: A Moral*

and Legal Analysis (Totowa, N.J.: Rowman and Littlefield, 1980); Kenneth L. Karst and Harold W. Horowitz, "Affirmative Action and Equal Protection," *Virginia Law Review,* 60 (1974): 965, 973.

62. For general discussions of stigma, see Regents of the University of California v. Bakke, 438 U.S. 265, 298 (1978) (Powell, J.); William Van Alstyne, "Rites of Passage: Race, the Supreme Court, and the Constitution," *University of Chicago Law Review,* 46 (1979): 775, 787.
63. See sources cited in Herbert I. Northrup, "Comparable Worth and Realistic Wage Setting," in United States Commission on Civil Rights, *Comparable Worth,* vol. 1; Cheryl Fields, "Comparable Worth and Affirmative Action Assaulted in Reagan's Budget Document," *Chronicle of Higher Education,* Feb. 15, 1984, p. 18; Senate Committee on Labor and Human Resources, *Committee Analysis of Executive Order No. 11246* (Washington, D.C.: Government Printing Office, 1982), p. 64 (administrative costs); Fernandez, *Racism,* pp. 118–119 (backlash); Herma Hill Kay, *Sex-Based Discrimination: Text Cases and Materials* 2nd ed. (St. Paul, Minn.: West, 1981), pp. 852–872 (academic freedom).
64. See sources cited in Fallon, "Merit," p. 818; Citizens Commission on Civil Rights, *Affirmative Action,* p. 168.
65. Martha Minow, "Foreword, Justice Engendered," *Harvard Law Review,* 101 (1987): 10; Mary Becker, "Prince Charming: Abstract Equality," *1987 Supreme Court Review* (Chicago: University of Chicago Press, 1988), p. 201.
66. U.S. Commission, *Affirmative Action,* p. 38; Michael H. Hitt and Barbara Wilceats, "Empirical Identification of the Criteria for Effective Affirmative Action Programs," *Journal of Applied Behavioral Science,* 20 (1984): 203; Barbara Babcock, personal interview, Stanford, California, Feb. 25, 1986.
67. See Ronald Dworkin, "De Funis v. Sweatt," in Cohen, Nagel, and Scanlon, *Equality and Preferential Teatment,* pp. 63, 68.
68. For a summary of psychological literature suggesting the importance of same-sex role models, see Mirra Komarovsky, *Women in College* (New York: Basic Books, 1985), pp. 306–307; Barbara Gutek, ed., *Sex Role Stereotyping and Affirmative Action Policy* (Los Angeles: Institute of Industrial Relations, 1982); Margaret Mooney Marini and Mary C. Brinton, "Sex Typing in Occupational Socialization," in Barbara F. Reskin, ed., *Sex Segregation in the Workplace* (Washington, D.C.: National Academy Press, 1984), pp. 192, 211; Lott, "Devaluation," and sources cited in Chapter 11.
69. See cases cited in Paul Mishkin, "The Uses of Ambivalence: Reflections on the Supreme Court and the Constitutionality of Affirmative Action," *University of Pennsylvania Law Review,* 131 (1983): 907; Fallon, "Merit," and Fullilove v. Klutznick, 448 U.S. 448 (1980) City of Richmond V. J. A. Croson Co., 109 S. Ct. 706 (1989) and note 70.
70. Regents of the University of California v. Bakke, 438 U.S. 265, 315 (1977) (Powell, J.).
71. Johnson v. Transportation Agency, 480 U.S. 616, 107 S. Ct. 1442 (1987). See Becker, "Prince Charming," and Minow, "Justice Engendered."
72. Johnson v. Transportation Agency, 480 U.S. 616 (1987).

73. See Laurence Tribe, *Constitutional Choices* (Cambridge, Mass.: Harvard University Press, 1985). For dangers of the "body count" approach, see Carl Hoffman, "Affirmative Action Programs That Work," *New Perspectives,* (1985): 16. For commentary sympathetic to affirmative-action programs that avoid quotas, see Derrick Bell, "*Bakke:* Minority Admissions, and the Usual Price of Racial Remedies," *California Law Review,* 67 (1979): 3; Vincent Blasi, "*Bakke* as Precedent: Does Mr. Justice Powell Have a Theory?" *California Law Review,* 67 (1979): 21; Hitt and Wilceats, "Affirmative Action."
74. Ronald M. Dworkin, *A Matter of Principle* (Cambridge, Mass.: Harvard University Press, 1985), p. 302; Alan D. Freeman, "Legitimizing Racial Discrimination through Antidiscrimination Law: A Critical Review of Supreme Court Doctrine," *Minnesota Law Review,* 62 (1978): 1049; Kathleen M. Sullivan, "Sins of Discrimination: Last Term's Affirmative Action Cases," *Harvard Law Review,* 100 (1986): 78.
75. Sakre Kennington Edson, *Pushing the Limits: The Female Administrator* (Albany: State University of New York Press, 1988), p. 166. See Law, "Affirmative Action" (noting need for organized groups to monitor compliance).
76. Claudia Goldin, "The Earnings Gap in Historical Perspective," in *Comparable Worth* (Washington, D.C.: U.S. Commission on Civil Rights, 1985); Sheila Tobias and Lisa Anderson, "What Really Happened to Rosie the Riveter? Demobilization and the Female Labor Force, 1944–47," in Linda K. Kerber and Jane De Hart-Mathews, eds., *Women's America: Refocusing the Past* (New York: Oxford University Press, 1982), pp. 367–368; Philip S. Foner, *Women and the American Labor Movement* (New York: Free Press, 1980), II, 355–357; Alice Kessler-Harris, "The Just Price, the Free Market and the Value of Women," *Feminist Studies,* 14 (1988): 235.
77. S. 882, 88th Cong., 1st sess. (see remarks of Senator Case, 109 *Congressional Record* 2780 [1963]); Michael Gold, *Comparable Worth,* p. 64 (quoting Representative Philip Landrum); Note, "Equal Pay, Comparable Work, and Job Evaluation," *Yale Law Journal,* 90 (1981): 657, 665–666.
78. Kirp et al., *Gender Justice,* p. 168; David Savage, "San Jose's Equal Pay Plan Survives," *Los Angeles Times,* Sept. 12, 1983, p. 3.
79. Treiman and Hartmann, *Women, Work & Wages,* p. 71; Ronnie J. Steinberg, "Identifying Wage Discrimination and Implementing Pay Equity Adjustments," in Civil Rights Commission, *Comparable Worth,* I, 99–101; Donald Schwab, "Using Job Evaluations to Obtain Pay Equity," in ibid., p. 84, 90.
80. Treiman and Hartmann, *Women, Work and Wages,* pp. 71–78; Carin Anne Clauss, "Comparable Worth: The Theory, Its Legal Foundation, and the Feasibility of Implementation," *Journal of Law Reform,* 20 (1986): 7, 18–25, 48–58; National Commission on Pay Equity, *Pay Equity,* pp. 77–105.
81. Helen Remick, "Major Issues in *A Priori* Application," in Remick, ed., *Comparable Worth,* pp. 106–107; and sources cited in note 80.
82. For an overview of state law and legislation, see Alice H. Cook, "Developments in Selected States," and Virginia Dean, Patti Roberts, and Carroll

Boone, "Comparable Worth Under Various Federal and State Laws," in Remick, ed., *Comparable Worth,* pp. 267–283, 240–266; Weiler, "Comparable Worth," pp. 1754–1756, nn. 104–109.

83. David Lauter, "How to Factor the Value of Worker's Skills," *National Law Journal,* Jan. 2, 1984, p. 24; Richard W. Beatty and James R. Beatty, "Some Problems With Contemporary Job Evaluation Systems," in Remick, ed., *Comparable Worth,* pp. 59–78; Donald P. Schwab, "Job Evaluation and Pay Setting: Concepts and Practices," in E. Robert Livernash, ed., *Comparable Worth, Issues and Alternatives* (Washington, D.C.: Equal Employment Advisory Council, 1980), p. 49; E. Killingsworth, "The Economics of Comparable Worth: Analytical, Empirical, and Policy Questions," in Hartmann, ed., *Comparable Worth,* p. 87; U.S. Commission on Civil Rights, *Analysis and Recommendations,* pp. 31–33.

84. See Lewin, "Women's Pay"; Michael Evan Gold, *A Dialogue on Comparable Worth* (Ithaca, N.Y.: ILR Press, 1983); Christensen v. Iowa, 563 F.2d 353, 356–357 (8th Cir. 1977).

85. See Judy Scales-Trent, "Comparable Worth: Is This a Theory for Black Workers?" *Women's Rights Law Reporter,* 8 (1984): 51 (quoting Michael Horowitz); National Commission on Pay Equity, *Pay Equity,* p. 16; Daniel Fishel and Edward P. Lazear, "Comparable Worth and Discrimination in Labor Markets," *University of Chicago Law Review,* 53 (1986): 891. But see Mary Becker, "Barriers Facing Women in the Wage-Labor Market and the Need for Additional Remedies: A Reply to Fishel and Lazear," *University of Chicago Law Review,* 53 (1986): 934.

86. Helen Remick and Ronnie Steinberg, "Technical Possibilities and Political Realities: Concluding Remarks," in Remick, ed., *Comparable Worth,* pp. 285–293; Donald Treiman, Heidi Hartmann, and Patricia Roos, "Assessing Pay Discrimination Using National Data," in Remick, ed., *Comparable Worth,* pp. 149–152; Treiman and Hartmann, eds., *Women, Work, and Wages,* pp. 82–90 (alternative statistical approaches).

87. Heidi Hartmann, "Comparable Worth and Women's Economic Independence," in Bose and Spitze, *Women's Employment Policy,* pp. 253, 256; Nina Rothchild, "Pay Equity—The Minnesota Experience," *Journal of Law Reform,* 20 (1986): 209. See George P. Sape, "Coping With Comparable Worth," *Harvard Business Review,* May–June 1985, pp. 151–152; Remick and Steinberg, "Technical Possibilities," pp. 299–300; Cook, "Developments," pp. 267–283; James D. Holzhauer, "The Economic Possibilities of Comparable Worth," *University of Chicago Law Review,* 53 (1986): 919.

88. See Clauss, "Issues," pp. 93–95; National Commission on Pay Equity, *Race,* pp. 18, 62, 71, 105–110; Kelly and Bayes, *Comparable Worth,* pp. 157–232; Julienne Malveaux, "Comparable Worth and Its Impact on Black Women," in Simms and Malveaux, *Black Women,* pp. 47, 53–61. But see Philip M. Holleran and Margaret Schwartz, "Another Look at Comparable Worth's Impact on Black Women," *Review of Black Political Economy,* 16 (1988): 97 (emphasizing that comparable worth cannot address discrimination that takes place prior to entry into the labor market).

89. County of Washington v. Gunther, 452 U.S. 161, 166.

90. Lemons v. City and County of Denver, 620 F.2d 288 (10th Cir., 1980); American Nurses Association v. Illinois, 783 F.2d 716 (7th Cir. 1986); AFSCME v. State of Washington, 578 F.Supp. 846 (W.D. Wash. 1983), *rev'd* 770 F.2d 1401 (9th Cir. 1985); Christensen v. Iowa, 563 F.2d 353 (8th Cir. 1977); Paul Weiler, "The Wages of Sex: The Uses and Limits of Comparable Worth," *Harvard Law Review,* 99 (1986): 1728, 1750, n.90.
91. AFSCME v. State of Washington, 770 F.2d 1401, 1405 (9th Cir. 1985).
92. For decisions granting only prospective remedies, see Arizona Governing Committee v. Norris, 463 U.S. 1073 (1983); City of Los Angeles v. Manhart, 435 U.S. 702 (1978). See also Clauss, "Issues."
93. Clauss, "Issues," pp. 77–83; Treiman and Hartmann, *Women, Work and Wages,* pp. 82–90.
94. See Spaulding v. University of Washington, 740 F.2d 686, 706 (9th Cir. 1984); Craik v. Minnesota State University Board, 731 F.2d 465, 480 (8th Cir. 1984); Wilkins v. University of Houston, 654 F.2d 388, 402 (5th Cir. 1981). See generally George H. Hildebrand, "The Market System," in Livernash, ed., *Comparable Worth,* pp. 79–106; Weiler, "Comparable Worth."
95. U.S. Department of Labor, Bureau of Labor Statistics, *Employment and Earnings,* January 1985, p. 210; Weiler, "Comparable Worth." For discussion of unions' traditional attitudes, see, for example, James J. Kenneally, *Women and American Trade Unions* (St. Albans, Vt.: Eden Press, 1978), Alice Kessler-Harris, "Where are the Organized Women Workers?" in Nancy Cott and Elizabeth Pleck, eds., *A Heritage of Her Own* (New York: Simon and Schuster, 1979), pp. 343–366. For contemporary campaigns, see Bob Drogin, "Comparable Worth at Center of Yale Strike," *Los Angeles Times,* Nov. 18, 1984, sec. 1, p. 5. For the risks and benefits of politicizing workers on pay-equity issues, see Sara M. Evans and Barbara J. Nelson, "Comparable Worth: The Paradox of Technical Reform," *Feminist Studies,* 96 (1989):171.
96. Joan Acker, "Sex Bias in Job Evaluation," in Bose and Spitze, *Employment Policy* (discussing Oregon Task Force); Bielby and Baron, "Undoing Discrimination," p. 225 (worker representation); Barbara F. Reskin, "Bringing the Men Back In: Sex Differentiation and the Devaluation of Women's Work" *Gender and Society,* 2 (1988): 58.
97. See Carol Lawson, "Women in State Jobs Gain in Pay Equity," *New York Times,* May 20, 1985, p. C12 (quoting Civil Rights Commission chairman Clarence Pendleton); Weiler, "Comparable Worth" p. 1729 (quoting Ronald Reagan's dismissal of the concept as a "cockamamie idea"); Michael Levin, "Comparable Worth: The Feminist Road to Socialism," *Commentary,* September 1984, pp. 13–19; Remick and Steinberg, "Technical Possibilities," pp. 289–290.
98. See Reskin and Hartmann, *Women's Work, Men's Work,* pp. 99–122.

9. Reproductive Freedom

1. The oldest known abortifacient was recorded between 2732 and 2696 B.C. in China. For historical overviews of abortion, see William P. Hawkinson,

"Abortion: An Anthropological Overview," in Abdel R. Omran, ed., *Liberalization of Abortion Laws* (Chapel Hill: University of North Carolina Press, 1976), p. 124; Rosalind Pollack Petchesky, *Abortion and Woman's Choice: The State, Sexuality and Reproductive Freedom* (New York: Longman, 1984); Anthony Nathan Cabot, "History of Abortion Law," *Arizona State Law Journal,* 67 (1980): 73, 74–83.

2. James C. Mohr, *Abortion in America: The Origins and Evolution of National Policy, 1800–1900* (New York: Oxford University Press, 1978), pp. 18–43; Petchesky, *Abortion,* p. 73–78.
3. For estimates on the frequency of abortion and the decline of the birth rate, see Linda Gordon, *Woman's Body, Woman's Right: A Social History of Birth Control in America* (New York: Grossman, 1976), pp. 45–53; David M. Kennedy, *Birth Control in America* (New Haven: Yale University Press, 1970), pp. 49–51. For estimates of contraceptive practices, see Barbara Bergman, *The Economic Emergence of Women* (New Year: Basic Books, 1986), p. 42, n.5.
4. See Chapter 11, and James Reed, *From Private Vice to Public Virtue: The Birth Control Movement and American Society Since 1830* (New York: Basic Books, 1978), pp. 40, 188 (quoting Alexander Skeene); A. Laphorn Smith, "Higher Education of Women and Race Suicide," (1905), reprinted in Louise Michele Newman, *Men's Ideas, Women's Realities* (New York: Pergamon, 1985), p. 147.
5. See Kristin Luker, *Abortion and the Politics of Motherhood* (Berkeley: University of California Press, 1984), pp. 27–28; Gordon, *Woman's Right,* pp. 59–60; Mohr, *Abortion,* pp. 32–33, 47–70.
6. Cabot, *Abortion,* pp. 85–86; Petchesky, *Abortion,* p. 80; Luker, *Motherhood,* pp. 58–59 (quoting Bishop Kenrick); Luker, *Abortion,* p. 15.
7. Gordon, *Woman's Right,* pp. 109–111, 238 (quoting Carrie Chapman Catt); Reed, *Private Vice,* p. 32 (quoting Catt). See also Petchesky, *Abortion,* p. 45; Mohr, *Abortion,* p. 111; congressional testimony of Marguerita A. Stewart, reprinted in Robert Bremner et al., eds., *Children and Youth in America: A Documentary History* (Cambridge, Mass.: Harvard University Press, 1971), II, 161–165. Of course, not all women's experience of sexuality was negative; see John D'Emilio and Estelle B. Freedman, *Intimate Matters: A History of Sexuality in America* (New York: Harper and Row, 1987).
8. Margaret Sanger, *Women and the New Race, and My Fight for Birth Control* (New York: Farrar and Reinhart, 1931).
9. See Kennedy, *Birth Control,* pp. 115–121 (quoting Sanger); Angela Davis, *Women, Race and Class* (New York, Vintage Books, 1981), pp. 210–219, and Petchesky, *Abortion,* pp. 87–93, for quotations from Sanger and discussions of sterilization; Gordon, *Woman's Right,* p. 344.
10. Buck v. Bell, 274 U.S. 200 (1927). See Petchesky, *Abortion,* pp. 130, 180; Thomas Shapiro, *Population Control Politics: Woman, Sterilization and Reproductive Choice* (Philadelphia: Temple University Press, 1985). J. Ralph Lindgren and Nadine Taub, *The Law of Sex Discrimination* (St. Paul, Minn.: West, 1988), p. 413 (discussing Stephen Jay Gould's analysis of *Buck*).
11. Petchesky, *Abortion,* pp. 130, 159, 179–180; Lindgren and Taub, *Sex Dis-*

crimination, pp. 413–418; Skinner v. Oklahoma, 316 U.S. 535 (1942); Hyman Rodman, Betty Sarvis, and Joy Walker Bona, *The Abortion Question* (New York: Columbia University Press, 1987), p. 74 (describing medical services conditioned on agreement to sterilization); Patricia J. Williams, "On Being the Object of Property," *Signs,* 14 (1988): 5, 7–8 n. 5.

12. Davis, *Class,* p. 210; Luker, *Abortion,* pp. 36–39. Petchesky, *Abortion,* pp. 45–50; Rodman, Sarvis, and Boner, *Abortion,* p. 154.
13. See generally Gordon, *Woman's Right;* Kennedy, *Birth Control,* viii, 218–271.
14. Griswold v. Connecticut, 381 U.S. 479 (1965), Eisenstadt v. Baird, 405 U.S. 438 (1972), Carey v. Population Services International, 431 U.S. 678 (1977).
15. Luker, *Abortion,* pp. 55–76; Kennedy, *Birth Control,* pp. 36–51; National Association for Repeal of Abortion Laws, in Gerda Lerner, *The Female Experience, An American Documentary* (Indianapolis: Bobbs-Merrill, 1977); Lawrence Lader, *Abortion II: Making the Revolution* (Boston: Beacon, 1973), p. 2; Frederick S. Jaffe, Barbara Lindheim, and Philip R. Lee, *Abortion Politics: Private Morality and Public Policy* (New York: McGraw-Hill, 1981), p. 24; D'Emilio and Freedman, *Intimate Matters,* pp. 253–255.
16. Kristin Luker, *Taking Chances: Abortion and the Decision Not to Contracept* (Berkeley: University of California Press, 1975); Sylvia A. Law, "Rethinking Sex and the Constitution," *University of Pennsylvania Law Review,* 132 (1984): 955, 1017, n. 221. Lader, *Abortion II,* p. 219.
17. Kennedy, *Birth Control,* p. 41; Raymond Tatalovich and Byron W. Daynes, *The Politics of Abortion: A Study of Community Conflict in Public Policy Making* (New York: Praeger, 1981), pp. 24–76; Barbara Hayes, "Abortion," *Signs,* 5 (1979): 307.
18. Jeffe et al., *Abortion Politics,* pp. 101–103; Judith Blake, "The Abortion Decision: Judicial Review and Public Opinion on Abortion; New Directions for Policy Studies," in Edward Manier et al., *Abortion* (Notre Dame, Ind.: University of Notre Dame Press, 1977); Lader, *Abortion II,* p. 186.
19. Roe v. Wade, 410 U.S. 113 (1973); Doe v. Bolton, 410 U.S. 179 (1973).
20. Roe v. Wade, 410 U.S. at 156–160; Ronald Reagan, "Abortion and the Conscience of the Nation," reprinted in J. Douglas Butler and David F. Walbert, *Abortion, Medicine, and the Law* (New York: Facts on File Publications, 1986), pp. 352–353. For discussion of more cautious alternatives, see Guido Calabresi, *Ideals, Beliefs, Attitudes and the Law* (Syracuse, N.Y.: Syracuse University Press, 1985); Paul Freund, "Storms Over the Supreme Court," *American Bar Association Journal,* 69 (1983): 1474, 1480; Laurence H. Tribe, "The Abortion Funding Conundrum: Inalienable Rights, Affirmative Duties, and the Dilemma of Dependence," *Harvard Law Review,* 99 (1985): 330, 342.
21. John Hart Ely, "The Wages of Crying Wolf: A Comment on *Roe v. Wade,*" *Yale Law Journal,* 82 (1973): 920–949. For discussion of the physician's role in determining viability, see Planned Parenthood of Central Missouri v. Danforth, 428 U.S. 52 (1976), and Colautti v. Franklin, 439 U.S. 379 (1979). For difficulties with the Court's trimester approach see Ely, "Crying Wolf"; Thornburgh v. American College of Obstetricians and Gynecologists, 476

U.S. 747 (1986) (White, J., dissenting); Nancy K. Rhoden, "Trimesters and Technology: Revamping *Roe v. Wade*," *Yale Law Journal*, 95 (1986): 639–697.

22. City of Akron v. Akron Center for Reproductive Health, Inc. 462 U.S. 416 (1983) (O'Connor, J., dissenting); Rhoden, "Trimesters," p. 668; Reproductive Health Service v. Webster, 851 F.2d 1071 (8th Cir. 1988) *cert.* granted—U.S.—(1988). For a summary of post-*Roe* restrictions, see Albert M. Pearson and Paul M. Kurtz, "The Abortion Controversy: A Study in Law and Politics," in Butler and Walbert, *Abortion*, pp. 107–136.
23. See Luker, *Abortion*, and Patrick J. Sheeran, *Women, Society, the State, and Abortion: A Structural Analysis* (New York: Praeger, 1987), pp. 125–127 (discussing right-to-life activists), Laurence Tribe, *American Constitutional Law* (Mineola, N.Y.: Foundation Press, 1978), p. 929 (discussing problems in the political process).
24. See Law, "Rethinking Sex," p. 1023, n. 245 (summarizing skepticism of experts concerning early fetal survival, including those cited by O'Connor); Petchesky, *Abortion*, p. 347 (92–96 percent of abortions at first trimester).
25. See commentary in Lindgren and Taub, *Sex Discrimination*, pp. 409–410; Stanley K. Henshaw et al. "A Portrait of American Women Who Obtain Abortions," *Family Planning Perspectives*, 17 (1985): 90, 91.
26. Note, "Technological Advances and *Roe v. Wade:* The Need to Rethink Abortion Law," *UCLA Law Review*, 29 (1982): 1194–1215; Robert N. Wennberg, *Life in the Balance: Exploring the Abortion Controversy* (Grand Rapids, Mich.: William B. Eerdmans, 1985).
27. Robin West, "Jurisprudence and Gender," *University of Chicago Law Review*, 55 (1988): 1; Sylvia Law, "Rethinking Sex," p. 1020; Palko v. Connecticut, 302 U.S. 319, 325 (1937). This is not to suggest that Good Samaritan analogies provide a wholly satisfying approach to the abortion issue. It is morally unsettling to defend women's right to abort a previable fetus on the same grounds that one would defend her refusal to risk physical injuries in aid of an existing child. It is also the case that most Americans do not extend Good Samaritan principles to exempt individuals from other life-threatening obligations, most notably the draft. Still, philosophers such as Judith Thompson and Donald Regan have made a persuasive case that such principles have some force in assessing abortion. Donald Regan, "Rewriting *Roe v. Wade*," *Michigan Law Review*, 77 (1979): 1569; Judith Jarvis Thompson, "Rights and Deaths," *Philosophy and Public Affairs*, 2 (1972): 146. For discussion of maternal bonds, see Robert D. Goldstein, *Mother Love and Abortion: A Legal Interpretation* (Berkeley: University of California Press, 1988).
28. Maher v. Roe, 432 U.S. 464, 474 (1977); Harris v. McRae, 448 U.S. 297, 316 (1980).
29. See dissenting opinions in *Maher* and *Harris;* Jaffe et al., *Abortion Politics*, pp. 143–145; Michael J. Perry, "Why the Supreme Court Was Plainly Wrong in the Hyde Amendment Case: A Brief Comment on *Harris v. McRae*," *Stanford Law Review*, 32 (July 1980): 1113; Tribe, *Constitutional Law*, p. 932, n. 77.

30. Jaffe et al., *Abortion,* pp. 143–146; Jimmy Carter, quoted in Law, "Rethinking Sex," p. 1016, n. 219; Brief for the National Abortion Rights Action League et al., in Thornburgh v. American College of Obstetricians and Gynecologists (1985), p. 14 (and sources cited therein); Laura Jefferson, "Reproductive Laws, Women of Color and Low-Income Women," in Sherrell Cohen and Nadine Taub, eds., *Reproductive Law for the 1990s* (Clifton, N.J.: Humana Press, 1988) (race); Catharine MacKinnon, "*Roe v. Wade:* A Study in Male Ideology," in Jay L. Garfield and Patricia Hennessey, *Abortion: Moral and Legal Perspectives* (Amherst: University of Massachusetts Press, 1984), pp. 45, 52.
31. See Mary Ann Glendon, *Abortion and Divorce in Western Law* (Cambridge, Mass.: Harvard University Press, 1987); Rodman, Sarvis, and Bona, *Abortion,* p. 59; Gina Kolata, "Any Sale in U.S. of Abortion Pill Still Years Away," *New York Times,* Oct. 30, 1988, p. 1 (noting U.S. companies' lack of investment in new birth-control technology because of high research and liability costs and potential profits).
32. Karen DeCrow, *Sexist Justice* (New York: Vintage, 1977), pp. 268–279; Elise F. Jones et al., "Teenage Pregnancy in Developed Countries: Determinants and Policy Implications," *Family Planning Perspectives,* 17 (1985): 53; Cheryl Hayes, ed., *Risking the Future: Adolescent Sexuality, Pregnancy, and Childbirth. Report of the Panel on Adolescent Pregnancy and Childbirth of the National Research Council, Final Report* (Washington, D.C.: National Academy Press, 1987), p. 1.2, 2.20–2.30; Janet Benshoof and Harriet Pilpel, "Minors' Right to Confidential Abortions: The Evolving Legal Scene," in Butler and Walbert, *Abortion,* p. 144.
33. DeCrow, *Sexist Justice,* pp. 268–279; Hayes, *Risking the Future,* pp. 2.3–2.20; Frank Furstenberg, Jr., J. Brooks-Gunn, and S. Phillip Morgan, *Adolescent Mothers in Later Life* (Cambridge: Cambridge University Press, 1987); Children's Defense Fund, *Teenage Pregnancy: An Advocate's Guide to the Numbers* (Washington, D.C.: January 1988); Dorothy J. Height, "What Must Be Done About Children Having Children," *Ebony* (March 1985), p. 77.
34. See Carole Joffe, *The Regulation of Sexuality,* (Philadelphia: Temple University Press, 1986), p. 45 (quoting Connaught Marshner); Sharon Thompson, "Search for Tomorrow: On Feminism and the Reconstruction of Teen Romance," in Carole Vance, ed., *Pleasure and Danger* (Boston: Routledge and Kegan Paul, 1984).
35. Hayes, *Risking the Future,* 6-5, 6-6; 42 U.S.C. Section 3003; Bowen v. Kenrick, 108 S. Ct. 2562 (1987).
36. Hayes, *Risking the Future,* 1.9 1.11; Bershof and Pilpel, p. 152, n. 60; Brigid Rentoul, "Cognitus Interruptus: The Courts and Minor's Access to Contraceptives," *Yale Law and Policy Review,* 5 (1986): 212; Planned Parenthood Federation of America v. Schweiker, 559 F.Supp. 658, (D.D.C.) *aff'd,* 712 F.2d 650 (D.C. Cir. 1983); *Accord,* State of N.Y. v. Heckler, 719 F.2d 1191 (2d Cir. 1983).
37. Belloti v. Baird, 443 U.S. 622 (1979); H. L. Matheson, 450 U.S. 398 (1981); Planned Parenthood of Central Missouri v. Danforth, 428 U.S. 52 (1976).

38. See studies cited in Bershof and Pilpel, *Minor's Rights,* pp. 144–145; Nanette Dembitz, "The Supreme Court and a Minor's Abortion Decision," *Columbia Law Review,* 80 (1980): 1251, 1255–1258; Robert M. Mnookin, "Bellotti v. Baird: A Hard Case," in Robert H. Mnookin, *In the Interests of Children* (New York, W. H. Freeman, 1985).
39. Petchesky, *Abortion,* p.270 (quoting Holder and Denton); Rentaul, "Cognitus Interruptus," n. 113; Ann L. Harper, "Teenage Sexuality and Public Policy: An Agenda for Gender Education," in Irene Diamond, *Families and Public Policy: A Feminist Dialogue on Women and the State* (New York: Longman, 1983); Eve Paul and Dana Lassel, "Minor's Right to Confidential Contraceptive Services: The Limits of State Power" *Women's Rights Law Reporter,* 10 (1987): 1; Hayes, *Risking the Future,* 6.60, 7.7; Harrell R. Rodgers, Jr., *Poor Women, Poor Families: The Economic Plight of America's Female-Headed Households* (Armonk, N.Y.: M. E. Sharpe, 1987), pp. 92–93.
40. Hayes, *Risking the Future,* pp. 17–18; Chapter 6; Kristin Luker, *Taking Chances: Abortion and the Decision Not to Contracept* (Berkeley: University of California Press, 1975); Maris A. Vinovskis, *An Epidemic of Adolescent Pregnancy: Some Historical and Policy Considerations* (New York: Oxford University Press, 1988), pp. 36–39, 194–203.
41. Catharine Chilman, "Feminist Issues in Teen Parenting," *Child Welfare,* 64 (1985): 225; Robert L. Barret and Bryan E. Robinson, "Teenage Fathers: Neglected Too Long," *Social Worker,* 27 (1982): 484; Vinovskis, *Epidemic,* pp. 166–168.
42. Marian Wright Edelman, *Families in Peril: An Agenda for Social Change* (Cambridge, Mass.: Harvard University Press, 1987); Kristin A. Moore, Margaret C. Simns, and Charles L. Betsey, *Choice and Circumstance: Racial Differences in Adolescent Sexuality and Fertility* (New Brunswick, N.J.: Transaction, 1986); Children's Defense Fund, *Advocate's Guide;* Jefferson, "Reproductive Laws."
43. For discussion of spousal consent requirements and relevant cases, see Stephen J. Schnably, "Normative Judgment, Social Change and Legal Reasoning in the Context of Abortion and Privacy," *New York Review of Law and Social Change,* 13 (1985): 715, 890; Lindgren and Taub, *Sex Discrimination,* p. 413.
44. Viviana A. Zelizer, "From Baby Farms to Baby M," *Transaction/Society* (March–April 1988): 23. See generally Michelle Stanworth, "The Deconstruction of Motherhood," in Michelle Stanworth, ed., *Reproductive Technologies: Gender, Motherhood and Medicine* (Cambridge, Eng.: Polity, 1987), p. 16.
45. Different reproductive techniques and market growth are surveyed in Lori Andrews, *New Conceptions: A Consumer's Guide to the Newest Infertility Treatments, Including In-Vitro Fertilization, Artificial Insemination, and Surrogate Motherhood* (Chicago: American Bar Foundation, 1984); Gena Corea, *The Mother Machine* (New York: Harper and Row, 1984), pp. 34–35, 120–125; Sevgi O. Aral and Willard Gates, "The Increasing Concern with Infertility: Why Now?" *The Journal of the American Medical Associ-*

ation (Nov. 4, 1983): 2327; George J. Annas, "Making Babies without Sex: The Law and the Profits," *American Journal of Public Health,* 74 (1984): 1415.

46. See statistics cited in *In the Matter of Baby M,* 217 N.J. Super. 313, 525 A.2d 1128 (N.J. Super. 1987); Wilson, "Adoption: It's Not Impossible," *Business Week,* July 8, 1985, p. 112. See Williams, "Property," pp. 7–8 (noting irony that a century after black babies were bought and sold, now it is white children who are in demand and minority infants have become "worthless currency" to adoption agencies).

47. Robyn Rowland, "Technology and Motherhood: Reproductive Choice Reconsidered, " *Signs,* 12 (1987): 513, 520; John A. Robertson, "Embryos, Families, and Procreative Liberty: The Legal Structure of the New Reproduction," *University of Southern California Law Review,* 59 (1986): 939.

48. See Joan Hollinger, "From Coitus to Commerce: Legal and Social Consequences of Non-Coital Reproduction," *University of Michigan Journal of Law Reform,* 18 (1985): 865.

49. Ruth Hubbard, "Some Legal and Policy Implications of Recent Advances in Prenatal Diagnosis and Fetal Therapy," *Women's Rights Law Reporter,* 7 (1982): 201; Marie Ashe, "Law Language of Maternity: Discourse Holding Nature in Contempt," *New England Law Review,* 22 (1988): 521, 542 (caesareans). See generally Helen Holmes, Betty Hoskins, and Michael Gross, eds., *Birth Control and Controlling Birth: Woman-Centered Perspectives,* (Clifton, N.J.: Humana Press, 1981); John A. Robertson, "Procreative Liberty and the Control of Conception, Pregnancy, and Childbirth," *Virginia Law Review,* 69 (1983): 405 (advocating regulation).

50. See generally Clifford Grobstein, *From Chance to Purpose: An Appraisal of External Human Fertilization* (Reading, Mass.: Addison-Wesley, 1981); Robyn Rowland, "Reproductive Technologies: The Final Solution to the Woman Question?" in Rita Arditti, Renate Duelli Klein, and Shelley Minden, *Test-Tube Women* (London: Pandora, 1984), pp. 356–369; Janice Raymond, "Feminist Ethics, Ecology and Vision," in Arditti, Klein, and Minden, *Test-Tube Women,* pp. 427–437; Helen Rodriguez-Trias, "Sterilization Abuse," in Ruth Hubbard, Mary Sue Henifen, and Barbara Fried, eds., *Biological Woman—The Convenient Myth* (Cambridge, Mass.: Schenkman, 1982), pp. 147–158.

51. Neil G. Bennett, ed., *Sex Selection of Children* (New York: Academic Press, 1983): Jalna Hamner, "Sex Predetermination: Artificial Insemination and the Maintenance of Male Dominated Culture," in Helen Roberts, ed., *Women, Health, and Reproduction* (London: Routledge and Kegan Paul, 1983); Betty B. Hoskins and Helen Bequaert Holmes, "Technology and Prenatal Femicide," in Arditti, Klein, and Minden, *Test-Tube Women,* pp. 237–255.

52. For a critical review of these policies, see Corea, *Mother Machine,* pp. 20–21, 42–51; Rebecca Albury, "Who Owns the Embryo?" in Arditti, Klein, and Minden, *Test-Tube Women,* pp. 54–67; Note, "Reproductive Technology and the Procreation Rights of the Unmarried," *Harvard Law Review,* 98 (1985): 669.

53. See Andrea Dworkin, *Right-Wing Women* (New York: Perigee Books, 1983), pp. 181–182; Susan Ince, "Inside the Surrogate Industry," in Arditti, Klein, and Minden, *Test-Tube Women,* pp. 99–116.
54. See Norma Juliet Wikler, "Society's Response to the New Reproductive Technologies: The Feminist Perspectives," *University of Southern California Law Review,* 59 (1986): 1043; Barbara Rothman, "The Meaning of Choice in Reproductive Technology," in Arditti, Klein, and Minden, *Test-Tube Women,* pp. 23–27.
55. In the Matter of Baby M, 217 N.J. Super. 313, 525 A.2d 1128 (N.J. Super. 1987).
56. Avi Katz, "Surrogate Motherhood and the Baby-Selling Laws," *Columbia Journal of Law and Social Problems,* 20 (1986): 1; Note, "Rumpelstiltskin Revisited: The Inalienable Rights of Surrogate Mothers," *Harvard Law Review,* 99 (1986): 1936; Ashe, "Law Language"; Symposium in *Georgetown Law Journal,* 76 (1989); 1717–1844.
57. See sources cited in note 49; "Baby M's Future," *New York Times,* April 5, 1987, p. 1; Hollinger, "Commerce"; Margaret Jane Radin, "Market Inalienability," *Harvard Law Review,* 100 (1987): 1849, 1930–1932. On this reasoning Britain has criminalized all but private uncompensated arrangements; see *Surrogacy Arrangements Act* 1985, sec. 1–3.
58. See, for example, Robertson, "Embryos," pp. 1012–1021; Note, "Redefining Mother: A Legal Matrix for New Reproductive Technologies," *Yale Law Journal,* 96 (1986): 187; Radin, "Market Inalienability," pp. 1932–1936. In the *Baby M* litigation, William Stern's desire for a biological legacy was amplified by the experience of losing the remainder of his family in the holocaust.
59. See Robertson, "Embryos," pp. 1012–1021; "Redefining Mother"; Laurence D. Houlgate, *Family and State: The Philosophy of Family Law* (Totowa, N.J.: Rowman and Littlefield, 1988), pp. 118–119. For a similar argument that "contracts should be fulfilled," see Lawrence Stone, quoted in Carole Pateman, *The Sexual Contract* (Stanford: Stanford University Press, 1988), p. 211.
60. In the matter of Baby M, 217 N.J. Super. 313, 525 A.2d 1128 (N.J. Super. 1987).
61. Ibid. See Martha A. Field, *Surrogate Motherhood* (Cambridge, Mass.: Harvard University Press, 1988), and studies summarized in Hollinger, "Coitus."
62. In the Matter of Baby M, 217 N.J. Super., 313, 525 A.2d 1128 (N.J. Super. 1987). See Chapter 7.
63. Ibid., Katha Pollitt, "The Strange Case of Baby M," *Nation,* May 23, 1987, pp. 61–82; Phyllis Chesler, *Sacred Bond: The Legacy of Baby M.* (New York: Times Books, 1988), pp. 177–183 (reprinting experts' reports).
64. Bruce Rosen, "Nasty Baby M Case Forced New Jersey Counsel to Look for Any Skeletons They Could Find," *Recorder,* Aug. 11, 1987, p. 1.
65. For comparable proposals, see Field, *Surrogate Motherhood;* Hollinger, "Coitus," Radin, "Market Inalienability," pp. 1932–1936, Katharine T. Bartlett, "Re-Expressing Parenthood," *Yale Law Journal,* 98 (1988): 291; and "The Baby M Contract," *New Jersey Law Journal* (Feb. 26, 1987), p.

27. See also Barbara Ashe, "Maternity," p. 557, and Barbara Hilkert Andolsen, "Why A Surrogate Mother Should Have the Right to Change her Mind: A Feminist Analysis of Changes in Motherhood Today," in Herbert Richardson, ed., *On the Problem of Surrogate Parenthood* (Lewiston, N.Y.: Edwin Mellen Press, 1987), p. 41. Compare Lori Andrew's "Surrogate Motherhood: Should the Adoption Model Apply?" *Children's Legal Rights Journal,* 17 (1986): 13; Diana Frank and Marta Vogel, *The Baby Makers* (New York: Caroll and Graf, 1988) (discussing the need for regulation of surrogacy agencies and describing abuses such as staff rewriting of psychologists' reports to make all potential surrogates sound like "Mary Poppins").

66. Ann Oakley, "Fertility Control—A Woman's Issue," *Journal of Obstetrics and Gynecology,* 4 (1984): Supp. 1, quoting Jacques Ellul, *The Technological Society* (New York, Alfred A. Knopf, 1964), p. vi.

10. Sex and Violence

1. Elizabeth Cady Stanton, quoted in Laura Lederer, ed., *Take Back the Night* (New York: Morrow, 1980), p. 22.
2. See Catharine A. MacKinnon, "A Feminist Political Approach: 'Pleasure Under Patriarchy,'" in James H. Geer and William T. O'Donahue, eds., *Theories of Human Sexuality* (New York: Plenum, 1987), pp. 65, 69.
3. Catharine A. MacKinnon, *Sexual Harassment of Working Women: A Case of Sex Discrimination* (New Haven: Yale University Press, 1979), pp. 159, 166. For accounts of the risks to nineteenth-century workers, see Harriet H. Robinson et al., *Women of Lowell* (New York: Arno Press, 1974), p. 19; Mary Bularzik, "Sexual Harassment at the Workplace: Historical Notes," *Radical America,* 12 (July–August 1978): 25–44.
4. See studies discussed in United States Merit Systems Protection Board, *Sexual Harassment in the Federal Government: An Update* (Washington, D.C.: Government Printing Office, 1988); Barbara A. Gutek, *Sex and the Workplace* (San Francisco: Jossey-Bass, 1985); Dail Anne Neugarten and Joy M. Shafritz, eds., "Overview," *Sexuality in Organizations: Romantic and Coercive Behavior at Work* (Oak Park, Ill.: More Publishers, 1980); Merit Systems Protection Board, *Report on Sexual Harassment in the Federal Workplace: Is It a Problem?* (Washington, D.C.: United States Government Printing Office, 1981); Donna J. Benson and Gregg E. Thomson, "Sexual Harassment on a University Campus," *Social Problems,* 29 (1982): 236.
5. For the absence of benefits, see Gutek, *Sex and the Workplace,* pp. 87, 159–168. For the costs, see Peggy Crull, "Sexual Harassment and Women's Health," in Wendy Chavkin, ed., *Double Exposure: Women's Health Hazards on the Job and at Home* (New York: Monthly Review Press, 1984), pp. 100–116; James E. Gruber and Lars Bjorn, "Blue Collar Blues: The Sexual Harassment of Women Autoworkers," *Work and Occupations,* 9 (August 1982): 271; Robert E. Quinn, "Coping with Cupid: The Function, Impact and Management of Romantic Relationships in Organizations," in Neugarten and Shafritz, *Sexuality,* pp. 38–51. For grievance procedures, see

Merit Protection Board, *Sexual Harassment;* "Overview," in Neugarten and Shafritz, *Sexuality,* pp. 7–9; Crull, "Sexual Harassment," pp. 67, 69–70; Eliza G. C. Collins and Timothy B. Blodgett, "Sexual Harassment: Some See It . . . Some Won't," *Harvard Business Review,* 59 (March–April, 1981): 76; Lynn E. Zimmer, *Women Guarding Men* (Chicago: University of Chicago Press, 1986), pp. 93–97.

6. Nancy E. McGlen and Karen O'Connor, *Women's Rights: The Struggle for Equality in Nineteenth and Twentieth Century America* (New York: Praeger, 1983), p. 186 (quoting Phyllis Schlafly); "A Clash Over Worker Sex Harassment," *San Francisco Chronicle,* April 22, 1981, p. 13 (quoting Phyllis Schlafly); Rosemarie Tong, *Women, Sex, and the Law* (Totowa, N.J.: Rowman and Allanheld, 1984), p. 66 (quoting Yale Official); Collins and Blodgett, "Sexual Harassment," p. 92 (quoting male respondent).
7. Zimmer, *Guarding Men* (quoting prison administrator), p. 97.
8. Corne v. Bausch and Lomb, 390 F.Supp. 161, 163 (D. Ariz. 1975), vacated and remanded, 562 F.2d 55 (9th Cir. 1977) (personal proclivity); Miller v. Bank of America, 418 F.Supp. 233 (N.D. Cal. 1976) (isolated misconduct; natural phenomenon); Barnes v. Costle, 561 F.2d 983, 1001 (D.C. Cir. 1977) (MacKinnon, J., concurring) (normal and expectable); Robert Meyers, "The File on Roarin Oren," *National Law Journal,* March 7, 1983, p. 32 (universal).
9. See Barnes v. Train, 13 Fair Empl. Prac. Cas. (BNA) 123, 124 (D. D.C., 1974); Tomkins v. Public Service Electric & Gas, 568 F.2d 1044 (3d Cir. 1977) (inharmonious); and Huebschen v. Department of Health, 32 Fair Empl. Prac. Cas. (BNA) 1582 (7th Cir. 1983) (incidental). See also the pregnancy cases discussed in Chapter 6.
10. Barnes v. Costle, 561 F.2d 983, 990, n. 55 (1977), Vinson v. Taylor, 760 F.2d 1330, 1333, n. 7 (D.C. Cir. 1985) (Bork, J., dissenting from denial of rehearing en banc) remanded, *sub nom.* Meritor Savings Bank, FSB v. Vinson, 477 U.S. 57 (1986); Heelan v. Johns-Manville Corporation, 451 F.Supp. 1382, 1389 (D. Colo. 1978).
11. 29 C.F.R. 1604. 11 (1981), Meritor Savings Bank, FSB v. Vinson, 477 U.S. 57 (1986).
12. Compare King v. Palmer, 35 Fair Empl. Prac. Cas. (BNA) 1302 (D. D.C. 1984), Katz v. Dole, 709 F.2d 251, 254, n. 3 (4th Cir. 1983) with Priest v. Rotary, 32 Fair Empl. Prac. Cas. (BNA) 1064 (N.D. Cal. 1983). For examples of failure to complain as a bar to recovery, see Walter v. KFGO Radio, 518 F.Supp. 1309, 1316 (D.D. 1981); Robinson v. DuPont Co., 33 Fair Empl. Prac. Cas. (BNA) 880 (D. Del. 1979), and Catharine A. MacKinnon, *Feminism Unmodified* (Cambridge, Mass.: Harvard University Press, 1987), p. 12.
13. Rabidue v. Osceo Refining Co., 805 F.2d 611 (8th Cir., 1986); see MacKinnon, *Sexual Harassment,* p. 50 (apology); Gutek, *Sex and the Workplace,* p. 12 (demotions or transfers); *On Campus With Women* 26 (1980): 11–12 (suspension); Billie Wright Dzeich and Linda Weiner, *The Lecherous Professor: Sexual Harassment on Campus* (Boston: Beacon, 1984), pp. 9–15.

14. Vinson v. Taylor, 760 F.2d 1330 (D.C. Cir. 1985) (Bork, J., dissenting from denial of rehearing), remanded, *sub nom* Meritor Savings Bank, FSB v. Vinson, 477 U.S. 57 (1986); Sand v. Johnson Co., 33 Fair Empl. Prac. Cas. (BNA) 716 (E.D. Mich. 1982); Bundy v. Jackson, 641 F.2d 934 (D.C. Cir. 1981). Zabkowicz v. West Bend Co., 585 F.Supp. 635 (E.D. Wisc. 1984); Katz v. Dole, 709 F.2d 251, 256 (4th Cir. 1983); Henson v. Dundee, 682 F.2d 897, 900, n. 2 (11th Cir. 1982).
15. Hearings Before the Senate Committee on Labor and Human Resources, 97th Cong., 1st sess. (1981) (of 130 pending cases, 118 presented corroborating evidence); MacKinnon, *Sexual Harassment,* p. 96 and n. 54; Claire Robertson, Constance E. Dyer, and D'Ann Campbell, "Campus Harassment: Sexual Harassment Policies and Procedures at Institutions of Higher Learning," *Signs,* 13 (1988): 792, 811 (fewer than 1 percent deliberate fabrications); Merit Systems Protection Board, *Update* (only 5 percent of those harassed filed complaints, and administrative process took almost a year).
16. Lynn Rubinett, "Sex and Economics: The Tie that Binds—Judicial Approaches to Sexual Harassment as a Title VII Violation," *Law and Inequality: A Journal of Theory and Practice,* 4 (1986): 245.
17. MacKinnon, *Feminism Unmodified.*
18. "Drexel President Quits in Harassment Dispute," *New York Times,* Oct. 25, 1987, sec. 1; see also William K. Stevens, "Harassment Change Poses Threat to Leadership of Drexel," *New York Times,* June 7, 1987, p. 13. In explaining his conduct, the president said: "I have made a deliberate attempt to be a more human caring person. I mean that in the best sense. This is new ground for me: where are the lines in this?" For grievance procedures, see Gutek, *Sex and the Workplace;* Alliance Against Sexual Coercion, *Fighting Sexual Harassment* (Boston: Alyson Publications, 1981); Collins and Blodgett, "Sexual Harassment," and note 5.
19. For estimates of domestic violence, see Murray A. Straus, Richard J. Gelles, and Suzanne K. Steinmetz, *Behind Closed Doors: Violence in the American Family* (Garden City, N.Y.: Anchor, 1980); Lenore E. Walker, *The Battered Woman* (New York: Harper and Row, 1979), p. ix, 19–20, Kathleen Waits, "The Criminal Justice System's Response to Battering: Understanding the Problem, Forging the Solutions," *Washington Law Review,* 60 (1985): 267, 273 (10–20 percent in any given year; 25 percent during the course of a given relationship). Some estimates suggest that more than half of all incidents of domestic violence are unreported. See Waits, "Battering," pp. 275–316; United States Department of Justice, Bureau of Justice Statistics and Bureau of the Census, *Intimate Victims: A Study of Violence Among Friends and Relatives* (Washington, D.C.: United States Department of Justice, 1980); Straus, Gelles, and Steinmetz, *Behind Closed Doors,* p. 35. For studies on homicides, see U.S. Commission on Civil Rights, *Battered Women: Issues of Public Policy* (Washington, D.C.: U.S. Government Printing Office, 1978), pp. 246–247, and Laurie Woods, "Litigation on Behalf of Battered Women," *Women's Rights Law Reporter,* 5 (1978): 137, n. 38 (in 85 percent of Kansas homicide cases, victims called the police once, and in the majority of cases five or more times, prior to death).

20. For male-female differentials, see Cynthia Diehm and Margo Ross, "Battered Women," in Sara E. Rix, ed., *The American Woman, 1987–88: A Report in Depth* (New York: Norton, 1987), p. 292; Maria L. Marcus, "Conjugal Violence: The Law of Force and the Force of Law," *California Law Review,* 69 (1981): 1657, 1676–1678; Susan Schechter, *Women and Male Violence* (Boston: South End Press, 1982), p. 214; Elizabeth A. Stanko, *Intimate Intrusions: Women's Experiences of Male Violence* (Boston: Routledge and Kegan Paul, 1985), pp. 50–51. For child abuse, see Diana E. H. Russell, "The Incidence and Prevalence of Intrafamilial and Extrafamilial Sexual Abuse of Female Children," *Child Abuse and Neglect,* 7 (1983): 133. For theoretical discussion, see Linda Gordon, *Heroes of Their Own Lives: The Politics and History of Family Violence* (New York: Viking, 1988), pp. 2–3. MacKinnon, "Patriarchy," and *Feminism,* and Robin L. West, "The Difference in Women's Hedonic Lives: A Phenomenological Critique of Feminist Legal Theory," *Wisconsin Women's Law Journal,* 3 (1987): 81.
21. Friar Cherubino of Siena's Rules of Marriage (1450–1481), quoted in Terry Davidson, *Conjugal Crime: Understanding and Changing the Wifebeating Pattern* (New York: Hawthorn Books, 1978), p. 99; William Blackstone, *The Common Law* I (7th ed., 1775), p. 445; Bradley v. State, 1 Miss. 156 (1 Walker) (1824). For nineteenth-century American law, see Chapter 1, and Sue E. Eisenberg and Patricia L. Micklow, "The Assaulted Wife: 'Catch 22 Revisited'," *Women's Rights Law Reporter,* 3 (1977): 138, 152; Nan Oppenlander, "The Evolution of Law and Wife Abuse," *Law and Policy Quarterly,* 3 (1981): 382, 393–400; Elizabeth Pleck, "Wife Beating in Nineteenth-Century America," *Victimology,* 4 (1979): 60–74. See also Chapter 1.
22. Robert L. Griswold, "Sexual Cruelty and the Case for Divorce in Victorian America," *Signs,* 11 (1986): 529; Pleck, "Wife Beating"; English v. English, 27 N.J. Equity Reports 71 (1876); Poor v. Poor, 8 N.H. 307 (1836); David v. David, 27 Ala. 222 (1855).
23. Gordon, *Heroes,* pp. 251–280; Pleck, "Wife Beating."
24. See Gordon, *Heroes,* p. 264; and Judith Lewis Herman, "Considering Sex Offenders: A Model of Addiction," *Signs,* 13 (1988): 695, 714–715.
25. Schecter, *Male Violence,* pp. 160–161; Federal Bureau of Investigation U.S. Dept. of Justice, *Crime in the United States* (Washington, D.C.: U.S. Department of Justice, pp. 333–339; U.S. Commission on Civil Rights, *Under the Rule of Thumb: Battered Women and the Administration of Justice* (Washington, D.C.: U.S. Commission on Civil Rights, 1982), p. 14; Eisenberg and Micklow, "Assaulted Wife," p. 138, n. 146 (police manual).
26. See police instructions quoted in Lisa G. Lerman, "A Model State Act: Remedies for Domestic Abuse," *Harvard Journal on Legislation,* 21 (1984): 68, 123; Lee H. Bowker, "Police Services to Battered Women: Bad or Not So Bad?" *Criminal Justice and Behavior,* 9 (1982): 479; Straus, Gelles, and Steinmetz, *Behind Closed Doors,* pp. 232–233 (stitch rule). For assumptions of male officers and law-enforcement officers, see Mildred Daley Pagelow, *Woman-Battering: Victims and Their Experiences* (Beverly Hills, Calif.: Sage, 1981), p. 71; Woods, "Litigation," p. 10; Eisenberg and Micklow, "Assaulted Wife," pp. 156–158.
27. See prosecutors quoted in Emily June Goodman, "Legal Solutions: Equal

Protection Under the Law," in Maria Roy, ed., *Battered Women: A Psycho-sociological Study of Domestic Violence* (New York: Van Nostrand Reinhold, 1977), p. 142; U.S. Commission on Civil Rights, *Under the Thumb,* p. 25; Tong, *Sex,* p. 138. For judges, see Elizabeth Pleck, *Domestic Tyranny* (New York: Oxford University Press, 1987), p. 125. For discussion of attrition studies, see R. Emerson Dobash and Russell Dobash, *Violence Against Wives: A Case Against the Patriarchy* (New York: Free Press, 1979), p. 219; Schecter, *Male Violence,* pp. 158–160; Maureen McLeod, "Victim Noncooperation in the Prosecution of Domestic Assault," *Criminology,* 21 (1983): 395, 407; U.S. Commission on Civil Rights, *Under the Thumb,* p. 36.

28. Pagelow, *Woman-Battering,* pp. 63–66; Walker, *Battered Women,* pp. 12, 36; Suzanne Prescott and Carolyn Letko, "Battered Women: A Socio-Psychological Perspective," in Roy, *Battered Women,* pp. 72, 76–78.
29. U.S. Civil Rights Commission, *Under the Thumb,* p. 63; Lisa G. Lerman, "Mediation of Wife Abuse Cases: The Adverse Impact of Informal Dispute Resolution on Women," *Harvard Women's Law Journal,* 7 (1984): 57; Woods, "Litigation," pp. 9–10. For a more positive assessment, see Charles A. Bethel and Linda R. Singer, "Mediation: A New Remedy for Cases of Domestic Violence," *Vermont Law Review,* 7 (1982): 15, 20–32.
30. Civil Rights Commission, *Under the Thumb,* pp. 47, 57; Marjory Fields, "Wife Beating: Government Intervention Policies and Practices," in U.S. Commission on Civil Rights, *Battered Women: Issues of Public Policy* (Washington, D.C.: U.S. Commission on Civil Rights, 1978), p. 20; Pagelow, *Woman-Battering,* pp. 79–82; Laura L. Crites, "Wife Abuse: The Judicial Record," in Laura L. Crites and Winifred L. Hepperle, *Women, the Courts and Equality* (Beverly Hills, Calif.: Sage, 1987).
31. Lynn Hecht Schafran, "Documenting Gender Bias in the Courts: The Task Force Approach," *Judicature,* 70 (1987): 280, 283–284; New York Task Force on Women in the Courts, Summary Report (March 31, 1986), p. 33; id., pp. 33–45; Ellen Goodman, "Equal Rights Award," *Boston Globe,* Aug. 25, 1982, p. A11.
32. See Schecter, *Male Violence,* p. 171 (discussing Illinois study); Tong, *Sex,* pp. 146–148; Elizabeth M. Schneider and Susan B. Jordan, "Representation of Women Who Defend Themselves in Response to Physical or Sexual Assault," *Women's Rights Law Reporter,* 4 (1978): 149, 153, and Elizabeth M. Schneider, "Equal Rights to Trial for Women: Sex Bias in the Law of Self-Defense," *Harvard Civil Rights–Civil Liberties Law Review,* 15 (1980): 623.
33. Walker, *Battered Woman,* pp. 45–51. See also Dobash and Dobash, *Wives;* Davidson, *Conjugal Crime.* For a critical review of such theories, see Wini Breines and Linda Gordon, "The New Scholarship on Family Violence," *Signs,* 8 (1983): 490; Christine Littleton, "Women's Experience and the Problems of Transition: New Perspectives on Battered Women" (unpublished manuscript, UCLA Law School, 1988).
34. Del Martin, *Battered Wives* (San Francisco: Glide, 1976), pp. 121–135; Schecter, *Male Violence;* Davidson, *Conjugal Crime,* pp. 89–90.
35. For discussion of the first battered women's shelter in Chiswick, London,

see Erin Pizzey, *Scream Quietly or the Neighbours Will Hear,* ed. Alison Forbes (Harmoundsworth, Eng.: Penguin, 1974), pp. 9–26; the U.S. movement is chronicled in Schecter, *Male Violence.*

36. See studies discussed in the Attorney General's Task Force on Family Violence, pp. 12–16 (Washington, D.C.: Attorney General's Task Force on Family Violence, 1984). For a summary of changes, see Schecter, *Male Violence;* Lerman, "Model Act," p. 61; Woods, "Litigation."
37. State v. Wanrow, 81 Wash.2d 221, 559 P.2d 548 (1977); Catharine A. MacKinnon, "Toward Feminist Jurisprudence," *Stanford Law Review,* 34 (1982): 703, 731; Elizabeth Schneider, "Describing and Changing Women's Self-Defense Work: The Problem of Expert Testimony on Battering," *Women's Rights Law Reporter,* 4 (1986): 195. For a critique of unreceptive cases, see Ann Jones, *Women Who Kill* (New York: Holt, Rinehart and Winston, 1980), pp. 281–321; and Phyllis L. Crocker, "The Meaning of Equality for Battered Women Who Kill Men in Self-Defense," *Harvard Women's Law Journal,* 8 (1985): 121.
38. Schecter, *Male Violence,* pp. 178–182; Tong, *Sex,* pp. 178–182; Waits, "Battering," pp. 305–326.
39. Senator Gordon Humphrey, quoted in Barbara Sinclair Deckard, *The Women's Movement,* 3rd ed. (New York: Harper and Row, 1983), p. 440, and Pleck, *Domestic Tyranny,* p. 197; Attorney General's Task Force on Family Violence, p. 60; Amendments to Family Violence Prevention and Services Act, Pub. L., no. 98-457, 98 Stat. 1749 (1984), Federal Register 51 (March 10, 1986), p. 8306 (allocating 8.3 million dollars to states); Hearings before Select Committee on Children, Youth, and Families, House of Representatives, 100th Cong., 1st sess. (Washington, D.C.: Government Printing Office, 1988).
40. Richard J. Gelles, *The Violent Home: A Study of Physical Agression Between Husbands and Wives* (Beverly Hills, Calif.: Sage, 1972); Straus, Gelles, and Steinmetz, *Behind Closed Doors,* p. 122; Dobash and Dobash, *Wives,* p. 22; Pagelow, *Woman-Battering,* pp. 15–16, 37–38, 163–169; Walker, *Battered Woman,* pp. 20–34; sources cited in Liane V. Davis, "Battered Women: The Transformation of a Social Problem," *Social Work,* 32 (1987): 306; Waits, "Battering," pp. 286–291.
41. Vivian Berger, "Man's Trial, Woman's Tribulation: Rape Cases in the Courtroom," *Columbia Law Review,* 77 (1977): 1 (quoting slogan). See generally Lorenne M. G. Clark and Debra J. Lewis, *Rape: The Price of Coercive Sexuality* (Toronto: Woman's Press, 1977), pp. 23–25.
42. Zella Luria, Susan Friedman, and Mitchel D. Rose, *Human Sexuality* (New York: John Wiley and Sons, 1987), p. 604 (and sources cited).
43. Andreas Capellanus, *The Art of Courtly Love* (1186), trans. John Jay Parry (New York: Frederick Ungar, 1959), p. 150; Susan Brownmiller, *Against Our Will: Men, Women and Rape* (New York: Bantam, 1976), pp. 230–232; Jennifer Wriggins, "Rape, Racism and the Law," *Harvard Women's Law Journal,* 6 (1983): 103; Marvin E. Wolfgang and Marc Riedel, "Race, Rape, and the Death Penalty," in Duncan Chappell, Robley Geis, and Gilbert Geis, eds., *Forcible Rape: The Crime, The Victim, and the Offender* (New

York: Columbia University Press, 1977); pp. 115, 122; Jacquelyn Dowd Hall, "'The Mind That Burns in Each Body': Women, Rape, and Racial Violence," in Ann Snitow, Christine Stansell, and Sharon Thompson, eds., *Powers of Desire: The Politics of Sexuality* (New York: Monthly Review Press, 1983), p. 328; John D'Emilio and Estelle B. Freedman, *Intimate Matters: A History of Sexuality in America* (New York: Harper and Row, 1988), pp. 30–35, 217 (quoting Senator Cole Blease and noting disparate enforcement of penalties according to the marital status of the victim and social class of the offender). For discussion of lynch mobs for "rape fiends," see Mary Frances Berry and John W. Blassingame, *Long Memory: The Black Experience in America* (New York: Oxford University Press, 1982).

44. See surveys discussed in Susan Estrich, "Rape," *Yale Law Journal,* 95 (1986): 1087, 1163–1166, and *Real Rape* (Cambridge, Mass.: Harvard University Press, 1987), pp. 15–18; Allan Griswold Johnson, "On the Prevalence of Rape in the United States," *Signs,* 6 (1980): 136, 145–146; Diana E. H. Russell, *Rape in Marriage* (New York: Macmillan, 1982), chap. 22; "Half of Rapes Are Unreported, U.S. Study Shows," *Washington Post,* March 25, 1985, p. A9. For discussion of the "not really" phenomena, see Russell, *Rape in Marriage,* pp. 44–48, 207, and MacKinnon, *Feminism Unmodified.* For a discussion of underreporting by minority women, see Kristen Bumiller, "Rape as Legal Symbol: An Essay on Sexual Violence and Racism," *Miami Law Review,* 42 (1987): 75.

45. Tong, *Sex,* pp. 104–105. For national statistics of pre-1980 rates, see Berger, "Man's Trial," p. 6; People v. Rincon-Pineda, 14 Cal. 3d. 864, 874 and n. 3, 538 P.2d 247, 257, and n. 3, 123 Cal. Rptr. 119, 129, and n. 3 (1975). For recent data, see Estrich, "Rape," pp. 1167–1172; Jim Galvin and Kenneth Polk, "Attrition in Case Processing: Is Rape Unique?" *Journal of Research in Crime and Delinquency,* 20 (1983): 126. See also Schur, *Deviance,* pp. 165–166 (8 percent complaint-conviction).

46. Berger, "Man's Trial," p. 8, and cases discussed in Estrich, "Rape," pp. 1116–1117.

47. Model Penal Code 213.6, Comment 6 (Philadelphia: American Law Institute, 1980), p. 429; U.S. Department of Justice, "Forcible Rape: A National Survey of the Response by Prosecutors," discussed in Margaret A. Clemens, "Elimination of the Resistance Requirement and Other Rape Law Reforms: The New York Experience," *Albany Law Review,* 47 (1983): 871, 872, and n. 6.

48. John Henry Wigmore, *Evidence in Trials at Common Law,* James H. Chadbourn rev. (Boston: Little, Brown, 1970), IIa, p. 744 sec. 924a (quoting Karl Menninger); Roberta J. O'Neale, "Court Ordered Psychiatric Examination of a Rape Victim in a Criminal Rape Prosecution—or How Many Times Must a Woman Be Raped?" *Santa Clara Law Review,* 18 (1978): 119; and sources quoted in Estrich, "Rape," pp. 1128–1129. For critical analysis of fantasy theories, see sources cited in Estrich, "Rape"; Berger, "Man's Trial," p. 28; Babcock et al., *Sex Discrimination,* p. 858.

49. Model Penal Code, 213.6.

50. Sir Matthew Hale, *The History of the Pleas of the Crown* (Philadelphia:

Robert H. Small, 1847), I, 635. For a representative endorsement of Hale's view, see Note, "Corroborating Charges of Rape," *Columbia Law Review,* 67 (1967): 1137, 1138. For underreporting and problems for rape complainants, see note 44; Cassie C. Spencer, "Sexual Assault: The Second Victimization," in Laura Crites and Wendy Hepperle, *Women in the Courts* (Beverly Hills, Calif.: Sage, 1987).

51. See lawyers and judges quoted in O'Neale, "Rape Victim," p. 143; judges quoted in Carol Bohmer, "Judicial Attitudes Toward Rape Victims," in Chappell, Geis, and Geis, *Forcible Rape,* pp. 161–164; Harry Kalven and Hans Zeisel, *The American Jury* (Boston: Little, Brown, 1966), pp. 249–254; Luria, Freidman, and Rose, *Sexuality,* p. 597; Gary La Free, *Rape and Criminal Justice: The Social Construction of Sexual Assault* (Belmont, Calif.: Wadsworth, 1989), pp. 95–107, 217–225.

52. People v. Abbot, 19 Wend. 192 (N.Y. Sup.Ct. 1838), cited approvingly in John Henry Wigmore, *Evidence in Trials at Common Law,* rev. Peter Tillers (Boston: Little, Brown, 1983), IA, sec. 62.1. See also Packineau v. U.S., 202 F.2d 681, 685–686 (8th Cir. 1953). For discussion of cross-examinations, see Berger, "Man's Trial," pp. 13–15.

53. Camp v. State, 3 Ga. 417, 422 (1847); Lee v. State, 132 Tenn. 655, 658, 179, S.W. 145, 148 (1915) ("spotless and pure"); Deckard, *The Woman's Movement,* p. 144 (citing CAL J1C 10.06 [1970 Rev.]).

54. Kalven and Zeisel, *Jury,* p. 251; La Free, *Rape,* pp. 95–107; Jane H. Aiken, "Differentiating Sex from *Sex:* The Male Irresistible Impulse," *New York University Review of Law and Social Change,* 12 (1984): 357, 376; Jeanne C. Marsh, Alison Geist, and Nathan Caplan, *Rape and the Limits of Law Reform* (Boston: Auburn House, 1982), p. 61; Babcock et al., *Sex Discrimination,* supplement (1978), p. 206; Shafran, "Gender Bias," p. 284 (discussing Wisconsin cases); New York Task Force, *Report,* p. 73 (discussing blue jeans and judicial censure).

55. Gilbert Geis, "Rape-in-Marriage: Law and Law Reform in England, the United States, and Sweden," *Adelaide Law Review,* 6 (1978): 284, 285 (quoting Hale). See generally Note, "To Have and to Hold: The Marital Rape Exemption and the Fourteenth Amendment" *Harvard Law Review,* 99 (1986): 1255.

56. See comments cited in Frances E. Olsen, "The Myth of State Intervention in the Family," *University of Michigan Journal of Law Reform,* 18 (1985): 835, 840, n. 9; Comment, "Rape and Battery Between Husband and Wife," *Stanford Law Review,* 6 (1954): 719, 725. See also Gilbert Geis and Robley Geis, "Rape Reform: An Appreciative-Critical Review," *American Academy of Psychiatry and the Law,* 6 (1978): 301, 307.

57. Catharine MacKinnon, "Feminism, Marxism, Method and the State: Toward Feminist Jurisprudence," *Signs,* 8 (1983): 635, 649 (discussing normalcy); Russell, *Rape in Marriage,* pp. 112–113 (injury, frequency); David Finkelhorn and Kersti Yllo, *License to Rape: Sexual Abuse of Wives* (New York: Holt, Rinehart and Winston, 1985), p. 6 (frequency); Estrich, "Rape," p. 1172 (injury); Andra Medea and Kathleen Thompson, *Against Rape* (New York: Farrar, Straus and Giroux, 1974); quoted in Russell, *Rape*

in Marriage (continuum), p. 73. See Irene Hanson Frieze, "Investigating the Causes and Consequences of Marital Rape," *Signs,* 8 (1983): 532.

58. Leigh Bienen, "Rape Reform Legislation in the United States: A Look at Some Practical Effects," *Victimology,* 8 (1983): 139, 144; Finkelhorn and Yllo, *Rape,* pp. 137–138, 141; Russell, *Rape in Marriage;* National Clearinghouse on Marital Rape (Berkeley, Calif., 1985), an unpublished fact sheet on marital rape, reporting 210 arrests between 1978–1985, of which 162 involved separations; Geis, "Rape-in-Marriage," p. 297.
59. California state senator Bob Wilson, quoted in Michael D. Freeman, "'But If You Can't Rape Your Wife, Who[m] Can You Rape?': The Marital Rape Exemption Re-examined," *Family Law Quarterly,* 15 (1981): 1; "New Laws Recognizing Marital Rape as a Crime," *New York Times,* Dec. 29, 1984, p. A5; Russell, *Rape in Marriage,* pp. 17–24; Aiken, "Differentiating Sex," p. 377.
60. For discussion of legal changes, see Patricia Searles and Ronald J. Berger, "The Current Status of Rape Reform Legislation: An Examination of State Statutes," *Women's Rights Law Reporter,* 10 (1987): 25; Kenneth Polk, "Rape Reform and Criminal Justice Processing," *Crime and Delinquency,* 31 (1985): 191; Janet Gornick, Martha R. Burt, and Karen J. Pittman, "Structure and Activities of Rape Crisis Centers in the Early 1980s," *Crime and Delinquency,* 31 (1985): 247; Schecter, *Male Violence,* p. 39.
61. March, Geist, and Caplan, *Law Reform,* pp. 52–61; Wallace D. Loh, "The Impact of Common Law and Reform Rape Statutes on Prosecution: An Empirical Study," *Washington Law Review,* 55 (1980): 543; Bienen, "Legislation," p. 147. For discussion of victims, see Kristin Bumiller, *Violence and Intimacy: The Social Construction of Rape* (Baltimore: Johns Hopkins University Press, 1987). For discussion of de facto corroboration requirements, see Estrich, "Rape," pp. 1173–1175; Schur, *Deviance,* pp. 154–155. See generally New York Task Force, *Report,* pp. 73–75.
62. See Jennifer Temkin, "Rape and Law Reform," in Sylvana Tomaselli and Ray Porter, eds., *Rape* (London: Basil Blackwell, 1987).
63. Spencer, "Sexual Assault"; Estrich, "Rape"; Bumiller, "Rape"; and Steven Katz, "Expectation and Desire in the Law of Forcible Rape" (unpublished, 1988).
64. Larry Baron and Murray A. Straus, "Four Theories of Rape: A Macro Sociological Analysis," *Social Problems,* 34 (1987): 467; Peggy Reeves Sanday, "Rape and the Silencing of the Feminine," in Tomaselli and Porter, *Rape;* Medea and Thompson, *Against Rape,* pp. 105–106; Diana E. H. Russell, *Sexual Exploitation: Rape, Child Sexual Abuse, and Workplace Harassment* (Beverly Hills: Sage, 1984), pp. 146–148; Katz, "Expectation" (summarizing studies).
65. Brownmiller, *Against Our Will,* p. 449.
66. Barbara J. Berg, *The Remembered Gate* (New York: Oxford University Press, 1978), p. 179; Elizabeth Pleck, "Feminist Responses to 'Crimes Against Women,' 1868–1896," *Signs,* 8 (1983): 451, 469; D'Emilio and Freedman, *Intimate Matters,* pp. 50–51, 130–135; Kathleen Daly, "The Social Control of Sexuality: A Case Study of the Criminalization of Prosti-

tution in the Progressive Era," in Steven Spitzer and Andrew T. Scull, eds., *Research in Law, Deviants, and Social Control,* vol. 9 (Greenwich, Conn.: JAI Press, 1988), pp. 171–206.

67. J. Wunsch, "Prostitution and Public Policy: From Regulation to Suppression, 1858–1920" (Ph.D. diss., University of Chicago, 1976), p. 101 (quoting Samuel Gross); John F. Decker, *Prostitution: Regulation and Control* (Littleton, Colo.: Rothman, 1979), pp. 37–48; Mark Thomas Connelly, *The Response to Prostitution in the Progressive Era* (Chapel Hill: University of North Carolina Press, 1980), pp. 4–5. Barbara Meil Hobson, *Uneasy Virtue: The Politics of Prostitution and the American Reform Tradition* (New York: Basic Books, 1987), pp. 50–51, 111. For discussion of anthropological data casting doubt on the "inevitability" of prostitution, see Robert W. Ferguson, *The Nature of Vice Control in the Administration of Justice* (St. Paul, Minn.: West, 1974), p. 77.
68. Caroll Smith-Rosenberg, *Disorderly Conduct: Visions of Gender in Victorian America* (New York: Alfred A. Knopf, 1985), pp. 109–128; Berg, *Remembered Gate,* p. 185;
69. Judith R. Walkowitz, *Prostitution and Victorian Society: Women, Class, and the State* (Cambridge: Cambridge University Press, 1980); Wunsch, *Prostitution,* p. 60; R. Wagner, "Virtue Against Vice: A Study of Moral Reformers and Prostitution in the Progressive Era" (Ph.D. diss., University of Wisconsin, 1971), pp. 25–27; D'Emilio and Freedman, *Intimate Matters.*
70. Connelly, *Prostitution,* pp. 3, 50–69, 97; Reginald W. Kauffman, *The House of Bondage,* discussed in Roy Lubove, "The Progressives and the Prostitute," *The Historian,* 24 (1962): 308, 316–318; D'Emilio and Freedman, *Intimate Matters,* p. 135 (Chinese). See also Jane Addams, *A New Conscience and Ancient Evil* (New York: Macmillan, 1912), pp. 108–110; William Thomas Stead, *Satan's Invisible World Displayed; or Despairing Democracy* (London: Clowes, 1898; repr. New York: Arno, 1974).
71. Caminetti v. United States, 242 U.S. 470 (1916). Note, "The White Slave Traffic Act: The Historical Impact of a Criminal Law Policy on Women," *Georgetown Law Journal,* 72 (1984): 1111.
72. Catherine Clinton, *The Other Civil War: American Women in the Nineteenth Century* (New York: Hill and Wang, 1984), p. 62 (quoting Rev. Samuel Akin); Ruth Rosen, *The Lost Sisterhood: Prostitution in America, 1900–1918* (Baltimore: Johns Hopkins University Press, 1982), p. 174; George Bernard Shaw, Preface, *Author's Apology From Mrs. Warren's Profession* (New York: Brentano's Press, 1905).
73. Vice Commission of Chicago, *The Social Evil in Chicago* (Chicago: Vice Commission of Chicago, 1911), p. 329. Connelly, *Prostitution,* pp. 11–44; Lubove, "Progressives," pp. 311–313 (quoting Philadelphia Vice Commission).
74. Leo Kanowitz, *Women and the Law: The Unfinished Revolution* (Albuquerque: University of New Mexico Press, 1969), pp. 16–17; Hobson, *Uneasy Virtue;* Rosen, *Sisterhood,* p. 35.
75. Hobson, *Uneasy Virtue;* Sylvia Pankhurst, quoted in Judith R. Walkowitz, "Male Vice and Female Virtue: Feminism and the Politics of Prostitution in

Nineteenth Century Britain," in Snitow et al., *Powers of Desire,* p. 433; Daly, "Social Control."

76. For discussion of social trends and motivations for seeking prostitutes, see Alfred C. Kinsey, Wardell B. Pomeroy, and Clyde E. Martin, *Sexual Behavior in the Human Male* (Philadelphia: W. B. Saunders, 1948), p. 59; Decker, *Prostitution,* p. 283; Lee H. Bowker, *Women, Crime, and the Criminal Justice System* (Lexington, Mass.: Lexington Books, 1978), p. 156; Harry Benjamin and R. E. L. Masters, *Prostitution and Morality* (New York: Julian Press, 1964). For estimates on numbers and revenues of prostitutes, see Carol Pateman, *The Sexual Contract* (Stanford: Stanford University Press, 1988), p. 190; Raymond I. Parnas, "Legislative Reform of Prostitution Laws: Keeping Commercial Sex Out of Sight and Out of Mind," *Santa Clara Law Review,* 21 (1981): 669, 673; Charles Winick and Paul M. Kinsie, *The Lively Commerce: Prostitution in the United States* (Chicago: Quadrangle, 1971), pp. 4–5.
77. Susan Brownmiller, "What Price Whoring?" *The Village Voice,* Jan. 13, 1972, p. 13 (quoting Holly Tanner); Friedrich Engels, *The Origin of the Family, Private Property and the State* (1884; repr. New York: International Publishers, 1942), p. 63; T. Grace Atkinson, quoted in Gilbert Geis, *Not the Law's Business* (Rockville, Md.: National Institute of Mental Health, 1972), p. 210; Frances Olsen, unpublished talk on prostitution, April 16, 1985 (UCLA Law School). See Pateman, *Sexual Contract,* pp. 189–209.
78. Gail Sheehy, *Hustling* (New York: Delacorte, 1973), pp. 197–199; Kate Millett, *The Prostitution Papers* (New York: Avon, 1973), p. 18; Decker, *Prostitution,* p. 318; National Organization for Women, 1973 Conference Resolutions, reprinted in California NOW, "Working Paper on Prostitution" (July 1983, unpublished), pp. 16–17.
79. Immanuel Kant, *Lectures on Ethics* (1780), trans. Louis Infield (London: Methuen, 1930), pp. 165–166; Nancy Erbe, "Prostitutes: Victims of Men's Exploitation and Abuse," *Law and Inequality: Journal of Theory and Practice,* 2 (1984): 609.
80. Gilbert Geis, *One-Eyed Justice* (New York: Drake, 1974), p. 174; sources cited in Barbara Milman, "New Rules for the Oldest Profession: Should We Change Our Prostitution Laws?" *Harvard Women's Law Journal,* 3 (1980): 1, 29; Mimi H. Silbert and Ayala M. Pines, "Occupational Hazards of Street Prostitutes," *Criminal Justice and Behavior,* 8 (1981): 395, 397; Erbe, "Prostitutes," p. 613; Schur, *Deviance,* p. 168.
81. Erbe, "Prostitutes," p. 611; Kathleen Barry, *Female Sexual Slavery* (Englewood Cliffs, N.J.: Prentice Hall, 1979); Jennifer James, "Answers to the Twenty Questions Most Frequently Asked About Prostitution," in Jennifer James et al., *The Politics of Prostitution* (Seattle: Social Research Associates, 1975), pp. 34–62.
82. Susan Brownmiller, quoted in Tong, *Sex,* p. 57; Model Penal Code, official comment, sec. 251.2; United States v. Betty, 208 U.S. 393, 401 (1908).
83. For discussion of cohabitation and homosexuality, see Chapter 7; Decker, *Prostitution,* p. 40 (quoting Saint Augustine); Gordon Rahray Taylor, *Sex in History* (New York: Vanguard, 1954), p. 21. For analogous contemporary

views, see generally Decker, *Prostitution,* and David A. J. Richards, "Commercial Sex and the Rights of the Person: A Moral Argument for the Decriminalization of Prostitution," *University of Pennsylvania Law Review,* 127 (1979): 1195. For poll data, see Parnas, "Legislative Reform," p. 671, n. 12; M. Anne Jennings, "The Victim as Criminal: A Consideration of California's Prostitution Law," *California Law Review,* 64 (1976): 1235, 1250; Milman, "New Rules," p. 45.

84. Decker, *Prostitution*, pp. 165–166; Paul H. Gebhard, "Misperceptions About Female Prostitutes: Medical Aspects of Human Sexuality," 3 (1969): 29–30, discussed in Geis, *Not the Law's Business,* pp. 176–177; Jennifer Jones, "Motivations for Entrance into Prostitution," in Laura Crites, ed., *The Female Offender* (Lexington, Mass.: Lexington Books, 1976); Geis, *One-Eyed Justice,* pp. 175–181; Sheehy, *Hustling,* p. 104.
85. See sources cited in B. J. George, Jr. "Legal, Medical and Psychiatric Considerations in the Control of Prostitution," *Michigan Law Review,* 60 (1962): 717 n. 6; "Recommendations and Report to the American Bar Associations House of Delegates by the Section of Individual Rights and Responsibilities Concerning Prostitution and Solicitation," *Human Rights,* 4 (1974): 77, 79.
86. For discussion of organized crime, see U.S. President's Commission on Law Enforcement and Administration of Justice, *The Challenge of Crime in a Free Society* (Washington, D.C.: U.S. Government Printing Office, 1967), p. 189, and Helen Reynolds, *The Economics of Prostitution* (Springfield, Ill.: Charles C. Thomas Press, 1986), p. 123. For zoning and harassment remedies, see Milman, "Prostitution"; Marilyn G. Haft, "Legal Arguments: Prostitution Laws and the Constitution," in James, *Politics of Prostitution,* p. 30. For problems regarding zoning, see Hobson, *Uneasy Virtue,* pp. 225–230.
87. James, "Twenty Questions"; Parnas, *Legislative Reform,* p. 671; Ex parte Carey, 57 Cal. App. 297, 207 P. 271 (Dist. Ct. App. 1922); NOW, "Prostitution," p. 7; Commonwealth v. King, 374 Mass. 5, 372 N.E. 2d 196 (1977).
88. Decker, *Prostitution,* pp. 90, 11–114, 142–181; Reynolds, *Economics,* pp. 86–124.
89. Decker, *Prostitution,* pp. 146–149; Winick and Kinsie, *Lively Commerce,* pp. 287–288; Hobson, *Uneasy Virtue,* p. 232; James, "Twenty Questions"; Reynolds, *Economics.*
90. Hobson, *Uneasy Virtue,* pp. 225–233; Margaret Jane Radin, "Market-Inalienability," *Harvard Law Review,* 100, (1987): 1849, 1921–1924.
91. Andrea Dworkin, *Pornography: Men Possessing Women* (New York: Putnam, 1981), pp. 199–200; Gloria Steinem, "Erotica and Pornography: A Clear and Present Difference," in Laura Lederer, ed., *Take Back the Night: Women and Pornography* (New York: William Morrow, 1980), p. 35. For critiques of the pornography-erotica distinction, see Dworkin, Preface, *Pornography*, and Ellen Willis, "Feminism, Moralism, and Pornography," in Snitow et al., *Powers of Desire,* pp. 462, 463. For a comprehensive discussion of pornography's etymological roots, which raises questions about

conventional linkages with prostitution, see Walter Kendrick, *The Secret Museum: Pornography in Modern Culture* (New York: Viking, 1987), pp. 1–32.

92. Edward Donnerstein, Daniel Linz, and Steven Penrod, *The Question of Pornography* (New York: Free Press, 1987), pp. 145–146; D. F. Barber, *Pornography and Society* (London: Skilton, 1972), Kendrick, *Secret Museum.*
93. Paul S. Boyer, *Purity in Print: The Vice-Society Movement and Book Censorship in America* (New York: Charles Scribner's Sons, 1968), p. 21 (quoting Comstock); Anthony Comstock, *Traps for the Young* (New York: Funk and Wagnalls, 1883); repr., ed. Robert Bremner (Cambridge, Mass.: Harvard University Press, 1967), p. 133; Felice Flannery Lewis, *Literature, Obscenity and Law* (Carbondale: Southern Illinois University Press, 1976), pp. 1–45.
94. Boyer, *Purity in Print,* p. 17 (quoting Julia Ward Howe); D'Emilio and Freedman, *Intimate Matters,* pp. 157–162.
95. L.R. 3 Q.B. 360, 371 (1868); Boyer, *Purity in Print,* p. 21.
96. Robert W. Haney, *Comstockery in America: Patterns of Censorship and Control* (Boston: Beacon, 1960), p. 66 (quoting Postmaster General Arthur E. Summerfield). See generally D'Emilio and Freedman, *Intimate Matters.*
97. D'Emilio and Freedman, *Intimate Matters,* pp. 280–283; Miller v. California, 413 U.S. 15 (1973).
98. Jacobellis v. Ohio, 378 U.S. 184, 197 (1964) (Stewart, J., concurring).
99. Catharine A. MacKinnon, "Not a Moral Issue," *Yale Law & Policy Review,* 2 (1984): 325 and sources cited in note 106.
100. See Stanley v. Georgia, 394 U.S. 557 (1969). For estimates on the pornography industry, see Catharine A. MacKinnon, "Pornography, Civil Rights and Speech," *Harvard Civil Rights–Civil Liberties Law Review,* 20 (1985): 30–31, n. 54; Carole S. Vance, "The Meese Commission on the Road," *Nation,* Aug. 2 and 9, 1986, pp. 80–81.
101. The Indianapolis, Indiana, May 1, 1984, ordinance provides in part: "Pornography shall mean the sexually explicit subordination of women, graphically depicted, whether in pictures or in words, that also includes one or more of the following: (1) women are presented as sexual objects who enjoy pain or humiliation; or (2) women are presented as sexual objects who experience sexual pleasure in being raped; or (3) women are presented as sexual objects tied up or cut up or mutilated or bruised or physically hurt, or as dismembered or truncated or fragmented or severed into body parts; or (4) women are presented as being penetrated by objects or animals; or (5) women are presented in scenarios of degradation, injury, abasement, torture, shown as filthy or inferior, bleeding, bruised, or hurt in a context that makes these conditions sexual; and (6) women are presented as sexual objects for domination, conquest, violation, exploitation, or possession, or use, or through postures or positions of servility or submission or display.

    "The use of men, children or transsexuals in the place of women in paragraphs (1) through (6) above shall also constitute pornography under this section.

102. President's Commission on Obscenity and Pornography, *Report* (Washington, D.C.: U.S. Government Printing Office, 1970), p. 27. For critiques of the Commission's findings, see, for example, Irene Diamond, "Pornography and Repression: A Reconsideration of 'Who' and 'What,'" in Lederer, *Take Back the Night,* pp. 187–203, Pauline B. Bart and Margaret Jozsa, "Dirty Books, Dirty Films and Dirty Data," in Lederer, *Take Back the Night,* pp. 204–238, and Donnerstein et al., *Pornography,* pp. 23–27.
103. Attorney General's Commission on Pornography, *Final Report* (Washington, D.C.: U.S. Department of Justice, 1986).
104. Vance, "Meese Commission," pp. 65, 76–82; Donnerstein et al., *Pornography.* See Brief of Feminist Anticensorship Task Force, *Amicus Curiae* in American Booksellers Association v. Hudnut, 771 F.2d 323 (7th Cir. 1985); Robin West, "The Feminist-Conservative Anti-Pornography Alliance and the 1986 Attorney General's Commission on Pornography Report," *American Bar Foundation Research Journal* (1987): 681, 685–686 (Symposium); Donald Downs, "The Attorney General's Commission and the New Politics of Pornography," ibid.: 641, 657–672; Daniel Linz, Steven D. Penrod, and Edward Donnerstein, "The Attorney General's Commission on Pornography: The Gaps Between Findings and Facts," ibid.: 713.
105. Russell, *Rape in Marriage,* pp. 84, 228; testimony reviewed in Paul Brest and Amy Vandenberg, "Politics, Feminism, and the Constitution: the Anti-Pornography Movement in Minneapolis," *Stanford Law Review,* 39 (1987): 611–661, and MacKinnon, "Civil Rights," pp. 55–58.
106. See studies reviewed in Neil M. Malamuth and Edward Donnerstein, *Pornography and Sexual Aggression* (Orlando, Fla.: Academic Press, 1984), pp. 589–602, and sources cited in notes 104 and 105.
107. See Malamuth and Donnerstein, *Pornography;* Linz, Penrod, and Donnerstein, "Gap"; Sunstein, "Pornography."
108. Brest and Vandenberg, "Minneapolis," p. 623 (quoting MacKinnon). See also Elizabeth Spahn, "On Sex and Violence," *New England Law Review,* 20 (1985): 629, 638–642; Eric Hoffman, "Feminism, Pornography, and Law," *University of Pennsylvania Law Review,* 133 (1985): 497.
109. Lisa Duggan and Ann Snitow, "Pornography Is About Images, Not Power," *Newsday,* Sept. 26, 1984 (quoting Suffolk County legislator); West, "Feminist-Conservative Alliance," pp. 698–702.
110. American Booksellers Association v. Hudnut, 771 F.2d 323 (7th Cir. 1985), *aff'd sub nom.* Hudnut v. American Booksellers Association, 106 S. Ct. 1172, *reh'g denied* 106 S. Ct. 1664 (1986). See Robert C. Post, "Cultural Heterogeneity and Law: Pornography, Blasphemy and the First Amendment," *California Law Review,* 76 (1988): 297; and Geoffrey R. Stone, "Comment: Anti-Pornography Legislation as Viewpoint-Discrimination," *Harvard Journal of Law and Public Policy,* 9 (1986): 461.
111. Willis, "Feminism," p. 462; Alice Echols, "The New Feminism of Yin and Yang," in Snitow, *Powers of Desire,* p. 446; Feminist Anti-Censorship Task Force, *Amicus* Brief, p. 131.
112. Willis, "Feminism," p. 467.

113. Commission, *Report,* II, 1505–1506, 1530, 1534, 1550–1551, 1557. See also Sunstein, "Pornography."
114. See Sunstein, "Pornography," pp. 609–617; Davis, "New Politics"; "The War Against Pornography," *Newsweek,* March 18, 1985, p. 58; Feminist Anti-Censorship Task Force Brief, pp. 19–21; Schur, *Deviant,* p. 179.
115. MacKinnon, "Civil Rights," p. 63; see also Dworkin, Preface to *Pornography,* and Kathleen Barry, "Beyond Pornography; From Defensive Politics to Creating a Vision," in Lederer, *Take Back the Night,* pp. 307, 310.

11. Association and Assimilation

1. Plessy v. Ferguson, 163 U.S. 537 (1896). A more extended version of this chapter with further supporting authority appeared in a 1986 symposium on the First Amendment. See Deborah L. Rhode, "Association and Assimilation," *Northwestern Law Review,* 81 (1986): 106.
2. Mississippi University for Women v. Hogan, 458 U.S. 718, 745 (1982) (Powell, J., dissenting). See Michael M. Burns, "The Exclusion of Women from Influential Men's Clubs: The Inner Sanctum and the Myth of Full Equality," *Harvard Civil Rights–Civil Liberties Law Review,* 18 (1983): 321, 324, n. 6 (quoting Robert Strub that the Los Angeles California Club has "no restrictions on any member except that it's a men's club. I don't consider that discrimination"); brief for the Appellee, Roberts v. Jaycees, 468 U.S. 609 (1984), p. 15 ("the fact that a few appellants do not like the [Jaycees'] policy does not convert a benign exclusion into an invidious discrimination"); "Free Association Right Said Unclear After Rotary Ruling," *Los Angeles Daily Journal,* May 26, 1987, p. 1 (quoting Bohemian President Harvey Scott: "We don't discriminate against anybody. We are a men's club, however").
3. Compare Richard Wasserstrom, *Philosophy and Social Issues, Five Studies* (Notre Dame, Ind.: Notre Dame Press, 1980), and Elizabeth H. Wolgast, *Equality and the Rights of Women* (Ithaca, N.Y.: Cornell University Press, 1980). See also chapter 12.
4. See sources cited in Rhode, "Association," p. 107. Even Hell's Angels has been subject to challenge. "The Other Reporter," *California* (February 1988), p. 6.
5. For discussion of pink frocks and tutus, see sources cited in Rhode, "Association," p. 8. See also Charlotte Low, "One 'Sexism' Excuse That Won't Wash," *Los Angeles Times,* Jan. 29, 1984, part IV, p. 5 (prohibiting male clubs "is on a par with forbidding men to . . . drink with their buddies or trade baseball statistics . . . [W]omen shouldn't delude themselves . . . that men's clubs are one of the burning civil-rights issues of our time").
6. See Burns, "Men's Clubs," p. 330, n. 29, and discussion in the text accompanying notes 25–28. See also J. Miller McPherson and Lynn Smith-Lovin, "Sex Segregation in Voluntary Associations," *American Sociological Review,* 51 (1986): 61 (finding that over half of all surveyed voluntary associations were sex-segregated).

7. Alexis de Tocqueville, *Democracy in America,* ed. Phillips Bradley (New York: Alfred A. Knopf, 1945), I, 191. See Michael Banton, "Voluntary Associations: Anthropological Aspects," *International Encyclopedia of the Social Sciences,* vol. 16 (New York: MacMillan and Free Press, 1968), pp. 357–362.
8. See sources cited in Constance Smith and Anne Freedman, *Voluntary Associations: Perspectives on the Literature* (Cambridge, Mass.: Harvard University Press, 1972), pp. 16–22. Although estimates of participation vary, most evidence suggests that associational activity is concentrated among a minority of the population and is correlated with income, education, and occupational prestige. See also Murray Hausknecht, *The Joiners: A Sociological Description of Voluntary Association Membership in the United States* (New York: Bedminster, 1962), p. 84. For discussion of the range of groups, see, for example, Arthur M. Schlesinger, "Biography of a Nation of Joiners" in *American Historical Review,* 50 (1944): 1, 10; Grant McConnell, "The Public Values of the Private Association," in J. Roland Penrock, and John W. Chapman, *Voluntary Associations,* Nomos XI (New York: Atherton, 1969), p. 147.
9. Thomas Jefferson, quoted in Martin Gruberg, *Women in American Politics* (Oshkosh, Wis.: Academia Press, 1968), p. 4. The rigidity of the public-private boundary should not be overstated. See Chapter 1.
10. See Karen J. Blair, *The Clubwoman As Feminist: True Womanhood Redefined, 1868–1914* (New York: Holmes and Meier, 1980). For discussion of the social club movement in the nineteenth and early twentieth centuries, see Barbara J. Berg, *The Remembered Gate: Origins of American Feminism* (New York: Oxford University Press, 1981), pp. 145–175. Some estimates suggest that by 1949 America boasted some 29,000 civic, professional, and luncheon groups, about a third of which were all female. Smith and Freedman, *Voluntary Associations,* p. 196. Although the remaining two-thirds were not classified by sex, the categories used (for example, luncheon, fraternal) suggest that a substantial percentage were all-male.
11. Gerder Lerner, *The Majority Finds Its Past* (New York: Oxford University Press, 1979), pp. 73, 83–108; See Elizabeth Davis, *Lifting as They Climb: The National Association of Colored Women* (Washington, D.C.: National Association of Colored Women, 1933); Gerda Lerner, "Early Community of Black Club Women," *Journal of Negro History,* 59 (1974): 158; Jeanne L. Noble, *Beautiful, Also, Are the Souls of My Black Sisters: A History of the Black Woman in America* (Englewood Cliffs, N.J.: Prentice-Hall, 1978).
12. Blair, *Clubwoman,* p. 21, n. 23, and p. 33, n. 66 (quoting Jane Croly); Ella Giles Ruddy, ed., *The Mother of Clubs: Caroline M. Seymour Severance* (Los Angeles: Baumgart, 1906), p. 42 (quoting Caroline Severance).
13. Blair, *Clubwoman* (quoting *Boston Transcript*), pp. 34, 70.
14. Estelle Freedman, "Separatism as Strategy: Female Institution Building and American Feminism, 1870–1930," *Feminist Studies,* 5 (1979): 512; Carroll Smith-Rosenberg, "Beauty, the Beast, and the Militant Woman: A Case Study in Sex Roles and Social Stress in Jacksonian America," in Nancy Cott

and Elizabeth Pleck, eds., *A Heritage of Her Own: Toward a New Social History of Women* (New York: Simon and Schuster, 1979), pp. 197–221.

15. See Moose Lodge No. 107 v. Irvis, 407 U.S. 163 (1972) (granting liquor license to a racially discriminatory club failed to constitute state action). For a critical assessment of state action theory, see Ira Nerken, "A New Deal for the Protection of Fourteenth Amendment Rights: Challenging the Doctrinal Base of the Civil Rights Cases and the State Action Theory," *Harvard Civil Rights–Civil Liberties Law Review,* 12 (1977): 297. Compare race-discrimination statutes and cases such as: I.R.C. 501(1) (West Supp. 1986); Coit v. Green, 404 U.S. 997 (1971); Bob Jones University v. United States, 461 U.S. 574 (1983); and Jackson v. Statler Foundation, 496 F.2d 623 (2d Cir. 1973), *cert. denied,* 420 U.S. 927 (1975), with sex-discrimination cases such as: Junior Chamber of Commerce v. United States Jaycees, 495 F.2d 883 (10th Cir. 1974), *cert. denied,* 419 U.S. 1026 (1974); Stearns v. Veterans of Foreign Wars, 394 F.Supp. 138 (D. D.C. 1975), *aff'd without opinion,* 527 F.2d 1387 (D.C. Cir. 1976), *cert. denied,* 429 U.S. 822 (1976).
16. 42 U.S.C. Sec. 2000a (1976); Ruth Bader Ginsburg, "Women as Full Members of the Club: An Evolving American Ideal," *Human Rights,* 6 (1975): 1, 15; Lisa Lerman and Annette Sanderson, "Discrimination in Access to Public Places: A Survey of State and Federal Public Accommodations Laws," *New York University Review of Law and Social Change,* 7 (1978): 215, 264.
17. Roberts v. United States Jaycees, 468 U.S. 609, 620–621 (1984); Board of Directors of Rotary International v. Rotary Club of Duarte, 481 U.S. 537 (1987).
18. New York State Club Association v. City of New York, 108 S. Ct. 2225 (1988).
19. See cases cited in Rhode, "Association," p. 117, n. 56.
20. See Jessie Bernard, *The Sex Game* (Englewood Cliffs, N.J.: Prentice Hall, 1968), p. 47 (noting different sexual dynamics); Chai R. Feldblum, Nancy Fredman Krent, and Virginia G. Watkin, "Legal Challenges to All-Female Organizations," *Harvard Civil Rights–Civil Liberties Law Review,* 21 (1986): 172, 175–179. For a general discussion of privacy interests, see sources cited in Ferdinand Schoeman, *Philosophical Dimensions of Privacy: An Anthology* (Cambridge: Cambridge University Press, 1984).
21. Roberts v. United States Jaycees, 468 U.S. 628.
22. See Chapter 12; brief of *Amicus Curiae,* American Civil Liberties Union and Minnesota Civil Liberties Union, in Roberts v. Jaycees, p. 15. See also briefs cited in Rhode, "Association," p. 120, n. 69.
23. See, for example, Reed v. Reed, 404 U.S. 71 (1971); Los Angeles Department of Water and Power v. Manhart, 435 U.S. 702 (1978), discussed in Chapter 5.
24. See sources cited in Burns, "Men's Clubs," pp. 327–329; brief of *Amicus Curiae,* National Organization for Women, in Roberts v. Jaycees, p. 21; Edith Lynton, *Behind Closed Doors: Discrimination by Private Clubs, A Report Based on City Commission on Human Rights Hearings* (New York: New York City Commission on Human Rights, 1975). Examples of private

clubs as locales for political discussions are summarized in G. William Domhoff, *The Bohemian Grove and Other Retreats: A Study of Ruling Class Cohesiveness* (New York: Harper and Row, 1974); David Alpern, "Clubs: The Ins and Outs," *Newsweek,* Jan. 10, 1977, pp. 18–19.

25. Heart of Atlanta Motel v. United States, 379 U.S. 241, 250 (1964).
26. Richard Wasserstrom, "Racism, Sexism and Preferential Treatment: An Approach to the Topic," *UCLA Law Review,* 24 (1977): 581, 608.
27. Lynton, *Behind Closed Doors,* p. 25; Burns, "Men's Clubs," p. 343; Perry Garfinkle, "Male Club Ponders the Unknown: Women" *New York Times,* Nov. 25, 1987, p. 19; Calvin Trillin, "U.S. Journal: Tampa, Florida: Four People Who Do Not Lunch at the University Club," *New Yorker,* April 11, 1977, p. 101; "Blackballed: Union League Bars Women," *Philadelphia Inquirer,* Jan. 12, 1983, pp. 1-A, 6-A; Lynn Hecht Schafran, "Private Clubs (Women Need Not Apply)," *Foundation News,* 23 (1982): 3, 7; Alpern, "Clubs," p. 19.
28. Brief of *Amicus Curiae,* Boy Scouts of America, in Roberts v. Jaycees, p. 10; see sources quoted in Rhode, "Association," p. 123.
29. Thomas F. Pettigrew and Joanne Martin, "Shaping the Organization Context for Black American Inclusion," *Journal of Social Issues,* 43 (1987): 41.
30. Compare Internal Revenue Code, section 501(C)(7) and section 501(i). Clubs that discriminate on the basis of race, color, or religion are not entitled to exemption. Catharine M. Goodwin, "Challenging the Private Club: Sex Discrimination Plaintiffs Banned at the Door," *Southwestern University Law Review,* 13 (1982): 255, n. 122.
31. See H.R. 875, 99th Congress, Equal Access to Public Accommodation Act of 1985, which would amend Title II of the 1964 Civil Rights Act to include sex discrimination as a prohibited practice in places of accommodation. The Act defines public accommodation to include any private associations used to a "substantial degree" for business purposes and defines "substantial degree" to include associations that have 20 percent of their gross receipts paid by trades or businesses. For a fuller discussion of such approaches and estimates of revenue, see Burns, "Men's Clubs," p. 219, Goodwin, "Sex Discrimination Plaintiffs."
32. See examples and sources cited in Rhode,"Association," p. 126.
33. "As Exclusive Clubs Open Their Doors, Women Draw Back," *New York Times,* Sept. 14, 1988, p. B2 (noting small numbers of women admitted).
34. Elaine Kendall, *Peculiar Institutions: An Informal History of the Seven Sisters' Colleges* (New York: G. P. Putnam's Sons, 1975), pp. 9, 15. See Mabel Newcomer, *A Century of Higher Education for American Women* (New York: Harper and Row, 1959), pp. 5–10. The most comprehensive history of women's education during this period is Thomas Woody, *A History of Women's Education in the United States* (New York: Octagon Books, 1929; 1974). For a good overview of recent literature, see Sally Schwager, "Educating Women in America," *Signs,* 12 (1987): 333; Linda K. Kerber, "'Why Should Girls be Learn'd and Wise?': Two Centuries of Higher Education for Women as Seen Through the Unfinished Work of Alice

Mary Baldwin," in John Mack Faragher and Florence Howe, *Women and Higher Education in American History* (New York: W. W. Norton, 1988), pp. 18, 21.

35. Nancy Woloch, *Women and the American Experience* (New York: Alfred A. Knopf, 1984), p. 276; Rosalind Rosenberg, *Beyond Separate Spheres: Intellectual Roots of Modern Feminism* (New Haven: Yale University Press, 1982).

36. Nancy F. Cott, *The Bonds of Womanhood: "Woman's Sphere" in New England, 1780–1835* (New Haven: Yale University Press, 1977), p. 115; Woody, *Woman's Education,* I, 329–459, 464, 492; Patricia Alberg Graham, "Expansion and Exclusion: A History of Women in Higher Education," *Signs,* 3 (1978): 759, 764. For statistics on colleges, see Newcomer, *Higher Education,* pp. 19–20; Louise Schutz Boas, *Woman's Education Begins: The Rise of the Women's Colleges* (Norton, Mass.: Wheaton College Press, 1935), p. 256. For a discussion of black women's experience, see Lerner, *Majority Finds Its Past,* pp. 67–76.

37. Jacqueline Jones, *Labor of Love, Labor of Sorrow: Black Women, Work, and the Family, from Slavery to the Present* (New York: Vintage, 1986); St. Clair Drake, "The Black University in the American Social Order," *Daedelus,* 100 (1971): 833; Jean Noble, *The Negro Woman's College Education* (New York: Columbia University Press, 1956); Linda M. Perkins, "The Education of Black Women in the Nineteenth Century," in Faragher and Howe, *Women and Higher Education,* pp. 64, 75–78; Rosalind Rosenberg, "The Limits of Access: The History of Coeducation in America," in ibid., pp. 107, 113.

38. See generally Henry Maudsley, "Sex in Mind and Education," in Louise Michele Newman, *Men's Ideas/Women's Realities* (New York: Pergamon, 1985), p. 79; Woody, *Woman's Education,* II, 151, 153 (quoting Noah Webster); Edward Clarke, *Sex in Education* (New York: Houghton Mifflin, 1873), pp. 31–60; Barbara Ehrenreich and Deirdre English, *For Her Own Good: 150 Years of the Experts' Advice to Women* (Garden City, N.Y.: Anchor, 1978), pp. 113–117; Carroll Smith-Rosenberg, *Disorderly Conduct* (New York: Alfred A. Knopf, 1984), pp. 259–260.

39. Liva Baker, *I'm Radcliffe! Fly Me!* (New York: Macmillan, 1976), p. 71. For discussion of marriage and reproductive roles, see Ehrenreich and English, *For Her Own Good,* p. 15; Sheila Rothman, *Woman's Proper Place* (New York: Basic Books, 1978), p. 46; and Kendall, *Institutions,* pp. 127–129.

40. Catherine E. Beecher, *Educational Reminiscences* (1874), p. 184, 78–79 (quoting Greely).

41. Woody, *Women's Education,* I, 30, II, 217; Benjamin Rush, "Thoughts upon Female Education, Accommodated to the Present State of Society, Manners, and Government in the United States of America," in Frederick Rudolph, ed., *Essays on Education in the Early Republic* (Cambridge, Mass.: Harvard University Press, 1965), pp. 27–40; Rothman, *Women's Proper Place,* p. 39 (quoting Vassar president John Raymond). Founder Sophia

Smith also hoped that educated women would "sweep the filth out of literature." Adele Simmons, "Education and Ideology in Nineteenth-Century America: The Response of Educational Institutions to the Changing Role of Women," in Bernice A. Carroll, ed., *Liberating Women's History: Theoretical and Critical Essays* (Urbana: University of Illinois Press, 1976), pp. 114, 118.

42. See Newman, *Men's Ideas,* p. 87; Barbara Miller Solomon, *In the Company of Educated Women: A History of Women and Higher Education in America* (New Haven: Yale University Press, 1985), pp. 53–59; Catherine Clinton, *The Other Civil War* (New York: Hill and Wang, 1984), pp. 77–78, 82–91, 127–130. For a discussion of Lynn White's proposals to replace courses in post-Kantian philosophy with preparation of well-marinated shish kebab, see Chapter 2, and Lynn White, *Educating Our Daughters* (New York: Harper, 1950), pp. 77–78, 82–91.
43. M. Carey Thomas, "Education for Women and Men," in Barbara M. Cross, ed., *Educated Women in America* (New York: Teachers College Press, 1965), p. 145; Elizabeth Schneider, "Our Failures Only Marry: Bryn Mawr and the Failures of Feminism," in Judith Stacey, Susan Bereaud, and Joan Daniels, eds., *And Jill Came Tumbling After: Sexism in American Education* (New York: Dell, 1974), pp. 279–292; Christopher Jencks and David Reisman, *The Academic Revolution* (Garden City, N.Y.: Doubleday, 1968), pp. 291–311, 306 (paraphrasing Diana Trilling).
44. Jencks and Reisman, *Revolution,* p. 309; Elizabeth Langland and Walter R. Gove, "Introduction," to *A Feminist Perspective in the Academy: The Difference It Makes* (New Haven: Soundings, 1981). See Adrienne Rich, "Toward a Women-Centered University," *On Lies, Secrets, and Silence* (New York: W. W. Norton, 1979), pp. 134–135; Barbara Sicherman, "The Invisible Women," in Warren Todd Furniss and Patricia Albjerg Graham, eds., *Women in Higher Education* (Washington, D.C.: American Council on Education, 1974), p. 156.
45. Helen Lefkowitz Horowitz, *Alma Mater: Design and Experience in the Women's Colleges from Their Nineteenth-Century Beginning to the 1930s* (New York: Alfred A. Knopf, 1984), pp. 59–60; Baker, *Fly Me,* p. 193; Kendall, *Institutions,* pp. 78–79; Solomon, *Educated Women,* pp. 111–113.
46. James Rowland Angell, "Some Reflections on the Reaction from Coeducation," in Newman, *Men's Ideas,* pp. 87, 93; and sources cited in Rhode, "Association," p. 134, nn. 130, 131.
47. United States Bureau of Education, quoted in Sara A. Burstall, *The Education of Girls in the United States* (New York: Arno, 1971; repr. of 1894 ed.), pp. 162–163; Woody, *Women's Education,* II, 264–265, 279–280, 290, 297; John H. Phillips, "Co-Education and Equal Suffrage," *American Education Review,* 34 (1913): 316; Horowitz, *Alma Mater,* pp. 232, 280 (quoting Calvin Coolidge).
48. For discussion of the financial advantages of coeducation, see sources cited in Woody, *Women's Education,* II, 257–262; Burstall, *Education of Girls,* p. 163. Disparities in resources between men's and women's schools are reviewed in Harris, "The Second Sex in Academe," *AAUP Bulletin,* 56

(1970): 283, 293–294; For discussion of Spellman and Bennett, see Solomon, *Educated Woman,* pp. 144–145.

49. Nathan Pusey, quoted in Ann Sutherland Harris, "Second Sex in Academe," p. 283; Dorothy Zinberg, "College: When the Future Becomes the Present," in Ruth Kundsin, ed., *Women and Success* (New York: William Morrow, 1974), p. 131; Newcomer, *Higher Education,* p. 37 (citing statistics), note 3. Since the Office of Education has not tracked the number of sex-segregated elementary and secondary schools, national statistics are more fragmentary. See statistics in *Congressional Record* 118 (Feb. 28, 1972), pp. 5804–5806.
50. See Comments of Senators Tower and Bentsen, *Congressional Record* 118 (Feb. 28, 1972), 558, 114–115, and 20 U.S.C.A. 1703(a) and 1681(a)(5). Title IX included a waiver for public undergraduate institutions that had traditionally and continually maintained single-sex admission policies. Certain sections of the Equal Educational Opportunities Act that apply to elementary and secondary education omit sex from the list of prohibited discriminations; other sections include sex. For discussion of these statutory ambiguities, see Vorchheimer v. School District of Philadelphia, 532 F.2d 880 (3d Cir., 1976), *aff'd* by an equally divided Court, 430 U.S. 703 (1977). See also Caren Dubnoff, "Does Gender Equality Always Imply Gender Blindness? The Status of Single-Sex Education for Women," *West Virginia Law Review,* 86 (1984): 295, 306, 309. In Grove City College v. Bell, 465 U.S. 555 (1984), the Supreme Court interpreted Title IX to apply only to programs actually receiving federal money, not to all parts of an institution receiving such funds. Congress subsequently reversed that holding by passage of the Civil Rights Restoration Act of 1988.
51. Heaton v. Bristol, 317 S.W.2d 86, 100 (Tex. Civ. Ap. 1958 A. P. 1958), *cert. denied,* 359 U.S. 230 (1959); Allred v. Heaton, 336 S.W.2d 251, 261 (Tex. Civ. App.), *cert. denied,* 364 U.S. 517 (1960); Williams v. McNair 316 F.Supp. 134, 136 n. 3 (D. S.C. 970), *aff'd mem.* 401 U.S. 951 (1971). See also Kirstein v. Rector and Visitors of University of Virginia, 309 F.Supp. 184 (E.D. Va. 1970), in which a three-judge court declined to strike down sex segregation by the University of Virginia, in part because one of the state's all-male campuses was "military in character" and the court was unprepared to contemplate requiring women to "wear uniforms and be taught to bear arms." For other decisions upholding single-sex schools, see Rhode, "Association," p. 137.
52. Vorchheimer v. School District of Philadelphia, 532 F.2d 880 (3d Cir., 1976), *aff'd by an equally divided Court,* 430 U.S. 703 (1977). See R. R. Dale, *Mixed or Single-Sex School* (London: Routledge and Kegan Paul, 1974), I, 21-25, 38–40; II, 22, 50, 198–203; III, 256, 293; Rhode, "Association"; *New York Times,* Oct. 19, 1976, p. 20 (discussing plaintiff's record in math and sciences). Compare Newberg v. Board of Public Education of Philadelphia, 9 Pa. 536, 565–566, 570 n. 124 (1983), *aff'd on other grounds,* 478 A.2d 1352 (1984).
53. Mississippi University for Women v. Hogan, 458 U.S. 718, 745, n. 18 (1982); brief of *Amicus Curiae,* National Women's Law Center et al., in Mississippi University for Women v. Hogan, pp. 22–23.

54. 458 U.S. at 744, n. 15, brief of National Women's Law Center et al., pp. 22–23 (any value in sex-segregated learning environments had been compromised by MUW's policy of permitting male auditors).
55. See 458 U.S. at 738–739 (Powell, J., dissenting), brief for Petitioner in Mississippi University for Women v. Hogan, pp. 12–19; Alexander W. Astin, *Four Critical Years* (San Francisco: Jossey-Bass, 1977), pp. 232–233; *Men and Women Learning Together: A Study of College Students in the Late '70s* (Providence: Brown University, 1980); Mirra Komarovsky, *Women in College* (New York: Basic Books, 1985), pp. 152, 154, 307; and sources cited in Roberta M. Hall and Bernice R. Sandler, *Out of the Classroom: A Chilly Campus Climate for Women?* (Washington, D.C.: Project on the Status and Education of Women; Association of American Colleges, 1984), pp. 3–4; Dubnoff, "Gender Equality," pp. 323–325; *A Study of the Learning Environment at Women's Colleges* (Washington, D.C.: Women's College Coalition, 1981).
56. See 458 U.S. at 738 (Powell, J. dissenting); Elizaeth M. Tidball, "Perspective on Academic Women and Affirmative Action," *Educational Record,* 54 (Spring 1973): 130, 132–133.
57. Sharp et al., *Learning Environment;* for critiques of the Tidball research, see, for example, Mary J. Oates and Susan Williamson, "Women's Colleges and Women Achievers," *Signs: Journal of Women, Culture and Society,* 3 (1978): 795. For subsequent research finding no statistically significant achievement differences between 1960 and 1980, see Joy K. Rice and Annette Hemmings, "Women's Colleges and Women Achievers: An Update," *Signs,* 13 (1988): 546, 555–556. It is also unclear whether women's opportunities for self-actualization are greater in the sheltered atmosphere of single-sex extracurricular activities than in more competitive coeducational environments, and whether all-female colleges encourage nontraditional careers. See Rice and Hemmings, "Womens Colleges," and Jencks and Reisman, *Academic Revolution,* pp. 307–308.
58. Mississippi University for Women v. Hogan, 458 U.S. 718, 735 (Blackmun, J., dissenting); President Bunting, and Maurice A. Jones, President of the Student Body at Hampden-Sydney College, quoted in Zoe Ingells, "Virginia's All-Male Hampden Sydney," *Chronicle of Higher Education,* Sept. 18, 1985, p. 3.
59. Mississippi University for Women v. Hogan, 458 U.S. 718, 720, n. 1 (quoting MUW charter).
60. Jencks and Reisman, *Academic Revolution.* For recent litigation, see sources cited in Rhode, "Association," and Susan S. Klein, ed., *Handbook for Achieving Sex Equity Through Education* (Baltimore: Johns Hopkins University Press, 1985).
61. Virginia Woolf, *Three Guineas* (New York: Harcourt Brace, 1966), pp. 62–63. For discussion of "woman-oriented" educational institutions, see Adrienne Rich, *On Lies*; Florence Howe, ed., *Women and the Power to Change* (New York: McGraw-Hill, 1975), pp. 27, 162–169. For discussion of specific reforms, see, for example, Hall and Sanders, *A Chilly Climate*; and

Margaret B. Wilkerson, "A Report on the Educational Status of Black Women During the United Nations Decade of Women," in Margaret C. Simms and Julianne M. Malveaux, *Slipping Through the Cracks: The Status of Black Women* (New Brunswick, N.J.: Transaction, 1986). See generally, Marian K. Chamberlain, ed., *Women in Academe: Progress and Prospects* (New York: Russell Sage Foundation, 1988).

62. See U.S. Commission on Civil Rights, *More Hurdles to Clear* (Washington, D.C.: Government Printing Office, 1980); Ellen W. Gerber, et al., *The American Woman in Sport* (Reading, Mass.: Addison-Wesley, 1974), pp. 4, 5–10; Betty Spears, "The Emergence of Women in Sport," in Barbara J. Hoepner, *Women's Athletics* (Washington, D.C.: American Alliance for Health, Physical Education, Recreation and Dance, 1974).

63. Kathleen McCrone, *Sport and the Physical Emancipation of English Women, 1870–1914* (London: Routledge, 1988), p. 84 (quoting Dorthea Beale); Helen Lenskyj, *Out of Bounds: Women, Sport and Sexuality* (Toronto: Women's Press, 1986).

64. McCrone, *Sport,* p. 135, 195 (quoting G. K. Chesterton); Lenskyj, *Out of Bounds,* p. 23; Jennifer Hargreaves, "Victorian Familialism and the Formative Years of Female Sport," in J. A. Managan and Roberta J. Park, *From 'Fair Sex' to Feminism* (London: Frank Cass, 1987), p. 130.

65. Lenskyj, *Out of Bounds,* p. 100; Susan Birrell, "The Woman Athlete's College Experience: Known and Unknown," *Journal of Sport and Social Issues,* 11 (1987): 82.

66. Charles R. Farrell, "Many Women Link Anti Sex-Bias Law to Outstanding Olympic Performance," *Chronicle of Higher Education,* Aug. 24, 1984, p. 31; Mary A. Boutilier and Lucinda San Giovanni, *The Sporting Woman* (Champaign, Ill.: Human Kinetics Publishing, 1982), p. 45. See also sources cited in note 62.

67. 117 *Congressional Record* 30407 (1971).

68. 45 C.F.R., sections 86.41(b) and (c).

69. Commission on Civil Rights, pp. 28–29; see Note, "Where the Boys Are: Can Separate Be Equal in School Sports," *University of Southern California Law Review,* 58 (1985): 1425; Karen L. Tokarz, "Separate But Unequal: Educational Sports Programs: The Need for a New Theory of Equality," *Berkeley Women's Law Journal,* 1 (1985): 201; Birrell, "Woman Athlete's College Experience," p. 86.

70. Hollander v. Connecticut Interscholastic Athletic Conference, Inc. No. 12497. (Sup. Ct. Conn., New Haven County, March 29, 1971; Petrie v. Illinois High School Associations, 74 Ill. App. 3rd 980, 394 N.E.2d 855 (1979); Buchanan v. Illinois High School Association, 351 F.Supp. 69 (ND Ill., 1972); Clark v. Arizona Scholastic Association, 695 F.2d 126 (9th Cir. 1982).

71. See Joyce A. Countiss, *Equity in School Athletics: A Guide* (New Brunswick: State University of New Jersey, 1977); Tokarz, "Unequal"; Susan Jewett, "The Equal Rights Amendment and Athletics, *Harvard Women's Law Journal,* 1 (1978): 53, 71–72.

72. See Commonwealth of Pennsylvania v. Pennsylvania Interscholastic Athletic Association, 334 A.2d 839, 842 (1975) and sources cited in Herma Hill Kay, *Sex-Based Discrimination* (St. Paul, Minn.: West, 1988), pp. 835–842.
73. Catharine A. MacKinnon, *Feminism Unmodified* (Cambridge, Mass.: Harvard University Press, 1987), pp. 74–120; Lyn Lemaire, "Women and Athletics: Toward a Physicality Perspective," *Harvard Women's Law Journal,* 5 (1982): 121.

Conclusion: Principles and Priorities

1. See Chapter 2. For a related discussion of issues in this chapter, see Deborah L. Rhode, "The 'Woman's Point of View,'" *Journal of Legal Education,* 38 (1988): 39.
2. See, for example, Ellen Hume, "Some Women Politicians Are Backing Away from Feminist Labels to Expand Base of Support," *Wall Street Journal,* April 3, 1985, p. 62; Anne Taylor Fleming, "The American Wife," *New York Times Magazine,* Oct. 26, 1986, p. 121; Dorothy Wickenden, "What Now?" *New Republic,* May 5, 1986, p. 19. For discussion of the "I'm not a feminist, but" syndrome, see Betty Friedan, "Where Do We Go From Here?" *Working Woman,* November 1986, p. 152.
3. Between 1970 and 1982, the number of women's studies courses in American colleges and universities had grown from 100 to over 30,000, and the total has continued to rise. See Catherine R. Stimpson, *Women's Studies in the United States: A Report to the Ford Foundation* (New York: Ford Foundation, 1986), p. 4. See also Marilyn J. Boxer, "For and About Women: The Theory and Practice of Women's Studies in the United States," *Signs,* 7 (1982): 661.
4. See Chapter 1; Karen Offen, "Defining Feminism; A Comparative Historical Approach," *Signs,* 14 (1988): 119.
5. See Chapters 2 and 4.
6. Offen, "Defining Feminism."
7. Betty Friedan, *The Second Stage* (New York: Summit Books, 1981); Betty Friedan, "How to Get the Women's Movement Moving Again," *New York Times Magazine,* Nov. 3, 1985, p. 26. For critical reviews, see Zillah Eisenstein, *Feminism and Sexual Equality: Crisis in Liberal America* (New York: Monthly Review Press, 1984), pp. 196–200.
8. Nancy Chodorow, *The Reproduction of Mothering: Psychoanalytic Feminism and the Sociology of Gender* (Berkeley: University of California Press, 1978), p. 206. See also Dorothy Dinnerstein, *The Mermaid and the Minotaur: Sexual Arrangements and the Human Malaise* (New York: Harper and Row, 1976). For an overview of the differences within psychoanalytic schools, see Nancy Chodorow, "Psychoanalytic Feminism and the Psychoanalytic in Psychology of Women," in Deborah L. Rhode, ed., *Theoretical Perspectives on Sexual Difference* (New Haven: Yale University Press, forthcoming).
9. Compare Alice S. Rossi, "Equality Between the Sexes: An Immodest Proposal," *Daedalus,* 93 (1964): 607, with Alice Rossi, "A Biosocial Perspective on Parenting," *Daedalus,* 106 (1977); Susan Griffin, *Woman and Nature:*

The Roaring Inside Her (New York: Harper and Row, 1978); Elizabeth H. Wolgast, *Equality and the Rights of Women* (Ithaca, N.Y.: Cornell University Press, 1980); Elaine Marks and Isabelle de Courtiuron *The New French Feminisms* (Amherst: University of Massachusetts Press, 1980); Jean Bethke Elshtain, "Feminism, Family, and Community," *Dissent,* 29 (1982): 442, 447.

10. Sara Ruddick, "Maternal Thinking," *Feminist Studies,* 6 (1980): 342; Mary O'Brien, "Feminist Theory and Dialectical Logic: Viewpoint," *Signs,* 7 (1981): 144; Nel Noddings, *Caring: A Feminine Approach to Ethics and Moral Education* (Berkeley: University of California Press, 1984); Carol Gilligan, *In a Different Voice: Pyschological Theory and Women's Development* (Cambridge, Mass.: Harvard University Press, 1982).
11. Gilligan, *Voice,* pp. 13–68; Lawrence Kohlberg, *The Philosophy of Moral Development: Moral Stages and the Ideology of Justice* (San Francisco: Harper and Row, 1981).
12. Gilligan, *Voice,* pp. 168–174.
13. See sources quoted in Kathy E. Ferguson, *The Feminist Case Against Bureaucracy* (Phildelphia: Temple University Press, 1984), pp. 185–186; Betty Lehan Harragan, *Games Mother Never Taught You: Corporate Gamesmanship for Women* (New York: Rawson Associates, 1977); Margaret Hennig and Anne Jardim, *The Managerial Woman* (Garden City, N.Y.: Anchor Press, 1977). One journalist, who gave up her full-time job to become a part-time columnist and mother of two, put the point directly: "I hope this is [having it] all because I can't handle any more." Victor R. Fuchs, *Women's Quest for Economic Equality* (Cambridge, Mass.: Harvard University Press, 1988), p. 1. For critical views, see Elizabeth Cagan, "The Selling of the Women's Movement," *Social Policy* (May–June 1978): 4; Suzanne Gordon, "Dressed for Success: The New Corporate Feminism," *The Nation,* Feb. 5, 1983, p. 129; Deborah L. Rhode, "Perspectives on Professional Women," *Stanford Law Review,* 40 (1988): 1163.
14. Compare Lawrence Walker, "Sex Differences in the Development of Moral Reasoning, A Critical Review," *Child Development,* 55 (1984): 667; Catherine G. Greeno and Eleanor E. Maccoby, "How Different Is the 'Different Voice'"? *Signs,* 11 (1986): 310; Cynthia Fuchs Epstein, *Deceptive Distinctions: Sex, Gender, and the Social Order* (New Haven: Yale University Press, 1988) pp. 76–94; Seyla Benhabib, "The Generalized and the Concrete Other: The Kohlberg-Gilligan Controversy and Feminist Theory," in Drucilla Cornell and Seyla Benhabib, *Feminism as Critique: Essays on the Politics of Gender in Late-Capitalist Societies* (London: Polity, 1987), pp. 77–79; Ann Colby and William Damon, "Listening to a Different Voice: A Review of Gilligan's *In A Different Voice,*" in Mary Roth Walsh, ed., *The Psychology of Women: Ongoing Debates* (New Haven: Yale University Press, 1987); see also the bibliography in Walsh, *Psychology,* pp. 275–277. For related criticism of psychoanalytic theories such as those found in Chodorow and Dinnerstein's work, see Nancy Fraser and Linda Nicholson, "Feminism and Post Modernism" (unpublished paper, 1986).
15. Carol Gilligan, "Reply," *Signs,* 11 (1986): 324, 329–330.

16. Pope Paul VI, quoted in Mary Daly, *Beyond God the Father: Toward a Philosophy of Women's Liberation* (Boston: Beacon, 1973), p. 3, and Chapter 4. See also Epstein, *Deceptive Distinctions.*
17. See, for example, Germaine Greer, *Sex and Destiny: The Politics of Human Fertility* (London: Secker and Warburg, 1984); Friedan, *Second Stage,* p. 319; Cagan, "Women's Movement." See also Chapter 1.
18. See Mary Ann Glendon, "The Probable Significance of the Bork Appointment for Issues of Particular Concern to Women," *Cardozo Law Review,* 9 (1987): 95, the discussion of employment discrimination against Sears Roebuck & Company in Chapter 8, and the pornography campaign in Chapter 10. See generally, Joan C. Williams, "Deconstructing Gender," *Michigan Law Review* 87 (1989): 797.
19. For discussion of leadership styles and political values, see Rosabeth Moss Kanter, "The Impact of Hierarchical Structures on the Work Behavior of Women and Men," in Rachel Kahn-Hut, Kaplan Daniels, Arlene and Richard Colvasol, eds., *Women and Work: Problems and Perspectives* (New York: Oxford University Press, 1982), pp. 234, 236–245, and sources cited in Rhode, "Woman's Point of View." See also Simone de Beauvoir, quoted in Eisenstein, *Equality,* p. 239.
20. Joan Scott, *Gender and the Politics of History* (New York: Columbia University Press, 1988) pp. 76–79; Catharine A. MacKinnon, *Feminism Unmodified* (Cambridge, Mass.: Harvard University Press, 1987). See Chapter 5, and Joan C. Tronto, "Beyond Gender Difference to a Theory of Care," *Signs,* 12 (1987): 644.
21. See Alison Jaggar, "On Sexual Equality," *Ethics,* 84 (1973–74): 275; Carolyn Heilbrun, *Toward a Recognition of Androgyny* (New York: Knopf, 1973); Joyce Trebilcot, "Two Forms of Androgynism," in Mary Vetterling-Braggin, ed., *"Femininity," "Masculinity," and "Androgyny": A Modern Philosophical Discussion* (Totowa, N.J.: Rowman and Littlefield, 1982); Jean Bethke, "Against Androgyny," *Telos,* 47 (1981): 5. For psychological data, see Sandra L. Bem, "Probing the Promise of Androgyny," in Alexandra G. Kaplan and Joan P. Bean, eds., *Beyond Sex-Role Stereotypes: Readings Toward a Psychology of Androgyny* (Boston: Little, Brown, 1976), p. 48.
22. Mary Anne Warren, "Is Androgyny the Answer to Sexual Stereotyping?" in Vetterling-Braggin, *"Femininity,"* p. 180; Ellen C. DuBois et al., "Feminist Discourse, Moral Values, and the Law—A Conversation," *Buffalo Law Review,* 34 (1986): 76 (remarks of Carol Gilligan); Heilbrun, *Androgyny,* p. 143; Chapter 4.
23. Janice Raymond, "The Illusion of Androgyny," *Quest,* 2 (1975): 57, 60; Elshtain, "Against Androgyny"; Christine A. Littleton, "Reconstructing Sexual Equality," *California Law Review,* 75 (1987): 1279.
24. See, for example, Wolgast, *Equality;* David L. Kirp, Mark G. Yudof, and Marlene Strong Franks, *Gender Justice* (Chicago: University of Chicago Press, 1985). See also Chapter 10.
25. Eisenstein, *Sexual Equality;* Jaggar, "On Sexual Equality."
26. See Audre Lorde, *Sister Outsider: Essays and Speeches* (New York: Crossing Press, 1984); Elizabeth Spellman, *Inessential Woman: Problems of Exclu-*

sion in Feminist Thought (Boston: Beacon, 1988); Gloria I. Joseph and Jill Lewis, *Common Differences: Conflicts in Black and White Feminist Perspectives* (New York: Doubleday, 1981); Phyllis Marynick Palmer, "White Women/Black Women: The Dualism of Female Identity and Experience in the United States," *Feminist Studies,* 9 (1983): 151.

27. Heidi Hartmann, "The Unhappy Marriage of Marxism and Feminism: Towards a More Progressive Union," in Lydia Sargent, ed., *Women and Revolution* (Boston: South End Press, 1981), pp. 1, 2. See Sandra Harding, "Why Has the Sex Gender System Become Visible Only Now?" in Sandra Harding and Merrill B. Hintikka, eds., *Discovering Reality: Feminist Perspectives on Epistemology, Metaphysics, Methodology, and Philosophy of Science* (Dordrecht, Neth., and Boston: D. Reidel, 1983), p. 321; Gloria Joseph, "The Incompatible Menage à Trois: Marxism, Feminism, and Racism," in Sargent, ed., *Women and Revolution,* p. 91.
28. See, for example, Alison M. Jaggar, *Feminist Politics and Human Nature* (London: Rowman and Allanheld, 1983); Nancy C. M. Hartsock, *Money, Sex, and Power: Toward a Feminist Historical Materialism* (New York: Longman, 1983).
29. See John Rawls, *A Theory of Justice* (Cambridge, Mass.: Harvard University Press, 1971), and Ronald Dworkin, *Taking Rights Seriously* (Cambridge, Mass.: Harvard University Press, 1977), and discussion in Chapter 6.
30. For comparable perspectives attentive to postmodern influences, see Jane Flax, "Postmodernism and Gender Relations in Feminist Theory," *Signs,* 12 (1987): 621, 633; Sandra Harding, "The Instability of the Analytical Categories of Feminist Theory," *Signs,* 11 (1986): 645; Rhode, "Woman's Point of View"; and Fraser and Nicholson, "Feminism."
31. See Chapter 1 (women lawyers); Chapter 2 (jury duty and occupational restrictions); Chapter 6 (pregnancy discrimination); and Chapter 11 (athletics); Deborah L. Rhode, "Definitions of Difference," in Deborah L. Rhode, *Theoretical Perspectives on Sexual Difference* (New Haven: Yale University Press, 1989).
32. Lynn Henderson, "Legality and Empathy," *Michigan Law Review,* 85 (1985): 1574; Judith A. Resnik, "On the Bias: Feminist Reconsiderations of the Aspirations for Our Judges," *University of Southern California Law Review,* 61 (1988): 1877.

Index